The Divine Consort

The Divine Consort

RĀDHĀ AND THE GODDESSES OF INDIA

EDITED BY
John Stratton Hawley
AND
Donna Marie Wulff

BEACON PRESS Boston

Beacon Press
25 Beacon Street
Boston, Massachusetts 02108

Beacon Press books are published under the auspices
of the Unitarian Universalist Association
of Congregations in North America.

First published in 1982 by Berkeley Religious Studies Series
in cooperation with Motilal Banarsidass Publishers

First published by Beacon Press in 1986 by arrangement with
the Graduate Theological Union

Printed in the United States of America

92 91 90 89 88 87 86 8 7 6 5 4 3 2 1

ISBN 0-8070-1303-X

Contents

Preface
JOHN STRATTON HAWLEY
xi

I. Introductory

Krishna Gopāla, Rādhā, and The Great Goddess
CHARLOTTE VAUDEVILLE
1

II. Rādhā

The Divine Duality of Rādhā and Krishna
BARBARA STOLER MILLER
13

A Sanskrit Portrait: Rādhā in the Plays of Rūpa Gosvāmī
DONNA MARIE WULFF
27

A Vernacular Portrait: Rādhā in the *Sūr Sāgar*
JOHN STRATTON HAWLEY
42

The Theology of Rādhā in the Purāṇas
C. MACKENZIE BROWN
57

Rādhā: The Play and Perfection of *Rasa*
SHRIVATSA GOSWAMI
72

Where Have All the Rādhās Gone?
New Images of Woman in Modern Hindi Poetry
KARINE SCHOMER
89

Comments: Rādhā and Erotic Community
NORVIN HEIN
116

Comments: The Reversal and Rejection of *Bhakti*
JOHN B. CARMAN
125

III. Other Goddess Figures

1. INTRODUCTORY

The Shifting Balance of Power
in the Marriage of
Śiva and Pārvatī
WENDY DONIGER O'FLAHERTY
129

2. INDEPENDENT GODDESSES

Blood and Death out of Place:
Reflections
on the Goddess Kālī
DAVID KINSLEY
144

Consort of None, *Śakti* of All:
The Vision
of the *Devī-Māhātmya*
THOMAS B. COBURN
153

Gaṅgā: The Goddess in Hindu Sacred Geography
DIANA L. ECK
166

A Theology of the Repulsive:
The Myth
of the Goddess Śītalā
EDWARD C. DIMOCK, JR.
184

Comments: The Goddess and the Polarity of the Sacred
RICHARD BRUBAKER
204

3. CONSORTS

Sītā: Mother Goddess and *Śakti*
CORNELIA DIMMITT
210

The Goddess Śrī: The Blossoming Lotus
and Breast Jewel of Viṣṇu
VASUDHA NARAYANAN
224

Pin̲n̲ai, Krishna's Cowherd Wife
DENNIS HUDSON
238

The Courtship of Vaḷḷi and Murugan:
Some Parallels with the Rādhā-Krishna Story
BRENDA E.F. BECK
262

Comments: The Divine Consort in South India
GLENN E. YOCUM
278

IV. Concluding Perspectives

Prolegomenon to a Psychology of the Goddess
DAVID M. WULFF
283

Types of Sexual Union and their Implicit Meanings
FRÉDÉRIQUE APFFEL MARGLIN
298

On Woman Saints
A. K. RAMANUJAN
316

Notes
327

Glossary
DONNA M. WULFF
369

Select Bibliography
DONNA M. WULFF
383

Contributors
405

Index
411

Illustrations

Black and White Photographs

Figure 1. Rādhā Remembers 21

Figure 2. Krishna Kneeling to Take Dust off Rādhā's Feet 33

Figure 3. *Varṣa Vihāra* (Rādhā and Krishna Sheltering from the Rain) 49

Figure 4. Union and Separation of Krishna and a Gopī 59

Figure 5. *Līlā Havā* (Rādhā and Krishna Exchanging Clothes) 85

Figure 6. *Dān Līlā* (Rādhā's Response to Krishna's Demanding Toll) 139

Figure 7. Folk Painting Representing the Goddess Kālī Straddled Over the Erect Lingam of the Corpse-Siva 149

Figure 8. Bathers in the Gaṅgā on Makarsankrānti in Benares 173

Figure 9. Śrī Sitting on a Lotus 229

Figure 10. Śrī on the Breast of Viṣṇu 233

Figure 11. Ekānaṃśā between Balarāma and Krishna 257

Figure 12. The Marriage of Vaḷḷi and Murugan 273

Figure 13. A Male Patient's Drawing in which the Mother Image Has Taken the Form of the Terrifying Mother Goddess 296

Figure 14. Lakṣmī in the Lap of Narasiṃha 299

Figure 15. Rādhā and Krishna Intertwined 301

Color Plates

Plate 1. *Virahitā Nāyikā* (The Beloved Waits)

Plate 2. *Upapati Nāyaka* (One Who Loves Another's Wife)

Plate 3. Illustration for a Verse of the *Satsaī* of Bihārī

Plate 4. *Ceṣṭa-Catura Nāyaka* (The Hero Clever Indeed)

Notes on miniature paintings are provided by Vishakha N. Desai, Joyce M. Paulson, Jitendrasinh of Wankaner, and John Stratton Hawley.

Preface

JOHN STRATTON HAWLEY

*H*indu society is overwhelmingly patriarchal. For the most part its defining structures relate males to males, and women find their place in society by their associations with the men in their lives. The overarching structures in Indian religion have also tended to be conceived in male terms. A traditional scheme that was devised to encompass the major forms of divinity (*trimūrti*) listed three males—Viṣṇu, Śiva and Brahmā—who vied with one another for supremacy.

Yet even as this formula was being articulated, Brahmā's actual position was tenuous, and as Hindus of later centuries reflected on their tradition they deleted him from the trinity and filled his place with what had been omitted: the Goddess. They ranked her power (*śakti*) alongside that of Viṣṇu and Śiva and classed themselves broadly as Vaiṣṇavas, Śaivas, or Śāktas. This too, however, only begins to suggest the extent of her real supremacy, for the act of placing her in a hierarchy misconstrues her distinctive force. Hers *is* a different sex, and she reigns as no male can. Hers is not the throne of structure, not the place of pride; she is rather the condition that makes structure itself possible.

To be sure, there are times when she is seen as that above which nothing can be conceived, but on the whole it is not her position that exalts her. Rather, she is the soul of relation. She connects, she communicates, she is warp to the woof. She makes the world organism live, speak, and love. Without her the ciphers in *dharma*'s complex equation would wander inert; she gives them life by connecting them. She mediates, she consorts.

The special nature of the hegemony of the Goddess (the very terms, biased toward hierarchy, seem inadequate: "supremacy," "hegemony") forces us to rethink the range of roles she plays in Hindu religion. To stimulate such a reconsideration the Center for the Study of World Religions at Harvard University sponsored in June of 1978 a conference entitled "Rādhā and the Divine Consort." In the hope of enriching the texture of discussion, the Center invited scholars of several disciplines and countries, varying ages, both sexes, and members as well as students of the traditions concerned. The papers collected in this volume are the fruit of that colloquy.

These articles comprise two main groups. Those in the first seek to describe and evaluate Rādhā, Krishna's cowherdess lover and consort. She is a figure neglected by Western scholarship, despite the fact that many devotees consider her coequal or even superior to Krishna. In a unique way she raises the question of the special role of the Goddess, for Rādhā is the consort *par excellence*. So crucial is her relationship to Krishna that theologians continue to argue about the structural backdrop against which one should conceive it: is she Krishna's wife or is she his mistress?

The second group of essays extends the range of discussion beyond Rādhā; with each paper another female divinity from the Indian spectrum makes her appearance. Some are consorts and some are primarily thought of as independent. Those that come from South India tend to be defined as consorts: indeed they unite with their gods in marriage. This tendency probably correlates with the fact that in the South, unlike the northern pattern, marriage confirms the status a woman's own lineage gives her. Cross-cousin marriage is the ideal; hence her lineage contributes to the marriage in a way that it does not in the north, where the woman's entire worth derives from the marital bond itself. The South Indian woman is assured a degree of parity in marriage that the North Indian wife only gradually achieves, if at all. Similarly, in the south, marriage does not compromise the power of the Goddess. The goddesses of North and Northeast India, by contrast, reflect a more volatile association with men. They tend to be much less moderate in their characteristics than their southern counterparts, mixing total rage with total compassion, and their relations to their consorts are looser.

In a certain way Rādhā, neither clearly married nor fully independent, mediates between these two types. Her status is ambiguous, as is her relation to the other cowherd girls, who are so often understood as exemplifying the souls of this world. She is one of them and yet she is not: one does not quite know whether she is human or divine. Her ambiguity highlights that feature that makes so many of the goddesses of India what they are, something beyond structure: call it auspiciousness, call it power, call it relationship, call it love.

Rādhā

Charlotte Vaudeville introduces the discussion by unmasking the persistent presence of the Goddess in the mythology and worship of the cowherd Krishna from earliest times. She traces progressive attempts to obscure the role of this paradoxical Mother-without-children in the later literature, but shows how the festival calendar and popular worship continue to bow to her. The relation between this overarching Goddess and Rādhā, however, remains enigmatic.

The next essays present three portraits of Rādhā. Barbara Miller establishes the primacy of Rādhā's relation with Krishna in the *Gītagovinda* by explaining how the twelfth-century poet Jayadeva portrays Rādhā and Krishna as a dual divinity: it is their memory of one another that binds them together. As the poet relates their mutual recollection the devotee is given access to the divine presence. Donna Wulff describes Rādhā as she is understood by the sixteenth-century theologian Rūpa Gosvāmī. It emerges that Rādhā in Rūpa's plays is not only a supreme model of devotion but also its object: both devotees and Krishna lose themselves in love for Rādhā. Wulff proposes that it is the transcendent quality of Rādhā's love that permits her this double role. John Hawley points to a similar phenomenon in the vernacular songs of Sūr Dās, Rūpa's contemporary. Much like the *Gītagovinda,* the early poems of the *Sūr Sāgar* insistently emphasize the relation between Rādhā and Krishna; as in Rūpa's plays Rādhā emerges supreme only on account of that relation, her love. Hawley suggests further that Rādhā's ambiguous status in relation to the other cowherd girls is the source of her religious power: she mediates between religious subjects and their object, not so much by virtue of her station as through her feeling.

Mackenzie Brown records the progressive elaboration of the figure of Rādhā and analyzes the means by which her exaltation is rationalized in the *Brahmavaivarta Purāṇa,* another sixteenth-century text in its final redaction. Here is an attempt to bridge the gulf that Vaudeville notes between the human lover and the universal Goddess. As in the plays of Rūpa, the theologian of the *Brahmavaivarta Purāṇa* supplies a secret, supernal marriage for Rādhā and Krishna, but at the same time he does not deny that at the human level they are lovers. This enables him to dignify the two of them with the terms traditionally accruing to the cosmogonic pair and to garland Rādhā with the attributes of the Goddess: *prakṛti, śakti,* and *māyā,* terms that appear in the later strata of the *Sūr Sāgar* as well. Through her theological transformation she finally becomes what she can never be as lover: a mother, indeed, Mother of the world.

Shrivatsa Goswami's contribution, unique in reflecting the point of view of a devotee, reveals a rather different understanding of Rādhā's transcendence. Drawing largely upon the philosophical writings of Rūpa's nephew Jīva Gosvamī, he asserts that the fundamental shape of reality itself involves the fusion of subject and object in a blissful union that manifests itself as aesthetic satisfaction (*rasa*) but is ultimately indescribable. Rādhā, as the summation of the experience of love and that which makes it possible for *rasa* to flow, is the only means by which humans can uncover this level of reality. As love, then, she transcends the gulf between human and divine, even making them in the final analysis reversible. By metaphysical necessity more than by virtue of any conflation of stories, she unites in herself the alienation that separated lovers can feel (humanity and divinity longing for one another) and the union of spouses (the final consummation of human and divine).

Karine Schomer illuminates quite a different contemporary perspective on Rādhā by showing how she has been replaced in modern Hindi lyrical poetry by other models of womanhood—from the "universal woman" of the Chāyāvād school to the individual and imperfect women of more recent writers. Schomer explains, however, that the Rādhā being rejected by this still rather limited "modern sector" of Indian society is not so much the Rādhā of religious devotion as the heroine of secular, courtly love, the *nāyikā,* with whom she became closely identified in the *rīti* poetry of the seventeenth and eighteenth centuries. In describing this *rīti* image of Rādhā, Schomer provides an important perspective for understanding much of the miniature painting that illustrates the volume.

Referring to this conflation of Rādhā with the *nāyikā,* and the uneasiness of recent generations with the resultant product, John Carman points out that radically immanentist theologies often run the danger of being set aside by subsequent generations with different world views. The rejection of a fully humanized Rādhā in twentieth-century India is no more surprising than the rejection of the nineteenth century's overly human Jesus by twentieth-century Americans. Remembering that it is a very specific Rādhā who is being put aside, however, one might ask further whether the secular theology of the Chāyāvād school, a eulogizing of relationship itself, was not in fact a reformulation of some of the familiar themes in earlier theologizing about Rādhā.

Whereas Schomer speculates on the reasons for recent shifts of attitude, Norvin Hein takes account of social factors surrounding medieval views of Rādhā. He suggests that her rise to prominence may have been a reaction of certain Hindus to the impoverishment of life that accompanied Muslim domination of their society. In order to soothe the wound, they identified with one another in non-structural ways. In *bhakti* communities the love of Rādhā and Krishna served as the model for that primal *communitas* which would regenerate society as a whole.

Other Goddess Figures

Wendy O'Flaherty prepares the way for the consideration of other goddess figures alongside Rādhā by demonstrating that in the wide sweep of Hindu mythology consortship need not imply the domination of the male. Both in pre-Vedic times and in recent centuries the Goddess has often predominated. In between there is a great deal of flux, and O'Flaherty illustrates this fact by calling particular attention to the multiple ways in which Pārvatī, the consort of Śiva, serves as mediator in the unequal marriages of humans with the gods.

In the essays that follow, four goddesses are described, each presenting a different way of understanding the supremacy of the Goddess. Kālī's transcendence is experienced as opposition. David Kinsley portrays her rages as power out of control. Once the Goddess (whether Durgā, Pārvatī, or Satī) gives vent to her wrath as Kālī, it surges over every boundary, threatening the very order it may have been intended to safeguard. There is a dimension, as Kinsley suggests, in which Kālī's excess makes her encompassing: she sets order in its context. But in the case of Devī, as Thomas Coburn shows in his study of three myths told in the classic sixth-century *Devī-Māhātmya,* this encompassing, summary nature is precisely the seal of the Goddess's supremacy. She incarnates in herself all the brilliance (*tejas*) and power (*śakti*) that the gods collectively possess, and her pervasive magic (*māyā*) gives them sufficient definition to be able to do battle with the powers of evil.

The supremacy of Gaṅgā, the River Ganges, is revealed less as summation than as connection. Diana Eck shows how as primordial river, the river in which all other rivers cohere, she signifies the symbolic bond that establishes the universe as a coherent ecosystem, both vertically and horizontally. Another dimension of her transcendence is seen in the fact that although she figures in the realm of narrative myth, she is not bound by it. She symbolizes organically, not merely with words. Edward Dimock takes us on another river journey in his discussion of an eighteenth-century Bengali *Śītalā-maṅgal*. Now, however, the river represents life's diachronic patterns, and Śītalā, goddess of smallpox, stands athwart it with paradoxical revelations that point to a synchronic structure eluding time. Here paradox is the lens through which one sees the Goddess's transcendence: when one understands Śītalā, disease is not disease. Richard Brubaker, commenting on this group of essays, extends the point and shows how elements of paradox and polarity are endemic in the portraits of each of these goddesses, revealing something at the core of the sacred itself.

Supreme and independent as these goddesses are, in only one case is the consort relation left entirely behind. True, these are challenging liaisons. Śītalā's companion is the virulent Jvarāsura, the smallpox demon. Kālī, far from domesticating Śiva as does his other consort Pārvatī, incites her mate to frenzy in a wild *pas de deux*. And Gaṅgā manages what no other goddess can: she is consort to both Śiva and Viṣṇu. Only the Devī of the *Devī-Māhātmya* stands above it all, and chiefly for the purpose of demonstrating that her relation to male expressions of divinity has an integrity, an internal logic, that might be missed if one construed them simply as her consorts.

In the case of the next four figures, three of which are indigenous to South India, consortship, even marriage, is primary. Sītā is the exception to the geographical rule, and as Cornelia Dimmitt shows she is exceptional in other ways as well. Sītā is far more than the dutiful wife of Rāma for which she is often taken. She bears the larger associations of earth and fertility; and when she returns to earth, rejected by her husband on the grounds that some may question her virtue, there is more than a hint that it is she who is leaving him and his little world of *dharma* to return to her indestructible divinity. Vasudha Narayanan examines another marriage, that of Śrī to Viṣṇu/Nārāyaṇa as seen by the thirteenth-century theologian Vedānta Deśika. Here too there is ambiguity, for Viṣṇu is understood as married not only to Śrī, but also to human souls, who approach him through her. In this respect her situation is not unlike Rādhā's. Narayanan also considers another problem that arises in understanding the relation of Rādhā and Krishna: their simultaneous unity and difference. In the case of Śrī the key to the puzzle seems to lie in the very meaning of her name. She is Viṣṇu's auspiciousness, hence inseparable from his own being, and their consortship has about it that particular sense: it is a marriage of true necessity.

Dennis Hudson treats Rādhā's most obvious counterpart in the south, Pinnai, Krishna's cowherdess consort and wife. Though she is familiarly known from the poetry of Āṇṭāḷ and others of the *ālvārs* as the mediator between Krishna and the *gopīs,* hence between God and human souls, Hudson sifts through the sources where she first appears and finds traces of a startingly different figure. No divinized cowherd girl, she may well be none other than Durgā herself in origin. Once again the great Goddess shows her intimate connection with the mythology of Krishna. Brenda Beck considers a possible parallel to Rādhā from the Śaiva mythology of South India: Vaḷḷi, the second consort of Murugan. She shows how popular religious pamphlets tell the story of the courtship of Murugan and Vaḷḷi in such a way as to resolve the tensions between human and divine levels and illicit and conjugal relations that fill the stories of Rādhā and Krishna. Nature is gradually transformed to culture as Murugan draws Vaḷḷi into marriage: she is divinized and the love she bears for him is sanctified. Similar attempts to rationalize and domesticate the meaning of Rādhā's consortship never quite succeeded in North India, and as Glenn Yocum suggests, perhaps this story too is as beloved for its raw beginnings as for its immaculate end. In relation to Śrī, Yocum stresses a point that we meet time and again in the study of the divine consort: the male may have a metaphysical or cosmological supremacy, but in matters of salvation it is the female who reigns.

Three essays of general import conclude the discussion, one by a psychologist, one by an anthropologist, and one by a litterateur. David Wulff begins the series by laying out perspectives in contemporary psychological theory that are relevant to an understanding of the goddess. He reviews the sparse experimental data and proceeds to delineate those aspects of Freudian and Jungian thought that provide a framework for comprehending the psychological processes that underlie Indian Goddess figures. Of particular interest are various observations about the polarization of good and bad in infantile conceptions of the mother and the projection of fears of castration upon the latter, and the Jungian distinction between the anima and the mother archetype.

Frédérique Marglin approaches a general typology for goddess and consort figures from another perspective. She derives a tripartite classification of types of sexual union from her field work in Puri and offers them as a possible schema for sorting out various kinds of consort relationships. Her first type, male-dominant, suggests most clearly the consorts of South India. Her third type, female-dominant, reminds one of many aspects of the independent goddesses of North and Northeast India. And, as her informants explicitly suggest, the second type, in which neither sex is dominant and love is pursued for its own sake, rings true for much of the mythology of Rādhā and Krishna.

A.K. Ramanujan, finally, shifts the ground from the divine to the human plane and analyzes the experiences of female saints. Because *bhakti* as a religious form is itself inherently antistructural, he finds that the relatively unstructured participants in society—women and outcastes—do not stand in the same need of conversion as do their male and caste counterparts. They are "natural" *bhaktas,* and their religious task is not to undo the entanglements of this world but simply to fend them off. In connection with this point, one remembers how difficult it frequently is to express in consistent structural terms the position and force of divine consorts. Like female *bhaktas,* these are the "once-born" of the gods. But because of their fluidity they also have a unique role to play in integrating the pantheon: Vaḷḷi, Mīnākṣī, and Gaṅgā are all responsible for forging a connection between Viṣṇu, Krishna and Śiva.

An exhibit of *pichvāīs* and miniature paintings drawn from the collections of the Boston Museum of Fine Arts, the Fogg Museum, and Stuart Cary Welch was mounted at the Fogg Museum to coincide with the Harvard symposium. Jitendrasinh of Wankaner from the Fogg Museum, Joyce Paulson and Vishakha Desai from the Museum of Fine Arts, and John Hawley have prepared notes on works of art from that exhibit which appear here. Donna Wulff has compiled a select bibliography, glossary, and index for the essays.

The editors wish to express their appreciation to Jan Fontein, Director of the Boston Museum of Fine Arts, and Stuart Cary Welch, Curator of Islamic Art at the Fogg Museum, for their support of the exhibit; to John B. Carman, Director of the Center for the Study of World Religions, for encouraging its sponsorship of the conference and to William Darrow for facilitating it; to Mark Juergensmeyer of the Graduate Theological Union for his guidance in preparing the volume for publication; and to Anita Miller for coordinating the book production. Thanks are also due to Linda Hess, who helped in standardizing the notes.

I.

Introductory

Krishna Gopāla, Rādhā, and The Great Goddess

CHARLOTTE VAUDEVILLE

*E*very Hindu male god has a distinct relation with at least one female deity, a *devī,* who usually stands as his wife or consort.[1] If the male god is conceived as powerful, the consort goddess tends to be conceived as the embodiment of the god's power or energy, his *śakti.* If the male deity is conceived as the supreme lord and master of the universe (*īśvara* in a Śaiva context) or as the Adorable One (*bhagavān* in a Vaiṣṇava context), his consort may be identified with the great cosmic *śakti,* the force or energy that sets the universe in motion. Whether identified with *prakṛti,* nature, as in the Sāṃkhya system of philosophy, or with *yogamāyā,* the power of illusion responsible for the emanation and development of the visible universe, this energy is personified as the great Goddess, Devī, and she is worshipped by gods and humans under a variety of names as the mother of the universe (*jagadambā*). Ultimately the great Goddess controls even the supreme male deity whose emanation she is supposed to be.

As rightly pointed out by Thomas Coburn in his contribution to the present volume, "although Devī is understood to bear a unique relation to each particular deity, this is no 'mere' consort relation; she is beyond being a consort to anyone." This point is to be kept in mind especially when discussing the Rādhā-Krishna couple. Rādhā herself, in indissoluble union with Krishna, is worshipped as his *hlādinī-*

śakti, his power of joy or blessedness, and she is represented with the bright, golden complexion usually attributed to Durgā.

The problem of Rādhā has been much discussed. Though she is frequently mentioned in Indian literature, at least from the time of Hāḷa, her emergence in the cultic and devotional sphere of Vaiṣṇavism as Krishna Gopāla's beloved and *śakti* is known to have taken place rather late, certainly not much earlier than the sixteenth century. From her character and her humble origin, as an obscure cowherd girl whose sole claim to fame was her total absorption in her love for Krishna, Rādhā appeared somewhat ill-fitted to take the place of the mother of the universe,[2] but this very discrepancy makes her elevation and ultimate transfiguration all the more striking.

The problem of Rādhā's relation to Krishna and of her divinization in medieval and modern Hinduism cannot be considered apart from the more fundamental problem of the relation between the Cowherd-god Krishna Gopāla and the great Goddess. I believe that it is in the interpenetration and interaction of these two great divinities of popular Hinduism that a solution to the problem of the emergence of Rādhā as Lord Krishna's *śakti* and divine consort must be sought.

For clues toward solving this problem, which, so far as I know, has been little investigated, I propose to draw upon two main sources: first, the Hindu calendar, and second, textual evidence from the Vaiṣṇava and non-Vaiṣṇava literature dealing with the legend of the Cowherd-god.

The Hindu Calendar

The Goddess occupies a central position in the Hindu calendar: she presides over both halves (*pakṣa*) of each lunar month, since the eighth days (*aṣṭamī tithi*) of both the dark (*kṛṣṇa*) and the bright (*śukla*) *pakṣas* are consecrated to her. The *aṣṭamī* of the dark *pakṣa* is dedicated to "Kālā," (Kālarūpiṇī or Kālī), the dark form of the Goddess, whereas the *aṣṭamī* of the bright *pakṣa* is dedicated to Durgā, the luminous form of the same Goddess. This dark/luminous duality is characteristic of the Goddess and central to her myth as cosmic deity. Both aspects are essential to the cult of Devī and manifest themselves in turn with the waning and waxing of the moon.

Under her dark aspect the Goddess is conceived as Ādyakālī, the primeval Kālī. She is the "Mother of Time" (Kālamātā), the night or sleep, the primordial waters from which creation arises, the cosmic

Mother from whose womb all beings including the gods arise. As such she is conceived as formless but she may be represented symbolically. Under her luminous aspect she usually assumes a human form, complemented by eight arms holding as many weapons, all of which symbolize her supreme power. In her primordial form as Ādyakālī she stands as mother not only of the whole cosmos but even of the luminous Devī, Ambikā or Durgā, the latter being born as her frightful aspect (*bhairavī*), an expression of her wrath and an instrument of her revenge. Yet, depending on the context, Kālī herself may be conceived as a secondary form of Durgā, or even as a kind of residue left by the manifestation of the Luminous One.[3] A study of the calendar shows that both forms of the Goddess are intimately connected with the Cowherd-god's origin and legend.

In stark contrast to the situation with respect to Devī, we find remarkably few specifically Krishnaite festivals in the Hindu calendar, apart from purely sectarian ones. Yet Krishna is naturally involved in nonsectarian Vaiṣṇava festivals such as those held on the eleventh *tithi* (*ekādaśī*) of each *pakṣa.* The most celebrated of these *ekādaśīs* is the festival of the going to sleep (*śayanī*) of Lord Viṣṇu on Āṣāḍha *śukla* 11, which marks the beginning of the *caturmāsya,* the four months of the rains. The Āṣāḍha festival is celebrated with great pomp and pageantry in Puri in Orissa, where it is known as the Rath-yātrā: on that day Jagannātha, Subhadrā and Baladeva, each on a monumental chariot (*ratha*), take a trip from their great temple to the Gundicā-devī temple and back. In Northern India Jagannātha is considered to be identical with Krishna, brother of Baladeva and of Subhadrā (another name for Ekānaṃśā, a form of Durgā).

It is a striking fact that all over India, and especially in Eastern India, the greatest Vaiṣṇava festival of the year is held not on the day Viṣṇu rises from his sleep (*devotthāna* or *prabodhinī*), on the eleventh *tithi* of the bright *pakṣa* of Kārttika (an arising that is closely followed by his marriage with goddess Tulasī), but on the day he goes to sleep, at the beginning of the dark season of the rains. This "going to sleep" of Viṣṇu most probably symbolizes his reentering the womb of the primeval Mother, who is the primordial Night (*nidrā*), that is, Kālī. There the god will lie as an embryo within the dark waters of the womb until he is manifested again at the end of the rainy season.[4]

The most important of the specifically Krishnaite festivals is Kṛṣṇa-janmāṣṭamī, Krishna's birthday, which is celebrated on the *aṣṭamī tithi* of the dark *pakṣa* of the month of Śrāvaṇa, the second month of the rainy season. The festival itself is admittedly a late one but its date is very suggestive. The month of Śrāvaṇa is entirely dedicated to the great Goddess, various vows in her honor being observed during the whole month, especially by women. The celebration of Krishna's birthday on the day of the month particularly sacred to Kālī clearly points to an ancient belief in the close connection between the two deities.

Even more suggestive of the Cowherd-god's parentage is the cluster of feasts collectively known as Dīpāvalī or Dīvalī, which occupies the last two days of the month of Aśvin and the first two days of the month of Kārttika (Aśvin *kṛṣṇa* 14-15 and Kārttika *śukla* 1-2). Aśvin *kṛṣṇa* 14 is sacred to Yama, the god of Death, and on that day lamps are offered to him. It is from this offering of lamps (*yamadīpādana*) that the festival takes its name. Once this is done, and that inauspicious deity, together with his principality Naraka (hell), is propitiated, Devī herself is honored as the goddess of wealth, Lakṣmī, together with the god of riches, Kuvera, on the night of the new moon (*amāvasyā*).[5] This is performed with great lavishness and brilliant display by the Vaiśyas, the merchant castes, who are largely responsible for making Dīvālī the most popular feast in Northern India. On the following day (Kārttika *śukla* 1), the festival of Annakūṭa or Govardhana-pūjā is celebrated, especially by the pastoral castes, in honor of the Govardhana hill and the cattle. The ceremony is performed by a cowherd and it is presided over by the goddess Gaurī, together with Gaṇeśa.[6] Even today this festival of mountain and cattle retains its primitive and pastoral character, though at least in the cities it is eclipsed by the pageantry and glitter of the Dīvālī festival patronized by the merchants. The day after the Annakūṭa festival, Kārttika *śukla* 2, is known as Bhāī-dūj (*bhrātṛ-dvitīya*). On that day, the goddess Yamunā (the Jumna river) is feasted, theoretically with her brother Yama, though the latter is not given much attention and the gifts of lighted lamps go to the holy river.

Thus the Dīvālī cluster brings forward successively three divine couples, two of which are not composed of a male god and his consort but of a female deity flanked by a male god who is conceived as her son or brother: Gaurī-Gaṇeśa and Yama-Yamunā. The feast in honor of Lakṣmī, falling on *amāvasyā*, the day of the new moon, and that of the black Yamunā river clearly refer to the dark form of the Goddess, whereas it is the luminous form of the Goddess, Gaurī, who presides over the Annakūṭa festival, in which Krishna Gopāla is celebrated as identical with the Govardhana hill. The feast of Bhāī-dūj on the following day in honor of Yamunā-devī (another dark form of the Goddess) is felt to be a continuation and culmination of Annakūṭa, the Yamunā being closely associated with the cult of the Cowherd-god in Braj.[7]

The most important celebration in honor of the great Goddess is Navarātrī ("Nine Nights"). Its culminating festival of Dasserā (*daśa-hara*), on the tenth and final day, commemorates the victory of the luminous war-goddess Durgā over the Buffalo-demon (*mahiṣāsura*); Durgā is honored on this last day, especially by the Rajputs, as Vijaya-lakṣmī. The whole celebration, collectively known as Durgā-pūjā, occupies the first nine *tithis* in the bright *pakṣa* of Aśvin (Aśvin *śukla* 1-9), ending on the morning of the tenth, the day dedicated to Vijaya-lakṣmī. On each night a *pūjā* is performed in honor of the Goddess under a different name. Though the festival as a whole is sacred to Durgā, the *pūjā* on the first night is offered to Mahākālī, the dark Mother, who stands for Ādyakālī. On each of the eight following nights the *pūjā* is offered to a secondary form of Durgā. The ninth and last night is sacred to Caṇḍikā or Caṇḍī, as Durgā *mahiṣamardinī.* On that evening a sacred fire is prepared, in which is thrown an animal offering (*bali*) that stands for the buffalo demon. To this fire, called "the fire of Kālī-devī," a special *āratī* is sung. It is from this very fire that the most effulgent form of the Goddess, Vijayalakṣmī, will be born in the middle of the night as an embodiment of the victory won by the great Goddess over the buffalo demon and the host of *asuras.*

What is characteristic of the Navarātrī sequence is that the eight nights sacred to Durgā are preceded by one night sacred to Mother Kālī, as Ādyakālī; Kālī also makes a brief but significant reappearance on the ninth night, on which she emerges from the flaming fire as *kālānalasamadyuti,* "Brilliant as the fires of the final dissolution," and Kālarātrī, "Night of Time" or "Night of Death."[8] Apparently her intervention is needed to ensure Durgā-Caṇḍikā's final victory.

Krishna Gopāla seems to play no part in the Navarātrī festival, though his birth is alluded to in a rather cryptic manner in the Caṇḍī-pātha (or *Devī-māhātmya*), which is sung during the ten-day celebration.[9] Yet the parallel between the myth underlying this performance and the story of the nine embryos as told in the *Harivaṃśa* account of Krishna's birth is, as we shall see, too striking to be ignored.

Textual Evidence

The most ancient textual evidence bearing on the Krishna Gopāla legend (if we except the reference found in Patañjali)[10] is found in the Pāli *Ghaṭa-jātaka.* In that Jātaka, Baladeva and Vāsudeva, sons of Upasāgara and Devagabbhā (Devagarbhā)—the latter clearly identical with Devakī—are said to live in the village of Govaḍḍhamana (Govardhana). The Govardhana region itself, which may be identified with modern-day Braj-bhūmi, is said to belong to Añjanī-devī, an elder sister of Baladeva and Vāsudeva. The very name of the goddess, which signifies her dark color, indicates that she is a form of Kālī.[11] Añjanī is otherwise known as a mountain goddess and as the mother of the divine monkey Hanumān, also a hill deity. In Braj tradition, Hanumān is credited with having brought the Govardhana hill from the Himalayas to the land of Braj.[12] As their elder sister and as the owner of the region in which they are born, Añjanī-devī's relation to the two male gods is one of dominance. Another potentially dominant figure is that of the two gods' mother, Devagarbhā (Devakī). It is to be noted that according to the Pāli version it is in the Govardhana area—in Braj itself—that Vāsudeva-Krishna, like his brother Baladeva, is born, and not, as in the purāṇic accounts, in Mathura.

In the *Harivaṃśa,* we find a detailed account of the circumstances in which Viṣṇu once took a double birth in the two brothers Balarāma (Baladeva) and Vāsudeva (Krishna). In chapter 45, Brahmā tells Viṣṇu that in order to save the Brahmins and the cows, Kaśyapa has been reborn as Vāsudeva (Krishna's purported father), and Kaśyapa's two wives, Aditi and Surabhī, have been reborn as Devakī and Rohiṇī.[13] The three of them now dwell on Mount Govardhana. There Viṣṇu himself should become incarnate in the wombs of both Kaśyapa's wives.

In *Harivaṃśa* 47, Viṣṇu goes to Pātāla in order to enlist the support of the great Goddess. The latter is portrayed under various names, such as Yoganidrā and Kālarūpiṇī, all of which refer to her dark form. Viṣṇu asks Kālī successively to place the six embryos she holds in her womb into the womb of Devakī. Viṣṇu will be the seventh and eighth embryos to be born from Devakī, whereas the Goddess herself should be the ninth, born from the *gopī* Yaśodā on the ninth day of the dark *pakṣa* of Śrāvaṇa. Viṣṇu adds that they will be born in the same month (Śrāvaṇa), and that they will change mothers. According to this account, the Goddess, under her manifestation as Durgā-Kātyāyanī, is Krishna's younger sister by one day.[14]

In what most manuscripts give as the following chapter but is treated as interpolative in the critical edition, Viṣṇu sings a hymn of praise to Devī, eulogizing her under a variety of names and epithets. Among others, she is addressed as twilight, night, day, sleep, and the night of death; the elder sister of Yama, clad in blue silken raiment (the Yamunā); without forms, (yet) having many forms; residing on peaks of mountains, by rivers, and in caves, forests, and groves; with peacock-feathered flags; living in the Vindhya mountains. She is also said to be the ninth day of the dark half of the month and the eleventh day of the light half;[15] Baladeva's sister; daughter of the cowherd Nanda; Aditi of the Devas; Surasā of the Nāgas; luster of light; Rohiṇī of the planets; receptacle of the Vasus; flame of fire; the supreme Brahman. Viṣṇu concludes with these words, which return us to the main text of the critical edition and conclude chapter 47:

> "Having deluded Kaṃsa, you enjoy the whole world,
> And I too shall live as a cowherd among kine:
> To accomplish my work, I shall be a cowherd of Kaṃsa."

Then Viṣṇu disappears and the Goddess gives her consent by saying, "So be it."

Why should the ninth day of the dark *pakṣa* be identified with the Goddess? The verse clearly distinguishes her dark form, associated with the dark *pakṣa*, from her luminous form, associated with the bright *pakṣa*. But according to the calendar it is the eighth day of the dark *pakṣa* that belongs to Kālī. The explanation must be sought in the Navarātrī sequence, analyzed above. We saw that the first night of Navarātrī belongs to Mahākālī or Adyakālī, the original Mother, whereas the ninth and final night is consecrated to Caṇḍikā and Kālī together, but especially to the latter, who is then associated with the terrible fire from which Vijayalakṣmī is born in the middle of the night. Careful scrutiny of the account of Krishna's birth as found in the *Harivaṃsa* shows that this account is based on the very same myth that underlies the Navarātrī performance. Ādyakālī, the original Mother of the eight embryos (corresponding to the eight "Durgās")[16] incarnated her full essence in the ninth, which was placed in Yaśodā's womb. Therefore the baby girl born of Yaśodā is the dark Goddess herself, who, significantly, is of the same hue as the baby Krishna born from Devakī. After Kaṃsa has killed the baby girl, however, the bright, terrifying form of the Goddess springs forth out of her dead body as out of a sheath.[17] In her luminous form, therefore, the Goddess is Krishna's younger sister, though under her essential Ādyakālī form she remains the "Eldest One,"[18] the source and holder of all the divine embryos and Krishna's original Mother. Thus it is only fitting that Krishna be born not in the bright *pakṣa* of Aśvin, which is dedicated to the luminous goddess Durgā, but in the dark *pakṣa* of Śrāvaṇa, a rainy month consecrated to the dark Goddess.

In the Vaiṣṇava Purāṇas, notably the *Viṣṇu* and the *Bhāgavata,* the role of Kālī in the Krishna *avatāra* is somewhat played down. In *Viṣṇu Purāṇa* 5. 1-2 Kālī, under the name Yoganidrā, is involved in the manifestation of Krishna, but she remains subservient to Viṣṇu. It is on his orders that she carries the embryos to Devakī's womb. Viṣṇu-Krishna is born on the eighth day of the dark *pakṣa* of Śrāvaṇa, as in the calendar and in the *Harivaṃśa,* and she herself is born on the ninth day from Yaśodā's womb. Viṣṇu, however, retains the initiative, and he does not sing a hymn of praise to the Goddess as he does in the *Harivaṃśa.* In *Viṣṇu Purāṇa* 5.2, the Goddess is called Jagaddhātrī, "Nurse of the universe," but this epithet applies to the effulgent form of Durgā-Kātyāyanī as she manifests herself to Kaṃsa after he has killed the baby girl. The role of Kālī is played down, whereas that of Durgā is emphasized. This emphasis is consistent with the Smārta tradition, which includes Durgā but not Kālī among the five great deities, and also with the Vaiṣṇava tradition, which tends to reject the cult of Kālī.

In *Bhāgavata Purāṇa* 10.2 the Goddess is called Kātyāyanī (Durgā) and Yogamāyā, and she is said to be Viṣṇu's own *śakti.* It is Viṣṇu himself who commands her to take birth in Yaśodā's womb and who prompts her to obey his orders by holding out inducements in the form of praise. In verse 10.19.6, in a different context, the Goddess is addressed as "Spouse of Viṣṇu, great Māyā, Śrī, Mother of the world": she is now identified with Śrī or Lakṣmī, Viṣṇu's own consort. In the *Bhāgavata* the domestication of the formidable Goddess is thus completed: her luminous form, Durgā, re-enters the Vaiṣṇava pantheon under the form of Lakṣmī. As Viṣṇu's consort, the Goddess all but loses her warlike attributes, which appear only in the scene of her encounter with Kaṃsa.

In the *Bālacarita* attributed to Bhāsa we can detect the same conflict between ancient traditions and Vaiṣṇava beliefs pertaining to Krishna's origins. In the second act Kaṃsa is confronted with the formidable Durgā-Kātyāyanī, who prepares to wreak her vengeance upon him. Durgā declares that she was "born into the house of

Kaṃsa" in order to destroy him, and that her followers have taken an oath to kill him. But how could Durgā be born in the family of Kaṃsa? It is by no means impossible. We know that Devakī is Kaṃsa's sister. A blood relation between Durgā and Kaṃsa, therefore, would imply that Devakī herself is a form of the Goddess. Devakī (alias Devagarbhā) is indeed said in the *Harivaṃśa* to be a reincarnation of Aditi, the Mother of the gods.[19] She is Krishna's subsidiary mother, as she receives in her womb his embryo, conceived by the original Mother, Kālī.[20]

The Emergence of Rādhā

The material analyzed so far suggests that long before the worship of Krishna Gopāla emerged as a distinct form of religion, the Vāsudeva-Baladeva cult included three distinct deities: beside Vāsudeva-Krishna and Baladeva (an ancient *nāga* or snake deity) stood a female figure who was a form of the great Goddess, either in her dark or her luminous aspect. In her dark form, as Kālī, she was conceived as the mother—or possibly the elder sister—of both male gods: she is thus definitely a dominant figure, connected with the dark world of primeval waters and *nāgas*. In her luminous form, an emanation from the dark, she is Durgā, the effulgent and terrifying goddess of war and victory, connected with both brothers as their sister but maintaining a special relation with Krishna as his protector. Dependent upon neither Krishna nor Baladeva, she therefore cannot have been conceived as the consort of either of them, at least in a Vaiṣṇava context.[21]

The relation of Krishna Gopāla with the great Goddess, both as Kālī and Durgā, together with the strong tantric flavor that pervaded his worship, must have contributed significantly to his gaining an ever greater popularity with the Hindu masses, but it also made more difficult his integration into the modern Vaiṣṇava pattern, with its profoundly mystical tendencies and its ethical sensitivity. On the one hand Krishna Gopāla, the much-beloved and much-married god, with his sixteen thousand *gopī* worshippers and his sixteen thousand wives, really had no divine "consort"—none at least who could be pictured as a devoted and obedient wife, as was Lakṣmī to Viṣṇu. On the other, he was plagued by the lingering presence of an all too powerful mother and/or a particularly warlike and ferocious sister, under whose protection he stood.

In various parts of India, wherever the cult of the Cowherd-god came to supersede the ancient non-sectarian Vaiṣṇavism of the Bhāgavatas, the problem of Krishna's connection with the Goddess had to be faced. Solutions, however, differed. Among the main centers of Krishna worship, Puri stands alone in retaining the archaic trio. The golden-complexioned female deity standing on the right of Jagannātha and now bearing the epic name Subhadrā (a designation of Arjuna's wife) is said to be the goddess Ekānaṃśā, a form of Durgā, and to be Jagannātha's sister.[22] Moreover, the Puri region is said to have belonged originally to the Mahā-bhairavī Ādiśakti (Durgā): even before Lord Jagannātha was established on the spot, the original temple was occupied by this goddess, under the name Vimalā-devī.[23]

As Jagannātha became ever more closely identified with Krishna Gopāla and as the archaic god Baladeva fell into oblivion as a separate deity, the original trio tended to become a pair: the dark-complexioned Jagannātha and the golden-hued goddess Ekānaṃśā-Durgā. In such a pairing the goddess inevitably came to be viewed as the *śakti* of Jagannātha, if not his consort. The immense popularity of Jagannātha in Northeastern India, especially among the low-caste population, and the fascination exerted on the masses by the Jagannātha-Ekānaṃśā pair, must have provided the pattern for the representation of the Rādhā-Krishna couple. It was in Eastern India, especially in Orissa and Bengal, and in Brindavan under the *gosvāmīs,* that the junction between the tantric and the Bhāgavata streams was accomplished in the early sixteenth century.[24] This fusion of the two great popular religious traditions of Northern India resulted in the near exclusion of Kālī from the new Vaiṣṇava synthesis in favor of the golden-skinned Durgā, and in the emergence of Rādhā as a substitute for Durgā-Ekānaṃśā, as Krishna's consort.

Caitanya, the founder of the Gauḍīya sect, was an ardent devotee of Jagannātha; it is well known that he spent the last part of his life in meditation within the Jagannātha temple. He does not seem to have made the Rādhā-Krishna couple the special object of his devotion, although in the *Caitanya-caritāmṛta* of Kṛṣṇadāsa (2.7) he is said to have revealed his true form (*svarūpa*) to Rāmānanda Rāya as the joint manifestation of "Rasarāja" (Krishna) and "Mahābhāva" (Rādhā). In other chapters of the same work (2.4-5), Caitanya's visits to two Krishnaite shrines are narrated. The Master is known to have paid devotional visits to the shrine of Gopīnātha in Remunā village in the Balasore district of Orissa and the Sākṣī-Gopāla of Kaṭak; Mādhavendra Purī's discovery of the Gopāla of Govardhana in the Braj country (i.e., Śrī Govardhannāthjī) is also narrated. In the first two shrines Krishna Gopāla is standing playing the flute in the pose known as *muralīdhāraṇa.* In the third he is standing in a cave underneath the Govardhana hill, which he lifts over his head with his upturned palm, in the *govardhanadhāraṇa* pose. In all three Krishna is standing alone; Rādhā is not represented, though in the Gopinātha shrine two *gopī* figures have been added later, one on each side of the god.

It was in Brindavan (Skt Vṛndāvaṇa), in the heart of the Braj country, that the *gopī* Rādhā, Krishna's sweetheart in popular tradition and the very embodiment of pure love (*mahābhāva*) for Krishna, came to be established as the latter's *śakti* and consort in the theological and cultic sphere. The treatises of the Gauḍīya sect, written by the *gosvāmīs* of Brindavan, disciples of Caitanya, conceived her as the supreme Lord's *hlādinī śakti,* his "energy of bliss," and elevated her to the rank of the Ādyaśakti, the cosmic energy, the primeval mother of the world. Such a metamorphosis took place away from Puri, where the cult of the Jagannātha trio or the Jagannātha-Ekānaṃśā pair was still dominant. Yet it could only take place in a tradition deeply imbued with tantric thought and practice, as was that of the *gosvāmīs,* who had come from Bengal to Brindavan.[25] It is well known that in Bengal Krishna devotion had developed under the prevailing influence of the *Gītagovinda* of Jayadeva and the songs composed by the Maithilī poet Vidyāpati: it is these two great poets (to whom the Bengali poet Caṇḍidās must be added) who had molded the character of Rādhā in Bengal and given expression to the strong emotionalism that characterizes the Gauḍīya form of *bhakti.* Their verses, the most brilliant Krishna poetry composed before Sūr Dās, demonstrate in a striking manner the absolute power of perfect love over the heart of Lord Krishna, a love that makes Rādhā his mistress in the full sense of the word. It is likely that Rādhā's popularity in Braj itself—as the "darling" (*lālī*) of all who dwell there—also played a part in her elevation to the rank she occupies today in Gauḍīya piety.

It is a well-known fact that in parallel Krishna sects, such as the *Puṣṭi-sampradāya* founded by Vallabhācārya in Govardhana, the presence of Rādhā at Krishna's side was not readily accepted.[26] But the lingering association of the Goddess with Krishna is acknowledged by modern Vallabhites, who interpret the water pot draped in a red cloth, which should always be placed before the god's image, as a symbolical representation of Devī; similarly, the round cushions placed on either side of the image are said to stand, when perceived with devotional feeling, for the breasts of Yaśodā. Krishna's consort is said to be Svāminījī, who may be interpreted as either Rukmiṇī or Rādhā or both, but who rarely stands by his side. It is the same with the other most popular forms of Viṣṇu-Krishna in Western India, Dvārakādhīśa of Dvārakā and Mathurā and Viṭṭhala or Viṭhobā of Paṇḍharpūr in Maharashtra: the god's wives stand in a separate shrine, next to or behind that of the god. Yet in Paṇḍharpūr as well as in Dvārakā, Krishna's first wife, Rukmiṇī, is said to have arrived on the spot *before* her Lord, a fact that is supposed to account for her special establishment in an older shrine outside the main temple.[27]

In the Rādhā-Krishna cult as it develops in Brindavan and Bengal in the sixteenth century, it seems that the worship of the Cowherd-god and that of the great Goddess have coalesced. The ever-youthful lover, Krishna Gopāla, ultimately comes to recognize in his fair lady-love, the *gopī* Rādhā, a new, more reassuring, and more bewitching form of the great Goddess Durgā, whom he had once known as a sister. His original link with the primeval Mother, Kālī, is more or less forgotten. Devakī herself tends to fade into oblivion, whereas the tender-hearted *gopī* Yaśodā is given pride of place in popular devotion as the child Krishna's doting mother. As the Lord's *hlādinī śakti,* Rādhā has renounced the fearsome *bhairavī* form that Durgā could still manifest, but she keeps Durgā's radiant beauty as the gentle milkmaid whose heart is aflame with love for Krishna. In modern times the Rādhā-Krishna pair of divine lovers has taken hold of the popular imagination, especially, but not only, in Bengal. Rādhā has won: but should her victory not be interpreted as the final victory of the ancient, all-powerful Goddess, mother, sister, and protector of the Cowherd-god?

II.

Rādhā

The Divine Duality of Rādhā and Krishna

BARBARA STOLER MILLER

Clouds thicken the sky.
Tamāla trees darken the forest.
The night frightens him.
Rādhā, you take him home!
They leave at Nanda's order,
Passing trees in thickets on the way,
Until secret passions of Rādhā and Mādhava
Triumph on the Jumna riverbank.

GĪTAGOVINDA 1.1

Who is Rādhā? A cowherdess who seduces the divine child Krishna? A worshipping woman abandoned by her divine adolescent lover? A goddess who triumphs over her consort? The images of her are varied and elusive throughout Indian literature, but they invariably reflect her unique relation to Krishna in his form as cosmic cowherd lover. The elaboration of her character in the *Gītagovinda* includes distinctive details mentioned in the stray verses about her that are preserved in anthologies.[1] Jayadeva's heroine is neither a wife nor a worshipping rustic playmate. She is a jealous, solitary, proud female who is Krishna's exclusive partner in a secret love, a union that is contrasted with his communal sexual play with the entire group of cowherdesses.

Her uniqueness and her pride are central to some of the earliest references to her, in Hāḷa's *Sattasaī* and Ānandavardhana's *Dhvanyāloka:*

> Krishna, removing cow-dust from Rādhikā
> with the breath of your mouth,
> you sweep away the high esteem
> these other cowherdesses have for you.
>
> "Gracious love, Rādhā is difficult indeed to please—
> her tears fall even as you wipe them away
> with the cloth that covered some true love's loins;
> woman's hearts are hard, so enough flattery! Leave me alone!"
> He was told this whenever Hari tried to placate her—
> May he grant you his blessing!

Though Rādhā has no known identity apart from Krishna, it is clear that her union with him basically alters the structure of Krishna's divine personality. The nature of the love that Krishna embodies to save the world in the Kali Yuga changes in the presence of Rādhā's demanding power. It is this relationship that I shall attempt to illuminate here by focusing on the dual form of Rādhā-mādhava, in which the drama of Krishna's encounter with Rādhā in the *Gītagovinda* is contained.[2] Let me begin by summarizing the aesthetic theory of memory (*smara, smaraṇa, smṛti*) that is dramatized by Kālidāsa and conceptualized by Abhinavagupta, in order to give a new perspective for viewing the aesthetic process by which this duality is resolved in the *Gītagovinda.*

The importance of memory in the thought process is universally recognized in Western and Indian epistemology.[3] What I am stressing here is the aesthetics of memory, linked to love, as a mode of knowing within aesthetic and religious experience. It is significant that memory (*smara*) is a major epithet of the god of love. The association between love and memory is known as early as the *Atharva Veda,*[4] whose hymns include a love-charm in which the female speaker asks the gods to send Memory to make a certain man burn for her. *Smara* and *kāma,* in fact, seem to be the only pre-epic names for love.

In Sanskrit poetry an act of remembering is a conventional technique for relating the antithetical modes of frustrated and fulfilled love (*vipralambha-śṛṅgāra* and *saṃbhoga-śṛṅgāra*). For example, in the *Caurapañcāśikā,* attributed to Bilhaṇa,[5] each of the formulaic verses is a miniature painting of the princess with whom the poet enjoyed an illicit love. For his recklessness in this love he was condemned to death. At the point of death, his final thoughts are details of his mistress's beauty:

> Even now,
> I remember her eyes
> restlessly closed after love,
> her slender body limp,
> fine cloths and heavy hair loose—
> a wild goose in a thicket of lotuses of passion.
> I'll recall her in my next life
> and even at the end of time!

By remembering the exquisite details of her physical beauty and her behavior in love, he brings her into his presence and they are mentally reunited.

Abhinavagupta's interest is in the aesthetic implications of the act of remembering. In his commentary on the *Rasasūtra* of the *Nāṭyaśāstra*[6] he cites the final verse from the opening scene of the fifth act of *Abhijñānaśākuntala.* The scene is a prelude to Śakuntalā's rejection by King Duṣyanta. In it Duṣyanta and his *vidūṣaka* Māḍhavya hear and discuss the song that is being sung by Haṃsapadikā, whom the king once loved and forgot. The king muses:

> Why, on discerning the meaning of the song, am I filled with such powerful longing—I am not separated (*viraha*) from anyone I love.

> Seeing rare beauty, hearing echoes of sweet sounds,
> even a happy man becomes strangely uneasy,
> then dim traces in his heart move him to remember
> loves of a former life, buried deep in his being.

Abhinava explains that Duṣyanta's experience is an aesthetic one in which his memory is brought to life by hearing the music; his present experience recalls vague, long-buried impressions of a former pleasure, heightened now by distance and artistic evocation.

Memory is recognized throughout Vaisnava literature as a way of knowing Krishna.[7] In the *Bhāgavata Purāṇa* (10.32.20), when the cowherdesses accuse him of cruelty for deserting them, Krishna answers:

> I, the embodiment of mercy—how can I be cruel, and especially to my devotees? No, never. My disappearance is only a veil

> that I draw in order to nourish yearning and love for me by the fire of separation. As a poor man hitting by chance on a treasure and again losing it is constantly brooding over it, so I wish that my devotee should not for a moment forget me.

Later, when Uddhava returns to Vraja with Krishna's message, it is the intensely detailed memory of him as the god of love that stimulates one cowherdess to sing the sensual *bhramaragīta,* which Uddhava hears as evidence of the cowherdesses' devotion (*Bh. P.* 10.47). In the later Vaiṣṇava theology based on the *rasa* theory of Sanskrit poetics, memory is an important way (*smaraṇa-mārga*) of knowing Krishna by inwardly contemplating his eternal and transcendental sports. [8]

In Jayadeva's *Gītagovinda,* memory is a complex set of mental processes that integrates religious, erotic, and aesthetic meaning, forming a whole through which the audience can share the poet's experience of the divine love of Rādhā and Krishna. This role of memory is made explicit in an opening verse of the poem (1.4) and again in the signature verse of the final song (12.19):

> If remembering Hari enriches your heart,
> if his arts of seduction arouse you,
> listen to Jayadeva's speech
> in these sweet soft lyrical songs.
>
> Make your heart sympathetic to Jayadeva's splendid speech!
> Remembering Hari's feet is elixir against fevers of this dark
> time.

It is by sharing in the mutual memories that Rādhā and Krishna have of their original secret meeting that the audience learns to appreciate and understand the unique relationship of the Rādhā-mādhava pair. Aesthetic memory breaks through the logic of everyday experience—it obliterates distances, reverses chronologies, fuses what is ordinarily separate. What makes Jayadeva's vision so powerful is that Krishna participates in the world of memory as subject as well as object. Krishna remembers Rādhā in the same kind of sensual detail in which she remembers him. His memory makes him as vulnerable to her possessive, overwhelming power as she is to his—as he again declares his love for her he gives no rationalization for the cruelty of his desertion because he too has suffered in the fire of separation.

The original encounter of Rādhā and Krishna in the dark forest flashes in the opening verse of the *Gītagovinda* like an enigmatic play-within-a-play. The imagery of the scene presents itself to the minds of the audience, leaving latent impressions that are intensified in the course of the lyric drama. The verse begins with an alliterative description of the clouds that veil the sky (*meghair meduram ambaram . . .*)

"Clouds thicken the sky.
Tamāla trees darken the forest.
The night frightens him.
Rādhā, you take him home!"
They leave at Nanda's order,
Passing trees in thickets on the way,
Until secret passions of Rādhā and Mādhava
Triumph on the Jumna riverbank.

The place and the time in which the action occurs in this verse are clear, but the characters and their relationship are ambiguous. This ambiguity has encouraged varied interpretations of Jayadeva's meaning in commentaries and later versions.[9] Most interpretations turn on the identification of the speaker of the first half of the verse and on the reference to Krishna's "fear" and Rādhā's role as his guide through the dark forest. The opening verse is variously attributed to Krishna, Rādhā, Nanda, and even the friend of Rādhā. The several voices that resonate in the verse all direct the sexual energies of Krishna toward Rādhā, but each voice shifts the quality of the darkness and the nature of Krishna's fear.

Kumbhakarna, the most influential literary commentator on the *Gītagovinda,* devotes considerable attention to every word in this verse in his *Rasikapriyā.*[10] He interprets the first half of the verse as the talk of the lover Krishna to Rādhā, to whom he speaks about himself in the third person (*imam* = *mām* according to Kumbha) in the veiled language of seduction, urging her to leave Nanda's presence with him. For Kumbha Krishna is not a child afraid of the dark, but a lover arousing emotions of fear to stimulate more intense passion.[11] This interpretation, like the Vaiṣṇava scholastic interpretation of Caitanyadāsa, is concerned with the impropriety of Nanda's active participation in the scene. Jayadeva is certainly not explicit here—*nandanideśataḥ* may mean "from the presence of Nanda" or "for the sake of joy" as well as "at Nanda's order." Yet I share with other commentators the view that Jayadeva intentionally places Nanda in the scene to add the dimension of Krishna's youthful vulnerability and to dramatize his transformation into a sexually potent adolescent through his encounter with Rādhā. This transformation is made explicit in the *Brahmavaivarta Purāṇa* version of the episode[12] and in a Garhwal painting of the opening verse, in which Nanda is depicted as a tall figure towering above the cowherd children and commanding Rādhā to take Krishna through the woods, and the scene of their love-making appears as a clearing among the dark trees.[13]

The darkness of the night in the forest is described in this verse in voluptuous imagery that is woven through the entire poem. It is in this secret, sexually stimulating environment that Rādhā and Krishna enact the initial triumph of their divine love and then suffer the long night of separation that ends in their reunion. They follow the path through the forest as a pair and the triumph of their passions occurs in this dual form (Rādhā-mādhava). The "home" to which Rādhā brings Krishna is a forest thicket (*kuñja*), the secret place of their divine love, in which they meet again at the end of their journey.

It is this encounter that Krishna returns to in his memory in the crucial opening verse of the third canto of the *Gītagovinda:*

> Krishna, demon Kaṃsa's foe,
> feeling Rādhā bind his heart with chains
> of memories buried in worldly lives,
> abandoned the beautiful cowherd girls.

The distance between the original experience and his memory of it is filled by a series of evocative songs that set Krishna's encounter with Rādhā in a definite religious and seasonal context.

The compounding of Krishna with Rādhā into a dual divinity is central to Jayadeva's conception of Krishna, not as an incarnation (*avatāra*) of Viṣṇu, but as the source (*avatārin, daśavidharūpa, daśākṛtikṛt*) of all the incarnate forms he himself assumes in order to save the world.[14] Jayadeva's Krishna is addressed as Jagadīśa, the loving compassionate "Lord of the World," a title that must be a variant of Jagannātha, the name of the complex composite Buddhist-Śaiva-Vaiṣṇava god of Puri.[15] Krishna's common epithet Bhagavān, Lord, which is prominent in the *Mahābhārata,* the *Harivaṃśa,* and various Purāṇas, and which is in the title of the *Bhagavadgītā,* is notably absent from Jayadeva's poem. Its absence, along with that of such basic Bhāgavata terms as *dharma, karma,* and *bhakti,* distinguishes Jayadeva's conception of Krishna from that of the divine object of the orthodox Bhāgavata cult. The orthodox theology that focused on the immeasurable superiority of the Lord, and on the human problem of relating to Bhagavān, was explored from this perspective. Devotion meant submission to Bhagavān in a loving relationship that was most powerful in the anguish of separation shared by all devotees. The orthodox cult was basically antithetical to Jayadeva's notion of Krishna's exclusive, erotic relationship with a single consort as the supreme expression of his love and as the model for the relation between Krishna and his devotee.[16]

In the song that follows the invocation of Krishna's cosmic power, events from various Vaiṣṇava myths are evoked to express Krishna's heroic prowess. Then Spring is described as the cruel time in which Krishna ignores Rādhā in his lust for all the beautiful women of the forest. This sensuous song is sung, as Jayadeva's signature verse says, "to evoke the potent memory of Hari's feet, coloring the forest in springtime mood heightened by Love's presence." It is followed by explicit descriptions of Krishna's sexual play with the cowherdesses of Vṛndāvana in the circular *rāsa* dance.[17]

It is the music and imagery of these songs that bring Krishna into dramatic focus and into intimacy with the audience, which is stimulated again and again by Rādhā's friend, a messenger who deepens our vision of Krishna:

> When he quickens all things
> to create bliss in the world,
> his soft black sinuous lotus limbs
> begin the festival of love
> and beautiful cowherd girls wildly
> wind him in their bodies.
> Friend, in spring young Hari plays
> like erotic mood incarnate.
>
> While Hari roamed in the forest
> making love to all the women,
> Rādhā's hold on him loosened
> and envy drove her away.
> But anywhere she tried to retreat
> in her thicket of wild vines,
> sounds of bees buzzing circles overhead
> depressed her—
> she told her friend the secret.

Rādhā's secret is her vivid memory of minute details of how Krishna looked as he danced in the *rāsalīlā* with the other cowherdesses (cf. figure 1) playing seductively to mock her, she says, and admits:

> My heart values his vulgar ways,
> refuses to admit my rage,
> feels strangely elated,
> and keeps denying his guilt.
> When he steals away without me
> to indulge his craving
> for more young women,
> my perverse heart
> only wants Krishna back.
> What can I do?

She sings her fantasy of making love with Krishna and remembers when he saw her watching him playing in the forest with the village beauties:

> The enchanting flute in his hand
> lies fallen under coy glances;
> sweat of love wets his cheeks;
> his bewildered face is smiling—
> when Krishna sees me watching him
> playing in the forest
> in a crowd of village beauties,
> I feel the joy of desire.

The power of Rādhā's memory is too strong for Krishna to resist. It penetrates his neglectful mind and binds him in chains of memories of their relations as Śrī and Vāsudeva in former incarnations, so that he in turn is made to suffer, haunted by details of her beauty in love when he cannot find her:

> Her joyful responses to my touch,
> trembling liquid movements of her eyes,
> fragrance from her lotus mouth,
> a sweet ambiguous stream of words,
> nectar from her red berry lips—
> even when the sensuous objects are gone,
> my mind holds on to her in a trance.
> How does the wound of her desertion deepen?

FIGURE 1.

Rādhā Remembers

Illustration for a manuscript of the *Gītagovinda.*
Mewar, Rajasthan, ca. 1660.

Figure 1.

Although no specific text accompanies this painting, it seems clearly to refer to one of the passages in the *Gītagovinda* in which Rādhā remembers Krishna's *rāsa līlā*. Rādhā, seated at the lower left, recalls the scene to her friend, and as she does so the landscape echoes the flow of her thoughts. The river on whose bank she sits, the Jumna, is the same whose banks hosted the circle dance, and the vine that arches over her head strains toward a nearby tree just as her memory reaches toward Krishna. Indeed the tree itself bends in his direction, as if in attraction or homage.

Homage comes from the opposite side of the painting as well, from two pairs of seers whose identity, aside from the fact that one pair is earthly and the other divine, is not plain. And in the middle, directly beneath the full moon and etched against a circular background (the *rāsamaṇḍala*) of brilliant red, is the unforgettable scene itself. Krishna strikes his flute-playing pose as the *gopīs* surround him with caresses, stretching their arms in his direction as do so many of the figures in this illustration. His peacock crown, pearl ornaments, and tinkling waistband are rendered with the most sensitive eye for detail, and the *gopīs'* vestments, like those of Rādhā and her confidante, are given a translucent quality that brings to life the contemporary *zenānā* costumes of Mewar.

— J.W. and J.S.H.

It is Krishna here who meditates on Rādhā and ironically reminds the god of love that it is not ash-smeared Śiva, but Krishna, his lovelorn body smeared with sandalwood powder, that he is tormenting. He tells Love that it is pointless to attack him, for Rādhā, the "living goddess of love's triumph" (*anaṅga-jaya-jaṅgama-devatā,* 3.15), has already defeated him. In his separation from Rādhā, Krishna, the embodiment of Love's creative sensuality, becomes the object of Love's arrows. The paradox of Rādhā's power over Krishna plays throughout the *Gītagovinda,* culminating in their reunion, from which she emerges as a triumphant "heroine whose lover is in her power" (*svādhīnabhartṛkā,* 12.11).

In view of the orthodox Vaiṣṇava insistence on the ultimate superiority of the Lord, it is significant that the sacred legends of Jayadeva's life invoke Krishna's own divine intervention to justify Krishna's submission to Rādhā at the end of the *Gītagovinda.* The legends relate that Jayadeva was a wandering mendicant whose ascetic life ended under the influence of Padmāvatī, a dancer in the Jagannātha Temple of Puri, in whose company he worshipped Jagannātha and composed the *Gītagovinda.* When Jayadeva conceived the climax of Krishna's supplication to Rādhā as a command for Rādhā to place her foot on Krishna's head in a symbolic gesture of victory, the poet hesitated to compose the verse, in deference to Krishna. Jayadeva went to bathe and in his absence Krishna himself appeared in the poet's guise to write the couplet; then Krishna ate the food that Padmāvatī had prepared for Jayadeva and left. When the poet returned he realized that he had received divine sanction to sing about his vision of Krishna's relation to Rādhā:

> Place your foot on my head—
> a sublime flower destroying poison of love!
> Let your foot quell the harsh sun
> burning its fiery form in me to torment Love.
>   Rādhā, cherished love,
>   abandon your baseless pride!
>   Love's fire burns my heart—
>   bring wine in your lotus mouth!
>
> Punish me, lovely fool!
> Bite me with your cruel teeth!
> Chain me with your creeper arms!
> Crush me with your hard breasts!

Angry goddess, don't weaken with joy!
Let Love's despised arrows
pierce me to sap my life's power!

The signature verse of the song (10.9) says that Jayadeva sang it to delight Padmāvatī. Padmāvatī may refer to the dancer of the legend, but the legend itself is probably a veiled allusion to Jayadeva's worship of Krishna's consort Padmāvatī, whose lotus feet are his acknowledged inspiration at the opening of the poem:[18]

Jayadeva, wandering king of bards
who sing at Padmāvatī's lotus feet,
was obsessed in his heart
by rhythms of the goddess of speech,
and he made this lyrical poem
from tales of the passionate play
when Krishna loved Śrī.

By portraying the emotion of Krishna's frustrated love and his worshipful submission at Rādhā's feet, Jayadeva establishes unusual correspondences among Krishna, himself, and his audience. The audience is able to feel emotion from Krishna's perspective and to share the delight he experiences in Rādhā's passionate triumph over him.[19] It is characteristic of Vaiṣṇava devotional texts that Krishna may be enticed by the love of the devotee and reciprocate in passionate ways, but the intensity of Krishna's expressed emotion in the *Gītagovinda* is quite different from the pranks and erotic play and preaching he uses to convince the cowherdesses of his love in more orthodox works like the *Bhāgavata Purāṇa*. After Rādhā's triumph over him, Krishna stays to ornament her according to her command. This scene is the final song of tee *Gītagovinda* and Jayadeva promises that those whose hearts are sympathetic to it and who remember Hari's feet have an elixir against fevers of the Kali Yuga. And the audience who has heard Jayadeva's song knows that Krishna's feet dance to Rādhā's rhythm.

The intense sexual experience between Rādhā and Krishna is Jayadeva's means of expressing the complexities of divine and human love. Sexuality is not merely a metaphor through which Jayadeva is speaking about something "spiritual." But the sensual eroticism of the poetry has led many commentators, medieval and modern, to interpret the relation between Rādhā and Krishna allegorically. Jayadeva's vision of their relationship occurred in an environment of religious complexity. The *Gītagovinda* resonates with images and concepts from a wide range of literature, including Śrīvaisnava theology, Caryagīti poetry, and Śākta mythology.[20] But the rich layers of form and meaning that characterize Jayadeva's work are lost in allegorical interpretations that reduce the relationship to a single idea: Rādhā as the paradigm of the devotee's love for the god, or Rādhā as the incarnation of heavenly wisdom whose purity is contrasted with the lasciviousness of the cowherdesses, who represent the senses diverting Krishna from wisdom.[21]

The great nineteenth-century Bengali writer Bankim Chandra Chatterji found in Krishna the perfect embodiment of the ideal culture-hero, and when he contrasted the representation of the life of Krishna in the *Mahābhārata*, the *Bhāgavata Purāṇa*, and the *Gītagovinda*, he regretted that the obvious allegory of the relation of spirit (*puruṣa*) to matter (*prakṛti*) represented by Krishna's love with the cowherdesses had vanished in the *Gītagovinda*.[22]

> From the beginning to the end, it does not contain a single expression of manly feeling—of womanly feeling there is a great deal—or a single elevated sentiment. The poet has not a single new truth to teach. Generally speaking, it is the poets (religious or profane) who teach us the great moral truths which render man's life a blessing to his kind; but Jayadeva is a poet of another stamp. I do not deny his high poetical merits in a certain sense, exquisite imagery, tender feeling, and unrivalled power of expression, but that does not make him less the poet of an effeminate and sensual race.

Bankim's unease over the sensuality and "effeminate" nature of the *Gītagovinda* must reflect his unstated perception of the androgynous voice with which Jayadeva aesthetically recreates the relationship of Rādhā and Krishna. Their parallel emotional states and fantasies express the emotional dependence that binds them into a dual divinity whose nature compromises Krishna's manly dominance.[23]

The dual character of Indian divinities is an ancient pattern whose examples are many and varied. With a few exceptions, like Heaven and Earth (*Dyāva-pṛthivī*) and Night and Dawn (*Naktā-uṣasā*), the oldest Vedic double deities are couples of male divinities, clearly distinguished from the post-Vedic pairs of gods and their consorts.[24] Krishna's composite forms include his pairing with his elder brother Balarāma as a single incarnation of Viṣṇu, one representing a white hair and one representing a black hair of the supreme god,[25] and his pairing with his cousin Arjuna as Naranārāyaṇa[26] Both these pairs reflect the Vedic model. The nature of Krishna's pairing with Rādhā is obviously different, but the Rādhā-mādhava duality resembles these other composite forms insofar as Rādhā functions as a vital complement to Krishna's cosmic power and dark color. In no case is the composite form made of absolutely balanced, symmetrical parts. The relations are always ambiguous, shifting, and intentionally paradoxical, as symbolized by Lord Krishna's being Balarāma's younger brother, Arjuna's charioteer, and Rādhā's worshipping servant.

Krishna's intimate relation to the cosmos is mystically expressed by Jayadeva's vision of the suffering that Krishna shares with Rādhā in the frustration of their love. Rādhā's sympathetic understanding of Krishna's emotions softens her angry pride and overcomes her psychic inhibition to express her sexual power over Krishna. Her triumphant, ecstatic reunion with him within the forest thicket in springtime consummates the experience of their separate passions emerging from and merging into the erotic mood of their relationship. For Jayadeva this erotic mood is the soul of Krishna's nature, fulfilled by his union with Rādhā:[27]

> All his deep-locked emotions broke when he saw Rādhā's face,
> like sea waves cresting when the full moon appears.
> She saw her passion reach the soul of Hari's mood—
> the weight of joy strained his face; Love's ghost haunted him.
>
> When her friends had gone,
> smiles spread on Rādhā's lips
> while love's deep fantasies
> struggled with her modesty.
> Seeing the mood in Rādhā's heart,
> Hari spoke to his love—
> her eyes were fixed
> on his bed of buds and tender shoots.
>
> Leave lotus footprints on my bed of tender shoots, loving Rādhā!
>
> Let my place be ravaged by your tender feet!
> Nārāyaṇa is faithful now. Love me, Rādhikā!

As sympathetic witnesses to the relationship of Rādhā and Krishna, Jayadeva's audience shares the poet's secret participation in the consummation of divine love—the culminating erotic, aesthetic, religious experience of their divine duality.

A Sanskrit Portrait: Rādhā in the Plays of Rūpa Gosvāmī

DONNA MARIE WULFF

The dramatic treatment of the love of Rādhā and Krishna by Rūpa Gosvāmī, a prominent disciple of Caitanya, departs in certain striking ways from the purāṇic and poetic accounts with which Western students of this tradition are familiar. Unlike the *Gītagovinda*, for example, Rūpa's *Vidagdhamādhava* [VM] gives a prominent place to Rādhā's mother-in-law Jaṭilā and to her son Abhimanyu, Rādhā's husband, whose repeated threat to take Rādhā to Mathura serves as an ever-present backdrop for the dramatic action. Moreover, Rādhā's jealousy of the women with whom Krishna dallies in the *Gītagovinda* is in the same play given concrete focus in the figure of a single rival, Candrāvalī. Even more conspicuously divergent from the standard purāṇic accounts is Rūpa's identification of Krishna's wives at Dvārakā with the *gopīs* of Vṛndāvaṇa, worked out elaborately in his longer and more complex *Lalitamādhava* [LM], in which he effectively collapses the two major phases of Krishna's career.[1]

In spite of such obvious differences, however, a sensitive reading of Rūpa's dramas reveals significant points of continuity with earlier accounts of Krishna's life. Rūpa's provision of a specific rival for Rādhā, for example, together with his detailed depiction of each successive phase in the unfolding love of Rādhā and Krishna, simply extends the process of increasing elaboration and specificity that one sees in the development from the *Harivaṃśa* through the *Viṣṇu* and the *Bhāgavata Purāṇas* to the *Gītagovinda*.

Rūpa's sources are many: although his position was that of private secretary to a Muslim ruler, Hussein Shah of Bengal, he clearly had accessible to him the entire range of Sanskrit learning, especially literature and poetics. His immense erudition is evident from the copious literary allusions and Sanskrit figures of speech that adorn his dramas, as well as from his highly elaborate theoretical treatises, in which he appropriated the complex structure and terminology of the *rasa* theory of the classical Sanskrit theater in order to articulate a new vision of the devotional life. He was also heir to the medieval lyrics in

Bengali and Brajabuli on the love of Rādhā and Krishna, and he may well have witnessed dramatic enactments of Krishna's deeds,[2] either in Bengal or in the sacred region of Braj, to which he repaired at Caitanya's direction, and in which he lived and wrote for the remaining decades of his life.

In his theory of *bhaktirasa,* Rūpa delineates five primary modes (*bhāvas*) through which the devotee may relate to Krishna: *śānta,* contemplative adoration of the transcendent Lord; *dāsya,* humble servitude to the divine master; *sakhya,* intimate companionship with the beloved friend; *vātsalya,* parental affection for the adorable child; and *mādhurya,* passionate love for the supreme lover. If one comes to the dramas with some knowledge of this general theory, which centers almost exclusively upon Krishna, one will naturally expect them to illustrate these five modes of relating to the Lord. One may well be initially perplexed, then, by the plays themselves. First, although the various *bhāvas* are indeed represented in them, it is not these, but the successive phases in the love of Rādhā and Krishna, that provide the major structuring principle. Furthermore, there are numerous indications throughout the dramas that Rādhā's significance for Rūpa goes far beyond that of a model of devotion. In what follows, we shall review this evidence as we explore Rūpa's vision of Rādhā and her relation to Krishna.

Rādhā as Model of Devotion

There is no disputing the fact that Rādhā is for Rūpa an ideal devotee. Indeed, it is hardly possible to speak of Rādhā in his dramas apart from her love for Krishna. In a telling verse (VM 3.49) in which she is spoken of as his ornament, an image that seems unambiguously to subordinate her to him, she is said to be herself rendered beautiful by her love. Moreover, throughout the plays it is the explicitly devotional quality of this love, together with its remarkable intensity, that elicits repeated comment. Through such comments the plays' main secondary characters—especially Paurṇamāsī, the venerable go-between who personifies the full-moon night; her granddaughter and companion, Nāndīmukhī; and Vṛndā, the goddess of the forest—communicate Rūpa's religious views and emotions to the audience or reader.

Throughout the two dramas, Rādhā's love expresses itself spontaneously in religious modes that bear considerable significance for devotion. A charming verse contrasts her incessant preoccupation with Krishna, whom she at first endeavors vainly to forget, with the transitory states attained by the arduous efforts of *munis* and *yogīs:*

> Seeking to meditate for a moment upon Krishna,
> The sage wrests his mind from the objects of sense;
> This child draws her mind away from Him
> To fix it on mere worldly things.
> The *yogī* yearns for a tiny flash of Krishna in his heart;
> Look—this foolish girl strives to banish Him from hers!
> (VM 2.17)[3]

The obverse of Rādhā's single-minded concentration is her utter obliviousness to the world: Lalitā notes with astonishment this sublime condition as she accompanies to a tryst the distracted Rādhā, who has put all her ornaments on wrong.[4] The image of a *yoginī* is similarly evoked by a tender scene toward the end of the second act of the *Vidagdhamādhava* in which Rādhā's intense desire to see Krishna culminates in a supreme effort to make him appear before her eyes by meditating (*praṇidhāna*).

Further indications of the intensity and devotional quality of Rādhā's love are the numerous passages in both dramas in which she expresses her inability to live if she cannot meet Krishna (e.g., VM 3.12; LM 3.27-28). At the end of the second act of the *Vidagdhamādhava,* as she contemplates suicide because of Krishna's rejection of her, she asks Viśākhā to allow her body to remain in Vṛndāvaṇa with her vine-like arm on the trunk of the *tamāla* tree.[5] Early in the next act, in response to Paurṇamāsī's words of discouragement, she expresses a similar aspiration: that she might die and be reborn as a bee on Krishna's forest garland, wholly intent upon his redolent face (VM 3.16). Classical Sanskrit dramas abound in examples of pining heroines who express the desire to take their own lives; here, however, the motif gains new significance, for Rādhā's utterances are indicative of a profound religious devotion that extends even beyond death.

Separation in the *Vidagdhamādhava* is always relatively short-lived, and Rādhā's morbid fantasies never materialize. Krishna's departure for Mathurā in the third act of the *Lalitamādhava,* however, proves to be too much for her to bear.[6] After giving expression to her extreme grief with such poignancy that Paurṇamāsī declares the entire world to be plunged into a vast ocean of pathos without an island (LM 3.23), the disconsolate Rādhā, at the urging of her friends, begins a desperate search.[7] In her complete obsession with Krishna, she longs for anything that has had contact with him. His necklace of *guñjā* berries becomes a companion in her misery: having graced Krishna's chest as has she herself, it too is now abandoned to roll in despair on the path (LM 3.37). Even Rādhā's former rival Candrāvalī is eagerly but vainly sought by her. All else having failed, Rādhā takes refuge in the dark waters of the Yamunā, which resemble Krishna's black limbs, and a voice from the heavens announces that she has pierced the orb of the sun.[8] Apparent death here is merely a change of form, and it is in the guise of the lovely Satyabhāmā, daughter of Satrājit, that Rādhā is subsequently reunited with Krishna in a new Vṛndāvana in the heart of Dvārakā, his western fastness. Clearly neither Rūpa nor Rādhā could tolerate the separation brought about by Krishna's departure from Vṛndāvana.

Rādhā's role as model *bhakta* is indicated even more clearly by her responses to the name Krishna. Even before her first meeting with him, she shows unmistakable emotion whenever her friends mention him by name, as they do deliberately. It is in this connection that Rūpa reveals most unambiguously the intimate relation between Rādhā's emotion and the experience of ardent Vaiṣṇava devotees. When Nāndīmukhī describes Rādhā's *pūrvarāga,* the first blossoming of her love, by enumerating the effects of Krishna's name on her (VM 1.14.30-31), Paurṇamāsī deems Rādhā's response fitting and eloquently expresses her own feelings in the following oft-quoted verse:

> Dancing on the tip of your tongue,
> they make you long for myriads of mouths,
> Alighting in the hollow of your ear,
> they make you wish for ears in plenitude,
> And when they reach the doorway to your heart,
> they still the turbulence of all the senses:
> "Krish-na"—just two syllables—
> yet how much nectar do they not contain? (VM 1.15)

By means of Paurṇamāsī's endorsement, Rādhā's response is explicitly established as an ideal for Vaiṣṇava devotion. That Rādhā also relates more actively to this name of her beloved is indicated by a punning verse in which her friend Viśākhā describes her as constantly uttering the name Krishna (VM 2.38). Rūpa thus links Rādhā with Krishna *bhaktas* not only on the level of emotion, but in the realm of ritual as well, for the repeated utterance or singing of Krishna's name has been a central element in Gauḍīya Vaiṣṇava practice, both individual and communal, at least since the time of Caitanya.[9]

Rādhā as Object of Devotion

Krishna's Devotion

The foregoing illustrations of Rādhā's devotion to Krishna, in which Rādhā is clearly portrayed as the ideal *bhakta,* represent only part of the picture. In the first place, for virtually every instance that I have cited, one can find a parallel passage attesting to Krishna's fervent devotion to her. We have observed above that Rādhā's single-minded concentration on Krishna is expressed in terms drawn from descriptions of yogic practice; Krishna, too, is on more than one occasion compared to a *yogī,* for he thinks incessantly upon Rādhā, losing sleep and renouncing all other enjoyments so long as he is deprived of her company.[10] Similarly, corresponding to Rādhā's reiterated expression of her utter inability to live without Krishna is a passage in which Krishna likewise acknowledges that he cannot live even for an instant without Rādhā (VM 3.22), and just as Viśākhā, addressing her, refers to Krishna as "the lord of your life" (*te jīvitapati*),[11] so Krishna calls Rādhā a life-giving herb, later confessing to her, "You are my life, O Rādhā!" (VM 2.46.1; 5.31). Such parallel expressions of emotion clearly have profound metaphysical implications, to which we shall shortly return.

The intense preoccupation of Rādhā and Krishna with one another is indicated by another set of parallel passages with similar metaphysical overtones. So obsessed with Krishna does Rādhā become that she sees him everywhere; when she mistakes a black *tamāla* tree for her dark lover, Viśākhā asks her how it is that the three worlds have become Krishna for her.[12] Krishna poses the corresponding question for himself as he eagerly awaits Rādhā at their point of rendezvous: "Rādhā appears before me on every side; how is it that for me the three worlds have become Rādhā?" (VM 5.18). Rūpa seems to have been especially taken with this mode of indicating Krishna's infatuation, for on two additional occasions he has other characters make virtually the same observation about Krishna's "delusion" (VM 3.18; 6.23.20-21). Moreoever, it is not only Rādhā in her obsession with Krishna who is explicitly termed "mad," but also Krishna in his unbridled passion for her. At one point, as Krishna is rushing headlong to meet her,

Madhumaṅgala, steadying him, asserts that he has been "maddened (*unmādita*) by an evil spell [uttered] by the wicked *gopīs*" (VM 6.14.3-4).

Just as Rādhā's devotion to Krishna at times assumes worshipful forms, such that she is aptly called his worshipper (*ārādhikā*[13]), so certain of Krishna's words and actions are clearly intended to suggest modes of adoration. In their first full meeting, Krishna expresses the desire to be in the nectar of Rādhā's favor (VM 3.43.3), using there the word *prasāda*, "grace," which has strong religious connotations. Lalitā's reply, that he may obtain her favor by serving her (*sevā*), is likewise significant, for *sevā* is the usual Vaiṣṇava term for service to the Lord.[14] Krishna is more than willing; his verse in response enumerates the ways in which he proposes to adorn and minister to her (VM 3.44). Later in the play, when he tries to appease Rādhā after spending the night with Candrāvalī, he indicates his penitence by making obeisance again and again, his peacock-feather crest touching the dust (VM 4.46; cf. figure 2). Still later, seeing his own worshipful gestures in the world of nature, he describes to Rādhā an expanse of lotuses rippled by the breeze as "doing *ārati* to your smiling face."[15]

Even in the case of the most explicitly worshipful element in Rādhā's relation to Krishna, her response to his name, there are remarkably close parallels. In the sixth act of the *Vidagdhamādhava*, when Madhumaṅgala promises to bring the hiding Rādhā to Krishna, and gives him instead a leaf inscribed with the two syllables of her name, Krishna expresses his utter delight at this gift, in a verse (VM 6.24) that is strongly reminiscent of Paurṇamāsī's rapturous words about *his* name. Paurṇamāsī herself, shortly after her verse exclaiming over Krishna's name, speaks of Rādhā's with no less enthusiasm as she proposes to entice Krishna with its auspicious syllables (VM 1.16.6-7). In the light of Paurṇamāsī's devotion to Rādhā, made explicit, as we shall see below, at numerous points in the dramas, this passage may reasonably be construed as signifying that Rādhā's name is sweet not only to Krishna, but also to Paurṇamāsī, and thus to Vaiṣṇava devotees as well.

Devotion Expressed by Others

The view of Rādhā as figuring in the dramas solely or even primarily as the ideal embodiment of devotion to Krishna is further challenged by a second body of evidence: the attitudes expressed by such secondary characters as Paurṇamāsī and Vṛndā, whose responses

FIGURE 2.

Krishna Kneeling to Take Dust off Rādhā's Feet

Detached illustration from a manuscript of
the *Rasika Priyā* of Keśav Dās.
Sub-imperial Mughul style, ca. 1610-1620.
(Courtesy, Museum of Fine Arts, Boston, 15.62F.
Ross Collection.)

Figure 2.

In a number of Vaiṣṇavite texts Krishna subordinates himself to his consort, Rādhā. He becomes her devotee and elevates her status, literally by touching her feet. Krishna's motivations for such an action are varied. Sometimes he tries to entice Rādhā and plays up to her; at other times he makes obeisance and asks for her forgiveness after spending the night with another woman. On still other occasions, bowing to Rādhā is simply an acknowledgement of his devotion to her. In the *Rasika Priyā*, an aesthetician's exposition of emotional and poetic delights, the image of Krishna touching Rādhā's feet is evoked several times, and always with different nuances.

This page is from the earliest illustrated text of the *Rasika Priyā* to come to light thus far.[1] Almost all the visual images in this set are generic in type and do not always reflect the subtle nuances indicated in the literary classification of heroes and heroines that the *Rasika Priyā* provides. Consequently an exact classification of this page without the accompanying text is extremely difficult. A small clue, however, is provided by the presence of a female attendant in the picture. She appears in the paintings only when she is specifically referred to in the text. Rādhā in this painting is clearly talking to her female confidante and not to Krishna. Thus it is possible that the *lajjā prāyarati mugdhā* — the young heroine who feigns bashfulness in the interest of stimulating love — is intended. In a properly bashful manner, she denies her love for Krishna and tells her friend, "He called and called, I did not speak/Then to win me my feet he touched. . . ."[2]

The illustration here, indeed the entire set of which it is a part, echoes the imperial Mughal trends in its use of a muted color palette, a sensitive line for the figures, and in its suggestion of the third dimension. Simpler and less aristocratic than their imperial Mughal counterparts, these *Rasika Priyā* paintings also differ from their Rajput contemporaries. Though brighter and flatter than imperial paintings, they have neither the brilliant palette nor the emotional intensity of the Rajput works that emerged from Rajasthan in the seventeenth century.[3]

— V.N.D.

---

[1]First published by Ananda Coomaraswamy in *The Catalogue of the Indian Collections*, part 4 (Cambridge: Harvard University Press, 1926). Approximately 45 illustrations in public and private collections are known today.

[2]K.P. Bahadur, trans., *The Rasika Priyā of Keshavadāsa* (Delhi: Motilal Banarsidass, 1972), p. 28.

[3]For further discussion of the sub-imperial Mughal style, see Pramod Chandra, "Ustād Sālivāhana and the development of the Popular Mughal Style," *Lalit Kalā*, 8, (1960), 25-46.

to Rādhā as well as to Krishna show strong devotional elements. In the introductory scene in Act I of the *Vidagdhamādhava,* Nāndīmukhī expresses envy of Paurṇamāsī's grandson Madhumaṅgala, who is privileged to enjoy Krishna's constant company. Paurṇamāsī's reply indicates that Nāndīmukhī's task, to increase Rādhā's passion for Krishna, is no less a privilege, for Rādhā, Paurṇamāsī confesses, means everything to her (VM 1.14.25). In a later conversation with Madhumaṅgala and Vṛndā, Paurṇamāsī reaffirms her deep love for Rādhā, comparing her feeling in its spontaneity and lack of motive with Rādhā's love for Krishna (VM 5.2.10-5.4.4).

The devotional significance of Rādhā for Paurṇamāsī, and by extension for the devotee who sees or reads this drama, is likewise evident from Paurṇamāsī's words of gratitude to Krishna at the end of the final act. When Abhimanyu is persuaded not to take Rādhā to Mathurā, Paurṇamāsī exclaims with considerable relief that she has been spared the pain of separation from Rādhā (*rādhikāviśleṣavedanā,* VM 7.59.3). Her expression and the threatened separation that it reflects constitute a reversal of the situation of the *gopīs* depicted in the *Bhāgavata Purāṇa* and the *Lalitamādhava,* in which it is Krishna who is taken to Mathurā and the *gopīs* who experience the anguish of separation.

Paurṇamāsī is not the only secondary character in the drama who expresses emotions toward Rādhā that are usually directed toward Krishna. A beautiful verse uttered in amazement by Vṛndā in the final act of the *Vidagdhamādhava,* in which she juxtaposes Rādhā's youth with her maturity in love, exhibits a parental tenderness (*vātsalya*) toward Rādhā that is reminiscent of Yaśodā's maternal affection for Krishna:

> Just yesterday she was playing in the dust,
> her ears newly pierced,
> Her hair, barely as long as a cow's ear,
> tied with a colored thread;
> Oh, where has this Rādhā learned such proficiency
> in the ways of love
> That she has conquered the unconquerable! (VM 7.44)

In the *Lalitamādhava,* Yaśodā herself expresses *vātsalya* toward Rādhā, whom she terms *vatsā laghvī,* "my dear little child," comparing her to Krishna in the delight that seeing her gives. Paurṇamāsī replies that all the inhabitants of Gokula feel a comparable delight (LM 1.42.15-19).

Vātsalya is not the only mode of devotion to Krishna in Rūpa's theory that is also exemplified by certain characters in their relations to Rādhā. Both *sakhya* and *dāsya,* friendship and servitude, are likewise directed toward Rādhā as well as toward Krishna. Indeed, although Krishna's fellow cowherds and his humorous companion Madhumaṅgala show *sakhya* toward him, this mode is most fully represented by the love for her of Rādhā's two close friends, Lalitā and Viśākhā. In addition to promoting her love affair with Krishna, they elicit expressions of her deepest feelings, as well as portraying externally, through their conflicting advice, aspects of her inner struggle. Their tender concern for her well-being is manifest especially at times of crisis, when her anguish leads to loss of consciousness and seems to threaten her very life (e.g., LM 3.18; 3.33.1-2). The strength of Lalitā's affection is revealed most fully in her expressions of grief at the loss of Rādhā: her distress is in fact comparable to Rādhā's own agony at Krishna's departure (LM 3.54.23-28).[16]

Although Rūpa gives considerable attention to the *sakhīs* (girlfriends, especially of Rādhā) in his *Ujjvalanīlamaṇi,* he speaks of *sakhya* in his *Bhaktirasāmṛtasindhu* exclusively in relation to Krishna. This is a puzzling fact, given the examples that we have just surveyed, as well as Rūpa's theoretical exposition of *dāsya.* In the *Bhaktirasāmṛtasindhu,* he identifies three kinds of servants, those devoted to Krishna and his beloved women, those devoted to one of these women, and those who serve Krishna alone.[17] When Satyabhāmā-Rādhā arrives in Dvārakā, she is entrusted to the care of Navavṛndā, who is requested to serve her, a duty that is said to be conducive to the welfare of all (LM 6.20). Lalitā's all-consuming desire in her separation from Rādhā and Krishna is also to serve Rādhā and to fan the two of them when they are together (LM 6.41). Both Navavṛndā's assignment and Lalitā's yearning for servitude anticipate the attitude of the *mañjarī,* the youthful maidservant of subsequent Vaiṣṇava tradition who attends Rādhā and Krishna in their lovemaking. Thus both the prominent role of the *sakhī* and the emerging figure of the *mañjarī* in Rūpa's dramas qualify, thrugh their primary relation to Rādhā, the virtually exclusive emphasis on Krishna represented by his theory of *bhaktirasa.*

Krishna as Model of Devotion

We have seen that Rādhā does indeed serve as a model of devotion to Krishna, but that her significance is not exhausted by this role, for she is also an object of the devotion both of Krishna and of certain important secondary characters. That the roles of model and object need not be mutually exclusive is clear from the fact that Krishna himself periodically serves as a model for the devotee. He several times expresses wonder at Rādhā's great love, most memorably on one occasion to Madhumaṅgala as he tearfully overhears Rādhā's expression to her friends of her unwavering devotion (VM 2.47.1). Moreover, after he is taken from Vṛndāvana, he repeatedly proclaims his preference for its qualities and inhabitants over those of any other realm. The most remarkable demonstration of this preference, which is clearly Rūpa's as well, is Krishna's response to the play depicting the Vṛndāvana *līlā* that is staged for him in Mathurā at Nārada's direction by a heavenly troupe of actors, in order to keep him from becoming disconsolate. Krishna's attraction to the actor playing the role of Mādhava, the Krishna of Vṛndāvana, is so strong that he utterly forgets who he is and has to be constrained from rushing headlong toward the stage to embrace his alter ego. As he watches the play unfold, he voices the desire to become a *gopī* in order that he might participate in the love sports,[18] and he later muses over the fact that the play afforded him the same bliss as the experiences it represented (LM 4.32.68-69). In each of these reactions, it becomes clear that not only Rādhā but Krishna too is a model for human *bhaktas:* in this respect they have a surprisingly parallel status.

Earthly yet Sublime: The Nature of Rādhā's Love

We have observed the devotional quality of Rādhā's love for Krishna as well as the wonder that it evokes in him. In order more fully to appreciate her significance for Vaiṣṇava devotion, we must now look more closely at the nature of her love.

Although Rūpa in his *Ujjvalanīlamaṇi* emphasizes the uniqueness of Rādhā's love, its course in his dramas reveals certain characteristically human qualities. Among these are her hesitancy to express her feelings even to her two close friends, her shyness especially in her early encounters with Krishna, and the unmistakably human apprehension that she will be found unworthy of his affection. Early in their courtship she is still sufficiently respectful to be initially horrified at Lalitā's suggestion that she play a joke on Krishna (VM 3.34.7-10), and only much later does she herself take the initiative in such teasing by hiding from him (VM 6.23.3-5; VM 7.36).

Likewise identifiably human are Rādhā's inner conflicts, which are sensitively portrayed by Rūpa. As her passion grows, she is torn between her love for Krishna and her *dharma* as a married woman (VM 1.34; VM 3.18; cf. LM 2.25). Subsequently, in response to his unfaithfulness, she comes to know the anguish of *māna*,[19] in which pride and jealous anger struggle in her heart against the intense desire for reconciliation. Suddenly bereft of her company when she is in this latter state, Krishna muses over her conflicting expressions in the following poignant verse:

> Now assuming a steadfast pose,
>   now showing signs of wavering,
> One moment uttering scornful sounds,
>   the next, words of eagerness,
> Now with a look of innocence,
>   now with glance bewitching
> Rādhikā is split in two
>   swayed now by anger, now by love. (VM 4.51)

Rādhā's warm humanness, evident throughout Rūpa's dramas, renders her eminently accessible to Vaiṣṇava devotees. Yet the plays themselves, as well as Rūpa's theory, also point in numerous ways to her transcendence. The remarkable intensity of her love makes it an object of perpetual wonder to those around her; she is by turns called foolish and mad.[20] Her agonized frenzy at Krishna's departure for Mathurā is designated by Rūpa *divyonmāda*, "divine madness."[21] Rādhā herself, as well as those who observe her, describe her state as fundamentally incomprehensible.

Two other terms applied to Rādhā's love in the *Vidagdhamādhava* are *sahaja* and *svābhāvika*, both of which mean "natural."[22] Rādhā's spontaneity is clearly of paramount importance for Rūpa. Her relative lack of conventional restraint allows her to be far more intimate with Krishna than her more docile rival. In his *Ujjvalanīlamaṇi*, Rūpa designates Candrāvalī's love by the term *ghṛtasneha*, love that is like clarified butter, and he repeatedly refers to the respect (*ādara*) that is its chief characteristic. Rādhā's love, by contrast, is called *madhusneha*, love that is like honey; instead of respect, it is characterized by a sense of possessing the beloved (*madīyatva*).[23] Its bold, playful ways and their effect on Krishna can best be seen from two successive verses in the final act of the *Vidagdhamādhava:*

> Words of protest filled with passion,
> Gestures of resistance lacking force,
> Frowns transmuted into smiles,
> Crying dry of tears—friend,
> Though Rādhā seeks to hide her feelings,
> Each attempt betrays her heart's
> Deep love for demon Mura's slayer. (VM 7.38)
>
> Bold employ of teeth and nails
> By one experienced in love sports:
> Rādhā's show of opposition
> Gives Hari immeasurable delight. (VM 7.39)

Unlike Candrāvalī, whose deferential reserve indicates greater awareness of Krishna's lordly majesty (*aiśvarya*) and constrains him to show similar courtesy toward her, Rādhā responds primarily to Krishna's sweet charm (*mādhurya*), and their more intimate love affords him the greater delight.

In addition to the wonder expressed repeatedly at her incomparable love, Rādhā's transcendence is indicated by certain adjectives and other designations found throughout the dramas. Krishna calls her *jagadapūrvā*, "unprecedented in the world" (VM 1.31.68), and her qualities are elsewhere termed *lokottara*, "extraordinary" or "transcendent" (VM 1.13; 3.21.19). Greatness in general is predicated of her by means of two synonymous terms, *mahiman* and *māhātmya* (VM 2.31.4; 3.12.1; LM 3.55) and her cosmic significance is strongly suggested by certain passages in the *Lalitamādhava* in which her effects, like Krishna's, are said to extend to the entire universe.[24] Finally, taking full advantage of the fact that the word *rādhā* designates a constellation, Rūpa several times puns on her name in a way that likewise hints at her cosmic stature (VM 1.31.58-59; 4.11; 5.29; 6.2.29-31; LM 2.22).

The metaphysical implications of the devotional parallels that we have noted earlier should by now have become clear. Just as Rādhā's demented state, in which she sees Krishna everywhere, perceiving nothing else in the three worlds, is a metaphysically accurate apprehension of reality—for Krishna, the Lord, is the reality behind everything in the universe—so the "deluding" effects of his parallel bewitchment may be taken as veridical if Rādhā is recognized as his *śakti*,[25] who, with him, pervades the whole world. The conviction of Rādhā and Krishna that each is the life of the other may correspondingly be interpreted as hinting at their metaphysical equality as well as affirming their intimate interdependence. Both Rūpa and his nephew Jīva assert in their theological treatises that Rādhā is the *hlādinī śakti* of Krishna, his "blissful potency."[26] Rūpa further states explicitly that Rādhā should be worshipped, indeed that her worship is as important as that of Krishna himself.[27]

Thus metaphysically Rādhā is understood as consubstantial and co-eternal with Krishna; moreover, in at least one important respect she is superior to him. Not only is her exclusive devotion to Krishna unique in Vraja; it is even declared to surpass Krishna's love for her. Just as the proud scholar Uddhava in the *Bhāgavata Purāṇa* comes to acknowledge the superiority of the *gopīs'* love for Krishna to his own more arid realization, so Krishna himself in Rūpa's dramas pays wondering homage to Rādhā's love. That love in fact wins a double victory, for it not only exceeds his, but it wholly captivates him, the "invincible" Lord to whom is subject the entire universe. As much as her love itself, the paradox of her inexplicable power over Krishna repeatedly evokes astonishment and delight.

That it is her love through which Rādhā surpasses Krishna is highly significant. It is this love, rather than Krishna or Rādhā alone, that is relished by the other characters in the dramas, certain of whom are clearly model *bhaktas*. In the final act of the *Vidagdhamādhava*, Vṛndā exclaims to Paurṇamāsī:

> What supreme enjoyment arises
> when Krishna and Rādhā are united!
> Who could cease to tell of that
> quintessence of erotic mood
> Save one speechless utterly
> with ecstasy? (VM 7.2)

Through her great love, made manifest in songs, in poems, in vernacular plays, and in dramas such as Rūpa's, Rādhā renders Krishna accessible to Vaiṣṇava *bhaktas*. She is necessary not because the Lord is conceived as unapproachable (as is often the case in religious traditions in which a mediator plays a prominent role), for it is not Krishna's majestic otherness (*aiśvarya*) that is paramount for Gauḍīya Vaiṣṇavas, but rather his exquisite sweetness (*mādhurya*). Something quite different is clearly at work here. Rādhā is necessary because love requires two, because sweetness needs "another" to taste it.[28]

There are several indications in Rūpa's works that love itself is what is absolute. Its experience by the *bhakta* is valued above all else; in the plays the importance of manifesting the mutual passion of Rādhā and Krishna outweighs all other considerations, even the pain that temporary deception may cause them. Furthermore, expressions used to designate Rādhā's emotion, such as *durūha* or *durvibodha,* "difficult to fathom" or "incomprehensible," are reminiscent of terms earlier applied to *ātman* or *brahman,* the "self" or the absolute referred to throughout the Upaniṣads and discussed in much subsequent Indian philosophy. It is significant that the absolute for Rūpa is not a metaphysical principle, but an emotion; it is with such love, and not with *brahman,* that unity is sought. Rādhā, as love embodied, is thus the supreme avenue of religious realization.

The love of Rādhā and Krishna is a subtle interplay of freedom and commitment, spontaneity and constancy. If we envision these poles as opposite ends of a continuum, we may place Krishna nearer to the freedom end and Rādhā nearer to that of commitment. Yet each partakes to some degree of the other's predominant quality. Rādhā's love as depicted in Rūpa's dramas incorporates elements of freedom in two ways. It is at least outwardly *parakīyā,*[29] love free from the contraints of marriage, for she is wed to Abhimanyu in the *Vidagdhamādhava,* and her love affair with Krishna in the *Lalitamādhava* must be concealed from his ever-vigilant queen. Moreover, as we have observed, her love shows spontaneity in its intimacy and its lack of deference. Nevertheless, its complete steadfastness puts it closer to the opposite pole.

Krishna, on the other hand, exhibits almost total freedom. Although his irresistible attraction to Rādhā leads to uncharacteristic single-mindedness, his love for her is never wholly exclusive. This perpetual fickleness on his part represents both the universality of divine love, which is as diffuse and varied as the many degrees and ways in which he is loved, and his transcendence of all conventional boundaries.

Why should commitment in love be preferred over freedom? For the Vaiṣṇava, the highest religious ideal is the sweetness of perpetual relatedness in *bhakti,* rather than the release from all bondage that is represented by the goal of *mokṣa.*[30] It is thus not surprising that Rūpa accords highest praise to Rādhā's love. If steadfast love is what is ultimate, then Rādhā, its supreme embodiment, can have no rival.

A Vernacular Portrait: Rādhā in the *Sūr Sāgar*

JOHN STRATTON HAWLEY

*I*n 1975 the International Society for Krishna Consciousness completed an impressive temple in Brindavan (Skt Vṛndāvana), a pilgrimage center for devotees of Krishna for five hundred years, for the town was founded on the site Caitanya clairvoyantly proclaimed was that of Krishna's circle dance with his milkmaid loves. The ISKCON temple has brought Westerners to Brindavan in dramatic numbers, and local residents have been quick to adopt for them and all Westerners the salutation ISKCON people use, the familiar "Hare Krishna!" The traditional Brindavan greeting, however, is quite different. "Rādhe!" one hears, the vocative form of Rādhā.

The change of name is significant, for by and large the people of Brindavan feel that it is Rādhā who is their queen, more even than Krishna their king. True, in many ways the two stand equal: her birthday celebrations balance his, and the town in which he grew up is venerated alongside her natal village.[1] But as the Rādhā-Krishna plays of Brindavan are performed it is at the mention of her name that hands are raised in adulation all over the audience: "Victory to Rādhā!" Simple men and women submit the vagaries of their lives to Queen Rādhā's will. Letters from Brindavan offer assurances that although much else in the world may have gone awry, there, where Rādhā rules, all remains peaceful and loving. And in the plays of Brindavan her ascendancy is explicitly celebrated, a supremacy she wields not only over all of Braj, but over Krishna himself. The moments when he comes to her with the humility of one who would place his head in the dust at her feet or wash those feet and even drink the water left over as a substance of grace (*prasād*) are greeted by their spectators first with hushed awe and then with shouts of excitement.[2]

Our task here is to understand how in the vernacular tradition of Braj (Skt Vraja), the region that surrounds Brindavan, all this came to be. One way to do so without introducing a bias in favor of any one of the several sects influential in Braj—for some accord Rādhā a more exalted place than others—is to choose a neutral figure, one revered by all, and study his Rādhā. Then we may note how tradition's gathering consensus about her left its mark on collections of poetry attributed to him as time went on.

I am thinking of Sūr Dās, the sixteenth-century poet generally acclaimed the greatest Braj ever produced, a man whose compositions are sung by members of every sect even if, as is normally the case, they accept the view that Sūr was affiliated with a community other than their own.[3] Sūr's poems had such a wide appeal that they came to serve as the core of the most catholic corpus of literature in Braj, and the largest: *Sūr Sāgar* it came to be called—the "ocean" of poetry that bears his name. Encompassing more than 5000 poems in the most recent printed edition, it contained only a thousand or so poems approximately a century after the poet's death.[4] The rest have been added over the years by other "Sūrs," not a few of whom were responding to the inspiration of their earlier namesake. Let us see how the image of Rādhā developed in this cumulative, remarkably nonsectarian tradition, restricting our attention to poems that apply specifically to her.[5] By separating out poems registered in the earlier manuscripts from those which appear only later we will be able to see how, at least in this one context, Rādhā's cult grew from the sixteenth century to the present in Braj.

Early Poems: An Intimate Rādhā

Modern-day critics have praised Sūr chiefly for two achievements in his portrayal of Rādhā: his attention to the many stages and vicissitudes of her love for Krishna, from the first time, as a young girl, he chanced upon her in her yard; and his extension of that portrait far beyond the time of their active love-making to include the long, aching years after Krishna had left to defeat the wicked king in the city of Mathurā.[6] How casually, how mischievously it all beings in the dialogue poem critics invariably cite:

"So pretty! Who are you?" he asks.
"And where is your family? your house?
    You've never been seen around here."
        "Never you mind—I stay in my place:
            right here in my yard where I play,

For Nanda's boy is out to steal
our curd and butter, they say."
"Now what would I possibly steal that you've got?
Come on, let's both of us play."
The charm of Sūr's Lord, his facile words,
disarm poor Rādhā, simple girl.[7]

How naturally we see the love of childhood sweethearts grow; how inevitably it turns to the solemnity, even the tragedy, of a woman's devotion to her man. Rādhā, archetypical wife,[8] suffers all, refusing to share her difficulties with the family and acquaintances of her chosen one.[9] Nobility itself, she endures the mockery broadcast by a world in which we cannot have what out hearts demand; she remains steadfast in love's perilous path.[10]

But the poet who gives pattern to all this, this "Sūr" whose comprehensive vision of Rādhā the critics praise, is in reality the *Sūr Sāgar* itself in its massive, current form. These writers give scant if any attention to problems of text criticism, and one fears that they, and some modern-day devotees along with them, may be disappointed to learn that in the earliest collections of Sūr's poetry Rādhā does not preside over every stage of Krishna's life to the extent that she does in later, fuller editions. She does not accompany him in his childhood. The poems that were later interpreted as describing the first meeting of these two special personages may or may not have originally pertained to Rādhā: the alluring girl in question is called only *bhāmiṇī* or *taraṅgiṇī,* a radiant, supple young woman, not specifically Śyāmā (i.e., Rādhā) as in much later versions of one of these early poems.[11]

Sūr, if we may use the term to designate collectively the authors of the thousand or so poems recorded under that name before about 1650 A.D., has no interest in chronicling Rādhā's youth. Evidently it is only her encounter with Krishna that he finds compelling, with all it entails, and in the only old poem describing their first meeting[12] there is nothing to suggest that it happens when they are still children, a point that becomes quite vivid in later poems such as the one translated above. We hear how Krishna used to grab Rādhā's clothes and steal them away[13] (in the modern plays of Brindavan she has risen too high to be the victim of such trickery on his part—it is the other *gopīs* instead) but all this is only recalled by a more seasoned Rādhā. We also hear how ever since Krishna first heard her name it has been his constant mantra: *hā rādhā hā rādhā*. But that too is refracted through a later vision: it comes from the mouth of one of Rādhā's friends, who is trying to draw her out of her disconsolate sulking.[14] Aside from that Sūr is silent: Rādhā's childhood per se does not appear. In this respect his Rādhā is much closer to the involved and suffering lover portrayed by Caṇḍidās and Vidyāpati than a later cross section of the *Sūr Sāgar* would suggest.

The case is similar at the other end of the story. Critics are apt to make a good deal of the reunion Rādhā has with Krishna long after he has left Braj, when both of them journey to Kurukṣetra on the occasion of a solar eclipse. In the oldest strata of the *Sūr Sāgar,* however, there is only one poem that could be construed as referring to this incident and in it Rādhā plays no active role. Instead all attention is focused backward in time as Rukmiṇī, Krishna's royal bride from the western city of Dvārakā over which he reigns after leaving Mathurā, surveys a group of *gopīs* and begs to know which of them is her erstwhile rival.

Rukmiṇī asks, "Which maid, my dear,
    is Bṛṣabhānu's child?
Come, let me know which one she is,
    your childhood sweetheart from long ago,
Who taught you to be so cleverly wise,
    and at such a tender age:
She taught you the art of being a thief—
    stealing even our peace of mind;
Whose virtues you've numbered and strung like beads
    that never abandon your breast.
You meditate, you memorize
    that beauty; your gaze never strays . . .
Look there—*that* girl!—standing out from the others,
    outstandingly fair and clad all in blue:
My mind has gone to her, Sūr Dās says,
    tied and tethered with the rope of the eye."[15]

It is important that the one clear early reference to Rādhā's having grown up so closely with Krishna comes at this point rather than at any other, for Sūr mentions this romance of early childhood in the interests of perspective, not of chronicle. Rukmiṇī, after all, has never been to Braj. For her it is all a matter of legend, a world in which she did not participate, a mysterious earlier affair. No wonder she tends to exaggerate, imagining Rādhā not only as the cause of all Krishna's mischief but also as his constant companion since infancy. When

Rukmiṇī envisions Braj, she sees Rādhā behind every tree. All this prepares the way for the ironic shift that concludes the poem. There is more than a hint of jealousy as Rukmiṇī describes Krishna's preoccupation with Rādhā, likening it to that of an ascetic who, wearing the necklace with which his guru would have initiated him, directs his attention totally to the object of his disciplines. In the course of this characterization, however, her own eye falls on a golden-complexioned, blue-clad girl whose identity she does not know, but we, from her description, do. And suddenly Rukmiṇī too is absorbed in the contemplation of the very one she was just disparaging.

This is no neutral historical account. There is nothing in the poem itself to suggest where the incident occurred, whether at Kurukṣetra or back at Dvārakā as the king and queen mused over a portrait someone had painted of Krishna's Braj acquaintances. If anything is chronicled it is a shift in perspective, and indeed Sūr's attention to perspective is one of the hallmarks of his portrayal of Rādhā. Rarely is anything seen point-blank. A poem that seems to proceed as a straightforward description of Rādhā's very unstraightforward beauty—the poet emphasizes her snake-like motions, the curvature of her eyebrows, her sidelong glances—turns out in the last line to be not only the poet's description but one offered also by Krishna himself.[16] Other times Krishna's vision, as he gazes at Rādhā, becomes hopelessly complicated: he is unable to believe his senses and wonders if it is all hallucination.[17]

Rarely does Sūr show us Rādhā and Krishna while they are actually making love. Again it is a question of perspective. They must be seen by some other figure in their world; hence we observe the moment when they emerge from their love nest (or Rādhā does so alone, Krishna having gone off while she slept).[18] Like the *gopīs* who witnessed such a sight, we look beyond their (or her) dishevelled state and imagine the battle of love that caused it. Or if the poet takes us to the battleground itself, he is apt to supply us with other perspectives from which to observe what we see, by turning the scuffles of Rādhā and Krishna into a match between the Love-god himself and his mate or comparing their encounter with the epic stand-off between Arjuna and Karṇa, a battle over which, ironically, Krishna himself presided in quite another guise.[19]

In other poems remembrance provides the perspective that preserves the dramatic integrity of Sūr's poetry. All his poems remain poems that could have been spoken by someone on the scene. There is no extraneous, neutral voice to stand between the audience and the drama itself: to hear the poem is to enter the world of Braj. Paradoxical as it seems, Sūr's attention to perspective, with the indirection it implies, is in fact intended to make this more direct access possible for the listener. As in the poem involving Rukmiṇī, he uses memory as his tool in this regard in the poems in which Ūdho returns to Krishna in Mathura and describes Rādhā's desolate state.[20] And discussions between the sulking, withdrawn Rādhā and her friends provide the occasions upon which entire phases of the affair between Rādhā and Krishna are recalled.[21]

Such use of perspective on the part of the poet permits the hearer a direct access to the world of Rādhā and Krishna at the same time that it shields its intimacy. And on the rare occasion when that intimacy is not otherwise present, Rādhā is apt to call for it herself, as she does when she asks for a heavy shawl in the following poem. The completed, blanketed scene, in which the divine couple are enclosed in a sheltered space that separates them from all possible viewers, is one that was often depicted in miniature painting (for example, figure 3).

> *"Give me, Kānh, a shawl for my shoulders.*
> Here and there the drops have started falling:
> the dye on my clothes will soon run red."
> Over and over Rādhikā seems concerned:
> "Look at that awesome event in the clouds."
> Laughing and smiling they cover and cuddle,
> Rādhā and yellow-clad Kānh, just the two.
> Śiva and Sanaka, Nārad, the sages,
> and beast-men creatures—none can come in;
> Sūr Dās says not even a glimpse is revealed,
> and the unknowing cowherds go on with their meal.[22]

As the Early Core Expands: An Exalted Rādhā

There is a tendency for this tart, intimate world of texture and perspective to become increasingly flat in the years up to about 1700 A.D. as other poems are added to the *Sūr Sāgar* that describe Rādhā and her relation to Krishna. In the earliest poems portraying Rādhā's beauty there is invariably some perspectival twist. As we have seen, the poet often asks us to envision her immaculate beauty through the perspective of her dishevelled state. Or if he describes her loveliness straight out, there will always be some gesture, some slight change that will alter the image and anchor the scene in its dramatic context. After some lines of description, for instance, Rādhā will respond with a little laugh, signaling the fact that the words we have been hearing are those of no removed narrator. They are Krishna's: more than description, they are lures to love.[23]

It is not long, however, before Rādhā's beauty per se becomes the sufficient subject of poetry in the *Sūr Sāgar,* and quite another style of poem emerges to do the trick. It is longer and, in that it involves no change of perspective, flatter; and it is self-consciously poetical. One verse will describe some feature of Rādhā's beauty and the next will introduce a simile. The living Rādhā has become an object of veneration; indeed the poet may be so direct as to offer his thanksgiving (*dhanya*) for her apparition.[24]

These poems are part of a tendency one can observe in the expanding *Sūr Sāgar* to raise Rādhā to the level of Krishna, a status she attained somewhat earlier in the plays of Rūpa Gosvāmī. Descriptions of Krishna's irresistible charm abound in the earliest levels of the *Sūr Sāgar:* now Rādhā's attractions are brought in line. Another aspect of the same development concerns explicit statements of the equality of Rādhā and Krishna. In the earliest poems this is only hinted at. We have only the words of Rādhā's friends assuring her that she and Krishna are equally refined, equally beautiful (*nāgari, nāgaravar; sundari, sundaravar*)[25] or that Krishna is infatuated with her;[26] he is her guest.[27] As in all poems of this early stratum, there is a dramatic rationale for utterances such as these: Rādhā's friends want to coax her out of her grim sulking.

Yet is is not long before the parity between Rādhā and Krishna becomes an independent datum, an article of faith. A poem attested before 1700 represented this vision poetically, balancing descriptions of one with descriptions of the other so as to imply the equal status of the two parts of the pair (*jorī*):

He's the bee, and she the lotus bud;
    a clever lad, and she's no foolish one.
So have them love one another, my friend,
    have them silently from their mothers steal away;
One a young sapphire, a dark *tamāl* sapling,
    the other a vine—fair, pure, and golden. . . .[28]

FIGURE 3.

Varṣa Vihāra

(Rādhā and Krishna Taking Shelter from the Rain)
Pahari Hills, Garhwal, ca. 1770-1780.
(Courtesy, Museum of Fine Arts, Boston, 17.2614.
Ross-Coomaraswamy Collection.)

Figure 3.

The motif of Rādhā and Krishna taking shelter from the rain under a cloak, an umbrella, or a tree provided a popular subject for painters from the Pahari Hills.[1] The literary milieu into which this motif would originaly have fit was a secular one: the *Bārahmāsā* ("The Twelve Months"), a cycle of poems in the Hindi vernaculars which describe the behavior and feelings of lovers during each of the twelve months. The *varṣa vihāra* theme depicts the dalliance of lovers during the rainy season. Devotional poets such as Sūr Dās and Bihārī, however, went beyond secular conventions and interpreted the different flavors of seasonal enjoyment through the narration of the love-sports of Rādhā and Krishna, crafting scenes such as the one that appears here.

Indeed, this painting is a kind of visual poem — one that can be enjoyed on several levels.[2] On the surface it can simply be viewed as Krishna providing Rādhā with shelter from the rain on a dark and stormy night. As the *gopas* and *gopīs* around them flee to take cover from the rain, the ardent lovers receive both privacy and protection in the enclosure of the cloak.

On another level, the cloak takes the shape of a nimbus enshrining and unifying the pair, isolating them so that they appear icon-like, and transforming them from the human realm to the divine. Indeed, amid all the scurry and bustle for shelter, only the flora and fauna seem to be aware of the divine presence. The peacock perched regally in the tree above the pair and delighting in the rain heralds the joy of their union, and the cow in the foreground pays homage by bowing. The rain itself is a libation to the trees and plants, which burst forth with spring green freshness, symbolic of fervent love, both human and divine.

— J.P.

---

[1]For the most updated and complete discussion of this painting, see W.G. Archer, *Indian Paintings from the Punjab Hills* (London: Sotheby Parke, Bernet Publications, 1973), vol. I, p. 116, no. 16.

[2]First published by Ananda K. Coomaraswamy in *Rajput Painting* (London: Oxford University Press, 1916), pl. 58.

Later poems can be more blatant. There is considerable effort, for instance, to depict Rādhā as no less ingenious than that renowned rogue, Krishna himself. Whole chains of poems—contrasting in every respect with Sūr's short, isolated compositions—are contrived to bear this out. She pretends, for example, to be taken deathly sick from the bite of a black snake and tells her mother that she can be cured only by the local *gāruḍī,* a physician who cures snakebite through his magical possession of the power of the divine bird Garuḍa, whose enmity for snakes is legendary. We can guess who this *gāruḍī* is, of course: Krishna, whose mythological vehicle is Garuḍa himself. One look at him and the stricken girl experiences an instant cure, which earns for him the indebtedness, at least temporarily, of her mother Kīrat.[29]

Other poems are even more forthright in directing praise to Rādhā that will raise her to the level of Krishna. In one of the earliest poems of this sort the exordium concludes with the request that the exalted Rādhā grant the poet-devotee the gift of devotion to her mate, who is by implication at least equally exalted.

Rādhikā, jewel of joy and of beauty,
    a treasure, a gem of the finest quality,
Those who bring to your lotus feet love
    through love attain also Krishna's.
Beloved of this world's lord and king,
    mother of the world, and its queen,
Who daily diverts the cowherd's darling,
    making Brindavan the center of your realm,
Your feet clear a path through the dead ends of life,
    Śrī Rādhā, dispenser of all that is blessed.
Taming life's terrors, raft to the bereft,
    you the Purāṇas and Vedas describe
Not with one tongue but with hundreds and millions—
    your measureless, boundless radiance they sing.
Grant us to share in the worship of Krishna,
    Śrī Rādhā, Sūr Dās comes to you begging.[30]

This is all theologically quite correct: the boon requested is devotion itself, faith is granted *sola gratia.* Also correct theologically is the term by which Rādhā is designated. For what may be the first time in the *Sūr Sāgar* she is given the honorific and called Śrī Rādhā, as in the community of faith today.[31] But the poetic cost of all this is notable. An extraneous voice, the poet's, intrudes upon the dramatic integrity with which Sūr is so careful to protect the intimacy of the relationship between Rādhā and her love. Rādhā is praised in those earlier poems too, but always through the voice of someone on the scene, normally one of her friends, as in the following example.

> Why this sudden burst to bloom?
> Rādhā, I wonder where have you been.
> What but Mādhav's tight embrace
> could bare a love so fathomless?
> What arrows strain at their bows, your brows,
> stretching over half your face!
> They gaze and pierce, they glance sidelong
> and force their own archer, Love, to dance.
> The experience craved by Śuk and the sages,
> the unattained object of Śiva's regime,
> That's what Sūr's Lord has showered on you—
> what even for Śrī was just prayer's charade.[32]

If it is a final truth that Rādhā is exalted beyond Śiva and all the sages, even beyond Śrī (Lakṣmī), that is for the hearer to decide. The poem only serves to make such an affirmation possible, but does so in such a brief, understated way that the leap of faith has all the more force. The prayer to which Śrī does not attain, as the Braj puts it (*śrī na lahati ārādhe*), contains the very name of Rādhā: *ā-rādhe*. This is the word, in fact, in its Sanskrit form as *ārādhita*, that has traditionally been interpreted as the one reference in the *Bhāgavata Purāṇa* to Rādhā, about whom it is otherwise silent.[33] Sūr repeats this play on words, inviting the hearer, in his guarded way, to perceive that the prayer of Śrī implies Rādhā herself.

Sūr's Rādhā and the Rādhā of Faith

It is a considerable journey from poems like this to the sort of composition one meets so frequently in the later strata of the *Sūr Sāgar*, in which the hearer is freely reminded that the young lovers being described are very incarnations of the eternal masculine and feminine polarities that provide the structure of reality as we know it. Over and over we are made to understand that they are the ancient correlatives *puruṣa* and *prakṛti*, hence really one, not two; two bodies with a single soul; inseparable as waves and water or trees and shade[34]—theological clichés that dominate the discourse of such works as the *Brahmavaivarta Purāṇa.*

A theological concern about the status of their union also begins to emerge: is Rādhā Krishna's mistress or is she his wife? The earliest poems in the *Sūr Sāgar* are entirely non-committal; it is only the intimacy of the two that counts, not what people think of it. There is more than a hint of irony when Sūr describes them as a "couple" (*dampati*) as they emerge dishevelled from the thicket where they have dallied. This is hardly the time for a serious comment about their marital status.[35] His mention of any engagement that might have taken place is similarly enigmatic, for the word that would be so interpreted in modern Braj parlance, *sagāī,* seems to have a greater ambiguity—it can mean "betrothal" or simply "liaison"—when he has one of Rādhā's friends assure her that Krishna has established no new *sagāī.* Rādhā is left wondering, as are we, just what her friend means.[36] Other terms that can have marital connotations are similarly vague, like *nārī* (woman, wife) and *var* (best, husband).[37] It is only in later strata of the *Sūr Sāgar* that they clearly mean husband and wife.[38] The earliest hints of such a nuptial (*svakīyā*) theology emerge, predictably, in long didactic poems that contrast in every way with the tone of the earliest poems in the *Sūr Sāgar.* Here for the first time Rādhā and Krishna are *dulah* and *dulahinī,* bride and groom,[39] as they were so clearly to be understood by later contributers to the *Sūr Sāgar,* and in consequence, by modern critics.[40]

Yet if Sūr was not interested in defining Rādhā as Krishna's wife, he was equally uninterested in the fact that she might have been any one else's (*parakīyā*). Unlike the plays of Rūpa Gosvāmī, the *Sūr Sāgar* nowhere mentions Abhimanyu, the husband whom Radha repeatedly abandoned for Krishna according to the Caitanyite tradition. True, there are frequent references to a family life, a world of social propriety, that has been left behind.[41] But this is true for all the *gopīs,* not just for Rādhā, and in both cases the marital offense involved is not stressed. Emphasis falls instead on the social dislocation their love for Krishna requires of them and the level of commitment entailed by their attraction to him. If anything, then, Sūr seems rather to relish the ambiguity of Rādhā's position somewhere between wife and mistress. Its lack of definition adds to her fascination and, I would argue, acts as a factor that makes her ultimately worthy of worship.

More of that in a moment. First let us observe a related phenomenon having to do once again with perspective. Rādhā's position in the early *Sūr Sāgar* is quite unique. On the one hand she is the only *gopī* who is singled out as the object of our attention; at least, she is the only one given a name.[42] She is the *gopī* who, by virtue of her especially heart-rending separation, is worthy of our attention. It is in such a role that we have described her thus far, for only in that role is she sufficiently objectified for Sūr to name her.

There are many more poems, however, that one could understand as having to do with Rādhā. These are the poems she might have spoken herself, whether in the awakening of her love, in her joy, or in her agonizing separation. Yet these are poems that have Krishna as their point of reference, and so absorbed is the speaker in what has happened to her as a result of *his* presence that her own identity becomes irrelevant and never intrudes into the poem. So intense is the subjectivity of these poems, in which the speaker either ruminates to herself or addresses some friend, that Sūr refuses to answer any question we might have as to whether this is Rādhā or some other of the women of Braj. In claiming some of these poems for Rādhā specifically, modern critics often take their cues from the groupings adopted by the Nagarīpracāriṇī Sabhā editors; but the most ancient manuscripts know of no such divisions, and in any case the poems were composed separately. The poet himself offers no help; he is always silent.

The reason, it seems to me, is that he understands the voice through which he speaks to be potentially that of any *gopī*. Her words express the satisfactions and longings—particularly the longings—of them all. In the subjective mood, this is who Rādhā is: she shares her perspective with that of the rest of the *gopīs* and, by extension, with all who have been touched by Krishna. If it is she who is speaking, then it is the voice of all. Only in the objective mood is she distinguished from the others: one sees her beauty, sees her dance, sees her sunk in a particular desperation.

In the ambiguity of this double perspective, the nameless subject and the named object, lies the legitimate basis in the words of Sūr Dās himself for the increasingly unreserved exaltation of Rādhā in the later portions of the *Sūr Sāgar*. As the one *gopī* to whom Sūr gives objective focus, she summarizes the states of all those whose nameless utterances of longing and praise for Krishna fill his poems. Hers is an exaltation born not only of a special intimacy with Krishna—that is obvious—but also of the summary role she plays in relation to the rest of the *gopīs* and hence to all of us. This latter, it seems, is Sūr's way of expressing the conviction to which the Brindavan *gosvāmīs* give theological voice by regarding the other *gopīs* as extensions (*vyūha*) of Rādhā.

Perhaps this poetic mode of expressing the connection gives a more pointed insight into the reason for Rādhā's exaltation than theology can do. For as the one objective figure who can be the possible subject of all the anonymous poems of love in the *Sūr Sāgar* she connects the two poles of the religious life, the self and God, the praising subject and the object praised. She is the bridge, and when we find that she was venerated with ever greater intensity as the *Sūr Sāgar* grew and the religion of Braj in general evolved, we may understand that this happened largely because as time passed people focused with increasing specificity upon the relation between ultimate subject (self) and ultimate object (God) and identified it—that is, her—as the stuff of religion itself. The object of worship became, in significant measure, that very relationship.

In worshipping Rādhā, then, one is worshipping love, and the only way to worship love is to love. Rādhā is love objectified—or should we say personified? But as the potential speaker of the anonymous poems that rise to the surface of the ocean of love for Krishna, she is also love subjectified. By refusing at any point to pigeonhole these outbursts of emotion as Rādhā's rather than any of the other *gopīs'* (or ours), Sūr holds her personality open to the subjective access of all. As such she becomes what Vaiṣṇavas have repeatedly said she is: *mahābhāva*, great feeling. She is not great in the hierarchical sense that she holds a position that mediates between Krishna's divine status and the *gopīs'* more human one. On the whole, tradition has denied this. Just as the early Christian councils labored against the notion that Jesus was half God and half man, arguing that he was fully both, so Vaiṣṇavas have held that Rādhā is both at one with the *gopīs* and at one with Krishna. And this is possible because the mediation she secures is a mediation of feeling, not of station.

This is what lies behind Sūr's unwillingness to confine Rādhā to the role of either wife or mistress. It is not her position that matters but her feeling, and the ambiguity of her position serves to underscore that fact. It is the same with Sūr's attention to perspective. He uses this tool draw his audience into a relationship, refusing to mediate that access by any neutral or commentarial voice. Thus the relations which obtain in the world of Krishna and his loves become immediately, dramatically available to his hearers.

As the patroness and paradigm of relationship per se Rādhā superintends this effort of Sūr's, and in just that role she superintends the piety of modern-day Brindavan. When the people of Braj bow down to Rādhā in love, declaring her their queen and captain of their emotions (*raseśvarī*), they acknowledge symbolically that true religion is a matter of relationship, of love. And when Krishna bows down to Rādhā in the plays of Brindavan, it signifies that same recognition.

In Brindavan it is considered a fault for Krishna to be worshipped in the absence of Rādhā, or her in his; images that outwardly represent only one personality are understood to imply the other as well. There is every good reason for this. It expresses the conviction that religion, and all life at its deepest, is not a matter of coming before any object, even if it be an object of piety. It is, rather, living in full relationship. That is what Rādhā and Krishna represent. But Rādhā represents it uniquely. Her claim to divinity rests especially there, not on any obviously divine ancestry such as Krishna has; and in this sense she is supreme even over Krishna in the piety of Braj. In this sense too she rules over the creativity of Sūr in a way that even he does not, symbolizing not only the love that is present when he is on the scene but also the love that persists when he is gone.

The Theology of Rādhā in the Purāṇas

C. MACKENZIE BROWN

In the beginning, Krishna, the Supreme Reality, was filled with the desire to create.
By his own will he assumed a twofold form.
From the left half arose the form of a woman, the right half became a man.
The male figure was none other than Krishna himself; the female was the Goddess Primordial Nature, otherwise known as Rādhā.[1]

In this summary of various passages from the *Brahmavaivarta Purāṇa*, a Krishnaite work of the fifteenth or sixteenth century, Rādhā appears not only as a goddess, but also as the highest embodiment of the divine feminine principle that pervades the universe. The account of creation continues as follows:

The Goddess, Primordial Nature, incited passion in the heart of the Supreme Being.
Krishna, infatuated with her beauty, embraced her in amorous sport for the lifetime of a Brahmā,[2]
At last discharging his seed into her womb.
From her exhausted limbs flowed perspiration which became the cosmic waters upon which the universe would float.
From her labored breathing arose the vital breaths that would sustain all living beings.
After a hundred eons, the goddess finally gave birth to a golden egg, which she kicked into the cosmic waters.[3]
From that egg arose, in due course, the entire universe.[4]

By means of the androgynous division of the Supreme Being and the subsequent reunion of the two parts in cosmogonic copulation, Rādhā and Krishna have become the parents of the world, including humankind. Rādhā, accordingly, is viewed as the Supreme Mother, and in this role she is not only the universal creator, but also the supreme mediator and redeemer for all ignorant and suffering beings.

This exalted status is remarkable in view of the fact that only a thousand years earlier, Rādhā was unknown in India, and even by the eleventh century A.D. she was still an obscure, low-class cowherd's daughter with no apparent marks of divinity whose sole claim to fame was her total absorption in love for Krishna.

The Development of Rādhāite Theology

The evolution of the Rādhā image or symbol was a complex process involving mythological, literary, devotional, and theological developments. In this historical context, I speak intentionally of the Rādhā image, in contrast to Rādhā herself, who, her worshippers could claim, transcends or lies behind the various historical manifestations of the Rādhā symbol. Thus, whereas the symbol of Rādhā may have had its origin only 1000 to 1500 years ago, Rādhā's real birth, according to many of her devotees, was at the beginning of creation, when she emerged from the left side of the Supreme Being.

Historically, Rādhā first manifested herself anonymously, at least in the great purāṇic tradition with which we shall be primarily concerned. In the earliest extended account of the Krishna legend, in the *Harivaṃśa* (the root of Krishnaite purāṇic literature, ca. 2nd c. A.D.), Rādhā is lost among the several unnamed *gopīs* (cowherd women) who seek amorous sport with Krishna. In the *Viṣṇu Purāṇa* (ca. A.D. 300-600) and the *Bhāgavata Purāṇa* (ca. A.D. 600-900), one of the *gopīs* is singled out as Krishna's favorite, with whom he disappears in order to teach the others humility, though she too is abandoned in turn, for the same reason (see figure 4). This favored woman remains without name, though in the *Bhāgavata Purāṇa* the other *gopīs* say that Krishna has been conciliated (*ārādhita*) by her.[5] Rādhā's name itself is clearly linked to this notion of conciliation, and later tradition identifies the favorite *gopī* of the *Viṣṇu* and *Bhāgavata Purāṇas* with Rādhā.

The name Rādhā appears in popular folklore and poetry as early as the sixth century A.D., long before its mention in purāṇic literature.[6] There are various scattered references to Rādhā up through the eleventh century, and in the twelfth her love for Krishna became immortalized in the *Gītagovinda*. During these centuries Rādhā, along with the *gopīs* in general, served on a symbolic level primarily as a model of the human soul longing for the divine. In this context, the

FIGURE 4.

Union and Separation of Krishna and a Gopī

Page from the fifth *Bhāgavata Purāṇa* series.
(Book 10, Chapter 30, verses 36-38.)
Basohli, ca. 1760-1765.
(Courtesy, Museum of Fine Arts, Boston, 61.382.
Gift of John D. McDonald.)

Figure 4.

A magical moment in the moonlit forest of Vṛndāvana, near the Jumna River, is captured in this illustration to the *Bhāgavata Purāṇa.*[1] The Sanskrit text accompanying it[2] describes the episode: To the right, the *gopī* (whom Krishna has singled out from the others at the first circular dance), intoxicated with pride and with arms outstretched, asks Krishna to carry her on his shoulders. (Rādhā is not specifically named, but she comes to be identified with this *gopī.*) Krishna, kneeling, appears to consent, but just as the *gopī* prepares to mount, he vanishes, leaving her in the same gesture, poignantly unfulfilled. To an adoring lover, the request is not unreasonable, but to God, it implies an excess of pride. Despite their impassioned lovemaking, the *gopī* must be humbled. It is interesting to note that as Rādhā's personality evolves through time her demands of Krishna become more effective (as in the concluding songs of the *Gītagovinda*), and he submits.

This painting derives much of its beauty from the manner in which the artist depicts nature — as mirroring the situation of the lovers. To the right, the union of the lovers is suggested by the entwined tree and flowering creeper, while to the left, the parted trees and the drooping willow tree reflect the abandonment of the *gopī* by Krishna.

— J.P.

[1]First published by Milo C. Beach, "A Bhāgavata Purāṇa from the Punjab Hills, *Bulletin Museum of Fine Arts,* Boston, LXII, no. 333 (1965), pp. 168-177. For a complete discussion of this painting, see W.G. Archer, *Indian Paintings from the Punjab Hills,* Vol. I, pp. 49-51.

[2]*Bhāgavata Purāṇa,* Tenth Book, chapter 30, verses 36-38.

question of Rādhā's marital status became highly significant, for it was a matter of considerable importance for human devotion to God whether Rādhā's love for Krishna was adulterous or conjugal.[7] In most early references to Rādhā she appears much like the other *gopīs*, her one distinguishing mark being her unrivaled love for Krishna. Accordingly, Rādhā, like the others, is often portrayed as, or at least implicitly understood to be, Krishna's mistress. There was, however, a tendency in certain later schools to make Rādhā the spouse of Krishna, despite the common notion, based on traditional legend, that she had a husband of her own.

In any case, it was by means of her all-consuming passion, whether as wife or mistress, that she came to occupy a seat of honor on Krishna's left side. In this position, she began to shed her human personality and assume that of a *devī* (goddess). Around the time of the *Gītagovinda* we begin to find references to Rādhā as *devī*, as in the writings of Nimbārka, where she is referred to as "the *devī* sitting on the left side of Krishna."[8] For Nimbārka, Rādhā is the eternal consort of Viṣṇu who, like him, has become incarnate on earth. Not long afterwards, in the *Śrīkṛṣṇakīrtan* of Caṇḍidās, we find the gods seeking Viṣṇu's help to destroy Kaṃsa, and after he agrees to incarnate himself, the gods ask Lakṣmī to be born as Rādhā, to be a companion to him.[9] The identification of Rādhā as the earthly incarnation of Lakṣmī may seem to subordinate Rādhā to Lakṣmī. But just as Krishna attained supremacy over Viṣṇu in many of the medieval Vaiṣṇava schools, such as those of Caitanya and Vallabha (sixteenth century and later), so too did Rādhā rise above Lakṣmī.

Returning to purāṇic literature, we find that the name Rādhā is specifically mentioned perhaps no earlier than the thirteenth century, in such late works as the *Devī-bhāgavata, Nāradīya, Padma, Brahmāṇḍa* and *Brahmavaivarta Purāṇas*.[10] In these works the Rādhā symbol has expanded from the earlier model of human longing for the divine to a revelation of feminine cosmic and redemptive power. In the *Brahmavaivarta Purāṇa* especially, a profound and relatively systematic theology of Rādhā is elaborated. The exact relation between the purāṇic elucidations of the Rādhā symbol and other popular or scholastic devotional movements is unclear. It is doubtful, for instance, that the *Brahmavaivarta Purāṇa* was the work of any single school, for some of its doctrines agree remarkably well with those of Caitanya, whereas others accord more closely with the teachings of

Vallabha's followers or of still other schools.[11] In large part it is precisely because of such a synthesizing approach toward various theological and philosophical viewpoints that the late Purāṇas represent a unique and significant strand in the process of reinterpreting the Rādhā symbol.

The purāṇic tradition, unlike the immutable Vedic tradition, retained its religious authority by constantly reconsidering and reinterpreting ancient doctrines and myths. It also sought to discover new symbols that might better reveal the meaning of the eternal Vedic truths for later generations. The image of Rādhā was one such symbol that particularly struck the imagination of the late purāṇic sages, who accordingly attempted to bring out her theological significance on a variety of levels.

Three Aspects of Rādhā as Goddess

Three basic factors were at work in the theologizing of the Rādhā image, corresponding to three roles or aspects of Rādhā as goddess. The first concerns the reworking and reinterpretation of the basic Rādhā legend, of the various events in the life of Rādhā and Krishna found in the traditional accounts. The result of this process was the transfiguration of Rādhā from the human mistress of Krishna dallying amorously in the earthly paradise of Vṛndāvana to the heavenly queen sporting in the eternal celestial sphere of Krishna's supreme world, Goloka. The second factor was the introduction and incorporation of general Hindu feminine theological ideas, such as *pṛakrti* (nature), *māyā* (creative mysterious power), and *śakti* (energy), taken over from more ancient goddesses such as Devī or Durgā. By such means the already transfigured *gopī* assimilated a great variety of cosmologic and cosmogonic functions. Finally, several ideals from the *bhakti* (devotional) tradition, such as *sevā* (service) and *kṛpā* (grace), came to be associated with Rādhā, who thus is perceived in a soteriological role, as the mediator of divine love and compassion. These three aspects, of course, are closely interrelated and are separated here merely for purposes of analysis. They are most clearly developed in the *Brahmavaivarta Purāṇa;* we shall therefore concentrate on this text in presenting the basic outlines of the purāṇic theology of Rādhā.[12]

Rādhā as Transfigured Gopī

In the *Brahmavaivarta Purāṇa,* the transfiguration of Rādhā through the reinterpretation of the traditional accounts of Krishna's life is typically manifested in the remarkable transformation of the *rāsa-maṇḍala.* In the *Bhāgavata Purāṇa* and earlier the *rāsa-maṇḍala* referred to the circle-dance of Krishna with the *gopīs* in the forests of the earthly Vṛndāvana.[13] In the *Brahmavaivarta Purāṇa,* it no longer refers primarily to a circle of dancers, but to a celestial orb situated in Krishna's eternal paradise, Goloka. It remains, however, a circle full of relish or enjoyment (*rasa*), for it is here that Rādhā sprang from Krishna's left side at the beginning of creation and proceeded at once to unite with him in sexual delight. The earthly *rāsa-maṇḍala* is now seen simply as a reflection or counterpart of the heavenly circle of ecstatic joy. Accordingly, in the celestial sphere, Rādhā is not any mere human mistress of Krishna; she presides over the *rāsa-maṇḍala* as the divine mistress or queen of the *rasa* (Rāsésvarī), for her essence is the supreme bliss (*paramānanda-rūpa*).

In the earliest textual layers of the *Brahmavaivarta Purāṇa,* Rādhā manifests herself in the *rāsa-maṇḍala* after the other major gods and goddesses have already evolved out of various parts of Krishna's body.[14] After Rādhā's own coming into being, there emanate from her body thousands upon thousands of other *gopīs;* thus she is clearly the head of all the cowherd women. Yet within this scheme of creation, there is an implicit subordination of Rādhā to the several primary deities. It is not surprising, then, to find in the later parts of the Purāṇa that the manner of evolution of these deities is somewhat different: Rādhā evolves from Krishna at the very beginning of creation, before any other gods are manifest, and afterwards all the other goddesses (as well as the *gopīs*) emanate from her body, while the gods issue forth from Krishna.[15] This latest recasting of the events transpiring in the *rāsa-maṇḍala* thus reveals Rādhā as the undisputed queen of the universe, the primoridal feminine principle that is the source of all divine as well as earthly female beings.

The transfiguration of Rādhā is also evident in the account of Krishna's reason for coming into the world. The traditional purpose for Krishna's descent, as found in the *Viṣṇu* and *Bhāgavata Purāṇa,* was to relieve the earth of her burden of tyrants, who were really demons in disguise.[16] The gods were to descend along with Krishna to help in the battle. The *Bhāgavata* adds the significant note that the divine damsels were to become incarnate as well (apparently as *gopīs*), for the sake of Krishna's pleasure, thereby suggesting another reason for his descent, namely his sport with the cowherd women.[17] In the *Brahmavaivarta Purāṇa*, this suggestion is elaborated further, and the original purpose of slaying demon-tyrants becomes merely a pretext for his incarnation. The real reason now is to make it possible for Krishna to accompany Rādhā to earth during her sojourn as a cowherd woman in Vṛndāvana.[18]

The occasion for Rādhā's human incarnation is itself of considerable interest. The author-compilers of the *Brahmavaivarta* took over most of the aspects of Rādhā's and Krishna's traditional love affair, including Krishna's unfaithfulness to Rādhā and the resultant quarrels, and transferred these incidents from earth to Goloka. In consequence of one of Rādhā's jealous rages, she is cursed by a servant of Krishna to descend to the world and thus to live in separation from her Lord. At this point, however, Krishna promises Rādhā that he will follow her to earth and sport with her in the forests of Vṛndāvana. This whole story, to be sure, hardly portrays Rādhā's greatness as the supreme Goddess of the universe, for she appears helpless against the curse of a mere servant of Krishna. Yet the text explains that these events were predestined and thus (the reader may assume) ordained by Krishna himself, the author of destiny. In any case the basic point that the Purāṇa is trying to make is that the amorous play of Rādhā and Krishna on earth is merely an interlude in the eternal play of the two in Goloka.

One final example of Rādhā's transfiguration is an episode during Krishna's infancy, when Rādhā was already a young maiden. Krishna's foster father, Nanda, had taken the baby Krishna out into the forest while grazing cows, when suddenly a thunderstorm threatened. Not wanting to abandon the cows, yet concerned for Krishna's safety, Nanda asked Rādhā, who happened by, to take Krishna home. Rādhā carried Krishna off to a jungle bower, where he transformed himself into a young man, and then the two proceeded to engage in love-play. Such seems to be the basic story that is briefly referred to in the first verse of the *Gītagovinda*.[19]

In the *Brahmavaivarta* the tale is considerably amplified. Most significantly, when Rādhā takes Krishna away into the forest, he disappears from her arms, to reappear as a handsome youth in a magically constructed house of gems that reminds Rādhā of the heavenly *rāsa-maṇḍala*. Krishna now causes Rādhā to recall her former existence in Goloka and indicates that he is presently fulfilling his vow to follow her to earth in order to sport with her. He also reveals to her their mutual interdependence and inseparability. Krishna declares that though he is male and she female, they are equal in all respects and that ultimately there is no difference between them. He can create the world only through union with her, for he is the universal form and she the universal energy (*sarva-śakti*) that activates and realizes the potentiality of form. Krishna also addresses her as the Goddess who is primordial nature (*mūlapṛakrtir īśvarī*). Following Krishna's disclosures the god Brahmā appears on the scene and unites the two in wedlock, having given his own eulogy of Rādhā as the co-creator of the world. After Brahmā discreetly takes his leave, Rādhā and Krishna turn their attention to the consummation of the marriage.[20]

This marriage has special significance in view of the fact that the *Brahmavaivarta* never denies the traditional notion that Rādhā has a human husband, though the Purāṇa at times rationalizes that only an illusory form of Rādhā is married to the first husband.[21] On a more profound and transcendent level, however, she belongs only to Krishna, and he to her. In performing the marriage rites Brahmā is thus simply rejoining the divine, primordial couple, who are none other than the eternal principles of form and power, spirit and matter, ever engaged in creative interplay.

Rādhā as Pṛakrti, Śakti, *and* Māyā

In the account of Rādhā's and Krishna's marriage, we find various important ideals of traditional feminine theology now being applied to Rādhā. One of the most basic of these ideals is that of *prakṛti* (nature). In the older Sāṃkhya school, *prakṛti* had been contrasted with *puruṣa,* spirit, not in sexual terms but rather as the material over against the efficient cause of the universe. Though *puruṣa* was regarded as a masculine principle, being masculine in gender and literally meaning ("man"), *prakṛti* was not thought of as specifically feminine in essence, despite its feminine gender. The term *prakṛti,* in fact, was often used interchangeably with the word *pradhāna,* neuter in gender, which signifies the first principle (of material existence). Gradually, however, *prakṛti* became 'feminized' as it was increasingly identified with the "womb of the world" (*jagad-yoni*),[22] and thus material nature was reinterpreted as maternal nature or Mother Nature. Finally, *prakṛti* came to be associated with various goddesses, such as Devī or Durgā. *Prakṛti* is no longer the insentient material principle, but a conscious, animating force within all matter. Furthermore, *prakṛti* is now related to *puruṣa* not so much as material to efficient cause, but as woman to man and as creator to procreator.

The sexual cosmogonic aspects of *puruṣa* and *prakṛti* were of special interest to the purāṇic reinterpreters of the Rādhā-Krishna legend. The amorous dalliance of Rādhā and Krishna in the forests of Vṛndāvana was readily assimilated to the cosmogonic interplay of *puruṣa* and *prakṛti*. This assimilation was made easier by the transformation of the *rāsa-maṇḍala* into the cosmic center where Krishna at the beginning of time split into male and female for the purposes of creation. It was almost inevitable that this female, who was none other than Rādhā, should come to be identified with *prakṛti,* as in the summary at the beginning of this article. By her identification with *prakṛti* Rādhā comes to be regarded not only as the amorous consort of Krishna but also as the maternal goddess of the world.

Throughout the *Brahmavaivarta Purāṇa* Rādhā's essential cosmogonic role as *prakṛti* is revealed in a number of analogies. For instance, Krishna himself often declares that just as a potter cannot make a pot without clay, so he cannot create the universe without Rādhā.[23] Such analogies, utilizing the notions of efficient and material cause, recall the older Sāṃkhya view of *puruṣa* and *prakṛti,* with its subordination of matter to spirit. The *Brahmavaivarta* itself is aware of this implication, pointing out that some people might argue for the superiority of the potter (*puruṣa*), since it is the potter who goes to fetch the clay and not *vice versa*.[24] Such a conclusion does not rest easily with our purāṇic philosophers, who usually prefer to stress the equality of Rādhā and Krishna and sometimes even suggest the superiority of Rādhā. Accordingly the *Brahmavaivarta* presents many other analogies that more clearly reveal Rādhā's non-subordinate status.

One especially important analogy that suggests the cosmogonic pre-eminence of Rādhā is that of *ādhāra* and *ādheya,* the "supporter" and the "supported." In traditional Krishnaite theology Krishna is seen as the suporter (*ādhāra*) of the entire world, the *ādheya*. Krishna himself is without support (*nirādhāra*). The *Brahmavaivarta* at times simply repeats this analogy, representing Krishna as the support of Rādhā, whom it identifies with *prakṛti* or the world.[25] However, Krishna himself declares in the Purāṇa that whereas the world indeed rests upon him, he in turn is supported by Rādhā and rests in her always.[26] Thus she is the *ādhāra* of Krishna, who is no longer *nirādhāra*. With this reversal of roles, another signification of the terms *ādhāra* and *ādheya* comes into play. *Ādhāra* can also mean receptacle or vessel, and *ādheya*, that which is contained therein. Rādhā as the *ādhāra* is the all-container, the receptacle and womb of the universe (*jagad-yoni*), a notion already associated with *prakṛti*. In this womb the cosmic germ, identified with Krishna, the *ādheya*, is implanted.[27]

The equality of Rādhā/*prakṛti* with Krishna/*puruṣa* is further indicated in the *Brahmavaivarta* in another, rather paradoxical way. The supreme reality in Hinduism has frequently been considered to be *nirguṇa*, without attributes or qualities. The term *nirguṇa* itself has been understood either in an absolute sense, or in the qualified sense of being without delimiting qualities, including especially the three *guṇas* of material nature (*sattva, rajas,* and *tamas*). In the Krishnaite schools it was natural enough for this ancient revered designation, *nirguṇa,* to be applied to Krishna, whose ultimate supremacy was thus attested. In the *Brahmavaivarta* the same term is also applied to Rādhā, even though as *prakṛti* her very essence is said to consist of the three *guṇas!*[28] In part the paradox can be explained by the fact that both Rādhā and Krishna are said to be beyond *prakṛti* and *puruṣa* in their highest, *nirguṇa* form, whereas in their lower form, as *prakṛti* and *puruṣa,* they become *saguṇa,* endowed with qualities.[29]

Another aspect of Rādhā's divine nature is brought out in a different kind of analogy, that of substance and attribute. Krishna is identified with substance, she with attribute. He is milk, she its whiteness; he is the moon, she its beauty; he is fire, she its burning.[30] Such analogies, while emphasizing the inseparability of Rādhā and Krishna,[31] may seem ontologically to subordinate her, as attribute, to the substance. Yet the *Brahmavaivarta* suggests the greater eminence of the attribute, for the latter is not merely a passive accident of the substance, but rather the essential, activating quality or force that allows the substance to realize its own nature. This is especially clear in the fire/burning example, where Rādhā is called not merely *dāhikā* (burning), but *dāhikā-śakti* (the power of burning).[32] Rādhā, then, represents the energy or power in all things, and Krishna is powerless without her.[33] Here we see the identification of Rādhā with *śakti,* perhaps the single most important feminine theological notion in Hinduism.

The term *śakti,* feminine in gender, had long been associated with the various male deities as their power or energy. Gradually the energy of each god became personified as his consort, and thus if a god was separated from his consort, he was powerless and inert. These notions were most fully developed in the Śākta school, in which the goddess Śakti, the active feminine element identified with Śiva's wife Devī (known also as Kālī or Durgā), was raised to pre-eminence over the masculine. In this context the relationship of *śakti* to *prakṛti* and to *puruṣa* is of special interest. In the old Sāṃkhya school, *prakṛti,* while ever unconscious, was solely responsible for activity; *puruṣa* was inactive and unchanging, though the superior principle, as it alone was conscious. It was natural enough, with the development of Śākta ideas, to identify the active *prakṛti* with Energy (*śakti*) herself. But since *śakti* was a *conscious* power, *prakṛti* was no longer merely the activating material force but also the power of consciousness. (Such a development reinforced the process of personifying and feminizing *prakṛti* that we saw earlier.) By logical extension, the male principle, *puruṣa,* would be unconscious without *prakṛti-śakti.* Accordingly, in Śākta views, Śiva without his wife Śakti is not only inactive but also unconscious, a corpse (*śava*).[34]

In the *Brahmavaivarta,* Rādhā assimilates much of the character of the goddess Śakti and is often identified with her.[35] Rādhā's consort, of course, is Krishna, so she comes to be known as *Krishna-śakti* (the Śakti of Krishna), and on the highest level she is said to be the *nirguṇa śakti* of the *nirguṇa* Krishna.[36] Her role as the energizing force of Krishna has both cosmogonic and redemptive aspects. Concerning the former, she not only bears the world-seed as his *śakti,*[37] she also activates his desire to create in the first place, for she is his *icchā-śakti* (power of desire).[38] In relation to the redemptive function, we are told that Śakti has a twofold power, that of discrimination and that of delusion.[39] As the power of discrimination, Śakti is the "sharp sword of Krishna" that cuts the bonds of *karma,* allowing the true seekers to differentiate the real and eternal (Krishna himself) from the impermanent (the desires and wealth of the world). Śakti's aspect as the power of delusion is more complex, for in this role she wields the power of *māyā* ('obscuring force'), or is actually identified with *māyā.* Whereas *māyā* may seem at first to be directly opposed to wisdom or discrimination, it has redemptive capacities of its own that merit consideration.

In the *Bhagavad Gītā māyā* is equated with the "world-illusion" composed of the three qualities or *guṇas* of material nature.[40] Deluded souls are unable to penetrate beyond this realm of *māyā-prakṛti.* The association of *māyā* and delusion with *prakṛti* is significant, for in the Sāṃkhya school bondage is said to arise from the involvement of *puruṣa* with *prakṛti* and from the subsequent confusion of the two principles. At the same time, according to the Sāṃkhya, *prakṛti* is active solely in order to effect the emancipation of *puruṣa*.[41] Similarly in the *Gītā*, although the ultimate reality, Krishna, is veiled by *māyā-prakṛti*, it is through *māyā's* power that Krishna, resorting to his material nature, *prakṛti*, is able to come into the world for the welfare and salvation of humankind.[42] *Māyā* is the power enabling Krishna to obscure his supreme nature and assume the role of a friend, master, child, or lover, thereby evoking a more intense, intimate response on the part of his worshippers.[43] When *māyā* became personified as a goddess, often called Viṣṇu-māyā, her redemptive functions were further elaborated.

In the *Brahmavaivarta*, the goddess Prakṛti, constituted of *māyā* (*māyā-mayī*), is likened to a boat for crossing the ocean of *saṃsāra*.[44] Krishna, who is full of compassion (*kṛpā-maya*), is the pilot guiding across his devotees. At times it is Māyā herself, or Viṣṇu-māyā, who is the pilot, using the boat of *Krishna bhakti* (devotion to Krishna), for she too is filled with compassion (*kṛpā-mayī*).[45] Accordingly, when Rādhā becomes identified with Viṣṇu-māyā, as well as with the discriminating power of Śakti, she soon takes on a new role as the supreme mediator and redeemer of the universe.

Rādhā as Supreme Redeemer

Rādhā's soteriological role is closely related to her status as Krishna's favorite. Through her devotion and service to Krishna, she becomes the mediator of his grace (*prasāda, anugraha*) and compassion (*kṛpā*). She is constituted of love for Krishna and is the main channel through which he sends his own love to his devotees. Thus she herself becomes a revered object of worship. As Krishna declares in the *Brahmavaivarta*, he will not grant *mokṣa* to anyone who does not revere Rādhā; he even affirms that the worship of Rādhā is more pleasing to him than his own.[46]

The particular devotional attitude that man should adopt toward Rādhā is significant. Among the five basic attitudes associated with the worship of Krishna,[47] *dāsya* (servitude) was taken over as the most appropriate for worshipping Rādhā. Her principal relation to humankind, at least in the *Brahmavaivarta,* is as Mother, and thus loving service is the most befitting mode of adoration on the part of her children-devotees.[48] As Mother, Rādhā is seen as especially forgiving of the faults of her offspring. She comes to be regarded as even more accessible and compassionate than Krishna, and as the mediator between her children and their Father. In this context it is of interest that Krishna had usually not been regarded as a father in traditional devotional terms. At times his role as creator of the world implied an abstract fatherhood that would most readily correlate with the attitude of *śānta* (extreme, impersonal awe). When, as a result of the cosmogonic copulation with Rādhā, his paternal role becomes more concrete, it is still perceived in terms of an awesome distance. Rādhā's motherhood thus emphasized the remoteness of Krishna, and she thereby gradually assumed the supreme redemptive role.

Although the Mother is regarded as more accessible and more intimately bound to her children than the Father, she is at the same time seen as deserving of greater reverence. As the *Brahmavaivarta* says:

> Prakṛti is the Mother of the world, and Puruṣa, the Father of the world.
> The Mother of the three worlds is a hundred times more venerable than the Father.[49]

It is not simply her greater compassion or accessibility that makes the Mother more revered, according to the *Brahmavaivarta.* She is also the supreme spiritual teacher:

> You [Rādhā] are the Mother of the world, Hari [Krishna] is the Father.
> The guru of the Father is the Mother, to be worshipped and honored as supreme.[50]

Rādhā has come a long way from the rustic *gopī* to the supreme amorous and maternal goddess. Ontologically, it is true, she never rises above Krishna, at least in the *Brahmavaivarta;* for she arises out of Krishna and ultimately will dissolve back into him. Yet in her cosmogonic and especially in her redemptive functions she attains preeminence. One final passage from the *Brahmavaivarta,* an injunction to one of her devotees, succinctly illustrates her soteriological supremacy:

> Worship that Rādhā who is without qualities.
> Quickly, by serving her, through her grace, you shall go to Goloka.

She has been served and worshipped by Krishna, who is propitiated by all.
Devotees, by serving him, unattainable by meditation,[51] hard to propitiate, without qualities,
In a long time, after many births, go to Goloka.
By serving her, full of compassion, devotees go there in a short time,
For she is the Mother of all,[52] representing all welfare.[53]

For all its power, the *Brahmavaivarta's* theology of Rādhā holds a somewhat paradoxical place in the history of medieval and modern Hindu devotionalism. On the one hand, it has a remarkable breadth. The *Brahmavaivarta* attempted a thoroughgoing synthesis of Krishnaite and Śākta ideas, fitting Rādhā into the outlines of Hindu feminine theology so as to accommodate important devotional-theological movements in North India during the fifteenth and sixteenth centuries. On the other hand, this same synthetic impetus led to an emphasis on Rādhā's maternal role that was largely peculiar to the *Brahmavaivarta* and was not acknowledged for the most part by the later Rādhā cults. To be sure, various notions about Rādhā in the *Brahmavaivarta* came to be widely accepted, such as the identification of Rādhā and Krishna with *prakṛti* and *puruṣa*. And such sects as the Rādhāvallabhīs, who worship Rādhā above Krishna, may be especially indebted to the *Brahmavaivarta*. Certainly other Purāṇas, such as the *Nāradīya, Padma,* and *Devī-bhāgavata,* as well as the *Nārada Pāñcarātra,* have elaborated upon Rādhāite notions that may well have been borrowed from the *Brahmavaivarta*. Yet in the final analysis it seems that the main significance of the *Brahmavaivarta's* interpretation of Rādhā is less its role in molding the religious attitudes of later generations than its status as a theological tour de force, aligning Rādhā with the great Goddess Devī.

Rādhā: The Play and Perfection of *Rasa*

SHRIVATSA GOSWAMI

Essense of beauty and *rasa*,
Quintessence of bliss and compassion,
Embodiment of sweetness and brilliance,
Epitome of artfulness, graceful in love:
May my mind take refuge in Rādhā,
Quintessence of all essences.[1]

As "quintessence of all essences" Śrī Rādhā is the ultimate answer to the human quest—philosophical, theological, existential. The following interpretation of her significance reflects the views of the religious community of which I am a part, the Caitanya Sampradāya, those who look to Śrī Caitanya, the Bengali ecstatic of the late fifteenth and early sixteenth century, as the complete avatar of both Rādhā and Krishna. It is fitting, therefore, that I begin with him.

'That,' the Object of Philosophy

The standard account of Caitanya's life tells of an extended encounter he had with Rāmānanda Rāya, the governor of a district of Orissa who was renowned for his wisdom. In the course of their discussion Caitanya put to him the perennial question: "What is 'that' which is to be attained?"[2] More than two thousand years earlier Gārgī Vācaknavī, Śvetaketu, Bṛhadratha, Kātyāyana and many others had raised the same query,[3] and in India the history of philosophy ever since has largely been shaped by attempts to find an answer. The question is put in many ways: Who am I? What is the cause of my existence, my world, my suffering? What is the way out, the final goal? No matter how it is expressed, the quest is fundamentally the same. Ultimately one wants access to that by means of which everything can be understood.[4] The natural desire of humankind is to be happy, to get rid of all suffering, and the search leads finally to the discovery of a state in which the very duality of happiness and suffering, pleasure and pain, is abolished.[5] Such a state must be infinite and absolute because nothing finite and limited can give uninterrupted happiness.[6] Thus the goal, the *summum bonum,* is the total knowledge or experience of that by means of which alone there is complete cessation of suffering. One finds that all worldly suffering stems from an aversion to this goal and that the aversion is in turn caused by ignorance of such an eternal principle. The remedy is found in conversion, in turning around to it, to 'that.'[7]

But what is 'that'? We are told that "knowers of reality (*tattva-vidaḥ*) declare reality (*tattva*) to be non-dual knowledge (*advaya-jñāna*)."[8] Such a definition, however, seems too general and abstract to be helpful. Hence the sages have specified the nature of reality according to its various manifestations, insofar as these correlate with the particular capacities of individual seekers.[9] Every person who desires to approach the transcendental reality, our 'that,' has a certain psychological constitution. Broadly, such character configurations may be classified as cognitive, conative, and affective; these correspond respectively to the three main paths (*mārgas* or *upāyas*) recognized in Indian spirituality; *jñāna, karma,* and *bhakti*.[10] As the sixteenth-century Vaiṣṇava philosopher Jīva Gosvāmī made clear, if one's point of departure is cognitive, then the absolute is apprehended (objectively) as Brahma, undifferentiated consciousness; if one's approach is conative, then the end to be attained (subjectively) is Paramātmā, the supreme innermost being of all beings; but if one's orientation is affective, reality becomes manifest in the fullest form of all, as Bhagavān, the Supreme Godhead.[11] Yet the three paths are not strictly equivalent, for Bhagavān in his twofold essence embraces both subjective and objective poles, whereas Paramātmā represents only the subjective aspect of ultimate reality, and Brahma, only the objective.

From the viewpoint of ultimate reality, which is non-dual knowledge, all distinctions are immaterial. Yet there are important differences among the three paths. The cognitive (*jñāna*) and conative (*karma*) paths have prerequisites, but the path of feeling (*bhakti*) does not. Anyone who has a genuine inclination (*śraddhā*) to experience reality-in-itself is fit for the path of *bhakti*. No ulterior motive intervenes: the dualities of pleasure and pain are transcended in this experience of greatest happiness, which is sufficient to itself.

The disciplines of *jñāna* and *karma* contrast with *bhakti* in respect not only to motive but also to effect. *Jñāna-yoga* has the effect of strengthening the seeker's longing for the ultimate experience of bliss by focusing attention on the supreme reality, and *karma-yoga* removes self-interest by inculcating the virtue of surrendering the fruits of action. *Bhakti,* however, is an integrated approach that makes the other two redundant. It is in no sense propaedeutic, as others have argued; for in human nature feeling integrates the cognitive and conative elements of personality, whereas these in themselves are exclusive and partial.[12]

Bhakti, then, comprehends the whole of human nature, and as such it corresponds and leads to the apprehension of reality in its total and essential manifestation.[13] This totality of Being is self-luminous consciousness overflowing with bliss: it is thus designated *sat-cit-ānanda,* being-consciousness-bliss.[14] Of these three, however, the accent lies upon the third. As the *Taittirīya Upaniṣad* puts it in a famous passage, "That (the ultimate reality), verily, is *rasa* (aesthetic experience); it and it alone causes supreme bliss."[15]

Rasa *and* Śakti: *Aesthetics and Power in Rādhā*

Because the Absolute is by nature blissful, it manifests itself in aesthetic experience, as *rasa.* Enjoyment itself, it implies subjective and objective poles, the enjoyer and that which is to be enjoyed. Without this duality there could be no joy. It is impossible to explain in precise logical terms how that which is by nature non-dual necessarily becomes dual. But analogy helps: a single non-dual Being effulgent with absolute bliss cannot enjoy itself any more than sugar can taste its own sweetness. Hence the absolutely blissful one, for the manifestation of its eternal self-enjoyment, polarizes its singularity into "he" and "she."[16] Non-dual in essence, it becomes dual in function.[17] Unspecifiable in essence, it becomes functionally specific. Thus scripture can say that "the absolute essentially triune entity, being-consciousness-bliss, the ultimate cause, is Krishna, the Cowherd God."[18] And again, "Krishna is Bhagavān Himself."[19]

From another point of view one can understand this self-differentiating action of the Absolute as a matter of divine potencies (*śaktis*). The Absolute differentiates itself in a threefold way, complementing its inherent form with two others, that of the material world and that of individual selves (*jīvas*). These three aspects—God, world and selves—are the manifestation of three potencies of Bhagavān, the essential (*svarūpa*), the deluding (*māyā*), and the intermediary (*taṭasthā*). When a seeker (*jīva*) moves beyond the range of the deluding potency, only the essential potency remains. The latter can be experienced because, though essential, it contains a potential differentiation within itself. Again it is threefold, in accordance with the three aspects of the divine essence, being, consciousness, and bliss. As powers or potencies (*śaktis*) these aspects are termed existential (*sandhinī*), conscious (*saṃvit*) and blissful (*hlādinī*). Here again, bliss is supreme among the three, for it is inherently encompassing, inherently fulfilling.

This *hlādinī-śakti* is joy itself and at the same time causes joy in others in that it has as its nature the fully conscious tasting of bliss (*ānanda-cinmaya-rasa*). The term I translate "tasting" here, *rasa*, is the same I earlier rendered as "aesthetic experience," and it is appropriate as a description of the blissful potency because it has a double meaning. It is regularly derived in two ways, one of which brings out the fact that it implies one who experiences (*rasayati āsvādayati iti rasaḥ*) and the other of which emphasizes the fact that it requires an object to be experienced (*rasyate āsvādyate iti rasaḥ*). Neither of the components of aesthetic experience can exist without the other; a duality is invariably involved.

On the transcendental plane this functional duality implies the split of the Absolute into power or potency (*śakti*), the subjective component, and the possessor of power (*śaktimān*), the objective one. On the phenomenal plane too there exists such a duality. In the realm of love it is the relation between the two poles, lover and beloved, that determines the nature of the experience. Unless the two approach one another, there can be no relation. In the religious realm a similar relation obtains between the devotee and the object of devotion. However hard a devotee may try, he or she cannot fully experience the bliss of Krishna unless he reveals himself, descends and becomes accessible. The reverse is also true: there must likewise be motion on the part of the devotee. This upward motion, brought about through spiritual discipline motivated by sincere longing, elevates a seeker to the level of the beloved.[20]

In such a discipline, however, it is crucial that expert guidance be available. This is the function of scripture and also of the guru: both reveal the transcendent and its relation to the phenomenal world. But because *rasa* is existentially a matter of experience, it is appropriate that the words of scripture become embodied in the form of *gopīs*, Krishna's beloved cowherd women, who function as gurus in the realm of concrete experience by exhibiting *rasa* in their very persons.[21]

Such a mediating presence is in fact necessary for the experience of *rasa,* which, as its literal translation ("juice") implies, is essentially flow. Whether the flow of aesthetic experience be from the ocean to a small pond or vice versa, a connecting stream (*dhārā*) is required to conduct it.[22] That stream is none other than Rādhā herself, the leader and exemplar of the *gopīs,* and the two syllables in her name (*rā-dhā*) suggest how reversibly the stream (*dhā-rā*) flows. It is her grace that makes the flow of *rasa* possible, connecting the human and the divine in a single liquid medium, submerging them in a world of *līlā* (play).

The play between Krishna and Rādhā or Krishna and the *gopīs,* who truly understood are only the various expressions of Rādhā's personality or the various outworkings of her potency (*śakti*), is no ordinary play. It is rather the spontaneous play that generates itself between the two aspects of the ultimate reality, the power or the potency on the one hand and the possessor of power on the other. This is a transcendental *līlā;* it is *alaukika,* not of this world. Indeed, it is what animates creation itself, for only as a by-product of the divine desire to enjoy itself through its essential potencies (*śaktis*) are revealed the differentiations constitutive of what we know as the world—the various forms of materiality and the individual selves that exist in relation to them. As the phenomenal world resonates to this supernal game, it becomes known as the gesture of grace,[23] and the hearts of devotees are attracted into the play.[24]

Such a revelation of grace takes place most palpably in Vraja, (sometimes pronounced Braj), the region around Mathura-Brindavan, where the Absolute comes down to earth as an ordinary human being to be the son of Nanda and Yaśodā: Krishna. This particular descent (*avatāra*) of the Divine is critically important. Its context is human and from the human seeker's point of view, says the *Mahābhārata,* "nothing is superior to being human.[25] Caṇḍidās is even more emphatic when he asserts, "Man is the highest reality; nothing else is higher."[26] No other form could have established a total loving relationship; anything else would simply have led to further estrangement. In the human arena as in the transcendental play Krishna's inherent *hlādinī-śakti* takes part: it accompanies him in this manifest play in Vraja by taking human form as Rādhā, daughter of Kīrti and Vṛṣabhānu.[27]

Because Krishna as the son of Nanda is without any of the grandeur (*aiśvarya*) normally associated with divinity, the ultimacy of his descent has been questioned. This, however, is a short-sighted objection, for as we have seen the absoluteness of the divine nature is most adequately expressed in its blissful aspect, and its only essential function is play. It is a play whose object is self-enjoyment, and thus sweetness (*mādhurya*) is even more integrally associated with the divine nature than is grandeur (*aiśvarya*). It is indeed in such a context that all the divine *avatāras* should be understood. The protection of virtue and the removal of unrighteousness, which are normally understood as their purpose, are really only by-products of this divine self-enjoyment.[28] The primary metaphysical function of Bhagavān also follows from this divine play. Metaphysically Bhagavān is a teacher: the drama of his self-enjoyment as one witnesses it in Vraja reveals the inner dynamic of the world at large.

The final adequacy of the Krishna *avatāra* has sometimes been likened to the sixteen degrees through which the moon waxes from nothingness to fullness in the course of a fortnight. These are called *kalās*, and it is asserted that Krishna contains them all, whereas other incarnations lack at least one. The *kalā* they lack is *kalā* in another of its meanings: fine art. They lack the fine art of love. Such *avatāras* may have been motivated by love, but they were never the enactment of love itself, its full play.

When one claims such a fullness of love for the Krishna *avatāra*, of course, it is not only Krishna about whom one is speaking. Without the highest *śakti*, Rādhā, it would all be impossible, for she is love's potency. Without the round dance that magnetizes the two of them—the *rasa* in which they equally participate—there would be no experience of *rasa*. There the divine grandeur plays a limited role at best: all melts away in the intensity of love. If it were not so the human seeker would remain far from the divine presence: there would be no common meeting ground.

The Levels and Varieties of Love

As we have seen, the love relationship within the divine nature is what makes every devoted search possible. Yet the essence of this love is rarely revealed immediately in all its fullness. Rather, love has its levels and varieties.

Although loving service for its own sake is the goal of the spiritual path of feeling, external factors may be helpful in generating an inclination towards the object of love, especially at the beginning.

Such helps to devotion may be grouped under the heading of *vaidhī bhakti,* which comprises acts of devotion that are enjoined on the devotee by scripture or by one's teacher. These include such practices as singing (*kīrtana*) and listening to the praises of Krishna, which induce a total absorption in the beloved.[29] As long as one maintains a focus on external things, ritualistic practices such as these may continue to be observed, until they lead to the emotional state of total self-surrender to the other. Divine grace is universal and unrestricted, but the contrary nature of the human heart often prevents such love from shining through. The formalization of the devotional life chastens the heart, making it ready to respond to the action of grace.

One must bear in mind that even this preparatory sort of *bhakti* is prompted by the eternal feeling immanent in the human soul in the form of Rādhā as atomic bliss-consciousness. Although it may be obscured for a time by the forgetfulness of our essential nature, the essence of both the devotee and the object of devotion is at bottom love. Devotional service on the part of humans, and grace on the part of the divine, are the natural expressions of their common essence, which is Rādhā. Thus ontologically the goal to which all *bhakti* leads exists from the very beginning. Human forgetfulness, however, necessitates a graded series of religious disciplines.[30] These practices of *vaidhī bhakti* help the devotee to develop a natural taste for loving service, and that intensifies into an eager desire (*lobha*) for love. Through a concentrated mental process (*smaraṇa*) all that was externally enjoined becomes spontaneous. It is unusual for these outward forms of *bhakti* to be abandoned even when such spontaneity is attained. When they are left behind, however, it is because internalized devotion (*rāgānugā bhakti*) follows the natural shapes of love itself, and love knows no bounds.[31]

Love is a form of relation grounded in the innate attraction of the human senses for their objects. This attraction builds upon a fundamental identity between subject and object; love is thus "a natural, intense desire of a subject for contact with its object."[32] Beings whose essences are mutually exclusive, by contrast, cannot be attracted to one another. Hence all love, following from a community of essence, is ultimately self-love. Yet in the process of love the distinction between subject and object does not collapse into total nondifferentiation. On the contrary, love is by nature a relation that presupposes a state of identity-indifference.

Human love may take any number of forms, but it finds its highest expression in the love of a man and a woman. Such love, in which two hearts melt into one, involves the highest degree of intensity, and it provides a more complete union than is found in other modes of relation, such as those of servant with master, parent with child, or friend with friend. Amorous love (*kānta-bhāva*) joins two lovers on the same level in mutual satisfaction. This equality coupled with intensity makes possible a level of *rasa* unknown elsewhere.

Because of its finite basis, however, this worldly love ultimately gives rise to feelings of disgust and aversion. It cannot lead to infinite and eternal bliss, and it is to this that the human quest tends. The limited phenomenal *rasa* must finally be transmuted into the transcendent, absolute *rasa*.[33] To attain to such a *rasa* the devotee chooses a personally suitable mode of relation with Krishna from those exemplified by the people of Vraja. The deep loving relation is crystallized in certain conceits that a devotee may adopt. One may regard Krishna as one's master, charge, friend, or beloved. Such conceits, remembered from dramatic situations in Vraja and gradually appropriated, give rise to permanent relationships. One comes to consider Krishna as a master (*dāsya*), a son (*vātsalya*), a friend (*sakhya*) or a beloved (*mādhurya*). When catalyzed by ancillary factors, these modes of intense attraction and attachment (*rati*), the substantive causes (*sthāyi-bhāva*) of love, culminate in the ultimate aesthetic experience of Krishna-*rasa*. Such realization is the highest form of love.[34]

These different modes put to use the variety of inclinations and capacities in individual seekers. In its own way each of them is adequate for the realization of Krishna, yet there are essential differences among them. *Śānta*, the neutral mode, implies a mere awareness of the object of its devotion; *dāsya*, servanthood, has an added quality of service. In *sakhya*, friendship, faith (*śraddhā*) is added to the former two, and *vātsalya*, parenthood, is further enriched by the added sense that one is a protector. *Mādhurya* is the culmination of them all, since it adds the quality of intense devotion (*sevā*) to the beloved and entails a total surrender on the part of the one who loves. This hierarchy of qualities in the modes of relation is reflected in the degree to which Krishna is realized: the total experience of his sweetness is possible only in the highest relationship, that of lover and beloved.[35]

At the level of *bhakti* that is characterized by these modes of relation, beyond the injunctions of *vaidhī bhakti*, there remains only one directive to be followed: to recollect and contemplate at the deepest level the play (*līlā*) that takes place eternally in Vraja. Devotees are to synchronize their lives with those of its inhabitants, observing the eight watches of the day as they are carried out in Vraja.[36] But this high state, warns one saint, is not open to those "who have not adored the dust of the lotus feet of Rādhā, who have not taken shelter in Vṛndāvana as stamped by her footprints, and who have not conversed with persons dwelling deep in Rādhā's emotion. How otherwise could they plumb the depths of the ocean of love that is Krishna?"[37]

Rādhā: Source and Personification of Love

What is the form of Rādhā adored by those who attain to such higher reaches of *bhakti*? On the one hand, Rūpa Gosvāmī tells us, she is "the supernal *hlādinī-śakti,* established in the scriptures and especially in the *tantras* as the greatest of all *śaktis.* Yet on the other hand that very *śakti* is Rādhā, daughter of Vṛṣabhānu. As such her form is exceedingly beautiful. She has sixteen ways of dressing and making herself up, and she bedecks herself with twelve different sets of jewels and ornaments."[38]

Raghunātha Dāsa Gosvāmī draws out the inner meaning of the various aspects of Rādhā's splendid appearance.

> Her body is the glowing touchstone of *mahābhāva* [the highest state of love], which further shines with the unguents of her friends' love for her. Having bathed in the ocean of the nectar of beauty that flows with the current of youth and ripples with compassion, Rādhā makes even Lakṣmī despair of her charms. Rādhā's inner silken garment is her modesty. Her body is delicately painted with the saffron of beauty and the musk of glowing *śṛṅgāra-rasa* [amorous mood]. Her ornaments are fashioned of nine most precious jewels: they are her trembling, tears, thrilling, stupor, sweat, stammering, blushing, madness and swoon. Her garland is prepared from the flowers of a select assortment of aesthetic qualities, and her garment is freshened with the pure, subtle perfume distilled from her exquisite virtues.
>
> Her hairdo is devious like her hidden pique, and she wears a bright mark of good fortune on her forehead. Her ears are adorned with the glorious sounds of Krishna's name. She reddens her lips with the betel-leaf of intense attachment, and the guile of love is her mascara. She is fragrant with the camphor exuded by her sweet smile and tinkling voice. Wear-

> ing on her heart the necklace of love's separation, weighted with a swinging pendant fashioned of the paradoxical feeling of separation-in-union, she reclines on a couch of conceit in the chamber of charm. Her breasts are covered with the blouse of anger and affection. The melody from the *vīṇā* of her glory drowns out the noise [of envy] from the hearts and speech of her co-wives. Her lovely hands rest playfully on the shoulder of her companion. Adorned in this way Rādhā offers the honey of amorousness, which maddens even the Love-god.[39]

Even when *bhakti* blossoms into the highest state of love (*premā*), there is a further internal intensification of feeling. This ripening process begins with the stage of being confident of one's love, flourishes in a complex of moods that express her stubborn annoyance at her lover's inconstancy, congeals into a state in which the heart melts with excessive longing for the beloved, and, in a love that is ever fresh, culminates in a supreme ecstacy (*mahābhāva*).[40] This process resembles the various stages required to refine the juice of the sugar cane until it becomes a transparent crystal, the quintessent concentration of sweetness. External agents may encourage this refining process, but their presence does not affect the essential flavor. The love of the *gopīs* of Vraja, and of Rādhā first and foremost, is of this highest type.

Love by its very nature is manifest, realizing itself in infinite ways and moods, and Krishna experiences it in its total variety through his relations with the panoply of *gopīs* that inhabit Vraja. Yet in a way that seems paradoxical he is satisfied only in the company of Rādhā, love's ideal. The paradox is resolved when one realizes that the many *gopīs* are but manifestations of the body of Rādhā (*kāya-vyūha*). She complicates herself thus in order to satisfy her beloved in all possible ways: her friends are but instruments of *rasa*. All that expresses the fact that the love of Krishna for his lovers remains the same, while yet it varies in accordance with the receptivity and preparedness of his devotees. The love of the *gopīs*, which symbolizes this devoted love at a higher level, is itself great. Yet in the last analysis there is a further height, a level at which all feelings are fully explicit. This manifests itself as an excess of unmotivated jealousy and a deep contemplative consciousness even in the actual eternal union with Krishna. It occurs only in Rādhā: it is possible for no one else, since she alone is the essence of *hlādinī śakti*.[41]

The basic feelings (*sthāyi-bhāva*) that constitute the raw material of love are spread abroad in the world, but they become substantial only in the relations between Krishna and the *gopīs,* and ultimately between Krishna and Rādhā. This supreme relation of subject and object—which also, we must remember, is the basis of all experience in the universe—is what makes the highest sentiment of devotion (*bhakti rasa*) possible in the human heart. Its specific qualities are determined by a hero, Krishna, who is clever, full of youth, high spirits and confidence, who is brave and sportive, yet who is controlled by love.[42] His relation to the *gopīs* in Vraja is that of a paramour: the *gopīs* are married to others.[43]

It may seem strange that the ideal of a spiritual discipline is presented in terms that are not acceptable even in the secular realm of aesthetics.[44] Ethically one may resist such a relationship—love outside of marriage—but it remains a fact that the energies of love are not constrained by socio-ethical norms. The force of this apparent scandalousness is not to be underestimated: it adds to love's intensity.[45] And it accords with the basic nature of love, for love presupposes two 'others' whom it binds together. In the same way, without a metaphysical alienation between humanity and Bhagavān, religion would be without any occasion whatever.

Yet the ontological value of this alienation (*parakīyā bhāva*) in both aesthetics and religion has its limit. If it were eternal it would preclude any possibility for ultimate realization. Furthermore, extramarital liaisons, being unethical, cannot serve as the ultimate moral standard; being obscene they destroy the value of any aesthetic experience of which they might form a part.[46]

This apparent dilemma posed by the fact that the *gopīs* are not Krishna's wives may be resolved in a deeper understanding of the phenomenon. One must realize that in their essential nature these *gopīs* are manifestations of the *śaktis* of Bhagavān, and as such they are eternally his own (*svakīyā*). It is only in the cause of generating intense longing that this ultimate belonging of one to the other is obscured and they appear separated, as illicit lovers. They later discover themselves to be husband and wife, in accordance with their deeper nature, and this produces a wonderful happiness. Their illicit status intensifies the bond of emotion that connects the two poles. Their separation is not the cause of *rasa,* for that subsists eternally; it only augments it.

In the final analysis such alienation is perceived only out of ignorance.[47] The possibility for such a misperception arises because the divine play takes place on two different planes. *Parakīyā* belongs to what is manifest; *svakīyā* to what is unmanifest. Although the illicit form of love is what is more immediately manifest, it is not ultimately different from the unmanifest play that undergirds it—a *līlā* in union. The manifest is contained in the unmanifest; their differences are only apparent.[48] The two categories are interconnecting, even redundant. Krishna is the possessor of power (*śaktimān*); the *gopīs* are his potencies (*śaktis*). The *vraja-līlā* is the play of Bhagavān and his blissful potencies, but it is graciously presented in a form comprehensible to the devotee.

The nearest counterpart to such aesthetic experience, *rasa,* in the human setting is that of sensual pleasure in the context of an amorous relationship.[49] This connection between intense longing and its most vivid worldly expression has led to a mistaken conflation of the two that obscures the crucial point of contrast. In the love that the *gopīs* and Rādhā bear for Krishna there is no element of longing for one's own gratification, which is the basic motive for sensual relationship in this world. Rather, their satisfaction comes only through the satisfaction of Krishna. Rādhā's love toward Krishna does have a sensual component but that sensuality is characteristically "an enjoyment in being enjoyed" and that makes its apparently sensual aspect dissolve in love per se.[50] Love is by nature a mutual satisfaction that is possible only when one negates oneself totally for the sake of other. This self-negation involves the negation of sensuality and constitutes the height of spirituality. Its other-directed delight both includes and transcends personal and subjective pleasure. Krishna seeks pleasure in heightening the *bhāva* of Rādhā and she is delighted in his delight.[51]

Thus Rādhā and Krishna, the subject and object of love, provide absolute bliss to each other through their lovely dalliance (*rāsa*). This supreme aesthetic experience is the ultimate stage of love, the goal of a devotee, where the two highest principles are coupled in one self-subsistent reality. Often this highest experience is described with the imagery of rain. Either Krishna is painted as the dark cloud pregnant with torrents of love's nectar (*rasa,* i.e., Rādhā) or Rādhā is envisioned as the receptacle and Krishna as the liquid content. Their mystical union is the ultimate *rasa.*[52] In it separation gives rise to the pleasure of union, and conversely union contains a loving feeling of separation. In such an intermingling the separate identities of lover and beloved dissolve into a single whole: two characters flow into each other; two separate entities become interchangeable.

The Perfection of Rasa: *Poetry Beyond Philosophy*

This state of *rasa* is at the limit of reason, for rational categories are predicated on the possibility of duality that is no longer possible here. "The ultimate essence of love is like the experience of the mute," as the *Nārada Bhakti Sūtras* proclaim;[53] it can be communicated only experientially, through the grace of Rādhā. She melts the highly condensed *rasa* and makes it available to the thirsty, through her eternal *rāsa* with Krishna. Here the realm of mind is replaced with that of the heart; feeling supersedes reason. Intellectual contemplation gives way to aesthetic participation and the medium of expression becomes poetry.

From age to age one essence, two names:
  the joy of bliss is Śyāmā,
  the bliss of joy is Śyāma.
From all eternity manifest
  as two in a single form
Two as one they come to Vṛndāvana,
  Rādhā-Krishna, Krishna-Rādhā,
  ever and unchanging,
Devastatingly beautiful.[54]

In this song of Harivyāsa Deva the two names are not only the obvious counterparts Śyāmā and Śyāma, Rādhā and Krishna respectively, but joy and bliss, words which translate interchangeably, *hlādinī* and *ānanda*. These two are not exactly identical, however, since the first is feminine and the second masculine, and the first specifically associated with Rādhā in theology and the second with Krishna. Yet the poet shows that they are indissolubly interlocked. In the same intense way Caitanya, who is both Rādhā and Krishna in a single body, is associated with the double manifestation of the single divine essence in Vraja, and it all shows that *rasa* always has the capacity to reverse its flow. In that moment the lover becomes the beloved, as if stone were to become water and water, stone. Gradually *rasa* matures until those who play at love lose themselves totally in the game. At that point the one becomes absorbed in the other, and the nature of the beloved washes back through the lover, replacing what was there before (*vaiparītya:* cf. figure 5).[55]

She wears his peacock feather,
  he dons her lovely, delicate crown;

FIGURE 5.

Līlā-Havā

(Rādhā and Krishna Exchanging Clothes)
Garhwal, ca. 1800.
(Courtesy, Museum of Fine Arts, Boston, 26.536.
Gift of Ananda K. Coomaraswamy.)

Figure 5.

Exchanging clothes is one of the favorite forms of love play in Indian literature. In this illustration it is symbolic of the intimacy between Rādhā and Krishna and of their identification with each other. Behind this simple sport is a complex concept in Vaiṣṇava philosophy. In Krishna's impulse to become Rādhā there is a fusion between the divine power, which reveals itself in earthly form, and the worshipper (with Rādhā as the archetype) who discovers his or her inner and ultimate divinity. This intrinsic identification of the worshipper and the worshipped is strikingly expressed in a verse of Sūr Dās, who speaks on behalf of Rādhā:

> You become Rādhā and I will become Madhava,
> truly Madhava; this is the reversal which
> I shall produce. I will braid your hair and will put
> (your) crown upon my head. Sūr Dās says: Thus
> the Lord becomes Rādhā and Rādhā the son of Nanda.[1]

That Rādhā walks on Krishna's left side may suggest some reference to the belief of some Vaiṣṇavas, reflected in the *Brahmavaivarta Purāṇa,* that Rādhā arose from the left half of Krishna's body and that there is no difference between them, since they originally formed one and the same body.

—J.P.

---

[1]Walter M. Spink, *Krishnamandala* (Ann Arbor, Mich: Center for South and Southeast Asian Studies, 1971), 88.

She sports his yellow garment,
he wraps himself in her beautiful sari.
How charming the very sight of it—
the Moon of Vraja has adorned her in the grove;
The daughter of Vṛṣabhānu turns Nanda's son,
and Nanda's son, Vṛṣabhānu's girl.[56]

The history of love matures completely in the two-in-one incarnation of Caitanya: he is both Rādhā and Krishna.[57] In Caitanya the pattern of love and devotion is reversed, for love's object has become its subject. God has come down as a devotee to settle his debt for all humanity's devotion.[58] The Dark One has become light-complexioned (*gaura,* an epithet of Caitanya); in Caitanya Krishna, the thief of love, has become Rādhā, the giver of love. Rādhā alone, the embodiment of the highest loving consciousness, stimulates this transformation. It was the intensity of her love that prompted Krishna to desire to shift the balance of forces between lover and beloved and to experience for himself the role of the longing lover. Rādhā's love made him see that the bliss of love lies not so much in being its constant object as in experiencing what it is constantly to give love.[59] Rādhā's greatness was that she was totally dedicated to fulfilling the wishes of her beloved. As such she became Krishna's preceptor in love, and he, taking her role in the person of Caitanya, instructs humanity at large in the art of love.

So strong is the beauty of Rādhā that she attracts the heart of the supreme attractor. So great is her power that she makes Krishna self-conscious (Kṛṣṇa-Caitanya, Caitanya's full name). So formidable is her love that it changes the standard color of love from dark (Krishna's color) to glowing light (her own: *ujjvala*).[60] So total is her grace that the Transcendental becomes immediately accessible in the phenomenal realm. In this totally blissful experience "lover, beloved and love itself dance in one body,"[61] as Caitanya among us, and he reflects back and makes knowable the glories of the love of Rādhā and Krishna in Vraja.

There is no end to singing the glories of Rādhā, who makes all this possible:

Rādhā's name is the greatest treasure.
Śyāma plays that name on his flute,
remembering it constantly.
She is the thread in every fabric,
each *yantra* and *mantra,* each Veda and Tantra.

Śukadeva knew this secret of secrets,
but decided it best stay unrevealed;
Krishna takes numberless forms to pursue it:
still its depths elude him.
But I, Vyāsadāsa, now shout it out openly,
throwing all caution to the winds.[62]

Śukadeva, in narrating Krishna's *līlās* in the *Bhāgavata Purāṇa,* maintained complete silence about Rādhā. His was an intentional silence, for Rādhā, as the quintessence of *rasa,* the supreme aesthetic experience, is the most valuable jewel in the treasure-house of love. Only a chosen few who know the code of love have access to that highest wealth: outsiders such as intellect and will are carefully kept away. Four centuries ago Jīva Gosvāmī, whose thinking I have quoted throughout, learned that code through her grace and opened the treasure-house for all to see. With painstaking scholarship he showed that the highest *rasa,* Rādhā and Krishna in their unified form (*rādhā-kṛṣṇa ekākāra-svarūpa*) is the true referrent of the very first verse of the *Bhāgavata Purāṇa,* and the implicit subject of it all.[63] His treatise on the *Bhāgavata,* by making clear how Rādhā's *rasa* permeates the whole, stood in danger of diluting this *rasa* in its crystallized form, yet for the sake of increasing understanding he dared to proceed. I too have dared, and take refuge in his prayer for having done so:

For whatever I may have distorted in the tiniest degree,
May the Beloved of Gokula, full of compassion, forgive me.[64]

All praise to Rādhā: *Jai Śrī Rādhe!*

Where Have All the Rādhās Gone?: New Images of Woman in Modern Hindi Poetry

KARINE SCHOMER

*I*n a poem entitled "Śrī Krishna Looking for Arjuna in an Antique Store," contemporary poet Lakṣmīkānt Varmā has a dispirited Krishna wandering about in the midst of carefully labeled and priced memorabilia of the *Mahābhārata* war, searching in vain for his lost identity. Suddenly, he stumbles upon a broken image of Rādhā, "stashed away in a silver casket,/brimming with emotion, swathed in a haze, body tarnished/and worn out,"[1] and doesn't even recognize her! This scene dramatically illustrates a striking characteristic of modern Hindi poetry as a whole: the conspicuous absence of Rādhā as a significant figure or symbol. Though there are some important exceptions, the general trend of the new poetry which began to be written at the turn of the twentieth century has been to abandon the Rādhā-Krishna story as poetic subject-matter, and to replace Rādhā with other, more universal images of woman. This represents a sharp break in tradition, for the love between Rādhā and Krishna had been one of the major themes of medieval Hindi poetry. Rādhā, though never as prominent in the Hindi area as in Bengal,[2] had nevertheless been a potent symbol in both the religious and the secular culture of the medieval period. The rejection of the symbolism of Rādhā and Krishna in modern poetry is indicative of major changes in beliefs, values, and sensibility on the part of the new Western-educated middle class by and for whom it has been written.

The Rādhā who has been rejected by the moderns is not so much the Rādhā of Krishnaite devotional religion as it is the other Rādhā, the Rādhā of courtly love. It is the Rādhā who was a cultural symbol of woman in love rather than a religious symbol for the soul seeking union with God. The tension between these two conceptions of Rādhā—a tension which itself demonstrates her power as a symbol—had been present in Rādhā-Krishna poetry from the very beginning. For example, in the lyrics of the fifteenth-century poet Vidyāpati, who wrote in the Maithili dialect of Eastern Bihar, the ambiguity is so profound that his lyrics have been variously understood as purely devotional or entirely secular; specifically, they were adopted by the Caitanya movement of Bengal as poetic expressions of Krishna *bhakti*, while in the Hindi area, they served as an inspiration to the secular tradition of poetry in the Braj dialect known as the *rīti* school. Over the course of the medieval period, this bifurcation between the devotional and the secular treatment of the Rādhā-Krishna theme became more marked, leading to two parallel traditions of Rādhā-Krishna verse, and thus two distinct, though interrelated, conceptions of Rādhā. As poetic creativity shifted from the aegis of religious movements to the environment of princely courts and aristocratic houses, the devotional Rādhā gave way increasingly to the secular Rādhā. In Bengali, this change can be seen in the difference between the devoted Rādhā of Caṇḍidās, whose life is "bound/in a loop of love/and firmly anchored to [Krishna's] feet,"[3] and the nubile maid of the eighteenth-century *kabivālās*, with her "hundred-petaled lotus, closed and warm,/ . . . opened/by the touch of time."[4] In the Braj poetry of the Hindi area, the contrast is even sharper because of the systematic elaboration of Rādhā's secular aspects required by the poetic aims of the *rīti* school. Thus, whereas the Rādhā of Sūr Dās was Krishna's faithful companion and, at times, his divine consort, the Rādhā of *rīti* poetry, as we shall see, was a heroine (*nāyikā*) relating to Krishna conceived as the ideal courtly lover (*nāyaka*).

What, then, was *rīti* poetry? In classical Sanskrit poetics, the term *rīti* simply meant "style," and was used descriptively to distinguish various qualities in poetry. In medieval Braj poetry, the meaning is quite different. Poet-scholars, the most famous of whom was the late sixteenth-century poetry Keśav Dās, developed a tradition of writing manuals of poetic theory illustrated by archetypal verses. In this tradition the word *rīti* had prescriptive import, referring to composition "in *proper* style," that is, in accordance with the concepts, categories, topics and rules set forth in the manuals.[5] Modern literary historians labeled poetry of this kind *rīti kāvya* ("*rīti* poetry"), and it is now customary to refer to poets of this tradition as *rīti* poets.

In the *rīti* tradition, which flourished under the patronage of the Hindu courts of North India, the principal genre of poetic work was something called the *lakṣaṇa-grantha* or "book of definitions." A *lakṣaṇa-grantha* is usually divided into separate sections dealing with the various categories and topics specified by poetic theory (e.g., figures of speech, poetic defects, the *rasas* or moods, the different kinds of heroes and heroines, the personnel of the king's court, the seasons, kinds of natural scenes, the meeting of lovers, love in separation, lovers' quarrels, etc.). Each chapter consists of brief verse definitions of particular elements, followed by illustrative examples. For example, the twelfth section of the *Rasikapriyā* of Keśav Dās, dealing with the kinds of women who serve as go-betweens for lovers, begins by listing twelve different categories of women who can function in this capacity, then gives examples of messages conveyed by these intermediaries.[6]

The subject-matter of *rīti* poetry was limited. Though in theory the *rīti* poets dealt with the whole range of *rasas,* in practice they focused primarily on *śṛṅgāra rasa,* the erotic mood. In the theoretical formulation of the *rasa* school of poetics, the successful evocation of *rasa* requires the portrayal of the various emotions (*bhāva*) associated with that mood, and this, in turn, requires the portrayal of the object which arouses the emotion (*ālambaṇa*) and the subject in whom it is aroused (*āśraya*). In the case of the erotic mood, the functions of *ālambaṇa* and *āśraya* were mutually fulfilled by the *nāyikā,* or woman in love, and the *nāyaka,* or courtly lover. Therefore, much of *rīti* poetry was devoted to descriptions of the various kinds of *nāyakas* and *nāyikās* and their interactions. The description of *nāyikās* was especially popular, and there developed an independent genre called *nāyikā-bhed* ("kinds of heroines") in which all the possible categories and sub-categories of *nāyikās* were enumerated and illustrated.

Being eclectic in their approach to tradition, the *rīti* poets drew from several sources for their schemes of classification. They borrowed freely from the *kāma-śāstra* texts on erotics, Bharata's *Nāṭya-śāstra* and its successors in the field of dramaturgy, and the whole *kāvya-śāstra* tradition of poetics. As a result, one finds many different typologies operating together, with heroines being variously classified according to physical type, situation, circumstances, emotional state, behavior, and so forth. However, two sixteenth-century works concentrating largely on the classification of heroes and heroines were especially influential. One was the *Rasamañjarī* of Bhānu Miśra, a work which attempted to harmonize all the prevalent typologies (and came up with a total of 384 possible kinds of *nāyikās!*). The other was the *Ujjvalanīlamaṇi* of Rūpa Gosvāmī, which was not purely a text of poetics dealing with *śṛṅgāra rasa,* but a brilliant and profound exposition of the theology of Krishna *bhakti* in terms of the categories of *śṛṅgāra rasa.* With the *Ujjvalanīlamaṇi,* the *nāyaka* of secular poetics became the Krishna of *bhakti,* and the *nāyikās* became Rādhā and the other *gopīs.*

The *rīti* poets adopted Rūpa Gosvāmī's Krishna-*nāyaka* and Rādhā-*nāyikā* equation, but not his devotional point of view; thus, in their poetry, Rādhā and Krishna came to symbolize the ideal courtly lovers who are the *ālambaṇa* and *āśraya* of the erotic mood. The devotional associations of Rādhā and Krishna were never entirely lost, and one finds occasional stanzas which are explicitly religious in their sentiment; but these are the exception rather than the rule, often appearing perfunctorily at the beginning or end of a *lakṣaṇa-grantha,* or interspersed in stray-stanza anthologies of the *satasaī* ("collection of 700 verses") type. Thus the Rādhā of *rīti* poetry was not primarily a devotee or divine consort, but rather the supreme model of the woman in love, the *nāyikā* par excellence.

Rādhā as Nāyikā:

The Heroine of Medieval Rīti *Poetry*

What kind of woman was she, this courtly heroine? To begin with, she was young and supremely beautiful:

The embodiment of beauty,
young, intelligent,
graceful, lovely, brilliant—
thus is the *nāyikā* described by all.[7]

It was a stereotyped outer beauty, often compared with that of the celestial nymphs (*apsarās*), and conveyed by means of all the conventional similes for describing the female anatomy. Much of the creative energy of the *rīti* poets went into detailed, often hyperbolic descriptions of the various parts of Rādhā's body. Her breasts, for example, were a never-failing source of inspiration:

Like two whirlwinds colliding,
her breasts swelled with the onrush of passion,
shattering the pride of haystack, dome, mountain and
even Himalaya.[8]

The emphasis on Rādhā's physical beauty was so great that *nakh-śikh,* the tradition of describing the human figure "from the toe to the top of the head," was adapted to her portrayal, and became an independent genre. In fact, of all the genres developed by the *rīti* poets, *nakh-śikh* was by far the most popular and, in terms of sheer quantity, represents the largest single category of *rīti* texts discovered to date.

It is difficult to characterize the Rādhā of *rīti* poetry in terms of any one set of physical, psychological, or behavioral traits beyond that of archetypal beauty. Because of the underlying schemes of classification and the illustrative purpose informing her representation as *nāyikā*, there is a certain protean quality about her. At times she is the *padminī* or "lotus-woman" of the *kāma-śāstra* tradition, "moderate in her desire, without anger or conceit, needing little food or sleep,"[9] while at other times she presents the very different personality of the *citrinī* or "art-woman,"

> fond of dance, song and poetry,
> with a roving glance but a steady heart,
> strong in her desire, liking to make love,
> exuding fragrance with her breath.[10]

Likewise, she may be portrayed as a *svakīyā* or properly wedded heroine, or as a *parakīyā* not married to the hero. She may be an adolescent (*mugdhā*) who "makes love with great bashfulness, and thereby increases her husband's affection,"[11] or an experienced adult (*prauṛhā*), "bold in her lovemaking, who holds her lover's heart by practicing the arts of the *kāma-śāstra*."[12] She may be *svādhīnapatikā* (having her lover well under control), *vipralabdhā* (separated from her lover), or *khaṇḍitā* (deceived by her lover). She may be a *vāsakasajjā* (one who dresses up and waits for her lover at the door of her house) or an *abhisārikā* (one who goes off in the night for a secret tryst with her lover), or any other of Bhānu Miśra's 384 kinds of *nāyikās*. By being so many different women, Rādhā becomes both depersonalized and universalized—a symbol rather than an individual. She is no woman in particular, but stands for every woman in love.

An important clue to understanding why the moderns felt uncomfortable with this Rādhā is to be found in the words for "woman" most commonly used to refer to her in *rīti* poetry. Besides "*nāyikā*," which automatically defined her in terms of her illustrative function and ruled out any other context than the erotic, two other words for woman stand out sharply: *kāminī* ("a desirable woman") and *ramaṇī* ("a [sexually] enjoyable woman"). Rādhā in *rīti* poetry is an exclusively sexual being and is thoroughly objectified as such. Her value lies not in her own subjective feelings, but in the objective behavior she manifests, and the pleasure it provides both to her lover and to the poetic connoisseur for whom it is artfully described. Whereas the Rādhā of *bhakti* often speaks in the first person, expressing her feelings with great poignancy, the Rādhā of *rīti* poetry is largely an observed Rādhā, described in the third person. Whatever her state of mind, she is charming and a source of delight to the observer, for both her joys and her sorrows help create the aesthetic mood of *śṛṅgāra*. Thus, Rādhā's eager anticipation as she "happily takes Krishna off to the woods, joking and flirting,"[13] and the pangs of jealousy she experiences when Krishna is with some other woman, are equivalent signs of love and portrayed with equal sympathy—or lack thereof. Rādhā in her jealous anger (*māna*) was considered particularly appealing, and descriptions of her jealousy constituted a distinct topic in *rīti* poetry. One of Rādhā's companions reports thus a scene between Rādhā and Krishna:

> Today, she was asking Gopāl in jest
> about other women's good qualities;
> The Lord of Braj gave one woman's name,
> calling her 'my friend.'
> The betel-leaf she was about to feed him stayed in her hand,
> the one in her mouth remained unchewed;
> Hearing that name, she felt hurt,
> and tears fell from her eyes.[14]

The question of jealousy brings up another important matter: the structure of Rādhā's relationship to Krishna in *rīti* poetry. This, too, is relevant to an understanding of the modern rejection of Rādhā, for it involves a conceptualization of the relationship between the sexes which was both untrue to modern social reality and unacceptable to modern ways of thinking. To begin with, Krishna in *rīti* poetry most often appears not as a cowherd, but as a prince. And Rādhā, though still referred to as a *gopī* and as the daughter of Vṛṣabhānu, is most frequently portrayed as a princess, one of the prince's many wives—usually the youngest. Thus much of the time we are in a polygamous situation where the *svakīyā-parakīyā* distinction breaks down, with each wife being at once the hero's "own" *and* "another woman"—especially to her co-wives. As a result, Krishna's "infidelities" are structurally sanctioned, and Rādhā has no choice but to swallow her grief and accept her lot:

Noticing lac disturbed on co-wife's feet, she secretly laughed;
Then, seeing co-wife shyly laugh, amid the laughs she sighed.[15]

She might occasionally let her jealousy get the better of her and reject him emotionally, but eventually she had to come around to accepting him again: after all, he was her husband.

This polygamous situation, and the absence of the mythological frame-story of the *Bhāgavata Purāṇa* in which Krishna eventually departs for Mathura, meant, among other things, that separation in *rīti* poetry was never more than a temporary matter. For the Rādhā of *rīti* there was no question of losing Krishna forever; hence the poignant cry of anguish present in the *viraha* poems of the *bhakti* tradition is largely absent. What we have instead is an alteration between *saṃyoga,* or union, and *viyoga,* or separation caused by some temporary impediment. Furthermore, we must remember that Rādhā is always a *nāyikā,* the description of whom is meant to evoke an aesthetic mood; therefore, the separation she endures and the union she enjoys are both simply means of creating *śṛṅgāra rasa.*

When separation from her beloved causes a woman great pain,
We have the mood of love-in-separation—so say all the poets.[16]

Typically, the *rīti* poets' descriptions of *saṃyoga* were much more successful than their attempts at depicting Rādhā in a state of *viyoga.* There is a world of difference between the sincere cry of the heart coming from the abandoned Rādhā of the *bhakti* poet and the theatrical display of frustrated passion described objectively by the *rīti* poet. Sūr Dās:

Without my beloved,
 the night is like a black she-cobra.
When lightning flashes in the night sky,
 she turns her body to sting me.
No talisman works, no mantra is of any use:
 my love grows cold.
Sūr says:
 deprived of Sūr's Lord, Rādhā tosses and turns,
 convulsed with anguish.[17]

Keśav Dās:

As the clouds scatter, her tears flow,
 as night deepens, her sighs increase;

Like a bird in flight, her laughter vanishes,
  lightning strikes and robs her of her sleep.
Like a *cātaka,* she cries out "Piu, piu!",
  waves of fierce heat rise up within her.
Listen, says Keśav, this is her condition:
  there is no fire, but her limbs are burning.[18]

The moderns, as we shall see, objected both to the polygamous court setting that structured Rādhā and Krishna's relationship and to the shallowness of their emotional bond. Valuing realism and sincerity of feeling, they found the stereotyped *nāyaka-nāyikā* relationship neither believable nor acceptable as a model for the many twists, turns, phases, moods and dimensions of love between man and woman.

Ultimately, however, it was not so much the artificiality and shallowness of the Rādhā-Krishna relation that caused the moderns to weary of it as poetic subject-matter, but its narrowness. The world of *rīti,* already limited socially and emotionally, was further narrowed by the fact that its two main protagonists had no concern about anything beyond their passion for each other. Rādhā is totally consumed by her infatuation with Krishna, to the exclusion of any other interest in life. She is completely vulnerable to him, exists only to be with him, has no life outside her relationship to him. Only at rare intervals does one ever get a hint that she may have other things to do than pine for Krishna all day, and this too serves only to confirm her single-minded desire for him:

The nearer comes the night, the greater the haste:
Jingling, jingling, the girl does chores, caught by desire.[19]

Krishna's world is somewhat broader, since he is involved with his other wives and with a variety of other women as well. Nevertheless, he too is only shown acting within the erotic sphere; for example, though a prince, he is never seen performing the duties of a ruler.

In terms of the aesthetic aims of *rīti* poetry, in which Krishna's role was to serve as an *ālambaṇa* or *āśraya* for the erotic mood, this one-dimensional portrayal was neither surprising nor illogical, but necessary, as was the similarly one-dimensional portrayal of Rādhā. But for the moderns, groping to embrace and express as broad and varied a reality as possible, this singleness of focus was stifling. The rejection of the Rādhā-Krishna theme and of the symbol of Rādhā by modern poets was partly a reaction against the narrowness of the poetic world of *rīti*—what the late poet Sumitrānandan Pant contemptuously referred to as "the three-foot world of *nakh-śikh*."[20]

Abalā: *The Helpless Woman of Early Modern Hindi Poetry*

The intensity of the modern reaction against the poetic world of *rīti* may be seen most clearly in the words of the poets themselves. A particularly impassioned and revealing statement is that made by Pant in the introduction to his 1926 collection *Pallav*. After having expressed a certain impatience with the Krishna *bhakti* poets, "whose whole life consisted of going back and forth between Mathura and Gokul,"[21] he takes on the real offenders, the *śṛṅgārapriya kavi* ("poets enamored of the erotic"), the *rīti* poets:

> What was there for them to do? Stimulated by desire, their infinite power of imagination spread out like Draupadī's veil and coiled itself around the *nāyikā's* every limb. From childhood to old age—i.e., until the moment when some "moon-faced deer-eyed beauty" pityingly addressed them as *bābā* ("old man")—their vision, rarefied and ever in search of *rasa*, travelled only from the toe (*nakh*) to the head (*śikh*), from the "south pole" to the "north pole." What an all-embracing sensibility! What astute genius! To be able to see the whole universe in a single limb! There need be no fear that their renown will ever fade or die: their *nāyikā*, a mere glimpse of whom caused their imagination to flower like a *tilak* branch, will surely bring her Satyavāns back from the jaws of death!
>
> Having had a vision of this great ineffable form, these poets, armed with bows of flowers, became victors in the new *Mahābhārata* battleground of love. Churning the ocean of desire, they brought the god of love back to life. (And he is not likely to turn to ashes again soon!) Loosing his powerful spell-binding arrow into the sky above our land, these brave warriors suffused all things with the presence of this *kāminī*, displaying the figures of a thousand *nāyikās* packed into one like Chinese boxes. By the magic of their poetry, they showed our land as a palace of mirrors belonging to the love-god, or as a curio-shop featuring cheap bits of glass coated with a shiny veneer of desire. As a result, the image of Indian woman—devoted, steadfast, chaste—became transformed into a riot of

gaudy, sensual reflections, and, caught up in this maze, we were unable to see our simple, modest Satī of old.[22]

This statement, delivered in the best bombastic style of the day, is interesting for several reasons. First of all, it clearly reveals a sense that the universe of *rīti* poetry is too constricting, and the desire for a broader reality—implicitly symbolized by the ancient *Mahābhārata* battleground, where the issues were more momentous then those dealt with by the "warriors of love." Secondly, it is filled with allusions to the older levels of Hindu mythology—the classical levels predating the medieval Rādhā-Krishna development. Thirdly, the geographical frame of reference, "our land," is India as a whole—a reflection of the new nationalist awareness of the time. Fourthly, the objection is clearly to the secular *nāyikā,* and not to the Rādhā of *bhakti* or to devotional religion as such. (In fact, the statement about all things being suffused with the *kāminī* of *rīti* poetry contains a subtle allusion to the *bhakti* outlook, for the expression used, *kāminīmaya,* echoes Tulsī Dās' familiar words about the whole universe being *rāma-sīyamaya* ["suffused with Rāma and Sītā"]). Fifthly, it is obvious that, for Pant, the rejection of the Rādhā-*nāyikā* figure is related to a desire for a more elevated and dignified image of Indian woman. Finally, there is a strong puritanical streak running through the whole statement.

We shall have more to say on each of these points, for this statement expresses in brief all the major tendencies in the early modern approach to the poetic inheritance of *rīti.* First, however, we must note the important fact that poetry such as Pant's came to be written in modern standard Hindi rather than in Braj Bhāṣā, since this was not at all unrelated to the rejection of Rādhā and Krishna as poetic subject-matter. Because of the strong hold of the Braj poetic tradition, the change to modern Hindi had been slow in coming, with poetry throughout the nineteenth-century continuing to be written in Braj even as the new standard dialect was rapidly becoming the language of communication and culture among the Hindus of the new middle class. Eventually, modern Hindi won out, but it was not simply because it made more sense for poetry to be in the language its readers habitually spoke. Rather, it was the impossibility of dissociating Braj from the traditional Rādhā-Krishna subject-matter of *rīti* which caused poets to make the linguistic switch. As the spirit and aspirations of the Indian Renaissance began to affect the Hindi area, and poets became interested in voicing contemporary concerns, ideas and experiences, it became necessary for them to express themselves in a language which was not hopelessly bound to the "three-foot world of *nakh-śikh.*" Reluctantly at times, they abandoned Braj, "that lovely maiden standing at the door of her house, unable to bear the weight of her own beauty,"[23] and began to use modern Hindi instead. In Pant's words:

> The bamboo flute of Braj was full of nectar; it sang of the springtime of Krishna's youth and his amorous adventures.... But now, Krishna has abandoned his flute and raised up the *pañcajanya* conch;[24] our sleeping land has awakened, and its drowsy voice has been replaced by the bright sound of the conch of modern Hindi. In Braj, there was the sweetness of sleep and the indolent dreaminess of moonlit nights, but in modern Hindi there is the vibrancy of awakening and daylight's call to action.[25]

What was the new poetry like? It has been described, not without justification, as "savorless, preachy, matter-of-fact and coarse,"[26] and in fact, it *was* earnest, puritanical, and more concerned with social ideals than with aesthetics. In other words, it was attuned to, and expressive of, the values of the new middle class. This new class, to which most modern poets belonged, was educated in schools and colleges where, on the one hand, it was forced to learn all the technical subtleties of *rīti* poetry but, on the other hand, and more significantly, it absorbed the puritanical attitudes of the Indian Renaissance. For these people, *rīti* poetry's overwhelming emphasiss on erotic love was anathema, and its heroine Rādhā hopelessly associated with a luxurious and permissive aristocratic life-style of which they disapproved. It is not surprising to discover, then, that the first generation of poets writing in modern Hindi not only turned their backs on the Rādhā-Krishna theme but, by and large, avoided the subject of love altogether. Instead, these poets turned to topics which, among other things, entailed images of woman very different from that of Rādhā as *nāyikā* or *kāminī.* The first of these was nationalism, just then becoming a potent force in the Hindi area. One of the main poetic forms which the new nationalism took was that of hymns of praise to Mother India:

> Hail to you! with gleaming Himalayan peaks,
> Rapt in the sound of rippling Gaṅgā,
> Limbs glistening under brilliant sun,
> Clothed in the glory of ascetic's garb!
>   Hail to you! beloved India![27]

Poems such as this drew their inspiration not from the figure of Rādhā, but from the more austere and awesome Śākta images of Devī—in this case, Pārvatī, doing penance to obtain Śiva.

Another form of nationalist poetry was the narrative recounting the deeds of heroic figures from India's historical past. This included women as well as men: the Rajput queen Padminī (who had led the women of Chitor in the rite of self-immolation when the fort fell to the Muslims), Durgāvatī, the queen of Gondwana (who had successfully resisted Akbar for some time), the empress Nūr Jahān (who had wielded great power in the affairs of the Mughal empire during her husband Jahāngīr's reign). The most beloved heroine, however, was the Rānī of Jhānsī, who had fought the British during the 1857 uprising, and the most famous poem of all Subhadrā Kumārī Cauhān's rousing "*Jhānsī kī rānī*":

Thrones trembled, monarchs frowned,
  youth came again to ancient India.
Recognizing the price of freedom lost,
  all resolved to chase the foreigners out.
  In the year of eighteen fifty-seven,
    the old sword flashed again.
  From the warriors of Bundelkhand,
    we heard the story—
    how she fought like a man,
      that Rānī of Jhansi![28]

There is obviously no trace of the Rādhā of *rīti* poetry here. In fact, far from being a *kāminī* or *ramaṇī*, the Rānī is described as a *mardānī*, from the masculine *mard* ("man")—a word that connotes strength, dauntlessness, valor and all the other "male" virtues.

A second topic of early modern Hindi poetry was nature. Description of natural scenes had not been absent from *rīti* poetry, but, as with the description of *nāyikās*, it was always illustrative of pre-defined archetypes (forests, mountains, rivers, lakes, oceans, etc.). In addition, nature in *rīti* poetry was not treated as an independent poetic subject, but instead performed the role of stimulant (*uddipāna*) to the emotion being portrayed. For example, description of the seasons (one of the conventional subjects) was always subordinated to the emotions of the *nāyaka* and the *nāyikā*, which they enhanced by providing setting and atmosphere. The modern poets made nature an independent subject, and began to describe it realistically in terms of the concrete details of particular scenes. The *rīti* poet, following the rule that

> moonrise saddens *cakravāka,* day-lotus, abandoned lover,
> darkness, sulking heroine and adultress,
> but gladdens
> night-lotus, ocean and *cakora,*[29]

had to subordinate his moonrise to *śṛṅgāra rasa* and his *nāyikā's* state of mind. A modern poet like Śrīdhar Pāṭhak, on the other hand, could describe it as a subject worthy of interest in its own right:

> The woods were deserted,
> the face of nature calm;
> It was nightfall—the time
> of the evening stroll;
> The new moon,
> swathed in the red afterglow of birth,
> rose slowly in the sky.[30]

Like the turn from erotic love to love of nation, this liberation of nature from the context of the *nāyaka-nāyikā* relationship also represented a rejection of Rādhā and Krishna's dominance over poetry.

A third characteristic topic of early modern Hindi poetry was the retelling of religious myths in a new way, giving them a humanistic slant that made them compatible with the new rationalist ethos of the times. Like the modern poets of Bengal two generations earlier, Hindi poets took to writing long narrative poems on mythological themes, recasting the gods as examplary human heroes and, through them, preaching some contemporary message. A good example is Maithilī Śaraṇ Gupta's *Sāket,* which recounts the events at Ayodhya from the marriage of Rāma and his brothers to Rāma's return from exile. Unlike all earlier retellings of the Rāma story, it emphasizes the nexus of family relationships at the court rather than the purposes of the gods or the workings of *karma,* and instead of being centered on Rāma, it focuses on Lakṣmaṇa's wife Urmilā and her undeserved suffering during the fourteen years of Rāma's exile. Likewise, Gupta's *Yaśodharā* takes the life of the Buddha and narrates it from the point of view of his wife Yaśodharā, transforming the familiar religious legend of the Buddha's struggle to achieve enlightenment into the story of his wife's struggle between resentment at being abandoned and love for their infant son.

Significantly, very few of these mythological poems dealt with the Rādhā-Krishna story. Most of the themes were taken from the *Rāmāyaṇa* or the *Mahābhārata*—a rejection of the medieval cultural past in favor of the more distant classical past of the epics. There was one exception, however, which, as such, deserves to be examined: the poet Harioudh's *Priyapravās.* It was the earliest of the new mythological narratives and therefore, presumably, closer in sensibility to the old Braj poetry. Nevertheless, instead of dwelling on Rādhā and Krishna's youthful romance, as did *rīti* poetry, it relates the story of Krishna's departure for Mathura and Rādhā's subsequent pining for him—a theme preferred by the *bhakti* poets. Furthermore, the account of Rādhā and Krishna's earlier relationship is stripped of its erotic tone. The two are portrayed as childhood playmates whose friendship gradually developed into love (a love which remained chaste), but who were separated by Krishna's departure before there could be any talk of marriage. Finally, the whole point of the story is transformed in light of the ideals of the Indian Renaissance. Whereas in the traditional account, Krishna's messenger Uddhav tries to console Rādhā with homilies on the omnipresence of Krishna as the God above all form, in *Priyapravās* he exhorts her to overcome her selfish desire for union with Krishna by exerting herself in the service of humanity:

> To engage in austerities for the sake of spiritual liberation
> is selfish, and cannot be called self-sacrifice:
> The greatest self-sacrifice in the world, O beloved,
> is to hold human welfare and service to humanity dearer
> than your own life.[31]

The poem ends with Rādhā and the *gopīs* taking a vow to remain unmarried and to devote themselves instead to serving the people and the nation. Thus the sexually desirable *nāyikā* is completely absent, and Rādhā is recast as a devoted and asexual *loksevikā* ("servant of the people"). That this new image of Rādhā was not found believable or appealing is apparent in the fact that no other modern reinterpretation of Rādhā was attempted for some forty years after the publication of *Priyapravās.* Instead of being reinterpreted, she was ignored.

The fourth and perhaps most important topic taken up by the first generation of modern Hindi poets was that of social reform. The social reform movement in those days was primarily concerned with injustices affecting women; the poetry reflected this emphasis by being largely about women and their problems. The evils of child-marriage and purdah, the cruelty of the upper-caste Hindu prohibition against widow-remarriage, the narrowness imposed on women by denying them access to education, and the drudgery of the life of the over-worked mother all became subjects of extensive poetic treatment. The plight of the Hindu widow, "that pitiful extreme of purity,"[32] was by far the most popular theme; Maithilī Śaraṇ Gupta's *Vidhvā* (The Widow") is typical of the genre as a whole:

Is this your sense of justice—
that you marry again and again, but widows are not allowed
to complain?

Even in old age, you indulge your senses,
But they, mere girls
whose bodies have never been touched
must renounce forever!

. . . .

Think how cruel you are,
how lacking in compassion and kindness:
How can you treat them with such contempt
and call it religious virtue?[33]

Earnest exhortations such as this alternated with melodramatic expressions of pity, as in Rāmnareś Tripāṭhī's *Vidhvā kā darpaṇ* ("The Widow's Mirror"), a poem in which the pathos of the widowed girl's situation is expressed by her abandoned mirror:

Alas, from that moment on, I never saw her again!
Where did that precious face disappear so suddenly?
The girl has never come near me again, even by mistake;
The wind has covered my face with dust and made me blind.

That sweet girl, nurtured in love, enveloped by affection,
The darling of the house—where is she now?
If there is anyone who can hear my pathetic cry,
Show me her face again! Give her another chance at life![34]

This overwhelming pity for women as mistreated and misunderstood creatures, the victims of social institutions and the selfishness of men, found its epitome in two lines from Maithilī Śaraṇ Gupta's *Yaśodharā* which became instantly famous:

Alas, this is the story of woman's life:
Milk flows from her breast and tears from her eyes![35]

Significantly, the word for "woman" used here, and throughout the reform-minded first phase of modern Hindi poetry, is *abalā,* "she who has no strength." Whereas the Rādhā of *rīti* poetry had been *kāminī* and *ramaṇī,* an object of desire, woman now became an object of pity instead, and the *nāyaka-nāyikā* relationship was replaced by that of helpless victim to either oppressor or protector.

Nārī: *The Universal Woman of the Chāyāvād Romantics*

If the first generation of modern Hindi poets tried to escape the hold of the Rādhā-Krishna theme by avoiding the subject of love, and replaced the image of Rādhā as *nāyikā* with that of oppressed woman or *abalā,* the second generation did something quite different. These poets, the so-called Chāyāvād group, were the young rebels of the 1920s and '30s. Inspired in part by Tagore and the English Romantics, they rejected the didacticism and the prosaic style of their predecessors and brought about a revolution in poetic sensibility. It was a romantic revolution, which involved, among other things, a subtle reformulation of the poet's relation to tradition. Like romantics elsewhere, the Chāyāvād poets were intent on expressing the individual's subjective truth, yet at the same time strove to establish a meaningful connection with their cultural past—especially the more distant cultural past. Likewise, although they placed infinite value on the individual human being, they saw human reality as organically related to natural reality, and they therefore tried at every point to "put life into the relationship between nature and the human heart."[36] And, typically romantic, they tended to prefer the abstract to the concrete, the distant to the near at hand, and to revel in subtlety, suggestiveness, and delicate shadings of feeling and form.

With Chāyāvād, love became once again the central subject of poetry, but it was a new conception of love. The lovers of Chāyāvād poetry are portrayed as soul mates, bound to each other in a relationship which is neither marriage nor the illicit love celebrated in Rādhā-Krishna poetry, but a spiritual relationship transcending all social definitions. As Pant says in his poem *Granthi* (The Bond):

A marriage-knot? The bond
we share is of gold, a gift
of fate containing
all of the longing, all
the abundance of
heaven and earth, unique,
infinitely precious.[37]

Unlike the *nāyaka* and *nāyikā* of *rīti* poetry, moreover, the Chāyāvād lovers are not single-mindedly intent on the goal of union, but see their love in its many phases of union and separation as a means to a fuller humanity and a deeper awareness of reality. Thus, Mahādevī Varmā, the foremost woman poet of the Chāyāvād group, wants her lover to remain ever hidden and inaccessible to her, and seeks to transmute the pain of separation into a universal empathy:

Settle in my heart,
    but hide behind my sorrow
        so that, in seeking you,
            I may find the whole world.

. . . .

Remain in my lite
    like the steady horizon,
        but let every attempt to hold you
            fail.

. . . .

Wait forever, while I walk
    with faltering footsteps
        on the road of separation,
            never reaching the end.[38]

Similarly, whereas love for the *nāyaka* and *nāyikā* was primarily a matter of intense sexual passion, the Chāyāvād lovers are moved by a subtle emotional attraction, a deep longing to know each other's innermost being. In his poem *Pragalbha prem* ("Mature Love"), for instance, the poet Nirālā says to his beloved:

Today I have but one desire,
beloved: enter
the half-open lotus of my heart,
leave behind
convention, triviality, wiles.
That path is too narrow
and full of thorns
for you,
who walk so gracefully.[39]

Above all, there is in Chāyāvād a certain abstract quality about love that contrasts sharply with the concrete eroticism of medieval Rādhā-Krishna poetry. Instead of showing the concrete Krishna

clasping Rādhā to his breast,
    lip touching lip, eye meeting eye,
        heart joined to heart in bliss,[40]

the Chāyāvād poet depicts the abstract emotion which binds the lovers to each other:

I am lost in my beloved,
    he is locked in my heart.
So call the night of separation
    the dawn
    of eternal union.[41]

However, if concrete eroticism is secondary to abstract emotions in the interaction of the Chāyāvād lovers, there is nevertheless a powerful sense of eros as the underlying force motivating all attractions. Eros is seen as pervading the universe, binding all things together, infusing life with creativity and exuberance, drawing beings to one another in love, and the love between man and woman is viewed as an intense participation in this ongoing erotic play of the universe.

Thus love in Chāyāvād is not devoid of sensuousness, but the sensuousness is made at once universal and abstract. It is expressed indirectly, by projecting human personality onto nature and depicting erotic love in terms of the interaction between natural objects. In Nirālā's poem *Juhī kī kalī* ("the Jasmine Bud"), for example, an encounter between lovers is conveyed through the natural personae of a jasmine bud and the fragrant southern breeze which rises up in the middle of the night. The breeze has come from afar and touched the bud lightly, but she has failed to wake up. Then,

> the ruthless hero
> violently shook her,
> raining down hard blows
> on her lovely, delicate body,
> bruising her pale round cheeks.
> Startled, the young woman
> glanced about her
> in bewilderment, then,
> seeing her lover by her side,
> lowered her eyes, smiled with delight
> and blossomed in his arms.[42]

This projection of the appearance, behavior, and emotions of lovers onto the different parts of nature was not only a way of expressing "the relationship between nature and the human heart," but also allowed the portrayal of erotic love in a way which would be less offensive to the puritanical values of the new middle-class society. In a sense, the canvas of nature replaced Rādhā and Krishna as the medium for expressing love between man and woman.

Though the Chāyāvād generation gave voice to a new conception of love, it should not be assumed that they cut themselves off entirely from the medieval poetic tradition. There are powerful echoes of *bhakti* devotionalism in much Chāyāvād love poetry, not only in the lyric form, the first-person voice, and the emotional intensity, but also in the fact that the lover is so abstract that he hardly appears to be human:

> He is a vast cloud, boundless and everlasting,
> and covers me with his breath.
> When he spread out over the sky
> and I became the object of his yearning,
> where could I hide from him,
> I the swift lightning that flashes and subsides?[43]

Likewise, though the illustrative purposes of *rīti* poetry have been abandoned, and the central poetic concern is the individual's personal vision rather than *rasa,* there are subtle evocations of the world of *rīti,* as when the woman speaking in Mahādevī's poetry expresses her mental state through the metaphor of the *nāyikā's* make-up and ornaments:

> Peering into the mirror of the moon,
> I have loosened the night's thick hair,
> Fastened in it a lotus from the stars,
> And put on a veil of endless rays;
>
> With a smile I have reddened my faded lips,
> And the lac on my feet is the speed of my steps;
> My eyelids are darkened with dreams,
> My hair-parting marked by a chain of tears.[44]

However, the whole thrust of Chāyāvād romanticism precludes the concretization that is possible with the figures of Rādhā and Krishna as *nāyaka* and *nāyikā*. The lovers address each other as *priya* and *priyā* (or *preyasī*), that is, by the most abstract possible masculine and feminine terms for "beloved," and are "half human, half imagination,"[45] hardly recognizable as flesh-and-blood men and women.

This new sensibility entails a strikingly new image of woman, which, once again, is signaled by a change in the word most often used to refer to her. In Chāyāvād poetry, woman is neither *kāminī* nor *abalā,* but is almost exclusively referred to as *nārī*—the most abstract Hindi (and Sanskrit) word for woman, one which indicates only that she is the female half of the universal man-woman ('*nara-nārī*') pair.

This abstract, universal woman is obviously very different from the conventional Rādhā. Whereas Rādhā the *nāyikā* was described largely in terms of her physical attributes, the *nārī* of Chāyāvād is described in terms of interior qualities of the spirit. In Jayśankar Prasād's epic poem *Kāmāyanī,* for instance, the central female figure Śraddhā is never once said to have a moon-shaped face, elongated fish-eyes, a wasp-waist or any of the other physical traits of the classical Indian beauty, but comes across as possessed of a deep and irresistible inner beauty:

> Radiant with never-aging beauty,
> a living image of universal desire,
> she attracts all things by her touch,
> bringing to inert matter
> the vibrancy of life.[46]

Often woman is made so abstract that she is little more than a constellation of qualities:

> You are longing, tears, laughter,
> a breath from the heart of creation,
> the object of all desires,
> a glimpse of heaven . . .[47]

Where she is concretized, moreover, it is through natural metaphors which elevate her to the status of a primal force and distance her from mundane human reality. This movement represents a return to the ethos of classical Sanskrit poetry and its association of woman with nature, but there is a change in emphasis: whereas the tendency in Sanskrit poetry was for woman to be a metaphor for nature (e.g., Kālidāsa's description of the Ganges in the dry season as a woman languishing for her beloved), Chāyāvād prefers to use nature as a metaphor for woman, or, more precisely, so to fuse the two that they are no longer distinguishable. Thus in Nirālā's poem *Sandhyā sundarī* ("Evening Girl" or "Evening as a Girl"), it is impossible to determine whether the object being described is a beautiful young woman or the natural phenomenon of evening:

> She comes under the mantle of darkness,
> no hint of flirtatiousness about her;
> Her lips are soft
> but rather serious,
> no playful laughter on them.
> Only a star smiles,
> fastened in her black curls
> to consecrate her
> queen of the heart's kingdom.[48]

This poem also reflects the Chāyāvād preference for portraying women as chaste, exalted beings to whom respect and reverence are due. The *nārī* of Chāyāvād is neither a sex object nor an object of pity, but an independent person, her lover's spiritual companion, "the queen of the heart's kingdom." Not only is the concrete eroticism of the Rādhā-Krishna relationship abandoned in favor of an interaction which takes place in the subtle realm of delicate, abstract feelings, but a new equality prevails. The one-sided self-surrender of Rādhā to a Krishna who is not exclusively devoted to her was not acceptable to the Chāyāvād romantics, and was replaced by a new relationship of mutual self-surrender. Even in poems that emphasize woman's self-surrender the principle of complementarity is never entirely lost, and the vision remains one of mutual self-fulfillment. Thus even though the woman in Mahādevī's poetry is often reminiscent of the medieval woman-who-waits, there is a difference in the way she thinks of herself vis-à-vis her lover. Though she waits for him, often in vain, she has pride ("This beggar-life of mine—/in what way/is it less than his?"),[49] and she is ultimately confident that he is as dependent on her as she on him:

> Silently, you enter my limited existence
>   to bind me with your love:
> But can the flame and the heat
>   ever be separated?[50]

How different the Chāyāvād poets felt this conception of universal woman was from the Rādhā of *rīti* poetry is evident in the following impassioned statement by Pant on the subject:

> Chāyāvād took the langorous woman of medieval *rīti* poetry, that concrete representation of sensuality, lying on a bed of flowers with hair dishevelled, oppressed by the heat of desire, drenched with sweat and scarred with nail marks, or slipping out at night for a secret rendezvous with her lover, and brought her out into the open air of nature, freeing her of the sycophancy of go-betweens and the stigma of adultery. It also raised her above the narrow confines of middle-class life and its unwholesome attitudes towards sex, and, clothing her half-naked form with the unsullied beauty of her most elevated feelings, put her next to man as an equal, giving her the dignity of an independent personality and social identity. In the woman of Chāyāvād, there is not only the moral strength of our age of national awakening, but also the universal feminine qualities of sympathy, sensitivity and wholesome affection. She doesn't come running out of her house, drawn to the Yamunā by her desire, slipping on the steps as she goes deeper and deeper into the water. Instead, she has ceased being self-conscious about her body, has removed the veil of bashfulness from her face, and, awake to her social responsibilities, walks forward in a dignified way on the high road of female independence. Love in Chāyāvād is a poem expressing the natural emotions of attachment and self-surrender, not a justification of unbridled eroticism by appeal to Rādhā and

> Krishna, or an enticement to sex in the form of catalogues of the emotions which strengthen the erotic mood. It is the voice of a new cultural consciousness which sees men and women in terms of their true value as members of society.[51]

Aurat *and* Strī: *Woman in Contemporary Poetry*

By late 1930s, the Chāyāvād movement had lost its impetus, and poetry began to take a new turn towards realism, an emphasis that became accentuated as time went on. Like contemporary poets elsewhere, the Hindi poets who have been writing in the quarter-century since India's independence have been dedicated above all to the ideal of authenticity—the belief that poetry should express the poet's actual feelings and concern itself with the actual world in which he or she lives. Unlike their Chāyāvād predecessors, who attempted to remain emotionally connected to their cultural past, contemporary poets consider tradition largely irrelevant, and try to write out of the experienced truth of their immediate circumstances. Likewise, rejecting Chāyāvād's predilection for the abstract and the universal, they concentrate on the particular, and the subject-matter of poetry becomes everyday human life in all its specificity. In this poetry, there is no room for the ideal types and conventionalized situations of *rīti* poetry, the didactic thrust of early modern Hindi poetry or the heightened vision of the Chāyāvād romantics. The poets see their task as the portrayal of actual human experience, unembellished by any idealized view of reality. As a result, contemporary Hindi poetry reflects the whole range of circumstances shaping post-independence life (especially middle-class urban life), and expresses the many currents of thought and feeling affecting this "New India."

In this poetry, the subject of love is neither central nor peripheral, but is treated as one of the many interwoven strands which make up the complex fabric of modern life. The Hindi poets of today are certainly concerned with man-woman relationships, but this is only one of their many concerns. They deal with the objective problems of poverty and injustice, industrialization and urbanization, and with their subjective counterparts of lost values and lost dreams, alienation, frustration and meaninglessness. They depict the most intimate and mundane details of domestic and workaday life as it unfolds within this overall context, and muse about the difficult moral, intellectual, and philosophical issues raised by the contemporary situation. And, instead of relegating the subject of love to an isolated realm set apart from all other human activity, they place it squarely within the context of these objective circumstances as well.

For contemporary poets, the love of Rādhā and Krishna is an objectionable theme not because it is erotic and concrete, but because it is not true to life. In the words of the poet Jagdīś Gupta,

> Today, that kind of idealized love, portrayed by means of religious figures and expressed in a special, stylized diction, is artificial and irrelevant, for it refuses to acknowledge all the problems which beset the real world.[52]

Instead their aim is

> to portray in the day-to-day circumstances of today the complex, infinitely powerful, and often contradictory feelings of attraction and rejection between the two eternal companions, man and woman.[53]

The result is a long, hard, and honest look at the real-life love relationships existing between actual men and women, in and out of marriage, each unique and fraught with ambiguities.

Thus we see the nostalgic memory of first love ("that first, pure surrender of the self"[54]) still alive in the midst of adult disillusionment and compromise; the comfort of a loving marriage with all its moments of affection (as when, in the midst of a man's demanding work, "suddenly a small, tender voice/comes over the phone,/calling me home"[55]); the conflicting pulls of romantic love ("that overpowering emotion in the deepest recesses of the heart") and domesticity ("my wife's love—symbolized by a cup of tea"[56]); the pathos of having to give up a love thwarted by circumstances ("clasping to your breast/ these dead dreams—/what good can it do?"[57]); the recognition of incompatibility ("that conflict which has gone on between us for years"[58]); the desolation following upon the loss of a beloved husband or wife ("How will my heart survive in this empty house?"[59]); the wonder at discovering one can love again ("Spring has struck me one more time!"[60]).

We also find expressed the whole range of the "infinitely powerful, and often contradictory feelings of attraction and rejection" occurring within a man-woman relationship. These are not the conventional feelings defined as topics by the *rīti* manuals nor the abstract emotional transports of Chāyāvād love poetry, but the mixed feelings of psychologically complex individuals with whom the poets' modern urban readers may be expected to identify. Sometimes simple physical attraction is described ("Those lips of yours/iridescent as opal/ravage my life"[61]), while at other times we see a more subtle psychic attraction ("You are a truth outside me/and I a truth within you"[62]). Sex is depicted in realistic physical detail and with a great deal of psychological realism as well. Thus, one finds both positive, lyrical descriptions of sex ("My manhood, aroused,/in your hand,/your face turned towards me,/your full lips reaching for mine"[63]) and attitudes of loathing and disgust ("that constant licking, the sour taste of kisses . . . etc."[64]). Anger and resentment are given expression ("I'm a man, not a god/who can put on a look of indifference,/sit wherever put/and say nothing!"[65]) as are the many faces of jealousy, from the first suspicion ("That day/on your averted face/I saw the expression of one caught/ doing something wrong"[66]) to the torment of certain realization.[67] Above all, there is an uncompromising fidelity to the complexity and ambivalence of man-woman relationships, a refusal to simplify by conventionalizing or romanticizing.

Woman, in this new poetry, is not reduced to a single image. There is neither a symbolic figure like Rādhā nor an abstract concept such as the universal woman of Chāyāvād; instead, what we find are individual women with unique personalities, engaged in a variety of mundane activities, related to men in a number of different ways. Once again, a change in vocabulary is indicative of the change in sensibility. Not only are the words *kāminī* and *abalā* almost entirely absent, but *nārī*, the abstract word preferred by Chāyāvād, stays in the background as the term against which a variety of particular women stand out. Thus, in a poem entitled *Yah ātmā kī khūkhār pyās* ("This Fierce Thirst of the Soul"), the poet Dharmvīr Bhāratī pointedly contrasts the idealized conception of woman as *nārī*, "in whose eyes I have seen . . ./an infinite pain concealing in its depths/a great unknown truth" with the pedestrian reality of an actual flesh-and-blood woman whom he must please by asking "with what color yarn will you embroider the edge of your sari?"[68] The term he uses here is the Perso-Arabic *aurat*, the most ordinary everyday word for woman and the one most free of any connotation other than gender, and it is this word, along with its slightly more dignified Sanskritic equivalent *strī*, which is most characteristic of contemporary Hindi poetry.

Rādhā could never be conceived of as *aurat* or *strī*, for she has no existence outside of her love for Krishna: hers is only a partial female personality. As a result, it has not been possible for modern poets to incorporate her into the poetry of authentic feeling and contextual realism. Even in poetry on the subject of love, allusion to her mythology is rare in comparison with the more "well-rounded" classical mythological figures of Sītā, Sāvitrī, Damayantī, Śakuntalā, or even Draupadī.[69] The inappropriateness of identifying the contemporary *aurat* or *strī* with the figure of Rādhā, or of using the symbolism of Rādhā and Krishna for the portrayal of contemporary love relationships, is so obvious to the poets of today that they tend to do so mostly in jest. For example, Prabhakar Machwe has a humorous exchange of letters between a Śrī Krishanjī of Mathura and a Mrs. Rādhā of Brindavan, in which Śrī Krishanjī propositions Mrs. Rādhā by suggesting that she read up on what Rādhā and Krishna do in the tenth book of the *Bhāgavata Purāṇa;* but Mrs. Rādhā replies that Krishna's Rādhā just got a bad name out of it all, and makes it clear that *this* Rādhā is not about to make herself dust at the feet of such a fool as a contemporary Krishna.[70]

The one major exception to this general tendency, Dharmvīr Bhāratī's long narrative poem *Kanupriyā*, is the only significant attempt since Harioudh's *Priyapravās* some forty years earlier to make the story of Rādhā and Krishna relevant to contemporary life. It is a controversial work which has won high awards on the one hand but, on the other hand, has been criticized as "so saccharine that our age cannot fully accept it."[71] Though Bhāratī recaptures in it some of the lyricism of medieval Rādhā-Krishna verse, his poem also reflects contemporary attitudes. Thus his Rādhā is no *nāyikā* confined to the "three-foot-world of *nakh-śikh*," but wants to understand the issues of the *Mahābhārata* war and, far from being pleased at being simply the dust at Krishna's feet, wants to play her part in the great events by being there for him when the war is over. She challenges Krishna as the medieval Rādhā never would have:

Listen, Krishna,
    am I just to be a bridge for you,
    an interval between your childhood playground
    and the battlefield?[72]

Nevertheless, the charm of the poem surely lies in its nostalgic evocation of the cultural past rather than in its contemporaneity;

despite its success, it stands as an isolated monument in the midst of a poetic world which continues to have no real use for Rādhā. For present-day Hindi poets, striving as they are to depict life as authentically as possible, love relationships cannot be subsumed under the mythology or the symbolism of Rādhā and Krishna. Nor can they be denied and replaced by mere compassion on the part of men for the sufferings of women, or sublimated into the abstract cosmic love of universal man and universal woman. They can be dealt with only in their concrete specificity, without the help of myth or ideal model, as part of the complex, ambivalent, bittersweet experience of actual human beings living at a particular time and in particular circumstances.

Comments: Rādhā and Erotic Community

NORVIN HEIN

My role here is that of a "respondent," but I can find nothing in my *dharmaśāstras* to describe a respondent's duty. It is not to present an independent study; that was the task of paper-writers. Nor is it to pronounce judgment on them; that I leave to the reader. As respondent, then, I have nothing to do but to play, and with the sanction of the Vaiṣṇava tradition I shall do my *līlā*. I shall sport with the materials of these excellent papers with no end in view but to draw you into my reckless generalizations. To use an old figure about the meaning of *līlā*, I shall be the devil-may-care polo player. Ideas from these papers will be my royal polo balls. I shall thwack them in all directions just to see how far they will go. If I can get you to dash off in the direction of any of these impulsive drives, my end will be accomplished.

A more modern metaphor might describe my rashness better. A theological war of the sexes is sweeping our religious world. The issue is the use of He or She in the language of religious thought, and the question of the motives and intentions of those who use one pronoun or the other. In a discussion of a goddess we meet inevitably on a great battlefield of that war. The gunsmoke of wider battles drifts in to us in one or two of our own papers. The role of this respondent? I am the moron in the powder-magazine, throwing matches about to see whether something will catch.

Trying to perceive the most noteworthy contributions of our papers, I have looked first for the basic questions that they ask. "Who is Rādhā?" is often their problem, in just those words. Sometimes, however, the question is rather "*What* is Rādhā?" because Rādhā's identity is found in forces, functions or values that go beyond the personal to generalities that cannot be anthropomorphically conceived.

"Who is Rādhā?" has been the easier question. It is a question that devotees of Rādhā can answer particularly well because it is in their hearts and minds that Rādhā can be found. It is the prerogative of the believers, not others, to describe the deity that they worship. Shrivatsa

Goswami has given us such a confessional description of Rādhā in a theological summary that is efficient and instructive. It is the Gauḍīya doctrine that he sets forth, and in one or two particulars he sets forth views held only by the followers of Caitanya. Overall, however, his sketch represents the belief of a high majority of those who worship Rādhā quite clearly as a deity. One could not hope for a doctrinal summary that would be truer to their understanding. His exposition from the theological works of the Brindavan *gosvāmīs* is supported by Donna Wulff's work on their dramas and by Mackenzie Brown's studies of the doctrine of the *Brahmavaivarta Purāṇa*. The poetry of the *Sūr Sāgar*, set forth so attractively by Jack Hawley, has an independent status as a popular supplement to this picture of the Rādhā of believers. But there is substantial agreement in all these metaphysical understandings, and our papers have presented them authentically. Who is Rādhā? She is the deity they have described. It is She who is our common focus.

When we ask, "*What* is Rādhā?" we face a more difficult question. Its language expresses our need, if we aim at a reasonably complete understanding, to observe what the worship of Rādhā means in the lives of her devotees. The tradition in this case provides no ready-made answer; its theologians have been intent upon the nature of the Goddess herself, not upon the affairs of human beings. So when we ask about the function of the Goddess in human life we are largely on our own. The tentative answers you are about to hear rest on no irresistible authority: they are illuminations that these papers have provided. Their validity, if they have any, depends on materials that you too have read, and on your agreement that my interpretations are plausible.

What is Rādhā? First, she is a revelation of what is at the heart of the universe, at the center of being where our existence culminates and life is most real. There, eternally existent in the triple being of God, is ideal *woman*. In the religious life, as in ordinary human experience, when man reaches woman, man is *home*. The creators of the Rādhā theology—as of every Indian theology—are men, despite their conception of themselves as cowherd girls—and when men attain to where woman is, they have reached home. The figure of Rādhā can be meaningful also to younger persons of any sex and to all those who remember childhood, when reaching the principal woman of one's life means the soothing of wounds, unquestioning acceptance, and supports that are not jealously reciprocal. For males in the prime of life, attaining to intimacy with woman has an additional blissfulness of meaning; and in the special Indian subculture on which our study focuses, the erotic and frolicsome aspects of man-woman relations, accepted and celebrated, provide the words and the emotional tone of the promise of final blessedness in salvation beyond time. The devotee will then be at home not merely with Krishna but also with Rādhā and all the security and delight she represents. This salvational hope that Rādhā expresses is spoken in the language of a special tradition, but the language springs out of the universal experience of mother and mate, and it expresses a longing common to persons of all religions. These devotees of Braj make moving use of the feminine aspect of divinity in this instance to utter a universal hope.

Universal strains in the religion of Rādhā soon run out, however. While pondering these papers I have been struck by the general sharp distinctiveness of this cult from all surrounding religious traditions. Rādhā is not interchangeable with any other well-known Hindu goddess. She is not polyvalent. We know how the great theological symbols found in most religious traditions are exploited and used in almost every possible religious meaning. Metaphors are turned this way and that like faceted gems, exposing for discussion this aspect and now that of the divine nature. Reflecting on God as Father, we think of Him in the role of creator, and then provider, or protector, or source of unfailing affection, but again as commander or judge. God as Mother is open to as many possibilities, and in the vast ranges of Indian religion all of them have been pressed into use again and again. It is remarkable how many of them the Rādhā-worshippers pass by. The positive discoveries of the papers gathered here are not more significant than their great silences. Rādhāism is not a minor variation on a familiar kind of Indian goddess-cult, set off from the others only by a special stress, and by the particularity of the myths and symbols by which it expresses values and hopes that are all but universal. The cult of Rādhā is distinguished first by the many things that Rādhā is *not.*

Notice first how little Rādhā is a mother goddess. The formal title is among her pedigrees, it it true. Deep in the Sanskrit theological books someone has called her Jaganmātā, Mother of the World. And one weak unpopular myth is known in which the origin of the universe is traced to her production of a cosmic egg—which she promptly brushed aside with her foot! When pressed, her theologians have resorted to her to answer the cosmogonic question, but her motherhood is otherwise ignored. Rādhā's heart is not in mothering, nor are her theologians and devotees seriously interested in that possibility. The fact of her creatorship is not significant in living religion. Not important as the mother of the universe, neither is Rādhā important as the mother of anyone in it. The goddesses are said to have come forth from her, but none thus born is ever named. The statement is not a genealogical one but a generality of which no further use is made. She is the progenetrix of no people, the beginning of no royal line, the mother of no one. Though she is a great sex goddess, she has never settled down to housekeeping.

Neither is Rādhā the ubiquitous Indian Earth-Mother, matrix of vegetable life, patroness of fertility, focus of India's perennial concern about germination and growth, prayed to in anxieties about food. Liturgically Rādhā is not an Annapūrṇā, nor does she appear to be any kin to the manifold village "Mothers" resorted to in agricultural crises by the people of innumerable farming communities.

If Rādhā is not the good Earth-Mother, even less is she the bad. Her anger, never insuperable, is felt by Krishna only. India's awareness of the stored-up anger of suppressed woman is not used theologically to explain in Rādhā the occasional sudden violence of the natural world. Cultic approaches to her are not efforts to control natural tragedy, nor can one see in them any systematic effort to domesticate tragedy in the emotional life. I do not see in Rādhā any functional relationship to Kālī whatsoever.

It is equally difficult to see in Rādhā the cosmologizing of womanly virtues, as seen in Sītā. It goes without saying that she is not the Hindu paragon of sexual propriety. The Bengal school makes a special point of the fact that she is not. She is a model—as Donna Wulff says—only in her passionate, persistent, and total dedication to her man. Her virtues are psychological, not social. Rādhā's support of life is not in the field of ethics.

If Rādhā represents any widely appreciated human value she would appear to do so as the divinization of ideal erotic love. A deep positive acceptance of sexuality—however controlled and limited—makes Rādhāism a most unusual Vaiṣṇava cult. The relation of the worship of Rādhā to the overt sexuality of her devotees is an inaccessible matter into which our papers cannot enter. There have been persons—some of them Hindus—who have charged that Rādhā is the very goddess of venery. In support of such a view the most that I could say is that Rādhā-worshippers do not regard sexual language as unusable, and that they dare to stir up erotic feeling deliberately and to use it in cultivating a distinctive kind of high emotion in groups. For some worshippers Rādhā may legitimize a hearty pursuit of *kāma*. But the interpretation of Rādhāism as hedonism with a capital "H" is not supported by my own information on the attitudes of the cult. The mating of Rādhā and Krishna is presented by theologians as a transcendental event not related to the carnal couplings of human beings. In the history of Rādhā worship, lechery has been an aberration, I believe, and far less common than rigid restraint. I surmise that the erotic emotions of religious assemblies are cultivated first for their own delightful tensions, and, beyond that, as happy experiential premonitions of a greater bliss, of kindred nature, that the faithful expect to know when present finally with Rādhā-Krishna in Goloka, watching the perpetual romantic sport of the deities and participating eternally in its joy. The sweetness of controlled erotic emotion on earth points to the quasi-erotic delight of an existence hoped for in salvation.

A further significance of Rādhā is suggested by Jack Hawley in the laconic but arresting remarks with which he concludes his paper. He says that Rādhā's blissful sexual union with Krishna means that religion is always a matter of loving relationship. Rādhā is a social being. As the feminine worldward side of the masculine-feminine Rādhā-Krishna she is the tie between deity and all souls, since she is one with the *gopīs* and thus with those whom the *gopīs* represent, namely all humankind. Rādhā is social also in the everlasting polarity of her metaphysical relation with Krishna. This interrelatedness of hers is never superseded metaphysically by disappearance into an undifferentiated One. Nor is her dualistic involvement in the pair Rādhā-Krishna ever set aside in religious practice in favor of a separate worship of Rādhā for herself alone. The dualistic implication of sexual language is seriously meant and fully maintained, as well as the implication of union. There is no Rādhā worship apart from Rādhā-Krishna worship. We speak of a Rādhā cult only in synecdoche, for convenience. Rādhā is not to be compared with the autonomous Durgā discussed in Thomas Coburn's paper, a goddess ever virgin and lonely in her power.

Hawley's suggestions have implications that go beyond theology to the supports of social unity. He all but says that the *socius* of Durkheim is involved in the cult of Rādhā, and that her sexuality has meaning as a social unifier. That the worship of Rādhā, or sexuality itself, for that matter, has anything to do with social unity is an interpretation of striking novelty. But the more I reflected on this proposition the less incredible it became. That the sex force is a social force is not biological nonsense, nor even political nonsense. A political community is securely united only when it is also an erotic community—an association of people whose males and females can look on each other as potential mates. I recall a biologist's plausible claim that sexual attraction was the cement of primeval human society and the factor that permitted civilization itself to begin to form. It was the continuing sexual receptiveness of woman—so different from the cyclic or seasonal heats of female animals—that drew man and woman into the lasting cohabitation that was the basis of the formation of the human family, and then of language and the transmission of learning and the rise of human culture. It is conceivable that human social groups are tied together still by the bond of erotic imagination. And if it is possible that an erotic tie facilitated the development of human society toward large-scale organization, it is also possible to see sexuality as a defensive resort of communities suffering from disorganization. Let us test the possibility that the blooming of the Rādhā cult reflected a problem of integrity in the Hindu society of the time.

The cult of Rādhā is especially open to historical interpretation because its fortunes rose and fell in recorded time. The papers before us provide data on the cult of Rādhā through many centuries, and reveal stratographic differences from which some striking inferences can be made. A sweep of fifteen centuries is involved, within which three periods can be discerned in which the cult of Rādhā had different constituencies and enjoyed quite different social favor.

Mackenzie Brown tells us about the six hundred years that preceded the appearance of the Sanskrit poet Jayadeva. The little that is known about this time is sufficient to show that the Rādhā of our earliest knowledge was established in the religious life of very humble people. For centuries mention of Rādhā is found only in Prakrit poetry, Apabhraṃśa works, and the writings of the Jains. The closest external associations of her cult are with low-class Śaiva movements. Rādhā belonged to the religion of the lower and middle classes, of simple people who were by no means the policy-makers of the Hindu society of the time, nor the enjoyers of its surplus.

Rādhā first appears in the mainstream of Sanskrit literature in the *Gītagovinda* of Jayadeva. She rises to prominence in the twelfth century as one whose time has come. The meanings seen in Rādhā deepened for a full six hundred years. Mackenzie Brown traces the magnification of Rādhā through the late *purāṇas;* Jack Hawley traces the same crescendo through the strata of the *Sūr Sāgar*. The Krishna and Arjuna of the *Bhagavadgīta* are replaced by Rādhā and Krishna in the ardent attention of the literature. Learned Brahmins now relate Rādhā's story and expound her theology. An erotic lore that had formerly delighted only the lower classes became the possession of a substantial cross-section of society.

In the late nineteenth century there was a reverse turn in the fortunes of Rādhā worship. Barbara Miller cites Bankim Chandra Chatterji's disdain for all that Rādhā represents. Swami Dayananda's hatred of the whole Krishna cult of Braj could be mentioned as a similar development of the time. Mahatma Gandhi's profound love of Krishna turns back again to the *Bhagavadgīta* alone. His silence about Rādhā is so complete that it is eloquent. Finally, we see the rejection of Rādhā in modern Hindi poetry, as traced by Karine Schomer. The adoration of Rādhā during the last hundred years has been swept out of the mainstream of Hindu religious life, to subsist once more in a religious subculture.

What may this scanning of history tell us about what Rādhā has meant in Hindu life? It suggests that Rādhā worship has been a hardtimes religion with a positive relation to the distresses of cultural and political bondage. This goddess who is "The Pleasing One" in the most ancient period pleased only the lowly, but in the middle centuries she met needs that existed in Brahmins and other twice-born Hindus. That the needs involved were the old needs is the most direct supposition: that the life of the Hindu elite in the high middle ages became like the life of the nobodies of the older period in some important way. The development, I suspect, was that the twice-born, too, had become nobodies, enjoyers no longer of the self-expression and the privileges of rule, deciders of no great issues, part of the suppressed. This is the age when, according to one Muslim historian, a sultan decreed that any Hindu accosted by a Muslim must stop and open his mouth so the latter might fill it with dirt. These were the Hindus who turned to Rādhā and built up her theology during the centuries of Muslim and British rule. When India in the late nineteenth century began to see her subjection as removable, religious nationalists began to pick themselves up out of the dust and the religion of Rādhā began to lose favor. Rādhā's work on the national scene was done.

Yet Rādhā had wide and deep significance for Hindus of all classes during those middle centuries. What was that significance?

Religion is a struggle toward such ideals as can be believed to be real possibilities. In modern Christianity, the social gospel and Barthianism have alternated with changes in our perception of the possible. Those who think that little blessedness is attainable in this world commonly seek salvation in the transcendent. But in the erotic there is a possibility for a last-ditch defense of satisfaction in the wordly life. Among mundane things that humans prize, erotic values are the possession hardest for external power to monopolize or take away. They are a common resort for demoralized societies like the contemporary West, whose members have lost all faith in their great cultural dreams. In the West, too, eroticists have engaged in metaphysical projection of sexuality, making it the basic process of the cosmos and the main value of existence. The medieval Rādhā cult can be understood to be a desperate defense of this kind. The diversion of the ancient Vaiṣṇava tradition's public hope into this unassailable private world can be seen in the Rādhā cult's revision of the ancient doctrine of *avatāra*. Brown and Goswami give us the essential information on this development, in which the divine intention to destroy evildoers, to protect the good, and to reestablish *dharma* in the world is no longer affirmed. In the medieval theology Krishna undertakes his descents to earth for the purposes of sport and self-enjoyment, and Rādhā becomes incarnate with him under the compulsion of a curse. The social and political overtones of the doctrine of the *Bhagavadgīta* have been surrendered. The expectation of the Kalkī avatar became another of these unconvincing old promises that could no longer support an immediate hope. Filling this gap, sexuality was required to bear such a heavy burden that the Rādhā's cult's religious sublimations could not suffice. In the seventeenth and eighteenth centuries the *Rasikapriyā* tradition, so often illustrated in art, as in figure 2 of this volume, led the Rādhā lore astray into purely secular eroticism that pointed to nothing but itself.

Should the sudden rise to prominence of the erotic Rādhā cult be understood as the diversion of hope in a frustrated people, and nothing more? Diversions of hope are sometimes unavoidable and even valuable. The deep emotion cultivated in this religious circle had a soothing and sustaining effect that was an important part not only of the attractiveness of this religion, but also of its constructive function. But this simplistic observation is not likely to exhaust the meaning of a faith widely held among such a complicated people as the Hindus. So I should like to attempt another extension of Hawley's notion about a socializing significance of the religion of Rādhā and Krishna. During the long centuries of alien control, Hindus had little opportunity to experience and develop any unity through organizational activity above the level of caste and village. My proposal is that a feeling of Hindu unity, and even practical organizing skills, continued to be cultivated in the life of Hindu sects and *sampradāyas,* a great many of which were devoted to Rādhā and Krishna. Events in which any intense, positive feeling is experienced collectively have a powerful integrating influence on the aggregations of people who share them. Occasions having erotic overtones are no exceptions. In these *sat-saṅgs,* filled with intense erotic emotion, a suppressed people sustained a hope of salvation, shared in the enjoyment of attainable satisfactions, and experienced a unity in a reality beyond village and caste. Milton Singer, in his article "The Rādhā-Krishna Bhajanas of Madras City," has shown how assemblies for singing the devotional songs of this cult bring a sense of social and cosmic support to isolated and lonely persons working in a vast modern urban center.[1] In earlier historical settings, when higher Hindu institutions were broken and civic sense was cold, the gathering of devotees, filled with the sweet *madhura rasa,* must have had the same sustaining and unifying function that they have now.

You may well think, in hearing all these bold remarks, that I have laid an egg—or dropped a bomb. Indeed, understanding myself to be your heedless theorist, I have not shrunk from taking risks. But the notion of trafficking in eggs and bombs seems a serious one to apply to my unresearched interpretations. I prefer to talk of polo balls. By lucky chance have I put some across the goal? Or have my drives been landing in the bushes? You have read the conference papers. *You* decide.

Comments: The Reversal and Rejection of Bhakti

JOHN B. CARMAN

I have been charged to comment especially on two of the papers you have before you, those of Barbara Miller and Karine Schomer. Let me begin by referring to the point on which Barbara Miller ends her extremely moving essay, that of opposite allegorical interpretations. The contradictions that the Western student often sees in the Vaiṣṇava tradition are not so different from the problems seen by the traditional commentator, who tries to resolve them with a more prosaic but perhaps more rational interpretation of a given verse. Different commentators, however, make sense of the verse in different ways, with the result that there emerge divergent prosaic resolutions of the central problems. I think it is the apparent incongruity between Rādhā as representative of human devotees and Rādhā as fully goddess that puzzles all of us who look from the outside at this tradition. What is significant in Miller's paper is the suggestion that the poet himself avoids coming down hard on either side; he wants to leave the matter ambiguous. Such a resolution as there is is aesthetic rather than metaphysical. This suggestion is largely correct, I think, but one should see the devotional poet in an ongoing dialogue with the theologian/philosopher.

For the theologian there is a shocking paradox here which is also shocking for the poet. According to tradition that is why Jayadeva could not bring himself to write the verse portraying Krishna's submission to Rādhā, and Krishna himself had to write it. Without the backdrop of hierarchy in which Krishna is not just a little bit superior, but immeasurably so, the whole punch goes out of what is said here about Rādhā's triumph. Thus this is a poet's language that deliberately does something different from that of the prosaic theologian or the prosaic commentator on the poetry. Yet without the theological backdrop the poetry would not produce the same dramatic effect.

Devotion is no mere attachment to any attractive object or entrancing personality, whether natural or superhuman. In both Śaiva and Vaiṣṇava traditions, *bhakti* is attachment to Ultimate Reality. But how can there be attachment or connection between the finite and the Infinite? And if a loving relationship is difficult between a superior and an inferior on the human level, how much more difficult must such a relationship be between the infinitely superior One and such miniscule beings as ourselves? The scriptures to which the poets so frequently refer affirm the hierarchy, yet they also recount the efforts of God to cut through the hierarchy and sometimes even to reverse human and divine roles. How do we make sense of such reversal? Does it, indeed, make any metaphysical sense?

Recently I heard Charles Hartshorne say how much he liked the Indian philosophies of *bhakti*. He complained, however, that Rāmānuja in particular was inconsistent: he did not follow through his emphasis on the devotional relationship by denying the infinity of God. Rāmānuja is therefore not a consistently relational theologian. I think Hartshorne is rightly pointing to what appears to be a striking inconsistency in Rāmānuja's system. Yet if Rāmānuja had shown the kind of consistency Hartshorne wishes he had, Rāmānuja would have denied one half of his *bhakti* tradition. Without the emphatic affirmation that *bhakti* is a one-sided relationship—God's supremacy and fidelity outdistancing anything humans can imagine—the devotee's confidence in resting on the ultimate ground of his or her own being would have no basis. On the other hand, without the dramatic and poetic expression of the reversal in God's love play, when Krishna is conquered by Rādhā and the divine bows to the human, the full reality that the devotee experiences would not be expressed. The *Gītagovinda* thus seems to me to point to the crux of this vision of reality, the heart of its philosophical difficulties but also the source of its remarkable power. This is, indeed, "amazing grace."

I was greatly instructed by Karine Schomer's treatment of the rejection of Rādhā in the Hindi heartland in modern times and would like to call your attention to a similar development that took place almost a century before this Hindi poetry. In the early nineteenth century there was a reaction against the Vaiṣṇava tradition in Bengal. The "father of modern Indian," Ram Mohan Roy, reacted against his father's Vaiṣṇava heritage, rejecting both its piety and its theology of incarnation, and looked for inspiration to the more distant "Vedic" past. Such bypassing of the more proximate *bhakti* past was a prominent feature of several nineteenth-century movements in India. Those engaging in them, as well as Western observers, were quite self-conscious about the analogy to European cultural developments. The new Hindu leaders were "reformers," and the reform movements collectively were seen by some as a "Hindu Renaissance." In Europe both the Renaissance and the Reformation had exhibited the same trait: a sharp critique of the immediate past and a harking back to an older and higher state of religion or culture. I am struck by the fact that what happened in the nineteenth century in Bengal happened and is even now happening in this century in Hindi-speaking areas. Clearly, however, there are many differences between the two, and the most important may be the "secularization" of Rādhā in modern Hindi poetry.

It occurs to me that the secularization of Rādhā is an unintended consequence of taking a theology of incarnation as far as is done in the Rādhā-Krishna tradition. Once the human is taken up so thoroughly to express the divine, and that assumption becomes such an important cultural value, it is only a small step for those somewhat separated from the orthodox tradition to conceive these incarnations as purely human figures.

Why did the same kind of development not take place in South India? Perhaps there are analogous developments of which I am not aware. As I think of the *āḻvārs'* hymns, however, with their constant movement back and forth in alluding to different divine forms and incarnations, and to different divine-human relationships, I am impressed by the poets' constant reminders to their audience that they are not talking at the merely human level. The *Gītagovinda* goes much further in its incarnational theology, and then there are those poems where it is not clear whether the poets intend to refer to this *bhakti* relationship or simply to a purely human love. Such developments can easily lead to a total humanization or secularization of the incarnations.

The modern Hindi reaction against Vaiṣṇava poetry can be paralleled in the modern American reaction against Protestant pietism. Liberal Protestantism in this country has gone through a period of sharp rejection of its pietist—if you like, *bhakti*—heritage, and the emotional reaction is often clearest in our negative feelings about pietist and evangelical hymns. Not only are they "out of date" theologically, but they are moralistic and they "drip with sentiment."

As this kind of pietism fades from the consciousness of liberal Christians, so does the emotional reaction to it. It is still the case, however, at Harvard Divinity School, where every conceivable form of religion is held up for sympathetic attention, that the one kind of religion no one has a good word for is the nineteenth-century pietism expressed in so many evangelical hymns.

When I was at Yale Divinity School a generation ago, the gospel song "In the Garden" was held up for scorn as typifying a socially irresponsible pietism with its scarcely disguised erotic emotions. In the Baptist church where I assisted on weekends, however, this hymn was quite popular and was often requested at the Sunday evening hymn sing, which was broadcast over the local radio station. That fact is a reminder that intellectuals' reactions may not be representative of those of other circles in society. Nevertheless, those responses are important, especially if they later stimulate a widespread change in religious sensibilities. In any case, such reactions are part of the individual or communal experience of many intellectuals in North America who are personally or academically interested in religion.

Many liberal Protestant theologians have developed a far more abstract language for expressing Christian faith in order to avoid the undesirable consequences of pietist theology. In India certain kinds of *bhakti* have been criticized on the grounds that they are morally deficient or even decadent. In North America the criticism is not that pietism is immoral, but that it is altogether too moralistic, being narrow and outmoded in its view of significant moral issues and moral values. There has also been criticism in both India and North America of the secular forms of enthusiastic piety. The Elvis Presley phenomenon is a good example, for in it we see the scorn or righteous indignation of religious intellectuals, but also the almost cultic adoration of Presley's numerous devotees.

Intellectuals have paid a high price, however, for turning away from *bhakti*. Neo-Vedantic and "post-liberal" Protestant theology draw on earlier theologies of incarnation—or at least of intermittent divine presence in our degenerate world—but they tend to be bloodless, unable to do justice to either the awesomeness or the mysterious sweetness of the divine-human encounter.

III.

Other Goddess Figures

1. INTRODUCTORY

The Shifting Balance of Power in the Marriage of Śiva and Pārvatī[1]

WENDY DONIGER O'FLAHERTY

Gods and goddesses (like kings and queens) are often said to have consorts. "Consort," though literally denoting a partner or spouse, is a heavily loaded term, for the consort is usually implied to be a mere appendage, far inferior in power and status to his or her spouse. Among animals, the ultimate male consort is the deep-sea angler fish, who affixes himself to the female, feeds off her body, and eventually atrophies until nothing is left of him but a bag of sexual organs to service the bloated female.[2] In divine hierogamies in India, one of the partners is generally a mere consort, far "less equal" than the other. In several significant cases, the stronger partner is the woman, who is a full goddess of the female angler-fish type; in others, the woman is a mere mortal who expresses, through her joyful subservience to her better half, the theological stance of the worshipper before the god. This essay traces Pārvatī's role in relation to the rise and fall of the dominant female figures in Indian hierogamies.

Male Dominance in the Rig Veda

The Rig Veda is usually taken as the beginning, in studies of Indian mythology, but in this case it would be misleading to begin in the Vedas, for by that time (1200 B.C.) a major power shift had already taken place. In the earlier Indo-European period, there appeared in myth and ritual an important goddess, associated with the moon and with mares, who chose a royal, human consort on whom she bestowed various powers for a limited period. She survives in the Rig Veda in the figures of Urvaśī, Saraṇyū, and Yamī, each appearing in a single, obscure hymn.[3] No worship is offered to this atavistic triad, for they are already pejoratively represented as sexually insatiable, immoral, dangerous, and cruel. Urvaśī herself admits that "Women have the hearts of hyenas," and the Vedic poet remarks, "The foolish woman sucks dry the wise man."[4]

There are several goddesses of great power in the Rig Veda, though relatively few hymns are devoted to them and they are certainly statistically far less important than the male gods who dominate the pantheon. Dawn and Night are personified and praised as beautiful women and sources of life; Indra is said to have done a heroic, manly deed by slaying Dawn, the woman who intended to do evil.[5] Aditi, personified as a female who gives birth by crouching with legs spread, is the cosmic origin of space itself and of earth, as well as being mother of the gods of the sky.[6] There is no question, however, that the Rig Veda casts goddesses in a secondary role; Indra's wife (simply called Indrāṇī, "Mrs. Indra") boasts of his sexual dimensions and prowess in true locker-room style, but one does not learn very much about *her*.[7]

Transition in the Epics

In the epics, we find both male-dominated and female-dominated hierogamies: that is, both Vedic and pre- (or non-) Vedic marriages. The *Rāmāyaṇa* shows traces of both; Rāma, a god incarnate and mortal king, marries Sītā, daughter of the earth and by implication herself a true earth-goddess.[8] But there is a serious ambiguity in the immortality of both partners, for Rāma is merely a mortal king in the early layers of the epic and only explicitly becomes a god in the later portions, whereas Sītā, on the other hand, shows traces of having *been* a goddess but is almost always treated as a mortal woman. (The fact that poetic imagery often likens her to a goddess who embodies beneficent nature is not necessarily significant for the theology of the myth, for it amounts to a poetic set-piece in literature of this type.) Thus both Rāmā and Sītā have ambiguous claims to divine status, and different parts of the epic bring out different aspects of this ambiguity. The first time that Rāma priggishly rejects Sītā after her long sojourn in Rāvaṇa's palace, he is reminded by the gods that he is a god, like them. Nothing is said here of Sītā's being a goddess, though the text does describe her as having a garland that has not withered, a possible hint of divinity, and she survives the ordeal of fire through divine intervention.[9] Rāma the god here taunts and rejects Sītā the mortal woman, who is helpless to defend herself against him. But when Rāma tries the trick a second time, the tables are turned: Sītā abandons Rāma and returns to the earth when he mistreats her[10] (just as Urvaśī abandons Purūravas when he violates his contract with her). At this moment, Sītā is clearly a goddess who will survive in her essential form in the earth, leaving behind a helpless mortal to mourn for her. Significantly, in this part of the epic Sītā has borne Rāma twin sons, the usual offspring of the Indo-European goddess; when she is a mother, he no longer treats her as a whore—but *she* rejects *him*.[11] A passage interpolated here has Rāma refer to Sītā as being "like Lakṣmī" and to himself as having the Earth as a mother-in-law,[12] phrases emphasizing Sītā's divinity; but such phrases do not occur in the earlier layers of the epic. Clearly Sītā is a transitional figure in this regard.

In the *Mahābhārata,* the Vedic model appears in the figure of Kuntī, wife of Pāṇḍu; when he is prevented by a curse from having intercourse with her,[13] she begs five Vedic gods to impregnate her (producing the five Pāṇḍavas, who all marry Draupadī, a multiform of Kuntī herself). Here is a dramatic instance of a mortal woman with five immortal consorts. But the pre-Vedic, Indo-European goddess also survives here in the form of Śrī, the fickle goddess of prosperity who plays fast and loose with a number of unfortunate mortal kings.[14] Many volumes have been written about these female figures; I cite them only to show that in the epic period the divine consort game (*līlā*) could still be played with either of two sets of rules.

Female Dominance in the Purāṇas

In the Purāṇas both male-dominated and female-dominated couples occur, and one can occasionally find them side by side in a single text, as in the epics. But by and large purāṇic sectarianism developed in such a way that it was almost always necessary to stand up and be counted on the side of the god or the goddess. When the female is ascendant we may be seeing traces of her origin, albeit murky and hypothetical, in the Indus Valley Civilization of 2300 B.C., with its crude terra cotta mother goddesses, or correspondences to much later Dravidian myths of a goddess who devours her consort.[15] On a different plane, one might see a contributing element in some of the basic precepts of Sāṅkhya philosophy that filtered down, on a *Reader's Digest* level, to the purāṇic texts: the concept of *prakṛti,* the female principle, more visible, immanent, and active than her constant companion, the pure and spiritual but inert *puruṣa,* the male. In purāṇic mythology (though perhaps not always in purāṇic theology) the Goddess often comes to affect her consort as *prakṛti* affects *puruṣa*—animating him and implementing his latent powers.

Change of Sex

Theologically, however, the concept of the dominance of the female divinity is in some ways a godsend—or perhaps a goddesssend. The passionate worship of God required by the *bhakti* movement that developed simultaneously with the emergence of the worship of the Goddess (during the first few centuries of the Christian era) often led the worshipper to imagine him or herself in an erotic relation with the divine. To do this in India (a country that has never acknowledged the existence of homosexuality) is to establish an erotic bond with an Other; one sex assumes the stance of the worshipper, while the other sex is cast in the role of God. When God is Krishna or Śiva, the female worshipper may respond naturally (though with Śiva this is a dangerous process, hedged with protective ritual), but the male worshipper may have difficulty in passing the physical; he must somehow become female, as is managed in various ingenious ways in the complex theology of Rādhā (particularly in the case of Caitanya). This change of sex is important for saints of both sexes, but for most *bhaktas* it applied to the man alone; just as androgynes are primarily male, so too male saints become female, but female saints generally remain female.[16] Although the motif of change of sex is widespread in mythology and folklore, and surfaces frequently in Dionysian rituals of reversal in which transvestism is a common occurrence,[17] as well as in the behavior of individuals who were inspired to renounce normal human conventions, as a permanent way of visualizing one's relationship with God it was an extreme step, and one not taken when there were other more convenient alternatives. How much simpler it all is if God is a woman, and we can all remain smugly male!

The problem, however, is that the blood-thirsty Devī is not the sort of lady to whom any but the most psychotic masochist would choose to make love. One ironic result of this problem was the tendency for worshippers of the Goddess to become transvestites or even eunuchs: for since only demons are dominated (and killed) by Devī in many mythologies, the worshipper avoids a sexual relationship with her and becomes female in order to be her servant or imitator.[18] By this logic men become women in order to escape the sexually threatening mother, not (as in the Krishna-Rādhā theology) in order to unite sexually with the erotic male consort.

Moreover, the overwhelming prominence of the image of the Goddess as mother made incest a barrier to a hierogamy grounded in this context. Incest is *denied,* and any explicit hierogamy with the Mother is out of the question. Thus, although an incestuous hierogamy underlies much of the motivating force and symbolism of cults of the Mother, the official mythology of hierogamy shied away from it. The resistance to any attempt to combine the images of divine female consort and divine mother may be seen in the mythology of Rādhā, who is almost never said to be a mother; when, on one rare occasion, she does give birth (to an egg), she kicks it away in anger, and her husband curses her to be barren evermore.[19]

The Transformation of the Consort: Pārvatī

Instead of the quest for the divine *Liebestod* with the dangerous Mother, another line was followed in the search for an approachable form of female divinity. A dominant, divine female "consort" was developed by inverting an already existing, acceptable, relatively peaceful marriage between a dominant male god and a subservient mortal woman. This took place primarily in the purāṇic mythology of Śiva and Pārvatī, from which most classical Śākta texts developed (though some did base themselves upon the Krishna-Rādhā mythology).[20] In the early layers of this corpus, Pārvatī, the daughter of the mountain Himālaya, is an ambiguous semi-divinity, like Sītā. Although poetic metaphors accorded her divine status,[21] she is the quintessence of the lowly mortal woman worshipping the lofty male god. She literally worships the phallus, as she is depicted doing on so many South Indian temples and as she is imitated by young girls in Bengal who make sand-*lingas;*[22] she undergoes physical torture to catch Śiva's attention; she purifies herself to be worthy of him. Like Sītā, she must enter fire (in her incarnation as Satī) to be reborn as Pārvatī, establishing the precedent for the very epitome of subservience to the husband: the institution of suttee.

Pārvatī's ambiguous mortal/immortal status is the pivot of the myth, the focal point of transition between male-dominated and female-dominated hierogamies. Below Pārvatī is the figure of the merely mortal worshipper of the God; but above her, and infusing her with power, is the figure of Devī, the Goddess herself, regarded not only as *a* divinity but as *the* divinity. Thus, depending upon the point of view of the particular text telling the story, Pārvatī may act more like her mortal counterparts (totally subservient to Śiva) or more like her immortal alter-ego (totally dominant over Śiva). In fact, all three levels are a single goddess, but as the context shifts different aspects are brought into play.

The first aspect, the mortal woman subordinate to the god, is developed at length in many purāṇic texts. Śiva expounds various tantric doctrines to Pārvatī, who responds either like one of Socrates' straight men ("Tell me more, O wise one") or by falling asleep. At this the narrator of the Purāṇa invariably remarks, "Naturally a mere woman could not be expected to understand a metaphysical discussion," but Pārvatī is nevertheless punished—usually by being cursed to become incarnate as a mortal and/or banished from the God's presence, two neatly appropriate fates for the consort who fails to match up to the theological majesty of her husband.

The myth of the *Liebestod* is removed from the Goddess in another way as well. The demon who lusts to marry the Goddess and is killed by her in an ecstasy of sexual/martial confrontation appears in a strangely garbled form in several later Śākta Purāṇas that depict Pārvatī as the loving wife even though she is an incarnation of the all-powerful Goddess. In this myth, the demon Āḍi seeks to seduce and kill not her but Śiva; to do this he must change into a woman (as must the worshipper who seeks union with Krishna) and he places teeth in "his" vagina. Śiva is on to him, however, in more ways than one, and places an adamantine weapon on his phallus, killing the demon in the most literal of love-deaths (*la morte douce*). It is perhaps significant that during this bizarre episode Pārvatī is out of town at a yogic beauty parlor having her complexion made lighter, to please her light-skinned husband; she does this by sloughing off her old, dark persona (the man-eating Kālī, who disappears conveniently into the Vindhya mountains until she is needed again) and returning as Gaurī, the Golden Girl—the pretty wife, the acceptable consort.[23]

The Mediation of Pārvatī

Curiously, the assumption of male dominance is maintained even in certain episodes that occur in the great Śākta Purāṇas, in which the Goddess is clearly more powerful than the uxorious divinity whom she deigns to marry. Such an episode occurs in the *Kālikā Purāṇa*. After the Goddess becomes incarnate as Pārvatī to marry Śiva, she consents to descend further to be born as the princess Tārāvatī, married to king Candraśekhara, an incarnation of Śiva. She does this in part to keep an eye on Śiva (who had been cursed to become incarnate as a mortal king as a result of trying to rape the goddess Sāvitrī, whom, he lamely insists, he had mistaken for Pārvatī); in part to do him a favor (for he begs her to become Tārāvatī so that he can fulfill the second part of the curse—to beget children on a mortal woman—without being unfaithful to Pārvatī, a possibility that suddenly seems less attractive to him than it did when he was chasing Sāvitrī, but that Pārvatī magnanimously takes at face value); and in part to do a similar favor for two of her immortal stepchildren (Bhṛṅgin and Mahākāla, who had been cursed to be reborn as monkey-faced mortals in punishment for having inadvertently caught sight of Pārvatī naked; as Tārāvatī, she will fulfill *their* curse as well as Śiva's, by giving birth to them).

Thus the Goddess appears on three levels in this myth. As Devī, she is the supreme divinity above all other gods and goddesses. As Pārvatī, she pretends to serve her husband Śiva docilely (and helps him out of a tight spot) but in reality controls the event through her higher aspect, Devī; this is a manifestation of the familiar syndrome in which omnipotent gods veil themselves with mortal attributes. And finally she appears as Tārāvatī, the mortal queen. Pārvatī knows that she is Devī and even has conversations with Devī, as is often the case when a Hindu god "becomes" a lower form of divinity while still continuing in existence as the "full" god. Though Tārāvatī experiences a confrontation with Pārvatī, she does not communicate with Devī at all and immediately forgets even her identity with Pārvatī. Pārvatī is therefore the mediator between the omniscient Devī and the ignorant Tārāvatī, who have no contact with one another except through her. Yet there are strong lines tying Devī to Tārāvatī. Such motifs as the birth of twins (particularly theriomorphic twins) and their implied incestuous relationship with their mother are remnants of the ancient myth of the mare-goddess,[24] a role here split, as it so often is, between a goddess and a mortal—Devī and Tārāvatī.

Despite the myth's firm grounding in the female-dominated hierogamy, the old Vedic pattern of male dominance surfaces in the central episode:

> One day when Tārāvatī was bathing in the river, a sage saw her and was overcome by lust for her. He said, "You must be a goddess or a demoness who has become mortal in order to enjoy the pleasure of the flesh. You must be Pārvatī, or Śacī, the wife of Indra." But she replied, "I am not a goddess, but merely a mortal queen, Tārāvatī, wife of king Candraśekhara." When the sage continued to make unwanted advances, she tricked him by substituting a look-alike sister, but the sage cursed her to be raped by Śiva in his terrifying form and to bear him a pair of monkey-faced sons.
>
> Hearing of this curse, Candraśekhara kept Tārāvatī in an inaccessible terrace on the top of the palace, where he himself made love to her. One day as Tārāvatī was worshipping Śiva she thought of Candraśekhara and did not distinguish between the two of them. Then, at Śiva's request, Pārvatī entered into Tārāvatī, and Śiva approached her in the form of a Kāpālika, wearing a garland of bones and disgusting clothing, with a deformed and evil-smelling body. Tārāvatī received him with great joy and afterwards gave birth immediately to two sons with monkey faces. Then Pārvatī left the body of Tārāvatī and deluded her so that she did not recognize herself [as an incarnation of Pārvatī]. When Tārāvatī saw the two boys she thought that she had been unfaithful to her husband, and she wept in grief and anger.
>
> Then the sage Nārada came to them and explained that they were incarnations of Śiva and Pārvatī, and he said to Candraśekhara, "Take Tārāvatī upon your lap and close your eyes and let her close her eyes, and when you open them you will see your divine nature." They did so, and when they had arrived at perfect understanding Nārada said, "Now you must close

> your eyes and return to mortal understanding until you give up your bodies." Then they closed and opened their eyes and they thought, "We are mortals." And as time passed they neglected the twins that had been begotten by the god.[25]

Despite the constant theological reminder that they are gods incarnate, Tārāvatī and Candraśekhara avoid the hierogamy at all costs and abhor the twins who remain as proof that it has in fact taken place. Tārāvatī is depicted as a trembling, ignorant woman visited by the uncanny, unsavory figure of the orgiastic god, possessed by him (rape, she calls it), and let fall, ruined, ashamed, and awkwardly unable to account to her husband for the two monkey-faced infants. Just as the Goddess appears on three levels, so too there are three men involved with Tārāvatī on the same three levels: Śiva (on Pārvatī's level), Candraśekhara (on Tārāvatī's), and the sage, who, by instigating the curse that is the counterpart of the curses set in motion in heaven, is the male figure in control of the event on earth, just as Devī arranges and disposes the curses from above.

Another point emerges from this complex myth, the implication that it is dangerous for a mortal to become an immortal or to have sexual contact with an immortal. Although Tārāvatī is reminded of her divine nature again and again, she denies it steadfastly. On one level this is an instance of metaphysical ignorance, lack of enlightenment;[26] but on another level it is an instance of the human preference for humanity over divinity, of the human fear of contact with the divine, the human inability to accept those moments when the dividing line between mortal and immortal dissolves or is revealed as mere illusion. So too Damayantī prefers Nala to all the gods who impersonate him, and Sukanyā prefers her decrepit old husband Cyavana to the glamorous divine Aśvins whom he resembles.[27] In each case, the woman rejects an immortal lover who is exactly like her human lover in every detail but the one essential distinction between human and god. She chooses her true love by spying out the specific qualities that distinguish the mortal from the immortal: mortals sweat, blink, cast shadows, have dust on them, wear garlands that wither, and do not (as the gods do) stand suspended ever so slightly above the ground. In each case the preference is for the lower end of the continuous spectrum from human to divine—in one's partner as well as in oneself.

As goddesses playing the role of mortal women, Pārvatī and Rādhā (and, to a lesser extent, Sītā) serve as mediators who intercede between the worshipper and the god, playing the role of docile and accessible servants. It is difficult to assess the precise components of mortality and immortality in any of these figures at a particular time; Rādhā is unknown to the *Bhāgavata Purāṇa,* a very human figure in the *Gītagovinda,* and the essence of the great female Godhead in the *Brahmavaivarta Purāṇa.* Subtle shifts may take place within a single text: thus despite her generally inferior position in the *Gītagovinda,* Rādhā triumphs in the end and assumes the "inverse" position in her love-play with Krishna. At this point she is called Caṇḍī, a name usually given only to Devī,[28] a possible indication that she has transcended the bounds normally assigned to Rādhā.

In popular traditions, also, Rādhā sometimes transcends her "place," as in the *dān līlā* illustrated in figure 6. Though the scene is unusually aggressive for Rādhā, it finds ample support in both secular and religious traditions, in the "love-battle" of bites and scratches described in all of the *Kāmaśāstras* and in the literal Liebestod of such demons as Mahiṣa, attacked by the object of his passion, the Goddess.

Pārvatī, too, may be regarded either as an appendage of the great god Śiva or as his controller. Similarly, as Satī and Sītā assume higher theological status, the same technique is used to distance both of them from embarrassing episodes in their pre-deified past: Satī no longer actually burns herself on her husband's pyre but merely creates a "shadow" Satī,[29] just as Sītā creates a "shadow" Sītā to be burnt when Rāma abandons her.[30] Both of these incidents are in imitation of the earliest Indian split goddess, Saraṇyū the mare, who leaves a "shadow" image behind when she abandons her mortal husband.[31]

Despite these variations it is usually clear at any given moment what the emphasis of the text is, and this emphasis bears strongly upon the balance of power between the two members of the unequal partnership. Richard Brubaker has discussed this problem with reference to the consorts of the village goddess: "The antagonists are sometimes gods rather than men or demons, but the antagonist . . . is the one who *responds* to the hierophany; his relationship with it therefore parallels the human relationship with the divine and, in so doing, has theological implications for human behavior."[32] If Krishna or Śiva is God, and if he is supplicated by his consort, the consort is thereby cast in the role of a mortal, even if she is technically a goddess. True, this unequal relation may be variously conceived. Thus the image of dancing on the prostrate body of a devotee, or dancing to control and dominate a

FIGURE 6.

Dān Līlā

(Rādhā's Response to Krishna's Demanding Toll)
Pahari Hill, Kangra, ca. 1825.
(Courtesy, Museum of Fine Arts, Boston, 25.524.
Gift of Ananda K. Coomaraswamy.)

Figure 6.

Among the rich variety of *dān līlā* episodes is the one depicted in this painting. Rādhā and the *gopīs*, disguised as Mathura guardsmen, surprise and capture Krishna, who with the *gopas* had been stealing curds and demanding toll from the *gopīs* en route to Mathura. As the *gopas* all take to their heels to escape, four *gopīs* with baskets containing curd jars stand to the left, along with Rādhā's armed companions.

Moreso than other painters illustrating this theme, the artist here has been extremely successful in conveying a sense of heightened drama. Surrounded by the greatly animated *gopīs* and *gopas*, Rādhā rushes aggressively forward to apprehend the youthful, almost shy Krishna. The *dān līlā* incident is not recorded in the standard Purāṇas, but appears in later poetry as another example of Rādhā and Krishna's mutual fun — teasing being an essential part of the lovemaking.

A text in Hindi on a now misplaced cover sheet, but documented in 1926 by Coomaraswamy, reads:

> Putting on Rādhā the guise of the king's body guard, the herd-girls brought her from Mathurā to Madhuban's grove:
>
> She says to Kānha, "Stop, stop, Kans Rai wants you; by whose leave, hark ye, are you stealing curds from the jars?"
>
> Away went the older herd-boys where they would, but Lord Śyāma being but a child was caught by the hand:
>
> But he got away by his wiles, and seeing his beauty, her frowns were dispersend and she smiled at his childish pranks.[1]

— V.N.D.

[1]Ananda Coomaraswamy, *The Catalogue of the Indian Collections* (Cambridge: Harvard University Press, 1926), pt. 5, pp. 154-55.

consort, takes two forms in the mythology of Śiva: in the image of the Naṭarāja, Śiva (the god) crushes the body of the lover (the devotee); in the tantric image of Kālī, the Goddess crushes the body of her lover (Śiva).[33] In the first image the relation between God and devotee is primary, the sexual (or martial) relation secondary (for no one is sure whether the figure under Śiva's foot is a demon or a devotee); in the second image the relation between Goddess and devotee is secondary, as the image is usually described in purely sexual terms. Nevertheless, Śiva is on top in the first, and on the bottom in the second, as he changes from God to devotee. This tendency to depict the consort as the devotee is enhanced by the overlapping patterns of devotion to a god, service to a husband, and supplication of a lover—particularly a lover who remains aloof and distant, as Krishna distances himself from Rādhā through erotic teasing and Śiva withdraws from Pārvatī through his ascetic meditation.

The Union of Mortals and Immortals

In this way the theoretical model of pairs ranked according to male/female dominance interacts with another model ranking them according to the mortal or immortal status of each partner. Several different patterns may be simultaneously present at any moment, though one is usually emphasized. First is the mating of a god and a goddess, the classical hierogamy, in which he may be dominant (Viṣṇu and Lakṣmī, Oberon and Titania) or she (Śiva and Devī). Second is the mating of the mortal and his mortal mistress, the tradition of Sanskrit court poetry, in which there is usually no marriage at all but merely an illicit liaison. In this groups, as in the first, the male is usually dominant. This human pattern pervades much of the mythology of Krishna and Rādhā, and it is interesting to note that when it was applied to that of Śiva and Pārvatī (in the eighth canto of Kālidāsa's *Kumārasambhava*, many centuries before the myth of Krishna and Rādhā) voices were immediately raised in protest: it was thought to be unseemly to depict in such human terms the love-play of gods (as unseemly as describing that of one's own parents).[34] Even Krishna's love-play proved an embarrassment to many a devout commentator once Krishna came to be regarded as God incarnate. Śrīdhara goes to great lengths to explain why, since Krishna is God, he could not actually have committed adultery with the *gopīs*, though other commentators went to even greater lengths to explain why, precisely because he *is* God, he can do things that mortals had better not imitate.[35]

Third is the mating of a mortal with an immortal. The dominated female figures in this group occupy a twilight zone, supplicating the god as a mortal would, but assuming a quasi-equality with the god when the marriage actually takes place. This pattern may be seen in much of the depiction of the myths of Sītā with Rāma and Śiva with Pārvatī, and it is relevant to the understanding of many manifestations of the cult of Krishna and Rādhā as well. This third group raises certain theological problems. Any sexual interaction is fraught with dangers; sex is auspicious (life-connected) but impure and dangerous [36] even when the partners are well matched. Indeed, when this is the case, and when both are powerful gods, the cumulative power of their sexuality places the entire universe in danger. Thus Śiva's seed must be kept away from Pārvatī when she is treated as a mighty goddess, lest the two forces together reach a kind of radioactive critical mass and blow up the universe.[37] When the partners are badly matched, the dangers are great indeed; and what could be more unequal than the mating of a mortal with an immortal?

When the female, the woman-become-goddess, is the dominated figure in this imbalance, the union is regarded as auspicious (i.e., hypergamous) and no danger is seen, for power flows the way it is supposed to, from male (divinity) to female (worshipper). Thus the worshippers of Krishna imagine themselves to be Rādhā (or, more modestly, one of her friends), for the consort is identified with the mortal worshipper and serves to mediate on his behalf with the god. The Purāṇas abound in instances of such mediation on a literal level; when Śiva is angry and wishes to destroy or punish a mortal, Pārvatī often intercedes and persuades him to be lenient. This means that the male worshipper must imagine himself to be the (dominated) female, and *bhaktas* seem often willing to do this, though Śiva-*bhaktas* usually identify with Śiva rather than with Pārvatī.[38]

When the female is dominant, as the Goddess, the male worshipper need undergo no change of sex to identify with her consort; but there are other problems inherent in this process, problems arising from the forbidding nature of the Goddess. In addition there are dangers inherent in the worshipper's identification with Śiva even when Śiva is not regarded as the all-powerful deity, dangers of overstepping boundaries between the human and the divine.[39] Moreover, there are complex problems arising from the flow of power in the "perverse" direction, from female to male, primarily the danger that the male worshipper will be overpowered by his Goddess. For this reason, though a man who worships divine couples in which the female is dominant may identify with the consort (as the tantric worshipper of Devī may identify with Śiva), other alternatives are usually preferred: the worshipper identifies with *both* the Goddess and her consort, or even solely with the Goddess herself; often the tantric visualization makes use of a human woman who is identified with the Goddess.

In this way, a balance of power is achieved between human and divine powers and, on each level, between male and female powers. Despite the danger to the male worshipper of the Goddess, benevolent forces flow to him. One way in which the danger is offset is by the splitting of spheres of ritual: power does not merely flow vertically, from the female divinity to the male worshipper, but it is also split so that it flows horizontally on two levels. In heaven, it flows from Śakti to Śiva, and on earth it flows between their two human incarnations, from female to male. Here at last, after three millennia, a new way has been devised for the Goddess to gain the upper hand in the Indian game of divine sexual politics.

2. INDEPENDENT GODDESSES

Blood and Death Out of Place: Reflections on the Goddess Kālī

DAVID R. KINSLEY

> She is dark as soot, always living in the cremation ground. Her eyes are pink, her hair disheveled, her body gaunt and fearful. In her left hand she holds a cup filled with wine and meat, and in her right hand she holds a freshly cut human head. She smiles and eats rotten meat. She is decked with ornaments, is naked, and is absorbed in drinking. Having conceived the deity in this way, one should propitiate her in the cremation ground. The householder will worship her at home, at dead of night, having partaken of fish, meat, and wine and being naked.[1]

So is described the fearful goddess Kālī, "the black one." Though most popular today in Bengal, she has been known in Hindu religious texts for more than 1500 years and has been worshipped at one time or another throughout the Indian subcontinent. This essay on Kālī does two things. First, and necessarily briefly, it summarizes her most common appearances and roles. Second, it attempts to make sense of Kālī within the context of the Hindu religious tradition.

Danger and Disruption in the Mythology of Kālī

Although Kālī is sometimes said to be beautiful,[2] and contemporary lithographs sometimes portray her as almost cherubic, Hindu texts referring to the goddess are nearly unanimous in describing her as terrible in appearance and as offensive and destructive in her habits. Her hair is disheveled, her eyes red and fierce, she has fangs and a long lolling tongue, her lips are often smeared with blood, her breasts are long and pendulous, her stomach is sunken, and her figure is generally gaunt. She is naked but for several characteristic ornaments: a necklace of skulls or freshly cut heads, a girdle of severed arms, and infant corpses as earrings. She is usually said to have four arms. The upper left hand holds a bloodied cleaver, the lower left hand, a freshly cut human head; the upper right hand makes the sign "fear not," and the lower right hand, the sign of conferring boons.

Her habits and associations reinforce her awful appearance. Her two favorite dwelling places are battlefields and cremation grounds. On the battlefield she is usually said to carry a skull-topped staff, to howl ferociously, and to consume her enemies by eating their flesh and drinking their blood. In the cremation ground she is described as being surrounded by snakes, jackals, and ghosts and is often described as sitting on a corpse. Unlike most other Hindu deities she does not have an animal vehicle but instead rides a *preta,* a ghost. And although Kālī's temples today may be found in the midst of cities and towns, her temples in earlier literature are described as being located on the fringes of civilization, in the woods or near cremation grounds.[3] Kālī also has a long history of association with criminals[4] and is notorious for having been the patron goddess of the murdurous Thugs. Finally, her appetite for blood is well attested. She is often said to drink blood, both on and off the battlefield, and at her temples she regularly receives animal sacrifices.

In the mythology of Kālī we find her associated primarily with three other Hindu deities: Durgā, Pārvatī, and Śiva. In each case Kālī's destructive habits and fearsome nature persist.

Two of Kālī's most famous deeds are recounted in the myth of the goddess Durgā's destruction of the demons Śumbha and Niśumbha. In the *Devī-māhātmya* version of this myth, Kālī is born when two demon generals, Caṇḍa and Muṇḍa, are sent to taunt and attack Durgā. Durgā loses her composure, grows furious, and from her darkened brow springs Kālī. She howls loudly, wades into the demon army crushing and eating her enemies, and finally decapitates Caṇḍa and Muṇḍa. Later in the battle she is summoned by Durgā to kill the demon Raktabīja. This demon has the magical ability to recreate himself every time a drop of his blood touches the ground. When Durgā wounds him she only makes her situation more desperate, and soon the battlefield is filled with Raktabījas. Kālī rescues Durgā by swallowing the swarm of blood-born demons and sucking the blood from the original Raktabīja until he falls lifeless.[5] In these myths Kālī seems to be Durgā's embodied fury, appearing when Durgā loses control or is confronted with a formidable task.

Kālī plays a similar role in her association with the goddess Pārvatī. In general, Pārvatī is a benign goddess, but from time to time she manifests destructive aspects. When she does, Kālī is often brought into being. In the *Liṅga Purāṇa* Pārvatī is requested by Śiva to slay the demon Dāruka, who has been granted the boon that he can be killed only by a woman. Pārvatī is then described as entering Śiva's body and remaking herself from the poison in his throat. She reemerges as Kālī, of terrible appearance, and with the help of beings who include *piśācas,* flesh-eating spirits, she begins to attack Dāruka and his hosts. However, due to her frenzy the universe itself is threatened with destruction and is only saved by Śiva's intervention.[6] Kālī is depicted in a similar way elsewhere in the same *purāṇa.* When Śiva sets out with his army to destroy the demons of the three cities, Kālī is mentioned as accompanying him. She is said to whirl a trident, to be adorned with skulls, to be intoxicated from drinking the blood of demons, to have her eyes half-closed in drunkenness, and to wear an elephant hide. She is also, however, praised as the daughter of Himalaya, thus being clearly identified with Pārvatī. It would seem that in the process of Pārvatī's gearing up for war, Kālī has appeared as Pārvatī's wrath personified, her alter-ego, as it were.[7]

In the *Vāmana Purāṇa* Pārvatī is called Kālī because of her dark complexion. When Pārvatī hears Śiva use this name, she takes offense and does austerities to rid herself of her dark skin. After she succeeds in this, she is renamed Gaurī, the golden one. Her dark sheath, however, is transformed into the furious battle queen Kauśikī, who subsequently creates Kālī herself in her fury. So again, although there is an intermediary goddess, Kauśikī, Kālī is shown to play the role of Pārvatī's dark, negative, violent nature.[8]

The myth of the creation of the *Daśa-mahāvidyās,* the ten awesome manifestations of the great Goddess, casts Kālī in a similiar role. The story is told that once upon a time the sage Dakṣa decided to undertake a great sacrifice. He invited all the gods except Śiva, excluding him because of his antisocial behavior. Śiva was not offended, but his wife Satī was. Becoming enraged at this social insult, she filled the ten directions with furious forms, the first of which was Kālī. Śiva, thus terrified, agreed to let Satī attend the festivities.[9]

In her association with the god Śiva, Kālī's tendency to wildness and disorder, although sometimes tamed or softened by him, persists, and at times she incites Śiva himself to dangerous, destructive behavior. In South India there is a tradition that tells of a dance contest between the two. After the defeat of Śumbha and Niśumbha, Kālī took up residence in a forest along with her retinue of fierce companions and terrorized the surrounding area. A devotee of Śiva in that area became distracted from doing austerities and petitioned Śiva to rid the forest of the violent goddess. When Śiva appeared, Kālī threatened him, claiming the area as her own. Śiva challenged her to a dance contest and defeated her when she was unable (or unwilling) to match his energetic *tāṇḍava dance.*[10]

Though Kālī is said in this tradition to have been defeated and forced by Śiva to control her disruptive habits, we find very few images and myths depicting a becalmed, docile Kālī.[11] Instead, we find references or images that show Śiva and Kālī in situations where either or both behave in disruptive ways, inciting each other, or in which Kālī in her wild activity dominates an inactive, sometimes dead Śiva.[12]

The former type of relationship is seen when the two are described as dancing together in such a way that they threaten cosmic order. In Bhavabhūti's *Mālātīmadhava* the divine pair are said to dance wildly near the goddess's temple, which is located near a cremation ground. Their dance is so chaotic that it threatens to destroy the world. Pārvatī is described as standing nearby, frightened.[13] Here the scenario is not that of a dance contest but one of a mutually destructive dance in which the two deities incite each other. In Bengali devotional hymns to Kālī this is a common image. In their madness and destructive habits they complement each other.

> Crazy is my Father, crazy my Mother,
> And I, their son, am crazy too!
> Shyama [the dark one, an epithet of Kālī] is my Mother's name.
> My Father strikes His cheeks and makes a hollow sound:
> *Ba-ba-boom! Ba-ba-boom!*
> And my Mother, drunk and reeling,
> Falls across my Father's body!
> Shyama's streaming tresses hang in vast disorder;
> Bees are swarming numberless
> About Her crimson Lotus Feet.
> Listen, as She dances, how Her anklets ring![14]

In iconographic representations of Kālī and Śiva, Kālī nearly always dominates the pair. She is usually shown standing or dancing on Śiva's prone body (figure 7), and when they are depicted in sexual intercourse, she is shown above him. Although Śiva is said to have tamed Kālī in the myth of the dance contest, it seems clear that she was never finally subdued by him and is most popularly represented as a being who is uncontrollable and is more apt to provoke Śiva to dangerous activity than to be controlled by him.

In general, then, we may say that Kālī is a goddess who threatens stability and order. Although she may be said to serve order in her role as the slayer of demons, more often than not she becomes so frenzied on the battlefield, usually becoming drunk on the blood of her victims, that she herself begins to destroy the world that she is supposed to protect. Even in the service of the gods, that is, she is ultimately dangerous and tends to get out of control. In her association with other goddesses she appears to represent their embodied wrath and fury, a frightening, dangerous dimension of the divine feminine that is released when these goddesses become enraged or are called upon to take part in war and killing. In her relation to Śiva she appears to play the opposite role from that of Pārvatī. Pārvatī calms Śiva, counterbalancing his antisocial or destructive tendencies. It is she who brings Śiva within the sphere of domesticity and who, with her soft glances, urges him to soften the destructive aspects of his *tāṇḍava* dance.[15] Kālī is Śiva's "other" wife, as it were, provoking him and encouraging him in his mad, antisocial, often disruptive habits. It is never Kālī who tames Śiva but Śiva who must becalm Kālī. Her association with criminals reinforces her dangerous role vis-à-vis society. She is at home outside the moral order and seems to be unbound by that order.

In nearly every respect Kālī would appear to be a classic example of a demoness whose blessing is realized only by her absence. To her devotees, however, she is the highest manifestation of the divine and is approached as "mother." It would seem that to understand the meaning of Kālī it is necessary to discover ways in which she might express truths that "fit" the Hindu vision of reality, and to look for ways in which she allows her devotees redemptive participation in those truths.

Chaos, Order, and Transcendence

In seeking to understand the meaning of Kālī for Hindus we are well advised to start with hints from the Hindu tradition itself. The great Goddess in medieval Hinduism is often said to be the embodiment of *māyā, prakṛti,* and *śakti.*[16] As a manifestation of this goddess,

FIGURE 7.

Folk Painting Representing the Goddess Kali Straddled over the Erect Lingam of the Corpse-Śiva

Orissa, nineteenth century. Gouache on cloth. (From *The Art of Tantra*, by Philip Rawson. Copyright 1973 by Thames and Hudson, Ltd., London. Used by permission.)

Kālī may be understood to express the nature of these realities, or the truths inherent in these ideas.

Māyā is typically associated with various Vedāntic schools, in which it means primarily superimposition grounded in ignorance. In purānic texts, however, it is more often described in terms of egocentricity (*ahaṁkāra*), the magical quality of creation, the very fabric of existence itself. *Māyā* lends to reality a mysterious and unpredictable quality that sometimes borders on the destructive. Egos, big and small, divine and human, in their self-importance and pique at real or imagined insults, set the whirligig of mythology and human events spinning, often seemingly out of control. The world as humans live in it, and the world of the gods, too, may be seen to be grounded in ego duels that threaten cosmic and human order. Kālī's wild appearance and behavior suggest, perhaps, the darker aspects of reality as *māyā*. She is the great bewitcher, embodying dramatically the inherent threat of *māyā* to the civilized order.

Kālī suggests meanings implicit in *prakṛti* and *śakti*, too. *Prakṛti* is also the created order, the "natural" order, consisting of three qualities: purity (*sattva*), energy (*rajas*), and lethargy (*tamas*). Together these threads (*guṇas*) constitute the fabric of the material world, the fabric of embodied existence. The inherent tendency of *prakṛti* is to specify and individualize, to assume grosser and more concrete manifestations, to serve its own ends of self-perpetuation. *Prakṛti* is usually considered smothering vis-à-vis human spirituality.[17] It binds the religious sojourner in a deterministic mesh from which escape is difficult.[18] *Prakṛti* is lush and teeming and is difficult to control. So is Kālī. She represents, perhaps, *prakṛti* uncontrolled. She is growth, decay, death, and rebirth completely unrefined.

She is *śakti*, too, I think, from the same perspective. *Śakti*, usually translated with such terms as "power" and "might," is often personified as a goddess. As *śakti*, various Hindu goddesses represent the tendency of the divine to action rather than inaction, the tendency to display and play. Kālī is that tendency in the raw, as it were, power out of control, or power in imbalance with stasis. In perhaps her most popular and well-known iconographic image, Kālī is represented as dancing on her consort Śiva, who lies still beneath her feet. She dominates the primordial tension between detached calm and frenetic display in such a way that creative action becomes threatening and dangerous.

Other things are clear in the mythology and imagery of Kālī. She is almost always associated with blood and death, and it is difficult to imagine two more polluting realities in the context of the purity-minded culture of Hinduism. As such, Kālī is a very dangerous being. She vividly and dramatically thrusts upon the observer things that he or she would rather not think about. Within the civilized order of Hinduism, the order of *dharma,* of course, blood and death are acknowledged. It is impossible not to acknowledge their existence in human life. They are acknowledged, however, within the context of a highly ritualized, patterned, and complex social structure that takes great pains to handle them in "safe" ways, usually through rituals of purification. For those inevitable bloody and deathly events in the human life cycle there are rituals (called *saṃskāras,* "refinements") that allow individuals to pass in an orderly way through times when contact with blood and death is unavoidable. The dharmic order is not naive and has incorporated into its refined version of human existence the recognition of these human inevitabilities.

But the Hindu *saṃskāras* are patterned on wishful thinking. Blood and death have a way of cropping up unexpectedly, fortuitously, tragically, and dangerously. The death of an infant, or spilt blood in any accidental and tragic circumstance, is an affront and a threat to the neat vision of the order of *dharma.* The periodic flow of menstrual blood or the death of an aged and loved old woman (whose husband has cooperatively died before her) is manageable within the normal order of human events. But a hemorrhage, the uncontrolled flow of blood, and untimely death are unmanageable. They are out of place and dangerous in the context of civilized order.[19] Yet they can never be avoided with certainty, no matter how well protected one thinks one is.

Kālī, at least in part, may be one way in which the Hindu tradition has sought to come to terms with the built-in shortcomings of its own refined view of the world. It would be nice if the system worked in every case, but it clearly does not, and it is perhaps best and even redemptive to recognize that it does not. Reflecting on the ways in which people must negate certain realities in their attempts to create social order, Mary Douglas writes:

> Whenever a strict pattern of purity is imposed on our lives it is either highly uncomfortable or it leads into contradiction if closely followed, or it leads to hypocrisy. That which is negated is not thereby removed. The rest of life, which does not tidily fit the accepted categories, is still there and demands attention. The body, as we have tried to show, provides the

> basic scheme for all symbolism. There is hardly any pollution which does not have some primary physiological reference. As life is in the body it cannot be rejected outright. And as life must be affirmed, the most complete philosophies . . . must find some ultimate way of affirming that which has been rejected.[20]

Kālī puts the order of *dharma* in perspective, perhaps puts it in its place, by reminding the Hindu that certain aspects of reality are untameable, unpurifiable, unpredictable, and always threatening to society's feeble attempts to order what is essentially disorderly: life itself.

To her devotees Kālī is known as the divine mother. In the light of what I have said, I would suggest that she is mother to her devotees because she gives birth to a wider vision of reality than the one embodied in the order of *dharma*. The dharmic order is insufficient and restricting without a context, without a frame, as it were. Kālī frames that order, putting it in a compelling context. As the alternative to the order of *dharma*, as *māyā*, *prakṛti*, and *śakti* out of control, as death and blood out of place, Kālī makes that order attractive indeed.

Yet the wider vision that she presents may be understood in a more positive way as well. The Hindu religious tradition consistently affirms a reality that transcends the social order. From the perspective of *mokṣa*, final release from the endless round of births and deaths, the order of *dharma* is seen as a contingent good, a realm that must finally be left behind in the quest for ultimate good. Standing outside the dharmic order, indeed threatening it, Kālī may be understood in a positive way as she who beckons humans to seek a wider, more redemptive vision of their destiny.

Depending upon where one is in one's spiritual pilgrimage, then, Kālī has the power either to send one scuttling back to the womb of *dharma* or to provoke one over the threshold to *mokṣa*. In either role she might be understood as the mother who gives her children shelter.

Consort of None, *Śakti* of All: The Vision of the *Devī-māhātmya*

THOMAS B. COBURN

It has long been recognized that the *Devī-māhātmya* is a text of unique significance in the Hindu religious tradition. The text forms a portion of one of the early Sanskrit Purāṇas, the *Mārkaṇḍeya,* and it was probably composed in or somewhat north of the Narmadā River valley sometime in the fifth or sixth century A.D.[1] Yet it is no mere antiquarian curiosity. The *Devī-māhātmya* has, through the centuries, been copied by the faithful with such regularity that it now exists in virtually innumerable manuscripts. Its recitation comprises part of the daily liturgy in temples of Durgā and occupies a central place during the great autumnal festival of Durgā Pūjā.[2] In a lecture delivered in 1840, H.H. Wilson placed it "amongst the most popular works in the Sanskrit language,"[3] and to this day its hymns, in particular, are familiar to vast numbers of Hindus. In 1823 it became the second purāṇic text ever to be translated into a European language (English).[4] By the turn of the century excerpts had appeared in French, and there was another full English translation as well as one in Latin and one in Greek.[5] The enormous stature of text has thus been recognized by both devotees and academics.

Of the various features of the *Devī-māhātmya,* one is preeminent. The ultimate reality in the universe is here understood to be feminine, Devī, the Goddess.[6] Moreover, the *Devī-māhātmya* appears to be the first occasion on which relentless and comprehensive articulation of such a vision is given in Sanskrit. There are, of course, various goddesses who are known in Sanskrit from the time of the Rig Veda onwards. But never before has ultimate reality itself been understood as Goddess.

Our collective investigations in this volume focus upon the divine feminine in varying and sometimes highly nuanced relationships to the masculine—as consort, as lover, as vanquisher, as mother, as sister. Accordingly, the feature of the *Devī-māhātmya* that most merits our attention here is the way in which it conceptualizes the relation between Devī and various masculine divinities.

The first part of this paper explores three "moments"—one from each of the three episodes in the *Devī-māhātmya*— in which this relation is presented in particularly vivid fashion. We shall see that although Devī is understood to bear a unique relation to each particular deity, this is not a "mere" consort relation; she is beyond being a consort to anyone. The second part of the paper relates the *Devī-māhātmya* to other topics in our collective inquiry by considering how certain of its myths and symbols had been employed in Sanskrit prior to the time of our text. Here it will be seen that there are certain affinities between the worship of Devī, as articulated in the *Devī-māhātmya,* and other, quite various theological currents involving Agni, Skanda, Śiva, and Krishna Gopāla.

Three Moments in Devī's Identity

The structure of the *Devī-māhātmya* is simple and beautifully symmetrical, consisting of a frame story and three myths that tell of Devī's various salvific activities. The first half of the frame story recounts how a king and a merchant, beset by mundane adversity, seek refuge from the turmoils of the world by retiring to the forest. There they encounter a sage who informs them that their woes are due to the power of *mahāmāyā,* a term that can mean either "she who possesses great deceptiveness" or "she who *is* the great illusion." Pressed for further details, the sage then recounts the three myths. The first, that of Madhu and Kaiṭabha, is a succinct delineation of the cosmic status of Devī. The second, a more extensive account of her origin on earth and her initial martial activity, culminates in victory over the dread buffalo demon (*asura*) Mahiṣa. The third and longest myth continues to exemplify Devī's mundane activity. It is an exuberant celebration of her various forms and their role in her victory over the minions of the *asuras* Śumbha and Niśumbha. The second half of the frame story finally tells how the king and the merchant worship Devī, meriting her appearance, and how their prayers are answered by her.

The feature of the first episode that commands our attention here is its characterization of Devī as *mahāmāyā.* This designation should probably be understood as a proper name, and a preliminary indication of its significance may be found in the words with which the sage introduces the two woebegones to her (1.39ff.):[7]

O best of men, human beings have a craving for offspring,[8]
Out of greed expecting them to reciprocate; do you not see this? Just in this fashion do they fall into the pit of delusion, the maelstrom of egoism,
Giving (apparent) solidity to life in this world (*saṃsāra*) through the power of Mahāmāyā.

. . . .

This blessed Devī Mahāmāyā, having forcibly seized the minds
Even of men of knowledge, leads them to delusion.

. . . .

She is (also) the supreme eternal knowledge (*vidyā*) that becomes the cause of release (*mukti*)
From bondage to mundane life . . . .

The *Devī-māhātmya* seems here to reflect the view of the early Upaniṣads that it is mystical knowledge of ultimate truth that extricates one from the rebirth process. But something else is clearly afoot as well, for Devī is not simply the knowledge that sets one free, but also the great illusion (*mahāmāyā*) that keeps one bound. The *Devī-māhātmya* is not given to systematic philosophical exposition, so it does not endeavor to resolve this paradox. Rather, it rejoices in it, for paradox is close to the heart of the *Devī-māhātmya's* view of Devī. In light of this fact we may note two features of earlier Sanskrit usage of the word *māyā* that help clarify what the *Devī-māhātmya* means when it calls Devī "Mahāmāyā."

First, the word *māyā* is as old as the Rig Veda, where it means "wile" or "magic power," a power that is frequently associated with the *asuras,* those beings who, in all but the earliest strata of Sanskrit literature, are understood as enemies of the gods (*devas*). If *māyā* is thus associated with the demons, we might expect the *Devī-māhātmya* to affirm that she who is Mahāmāyā is also the great demoness. These turn out to be precisely the terms in which Devī is hymned later in this same episode.[9] To say that Devī is Mahāmāyā is thus to affirm that she is, indeed, Goddess, but it is also to affirm that she transcends the conventional distinction between *devas* and *asuras.*[10]

The second conceptual formulation that prior usage bequeaths to the *Devī-māhātmya* is the equation of *māyā* with *prakṛti,* the primordial matter that evolves into the manifest universe. It is in the philosophical school of Sāṃkhya that *prakṛti* receives its classical development as one of the two fundamental principles of the universe, the other being *puruṣa* (spirit). This atheistic dualism had, however, been adapted to theistic philosophical needs long before the *Devī-māhātmya*. In particular, that watershed of theistic speculation, the *Śvetāśvatara Upaniṣad,* formulates the crucial issues in an illuminating way. Having articulated the distinction between the Lord and the individual soul, that text proceeds to relate them both to *māyā:*

> The Vedas, the sacrifices, the ceremonies, the acts of devotion, the past, the future, and what the Vedas declare—
> All this does the Lord (*māyin,* the possessor of *māyā*), pour forth out of this (Brahmā), and in it is the other (the individual soul) confined by *māyā.*
> Know *māyā* to be *prakṛti,* and the possessor of *māyā* to be the great Lord.
> This whole world is pervaded by beings that are part of him.[11]

Although it would be risky to rely on a narrow interpretation of such philosophically pregnant concepts as *māyā* and *prakṛti,*[12] we may note that the *Devī-māhātmya* is inclined to favor their identification in a way that is reminiscent of the *Śvetāśvatara.* Thus in the first episode Mahāmāyā is hymned with the affirmation, "You are the *prakṛti* of all, manifesting the triad of constituent strands (*guṇas*)" (1.59) and, later on, with the confession, "You are the supreme, original, untransformed *prakṛti*" (4.6). On the basis of such passages it seems safe to say that the *Devī-māhātmya* has shifted the focus of Sāṃkhya and the *Śvetāśvatara* by understanding *prakṛti,* not as the material shroud or possession of spirit, but as itself supremely divine, as Devī herself.

By way of summarizing these various implications of the designation "Mahāmāyā," we may consider the myth that is recounted in this first episode. As part of his introduction to Devī, the sage declares: "The yogic slumber (*yoganidrā*) of the lord of the worlds, Viṣṇu, is (this same) Mahāmāyā, and through her is this world being deluded" (1.41). Such a declaration enables him to move directly to the myth, which involves Viṣṇu, *yoganidrā,* and the *asuras* Madhu and Kaiṭabha. In order to appreciate the unique features of the *Devī-māhātmya's* version, we must ascertain the resonance of this particular myth at the time of the *Devī-māhātmya.*

Throughout the *Mahābhārata,* the Madhu-Kaiṭabha myth is associated, virtually without exception, with the figure of Viṣṇu. The myth is recounted in full on several occasions, and Viṣṇu's epithet *madhusūdana,* "slayer of Madhu," is used in the epic on more than two hundred occasions. The classical version of the myth may be summarized as follows.[13] It is *pralaya,* the state of universal dissolution that occurs at the end of a cosmic cycle. All that exists is the universal ocean. On the ocean, Lord Viṣṇu sleeps, reposing on his serpent Śeṣa, who is coiled in the shape of a couch. While he is sleeping, two *asuras* named Madhu and Kaiṭabha arise from the wax in Viṣṇu's ear and, puffed up with pride and egoism, begin to assail the god Brahmā, who is seated on a lotus that grows from Viṣṇu's navel. Brahmā arouses Viṣṇu by shaking the lotus, and Viṣṇu engages the two demons in battle, sometimes physically, sometimes in a battle of wits. Madhu and Kaiṭabha think they have outwitted Viṣṇu by asking to be slain in a dry place. But Viṣṇu raises his thighs and kills the demons on them. From the fat of the two *asuras,* which permeated the waters, the earth was created.

When the *Devī-māhātmya* retells this thoroughly Vaiṣṇava myth, there are several crucial modifications. The setting is exactly the same, but Viṣṇu is described as having entered into *yoganidrā,* the twilight slumber of tranquillity, a term that is not used in the epic versions. The demons begin their assault upon Brahmā, who endeavors to awaken Viṣṇu. He does so here, however, not by shaking the lotus, but by invoking Devī, who is addressed as Yoganidrā, that is, as the personification of the state of sleep into which Viṣṇu has entered. The climax of the invocation reads (1.63-67):

> Whatever and wherever anything exists, whether it be real or unreal, (you) who have everything as your very soul,
> Of all that, you are the power;[14] how then can you be (adequately) praised?
> By you the creator of the world, the protector of the world, who (also) consumes the world,
> Is brought under the influence of sleep; who here is capable of praising you?
> Since Viṣṇu, Śiva, and I have been made to assume bodily form
> By you, who could have the capacity of (adequately) praising you?
> May you, thus praised, Devī, with your superior powers
> Confuse these two unassailable *asuras,* Madhu and Kaiṭabha,

And may the imperishable Lord of the world be quickly awakened,
And may his alertness be used to slay these two great *asuras.*

Devī then accedes to Brahmā's request by withdrawing from Viṣṇu's various limbs, Viṣṇu awakens, and the *asuras* are dispatched as in the earlier versions.

Several conclusions seem to follow from such an account. First, the *Devī-Māhātmya* clearly suggests that it is solely through the grace, the graceful withdrawal, of Devī that Viṣṇu can fulfill his familiar role of slaying the *asuras.* In fact, it is only through this grace that he can act at all. If this is true of Lord Viṣṇu, the implication is that each of us human beings is similarly indebted to her.[15] Second, Devī is affirmed to be the primary ontological reality. From her the gods explicitly derive their bodily form. From her, also, all material existence proceeds. This is evident both from the prior affirmation that Devī is *prakṛti* and from the suggestion that it is the substance of the *asuras* that comes to form the earth, for Devī is, we have noted, the great *asurī.* One might go so far as to say that whatever *is* is Devī. Finally, the text demonstrates the paradoxical action of Devī Mahāmāyā. It suggests, on the one hand, that it is she who deludes the two self-important demons into thinking they can outwit the divine. But, on the other hand, it is also she who shows how, through the frustration of their egotistical desires and through their apparent death, those demons come to participate in a divine plan far larger than themselves, indeed in the cosmic process of creation. Devī is both the great deluder and the one who redeems the victims of her magic tricks by incorporating them into the life divine.

The event that is of interest to us in the second episode may be dealt with more briefly. This is the point at which the text, having established Devī's cosmic status, turns to the account of her career on earth. It is apparent from the outset that the event precipitating that career is the severe dislocation of the mundane equilibrium. Thus the second episode begins (2.1-2):

Once upon a time, a battle between the gods (*devas*) and *asuras* raged for a full hundred years,
When (the buffalo demon) Mahiṣa was leader of the *asuras* and Indra (was leader) of the gods.
The gods' army was conquered there by the mighty *asuras,*

> And having conquered all the gods, the *asura* Mahiṣa became lord (lit., "Mahisa became Indra").

Faced with this quandary, the remnants of the *devas'* army seek out Śiva and Viṣṇu and recount the course of events. There follows the famous account of Devī's mundane origin (2.8-12):

> Having listened to the words of the gods, Viṣṇu
> And Śiva became angry, their faces distorted, with furrowed brows.
> Then from the face of Viṣṇu, filled with rage,
> And (from that) of Brahmā and Śiva came forth a luminous brilliance (*tejas*).
> Also from the bodies of Indra and the other gods
> Great brilliance came forth, and it coalesced into a unity.
> There the gods saw a mass of brilliance,
> Blazing like a mountain, filling the firmament with flames.
> That peerless, unified brilliance, born of the bodies of all the gods,
> Became a woman, pervading the three worlds with her splendor.

Our text then recounts how this woman, who is, of course, Devī, received her various limbs and weapons from different gods and how, thus constituted, she proceeded to vanquish Mahiṣa and his hordes.

From the perspective of our concern with Devī's relation to certain male deities, two comments are in order. First, whereas there is justification for saying that Devī is here conceptualized as subordinate to the gods, because she is derivative from, and indebted to, each of them, it can also be argued that the reverse is true. It is she who succeeds in restoring the mundane equilibrium, a feat that the gods individually and collectively had been unable to accomplish. Moreover, it is clear that Devī, for all her original mundane derivation from the gods, is subsequently understood to be a continuing salvific presence in the world. Thus at the end of this episode she consents to bring relief to those who call upon her in future calamities, and the episode concludes, not by having her rediffused into the bodies of the gods, but by saying simply, yet suggestively, "She vanished" (4.30-33).

Second, we must note the conceptual model that the *Devī-māhātmya* is here employing in describing Devī. In the first episode the text has established her primacy in the cosmic context. Now, in the second, it endeavors to demonstrate not only that Devī also has an earthly career, but that she is supreme ruler of earthly creatures. To portray Devī in this role, the text draws on a classical Indian model, that of the king. In his vision of social order, Manu begins his account of the king as follows:

> . . . when these creatures, being without a king, through fear dispersed in all directions, the Lord created a king for the protection of this whole (creation),
>
> Taking (for that purpose) eternal particles of Indra, of the Wind, of Yama, of the Sun, of Fire, of Varuṇa, of the Moon, and of the Lord of Wealth (Kubera).
>
> Because a king has been formed of particles of those lords of the gods, he therefore surpasses all created beings in lustre [*tejas*];
>
> And, like the sun, he burns eyes and hearts; nor can anyone on earth gaze on him.
>
> . . . .
>
> Having fully considered the purpose, (his) power, and the place and time, he assumes by turns many (different) shapes for the complete attainment of justice.
>
> He, in whose favour resides Padmā, the goddess of fortune, in whose valour dwells victory, in whose anger abides death, is formed of the lustre of all (gods).[16]

The conclusion that this model of secular power underlies the *Devī-māhātmya's* vision of Devī's earthly origin seems inescapable. That such a model is utterly appropriate seems equally obvious, for only one who is of unrivaled power on the world's own terms can cope with the great disturber of the mundane equilibrium, Mahiṣa. What the *Devī-Māhātmya* thus affirms is that the effective agent on earth, as in the cosmos, is not masculine but feminine, not king but Queen.

We must finally examine the *Devī-māhātmya's* use of the term *śakti*, "power," with regard to Devī, and, in particular, its use of this term in the third episode. We have already seen that the *Devī-māhātmya* has an understanding of *śakti* as a singular and universal phenomenon, as a phenomenon that Devī *is*.[17] In addition, it has an understanding of *śaktis* as plural and particular phenomena, as something that each individual deity *has*. This latter conceptualization emerges in the course of Devī's martial engagement with the *asuras* Śumbha and Niśumbha. When Śumbha, incensed at the destruction of two of his generals, sends forth his legions against Devī, she multiplies her own forces (8.11-13):

At that very moment, king, in order to destroy the enemies of the gods,
(And) for the sake of the well-being of the gods, very valorous and powerful
Śaktis, having sprung forth from the bodies of Brahmā, Śiva,
Skanda, Viṣṇu, and Indra, (and) having the form of each (of them) approached Devī.[18]
Whatever form, ornament, and vehicle a (particular) god possessed,
With that very form did his *śakti* go forth to fight the *asuras.*

The text then describes how seven *śaktis* emerged from seven gods, each possessing the distinctive iconographic features of its source. These *śaktis*—named Brahmāṇī, Māheśvarī, Kaumārī, Vaiṣṇavī, Vārāhī, Nārasiṃhī, and Aindrī[19]—together with another figure whom we shall consider in a moment, are referred to collectively in the ensuing combat as "the Mothers."

Four features of this passage and its consequent development in our text deserve our attention. First, although it is tempting to conclude that the text views each god as having a consort who is called a *śakti* and is a form of Devī, closer examination reveals a quite different situation. In fact, the *Devī-māhātmya* is careful to avoid using language that would imply that the *śaktis* are consorts of their respective gods. This is evident from the fact that, in the mythology that was current at the time of the *Devī-māhātmya's* composition, two of the gods who here put forth *śaktis,* Indra and Śiva (Maheśvara), are known to have consorts. Indra's spouse has been known since Rig Vedic times as Indrāṇī or Śacī. Śiva's spouse is known throughout the *Mahābhārata* as Umā or Pārvatī. But Indra's spouse has never before been designated by the word *aindrī,* and Umā has been called *māheśvarī* on only one known occasion.[20] Consesequently, when the *Devī-māhātmya* calls Indra's *śakti* Aindrī, "the one related to Indra," and Śiva's *śakti* Māheśvarī, "the one related to Maheśvara," it apparently wishes to make it clear that a god's *śakti* is not the same as any previously known consort of his. A *śakti* does not have a mere formal, external, consort relation with her god. Rather, she is far more fundamental, more internal, to his identity, for she is, in fact, his power (*śakti*).[21]

Second, it is clear that although the polarity of Śiva and Śakti is well known in later Śākta and tantric circles, the *Devī-māhātmya* shows no preference for Śiva when it is discussing Devī as *śakti.* The only unique attention that is paid to Śiva at this juncture is that after their emergence the *śaktis* are said to gather around him (8.21). However, no particular importance is attached to this fact.

Third, an even more striking contrast with later views is found in the fact that the *Devī-māhātmya* does not know the conceptualization that a *śakti* is feminine and its possessor or vehicle masculine, for Devī herself possesses a *śakti*. Immediately after the previously named *śaktis* have gathered around Śiva, the text declares (8.22):

> Then from the body of Devī came forth the very frightening *Śakti* of Caṇḍikā (Devī), gruesome and yelping (like) a hundred jackals.

In the subsequent combat, this *śakti* is treated as kindred to the other *śaktis*, as one of the Mothers.

Finally, for all this proliferation of forms of Devī, and for all the involvement of some of them with male deities, our text never loses sight of the fact that Devī is the primary reality and that her agency is the only effective one. This fact is indicated at the very end of the episode, where the text sets the stage for the final dramatic encounter by reducing the combatants to the bare minimum. The demon Śumbha has accused Devī of false pride and haughtiness, for in the foregoing encounters she has relied not on her own strength, but on that of others. Thereupon Devī proclaims her relation to the apparently heterogeneous forms (10.3):

> I alone exist here in the world; what second, other than I, is there?
> Wicked one, behold these my hierophanies[22] entering (back) into me.

The text continues:

> Thereupon, all the goddesses, led by Brahmāṇī,
> Went to (their) resting-place in the body of Devī; then there was just Devī[23] alone.

Subsequently, Devī throws down the gauntlet for the final combat:

> When I was established here in many forms, it was by means of my extraordinary power.
> That has (now) been withdrawn by me. I stand utterly alone.
> May you be resolute in combat.

Our text thus concludes as it began, with the affirmation that there is but one truly ultimate reality, and that it is feminine; with the indication that this reality takes on different forms, to which the ignorant impute independent and permanent existence, but which the wise recognize as grounded in Devī; and with the demonstration that this reality is related to male deities, as to all that exists, not externally but internally, not as consort, but as *śakti*.

Four Cross-Currents Involving Devī

We have seen that one way in which the *Devī-māhātmya* establishes the identity of Devī in the Sanskrit tradition is by incorporating the familiar Vaiṣṇava myth of Madhu and Kaiṭabha. That this incorporation reflects historical interaction between Vaiṣṇavism and the worship of Devī, however, seems doubtful. It appears more likely that the *Devī-māhātmya* is offering a reinterpretation of a familiar myth in order to capture the attention of those who should chance to hear the text. It is virtually alone, among the fourteen or fifteen later puranic accounts of this myth, in relating the story to Devī.[24] Similarily, although the use of regal imagery in the second episode has a Vaiṣṇava aura, the *Devī-māhātmya* uses the distinctively Vaiṣṇava epithets Lakṣmī and Śri almost casually, without drawing out their theological ramifications.[25] Because the *Devī-māhātmya* is effecting a synthesis of diverse strands in the Sanskrit tradition, the presence of Vaiṣṇava motifs is hardly surprising. But this can scarcely be taken as reflecting a more fundamental rapprochement between Vaiṣṇavism and the worship of Devī.[26]

There are other features of the *Devī-māhātmya*, however, that suggest historical and symbolic connections between the worship of Devī and other religious movements in classical India.

First, scholars are virtually unanimous in the opinion that the basic impulse behind the worship of the Goddess in India is of non-Aryan, non-Sanskritic origin. For all its brilliance in incorporating diverse Sanskrit motifs into its vision of Devī, the *Devī-māhātmya*, too, seems to support this view. Thus, for instance, the most common designation for Devī in this text (other than the word *devī* itself) is Caṇḍikā, which probably means "the violent and impetuous one," but which is used throughout as a proper name. Although feminine forms of the adjective *caṇḍa* are found in earlier texts, never before has the word *caṇḍikā* appeared in Sanskrit.[27] Since the *Devī-māhātmya* attests to the existence of a cult of Devī,[28] it seems likely that we should look for the historical origin of her worship in non-Sanskritic circles, in the worship of a deity known as Caṇḍikā.

Second, although the *Devī-māhātmya* does not understand Devī as the consort of Śiva, there is some evidence that her worship and identity are intertwined with those of Śiva. The second most frequent designation of Devī in the *Devī-māhātmya* is Ambikā, a name that is found in late Vedic texts in association with the nascent figure of Rudra-Śiva.[29] In addition, there is the intriguing fact that the destruction of Mahiṣa, which the *Devī-māhātmya* and subsequent purāṇic literature clearly ascribe to Devī, had been previously known in the *Mahābhārata* as the crowning event in its first account of the birth and early career of Skanda.[30] The latter is, of course, known throughout the Purāṇas as the offspring of Śiva and Umā. The epic account is extraordinarily complicated—largely because at this juncture Skanda is a new figure in Sanskrit mythology and his genealogy is unclear—but it is also enormously suggestive. Throughout the account, Agni's claims to the paternity of Skanda predominate over those of Śiva, but it is immediately after Śiva's claims are introduced (3.220) that the narrative reaches its climax by telling of Mahiṣa's defeat at the hands of Skanda. Moreover, although the identity of Skanda's rightful mother is never clearly determined, embryonic "Goddess motifs" abound: one candidate for motherhood is a horde of ogresses euphemistically called "the Mothers," and there are several momentary appearances by a goddess named Śakti. One cannot help but feel that, at least mythologically and perhaps liturgically as well, Devī's identity emerges out of a matrix in which Śiva, Skanda, and Agni also figure prominently.

Third, in addition to this convergence of Devī with Agni by virtue of the latter's relation to Śiva,[31] there are several still more direct connections. If one pursues this notion of "the Mothers," one finds a number of mothers attributed to Agni as far back as the Rig Veda.[32] One of the distinctive forms of Devī in the *Devī-māhātmya* is Kālī, a name that also appears in *Muṇḍaka Upaniṣad* 1.2.4 as the designation for one of Agni's seven quivering tongues. To investigate Devī's names Śrī and Lakṣmī is to discover that they are intertwined with the figure of Agni in an appendix (*khila*) to the Rig Veda known as the *Śrī Sūkta*.[33] Another of the *Devī-māhātmya's* common names for Devī is Durgā, a name that is a play on words: she is the great protectress from worldly adversity (*durga*) and is at the same herself unassailable and hard to approach (*durgā*).[34] This same play on words is found in earlier texts: *Taittirīya Āraṇyaka* 10.1, for example, quotes *Rig Veda* 1.99, a one-verse hymn to Agni in which he is praised for leading us through difficulties (*durgāṇi*), and then declares:

> In her who has the color of Agni, flaming with ascetic power (*tapas*), the offspring of Virocana, who delights in the fruits of (one's) actions,
> In the goddess Durgā do I take refuge; O one of great speed, (well) do you navigate. Hail (to you)!

In the Sūtra literature, this same Vedic hymn to Agni becomes known as the Durgā Sāvitrī.[35] Although it would be unwise to consider the post-Vedic figure of Agni in sectarian terms, at least we may say that there is a certain homology between Devī and Agni, in the conceptualization of the divine as "the flaming one."

Finally, the *Devī-māhātmya* provides further evidence for the relation that Charlotte Vaudeville has perceived between Devī and Krishna Gopāla, for references to the myth of Śumbha and Niśumbha are found earlier only in Krishnaite documents. In the *Harivaṃśa's* account of Krishna's childhood, Viṣṇu descends to hell (*pātāla*) to solicit the aid of the goddess Nidrā. He proposes a plan for his birth and that of the goddess to Devakī and Yaśodā, and then foretells the future course of events. He predicts among other things that this goddess will slay the demons Śumbha and Niśumbha.[36] Later (65.51) the *Harivaṃśa* asserts that she has, in fact, slain them. This connection between a Śumbha-Niśumbha-Goddess myth and the Krishna Gopāla cycle is evidently more than chance, for reference to such a myth also occurs in the Krishna story as told in the *Viṣṇu Purāṇa* (5.1.81) and in Bhāsa's *Bālacarita* (2.20-25).[37] Since Vaudeville has argued persuasively that the Krishna Gopāla cycle originated as a cycle of hero stories among the non-Aryan castes of north India who were predominantly worshippers of Devī,[38] the implications for our understanding of the *Devī-māhātmya* seem clear. What we have in the Śumbha-Niśumbha myth is a fragment of the mythology of Devī as it was current among certain north Indian peoples who came to know of the heroic exploits of Krishna Gopāla. Just as those exploits went on to receive sophisticated religious elaboration in various ways, some of which are examined in other papers in this volume, so, too, did the Śumbha-Niśumbha-Goddess story become integrated with other mythological motifs and receive *its* elaboration in such texts as the *Devī-māhātmya*.

Gaṅgā: The Goddess in Hindu Sacred Geography

DIANA L. ECK

O Mother Gaṅgā, may your water,
abundant blessing of the world,
treasure of Lord Śiva, playful Lord of all the earth,
essence of the scriptures and
embodied goodness of the gods,
May your water, sublime wine of immortality,
Sooth our troubled souls.[1]

The pursuit of the Goddess in the Hindu tradition leads one to the bank of the river that Hindus revere as Mother—Gaṅgā Mātā, Mother Gaṅgā. Here the mythology of the Hindu tradition and the sacred topography of the land of India flow inseparably together. The Gaṅgā is both goddess and river. She is claimed as the consort of Śiva and Viṣṇu alike. Her waters are said to be the liquid embodiment of *śakti* as well as the sustaining immortal fluid (*amṛta*) of mother's milk. And her *avataraṇa,* her "descent" to earth, brings both her power and her nurturance to incarnation on the plains of India.

Along her entire length the Gaṅgā is sacred, and just as a temple or a holy city might be circumambulated, so is this entire river circumambulated by a few hardy pilgrims who walk her length from the source to the sea and back again on the other shore. Many *tīrthas,* sacred "crossings," pilgrimage places, mark her course: Gaṅgotrī, her source in the Himālayas; Hardvār, also known as Gaṅgādvāra, "Door of the Gaṅgā," where she breaks out of the mountains into the plains of North India; Prayāg, where she joins the Yamunā River as well as the mythical underground Sarasvatī; Kāśī, the city of Śiva, where she makes a long sweep to the north as if pointing to her Himālayan source; and, finally, Gaṅgā Sāgara, where the river meets the sea in the Bay of Bengal.

All along the river, and especially at her great *tīrthas,* devout Hindus bathe in the Gaṅgā, taking the waters cupped in their hands and pouring them back into the river as offerings to the *pitṛs* and the *devas*. They present in the river, as in the sanctum of a temple, offerings of flowers. On great occasions they ford the river in boats, shouting, "Gaṅgā Mātā kī jai!" ("Victory to Mother Gaṅgā!") and trailing garlands of flowers hundreds of feet long to adorn the neck of this Goddess River. They return to their homes, perhaps hundreds of miles away, carrying vessels of her water. And they come again that distance to bring the ashes of their dead to her care.

The *māhātmyas* ("praises") of the Gaṅgā, which are found in the Sanskrit epics and Purāṇas, extol the greatness of the river and describe her many glories. On the most mundane level, the chanting of her name alone is said to relieve poverty, banish bad dreams, and vouchsafe perpetual protection from the falling dung of flying crows.[2] On a more exalted plane, *mokṣa* itself is said to result from bathing in the waters of the Gaṅgā or being cremated on her banks.[3] This is especially the case in the Kali Yuga, when the traditional means of gaining release are too difficult for ordinary people.[4] The Gaṅgā, it is said, is supreme among rivers, as Kāśī is supreme among holy cities and the Himalayas are supreme among mountains.

The Gaṅgā as Goddess is more than a single river. She functions in India as the archetype of sacred waters. Other rivers are said to be like the Gaṅgā, others are said even to be the Gaṅgā (such as the River Kāvērī, the "Gaṅgā" of South India)[5] but the Gaṅgā remains the paradigmatic sacred river to which they are likened. The River Gaṅgā is not confined to the course she takes across the plains of North India but participates in that spatial transposition which is so typical of Hindu sacred topography, pervading the sacred waters of all India's great rivers.[6]

If a person elsewhere in India cannot go to the Gaṅgā, going to another sacred stream *is* going to the Gaṅgā. There are said to be seven rivers of such great sanctity: Gaṅgā, Yamunā, Godāvarī, Sarasvatī, Narmadā, Sindhu, and Kāvērī. If such rivers as these are out of reach, one might simply go to the nearest stream. In fact, in every temple and home the Gaṅgā is called to be present in the waters used in ritual, either by mixing those waters with a few drops of Gaṅgā water or by uttering the name and *mantras* of the Gaṅgā to invoke her presence. The Gaṅgā is the quintessence and source of all sacred waters, indeed of all waters everywhere.

Not only is the Gaṅgā said to be present in other rivers, but others are also present in her. Bathing in this one river, one bathes in all rivers. As a contemporary Indian author writes, "When a pilgrim dives into the sacred waters of the Gaṅgā, he feels the thrill of plunging into the waters of all the rivers of India."[7] The *māhātmyas* claim that the Gaṅgā concentrates in her waters some thirty-five million *tīrthas*. More simply, it is said that every wave of the river is a *tīrtha*.[8]

There are few things on which Hindu India, diverse as it is, speaks with one voice as clearly as it does on Gaṅgā Mātā. She carries an immense cultural and religious significance for Hindus, no matter what part of the subcontinent they call home, no matter what their sectarian leaning might be. As one Hindi author writes, "Even the most hardened atheist of a Hindu will find his heart full of feelings he has never felt before the first time he reaches the bank of the Gaṅgā."[9]

Some of those "feelings" were eloquently expressed by Jawaharlal Nehru, who was at the most westernized end of the modern spectrum of Indian life and who loved the Gaṅgā deeply:

> My desire to have a handful of my ashes thrown into the Gaṅgā at Allahabad has no religious significance, so far as I am concerned. I have no religious sentiment in the matter. I have been attached to the Gaṅgā and the Jumna rivers in Allahabad ever since my childhood and, as I have grown older, this attachment has also grown. I have watched their varying moods as the seasons changed, and have often thought of the history and myth and tradition and song and story that have become attached to them through the long ages and become part of their flowing waters. The Gaṅgā, especially, is the river of India, beloved of her people, round which are intertwined her racial memories, her hopes and fears, her songs of triumph, her victories and her defeats. She has been a symbol of India's age-long culture and civilization, ever-changing, ever-flowing, and yet ever the same Gaṅgā. She reminds me of the snow-covered peaks and the deep valleys of the Himalayas, which I have loved so much, and of the rich and vast plains below, where my life and work have been cast.[10]

It is in part the province of scholars to see and uncover those affirmations that have been explicitly denied. As one who considered himself thoroughly secular, Nehru denied that the Gaṅgā had any "religious" significance for him, meaning "supernatural" significance. His attachment to the river and his desire to have his ashes thrown into it was, on the contrary, as natural and organic as his love for the land of India. In this, one might say, he was thoroughly Hindu, and his affirmation of the land, its waters, its mountains, was a thoroughly Hindu religious affirmation. For the natural *is* the religious. Although the river has attracted abundant myth and *māhātmya*, it is the river itself, nothing "supernatural" ascribed to it, that has been so significant for Hindus. The river does not stand for, nor point toward, anything greater, beyond itself; it is part of a living sacred geography that Hindus hold in common. It is with certain presuppositions about that common geography that Hindus, even such as Nehru, behold the Gaṅgā. The Gaṅgā is one goddess we cannot consider apart from the land in which she flows and the pattern of symbols that this land embodies.

Living Land

Leaving the river for a moment, let us look at some of the mythic images of the cosmos in which the Gaṅgā moves. One of the most striking aspects of the multitude of Hindu cosmogonic myths is the organic, biological vision that they express. The completed universe is imaged as a living organism, a vast ecosystem, in which each part is inextricably related to the life of the whole. And the whole is indeed alive: it is in constant process and movement, growing and decaying. There is no such thing as objectified "nature" or lifeless "elements," for everything belongs to the living pattern of the whole.

One well-known image is that of the sacrifice of the primal giant Puruṣa, a cosmogonic event in which each part of this macrocosmic being became an element of the natural world.[11] From his feet came this earth; from his torso the *antarikṣa,* the mid-region of the sky, extending as far up as the blue extends; and from his head came the heavens above the sky. More particularly, from his eye came the sun; from his mind, the moon; from his mouth, the gods Indra and Agni; from his breath, the winds.

Another image is that of the Golden Embryo, Hiranyagarbha, called in the Rig Veda the "first-born of creation," the egg or embryo that contained within it all the vast and particular life of this cosmos.[12] When it had incubated for a long time, it split open; the top half became heaven; the bottom, earth; and the space between, the mid-region of the sky. The outer membrane became the mountains; the inner membrane, the clouds and mists; the veins of the egg, the rivers;

the interior waters, the oceans. Every atom of the universe came from the life of that embryo. In a later myth, the egg is replaced by Viṣṇu, reclining asleep on the cosmic waters, containing within his body the whole of the universe in unmanifest form. When the time is ripe, the lotus springs from his navel, unfolds, and gives birth to Brahmā, the agent of creation.[13]

These are images of a biological world-view, grounded in the Vedas, strengthened by the indigenous *yakṣa* and *nāga* traditions, and persisting still in the Hindu mythic imagination. It is a view in which the universe, and by extension the land of India, is alive with interconnections and meanings and is likened to a living organism. There is no nature "worship" here, but a sacramental natural ontology. In an excellent essay, Betty Heimann writes: "In India the veneration of Nature has never been discarded as outdated and primitive. On the contrary, primitivity is here appreciated in its productive ambiguity and inexhaustible potentialities. Nature cult is the fundament of the earliest forms of Indian religions and remains the basis of even the highest and most exalted speculations of Indian philosophy."[14]

In this organic ontological vision, the term "symbol," if we are to use it at all, describes the vehicle of movement from meaning to meaning. Symbols enable one to follow certain strands of the complex interrelatedness of the whole, up and down, back and forth, from heaven to earth, from place to place. The image of the loom is utilized by the poets: the universe is woven on the loom, as it were, by two maidens, Night and Day, who lay and draw the threads.[15] Gārgī asks the sage Yājñavalkya, "What is the warp and woof on which this all is woven?"[16] For this "All" is a woven fabric. One may follow any thread, horizontally or vertically, seeing it slightly differently in one woven context and then another. One thread runs along the warp from the sun above to the fire here below, to the eye of the sacrificial horse, to the human eye, to the Yamunā River, to the subtle channel called *piṅgalā* within the body-cosmos. Another thread runs from the Moon above, to the Soma that dwells as waters in the vault of the heaven and as plants on earth, to the earthly waters, to the human mind, to the River Gaṅgā, to the subtle channel called *iḍā* within the body-cosmos.[17]

In a sense, everything is a symbol in that it leads into the living web of relationships that constitutes the whole, for symbols do not live alone, but in a pattern of meaning shaped by other symbols. But here the symbol does not, as in some Western interpretations, point beyond itself to some other reality. The Holy is constituent of the life and fullness of the whole. The symbolic referent in this organic ontology is not the Holy, but the Whole, which each symbol, each thread, helps to constitute.

Just as the cosmos is a biological whole, so on the microcosmic level the land of India is pictured as an organic whole, a full sacred geography. The living landscape is dense with significance. Each village has its *grāma-devatā,* the lord of its place. The sacred literature is full of *māhātmyas* of place: the Naimiṣa forest, the Gaṅgā, Yamunā, and Godāvarī rivers, the Himalaya and Vindhya mountains. Such places have been affirmed to have particularly strong strands of connection to the macrocosm. They are called *tīrthas,* a word that originally meant "ford" or "crossing place" and has come to mean a "spiritual ford," a place of pilgrimage.

The earth, like the macrocosmic Puruṣa, is a body, both in its wholeness and its diversity. In the *Mahābhārata* it is put this way:

> Just as certain parts of the body are called clean, so are certain parts of the earth and certain waters called holy.[18]

Those "certain parts" of earth that give ready access to the heavens are *tīrthas.* They are thresholds, doorways upward, where one's prayers are more quickly heard, one's desires more readily fulfilled, one's rituals bound to bring more abundant blessings. And it is precisely because these doorways were opened by some hierophany, some *avatāra,* that they are *tīrthas* for human beings. *Avatāra* and *tīrtha,* both coming from the root *tṛ,* "to cross over," are the dynamics of movements along the warp of the cosmic loom: crossing down, and crossing up.

There are thousands of *tīrthas* in India, some well-known through the whole land and some of but local prominence. The great *tīrtha* cycles include the *saptapurī* (the seven sacred cities);[19] the *cār dhām* (the four divine abodes, one at each compass point);[20] and the *pīṭhas* (the "seats" of the goddess, each corresponding to a part of the body of the goddess Satī).[21] The whole of India adds up to a body-cosmos.

Pilgrims circumambulate the whole of India as a sacred land, visiting the *dhām* at each compass point, marking with their feet the perimeter of the whole, bringing sands from the southern tip of India at Rāmeśvaram to place in the Gaṅgā when they arrive, and returning with Gaṅgā water to sprinkle the *liṅga* at Rāmeśvaram. This network of *tīrthas* constitutes the very bones of India as a cultural unit. Considering its long history, India has had but a few hours of political and administrative unity. Its unity as a nation, however, has been firmly constituted by the sacred geography it has held in common and revered: its mountains, forests, rivers, hilltop shrines, and sacred cities. It is no surprise, then, that the national anthem of Nehru's independent India is a litany of the great place-names of her sacred geography. This hymn expresses a Hindu view of the living land that is as old as India itself.

Living Waters

India's rivers have been the life-giving arteries of this living land. The waters of this earthly realm, the rivers and oceans that course through, surround, and support the continents, have, in the Hindu view, their counterparts in heaven, above the vaulted blue of the sky. In the beginnings, they were set free to run upon the earth by the gods themselves. The seers of the Rig Veda envisioned the connection in this way:

> Forth from the midst of the flood they flow,
> The sea, their leader, purifying, never-sleeping,
> Indra, the thunderer, the bull, dug out their channels.
> Here may these goddess waters bless me!
>
> Waters that flow from heaven,
> Or spring from the dug earth, or meander freely,
> All of which, bright and pure, head for the ocean,
> Here may these goddess waters bless me!
>
> In whose midst King Varuṇa moves,
> Observing men's truth and falsehood,
> Nectar they are, and bright and pure,
> Here may these goddess waters bless me!
>
> In which King Varuṇa, in which Soma, in which all the gods
> Became drunk with strength,
> In which Agni Vaiśvānara entered,
> Here may these goddess waters bless me![22]

The waters are identified here as divine, as goddesses set free from their heavenly source by Indra, who dug their channels. They are rivers of blessing and purification. Elsewhere in the Rig Veda the seven rivers

FIGURE 8.

Bathers in the Gaṅgā on Makarsankrānti in Benares

Photograph Diana L. Eck.

are said to be set free when Vṛtra is slain.[23] There are the great Sindhu, now called the Indus; the Sarasvatī, a river that since Vedic times is said to have disappeared; and the five rivers of the Punjab. Since then, the names of the seven have changed, and the Gaṅgā has become their leader, but the tradition of seven divine rivers has persisted.[24]

The poet seers of the Vedas launched a tradition of praise for the blessing and purifying energy of the "goddess waters" that continued for more than two thousand years, through the many purāṇic *māhātmyas* and *stotras* to the great poetic hymns to the Gaṅgā, such as Jagannātha's "Gaṅgā Laharī." It is particularly the life, the movement, the activity of the waters of the Gaṅgā that has attracted poets and devotees through the ages. Hers are not the motionless waters of the pre-creation seas, but running, energetic waters of life. The traditional etymology of Gaṅgā is from the verb *gam*, "to go."[25] Her hymns constantly emphasize the running, flowing, energetic movement of her waters, and they do so at times with elaborate alliteration and onomatopoeia, as in this line from the famous "Gaṅgā Laharī": *marullīlā-lolallaharī-lulitāmbhoja-paṭala.* (May your running waters . . . "covered with lotuses that rock in your waves and roll playfully in the wind" . . . weaken the web of my earthly life.)[26]

It is running water that is the chief agent of purification in the complex Hindu scheme of purity and pollution. Water absorbs pollution, but when it is running, it carries pollution away as well. It is in part because they are "Never-sleeping" that these goddess waters bring purification. The Gaṅgā *māhātmyas* proclaim her purifying powers in elaborate detail: even to be touched by a breeze bearing a tiny droplet of Gaṅgā water will erase the sins of lifetimes in an instant!

Avataraṇa

Each year as the hot and dry season reaches its peak in May and early June, Hindus celebrate the descent of the Gaṅgā from heaven to earth in anticipation of the monsoon rains. The day is Gaṅgā Daśahara, the tenth day of the bright fortnight of the month of Jyeṣṭha. It is called the "birthday" of the Gaṅgā, and on that day her banks are crowded with bathers. A dip in the Gaṅgā "destroys ten [sins]" (*daśahara*) or ten lifetimes of sins; but as festival manuals confirm, even those far from the Gaṅgā may gain similar benefits from bathing in whatever "Gaṅgā" is near at hand.[27]

The descent—*avataraṇa*—of heavenly waters to earth is an ancient theme with many variations in Hindu mythology. In one of the great Vedic myths, Indra, who has pillared apart heaven and earth and established the sky between them, engages in combat with the great serpent Vṛtra, who has coiled around the vault of heaven and closed up the celestial waters.[28] The waters stored in the vault of heaven are often identified with *soma,* the nectar of the gods and the strengthening elixir of immortality. In defeating Vṛtra, Indra sets free these divine waters for the nourishment of the earth.

In the many Vaiṣṇava versions of the myth, the river is called Viṣṇupadī, after its origin in Viṣṇupada ("the celestial realm of Viṣṇu" or "the foot of Viṣṇu"). Viṣṇu, who in the Rig Veda was Indra's helper in releasing the nectarous waters, is here the primary cause of their descent to earth. In taking his famous three strides, Viṣṇu, the dwarf-turned-giant, stretched through and took possession of the three-fold universe. With his third stride he is said to have pierced the vault of heaven with his toe and released the heavenly waters.[29] Through this opening in the shell of the universe, the Gaṅgā, which had hitherto flowed around the cosmic egg, flowed into the heavens, landing first in Indra's heaven, where she was caught by the steady pole-star Dhruva. From there she ran down the sky to the moon as the Milky Way, and from the moon to the realm of Brahmā situated just above Mount Meru, rimmed by the peaks of the eight directions and forming the calyx of the lotus of this world. From Meru, the river split into four parts and ran out upon the various lotus-petal continents. One branch, the Alakanandā, flowed into Bhārata-varṣa (India) as the Gaṅgā.[30]

In the most celebrated myth of the Gaṅgā's descent to earth, it is Śiva whose role is predominant. The story, which is told in the *Rāmāyaṇa,* the *Mahābhārata,* and in many Purāṇas,[31] is too long to recount here. What is significant for our understanding of the goddess Gaṅgā, however, is that the Gaṅgā fell from heaven in order to revive the sixty thousand sons of King Sagara, burned to ashes by the scorching heat of the glance of the sage Kapila, whose meditation they had rudely disturbed. It was Bhagīratha whose *tapas* finally won the favor of Gaṅgā. She agreed to come to earth, but was certain that the earth would shatter under the force of her fall. Śiva promised to catch her on his head and tame her in the thicket of his ascetic's hair before releasing her to flow upon the earth. Thus did the Gaṅgā fall, winding her way through Śiva's hair and out upon the plains of India, where

Bhagīratha took charge of her and led her to the sea. From there she reached the netherworld and became the saving funereal waters for the sons of Sagara.

According to some accounts, the Gaṅgā split into seven streams as she emerged from the hair of Śiva, three flowing to the east, three to the west, and the Bhāgīrathī to the south. This tradition recalls the seven rivers of the Vedic hymns and reminds us that the Gaṅgā in essence waters the whole earth. Indeed, when Bhagīratha brought the Gaṅgā to earth, her waters not only restored the ashes of the dead, but also replenished the ocean, which had been swallowed by the sage Agastya.[32]

It is because the Gaṅgā descended in her *avataraṇa* that she is a place of ascent as a *tīrtha*. She, as *triloka-patha-gaminī*, "flowing in the three worlds," has crossed over from heaven to earth to the netherworlds and has thus become a place of crossing for human beings, both the living and the dead. As she quickened the ashes of the sons of Sagara, so will she quicken the ashes of all the dead. Thus it is that the story of the Gaṅgā-*avataraṇa* is read in *śrāddha* ceremonies, that Gaṅgā water is used in *śrāddha* and *tarpaṇa* rites, and that the place where the Gaṅgā skirts the Mahāśmaśāna, the "Great Cremation Ground" of holy Banāras, has made that place the best place to die in all of India. For the dead, the Gaṅgā has the epithet *svarga-sopana-saraṇī*, "the flowing staircase to heaven." There is no theme more pervasive in Gaṅgā hymnody than the yearning for the lap of the Gaṅgā at the time of death. The popular "Gaṅgāṣṭakam," for instance, begins with the following verse:

> O Mother! Co-wife of Pārvatī! Necklace adorning the worlds!
> Banner rising to heaven!
> I ask that I may take leave of this body on your banks,
> drinking your water, rolling in your waves,
> remembering your name, bestowing my gaze upon you![33]

Liquid Consort

The mythology of the *Devībhāgavata* and *Brahmavaivarta Purāṇas* relates the Gaṅgā closely to Viṣṇu and more specifically to Krishna as one of the forms of the female *pṛakṛti*, "Nature," or in some instances as one of the forms of Rādhā herself.[34] In one instance, the Gaṅgā in human form, sitting with great adoration next to Krishna, arouses the jealousy of Rādhā, who threatens to drink her up. Gaṅgā immediately disappears, taking refuge inside the foot of Krishna. The earth is then distressed by the draught that results from Gaṅgā's disappearance. It is only when the gods supplicate Rādhā and calm her jealousy that Gaṅgā emerges from the foot of Krishna and flows forth again.[35]

In another myth, the three co-wives of Viṣṇu—Gaṅgā, Sarasvatī, and Lakṣmī—quarrel among themselves over the attentions of their common husband. Both Sarasvatī and Gaṅgā curse one another to become rivers on earth and to bear the burden of human sins. At this point, Viṣṇu intervenes and specifies that in their lives as rivers Sarasvatī will become the wife of Brahmā and Gaṅgā will become the wife of Śiva. Lakṣmī, who had done nothing but try to mediate in the quarrel, will become the sacred *tulasī* plant and will remain his wife.[36] Gaṅgā and Sarasvatī, however, lament so loudly that Viṣṇu finally agrees that while they go their separate ways they will remain, in essence, with him.

If Gaṅgā is a co-wife of Viṣṇu and a form of Rādhā, it is clear that her relationship to the Lord is intimate, so much so, in fact, that she flows out of his very body. And as Krishna and Rādhā share one body, so do they mingle in the waters of the Gaṅgā. One striking account tells of the full harvest moon of Kārttika, the night of the *rāsa* dance. All the gods have assembled and watch in awe as Krishna and Rādhā dance. As Śiva sings rapturous songs, they all fall into a swoon, and when they come to their senses, the magic circle of Rādhā's and Krishna's dance has become a sea of water. The two have liquified to become the waters of the Gaṅgā.[37]

Liquid Śakti

From the Śaiva point of view, it is Śiva whose relationship with Gaṅgā is most prominent and most intimate. If she is consort of Hari, so is she *śakti* of Śiva; if she flows from the foot of Viṣṇu, so she meanders in Śiva's hair.

Śiva as Gaṅgādhara, "Bearer of the Gaṅgā," is commonly depicted wearing the Gaṅgā in his hair, either as the mermaid who clings to the crescent moon in his topknot or as the stream of water spurting up like a geyser. The Gaṅgā, therefore, is Śiva's constant companion, making his tangled ascetic's locks her way-station on her perpetual fall from heaven to earth. Her *avatarana* is a continuing process, not a single event; each wave of the Gaṅgā falls upon Śiva before reaching the earth. In agreeing to bear the Gaṅgā, Śiva involved himself in a relationship rather than a simple project.

So close is the relationship of Gaṅgā and Śiva that she is called his wife and is occasionally depicted in sculpture approaching him as a bride.[38] Naturally, as co-wife and rival, she arouses the jealousy of Pārvatī, much as she does that of Rādhā. Gaṅgā, born of Himālaya, the Mountain, and his wife Menā is, in fact, Pārvatī's sister; but she is also Pārvatī's rival. Pārvatī's jealousy became a favorite theme of both poets and artists. The poet Jagannātha, for instance, writes:

> Who here can speak the greatness of your gracious form,
> which vanquishes our worldly fears
> by its mere beholding,
> which Śiva ever holds upon his head,
> despite the strong entreaties of the Mountain's Daughter
> who grows faint with envy.[39]

Śiva is called Umā-Gaṅgā-patīśvara, "Husband and Lord of Umā (Pārvatī) and Gaṅgā," and is depicted as such by artists, who show Gaṅgā clinging to his hair and a frowning Pārvatī turning her face away in jealousy.[40]

In the *Skanda Purāṇa* Śiva, speaking to Viṣṇu, resolves the issue by identifying Gaṅgā with Pārvatī as the female aspect of the Divine, however construed:

> As Gaurī (Pārvatī) is, so is the Gaṅgā. Therefore whoever worships Gaurī properly also worships the Gaṅgā.
>
> And as I am, so are you, O Viṣṇu. And as you are, so am I. And as Umā (Pārvatī) is, so is the Gaṅgā. The form is not different.
>
> And whoever says that there is some difference between Viṣṇu and Rudra, between Śrī (Viṣṇu's consort) and Gaurī, or between the Gaṅgā and Gaurī is a very foolish person.[41]

The Gaṅgā embodies the Supreme Sadā Śiva's active energy or *śakti*. *Śakti* is that life energy, conceived as female, through which the qualityless, unspeakable Sadā Śiva manifests himself in the world. This *śakti* can be apprehended, praised, and loved. She can even be touched in this, her liquid form. A contemporary Hindi religious writer speaks of the Gaṅgā as the "liquid (*drava*) *mūrti*" of Parabrahma, Paramātmā.[42] Kālidāsa, in the *Kumārasambhava*, calls her *śambhor ambumayi-mūrti:* Śiva's water-form.[43] It is a female form, flowing out upon the earth for the blessing of all. Says the *māhātmya* from the *Skanda Purāṇa:*

> She, the Gaṅgā, is my supreme *mūrti,* having the form of water, the very essence of Śiva's soul. She is Nature (*prakṛti*) supreme and the basis of countless universes.
>
> For the protection of the world do I playfully uphold the Gaṅgā, who is Mother of the world, the supreme Brahman's very embodiment.[44]

As this "embodiment" the Gaṅgā makes Śiva's activity in the world possible. Śiva-in-action indeed is *śakti,* the energy that creates and nourishes all the manifest universe. Without this energy, that One is unnameable, qualityless, and without expansion. *Śakti* bodies forth the living cosmos; and the Gaṅgā is liquid *śakti.* Her fall from heaven to the head of Śiva is repeated countless times daily in the simple ritual act of pouring water upon the Śiva *liṅga.* The unutterable incandescence of the *liṅga* of fire is joined with the torrential energy of the celestial waters. Without the Gaṅgā, Śiva would remain the scorching, brilliant *liṅga* of fire; without Śiva, the Gaṅgā would flood the earth.[45] Bearing her on his head, Śiva became the vehicle for the Gaṅgā's fall. But if Śiva is a vehicle for the Gaṅgā, she is also a vehicle for Śiva: for it is through her liquid *śakti* that Śiva is able to enter into the world as an active agent of salvation. As Skanda explains to Agastya in one of the Gaṅgā *māhātmyas:*

> O Agasyta, one should not be amazed at the notion that the Gaṅgā is really Śakti, for is she not the supreme energy of the eternal Śiva, which has taken the form of water?[46]

The Śiva we speak of here, however, is not Rudra-Śiva, but the One called Sadā Śiva, who includes and transcends Brahmā, Viṣṇu, and Rudra-Śiva. The Gaṅgā as the liquid *śakti* of this Supreme Śiva embodies all these gods, just as in another context she is said to embody Krishna and Rādhā together. The opening stanza of one hymn makes this clear:

> Om. Praise be to the auspicious Gaṅgā, gift of Śiva, O praise!
> Praise be to her who is Viṣṇu embodied, the very image of Brahmā, O praise!

> Praise to her who is the form of Rudra, Śaṅkara, the embodiment of all gods, the embodiment of healing, O praise![47]

Likewise, the opening stanza of the "Gaṅgā Laharī" calls her the "essence of the scriptures and embodied goodness of the gods."[48]

Mother Gaṅgā

It is significant that Gaṅgā is the embodied "goodness" of the gods, for hers is an energy perpetually praised as good. Her destructive force is utterly purified and calmed in the hair of Śiva. As she flows out upon the plains, she is Mother, and she is the perfect dream-mother: embracing, nourishing, and forgiving, without a trace of anger. In India, where virtually every manifestation of female divinity is tinged with ambiguity, it is noteworthy that this river, with such tremendous potential for destruction, is acclaimed in such unambiguous terms.

The image of rivers as mothers is ancient and widespread. The Vedic poets say, for instance, that when Indra released the waters of heaven, they ran out upon the earth like mother cows to suckle their young, like milk cows rich in milk.[49] The poets beg of the rivers, "Like longing mothers give to us here on earth the most blessed nectar that you have!"[50] When the cow-rivers run upon the earth they are pregnant with the sun; they are also called the mothers of Agni, fire.

The Gaṅgā inherits her mothering capacities from those ancient waters. It is she who accepts from Agni the burning seed of Śiva and becomes the mother of the War-god, Skanda.[51] Elsewhere, as the wife of Śantanu, she is the mother of the eight Vasus and of the hero-sage Bhīṣma. When Bhīṣma finally dies in the great battle of the *Mahābhārata*, she rises in human form from the river, weeping as bitterly as any mother.[52]

The waters of the Gaṅgā are the drink of life. As the gods drink *soma* for life, so do humans drink Gaṅgā water.[53] It is as nourishing as mother's milk, and indeed the *Mahābhārata* compares human thirst for her waters to that of hungry children thirsting for their mothers' milk.[54]

It is as Mother Gaṅgā that this river is most universally known to Hindus, and, like a mother, the Gaṅgā can be trusted to render unconditional love to her children. Even those utterly unfit for salvation by brahmanical standards will be embraced and saved by the Gaṅgā.

In India today the most widely known hymn to the Gaṅgā is the "Gaṅgā Laharī" of the seventeenth-century poet Jagannātha, who was patronized by the Mughal emperor Shāh Jahān and his son, the *littèrateur* prince Dārā Shikoh. The poet was outcasted by his Brahmin subcaste for his long love affair with a Muslim woman at court. According to legend, Jagannātha went to Banāras to try to restore his status by proving himself acceptable to Brahmins there, but he was unsuccessful. As the story goes, he sat with his beloved atop the fifty-two steps of Pañcagaṅgā Ghāṭ and, with each of the fifty-two verses he composed, the river rose one step. At the conclusion of the hymn, the waters touched the feet of the poet and his beloved, purified them, embraced them, and carried them away.[55]

In the "Gaṅgā Laharī" Jagannātha addresses the river as Mother, the one who will love and claim the child rejected by everyone else. He is so despicable that he is shunned even by outcastes; he is criticized even by madmen; he is so filthy with sin that all the *tīrthas* hang their heads in shame at their inability to cleanse him. There are plenty of gods who will care for the good, but who except the Gaṅgā will care for the wicked?[56] He approaches the Gaṅgā with complete trust and faith:

> I come to you as a child to his mother.
> I come as an orphan
>   to you, moist with love.
> I come without refuge
>   to you, giver of sacred rest.
> I come a fallen man
>   to you, uplifter of all.
> I come undone by disease
>   to you, the perfect physician.
> I come, my heart dry with thirst,
>   to you, ocean of sweet wine.
> Do with me whatever you will.[57]

Above all, it is mercy and compassion that flow out from the foot of Viṣṇu or from the hair of Śiva in the form of this mothering river. It nourishes the land and all its creatures, living and dying. The hymns repeatedly affirm that this river is intended as a vehicle of mercy:

> This Gaṅgā was sent out for the salvation of the world by Śambhu, Lord of lords, filled with the sweet wine of compassion.

> Śankara, having squeezed out the essence of *yoga* and the *upaniṣads,* created this excellent river because of his mercy for all creatures.[58]

In earlier ages and better times *mokṣa* could be had only by means of meditation (*dhyāna),* austerities (*tapas*), or ritual sacrifice (*yajña*). But now, it is said, in this Kali Yuga, these are no longer viable. Only the Gaṅgā can bring the blessings of salvation.[59]

The River

The Gaṅgā's history in the Hindu mythological tradition is long and rich. Here we have only pointed to some of its various aspects. As a celestial stream flowing upon the earth she has her mythic origins in the world of the Vedas. As the tradition developed, she wound her way into the myth and ritual of Vaiṣṇavas and Śaivas alike. She is hardly the best-known consort of either Viṣṇu or Śiva, but she has acquired the position of consort to both of them, something no other goddess can claim. Even Brahmā keeps close company with her, carrying the river in his water pot.

The river's accumulation of mythological traditions demonstrates the distinctive persistence of natural geographical symbols in India. For the Gaṅgā is most certainly not loved and worshipped because she is spouse of Śiva, co-wife of Pārvatī, consort of Viṣṇu, or the liquified Rādhā-Krishna. Rather, she has attracted this mythology over the years precisely because *she* is worshipped and loved. Here one sees the difference between the organic myth or symbol and the narrative one. For the Gaṅgā's significance as a symbol is not exhaustively narrative. First, she is a river that flows with waters of life in a vibrant universe. Narrative myths come and go in history. They may shape the cosmos and convey meaning for many generations, and then they may gradually lose their hold upon the imagination and finally be forgotten. But the river remains, even when the the stories are no longer repeated. The river flows on, bringing life and conveying the living tradition, even to those of this age for whom everything else is demythologized.

In the Hindu tradition, any place can become the sacred abode of the gods, if the proper rites are performed. When a temple is consecrated and its image installed, the great rites of *pratiṣṭhā* serve to call the presence of the divine to that place. With any *mūrti* fashioned of wood or stone or rudely crafted of clay, rites of *āvahana* or "invitation" are observed at the beginning of worship, inviting the deity to be present, and rites of *visarjana* or "dismissal" are observed at worship's end, giving the deity leave to go. With the worship of the Gaṅgā no such rites are ever observed. This river is no ordinary *mūrti* in which the divine has come to dwell. She is celestial—unmediated and immediate. Whatever is holy, whatever is merciful, whatever is utterly auspicious is already there.

A Theology of the Repulsive: The Myth of the Goddess Śītalā*

EDWARD C. DIMOCK, JR.

> When the sacrifice was completed, the sacrificial fire was extinguished, and in it was born a girl most radiant; she emerged, holding a winnowing fan on her head. When he saw her, Prajāpati asked solicitously: "Who are you, O beautiful girl? Whose daughter are you, and whose wife? For what reason were you in the fire? Tell us that story." And the goddess said: "My birth was in the fire-pit. Where shall I go? What shall I do? My heart is troubled." And when he heard, Brahmā said: "Your birth was at the time of the cooling of the sacrificial fire. Thus, your name is Śītalā."

*H*ence the etymology of the name Śītalā, "the Cool One," as it is given in the *Śītalā-maṅgal* of Dvija Nityānanda (Cakravartī), an eighteenth-century text in Bengali.[1] *Maṅgal,* "auspiciousness" or "beneficence," is the name given to a eulogistic type of Middle Bengali text devoted to one or another of the gods, or, more often, goddesses. Śītalā is the goddess of pustular diseases in Bengal and of malaria, and it is possible that her name is a euphemism, an attempt to ward off the goddess's fire as she rages through the Bengali countryside with her virulent companion Jvarāsura, "the Fever Demon" (as he is known to Nityānanda), or Basanta-rāy, "Lord of Smallpox," (as the writer of another of her *maṅgal* poems, Kṛṣṇarām-dās, would have it).[2] She is a fierce goddess, of course, though she is called Karuṇāmayī, "She who is full of mercy" and Dayāmayī, "She who is full of grace": in her *līlā* she sweeps through villages and cities, like fire leaving one house unscathed to destroy the next, searing with her fevers good people and bad without distinction.

How may we understand this *līlā* of the goddess Śītalā? The etymology of the term presents a problem. In an article entitled "Līlā," A.K. Coomaraswamy makes a series of interesting suggestions. He first presents the notion of *līlā* as divine playing, the usual

*I am greatly indebted for many of the thoughts contained in this paper to my student, friend, and now colleague Aditinath Sarkar.

interpretation, citing occurrences in Rig Veda 9 and 10, and then he writes:

> It is obvious that Agni [the god of fire] is thought of as "playful" inasmuch as he "flares up and dies down" . . . and that the designation of his tongues as the "flickerers" (*leläy-amānāh*) in Muṇḍaka Up. I.2.4. corresponds to their designation as the "playful ones" in RV.X.3.5. At the same time Agni is constantly spoken of as "licking" (*rih, lih*) whatever he loves or devours. . . .[3]

Yet although the etymology is not clear, Burrow also suggests[4] that the root *lih* has cognate forms that yield such terms as the modern English "lick," which the Oxford Universal Dictionary defines as "to play lightly over, as of waves or flame." Another suggestive possibility is the root *lī-*, "to hide in." For the fire, especially the sacrificial fire, consumes and does not consume.[5] It flames up and subsides again. Now it is seen, now it is not seen. The fire is endemic. As the Baul song has it, it is latent in the wood, and in the flint and steel:

> There is yet fire in the ashes.
> and it will burn again, if the ashes are stirred.
> They say that burning is a quality of wood,
> that in the flint and steel the fire dwells.
> But fire does not burn a brick-built house,
> nor does the wall of earth around the fire burn.[6]

Or, from time to time, the fire is epidemic, and then it flames; it rages and consumes.[7] Fire is a quality of wood, and, as the Baul song suggests, of the flesh, in the innate lustfulness and disease- and fever-proneness of that substance; and flame is the quality of fire.[8] Fire is the persistent condition; flame is sporadic. Yet the connection between the two is intrinsic: one cannot exist without the other. Fire is the source of flame; but fire is unmanifest, and thus ineffective and even meaningless, without the flame. Fire is the latent principle; flame, its manifestation. The analogy, of course, is that disease of certain types is endemic in Bengal, and a smallpox or cholera outbreak is a manifestation of this latent principle. Mother Śītalā, who is "full of grace," is always present, and from time to time she manifests herself in her *līlā*, and humankind suffers. Or perhaps there is a question as to whether or not such manifestations are finally understood as suffering.

Līlā, then, might describe the fiery and seemingly random visitations of the goddess. But there is another way to interpret the term, also suggested by Coomaraswamy.[9] For he points out that the Prakrit word *līḷhā*, referring to the Buddha's manifestation, is glossed in the Pali Text Society's lexicon as "grace."

Again, etymology is suggestive, if not conclusive. For if grace is *charis*, as it is defined by *Thayer's Greek-English Lexicon of the New Testment*, then the quality of grace, i.e., *charisma* in its Pauline sense, is the investiture of certain individuals with particular authority from above, or, in Thayer's words, "extraordinary powers, distinguishing certain Christians and enabling them to serve the Church of Christ, the reception of which is due to the power of divine grace."[10] Charisma, then, is the manifestation of grace, and there would seem to be a parallel by which disease could be called the charisma, or the grace, or the *līlā*, of the goddess Śītalā. And those who are "afflicted" by her from one point of view, from another become the recipients of her grace.

There are problems with this interpretation in addition to those attendant upon inter-language etymological speculation. One such problem is pointed up by Thayer's use of the term "certain Christians." In the Jewish, Christian and Islamic traditions, with their millenarian and messianic expectations, charisma is that which invests an individual with particular authority. The charisma of Śītalā, on the other hand, is democratically distributed. Not only is she always there, embedded and latent in human society and in the substantial world, but when she manifests herself in *līlā* she will touch the better part of Burdwan district, or Jessore, or all Bengal. As she is latent, whether people are healthy or an epidemic is raging, the degree of her charisma is the same; her grace is there. This is quite a different attitude, it seems, from the one frequently encountered in Judaeo-Christian thought, in which humanity is visited by disaster as retribution, as in the case of the plague on Egypt, or testing, as in the oppression of Job.

It might further be observed that the reception of the grace of Śītalā is in chronologically discrete events. It is through these events, called epidemics, that people, knowing little, wishing to know less, and tending to forget much, are made aware of her constant presence. The event takes place in chronological time. But the meaning of the event places it outside time: the grace of the goddess invests not only individual people in Burdwan district, for example, but time itself. Time becomes a series of changing forms of a single essence—that of the goddess Śītalā.

Time and the Śītāla-maṅgal

In their paper "The Fever Demon and the Census Commissioner,"[11] Ralph Nicholas and Aditinath Sarkar point out that in certain specific cases the worship of Śītalā and the writing of her poems follow upon the outbreak of epidemics. They also note, however, that there is more than a simple cause-and-effect relation at work here. For although the epidemic is a diachronic event, the *maṅgal* poems are meant to describe its synchronic source, the endemic goddess herself. The epidemic is the *līlā* of the goddess, but it is also information. The *līlā* seems random, and thus without meaning for human society, unless it is related to the synchronic structure that underlies it. It is for this reason that *maṅgal* poems are written: taken together, they constitute the synchronic structure of truth. This is also why they are *maṅgala,* imparting "well-being, beneficence." They enable us mortals, with limited vision and small intelligence, to learn from discrete experience, to fit that experience into the larger divine scheme of things. We are kept aware of the presence of the goddess, and of her grace, and by devotion to her we are blessed.

The *Śītalā-maṅgal* differs from most other *maṅgals* in that it is locatable in historical time.[12] This is not to say that the others take place in a world completely apart from the immediate one. To the contrary, the river that is such a prominent feature in most of the *maṅgals* is, like the Gaṅgā flowing from the head of Śiva, a link between immediate time and space and the realm of the divine. In the *maṅgals* of Caṇḍī, Manasā, and Kamalā, for example, the protagonist sails down this river, past *ghāṭs* that can be seen today, past places with names that are known, if not from maps of present-day Bengal, then from those found in Rennell.[13] But as the ships move out of the river and beyond the comforting sight of land, they begin to pass mysterious, unworldly places with names like Māyāpur, "the place of transformations," and Kālidaha, "the whirlpool of time." And in these places strange and grotesque things take place:

> Crossing the grievous seas, the merchant arrived at Māyādaha, and happily cooked his meal and ate. When she heard of this from her attendant, Śītalā came there to deceive the merchant. A palace appeared in the middle of the sea. It was a place of wonderful delight. Around a beautiful throne twelve *vidyādharīs*[14] sang and danced, and there were dancing girls. And behind them, men played with tigers. Everything was orna-

> mented with gems. The predator and prey roamed together, and one did not attack the other, such was the enchantment of *māyā*. In front there could be seen a hundred men in battle dress.[15] Crocodiles and lions were there together. Hooded serpents were in the palace arbors, the gems on their heads flashing fire, playing with peacocks. The many sides of the palace were adorned with mango and other trees, in untimely bloom. Birds flew in flocks, singing sweetly, and played in delight. Inside the palace courtyard was a huge *bāici* tree, with coral blooming on it. Beneath it sat Śītalā, with many maids in waiting and many children.[16] Who can understand this causing a *bāici* tree to grow in the middle of the sea by *māyā*?

And so the merchant goes to relate this marvelous vision to the king:

> There is a heavenly palace there; it is a most wonderful tale! I saw a cat and mouse together, and a snake and peacock at play. Before everyone, horses and buffaloes, men and tigers played together. Coral blossomed on a *bāici* tree, and near it was a most lovely lady.

The king, understandably, does not believe him, so he takes the merchant and all his retinue, and they embark for Māyādaha. When they reach the place, the king sees only water, and threatens to kill the merchant. But the merchant replies:

> Look! There is the jeweled palace. There is the beautiful lady seated beneath the coral tree. If you do not see even when you see, what am I to do?

The king, furious, is about to have the merchant beheaded. But the merchant prays to Śītalā, who is ready to answer her devotee's prayer with her army of diseases. She is dissuaded from doing so by Nārada, who suggests instead that she appear to the king in a dream and instruct him to release the merchant and worship her. So the king dreams, and when he awakes he describes his dream to the courtiers, who reply:

> Who is this Śītalā? You must have dreamed this because of gas on the stomach.

So the king orders the execution of the merchant. And Śītalā, her patience exhausted, strikes with her army of diseases. The king himself was afflicted

> with leprosy, and glaucoma in both eyes.[17] "Ah," he cried, "what has happened? What can I say, that my fate has turned like this?" Then, faintly, he saw the *māyā* of Śītalā. Upon it[18] there were luminous divine beings, attendants of the goddess, making the whole place glow as they plucked red coral from the *bāici* tree. The predator and prey grazed together, numerous and wonderful to see. . . . The glaucoma cleared from the king's eyes [and he said to the goddess]: "I will wed my daughter to the merchant. Remove all these afflictions from my land. I know you now to be the goddess Śāradā,[19] full of mercy. I worship your lotus feet; grant right-mindedness to us all.[20]

In other *maṅgals* equally wondrous things occur, once one clears familiar shores. In the *Caṇḍī-maṅgal,* the goddess in the form of a beautiful, sexually exciting lady sits on a lotus in the middle of the sea swallowing and disgorging elephants:

> Behold, O helmsman, the *avātara* of a beautiful lady on that lotus. Holding a bull elephant in her left hand, she regurgitates it and again consumes it. . . . She is slim-waisted, heavyhipped with firm buttocks. She parts her lips a little, and swallows and regurgitates an elephant.[21]

The merchant and his helmsman remain human, though moving now in worlds no longer known and comforting. But they meet the gods, and are taught by them, and with their help they return again into the mortal world, against the river's current. The river is the continuum of time and space; it links time and the timeless. It links the world that follows comprehensible laws with that in which laws are suspended, the place of the *līlā* of the gods.

Mircea Eliade points out that such *coincidentia oppositorum* as in the passage above, the lion lying down with the lamb, are often features of Paradise, in fact features of divinity itself, "simultaneously, benevolent and terrible, creative and destructive." They reveal, he says, "the actual structure of the divinity, which transcends all attributes and reconciles all contraries,"[22] thus showing how utterly different divinity is from humanity. This is not to say that certain types of people cannot gain the experience of the coincidence of opposites. That very experience is the aim of the ascetic and the sage, and transcends all attributes. "The consciousness of such a man knows no more conflict. and such pairs of opposites as pleasure and pain, desire and repulsion, cold and heat, the agreeable and the disagreeable are expunged from his awareness, while something is taking place within him which parallels the total realization of contraries within the divinity."[23] The merchant, and the king too when he has become temporarily blind, see this reality of the integrated dual nature of Śītalā. They have known lions and they have known lambs, but the playing of the two together is not in their ordinary experience. They have known beneficence and they have known virulence, but the consorting of the two together they have not known before. This is the *māyā*, the illusion, of the goddess. And if the word "illusion" can be derived from *in ludere,* it is indeed her play that is revealed to them, her *līlā.*

Another interesting facet to the episode of the vision is that the epidemic which ravages the good king and his kingdom has a pedagogic purpose. Śītalā, like Caṇḍī, reveals herself, to those who have eyes to see, as beautiful, benign, and the locus of the *coincidentia oppositorum.* To the king, who does not, at least at first, have eyes to see, she is malevolent. Only when his eyes become diseased, through the good offices of the goddess, does the king see that she is the totality of things. It could be concluded that only by what is deviant in ordinary experience can true normality be seen; only by what is "diseased" by human perception, or by what is called "strange and mysterious," is reality perceived. A Baul song says:

> I am blind. I can see no one.
> You who are on the path,
> move aside a little.
> Because of my past faults
> God has taken away my eyes.
> Because of the sins of some former birth
> God has taken my eyes.[24]

In fact, however, his blindness is not a curse, but a blessing. For the Baul must look within, to find the Man of his Heart. And he can do so only when his outward-looking eyes are sightless, no longer captivated by the glittering bauble that is the world. And, too, looking with the outer eyes of particular and ordinary experience, one sees either one form or the other of the deity's bivalent nature. Beneficence and virulence are familiar and therefore acceptable separately. But the special nature of the lady on the lotus or the palace of transformations is that in them the one who has the eyes to see is allowed a simultaneous vision. He sees at the same time what creates and what destroys. He sees that, so far as the deity and the realm of the divine are concerned, creation and destruction are not separated by time at all. And thus he sees that time has no reality of its own. What is life and what is death exist at the very same moment: the vision then teaches the illusion of time, the play of the goddess. It might be added that this is also the force of some of Freud's thought: opposites such as love and hate exist simultaneously in the unconscious, but cannot be expressed simultaneously. It is only in dreams or in imaginative pictorial representation that logical temporal sequence is not demanded.[25]

The question, of course, is how all this relates back to particular experience: does the ordinary person in Burdwan perceive fever and pustules as *māyer dayā,* "the mother's mercy?" The answer is probably no: probably such a person takes the mother's mercy as freedom from those very afflictions. It is to teach him or her that this is only half the truth that the myth exists. The king is taught to see by his blindness. The merchant, already a devotee, does not require such affliction to learn. This is the lesson of the *maṅgal,* and it is in fact an aspect of the goddess's grace that she allows us to learn—if we have the eyes to see—through poetry and myth rather than through her ignorance-destroying and otherwise edifying visits. To assure the goddess of their enlightenment the *maṅgal* poets invite her, at the beginning of their poems, to come down onto the stage, witness the play, approve of the music, and be pleased by the verse.

A myth puts events outside secular time. An epidemic in 1877, which, as Nicholas and Sarkar show, is immediately followed by the production of *Śītalā-maṅgal* poems, has, when taken up into the myth, relevance to an epidemic that may have occurred in 0077 and to one that may take place in 2077.[26] The myth states, in other words, the principle of the endemic, the perpetual presence of the goddess. The existence of a Śītalā text thus both places an event in time and removes it beyond time. The text, the event, and the individual become the same. The realm of the Śītalā myth is the divine realm, which both collapses time into simultaneity and expands it into infinity. Three separate human events, which spawn three different texts, are three forms of the goddess, placed perhaps differently according to human conceptions of time and space, but not in essence different. This is a view not unfamiliar to Vaiṣṇava theology: the avatars of Viṣṇu differ in form, in time, and in space, but they are all fully godhead, existing eternally in one divine essence. There are many *rūpas,* ("forms") but only one *svarūpa* ("true form"). Similarly, Caitanya can say that on the level of the real, he is Krishna, and that which surrounds him is not sixteenth-century Bengal but the eternal Vṛndāvana. And Ramakrishna can say in his turn that he is Caitanya and therefore also Krishna. Time and space have collapsed.

This is an interesting view of history. A text is written because of an event. Yet by the act of being narrated, of being made specific, the event is put beyond time. It is there forever, and in fact has been, like the Veda, there for all time past. In the divine realm there is no history. The goddess in her mercy, however, sees that we are trapped in our humanity and ignorance and cannot deal with this reality. The view of history presented in the *maṅgals* is therefore a mediating one. It is a kind of cinematographic view: one frame succeeds another in unending sequence. The former frame is replaced, but its image is not eliminated. The second frame does not make sense without the first. The image of the first lingers and remains effective, and is to that extent simultaneous. The *maṅgal* poem is a frame, lingering a while upon the screen, leaving an image of pain and destruction—as it is seen by human eyes—which is the goddess's mercy, to be replaced by an image of prosperity and freedom from disease. Embedded in what we see as sequence, as history, is the divine pedagogy. If there were no epidemic, there would be no awareness of the presence of the goddess. And if there were no *maṅgal,* the image of that frame would fade too quickly. The human view is that affliction can be replaced by prosperity, but prosperity can also be replaced by affliction. The fact is that both are present all the time. The opposite sides of existence are coincident in the unconscious, and in Śītalā.

We need constant reminders that prosperity can be replaced by affliction. The kingdom of Virāta is a most idyllic place:

> [The king] Virāta is very devoted to Śiva. He is a Vidura[27] in politeness, an inflamed Duryodhana in haughtiness, a Kaṃsāsura in pride. The king is swift as the wind, like him whose refuge is Rāma.[28] He maintains his kingdom like [that of] Rāma, but is death to his foes. He is a Karṇa in generosity, a Kuvera in wealth, an Arjuna in battle. The daily recitation of his eulogy brings merit, for he is a Yudhiṣṭhira in truthfulness. He is like Agni in ardor, like the ocean in his qualities, like Bṛhaspati in wisdom. His queen-consort is the faithful and benevolent Sudeṣṇā.

> The king's minister Kicaka is a wrestler like Bhīma, and a living double of the king of death. The king's daughter is Uttarā, and Uttara is his son. Great wealth and many cattle are in his household. Every king would like to conquer Virāta, but none dares go there for fear of Kicaka.
>
> There is no injustice or unrighteousness there. All speak the truth and abjure falsehood. The policy of the king and the kingdom is devotion to Śiva. There is no mischief, nor peril, nor untimely death.[29]

Virāta, happy and righteous as it is, is a place that can be devastated in a moment. Śītalā, appearing in the previously mentioned dream, points this out to the king:

> In the last period of the night, Śītalā appeared in a dream. Seated at the king's head, she was in a most terrifying guise: naked, quelling all vanity, huge and wide, with terrible eyes. Before her danced Jvara, in his deadly form—six eyes, six hands, three heads, and three feet.[30] Holding aloft arms severed at the shoulder, crying "Śītalā!" as she danced, Raktāvatī[31] roared like a lion. On all four sides the king saw beautiful pulses—red, blue, white, and yellow.[32] And suddenly he saw the royal palace ablaze, and he saw freshly severed heads. One hundred and twenty diseases were spread all over,[33] and assuming terrible form, these devoured the king in his dream. There were uncountable [inauspicious] shooting stars and rivers flowing with blood, while the diseases sucked blood.
>
> Seeing all this, the king shuddered in terror. Śītalā, seated at his head, said: "Listen with a calm mind, O king. It is my grace (*dayā*) to extend this my *māyā* to you. I am the mistress of all diseases. I will give you the four great goals of life, I will be your final deliverance, and I will prevent untimely death. Rise in the morning, O king, and worship Śītalā with offerings of countless male goats and rams.[34]

The king, unfortunately, did not heed this very clear warning, and Śītalā reduced his kingdom to shambles. The situation was so serious that one does not know whether to translate *virāta-śmaśāna* as "the cremation ground of the city of Virāta" or "Virāta, the cremation ground." In the marketplace, where there had been joyous and fair commerce, Śītalā established a rather different trade:

> In Virāta, at the foot of a banyan tree, on an extensive piece of ground eight miles in length and breadth, Śītalā, in great good humor, attended by her male and female servants, established a marketplace for ghouls. In heaven, the sun, the moon, Death, and the gods of the ten directions trembled when they observed her play. Demons sounded drums, a great uproar arose, and with arms uplifed the diseases danced. Having gathered all the corpses, male and female ghouls put them on abundant display in shops, and bought and sold. Getting the stench, crows and kites in hundreds of thousands came, and flies buzzed around. An old grandmother ghoul sold intestines of corpses, calling them jackfruit . . . and human heads as coconuts and rotting heads of elephants as ripe palmyra fruit. The ears of corpses were sold in the market as *pān,* and the pupils of their eyes as *śāli*-rice. Female ghouls bought bags of brains of corpses as lime, and rotten melting corpses for perfume. Pairs of ears were sold as incense, [finger and toe] nails as husked rice, and the penises of boys as enticing dates. Palates were sold as ripe cantaloupe, and human heads as vegetables. Vomited blood is the best loved drink of male and female ghouls; human blood is sugar-cane juice for them. Demons bought and ate the breasts of dead women as if they were custard apples or pomegranates, with great delight. . . . And the female ghouls all bought and wove garlands made of human heads and fingers and toes and hands and feet. Blue and yellow ghouls sold brains, having broken open skulls and emptied them. Heads of men and women were lined up, and heads of children, and elephant tusks were sold as radishes. Human ears were hibiscus flowers, fly-whisks were made of skin with hair, and blood and pus were sold as sandalwood paste.[35]

In the same space where once flourished the *rām-rājya* of Virāta, ruled by a dharmic king, its fifty-two marketplaces brimming with prosperity, the divine person "in a mood of supreme playfulness (*paramaraṅge*)," establishes this horrid scene, in which all that is usual and attractive to mortals is substituted, parodied, and travestied.

The problem, of course, is one of form. Thus the conclusion arrived at by the Bengali Vaiṣṇavas when they reflected on the form of the deity may also be instructive here: in their view the fact that the deity is infinite means that he can have all forms at all times, any form at any time, and various forms at any and all times, without being in any way affected in his true essence. A corollary to this point is that the concept "totally manifest" includes the concept "unmanifest." The deity need not be manifest at all; manifestation is a function of *līlā*. If this logic does indeed apply, it is clear that Śītalā is present at all times in a variety of ways. The epidemic marks the presence of the goddess. Yet times during which disease is absent also signify her presence. The *maṅgal* poems teach us not to conclude that she is absent simply because she does not show herself in manifest epidemic form.

Thus the *maṅgal* poems are attempts to merge the diachronic event with the synchronic structure, the all-pervasive presence. In them, views of time become quite complex. For on the level of divine perception, as we have seen, there is no such thing as time at all: opposites exist simultaneously, with no temporal gap between them. This is not a concept that is congenial, or even comprehensible, to the human consciousness; that it is inexpressibly present in the unconscious may be one of the problems of the human condition.[36] Nor is it a concept limited to the *maṅgal* poems and to Freudian psychology, for, as I point out in a paper on a poem by Jibanānanda Dāś,[37] in that poet's eyes the Bentinck Street section of Calcutta is at least two realities: it is full of Bengali businessmen by day, and swarming with whores and foreign sailors by night. It is not the change from day to night that makes the difference, though it seems so to our experience, for both Calcuttas are present all the time. It is like the famous Orissi painting of the deer, one head grazing, the other staring fearfully backwards. Two-headed deer are not in our experience. Or it is like a Picasso painting of a woman with two eyes on the same side of her head. This also is not in our experience, yet the artistic statement is clear. Our consciousness must define time in terms of particulars: a human year, or a million human years, are but a day to the gods. Beware of such constructions designed to make things comprehensible, say the *maṅgals*. The truth is that all things are present all the time.

It is the replacement of one frame by another that is experienced as time by humans, for only in the gods are the extremes combined. The Bengali term is *āndalan*, "oscillation," and it carries with it the idea of a single but continuously varying form. For humanity, immersed in this rotten Kali Yuga (yet another concept of time), when ignorance is a constant condition and memory and perception are limited, it may be that searing cataclysms are necessary for the divine pedagogy. But they are to be understood as oscillation from the implicit to the epidemic forms of grace: these are the avatars of the goddess in the Kali Yuga.

As all forms of the divine are possible, there is no difference, except to limited human sight, between what is beautiful and what is repulsive. In the divine realm of the goddess, in her avatars, and in the texts that describe them, these opposites do not exist. The marketplace of ghouls is merely another aspect, equally real, of the marketplace of everyday consciousness and sight. The repulsive, horrifying form, as it seems to our eyes, is latent in good times; or perhaps it would be better described as repressed, for, poor weak creatures that we are, we see an untrue distinction between beauty and ugliness. We cannot see that the distinction is false, and could not stand it if we could. The lady on the lotus eating elephants is both beautiful and grotesque in the extreme. But what is grotesque is what is exaggerated, and in the divine realm the concept "grotesque" cannot exist. There can be no hyperbole, for in the realm of the divine, the most extreme concepts of which the human imagination is capable are simply and utterly true.

It must be remembered that *maṅgal* poetry, like most Bengali poetry of the middle period, is not only pedagogy but revelation. The poet is literally the mouthpiece of the deity, and what he says, therefore, is true. The difficulty, of course, is that whereas to the Vaiṣṇavas beauty is truth and truth beauty, an understandable proposition, in the *Śītalā-maṅgal* the truth is sometimes repulsive: there is nothing beautiful about the marketplace of ghouls. But it is again a matter of form, not of essence. The human view is that there are distinctions between pain and pleasure, or between the beautiful and the ugly. The true view is that in essence no such distinctions exist. Disease and health are both aspects of the mercy of the goddess, and are her *līlā*. Śītalā, in her *maṅgal,* comes to the city and sees no pock-marks on the faces of the children. "There are no signs of *māyer dayā*— the mercy of the Mother—in this place," she says.

As we have seen, the *maṅgal* texts are precisely that: blessings of the goddess. By hearing of suffering, by realizing the extent of human frailty, one with the eyes to see may be spared the necessity of more particular pain. Śītalā allows us cognition of our position in the universe, and recognition of herself as Mother. Her grace is that she allows us restitution in return for the understanding of her constant presence, for worship, and above all for realization by humans of where they stand, and where stand the gods.

Śītalā and Eschatology

Another line of thought might be stimulated by all this, and that has to do with the examination, and possible modification, of the commonly expressed position that there is no eschatology or millennialism in Hindu thought. The most recent and lucid statement of the position is in the Nicholas and Sarkar paper "The Fever Demon and the Census Commissioner":[38]

> Many students of millennial movements have commented on their absence from Hindu India. In situations of widespread distress, such as deadly epidemics, and particularly where there is general social disorder, such as existed in the latter half of the 18th and 19th century Bengal, large numbers of people have responded to the visions of millennial dreamers with a kind of total enthusiasm unprecedented in their own experience. Bengali Hindus (and Hindus in general) have not had millennial visions nor the kind of sweeping enthusiasms characteristic of movements in other parts of the world. There are many approaches to the explanation of the absence of millennialism from India, but they all come down to a single point: integral to Hinduism is a non-eschatological conception of the universe.

One might of course adduce as counter-evidence the doctrine put forth in *Gītā* 4.7-8[39] or Kalkī, the avatar-to-come; or, extending Hinduism a bit, one could cite the expectation of the Buddha-to-be. And to be sure these items do suggest that there is at least a strand of what we might call eschatology in Hindu thought. But the Nicholas-Sarkar statement and others like it seem to have a general ring of truth. There are indeed none of the enthusiasms or hysteria one finds in some other cultures. Yet is it bothersome that in this view there is an underlying suggestion that in all situations of "widespread distress," such as epidemics, the type of millenarian response familiar to the West is to be expected. The problems are two. The first is the definition of distress; and we have seen that from certain points of view, at least theoretically, epidemics can be viewed as something other than disasters. The second is related to it, and has to do with the appropriateness of applying concepts and systems derived from one cultural context to an entirely different one.

There has been a spate of books written on millennialism lately, and if one looks through an anthology of essays such as *Millennial Dreams in Action*,[40] one is struck by two contrasting approaches. The first is rather sociological, and seeks to generalize such ideas, ritual and organizational, as can be abstracted from cultural traditions, and to construct typologies. Somewhat typical of it is the essay by Howard Kaminsky called "The Problem of Explanation."[41] After calling for a synthetic method for interpreting millennial movements, he writes:

> Another way, which I think would be more fruitful, could be termed "analytic"; it would take the evidence of the movement itself as grounds for inference about the relationship of the movement to society, and about the psychology of the members. The movement always subscribes to an ideology that empties the existing social order of all value; it also invariably takes the form of a physical movement—a withdrawal from the existing order. Thus on the one hand its ideology is arbitrary, extravagant, and fantastic; on the other hand its social structure is all but non-existent: it is a perfectly plastic mass, without the solidity that comes from a practical working relationship to reality.

Application of these principles to the efflorescence of the worship of Śītalā in eighteenth- and nineteenth-century Bengal would obviously lead Kaminsky to conclude, as Nicholas and Sarkar have done, that it was not a millennial situation at all. Religious response to the epidemics was not "abritrary, extravagant, and fantastic," but was in fact the writing of texts, a response well within the existing order and one that might be expected from Bengali culture. This is of course precisely the problem: if one attempts typologies, in this case one separates the characteristics of the response to disaster from the characteristics of the response to non-disaster, and one's view of the culture involved is fragmented.

The second approach is exemplified by Anthony Wallace, who comes close to meeting this objection.[42] For he places great emphasis on the notion of "stress," stated in almost physiological terms. Stress is a condition that threatens a part or the whole of a social organism with serious damage or even annihilation. When this occurs, and the mechanisms that individuals and the society have devised are no longer able to meet the threat, either what he calls a "revitalization movement" occurs or the society dies. He sees a consecutive process of steady state—crisis—revitalization—steady state, a pattern reminiscent of the oscillation implied by the term *āndolan*. In the Bengali context, the *maṅgals'* reminders of Śītalā's presence might be interpreted as revitalization.

The basic text of Christian millenarian movements is found in *Revelation* 20.4-6:

> Then I saw thrones, and seated on them were those to whom judgment was committed. And I saw the souls of those who had been beheaded for their testimony to Jesus and for the word of God, and who had not worshipped the beast or its image and had not received its mark on their foreheads or their hands. They came to life again, and reigned with Christ a thousand years. The rest of the dead did not come to life again until the thousand years were ended. This is the first resurrection. Blessed and holy is he who shares in the first resurrection! Over such the second death has no power, but they shall be priests of God and of Christ, and they shall reign with him a thousand years.[43]

There are two particularly striking things about the passage. The first is that the Messianic kingdom is to be of limited duration. The second is that it is to be shared only by the martyrs, those relatively few who, presumably, drew the strength for martyrdom from charisma or grace. Both ideas, says von Harnack, come from quite late Jewish apocalyptic literature, neither being mentioned in either the discourses of Jesus or the apostolic epistles.[44] The earlier belief was that the kingdom would not be of fixed duration, and that all believers would be included in the first and only resurrection.

The older belief is much closer to the situation with which we are dealing in Bengal, where a segment of linear time has no meaning except as metaphor or as a way to comprehend particular experience. There is of course some question as to whether the older Jewish forms of the Messianic hope can be called "millennialism" at all, since the term itself refers to the thousand years. But it is also true that the application of the term has been expanded, as Norman Cohn points out, so that it is now "simply a convenient label for a particular type of salvationism."[45]

It is at this point that arguments regarding Buddhist soteriology, the *mokṣa* or *mukti* offered by most Hindu deities (even Śītalā) and gurus, the future avatar of Viṣṇu, and so forth, could be advanced as examples of "Messianism" in Indian culture. Cohn characterizes the ultimate state envisioned by millenarian movements as: 1) collective, to be enjoyed by the faithful as a group; 2) terrestrial, to be realized here and not in an other-worldly heaven; 3) imminent, to come both soon and suddenly; 4) total, in the sense that the transformation of life on earth will be no mere improvement of present conditions, but rather perfection itself; and 5) "accomplished by agencies that are consciously regarded as supernatural."[46] What Śītalā promises in return for recognition and worship fulfills all these conditions.

Yet the impression is strong that what Cohn is describing and what the Śītalā texts suggest are not really the same thing. One simply does not, in Hindu India, have groups of white-robed people standing around on mountaintops awaiting the cataclysm. It may be that Michael Barkum brings us a step closer to the proper position in pointing out that "virtually all cultures turn out on close examination to harbor motifs capable of a place in a new millenarian synthesis."[47] The white-robed cultists represent the flowering of a seed planted by the Apocalypse, a seed of an even older species. The seed nourished by the soil of India is of a different species, though the genus may be the same.

To quote Barkum again:

> Yet relative deprivation, decremental or otherwise, fails to provide a full explanation of millenarianism. As David Aberle notes, "It would seem . . . that a knowledge of the severity and type of deprivation, and of the date and place of its occurrence, would make it possible to predict when, where, and with what ideology a social movement would arise. Such a claim cannot be sustained." Why do some depressed conditions produce volatile political activity, while other circumstances, at least as bleak, yield only political apathy? Why do millenarian movements occur at some times of relative deprivation and not at others: What triggers them, and why does their content depart so significantly from conventional forms of political action? Finally, what explains the bizarre features so often remarked upon in descriptions of millenarian discontent? . . . Millenarian movements, while widespread, are by no means universal, and it remains to separate those relative deprivations that induce millenarianism from those that engender apathy, reform, or unfocussed rioting.[48]

Deprivation, then, engenders either millenarianism or apathy, reform, or unfocussed rioting. It may also, as is clear from the Śītalā texts, engender a religious interpretation that says, "This too is the mercy of the goddess, and her nature."

Barkum does not ignore religious interpretations of disaster. He mentions five of them: 1) as the mark of an evil or angry deity who has not been appeased; 2) as a situation where the universe is a matter of competition between good and evil forces, in which disaster is a sign of at least a temporary victory of evil; 3) as God's punishment on evil people; 4) as God's will, even though the victims are not especially evil; and 5) as a case in which "God is not assessed clear responsibility, nor is man guilty of provoking him. . . . God is seen in a similar role as a physician. He does not assume responsibility for the outbreak of the epidemic, but he deserves the credit for mitigating its worst effects."[49] Although the last of these is not too far from describing the Bengali situation, none of the points precisely recognizes what the Śītalā texts say. She is not evil, though as Mother she may be occasionally angry; nor is there, on the level of the divine, any distinction between good and evil. Her visitations are not "willed," but are manifestations of her *līlā;* God as having a "will" is an anthropomorphism that makes divine action somewhat more comprehensible, while if *līlā* has pattern and structure we mortals are too limited to see it. And Śītalā is certainly responsible for both epidemics and freedom from them. But Barkum goes on:

> Why does disaster have these [i.e., various psychological reactions that go under the rubric of "disaster syndrome"] effects? We normally harbor assumptions concerning the general stability of true society, and the rate at which it can be expected to change. Cultures differ in the matter of size and frequency of incremental change. When changes occur within culturally defined limits, explanations for them come readily to hand. It is a major function of the mazeway to provide these explanations, and the internalized conception of the true society is predicated on the continued existence of limits on change. The disaster syndrome occurs precisely because these limits have been abruptly violated.[50]

The "mazeway" referred to is Wallace's ordering principle in an individual, an individual's "cognitive map," made up of such elements as nature, culture, and society. A society, then, is made up of individuals whose cognitive maps are isomorphic or largely so. When these mazeways overlap, there is inner consistency and correspondence to reality to a high degree. When external threats confront an individual or a society, the mazeways become diffused, and revitalization is necessary or the society dies. The texts of Śītalā, her worship, beliefs concerning her, and knowledge of her presence, constitute such a mazeway. The vital distinction is that an epidemic or the threat of one does not disrupt, but strengthens, this mazeway. Periodic epidemic flare-ups of disease are not unexpected events, but are well within the known and accepted limits of possible change. And an epidemic is not in the last analysis a disaster at all.

The epidemic is thus not a threat to the culture. If anything, it is an affirmation, in the same way in which what Mircea Eliade calls "the periodic retrogression of the cosmos into chaos" [51] is an affirmation: the chaos engendered by reversal enables the society to emerge renewed and refreshed, but not changed. One is almost forced to contrast the reactions of the *maṅgal* poets and their listeners with the unforgettable scenes in Ingmar Bergman's *The Seventh Seal,* in which penitents scourge themselves all the way across Europe, presumably to cause the Almighty to relent. In a recent and perceptive article, Harold Gould has argued that the Sepoy Mutiny was in fact a millenarian movement that failed because of a lack of "institutional precedents for the kind of social structures needed to deal with the adversary at hand."[52] In the case presented to us by the *Śītalā-maṅgals,* the structures are there, and the society is revitalized, though threat and response are enclosed entirely within the system. The goddess is not really an adversary: rather, an unpredictable acquaintance. She is not a threat to, but a part of, the culture. A friend once told me that the proper attitude toward the Goddess is defined best in terms of religious, and social, ritual: "As with any guest, you invite her to your house, even though you hope she will not come. If she does come, you treat her well, mindful of the rules of hospitality and the consequences to those who do not follow them. And she, like any good guest, will not stay too long, nor come again too soon."

Finally, if one considers that the *maṅgals* of the goddess Śītalā are quaint and fanciful, one needs only to read the final lines in Camus' *La Peste* to be brought back to chilling reality:

> Hearing the cries of gaity which rose from the city, Dr. Rieux reminded himself that this gaity has always been menaced. For he knew that this madness in joy was ignorant, and that one could read in the books that the bacillus of the plague did not die nor ever disappear, and that it could remain dormant for dozens of years in furniture and linen, that it would wait

> patiently in bedrooms and cellars, in suitcases and handkerchiefs and waste-paper, and that, perhaps, the day would come when, for the misfortune and instruction of men, the plague would awaken its rats and send them forth to die in a happy city.[53]

Dr. Rieux had the eyes to see.

Comments: The Goddess and The Polarity of The Sacred

RICHARD L. BRUBAKER

One theme appears in all five of these papers, sometimes as a background motif, sometimes dominating the foreground. In David Kinsley's paper it appears as the power of Kālī "either to send one scuttling back to the womb of *dharma* or to provoke one over the threshold to *mokṣa*." In the *Devī-māhātmya* discussed by Thomas Coburn the theme appears similarly in the capacity of the great Goddess to be the source both of *māyā* and its bondage and of the knowledge that sets one free. In the Bengali *maṅgals* described by Edward Dimock it appears as a river linking "the world that follows comprehensible laws" with the realm of divine *līlā* "in which laws are suspended." In Diana Eck's discussion of *the* river, our theme appears in Gaṅgā's opposite relations with Viṣṇu and Śiva: she flows dutifully from Viṣṇu's foot but crashes down upon Śiva's head. And it appears in Wendy O'Flaherty's guide to "the divine consort game" as Pārvatī plays proper devotee to her lord while being in reality the awesome source of all his power.

All these are variations on a single theme, and to identify that theme we may take a clue from Kinsley's title, "Blood and Death Out of Place." "Being in their place," says Lévi-Strauss, "is what makes [things] sacred."[1] And so it does; but so, equally, does being out of place. *Dharma,* for example, is very much a matter of things being in their proper place, whereas *mokṣa* shatters all such fixations. India knows both the sacredness of order and the sacredness that abandons order; in fact she has given extraordinary emphasis to both and hence has a lively sense of their polarity. And it is this polarity that constitutes the theme appearing in various forms in these five papers.

It is important to emphasize the reciprocity between these two visions of sacred reality. To say, with Kinsley, that "Kālī is a goddess who threatens stability and order" is to say that when one emphasizes the sacrality of a well-ordered universe, everything Kālī represents is distressingly and dangerously out of place. But from the perspective of *mokṣa* "Kālī puts the order of *dharma* . . . in its place"—as only half of the way things are. There is more to the reciprocity than this, however. The stronger either side of this polar tension becomes, the greater strength it calls forth on the other side. Thus it is surely true and important to say, as Kinsley does, that Kālī wildly throws around so much blood and death because the dharmic system works so hard to keep them safely in their place. Yet it seems equally true and important to suggest that the system works so hard to keep everything it can under control because India has received such a stunningly clear revelation of the ultimately uncontrollable Śakti.

The same polarity, of course, is reflected in numerous tales of the gods. There is an obvious parallel between the calming, domesticating activities of certain deities toward each other and the effect on human beings of the structuring, refining system of *dharma*. There is likewise a clear relation between deities' inciting of one another and a shattering vision that provokes one, as Kinsley says, "over the threshold to *mokṣa*."

In the *Devī-māhātmya* several changes are rung on the inciting motif. In the process the text clearly presents the phenomenal world (including its dharmic order) in two lights: both as sacred and as ultimately imprisoning. Devī seduces us into delusion, craving, and bondage, just as she seductively provokes the *asuras* Śumbha and Niśumbha to attack her and be killed. The reaction in both cases is divinely incited for the sake of the world, that it may thrive and be perpetuated, being neither abandoned by humans nor devastated by demons. But the world thus valorized by the Goddess is none other than the realm of *saṃsāra*, from whose fertile yet fatal embrace she would also release us. In her hands even the sacred law of this world can be an instrument of our delusion. "[H]uman beings have a craving for offspring,/Out of greed expecting them to reciprocate"[2]: even the dharmic duties to produce children and to perform *śrāddha* rites for parents are revealed to be rooted in egoism and to bear the fruit of bondage.

An even more striking interplay of these opposites emerges from Coburn's discussion of Devī as *yoganidrā*. Here the demon-slaying *śakti* present in Viṣṇu can be activated only when the *śakti* producing his "yogic slumber" withdraws. Yet it is the latter that has enabled him, without his knowledge, to produce the demons in the first place, and that has incited their egocentric desires and powers to the point where they would be killed and from their bodies a world would be fashioned—our sacred world again—whose every inhabitant would be empowered by the *śakti* of bondage *and* the *śakti* of liberation, the Divine playing hide-and-seek with Herself. And with us.

Here the reciprocity is delicately balanced, for it lies in the two hands of the One Devī. Her left hand continually takes away what her right hand puts in place and her right hand continually replaces what her left hand removes. Thus she offers a choice—apparently between opposite visions of the sacred, but ultimately between experiencing them as schizophrenically split and (with the *Devī-māhātmya,* indeed with the Devī herself) rejoicing in their paradoxical oneness.

It is easy to miss that oneness when viewing what O'Flaherty calls "the Indian game of divine sexual politics" (to say nothing of participating in its human counterpart). But that the situation is highly polarized is obvious. The pattern of male dominance and female submission is so much the norm in Hinduism, on both divine and human levels, that it provides a popular model for the proper relations between those two levels. And vice versa: the divine/human hierarchy provides a model for relations between the sexes and thereby sacralizes the male/female hierarchy, among deities as well as humans. Male subordination and female insubordination are decidedly out of place. They are adharmic, and dangerously so. And on precisely this account they may be powerful instruments of *mokṣa.*

As O'Flaherty points out, there is danger in any union between mortal and immortal. There is danger because of the power involved; but there is also power because of the danger. Thus when a devotee relates to a deity in the mode of lover, the very audacity of the act heightens the ecstasy: one could be destroyed but instead is transformed or at least transported. The erotic forms of Krishna *bhakti* are familiar examples, with devotees of either sex identifying with Rādhā. But when, as O'Flaherty says, power flows not only from deity to mortal but at the same time "in the 'perverse' direction, from female to male," it is doubly dangerous. Such power is therefore precisely what the tantric adept (*vīra*) opens himself to in his quest for radical transformation here and now. "The blood-thirsty Devī is not the sort of lady to whom any but the most psychotic masochist would choose to make love"—*or* the most knowing of her children, to whom both terror and illicit eroticism, even incest, by their very power to inhibit, are all the more powerful invitations to liberation.

Śiva is our model here.[3] He is the great yogi, the great knower. And although he knows well how to play supreme lord and master to a

Color Plates

Rajput Paintings of Rādhā and Krishna

The term Rajput painting has two distinct meanings. On the one hand it refers to the patronage and provenance of a group of paintings made primarily for the Hindu patrons—kings, royal families, and courtiers—in the small kingdoms in Rajasthan, central India, and the Punjab Hills from the sixteenth through the nineteenth centuries. On the other hand, the term connotates a definite style. In this context, Rajput painting refers to small album pictures with relatively flat, bold compositions, vivid colors, and symbolic landscapes in which divine and human figures convey the primary meaning of the painting.

Rajputs, "sons of kings," had originally entered India from the northwest in the early centuries of the Christian era and were assimilated in the Hindu social structure as members of the warrior caste. Throughout history they are known for their intense passions, romantic lores, and for their codes of honor and chivalry. As a group, they were chiefly responsible for preserving the Hindu character of Indian society in medieval times when the subcontinent was overrun with frequent attacks by Muslim invaders from the northwest.

In addition to preserving earlier scholarly and artistic traditions in painting, Rajput rulers were responsible for initiating new themes and styles of painting, beginning in the fifteenth century. A variety of factors made the development of this new genre of painting possible. One of the most significant elements was the rise of the devotional cults centering around Krishna in northern India. In fact, although the subject matter of Rajput painting can be divided roughly into three categories—religious, literary, and aristocratic—even the latter two categories are infused with the spirit of the adventures and lives of Krishna. In Rajasthan, the first two groups of paintings predominate in the seventeenth century, whereas the next century is filled with rather decorative paintings of Maharajas in their favorite pastimes, such as boar hunting or playing with the palace ladies. In the Punjab Hills, all three themes seem to be popular from the beginning, in the late seventeenth century, through the decline in the nineteenth century.

The selection that follows focuses on various religious, literary, and human aspects of Krishna and his consort, Rādhā, in Rajput painting. Some of the works illustrate themes from the *Bhāgavata Purāṇa* and can be considered purely religious. Even so, however, they have an earthly vitality and directness of meaning, for they accurately convey the interplay of religious and human elements that is so characteristic of the *bhakti* movement. In other paintings Krishna is portrayed as a royal hero or cosmic lover—a *nāyaka*—the sort of figure one meet in literary and poetic texts such as the *Rasamañjarī*, *Rasika Priyā*, or *Gītagovinda*. It is significant that in both the *Rasikamañjarī* and the *Rasika Priyā*—texts describing various classifications of heroes and heroines—Rādhā plays a variety of roles. Sometimes she is seen as a *svakīyā nāyikā*, a woman who legitimately belongs to her lover and is publicly recognized as such. More frequently, however, she is the *parakīyā nāyikā*, the woman who belongs to another and therefore takes part in a clandestine love. In either case, Rādhā and Krishna are seen as archetypal lovers. They symbolize all aspects of relations between heroes and heroines, between males and females. Some paintings of Rādhā and Krishna add to these universal ideals a particular dimension by injecting depictions of Rajput patrons who wanted to have themselves cast in the role of the ultimate and divine lover, Krishna.

The stylistic variations in Rajput painting are generally attributed to the fact that these works of art were crafted in a variety of regional centers in Rajasthan and the Punjab Hills and are seen against the background of the political and cultural connections that tied a particular Rajput court with the neighboring Mughal power. A more lively sense of the style presented by these paintings, however, can be attained by means of a different classification, one that takes as its point of departure the types of subjects portrayed. When the theme of a given painting was secular, when its purpose was to depict the courtly realities of the Rajput world, the painters tended to adopt a naturalistic treatment of the figures and to use the soft tonalities of the seventeenth-century Mughal palette. If the theme was religious or semi-religious, however, they preferred to follow age-old customs, using unmodulated bright colors, dividing their compositions into distinct compartments, emphasizing the symbolic quality of the narrative, and portraying general types of heroes rather than individual personalities. This traditional Indian preference for the mythical over the historical and for the universal truth over any specific, observable reality makes Rajput painting abstract and conceptual and renders it particularly attractive to modern viewers, for whom just these qualities have a special appeal.

—V.N.D.

In this vivid painting from Bundi, the beloved, decked in the finery of a bride-to-be, squats on a stepped dais (*oṭā*) and converses with her confidante. The halo around her head indicates that she is no anonymous *nāyikā*, but Rādhā herself. It signifies her exaltation with the same subtlety that one finds in the shading that Bundi artists typically applied to the profile, as it is here to hers. The sacred conversation takes place in a bower in which the heroine is effectively framed by a plantain tree whose banana stock is in bloom. The burnt orange skyline ushers in dusk, and the thicketed area is enveloped in the darkness of a *tamāla* tree. This is the tree whose black bark so often suggests the color of the skin of Krishna himself.

As the bereft lady stammers out her longing lamentations, the landscape resonates with gurgling waterfalls: they guide the eye past crystalline rocks toward a misty pool that suggests the heroine's tears. An army of monkeys enlivens the setting with animated chatter, and the sylvan foreground is peopled by a mated pair of white cranes and that ever-present mythical watery creature, the *makara*.

Nothing certain can be said about the identity of the confidante. Perhaps the artist knew her as Lalitā or Viśākhā, or another of the eight *sakhīs* conceived by the Vallabha Sampradāya to have a particularly intimate relation to Rādhā. Perhaps she is one of the greater number Rūpa Gosvāmī names, women who provide such a fitting audience for Rādhā's feelings because they are, theologically, expressions of Rādhā herself. Or perhaps the confidante was as anonymous to the artist as she is to us today.

—J.W.

PLATE 1

Virahitā Nāyikā (The Beloved Waits)
Bundi, Rajasthan, ca. 1750.
(Courtesy, Fogg Art Museum. Private Collection.)

From one of the finest sets of Indian paintings, this *Rasamañjarī* page from Basohli with its dazzling colors and sharp angles beautifully conveys the inherent tension of a clandestine union of lovers. The Takri superscription in the upper border identifies the painting as an illustration of the *upapati nāyaka*. In the verse from Bhānudatta's *Rasamañjarī* (a Sanskrit text written in the late fifteenth century in Orissa) that appears on the back of the painting, the secret loves of an *upapati nāyaka* are described.

> Fear of detection does not permit the eager lovers' gaze to meet. Scared of the jingling sound of the armlets, they desist from embracing. They kiss each other's lips without the contact of their teeth. Their union is hushed too. Such a love is, indeed, void of joy.[1]

The painter successfully conveys the essence of the verse. A slightly asymmetrical placement of the couple in the center of the composition agitates the flat surface and creates a degree of tension. By juxtaposing dark and light expanses of color, the artist keeps Krishna in a strong frontal position while relegating his lady love, with her darker clothes, to a more distant, secondary role. The lovers are not entirely absorbed in one another. They look at one another, but as if in a daze. Their eyes move past one another without establishing contact, and their arms, placed around each other diagonally, add to their air of uncertainty.

Nowhere in the verse is there a reference to Krishna, yet there is no question about the identity of the dark-skinned, lotus-crowned hero in the painting. It is difficult to identify the heroine as Rādhā with the same degree of certainty, since Rādhā has no characteristic iconographic features. But she is not unlikely: Rādhā was indeed someone else's wife, and many Vaiṣṇava texts emphasize the secretive nature of her affair with Krishna, the theme of the *upapati nāyaka* as it is represented here.

Basohli, a small but powerful kingdom in the Punjab Hills, produced a unique style of Indian painting in the late seventeenth century. This page comes from the earliest of three known sets of *Rasamañjarī* paintings from Basohli; on stylistic grounds this set is datable to about A.D. 1660-70.[2] Basohli painting embodies the bright colors and persistent two-dimensionality of earlier Rajasthani painting and integrates these elements with the predilection for meticulous detail and refined line that characterizes the Mughal tradition. This combination makes early Basohli painting unique in the history of Rajput art.

— V.N.D.

---

[1]M.S. Randhawa and S.D. Bambri, "Basohli Paintings of Bhanudatta's Rasamanjari," *Roopa-Lekha* 36 (n.d.), p. 99, verse 105. Randhawa's and Bambri's identification of this painting supersedes that of Coomaraswamy.

[2]Of the 136 verses of the *Ramamañjarī*, only 20 verses allude to divine couples — Rāma-Sītā, Śiva-Pārvatī, or Rādhā-Krishna — in describing the ideal lovers. Krishna and Rādhā appear in only eleven of these 20, yet a majority of the heroes in this set of paintings are clearly identified as Krishna. In subsequent sets of *Rasamañjarī* paintings from Basohli, however, the hero is secular. See W.G. Archer, *Indian Paintings from the Punjab Hills*, vol. 1, London: Sotheby Parke Bernet, 1973, p. 39.

PLATE 2

Upapati Nāyaka (One Who Love's Another's Wife)
A page from the illustrated manuscript of the *Rasamañjarī* of Bhānudatta.
Basohli, Punjab Hills, ca. 1660-1670.
(Courtesy, Museum of Fine Arts, Boston. 17.2781.
Ross-Coomaraswamy Collection.)

The main scene, stretching across the upper register, depicts a familiar moment in which one of Rādhā's confidantes shows Krishna to the door after a rendezvous. Two additions to the central motif, however, make this painting quite individual. One is the inclusion of the flowery Kāma as a visitor to Rādhā's chamber, and the other is the rustic forest scene in the lower register, which provides an unusual juxtaposition to this refined drama of love. These additions are by no means accidental. They draw out suggestions in the verse of Bihārī to which they are appropriate:

> Cuckoo-*ḍākūs* on forest roads, seeing the parted unmindful,
> Continually redden their eyes and raise the cry, "Kill, kill."[1]

The verse gains its force from a pun. The cry "*kuho-kuho*" is that of the red-eyed cuckoo, calling in love to its absent mate. But in Spring, when this scene occurs (as the preceding verse in the *Satsaī* makes clear), the cry of the cuckoo cuts into the newly separated woman's heart with particular force, for Spring (Vasanta) is Kāma's closest associate, his captain-at-arms. To venture into the forest in Spring is especially dangerous business for those whom love has touched.

And so it is: to the *virahiṇī* the calls of the cuckoo announce Kāma's destructive side. The birds seem dacoits (*ḍākū*). They set upon her with frightful red eyes — they will soon lend to hers their color by causing her to weep — and they shout, "Kill, kill!" for Kāma is the great slayer. The *virahiṇī* hears the haunting "cuckoo-cuckoo" (in Braj Bhāṣā "*kuho-kuho*") not just as animal sounds but as words, variants on the root *kuṣ/kukh,* and therefore having to do with killing and destruction. Thus the delicate attack of Love pictured in the upper register seems to her, on parting, armed robbery, and is depicted as such in the lower register. The painting, like the verse, has it both ways.

— J.S.H.

---

[1] *Satsaī* 475 in the *Bihārī-Ratnākar* edition, in *savaiyā* meter, tr. Baron Holland, *The Satsaī of Bihārī,* Ann Arbor: University Microfilms, 1969, p. 163.

PLATE 3

Illustration for a Verse of the *Satsaī* of Bihārī

Mewar, Rajasthan, ca. 1750.

(Courtesy, Fogg Art Museum. 1973.155.

Gift of John Kenneth Galbraith.)

This page comes from the same *Rasamañjarī* series as the *upapati nāyaka,* and here as there the correlation between the poetic spirit and its visual expression is close. Bhānudatta's verse describes the clever deeds of a hero as follows:

> When the lover holds in his hand the golden lime
> fruit, the moon-faced Nayika puts a dot on the sun,
> painted on the wall.[1]

Randhawa and Bambri have suggested a plausible meaning for this seemingly opaque verse. The clever *nāyaka,* Krishna, arrives with a lime fruit — symbolic of a woman's breasts and therefore of the erotic pleasures of the world — and thus proposes a secret tryst. The heroine in turn consents by pointing to a dot on the painted sun, indicating sunset: she will rendezvous after dark. Curiously, there is another white circle with a dark dot near the *nāyaka* that is not explained in the verse. Perhaps the two circles together indicate the sun and moon, but they likely suggest a woman's breasts as well, thereby enhancing the erotic flavor of the picture.

An ingenious sense of composition and color arrangement is evident here. The Basohli painter articulates large rectangular surfaces by juxtaposing pure colors and intricate patterns, and uses the curves of the fluttering scarves and the counter-curves of the moving arms to encourage the eye to travel through the entire composition. Even the gargoyle at the bottom and the palace pavilions at the top help to activate the composition, extending the painting beyond its formal boundary. This is one of the finest achievements of Indian painting: it exhibits a perfect rapport between boldness and delicacy and realizes an exceptional clarity of narrative by means of bright colors, economy of line, and abstract but emotionally charged characters.

— V.N.D.

---

[1]Randhawa and Bambri, "Basohli Paintings," p. 104, verse 112.

PLATE 4

Ceṣṭa Catura Nāyaka (Clever Hero)
A page from the illustrated manuscript of the *Rasamañjarī*.
Basohli, Punjab Hills, ca. 1660-1670.
(Courtesy, Museum of Fine Arts, Boston. 17.2785.
Ross-Coomaraswamy Collection.)

The editors wish to express their gratitude to
the Museum of Fine Arts, Boston,
to the Fogg Art Museum at Harvard University,
and to Professor Stuart Cary Welch
for their kindness in allowing paintings
in their collections
to be reproduced in this volume.

compliant and adoring Pārvatī, he also knows to submit totally to her in her form as Devī. Indeed his submission is far greater than that of dutiful divine wives. Like the deep-sea angler fish, who "atrophies until nothing is left of him but a bag of sexual organs to service the bloated female," he is "the ultimate male consort"—as witness those paintings of him prostrate beneath the awesome Devī's dancing feet, lifeless but for a very lively *liṅga*. A divine wife tenderly massaging her lord's foot may be a satisfying model for human *bhakti;* it is certainly a properly domestic one. The model Śiva offers is rather more radical: the ecstatic death of all that the Goddess does not require.

The foot of the Lord Viṣṇu appears in Eck's paper, in contact with Gaṅgā. And although this is not a massage scene, the import is the same in terms of male dominance. It is exquisitely appropriate that the two great myths of Gaṅgā's descent are such mirror images of each other, and reflect typically opposite roles for Viṣṇu and Śiva in relation to a goddess. Gaṅgā's flowing from Viṣṇu's foot (and again later from Krishna's) can certainly be seen as an image of her subordination to him, whereas we see Śiva humbling himself before her, standing beneath her and offering his matted hair to cushion her crashing descent. And of course the gods' opposite roles reflect the dual nature of the Goddess: she can be, as Eck notes, both the placid consort of Hari and the powerful *śakti* of Śiva.

Śiva as Gaṅgā's cushion is reminiscent of him as Kālī's dance platform. In both cases her wild force falls upon his inert form, for she is Śakti—his and ours. When Kālī dances, Śiva is the one who is energized (as well as crushed) by her; when he breaks Gaṅgā's fall, we are the recipients of this "liquid *śakti*." It is indeed striking, as Eck remarks, that "this river, with such tremendous potential for destruction, is acclaimed in such unambiguous terms" as perfectly "embracing, nourishing, and forgiving. . . ." But this is another way of polarizing the situation, for she is, on the far side of Śiva's restraining locks, simultaneously a violently raging torrent. And, again as Eck points out, Śiva is also the searingly incandescent *liṅga* and Gaṅgā the enveloping waters soothing him and protecting us: each is a vehicle for the other's entrance into our midst. Female or male, God veils God that we may live—then rends the veil for our salvation.

It is well that these papers include one concerned with a goddess closer to village life than to the Sanskrit tradition; for it is not always recognized that these same profound and crucial religious paradoxes are equally manifest at that humbler level, as Dimock eloquently demonstrates in the case of Śītalā.

If Gaṅgā manifests herself in this world as healing, life-giving waters, Śītalā does so as feverish ravaging disease. Yet the mythology of each goddess reveals her reverse side as well, and invites us to see that the two sides are the same. In her upper (celestial) reaches, Gaṅgā has a force that would shatter the earth but for Śiva's gracious intervention, whereas here below it is she who is ever gracious, earth's tenderly nurturing mother. Similarly but in reverse, the river in the Bengali *maṅgals* flows from the familiar and dependable landscape of a world with comprehensible laws into the unworldly sea of marvelous/grotesque divine *līlā*. And in each case it is only our finite perspective that hides the simultaneity of the two kinds of flow, the eternal coincidence of apparent opposites. Similarly with Śītalā herself: freedom from disease is evidence of her power, but so equally is a raging epidemic. As with Viṣṇu's *yoganidrā* and his demon-slaying power, so with Śītalā and the presence and absence of disease: it is the withdrawal of her "negative" *śakti* that activates her "positive" *śakti* and vice versa. Furthermore, what is negative and what is positive depend on one's viewpoint, for affliction by the goddess is a special grace, suffering at her hands a special mercy.

Just as Kālī offers a "more redemptive vision" by "standing outside the dharmic order—indeed threatening it" most horrendously, Śītalā's dread visitations grant that same vision, opened to us "only by what is deviant in ordinary experience." Her devotee welcomes her intense fevers flickering over the flesh as Śiva receives Śakti dancing wildly on his body and the tantric adept glories in the fiercely erotic *līlā* of his divine Mistress. But Śītalā's impact is more "democratically distributed," as Dimock says: one need be neither a deity nor a devotee to stand a good chance of receiving her terrible blessing. And if her transcendent truth has not been appropriated through myth or ritual, one may well come to experience it in the flesh.

Again one is faced with a choice. As with the disease-dousing goddesses so important to the villages of South India (i.e., goddesses who alternately douse the community with an epidemic and douse the flames of the disease),[4] the choice Śītalā offers is not between health and disease, well-being and devastation: these, in Dimock's image, are but swings of the pendulum of time. One's choice is between knowing and failing to know them as "an oscillation [between] implicit [and] epidemic forms of grace" and thus as expressions of a single divine *rasa*.

These five papers add to our knowledge and insight in many other matters as well. But to this respondent, at least, their special value as a group is to show in a great variety of ways Hinduism's genius for heightening the tension between opposite visions of the sacred—stretching the spirit to the point where the tension suddenly snaps and, for an eternal instant, Reality is seen whole, as with divine eyes.

3. CONSORTS

Sītā: Fertility Goddess and *Śakti*

CORNELIA DIMMITT

Sītā in the Vālmīki *Rāmāyaṇa* is usually thought of as a model Hindu wife. Following Rāma into his forest exile, living the life of a forest-dweller without complaint, enduring with fortitude her captivity at the hands of the evil king Rāvaṇa, she appears to exemplify the injunctions of the Hindu civil law codes regarding women, as, for example, the Laws of Manu:[1]

> Though destitute of virtue, or seeking pleasure (elsewhere), or devoid of good qualities, yet a husband must be constantly worshiped as a god by a faithful wife. (5.154) Her father protects (her) in childhood, her husband protects (her) in youth; and her sons protect (her) in old age; a woman is never fit for independence. (9.3)

In the *Rāmāyaṇa,* Sītā repeatedly announces her wifely fidelity, claiming there to be no life for her apart from Rāma, her husband and master. This is why she follows him into exile.[2]

> A wife wins the fate of her husband, and not her own, O bull of a man. Knowing this, I shall live in the forest from now on. Here and hereafter there is only a single goal for a woman: her lord, and not her father, her child, herself, her mother nor her friends. . . . O take me with you, noble husband! Do as I ask, for my heart is devoted only to you. If you leave without me, I shall die! (2.24.3, 4, 18; Sh. 2.27)

Yet there is evidence that Sītā's character possesses another, more profound dimension; a deeper study of Sītā in the *Rāmāyaṇa* yields another picture of her from that of the dutiful wife. She can be seen to display the qualities of a goddess in two different modes: as mistress of the plants and animals she is intimately related to the fertility of the earth, and as *śakti,* the energy that inspires the hero Rāma to action, she is the source of his power as king. Two sorts of evidence can be found to support this view: the testimony of Vedic literature and the contents of the *Rāmāyaṇa* itself.

Goddess of Fertility

Sītā makes her appearance in Vedic literature as a fertility goddess of the fields, worshipped by farmers (literally, "ploughmen," *kṛṣaka*). This theme was evidently borrowed intentionally by Vālmīki, for in the epic Sītā is born from a fresh furrow while her adoptive father Janaka is ploughing in the field. She says of her own origins:[3]

> Truly, when [Janaka] was ploughing a round field (for the sacrifice), I appeared, splitting the earth, as the daughter of the king. While that lord of men was distributing handfuls of soil, he saw my body all covered with dirt and was amazed. Having no children himself, he put me affectionately on his lap and said, overwhelmed with love for me, "this is my child!" (2.110.27-29; Sh. 2.118)

Sītā literally means "furrow," as in a ploughed field, or the parting of the hair on the head; it also implies the female vaginal furrow as the source of life. A hymn to Kṣetrapati (the "lord of the fields") in the Rig Veda is the earliest mention of Sītā; here she is simply the earth's furrow, propitiated for her potential fruitfulness:[4]

> Auspicious Sītā, come thou near:
> we venerate and worship thee
> That thou mayst bless and prosper us
> and bring us fruits abundantly.
>
> May Indra press the furrow down,
> may Pūshan guide its course aright.
> May she, as rich in milk, be drained for us
> through each succeeding year. (R.V. 4.57.6, 7)

Three hymns to Sītā, one in the *Kauśika Sūtra,* one in the *Parāskara Sūtra,* and one in the *Harivaṃśa,* show that she was worshipped as a goddess, the furrow personified. In the *Kauśika Sūtra,* Sītā is called "wife of Parjanya, god of rain" and "mother of gods, mortals and creatures," and she is invoked for produce:[5]

You are intelligence; you are growth;
Among the Prajāpatis, you are increase!
Desiring prosperity for myself, I cry out 'Svāhā'!

The *Parāskara Sūtra* describes an offering made to Sītā in the sacrificial fire, accompanied by *darbha* grass and *ghī.* First "Indra, slayer of Vṛtra" is summoned and then Sītā, designated "wife of Indra," is called; after this, cooked rice and barley are offered to the pair, to the accompaniment of *mantras*.[6]

In the *Harivaṃśa* a goddess is hymned at length under a variety of names and personalities, both horrific and beneficent, of which Sītā is only one. This goddess is called Āryā, Nārāyaṇī, Kātyāyanī, Success, Fortune, Wealth, and Prosperity; also Sāvitrī, Rohiṇī, and Sarasvatī, as well as Death, mistress of the *bhūtas* and the goddess of ascetics. The abode of the goddess is said to be mountain caves and forests; she is attended by wild barbarians and by cocks, goats, bees, lions, and tigers. Finally, she is sought for protection in battle, in the presence of thieves, in the wilderness, and in all life's dangers.[7] It is evident that the goddess of this hymn is an amalgamation of a number of deities and that she is more comprehensive in personality than the Sītā of the Rig Veda and the Sūtras. But Sītā as the deity of farmers is included as one aspect of the composite goddess depicted in this hymn:

O goddess, you are the altar's center in the sacrifice,
The priest's fee,
Sītā to those who hold the plough,
And Earth to all living beings. (*Harivaṃśa* 2.3.14)

No doubt Vālmīki chose his heroine Sītā for her divine qualities; by giving her a chthonic origin rather than a human birth he clearly emphasizes this dimension of her nature.[8] But there is a second mode to Sītā's personality that also finds its origin in Vedic thought: the kidnapped bride whose feminine powers include fertility.

Indra's mighty feat, retold frequently in the hymns of the Rig Veda, is to slay the demon Vṛtra, the "encloser" or "container" who withholds the sources of life from humanity. These sources of life include water from rains and rivers, cows, the sun, and even the land itself—all elements necessary to the prosperity of the Aryans as they encountered and eventually dominated the indigenous agricultural peoples who were settled along the Indus River in northwest India, from about 1500 B.C.E. Thus Indra as both god of the thunderstorm and culture hero defeats Vṛtra to release all the goods from the confining clutches of the enclosing demon:[9]

I will declare the manly deeds of Indra,
the first that he achieved, the Thunder-wielder.
He slew the Dragon [Vṛtra], then disclosed the waters,
and cleft the channels of the mountain torrents.

He slew the Dragon lying on the mountains:
his heavenly bolt of thunder Tvaṣṭar fashioned.
Like lowing kine in rapid flow descending
the waters glided downward to the ocean.

Guarded by Ahi stood the thralls of Dāsas,
the waters stayed like kine held by the robber.
But he, when he had smitten Vṛtra, opened the cave
wherein the floods had been imprisoned. (R.V. 1.32.1, 2, 11)

Clearly Indra's act effects both the fertility of the land via riverine floods and the prosperity of the people via cattle, the means of their livelihood.

This same theme is more clearly specified in the story of Saramā and the *paṇis*, who have stolen the cattle and concealed them in a cave. The bitch Saramā, as a messenger of Indra, finds them after making her way "o'er Rāsa's waters" so that Indra may release them from their prison, by battle.[10] The feats performed by Indra as culture hero of the Aryan people form a metaphorical parallel to the Vedic sacrifice itself. Just as Indra destroys his enemies in battle, so are the offerings destroyed on the altar by fire; both Indra's exploits and the Vedic sacrifice are, in the end, creative acts.

Indra, as the thunderstorm personified, is a masculine fertility deity of the Aryan people, who fructifies earth with floods of water. As such his function is closely related to that of the deity Parjanya, the rain-cloud, whose main activity is to pour down the rain that nourishes vegetation by impregnating earth:

Forth burst the winds, down come the lightning flashes:
the plants shoot up, the realm of light is streaming.
Food springs abundant for all living creatures,
what time Parjanya quickens earth with moisture.
(R.V.5.83.4)

Sītā, on the other hand, is the feminine productive furrow thus fertilized. In the *Kauśika Sūtra* she is propitiated as the "wife of Parjanya, god of rain," and in the *Parāskara Sūtra*, as the "wife of Indra," there called the "slayer of Vṛtra." Two modes of fertilizing power are united in these passages in a sexual metaphor: the male thunderstorm mates with the female earth; Indra/Parjanya, god of rain, unites with Sītā, goddess of the furrow.

These Vedic themes related to Sītā appear in attenuated form in the *Rāmāyaṇa* itself, where in a variety of ways the hero Rāma is associated with Indra, the demon Rāvaṇa with Vṛtra, and Sītā with the powers of fertility and prosperity that are withheld from earth for the duration of her captivity in Laṅkā. First, Sītā shows many characteristics of a goddess who is intimately related to the fertility of the earth. She is called *ayonijā,* born without benefit of a human womb (*yoni*), for she springs directly from the ground while her father is ploughing land for the sacrifice. And at the end of the epic she does not actually die, but she reenters the earth on a throne sent up from the netherworld by her mother, Mādhavī Dharaṇī, "Earth, the Upholder" (7.88; Sh. 7.97). Throughout the epic, nature consistently echoes Sītā's actions and moods as if she were the divine mistress of the plants and animals.[11] For example, when she leaves Ayodhyā, along with Rāma and Lakṣmaṇa, all of nature is disordered.[12]

> No sacred fires were ordered; the sun was hidden; elephants spat out their food and cows refused to suckle their calves. Constellations dimmed; planets lost their luster and, leaving their customary paths, stood in the sky shrouded in mist. . . . Crushed by the burden of fear, earth quaked violently while herds of elephants, warriors and horses roared aloud.
> (2.36.9, 11, 17b; Sh. 2.41)

When Rāvana kidnaps Sītā, nature again responds:

> Struck by the rising wind, trees filled with flocks of birds of different kinds tossed their tops as if to say, "Fear not!" Ponds with blown lotuses, with waterfowl and quivering fish mourned for Maithilī as for a joyless friend. Gathering together from all sides, lions, tigers, deer and birds, running after in fury, followed Sītā's shadow. (50.32-35; Sh. 3.52)

And when Sītā returns to mother Earth in the end, the narrator says that "a mighty tremor passed through the entire earth" (7.88; Sh. 7.97).

Sītā is intimately related both to the trees and plants and to the forest animals; they protect and help her in the forest, which she finds a congenial, not a terrifying place to live:

> Just as Sītā used to delight in going through the city parks, so is she now content in the forest solitude. The virtuous Sītā, her face like the new moon, plays in the lonely forest like a child, where Rāma is, her heart filled with joy.
>
> 2.54.9, 10; Sh. 2.60)

At the departure of the couple from Ayodhyā, "the city seems like a forest of leafless trees that are lamenting as if abandoned by their lovers" (2.65.19; Sh. 2.71). They do the same when she is kidnapped from the mountain hermitage at Pañcavaṭī in the Daṇḍaka forest:

> When [Rāma] saw his leaf-hut empty and desolate, the trees nearby that seemed to be weeping, the melancholy birds, miserable deer and faded flowers, deserted by his beloved and abandoned by the forest spirits . . . he cried out, lamenting bitterly, over and over again. (3.58.6, 7; Sh. 3.60)

In fact, like many other heroes and heroines of Indian literature in similar circumstances, Rāma cries out to a whole series of trees, each one by name, asking them where Sītā has gone; getting no answer, he asks the wild beasts in turn, also to no avail. Previous to this, during their travels through the forest, Sītā made a sacrificial offering under a "green-leafed Nyagrodha tree," where all the growing plants were brought for her inspection, as if she were truly the mistress of vegetation (2.49; Sh. 2.55).

While Sītā and Rāma are absent from Ayodhyā, the city appears to be in a state of suspended animation. Bharata, as ruler, lives an ascetic life while the prosperity of the realm is in abeyance. Wherever Sītā appears, however, flowers abound. At her wedding, there are flowering branches and showers of flowers (1.72; Sh. 1.73). In the Citrakūṭa mountains and along the Godāvarī River where she and Rāma camp, blossoming trees abound (2.50 and 3.14; Sh. 2.56 and 3.14). Even the Aśoka grove where she is held captive by Rāvaṇa at his palace in Laṅkā is full of blooming trees (5.16; Sh. 5.18). And when Sītā is rescued and her exile over, on the return road to Ayodhyā trees blossom and flower out of season:

> Fruitless trees became fruitful; trees without flowers abounded in blossoms; those that were withered sprouted leaves, and the foliage dripped honey. (6.112; Sh. 6.126)

In all these ways Sītā appears to be the mistress of the plants and trees. This is poetically suggested by the sorrowing Rāma who in her absence even likens her body to a plant:[13]

> O thou, whose youthful flowering is more graceful than the Ashoka branches, do not conceal thyself and increase my pain! O Darling! thy thighs resemble the plaintain boughs which conceal thee, yet, O goddess, thou canst not hide from me! . . . Return, O Large-eyed Damsel, thy hut is desolate!
> (Sh. 3.62)

Sītā is also mistress of the animals, who like the trees and plants echo her moods, but in addition come actively to her aid. When she and Rāma leave Ayodhyā, elephants and cows neglect their functions (2.36; Sh. 2.41; see also above). At her kidnapping, lions and tigers follow her shadow (3.50; Sh. 3.52; see also above). Jaṭāyu, the vulture, becomes her particular guardian and even gives up his own life in an attempt to save her from capture (3.14; Sh. 3.14). Deer give the clue to Rāma and Lakṣmaṇa by turning their heads in her direction, to the south, as if pointing the way (3.60; Sh. 3.64), and a cawing crow portends the reunion of Rāma and Sītā, showing Rāma and Lakṣmaṇa that they are on the right path (4.1; Sh. 4.1). Finally, the army that eventually rescues Sītā consists mostly of monkeys and bears. And it is the loyal monkey Hanumān who discovers her in the Aśoka grove where she is held captive, and who leads Rāma to her hiding place, aided by Sampāti, the vulture brother of Jaṭāyu.

Thus in a variety of ways is the career of Sītā in the *Rāmāyaṇa* closely tied to nature. Her birth, death, and the events of her life suggest her role as goddess, in particular as the mistress of plants and animals and source of the fertility of the earth. This dimension of her character is emphasized in a different way in Books 1 and 7 (possibly later additions to Vālmīki's original version), where Sīta is implicitly identified as the wife of lord Viṣṇu, Śrī or Lakṣmī, who is the official patroness of good fortune and prosperity in later Hindu tradition.

The second mode of Sītā as a goddess in the *Rāmāyaṇa* can be seen in her role as the kidnapped bride whose sojourn in the stronghold of Laṅkā may be likened to the entrapment of the life-giving cows in the cave by the *paṇis* in the Rig Veda, and to the containment of the waters by Vṛtra, the creature of drought. This analogy would liken Sītā to the cattle and the waters, both sources of life in the Rig Veda; these fertile powers are symbolized in feminine terms in the epic in the person of

Sītā. There is in fact clear evidence that Vālmīki used the Indra-Vṛtra theme intentionally with this metaphor in mind.

Rāma is frequently likened to Indra in his capacity as a hero, especially in the battle scenes where he finally destroys the demon king Rāvaṇa. Their struggle is likened to "the contest between Vṛtra and Vāsava (Indra)" (6.86; Sh. 6.100). And when Rāvaṇa dies, he falls "from his chariot like Vṛtra felled by Indra's thunderbolt" (6.97; Sh. 6.110). A double of this theme is found in the simultaneous contest between Lakṣmaṇa and Rāvaṇa's son Indrajit, "conqueror of Indra." The battle between Rāma and Rāvaṇa is punctuated by Vedic elements: Indra lends Rāma his chariot for the fight; Hanumān, Rāma's servant and loyal follower, is the son of Vāyu, the wind, and is usually nicknamed Maruti, a designation reminiscent of Indra's company of attendants, the Maruts, or storm winds. Rāma defeats Rāvaṇa attended by the Vedic deities Vāyu, Sūrya, and Agni; his Brahmaśiras weapon was "created long ago by Brahmā for Indra. . . . The Wind stood in its wings, and in its tip, the Fire and Sun" (6.97; Sh. 6.110). Loosed to the accompaniment of Vedic *mantras* and composed of Vedic deities, its force is irresistible; by it Rāvaṇa is slain at last. Thus Rāma kills Rāvaṇa as Indra slew Vṛtra, and for the same purpose: to release the obstructed powers of fertility and prosperity for his people.

Sītā appears to embody those powers of fertility and prosperity that are withheld from earth, for as long as she is held prisoner in Laṅkā, Ayodhyā remains in a state of suspended animation, and the plants and animals refuse to perform their usual functions. Rāvaṇa, as the kidnapper, plays a role in the epic similar to that of Vṛtra, the "encloser" in the Rig Veda: he has obstructed the growth processes of nature by confining their source, the goddess Sītā, in his palace, where she refuses to consent to sexual relations with him. This theme of enclosure is evident in the descriptions of Laṅkā as an impenetrable fortress where Sītā's beauty fades, out of misery, while she is held captive:

> The vast golden walls [of Laṅkā], studded on the inside with jewels, coral, cat's-eye gems and pearls, are impregnable to attack. There are deep and forbidding moats on all sides, of magnificant proportions, filled with crocodiles and inhabited by fish. At the gateways four bridges extend across [the moat] equipped with rows of huge war machines set side by side. The bridges form a defense against the approach of enemies who are scattered by these weapons into the ditches on all sides. . . . With its four-fold defenses—rivers, mountains, forests and man-

> made walls—Laṅkā is a formidable fortress, inaccessible even to the gods. (6.3.13-16, 19; Sh. 6.3)

Furthermore, Rāvaṇa threatens to eat her up if she will not yield sexually to him; at this she threatens suicide (5.20 and 24; Sh. 5.22 and 26). That her death would mean the end of the world is echoed in Rāma's expressions of despair at the thought of her loss. When he discovers that Sītā has been kidnapped, he cries out that he cannot live without her, and further, that he will annihilate the universe if she does not return:

> If the gods do not bring Sītā back to me in full health, then, son of Sumitrā, they shall see my power! . . . Neither gods, nor demons, nor Piśācas, nor Rākṣasas shall survive my fury when I annihilate the three worlds. . . . If they fail to restore my beloved and blameless Sītā to me, I shall topple the entire earth with its mountains, gods, Gandharvas, human beings and Snakes! (3.60.44, 49, 52; Sh. 3.60)

The threat that the demonic powers that impede fertility, growth, and prosperity will prevail motivates the entire story of Sītā's capture and imprisonment, as it also motivates the myth of Indra in the Rig Veda. In the epic this fact is made plain not only in Rāvaṇa's threat to consume Sītā, but also in the character of the demon brother of Rāvaṇa, Kumbhakarṇa ("Pot-Ear"), whose voracious appetite continually threatens the universe. In fact, he sleeps six months and awakens only for a single day to eat, lest, presumably, he consume the three worlds entirely in his greed (6.49; Sh. 6.61). This is the nature of the demons' threat in the Rig Veda, in the *Rāmāyaṇa,* and in the Purāṇas as well: that they will obstruct the powers of fertility, growth, and prosperity on the earth and so prevent the universe from fulfilling its natural course. Indra's feat as fertility god is to thwart the powers of drought embodied in Vṛtra; Rāma's feat as hero is to rescue Sītā and thwart the demon Rāvaṇa; the continuing battle between gods and demons in the Purāṇas, in which the great gods Viṣṇu and Śiva periodically intervene on the side of the lesser gods, has the same theme and purpose: the restoration and preservation of the powers of fertility and growth from the threat of sterility and death.[14]

Sītā as Śakti

In the *Rāmāyaṇa,* however, it is not only Rāma who acts, as the hero, to restore and maintain the powers of fertility, but it is Sītā, as a goddess in the mode of *śakti,* "energy," who actually instigates the action herself, forcing the hero again and again to acts of heroism. Without Sītā there would be no story, not simply because she is a passive victim requiring rescue, but rather because she is instrumental throughout the epic in making the critical events of the story occur. First, it is she who insists on going into the forest with Rāma by protesting vociferously against his decision to leave her behind, supposedly for her own good:

> O Rāma, what need have I of anyone but you? You shall protect me in the forest where I will be happy eating fruits and roots. Surely I will be no trouble to you at all. . . . I shall go to the impenetrable forest full of deer and wild monkeys, where I shall live as happily as in my father's house, devoted to your feet. Take me along, noble lord, for my heart is given only to you. I am resolved to die if you leave me! Grant my request, for I shall not be a burden to you. (24.11, 12, 17, 18; Sh. 2.27)

Ostensibly Sītā is behaving like a loyal and devoted wife; actually she is insisting on her rights to be protected and cared for by her husband: she is forcing him to do his duty.[15]

Second, Sītā insists on possessing the illusory golden deer sent by Rāvaṇa to trick Rāma. In fact, Rāvaṇa plays this trick only because he knows that "Rāma will not survive without Sītā" (3.29; Sh. 3.31). Not only does she send Rāma after the deer, but when Rāma's voice is heard crying for help, she mercilessly taunts Lakṣmaṇa, who has remained behind to protect her, in order to force him to leave her unguarded:

> You only pretend to be your brother's friend, son of Sumitrā, while you are full of hatred for him. As long as I stay here you refuse to help your brother. O Lakṣmaṇa, you want Rāma dead because of me! (3.5b, 6; Sh. 3.45)

It is clear that without her complicity, no kidnapping could have occurred. It is because of her own actions that Sītā finds herself alone, unguarded in the forest, ripe for capture by the wicked Rāvaṇa.

And finally, when Hanumān discovers her in the Aśoka grove on Laṅkā, he offers to rescue her then and there with his magical powers. Ostensibly disdaining to be touched by anyone other than her husband

Rāma, she refuses to be rescued by the servant monkey. Actually she is compelling Rāma to be a hero by insisting that he alone must save her. She replies to Hanumān:

> I cannot go with you, enemy-destroyer. . . . For even if you are willing and able to kill all the *rākṣasas,* if you destroy the demons, Rāghava's glory will be diminished. . . . So there is no point in rescuing me by yourself. But if Rāma comes with you, his glory will increase! (5.35.48a, 57, 59; Sh. 5.37)

> When you deliver my message to Rāghava, that brave man will be compelled by law to do this heroic duty. (5.37.11; Sh. 5.39)

Thus does Sītā, as Rāma's *śakti,* his motivating power, actually move the story forward by her actions. Not the passive victim she appears to be at first, Sītā is rather the subtle *provocatrice* whose actions inspire the heroism of her spouse.

The *śakti* theme is interestingly echoed in the critical actions of two other females in the story, both of whom are also indispensable to the plot: Kaikeyī, king Daśaratha's wife, and Śūrpaṇakhā, king Rāvaṇa's sister. Kaikeyī's selfishness in wanting her son to be on the throne of Ayodhyā starts the whole story moving when she insists on the banishment of Rāma, an event that leads to Sītā's kidnapping and eventual rescue. Śūrpaṇakhā, however, is also necessary to the plot, for it is because of her sexual advances toward Rāma, another instance of unbridled desire, that Lakṣmaṇa cuts off her ears and nose in the forest (3.17; Sh. 3.18). Because of this mutilation she demands that Rāvaṇa avenge her. The demon's kidnapping of Sītā, then, is due not simply to his inordinate lust for fresh women, but it is rather an act of revenge on Rāma for the harm done his sister. As Kaikeyī prods Daśaratha to put her son on the throne, and as Sītā persuades Rāma first to take her to the forest with him and then to chase the golden deer, so does Śūrpaṇakhā needle Rāvaṇa into an action he otherwise would not have taken. Thus do all three females energize their men. They are *śakti* figures, and together they provide the motivations central to the epic's plot.

A final way in which Sītā can be seen to be Rāma's *śakti,* his very strength, is as his virtuous wife whose chastity or fidelity is the source of his royal power as king. Ayodhyā suffers a power vacuum while the pair is in exile. Bharata, Rāma's brother, simply refuses actively to rule; he puts Rāma's sandals on the throne in his stead and lives an ascetic life. This appears to be a symbolic gesture on Bharata's part, showing that the prosperity of the kingdom is in a state of suspension during the absence of the rightful royal couple. That Rāma and Sītā are to be regarded as one being, her virtue the source of his power, is suggested in the epithets applied to Sītā throughout the epic: *ardhāṅginī,* the "half-body (of her husband)," and *pativratā,* "devoted to her lord." This theme is also revealed in the language with which Sītā refuses the advances of Rāvaṇa, in which she asserts her own virtue and her unswerving loyalty to Rāma:

> I cannot be seduced by wealth or glory. I belong only to Rāghava as light belongs to the sun. After having leaned on the honored arm of that world-protector, how could I ever turn to anyone else? I am the proper wife of the lord of the earth; I belong to him as the law belongs to a self-aware brahmin who has faithfully kept his vows. (5.19.14-16; Sh. 5.21)

The power of her chastity while in captivity, proof of her fidelity to Rāma, is similar to the power of *tapas* won by the celibate seer. This is the source of the power by which Sītā compels Rāma to rescue her.[16]

That Rāma's right and power to rule are dependent on Sītā's virtue is made abundantly clear during the fire-ordeal in Book 6 (and its double in Book 7), where Rāma is reunited with Sītā at last, only to repudiate her because of the suspicion that she has lost her virtue at the hands of her abductor:

> I have done all that a man must do, O Sītā, to wash you clean of this outrage; you have been redeemed from the impatient clutches of the enemy! . . . Now, however, your reputation is in doubt and your presence hurts me as lamp-light offends a man with eye-disease. . . . What noble man born in a good family, even with his heart torn by affection, would take back a woman who had lived as the wife of another man? You were seen fleeing from the lap of Rāvaṇa as he looked lustfully at you. How could I take you back again without falsely representing my great lineage? I have accomplished the purpose for which I rescued you—my own glory. Now I no longer have any attachment to you, so go wherever you desire!
>
> (6.103.13, 17, 19-21; Sh. 6.117)

But Sītā announces the abiding purity of her intentions by a truth-vow, and steps into a funeral pyre to prove her virtue. Because of the truth of her claim, the god Fire refuses to burn her, and Rāma accepts this as proof of her fidelity to him, as much to convince the gossiping populace as to convince himself. But it appears that he regards her presence as indispensable to him: "Sītā is to me what light is to the sun. Before the three worlds, Janaka's daughter Maithilī is pure; therefore I can no more forsake her than an honorable man can renounce his honor" (6.106.17b, 18; Sh. 6.120). After the ordeal, Sītā is likened to *ghī* poured into the sacrificial fire, whose purity occasions both the prosperity of the earth in general and that of the kingdom of Ayodhyā in particular. Rāma fully accepts his wife, half of himself, and the happy couple rule over Ayodhyā for ten thousand years.[17]

The ensuing reign of Rāma and Sītā is described as a perfect kingdom, a kind of paradise on earth. The rescue of Sītā has resulted in the restoration of earth's fertility and the reestablishment of an idyllic kingdom in Ayodhyā where prosperity and happiness abound for everyone:

> At the coronation of the worthy and glorious Rāma gods and *gandharvas* sang and troops of *apsarases* danced. Earth was filled with grain, trees with fruit, and flowers with sweet perfume at Rāghava's celebration. (6.116.62, 63; Sh. 6.130)

And thereafter, for the duration of Rāma's reign:

> While Rāma ruled his kingdom, men lived a thousand years and sired a thousand sons. Tall trees bore flowers and fruit without ceasing, Parjanya rained in due season, and Maruta blew sweet breezes. All did their own work; persons were contented with their lot. All creatures were filled with *dharma* and no one was unlawful when Rāma reigned. Everyone was steadfast in the pursuit of *dharma* while Rāma ruled his kingdom for ten thousand years. (6.116.87-90; Sh. 6.130)

Sītā, as fertility goddess and *śakti,* rescued and protected by the hero Rāma, contributes her divine powers to his realm as his devoted consort, wife, and other half. The source of this fertility theme exemplified by Sītā in the epic is to be found in Vedic literature, for it appears that the author consciously appropriated certain Vedic motifs for his purposes. Yet he greatly expanded this theme, working what was a sacrificial motif into the central strands of the epic drama. And within the epic there occurs a further amplification of the two main characters themselves, Rāma and Sītā, for in the (possibly later) first and last books of the epic, the two are identified with the great deities of the Hindu tradition, Viṣṇu and Śrī or Lakṣmī, the god who "preserves" the universe and his consort, the goddess of wealth and prosperity.

Thus, Sītā, who in one dimension is the dutiful and obedient wife of Rāma, may also be viewed as a goddess whose power is the source of earth's fertility, and as the *śakti* of the hero Rāma whose energy motivates him to perform feats of heroism and whose fidelity underlies the strength and enduring qualities of his reign as king. United with the hero/god, Sītā is the source and support of the continuing prosperity of the world, as symbolized in the extraordinary qualities of the rule of Rāma, his divine ten-thousand-year reign.

The Goddess Śrī: Blossoming Lotus and Breast Jewel of Viṣṇu

VASUDHA NARAYANAN

Among the devotees of Viṣṇu in South India the most influential group historically and theologically speaking have been the Śrī Vaiṣṇavas. This community crystallized in the generations immediately following the eleventh-century preceptor Rāmānuja and looked to both Sanskrit scripture and the songs of the Tamil mystics (*āḻvārs*) for the basis of its theology. Its name is significant, for it contains not only that of Viṣṇu, the masculine God, but also that of His consort, Śrī. Śrī Vaiṣṇavas distinguish themselves from other Vaiṣṇava groups by insisting on the importance of the intimate tie between these two for the life of faith and the logic of salvation: without Śrī there is no deliverance. They differ among themselves, however, in the way in which they construe this relation. In what follows, I would like to present principal contours in the conception of Śrī held by Vedānta Deśika, the theologian of the late thirteenth century whose views are representative of that portion of the Śrī Vaiṣṇava community who call themselves Vaṭakalais.

For Deśika, Śrī is the great mediator between God and the human soul. She has her own particular nature, distinguishable from that of Viṣṇu, for she is auspiciousness itself; yet at the same time she is inseparably bound to Him. Deśika discerns that Śrī's uniquely salvific power has to do with the concomitance of these two roles: a certain distinctness and a distinct inseparability. As we shall see, these two roles are symbolized by Śrī's associations on the one hand with the lotus and on the other with the breast of Viṣṇu.

In sculpture and verse, Śrī is pictured as seated on a lotus or on the breast of Viṣṇu. For instance, in a verse recited every day by Śrī Vaiṣṇavas, Viṣṇu is spoken of as one from "whose breast the lady of the blossoming lotus is inseparable."[1] But it is primarily Śrī's role as the mother and mediator that preoccupies Deśika, and we shall focus on these aspects first.

Śrī as the Mediator

Listen to the following verses of Deśika:

> O incomparably glorious Śrī, who grants auspiciousness to everything that is auspicious! You grace the breast of Viṣṇu with your radiance, . . . you are the protector of those who seek your refuge, . . . and I, who am without any other refuge, now surrender myself to you. . . .
>
> O Mother who resides on the lotus, hearken to my plea! I babble like a child; with your grace (*prasāda*) make the Lord who is your beloved listen to my [petition]. . . .[2]

Śrī is mother, just as Viṣṇu is father, a point that Deśika often makes: "O Goddess, You are my mother; the Lord with auspicious qualities is my father!"[3] In the Indian family it is the special province of the mother to be gracious, to forgive. When human devotees stray from the right path, then, Śrī's role becomes crucial. She is the one who can mediate between the errant child and the just father.

Viṣṇu too is innately gracious, but his is an initial, prevenient grace, which Deśika designates with the name *kṛpā*. It is a grace common to all human beings: that in human nature which enables each of them to seek refuge with Viṣṇu and thus become his devotee. There is also, however, a further and more specific grace, which Deśika designates as *prasāda*. *Prasāda* is saving grace, that action of divine self-extension which permits an individual to be released (*mokṣa*) from the confining conditions of humanity. Out of considerations of justice—an aspect of life of which it is a father's duty to be aware—Viṣṇu cannot offer this act of generosity indiscriminately: there has been too much wrong-doing in the world. For him *kṛpā* and *prasāda* are distinct, and justice prevents the latter from being a reflex of the former. As a father may wish he had some pretext for ignoring the misdeeds of his children, so Viṣṇu longs for a pretext to ignore human infractions of the divine order; but without some excuse, even the least sign of faith, he cannot rightly act.[4]

A mother's nature, however, is different from a father's. In a family it is often she who mediates between the children and the father, and the reason is that she is not so firmly bound by considerations of justice and order. Deśika expresses this fact in relation to Śrī, the archetypal case, by saying that in her nature there is no distinction between *kṛpā* and *prasāda*:[5] she is always, pervasively, immediately gracious, always ready to save. The Lord relents if he is solicited for help; with a prayer his *prasāda* is available. But Śrī forgives voluntarily; she needs no reason to forgive. Hence Śrī becomes the first and primary refuge of all who err: not only is it preferable to turn to her, it is necessary. As Deśika says, quoting Śaunaka,

> The person who craves to reach the Lord should, out of necessity, seek the protection of Lakṣmī [i.e., Śrī]. It does not suffice to seek refuge with the Lord. . . .[6]

For she is that aspect of the Godhead that forgives necessarily, whose essence is unqualified grace.

Deśika expresses this fact in several ways. He calls Śrī simply the most compassionate one: *kāruṇyasīma,* the ultimate in compassion.[7] He says that she is the very personification of grace, *anugrahamayī,* using yet another Sanskrit term for grace (*anugraha*) to do so. He goes on to say that she does not even know what punishment is (*nityam ajñātanigraham*).[8] While commenting on a verse of Ramanuja's predecessor Yāmuna, he says that he is surrendering himself to Śrī because she is possessed of compassion, mercy, and maternal affection (*dayā, karuṇā, vātsalya*).[9] Elsewhere he remarks that along with the innumerable auspicious qualities that attend her there is a dominant extra one, accessibility.[10]

The importance of all this for the devotee becomes clear in Deśika's *Cillarai Rahasyaṅkaḷ* ("Minor Secrets"):

> The mother (Tamil: *piraṭṭi*) who is the owner (*śeṣī*) of all except the Supreme Owner (*sarvaśeṣī*), whose nature is such that her grace is unmixed with any anger and is showered on all, does not spare any effort to make the punishing Lord be pleased with those who have committed several faults. She cools the heat of His anger, which arises because He is the father. Bhaṭṭar said, "O Mother! When your Lord gets angry with a man as a father does with his son, you ask, 'What is this? Who is not at fault in this world?' and make Him forget the offences; . . . therefore you are indeed my mother!" Thus she unites [the individual] with His auspicious feet and brings the Lord to the state of saying [as Periyāḻvār put it], "Even if the Lady of the lotus [i.e., Śrī] finds fault with the devotee, I would say that My devotee does no wrong; why, if he does, then *that* act would be right. . . ." We pray to her to be the mediator, for the Lord punishes. . . .[11]

Śrī, by contrast, never punishes.[12] Deśika underscores this point in his writings by frequent references to Śrī's incarnation as Sītā, for in the narrative of the *Rāmāyaṇa* one is made pointedly aware that Sītā was ready to forgive even those who would harm her. He recalls several times that Trijaṭā could confidently encourage the demonesses who had frightened Sītā, saying that they had but to bow down to her and she would protect them from Hanumān's just revenge.[13] He also quotes a verse of Parāśara Bhaṭṭar, a younger contemporary of Rāmānuja; this verse is in the form of a prayer to Sītā:

> O Mother Maithilī! Even while the demonesses were harming you, you saved them from the wrath of Hanumān. Because [of this act] Rāma's side seems small (*laghu*), for He only protected Vibhīṣaṇa [Rāvaṇa's brother, who had not specifically offended him] and the crow which had sought refuge. But you protected the demonesses at the very time they were tormenting you, even though they did not ask for protection. . . .[14]

Finally, Deśika finds all this salvific potential implicit in the very name of Śrī. He derives it in six different ways, each having to do with her graciousness:

> *śrīyate:* she who is resorted to
> *śrayate:* she who resorts [to the Lord]
> *śṛṇoti:* she who listens [to humans]
> *śrāvayati:* she who makes [the Lord] listen
> *śṛṇāti:* she who removes [the past *karma,* faults and the hindrances in the way of the devotee]
> *śrīṇāti:* she who makes [human] perfect [for *mokṣa*][15]

In the *Cillarai Rahasyaṅkaḷ* he goes on to explain how these various meanings are integrated in her personality. He is commenting on the *dvaya mantra,* the most important of all *mantras* for Śrī Vaiṣṇavas, the object of repeated meditation and the focus of several theological treatises. In it the word Śrī occurs.

> In the first line [of the *dvaya mantra*] the word "Śrī" indicates the wonder of her maternal affection towards her subjects and the wonder of her love for her husband; the mother by virtue of being the refuge and the rightful wife of the Lord by all; she seeks refuge with the Lord; she listens to the petitions of the devotee and makes the Lord listen; she takes away the faults [of the devotee]; through her grace (Tamil: *aruḷ*), she makes

> wisdom and other qualities rise in the [devotee]. These are the meanings of the word "Śrī" denoted by scripture.[16]

As wife to Viṣṇu, then, and as mother to humans, Śrī is by her very nature a mediator.

Śrī and the Lotus: Her Auspiciousness

One of the striking aspects of the iconography of Śrī is her persistent association with the lotus. She is said to dwell on the lotus or, indeed, in a "forest of lotuses" (*padmavanālayām*),[17] and lotuses are all about her. She shares their hue and particularly their fragrance, for the scent of the lotus is as inseparable from its source as is Śrī's grace from its author, and as constant.[18] Deśika is fond of quoting the mythological passage from the *Viṣṇu Purāṇa* that explains how all this came to be, a passage that ends in a prayer:

> . . . from the ocean of milk then arose the Goddess Śrī. Seated on a blossoming lotus, bearing a lotus on her hand, she appeared [before all] . . . . the ocean of milk then manifested itself as a person and presented her with a garland of full-blown lotuses. . . . And Śakra praised the goddess who bears a lotus in her hand, saying: "I bow down before Śrī, the mother of all, who resides on the lotus, has eyes of blossoming lotuses, and who reclines on the heart of Viṣṇu. . . ."[19]

It is a perception too basic, evidently, ever to have required comment either on the part of Deśika or other Śrī Vaiṣṇava theologians that the association between Śrī and the lotus is based on the fact that both are pure forms of auspiciousness (*kalyāṇa, maṅgala*). To a large extent they simply rely on scripture to establish this association. Deśika merely says:

> The auspicious lotus is to be seen as an important example of auspiciousness; . . . this is stated in scripture: verses in the *Viṣṇu Smṛti* and other works make it clear.[20]

This theme is echoed by several Śrī Vaiṣṇava theologians even today.

Śrī is all-pervasive, latent in everything. She manifests herself, however, only in auspicious places, of which the lotus itself is the great exemplar. In a brief verse Deśika says that because Śrī has the quality of

FIGURE 9.

Śrī Seated on a Lotus

Wall calendar. Photograph College of Du Page.

pervasion she can be said to be everywhere, and everything is her body, but he adds that her own auspicious form is in the Lord.[21]

This note of qualification indicates that Śrī should not be understood as the immanent pole of divinity, with Viṣṇu as the transcendent pole. The purity of her auspiciousness sets her apart from creation as such: she is not simply *prakṛti,* as in the tantric view. Deśika is aware that she is hailed as *prakṛti* in the text that recites her thousand names, the *Lakṣmī Sahasranāma,* but he interprets this name as meaning "she who partipates in the creation of *prakṛti.*" This he argues by analogy to another of her names, *vidyā,* knowledge, which he alleges really means "the one who grants knowledge."[22] Similarly, she is not only the fulfillment of all desires but the one who fulfills all desires. Deśika says:

> She fulfills all desires of all people. She is noble (*āryā*); she gives prosperity; she is filled with good thoughts; she gives virtue, pleasure, attainment, and liberation (*dharmakāmārthamokṣadā*).[23]

These are the four aims or ends of human life, and the fact that Śrī grants the fourth along with the rest, liberation from the encumbering conditions of life itself, is especially significant. It indicates how far her auspiciousness extends: utterly beyond the realm of this world.

> . . . she gives the highest state (*parinirvāṇa*), . . . she helps one cross *saṃsāra.* . . . O Śrī you give one knowledge of the sacrifices, the great knowledge, the secret knowledge, knowledge of the self, and through these you give their fruit . . . liberation (*vimuktiphala*). . . .[24]

Śrī's fulfilling of desires that may bind one to earth and her helping one to cross the ocean of *saṃsāra* are never seen as irreconcilable by the theologians themselves. Deśika, for instance, sees Śrī's granting of wealth and liberation as a natural outcome of her sovereignty and compassion. It is but the natural result of her generosity and grace. Easily pleased, she bestows overwhelming gifts. Deśika quotes Bhaṭṭar:

> O Mother! To those who take the trouble of but joining their palms together in salute (*añjali*), you give wealth, the state of enjoying one's Self (*akṣaragatim*) and the supreme state (*paramapadam*). And still seeming ashamed, you exclaim, "Oh, I have done nothing for him!" What is this generosity?[25]

It is stressed that we need Śrī initially to qualify ourselves to approach the Lord, and later as a means to liberation (Skt.: *mokṣopāya*).[26] It is, in fact, in this capacity that she is called "ausipicious" by Deśika. Śrī is known to be auspicious (*kalyāṇa*) for two reasons: she gives the auspicious knowledge of reality (*tattvajñāna*) that leads one to *mokṣa,* and she is always accessible to everyone.[27] Śrī is the source of all auspiciousness (*maṅgalam maṅgalānām*).[28] Again Deśika quotes Bhaṭṭer on this point:

> O Lady of the Lotus! Because of your touch, the Lord is filled with auspiciousness. Your auspiciousness is not caused or conditioned—it exists on its own, for is not your name Śrī?[29]

The concept that Śrī's auspiciousness is self-caused leads us to yet another nuance involved in depicting Śrī on the lotus, for this image shows her existing on her own, and not as just a part of Viṣṇu. It affirms her distinct personality and existence as a goddess who is the source of auspiciousness and glory. This identity of Śrī is an important aspect in Deśika's understanding, and one that distinguishes the Śrī Vaiṣṇava position from others. He categorically affirms—with scriptural authority—what Śrī is *not.* She is not insentient matter (any form of *prakṛti*); she is not just a form that Viṣṇu takes; she is not part of the same body as Viṣṇu; she is not just a personification of his grace (*dayā*).[30] Deśika elaborately argues that Śrī has a distinct personality, that she is the perfect consort of Viṣṇu, equal to him in every way and subservient to him only because she herself wills it so:

> Through your own will you belong to the Lord. . . . O Goddess, though both you and the Lord have such qualities as youthfulness, He has the masculine characteristics of not being controlled by others, controlling enemies, and valor . . . [whereas] you have the feminine qualities of tenderness, being submissive to your husband, mercy, patience. . . . You two have thus split up the functions to enjoy [creation]. . . .[31]

Śrī is seen as a distinct person; the wife of Viṣṇu and the mother of the universe. "Scripture affirms that [the Lord and Śrī] are a couple," says Deśika, "and it is not [ours] to ask why. . . ."[32]

Śrī Vaiṣṇavas have always emphasized their exclusive devotion to Viṣṇu. Their faith rests on the promise made in the *Bhagavadgītā* by Viṣṇu incarnate as Krishna: "Abandoning all other *dharma,* take refuge in me alone (*mām ekam*); I shall save you from all sins, do not grieve."[33] The stress is on "one-pointed" or exclusive devotion. The question then arises: does the worship of Śrī—a distinct person—compromise the exclusiveness of this devotion? The Śrī Vaiṣṇava answer is that it does not, and one way to understand how this is possible is to consider another of the dominant Śrī Vaiṣṇava images for Śrī.

Śrī as Breast-Jewel: Inseparable From Viṣṇu

The lotus, as we saw, provides an image for Śrī's distinct identity. But there is another image that poets, artists and theologians alike have associated with Śrī, one that represents quite a different facet of her character. Śrī abides on the breast of Viṣṇu, adorning it; and when Deśika speaks of this image, he is thinking of the inseparable connection (*apṛthak siddhi*) that binds them to one another. Śrī is described as one who is "eternally united" with Viṣṇu.[34] Even when the Lord incarnated himself as a young unmarried man, in his incarnation as Vāmana, the Brahmin, Śrī was hidden on his breast. Deśika refers to the simple cloth that Brahmins wear on their upper bodies when he says, "The Lord covered His breast with a shawl to hide Śrī, who is inseparable from Him."[35] In commenting on the verse from the *Gītā* quoted above, he marshals twenty-five verses from elsewhere in scripture that testify to Śrī's eternal connection with Viṣṇu and concludes that the words "me alone" must include Śrī as well.[36] Elsewhere, in discussing the word "alone," he comments:

> Some say that the word *eka* (alone) refers to the singleness of the Refuge. [But we say] that Śrī is always with Him as an attribute (*viśinaṣṭi*), just as His qualities (*guṇa*) are inseparable from His form. She is the goddess of all and the beloved one of the Lord; with Him she protects the devotees as a rightful wife performing her duty (*sahadharmacārī*). Even though scripture says that the cause of the universe is one, it is implied that other requisites [like souls and matter] exist as the Lord's attributes. Similarly, Śrī is also implied. . . . The Lord is the single means to the goal (*siddhopāya*), but His qualities always exist with Him. And so it is seen by those who have the eyes of scripture that the Lord is always with His wife. When one says "light" or "the object which is the source of light" (*prabhā prabhāvato*), the connection of one with the other is always implied; similarly, when either of the two [the

FIGURE 10.

Śrī on the Breast of Viṣṇu

From the jacket of M.S. Subbulakshmi,
"Bhajagovindam and Vishnusahasranamam"
Odeon Records, The Gramophone Company of India, Ltd.

> Lord or Śrī] is mentioned, the other is always included. . . . In the *dvaya mantra* it is said that the two are owners [of this universe]; when the Lord is the means [of salvation] and the goal itself (*upāya upeya daśayo*), Śrī is also with Him . . . so when we say that we ought to take refuge in the Lord alone, we mean the Lord who is with His wife. . . .
> The words "feet" [of the Lord] and "Nārāyaṇa" imply the Lord with all His qualities, attributes, and forms: yet we consider Him to be the single means of salvation. Similarly it becomes clear from the usage of the word Śrīmat [which invariably precedes the word Nārāyaṇa] that Śrī, because of her eternal relation to Viṣṇu as His wife, is inseparable from Him, and the exclusiveness of the path to liberation (*upāyaikyatvam*) is not impaired. . . .[37]

In this passage Deśika is carrying forward Rāmānuja's theological method. Rāmānuja had held that Brahman is qualified by souls and matter (*cit* and *acit*) but that this fact does not falsify the unity of Reality or its encompassing nature, since souls and matter are its attributes (*viśiṣṭya*). Here Deśika characterizes Śrī as an attribute of the Lord. As Rāmānuja had insisted that Brahman, souls, and matter are inseparable, so does Deśika argue in the case of Śrī.[38] All this does not, however, imply that for Deśika Śrī's status is essentially the same as that of sentient souls. On the contrary, she, like her mate, is the owner of the universe (*śeṣī*) whereas they are owned (*śeṣa*). She is no more separable from Him than are the sun's rays from the sun itself in the eye of the perceiver.

> Inseparable, they create, rule, and sustain the universe together: the Lord, looking at Śrī's face, and following her will, creates, destroys and sustains the worlds, grants hell, heaven, or the supreme state. Since the two are engaged in the same work and experience the same delight, the Lord would not feel happy without Śrī's participation in the sport (*krīḍā*) [of creation]. May that Śrī be benevolent toward us.[39]

It is in this inseparability that one can talk of the "oneness" of the deity:

> Poykay Āḻvār said, "We only know of the Lord of the Lady of the Lotus" (*Mutal Tiruvantāti*, vs. 67). We have also heard from Namjiyar who heard from Āccān that Rāmānuja used to say that wherever the Lord is referred to, we refer to Śrī also. . . . Since the Lord and Śrī form single owners (Maṇipravāla: *eka*

> *śeṣitva ttālum*), since they are of the same mind, intimately attached to each other in their very essential nature and in their forms, we know of the inseparable nature of the "qualified Reality" (Maṇipravāla: *viśiṣṭa tattvam*)—that is, the Lord and Śrī. . . .[40]

So inseparable are Śrī and Viṣṇu that Deśika is unwilling even to frown on those who worship Śrī as if she were a divinity separate from her Lord:

> Those whose goal is only liberation and who worship with no ulterior motive, worship Śrī in union [with Viṣṇu: i.e., as portrayed on the breast of Viṣṇu]; or, as the one enjoyed by the Lord [portrayed at His side]. Those who desire worldly benefits worship her separately. But there is no impropriety . . . for she is our mother, and in all forms, her being this wife of Viṣṇu is an established fact. . . .[41]

More desirable, however, is not to forget the connection, which her position on His breast so vividly symbolizes.

Bathing in the Place of the Lotus

Our focus here has been on Śrī, but Śrī Vaiṣṇavas do not consider her to be the only consort of Viṣṇu. Indeed, he has innumerable other brides: Bhūdevī (the Earth Goddess) and Nīḷādevī (or Nappiṉṉai), as well as all human beings. The relations are, however, ordered hierarchically. The one consort who is equal in every way to Viṣṇu, who because of her accessibility is in fact superior to Viṣṇu, is Śrī. Bhū and Nīlā, Viṣṇu's other divine consorts, are certainly goddesses and thus superior to human beings, but their status is less exalted then Śrī's. For Śrī, according to Deśika, is the only one apart from Viṣṇu who can be called *śeṣī*, the owner and mistress of the universe. All of creation is *śeṣa* (owned by or vassals of) Viṣṇu and Śrī. Bhū and Nīlā cannot be called *śeṣī*. Instead, they are described as being part of Śrī, or poetically compared to an organ or limb (*aṅga*) of her body.[42] Iconographically, in temples, Viṣṇu is portrayed as having two main consorts, Śrī and Bhū.[43]

So far we have portrayed the human soul as a truant child and noted that Śrī has a unique role to play as consort and mother in bringing the soul to salvation. We have seen that her power to mediate between the divine and human standpoints follows from both her own distinct identity and her inseparability from Viṣṇu. We must note however, that this is not the only way in which Śrī Vaiṣṇavas have conceived the divine-human relation. Often the *āḻvār* poets pictured the soul as the beloved woman and the Lord as the lover, and this image would appear to cast Śrī's position in quite a different light. One might think that the metaphor would imply that Śrī and the soul would become rivals in some way, but the *āḻvārs* are at pains to state that this is not so. In the following verse of Tirumaṅkayāḻvār, for instance, the mother of the woman involved—representing the soul—marvels that there is no envy. Speaking of her daughter, she says:

> She who has the face of a shining moon knows that on Your heart resides the damsel born of the nectar of the billowing sea; and yet she does not stop loving You. [My daughter], with eyes like flowers, is beauteous; she longs for Your feet. . . . O my Lord of Iṭaventai, just what are Your intentions?[44]

Śrī Vaiṣṇava theologians went so far as to portray the soul as the bride of Viṣṇu, and still there is no enmity between the bride-to-be and Viṣṇu's eternal bride. On the contrary, Śrī's marriage to Viṣṇu makes him all the more lovable. Deśika turns, as had Parāśara Bhaṭṭar before him, to the *Rāmāyaṇa* for a clarification of the sentiments involved. He points out that the people of Mithilā loved Rāma both because he was the exemplary bridegroom and also because they were all so devoted to his chosen bride, Sītā. Similarly, we love the Lord not only because he is the bridegroom of all creation, the ultimate match for every soul, but also because he is the consort of Śrī, whom everyone loves. Here is the passage, in which Deśika quotes Bhaṭṭar:

> O Mother Lakṣmī [Śrī]! In Mithilā, people looked upon Rāma as their bridegroom, and also as the husband of Sītā. . . . We approach the Lord, gaze at Him, and serve Him [since we are committed to Him] and also because of His relationship with you. . . .[45]

Deśika expresses all this in a different way in poetry. He makes use of a figure of speech that he shares with a number of Śrī Vaiṣṇava theologians and poets, in which union with the Lord is described as if it were an intimate union of a man and a woman. This was euphemestically called "bathing" (in Tamil, *nīrāṭal*).[46] The *āḻvārs* often used the term to describe the overwhelming nature of their immersion in the

Lord, and often a lotus is present. Tirumaṅkayāḻvār, for example, speaks of bathing in "the pond of the golden lotus": the pond is Viṣṇu, and the lotus, of course, is Śrī. It is not merely the coolness of the pool that attracts, but also the glory that the presence of the lotus infuses into the scene: the shining, fragrant auspiciousness of Śrī. In a poem of Deśika with which I would like to close, not only is all this clear, but one has as well an allusion to Śrī's nature as breast-jewel, she whose resort and resting-place is Viṣṇu. Here she plays her role not only in reconciling God's lost children, but in attracting God's brides: so full is her mediation.

> My Lord! form is like
> a broken bit of emerald, a lake
> on which resides Lakṣmī.
> The waters are the resort
> for the lotus.
> Flawless and entrancing
> is Your form. Deep
> and sweet are the waters.
> They soothe away
> the exhaustion and strain
> of those who bathe in You.[47]

Piṉṉai, Krishna's Cowherd Wife

DENNIS HUDSON

The development of Rādhā's place in Vaiṣṇava myth and ritual has occurred largely in North India, in the literature of its Indo-Aryan languages. A full consideration of that development, however, will need to take into account her closest analogue in the South, Piṉṉai, the cowherd lover of Krishna and a significant figure in Tamil literature. In the form of Nīlā, the Dark Goddess, she has come to be seen by Śrī Vaiṣṇavas as another of the consorts of Viṣṇu: her position, along with that of Bhū, the Earth Goddess, is secondary to that of Śrī. This study will present a historical profile of Piṉṉai. We shall begin with the Piṉṉai story as it first appears in Tamil literature, then survey its development by the Tamil poet-saints, the āḻvārs, and finally consider the theological interpretations of Piṉṉai given by the commentators on the āḻvār poetry, the early Śrī Vaiṣṇava ācāryas. We shall conclude with some speculations on Piṉṉai's origin in South Indian Krishna lore.

The Piṉṉai Story

The earliest literary reference to Piṉṉai appears to occur in the *Cilappatikāram,* a Tamil courtly epic of about 450 A.D.[1] The epic's narrative describes a variety of religious practices as it portrays the kingdoms of three Tamil dynasties, the Chōḷas, Pāṇḍyas, and Chēras. In one scene set in a cowherd settlement (*āyarpāṭi*) outside the walls of the Pāṇḍyan capital of Madurai, seven cowherd girls (*āycciyar*) perform the circular *kuravai* dance to enact an episode in the story of Krishna's life.[2] In that episode the cowherd (*āyar*) Krishna conquered seven bulls and won a bride, the cowherd girl variously called "Piṉnai," "Piññai," and "Nam Piṉṉai" (and later "Nappiṉṉai"). In celebration, Krishna, his brother Balarāma, and Piṉṉai danced the *kuravai,* and that dance the seven girls reenact.

The occasion for this scene in the epic is the need to provide the heroine with an auspicious diversion, for she is faced with inauspicious omens regarding the fate of her absent husband. A cowherd woman assembles the seven girls and points out a specific bull associated with each of them, probably to represent the seven bulls Krishna conquered, though this is not stated by the text. She then assigns each girl two identities, a tone in the musical octave and a character in the *kuravai* dance. One girl plays the cowherd girl Piṉṉai (*āymakal piṉṉai*), one plays Krishna (*māyavaṉ*), and one plays his elder brother (*tammuṉōṉ*) Balarāma, while the remaining four play other unnamed cowherds. Then, while the seven bulls stand in the background, the girls assemble themselves, sing their songs, and dance.

Their songs begin with recollections of Krishna's heroic deeds and of his special fondness for the bewitching Piṉṉai, a fondness seen, for example, in his repentance when he realized her distress after he had stolen her clothes, along with those of the other cowherd girls, while they were bathing. Then follows a song about the *kuravai* that Krishna, Piṉṉai, and Balarāma danced while the sage Nārada kept the rhythm and during which each of them stood in a specific position: Piṉṉai in the middle, Krishna at her left, and Balarāma at her right. The girls then sing songs praising the Pāṇḍyan, Chōḷa, and Chēra kings, follow them with more praise of Krishna's deeds, and then end the dance and the scene.

In an important article on the figure of Piṉṉai, Erik Af Edholm and Carl Suneson suggest that this story of Krishna's conquest of seven bulls and his claiming of Piṉṉai as bride developed as a Tamil oral tradition from the ancient custom among Tamil cowherds of heroic men fighting bulls to win brides.[3] They point out that *Kalittokai*, a text earlier than the *Cilappatikāram*,[4] portrays such a bull-fighting scene together with the *kuravai* dance performed in the common meeting ground of a cowherd village.[5] There the cowherds also praise their god (unnamed) and their king, but in their activity they do not imitate anyone: they conquer the bulls, embrace the women they have won, and dance, but they are not themselves gods nor are they imitating gods.

The scene in the *Cilappatikāram*, therefore, represents a development in literature of a theme derived from a social ritual of Tamil cowherds. By the time of the epic the theme has become so much a part of the vernacular Krishna story that the narrator feels no need to tell it directly. The audience, he seems to assume, already knows it. This fact and the way the author portrays this version of the *kuravai* dance as a characteristic practice of the Krishna-worshipping cowherds at Madurai suggest that he intends to portray an actual custom of his time, as his predecessor had done in *Kalittokai.*

Scenes where cowherd girls imitate Krishna's deeds also appear in the Sanskrit *Harivaṃsa* and *Viṣṇu Puraṇa,* which are probably earlier than the *Cilappatikāram.*[6] It is possible, of course, that they influenced the author of the Tamil epic to create that scene outside the walls of Madurai and that the scene in fact had no basis in any practice of Tamil Krishna worshippers in the fifth century. It is more likely, however, that the scenes in both the Sanskrit texts and the *Cilappatikāram* are themselves based on ritual performances in which Krishna devotees dramatized for devotional purposes the stories of Krishna. Edholm and Suneson note that the author of the *Cilappatikāram* uses in his scene the Sanskrit phrase meaning "dramas about the story of the child (Krishna)" (*bālacarita nāṭaka*) in a Tamilized form (*vāla caritai nāṭaṅkaḷ*), a usage suggesting, they say, "the existence of a quite early non-regional dramatical element in the South Indian Kṛṣṇa tradition."[7] The use of this phrase also calls to mind Norvin Hein's well-reasoned conjecture that vernacular dramas present in the region of Mathurā as early as the second century B.C. may have been the source of much devotional material about Krishna that later emerged in Sanskrit and other texts.[8] The scene in the *Cilappatikāram* may itself be an example of one such vernacular drama about Krishna's childhood, representing a continuation in Madurai, the "southern Mathurā," of vernacular devotional practices originally derived from the "northern Mathurā."[9] The epic also suggests that Pāṇḍyan Madurai was by the fifth century the locale of the Bhāgavata cult of Krishna and Balarāma, in which such dramas were performed.[10]

The Pinnai story in the *Cilappatikāram* is the most complete version found in early and medieval Tamil literature, though other poets allude to it frequently as if they assumed their audience knew the whole story. For example, in *Maṇimēkalai,* the sixth-century sequel to the *Cilappatikāram,*[11] the author refers to Pinnai as Krishna's lover, and to their dancing the *kuravai* together with Balarāma in a scene in which a king and queen stroll in a garden. In this setting, alive with symbols of erotic desire, they see

> a peahen and peacock together, spreading both wings, rising and circling, while on one side [a male] watches with increasing joy. And they say, "This is surely the *kuravai* danced by him, the color of dark gem, by his elder brother, and by Piññai."[12]

The three are also alluded to in a poem in the collection, *Paripāṭal,* addressed to Vishnu in the Madurai region and dating from 400-550 A.D.[13] In one verse of the poem (3.83) the poet refers cryptically to Krishna and Balarāma by the phrase "right and left, pot and plough, herder and guardian." The presence of Piṉṉai is implied in the words "right and left," for, as we saw, during the *kuravai* as portrayed in the *Cilappatikāram,* she stands to the right of Krishna (who once danced with a pot and is a herder) and to the left of Balarāma (who carries a plough and is a guardian).[14] This cryptic allusion suggests that the positioning during the dance was established as a characteristic icon of the three by this time.

A change in these references occurs, however, after the mid-sixth century, probably indicating a change in the oral version of the story itself. Balarāma drops out of the scenes in which Piṉṉai is present, and her explicit connection with the *kuravai* dance is made only once. She remains, nevertheless, the bewitching woman for whom Krishna conquered the seven bulls and with whom he is erotically entangled. This change in story may reflect a development within the Bhāgavata movement itself, in which Balarāma recedes in favor of Krishna as the primary focus of cultic attention.

There may also be a connection between this change in the Piṉṉai story in Tamil literature and the appearance of forms of it in two Sanskrit texts, both of which were composed in the South probably between the seventh and the tenth centuries. One text is an interpolation into the southern recension of the *Harivaṃśa* of the story of Piṉṉai and the seven bulls.[15] Piṉṉai, however, is known by the Sanskrit name Nīlā, "the dark one," and not by her Tamil name. According to this version, Krishna's cowherd mother Yaśodā has a brother named Kumbhaka who herds cows in Mithila. His wife is named Dharmadā and they have a daughter Nīlā and a son Śrīdāman. Seven demons enter Kumbhaka's herd disguised as bulls and create havoc. Unable to bring them under control, Kumbhaka promises to give Nīlā in marriage to the person who can. At this point Krishna's cowherd father Nanda takes him and Balarāma to Mithila, where Krishna proceeds to kill all seven bulls, thereby winning Nīlā as his bride. However, they do not dance the *kuravai.*

This version of the story makes it clear that Nīlā is Krishna's maternal uncle's daughter, and in Tamil kinship terms this means he is her cousin-to-be-married (*maṉālaṉ*).[16] Probably an older Tamil oral tradition is recorded in this Sanskrit interpolation, for this identity of

Krishna and Piṉṉai as marriageable cousins is assumed by *āḻvār* poets in the ninth century and may already have been part of the oral tradition that the author of the *Cilappatikāram* drew upon in the fifth century. The importance of the *Harivaṃśa* for the Tamil Bhāgavatas, especially the *āḻvārs*, no doubt explains why this story appeared in the southern recension of that text: a highly authoritative Sanskrit biography of Krishna would have been incomplete if it did not contain an episode so widely known in the vernacular oral tradition of Krishna worship.

Such was not the case, it seems, with the other text, the *Bhāgavata Purāṇa*. It may have received its first form somewhere in the South as early as 750 A.D.,[17] but it is not yet clear what connection if any it had with the Tamil Bhāgavatas. It seems to have incorporated two fragments of the Piṉṉai story in ways suggesting that the author either did not know the original version or revised it radically.

The *Bhāgavata Purāṇa* tells of a nameless *gopī* whom Krishna favored. She may indeed be an echo of Piṉṉai, but there is nothing about her portrayal that suggests Piṉṉai rather than any other cowherd girl.[18] The text does include the story of Krishna's conquest of seven bulls to win a bride, but not in connection with this nameless *gopī*, or, for that matter, with any of the others. The feat is placed during Krishna's life as a *kṣatriya* and has the purpose of adding to his already sizeable harem Satya, the daughter of a king in Ayodhyā named Nagnajit.[19] Krishna's mode of conquest has also changed. To conquer the bulls, we are told, he divided himself into seven forms, held them, bound them with a rope, and "then drew those bulls as easily as boys sportively draw the wooden bulls by strings."[20] In the Tamil *āḻvār* poetry and in the *Harivaṃśa* interpolation Krishna does not play with the bulls, but kills them all at once, and not by dividing himself into seven forms.

The *Bhāgavata Purāṇa* thus seems to stand on the periphery of the Piṉṉai tradition; wherever it was composed, it was probably not composed in Madurai, nor anywhere else in the realm of the Tamil dynasties, and it tells little about how the Piṉṉai tradition developed at its core. For that we must turn now to the Tamil poetry of the *āḻvārs*.

Piṉṉai in Āḻvār *Poetry*

The Piṉṉai story continues to be important in the *āḻvār* poems, the earliest of which appeared in the seventh century. It was also known to contemporary Śaiva poets, for Appar and Campantar each make at least one reference to Piṉṉai as the object of Krishna's love.[21] But the *āḻvārs* are the ones who develop her place in Tamil Vaiṣṇava devotion, since their poems serve as sacred scripture for the Śrī Vaiṣṇavas. The earliest *āḻvārs* were Poykai, Pūtam, and Pēy, who belonged to the region of Kāñcipuram. They date to about 650-700 A.D.,[22] the time of the vigorous expansion of the Pallava dynasty, which used Kāñcī as its capital. In 642, for example, the Pallavas conquered the Chālukyan fortress at Bādāmi, and throughout the century they conducted wars with the Pāṇḍyas of Madurai, using their plunder and tribute to renovate, build, and carve Hindu temples. Their port town of Māmallapuram, the present Mahābalipuram, contained their most noteworthy sculpted works. As Pallava sculpture shows, the Bhāgavata movement was vigorously present in the region during this period, as were two of its liturgical schools (*āgamas*), the Pāñcarātra and the Vaikhānasa. The poems of Poykai, Pūtam, and Pēy represent early vernacular expressions of this Bhāgavata devotion in the Pallava kingdom.

Out of their 300 verses,[23] seven refer to Piṉṉai and/or to the seven bulls, but none of the seven refers to the *kuravai* dance. When they speak of Piṉṉai and the bulls, however, the focus of their attention is on Krishna. For example, Pūtam refers to "my Lord who conquered and destroyed all seven bulls, their curved [horns] fully grown; he deliberated, then ended their prowess."[24] This feature will be true of almost all *āḻvār* poetry: Piṉṉai and the seven bulls are used to enhance the nature of Krishna, who stands at the center of attention.

One verse by Poykai merits our special attention, for it introduces Piṉṉai into a new context and implies a change in her story that is continued by later *āḻvārs*. Piṉṉai is portrayed as one of Nārāyaṇa's three consorts in his Supreme Realm:

Though united with Lady Śrī (*tirumakaḷ*),
With Lady Earth (*maṉmakaḷ*),
And with the Cowherd Lady (*āymakaḷ*),
How can he separate from Lady Śrī (*tirumakaḷ*)?
His mind is on Lady Śrī (*tirumakaḷ*),
He the color of the Great Sea

> Lying on the Cobra Bed
> With its raised hood
> Spilling drops of milk.[25]

This verse makes it clear that while Nārāyaṇa loves Bhū, the earth goddess, and Piṇṇai, the cowherd goddess, he is especially fond of the goddess Śrī. This idea, we shall later see, is consistent with subsequent Pāñcarātra liturgical texts and statements of Śrī Vaiṣṇava *ācāryas*, in which Śrī is portrayed as the primordial goddess from whom the others emerge in the process of creation.

The question to be raised here, however, concerns the way in which the Cowherd Lady (*āymakaḷ*) is to be understood in this new context. Is she a goddess who once descended from the Supreme Realm as Piṇṇai the cowherdess, became Krishna's lover, and now has returned to the Supreme Realm where she serves Nārāyaṇa? Or is she a cowherd girl who became Krishna's lover and subsequently ascended to the Supreme Realm in some form of "assumption"? The former would be consistent with purāṇic *avatāra* myths, but the latter would reflect a pattern that is evident in the case of the heroine of the *Cilappatikāram*, who became the goddess of wifely faithfulness because of her faithfulness as a wife on earth. Whatever the reason, from this point on the *āḻvārs* refer to the Cowherd Lady (*āymakaḷ*) as either in the Supreme Realm with Nārāyaṇa or in Gokula with Krishna, and it is clear that in both places she is the same Piṇṇai of the Tamil oral tradition used by the author of the *Cilappatikāram*. But they never call her by her Sanskrit name Nīlā, and they never say how she got to the Supreme Realm. What they do say is that in both realms she is loved by the Lord.

The six *āḻvārs* after Poykai, Pūtam, and Pēy who concern us do not appear for about a century. One of them, Kulacēkara (ca. 800), was associated with the Chēra region on the west coast and is noted for his devotion to Rāma.[26] Among his 105 verses he makes no reference to Piṇṇai and only one unambiguous reference to Krishna as the slayer of seven bulls.[27] When poets refer to Krishna as a bull-slayer, it is at times unclear whether they allude to the story of the seven bulls, or to the story in the *Harivaṃśa* of the demon Ariṣṭa, who took on a bull form to kill Krishna but whom Krishna slew instead.[28]

The other five *āḻvārs* date to about 800-930 A.D. and are associated with regions dominated by contending dynasties at Kāñci, Tanjore, and Madurai. The conflict between the Pallavas and the Pāṇḍyas intensified in these years, but both dynasties were finally eclipsed by the ascending Chōḻas. In 850 A.D. they captured Tanjore; by 897 they had taken over Pallava territory completely; and in 910 they seized Madurai. By the beginning of the Chōḻas' period of paramount strength, in 985, however, *āḻvār* expression of Bhāgavata devotion had ceased and the commentarial work of the Bhāgavata *ācāryas* of the Pāñcarātra school had begun.

The earliest of these five was Tirumaṅkai (ca. 800-870), who wrote most of his poetry in connection with temples in the regions of Kāñci and Tanjore.[29] Out of his 1361 verses, 42 refer to Piṉṉai and/or to the seven bulls,[30] with the focus throughout on Krishna as hero and lover. Here are some examples. "For the sake of Piṉṉai, her feet soft as cotton, he once slew seven leaping bulls." "For the sake of her with the slender waist, shaped like the hourglass drum, hair coiled in a circle, teeth sparkling—a young creeper—he killed the cowherd's bulls, their fierce bellows thundering." There is also the following testimony to the motive for Nārāyaṇa's descent into this world: "Though he knows all seven rare worlds of pure gold, yet in the cowherd village he killed bulls in order to unite with the beauty of Piṉṉai, her waist slim as a stem."[31]

In one of these 42 verses he mentions Krishna's dancing the *kuravai* after killing the bulls, the only mention of the two events together, so far as I can determine, in any *āḻvār* poetry.[32] In four verses he refers to Krishna with forms of the word *maṇāḷaṉ*,[33] making it clear that Krishna and Piṉṉai are cousins-to-be-married and suggesting the same Piṉṉai story that emerged in the *Harivaṃśa* interpolation and that may have been known to the author of the *Cilappatikāram*.

Tirumaṅkai also speaks of Piṉṉai together with Śrī and Bhū. In one verse he refers to Krishna as "the darling of the Lady of the lotus flower [Śrī] and her sweet companion," as "the master of the good earth," and as "master of the cowherd's daughter (*āyarpāvi*) Nappiṉṉai."[34] In another he portrays a scene in the Supreme Realm and says of Nārāyaṇa, "He comes with the incomparable Cowherd Lady (*makaḷāyar*), with the Lady Earth—a young woman—and with the other one, the Lady Śrī."[35] In two others he refers to Piṉṉai together with Śrī but not Bhū, and once with Bhū but not Śrī, and each time to Nārāyaṇa as the lover of both.[36] These references to the three goddesses indicate a continuity with Poykai's thought a century earlier, based most likely on their participation in the same Bhāgavata liturgical school.

Another *āḻvār* associated with the Tanjore region is Tirumāḻicaippirāṉ (ca. 850).[37] He refers to Piṉṉai and/or to the seven bulls in ten of his 216 verses, and in one he speaks of the three goddesses together with Nārāyaṇa.[38] Yet there he makes a clear distinction between Śrī and Bhū in the Supreme Realm and Piṉṉai on earth. Addressing the Lord at Śrī Raṅgam, he says, "You parted from the eternal Great Flower [Śri] and from the Lady Earth, became a youth, and then united in marriage (*maṇam*) with the shoulders of the cowherd's Piṉṉai (*āyar piṉṉai*)." Perhaps she is understood here not as an avatar of one of the three goddesses but as a cowherd girl who would later be taken to the Supreme Realm to become one of the three. As a simple cowherdess she underscores the wonder of Nārāyaṇa's lowly presence in this world and points to a tension in the Lord's own being upon which later *ācāryas* dwell, namely, the tension between Nārāyaṇa's majesty in the Supreme Realm where he loves Śrī and Bhū but seems personally inaccessible to his devotees, and his accessibility as the lover of Piṉṉai.

The remaining three *āḻvārs* belonged to the southern Tamil kingdom ruled by the Paṇḍyaṉ dynasty at Madurai, but none of them came from the capital itself. The home of Periyāḻvār and of his daughter Āṇṭāḷ was Śrīvilliputtūr, a town about 40 miles southeast of Madurai, and the home of Nammāḻvār was Kurukūr, a village about 100 miles southeast of Madurai on the Tāmraparṉi River.

Periyāḻvār (ninth century)[39] refers to Piṉṉai and/or to the seven bulls in only seven verses of 473, and makes no reference to Piṉṉai together with either Śrī or Bhū. His daughter Āṇṭāḷ (ninth century)[40] composed 173 verses and in only three does she present Piṉṉai, but with no reference either to the bulls or to Śrī and Bhū. This seemingly slight attention, however, does not reflect Piṉṉai's importance to Āṇṭāḷ, for she is in fact the only poet who directly addresses Piṉṉai herself. The three verses in which she does so occur sequentially in her 30-verse poem *Tiruppāvai,* a portrayal of cowherd girls setting off to fulfill a vow made to the goddess Kātyāyaṉī. The vow is to perform a bathing ritual, for which they need ritual implements that only Krishna, as son of the chief cowherd, can provide. In the course of the poem they proceed to Nanda's house, where Krishna sleeps, and call to members of the household to wake up and let them gain access to him. First they address the guardian of the door, then Nanda and Yaśodā, and then Krishna and Balarāma. None of these efforts succeeds, so they address Nappiṉṉai and Krishna together, beginning with Nappiṉṉai:[41]

> Juices flowing, a bull elephant is he,
> Shoulders never fleeing, mighty is he,

Nanda, the protector of cows.
And his daughter-in-law are you,
O Nappinnai.
Will you, with coiled hair wafting scent,
Open the gate, please?
Look, all around us cocks crow.
Look, on the *mādhavī* bower flocks of *kuyil*
Cry out over and over.
That we may sing the names of your husband
Will you, with fingers holding a ball,
Come, and with your red lotus hand,
Its graceful bangles tinkling,
Open up, please, rejoicing,
O my Lady.

A standing lamp burns,
While spread out on a smooth bed
Of the five finest qualities
Over a frame with tusks for legs
You rest,
Holding on your full-blown chest
The breasts of Nappinnai,
Clusters of blooming flowers
Coiled in her hair.
Speak to us, please.
And you there with those shadowed long eyes,
Won't you let your husband awake from sleep
Even for a moment?
Look, can't you stand separation
Even for a second?
That's not your nature, not your way,
Open up, please, rejoicing,
O my Lady.

The thirty-three Immortals you led,
Dispelling their fear:
Such strength is yours!
Please awake from sleep.
You are faithful, you are brave,
You are the Uncorrupted
And give sorrow to your foes!

Please awake from sleep.
Breasts soft, small like pots,
Mouth red, waist slender,
O Nappiṉṉai, best of women,
O Beauty!
Please awake from sleep,
Give us a fan, a mirror, your husband,
And let us bathe this very moment,
Open up, please, rejoicing,
O my Lady.

The effort finally succeeds and in subsequent verses they address Krishna directly without reference to Piṉṉai.

In these three verses Āṇṭāḷ has retained the heroic and erotic qualities of Krishna's relation to Piṉṉai, though she makes reference to his heroism not by recalling his defeat of the seven bulls but by mentioning other deeds. His eroticism is not that of the forest lover but of the domestic husband enjoying the pleasure of the marriage bed with his wife. And his wife is a person in her own right whom other cowherd girls must enlist on their side if they are to gain access to him. This is the only instance in *āḻvār* poetry where Piṉṉai's role in relation to Krishna's devotees is made explicit: she is the mediator between the cowherd girls and Krishna, and by implication the mediator in the metaphysical relation of devotees to Nārāyaṇa.

The final poet to consider is Nammāḻvār (880-930),[42] whom the *ācāryas* consider the most profound of all the *āḻvārs*. Out of his 1296 verses, 23 refer to Piṉṉai and/or to the seven bulls. For example,

Though he cast me off,
Even he cannot now escape
My abundant love,
For he with exultant might,
Desiring Piṉṉai's shoulders,
long and soft,
Of all the ancient immortals
Is the First.[43]

Nammāḻvār is the only *āḻvār* to state explicitly that meditation on the erotic union of Krishna and Piṉṉai produces bliss for the devotee, a tantric method consistent with the Pāñcarātra liturgy. One verse reads,

Playing sweet songs on the flute,
Herding cows,
Uniting with the shoulders of Pin̲n̲ai,
her eyes flashing like silver,
hair coiled with scented flowers—
When I think of these and many other deeds
Of that beautiful Lord,
My heart melts with love
and I am undone.
What world then will satisfy me?[44]

Another verse ends, "O great Lord united with the shoulders of Pin̲n̲ai," suggesting, as an early commentator points out, that the speaker obtains bliss from beholding the coupling of Krishna and Pin̲n̲ai.[45]

The three goddesses appear together in six of Nammāl̲vār's verses[46] and one of them expresses a dazzling vision of the Lord's mysterious powers:

> The Ladies who long to abide with him are these three called Lady Śrī, Lady Earth, and the cowherd's simple daughter. All three worlds he alone rules and he, my Lord, swallows them all together and lies on the banyan leaf. That great Lord whose *māyā* exceeds the sea—Krishna—it is he who is in my womb.[47]

Another verse explicitly links the three goddesses with the method of obtaining release from *saṃsāra,* known as *śaraṇāgati,* going to the Lord for refuge (*śaraṇam*):

> There, here, and everywhere gods and foes, everyone, cry out, "We cannot understand this nature of yours." And [thus] they say, "We take refuge in the Holder of the conch and the disk, who joins his body to the Lady of the Flower, to Lady Earth, and to the Cowherd Lady.[48]

The meaning seems to be that the devotee is to take refuge in the Lord in his fullness, that is, as the majestic ruler conjoined with his three consorts. These serve as mediators between the refugee and the Lord, who bears the emblems of power and justice.

The *ācāryas* reflect further on the nature of the goddesses' mediation, and they stress the erotic relation between Pin̲n̲ai and Krishna as the basis for her particular mediating activity. Their commentarial work began immediately after the period of the *āḻvārs,* which closed with Nammāḻvār.[49]

Pinnai in the Commentaries

The earliest *ācāryas* who refer to Pinnai appear in the eleventh and twelfth centuries, but they write in Sanskrit and refer to her always as Nīlā and as a transcendent goddess along with Śrī and Bhū. As Vasudha Narayanan points out,[50] when the *ācāryas* write in Sanskrit they seem to avoid using the Tamil names Pinnai and Nappinnai and seldom if ever speak of Nīlā in a context that suggests Gokula. The great *ācārya* Rāmānuja, for example, refers to the Beloved of Śrī (*Śrīvallabha*) as also the Lord of Bhū and Nīlā (*Bhūmi-nīlā-nāyaka*),[51] and his foremost disciple, Kūrattāḻvān, speaks of the Lord at Āḻakar-kōyil as the lover of Śrī, as well as of Bhū and Nīlā, who share in Śrī's qualities.[52]

Explicit identification of the Sanskrit Nīlā and the Tamil Pinnai was made in a Sanskrit text written in the late twelfth century by the *ācārya* Parāśara Bhaṭṭar.[53] In his Sanskrit verse introducing Āṇṭāḷ's *Tiruppāvai,* he refers to Krishna's "sleeping on the mountain slope of Nīlā's swelling breasts,"[54] and thus he avoids using the Tamil name while making it clear that Nīlā refers to both the transcendent goddess and the mundane cowherd girl. Elsewhere he follows his predecessors by speaking of Bhū and Nīlā as if they are derivatives of Śrī: they are like the breast, hands, feet, and glance of Śrī and thus please the Lord.[55] From this time on commentators writing in Tamil or in the Tamil-Sanskrit mixture known as Maṇipravāla use these names interchangably; however, they follow the general pattern of speaking of the cowherd girl in Gokula as Pinnai and the Cowherd Lady of the Supreme Realm as Nīlātēvi, "the goddess Nīlā."

In our examination of the treatment of Pinnai in the *ācāryas'* commentaries we shall limit our discussion to the two *ācāryas* of thirteenth-century Śrī Raṅgam who represent the flowering of the Maṇipravāla commentaries.[56] Vaṭakkuttiruvītippiḷḷai (1217-1312?) wrote a long commentary on Nammāḻvār's *Tiruvāymoḻi* commonly known as the *Īṭu.* His contemporary Periyavāccāṉpiḷḷai wrote commentaries on all the *āḻvār* poems, but his exposition of Āṇṭāḷ's *Tiruppāvai* will be the focus of our attention.

In the *Īṭu,*[57] Krishna's heroic and erotic qualities in relation to

Pinnai are brought out in comments on the portion of verse 3.5.4 that reads, "For the sake of the garland wafting scent he destroyed the huge bulls, all seven, he the bearer of Śrī, [he] with lips ripe like red coral." The commentator gives this interpretation of the statement:

> For the sake of Lady Nappinnai, whose hair bore a garland emitting fragrance. . . . [The Cowherds] had resolved to hand over Lady Nappinnai, saying, "We should give her to the one who conquers these bulls." When [Krishna] saw the beauty of her adornment and her coiled hair, he desired her, and saying, "*Tavāsmi*—I am yours," he gave himself to her . . . . [But] just as it is said that even for great people there are many obstacles to good deeds, for him there were not one or two but seven enemies. . . . But since he could begin embracing her shoulders [right] after [conquering the bulls], he did not break their necks one at a time; [he broke them] all at once. . . . Then when those obstacles to his desire were gone, he smiled gently. Or the verse could mean that because those lovely shoulders had no flaw, he smiled gently. He conquered all seven of these bulls and is together with the good fortune of a hero (*vīra-lakṣmī*). Or it can mean that she embraces him: just as the Lady [Sītā] embraced the Lord [Rāma], Lady Nappinnai embraces [Krishna].

The commentator brings out the intensity of Krishna's desire for Pinnai in the following interpretation of "He seized seven bulls" from verse 4.2.5:

> He expects in the next moment to grasp her and therefore, just as if he is embracing her, he joins [himself] to the bulls. . . . Because [killing them] is the means by which he obtains her, he is joined to their horns (*kompu*) just as if he were united with this [girl slim as a] twig (*kompu*), and [he] enjoys it.

The commentator goes on, however, to point out that crucial to their union was the fact that they belonged to the same caste. Commenting on two of Krishna's epithets, "the guardian of cows," and "the dancer with pots," he says,

> He has the proper family birth and daring for obtaining her. Just as Janaka would not give his daughter [Sītā] to anyone not of the lineage of Ikṣvāku, even if [he had] broken the bow, would the cowherds then give the girl [Pinnai] to anyone not of the cowherd caste (*kulam*), even if [he had] killed the seven bulls?

This statement recalls the observation made by the commentator's father, Kūrattāḻvāṉ, that Krishna had two ladies suitable to his two caste identities, Nappiṉṉai while he was a cowherd and Rukminī while he was a *kṣatriya*.[58]

Piṉṉai's attractiveness to Krishna is highlighted in what the commentator says about a phrase in verse 9.8.2, "the husband of simple Piṉṉai, her eyes broad like sharp spears":

> Like a sharp spear she attacks in one glance [as does] an incomparable warrior, [for] she has eyes with a sweetness not [found] among the qualities possessed by the experiencer [Krishna]. He was born to taste Lady Nappiṉṉai, who is full of the qualities of the self.

The "qualities of the self" (*ātma guṇaṅkaḷ*), which all individual selves possess, are fully possessed by Piṉṉai, and they make her bewitching to Krishna. They include feminity (*strītvam*), restraint of the mind (*sama*), and control of the body (*dama*).[59] She represents the true, though unrecognized, nature of all selves in relation to the Lord, and the implication seems to be that all selves are at least potentially bewitching to him.

It is precisely Piṉṉai's attractiveness to Krishna that is the basis for her influence as intercessor with him. The commentator points out with regard to verse 1.9.4 that each of the three goddesses who mediate has her own approach. Śrī holds the highest position of the three, for she serves as the preeminent wife to the Lord of all. When imperfect devotees approach her for help in mitigating the Lord's strict application of justice she mediates, as Sītā does in the *Rāmāyaṇa,* by reminding him, "There is no one who has not done wrong." The patient Earth, by contrast, teaches him forbearance by asking him right away, "Ought one look at faults?" But the cowherd's simple Piṉṉai, being the very source of his enjoyment, gives no advice, but engrosses the Lord by the beauty of her form so that he is not even aware that the devotee has any faults.

Piṉṉai's connection with the Lord's pleasure is brought out more clearly when the commentator finds further meanings in these goddesses: Śrī is the Lord's wealth (*aiśvarya*); Earth is the producer of it; and the cowherd's daughter is the enjoyer who eats it. In another interpretation (5.6.11) she is the Lord's wealth in its many enjoyable forms. The implication is, then, that Nārāyaṇa's erotic entanglement with Piṉṉai, whether in the transcendent or the mundane realm, is a mode of his enjoyment of his own quality of *aiśvarya,* a term meaning both wealth and lordliness. And Krishna's conquest of seven bulls to gain Pinnai suggests both meanings of the word: as we noted earlier, she is *vīra-lakṣmī,* the good fortune of a hero.

Periyavāccānpiḷḷai, our second commentator, goes still further in delineating the mediating role of Pinnai as he expounds upon the three verses from Āṇṭāl's *Tiruppāvai* that we examined earlier. In his introduction to verse 18, where the cowherd girls address Nappinnai and Krishna as they lie in bed, he observes that up to this point the girls have not been able to arouse anyone in Nanda's house, although they have appealed to Nanda and Yaśodā and to Krishna and Balarāma. The reason, he says, is that to arouse Krishna no one suffices as intercessor except Nappinnai. With her as mediator, however, they will surely gain him. He points to several incidents in traditional lore to demonstrate this fact.[60] In the *Rāmāyaṇa,* for example, there is the crow who transgressed the moral boundary with regard to Rāma but received protection from Sītā. There are also the demons of Śrī Lankā: Sūrpaṇakhā, who scorned Sītā but sought Rāma and thereby lost her nose and ears; her brother Rāvaṇa, who scorned Rāma but sought Sītā and thereby lost his ten heads; and their brother Vibhīṣaṇa, who, by contrast, sought both Rāma and Sītā for refuge and prospered. The problem in the *Tiruppāvai* is that the *gopīs* act on their zealous urges and begin falling directly at the feet of Krishna without first going through Nappinnai, and that does not work. They then decide to follow the proper course of conduct in order to arouse him, and when they approach him through her auspices, they are successful.

Aṇṭāḷ describes Nappinnai in verse 18 as holding a ball in one hand: this the commentator sees as expressing her mediating position. In effect, he notes, what the cowherd girls are saying as they stand at the door appealing to her is, "We have left our intelligence behind and are insensible. Our fate rests in your hands." And the ball she holds in her hand, to which they make their appeal, signifies that she will mediate on their behalf:

> She played ball with Krishna, defeated him, and [now] lies embracing him with one hand and the ball with the other. He is the means of her pleasure (*bhoga*) and the ball is the means of her play (*līlā*). In one hand is Nārāyaṇa and in the other hand is the glorious universe. In this is illustrated the quality of intercession that derives from her double relation. It is just

> as [the *Nīlāsuktam*] says, "The wife of Viṣṇu is the mistress of this universe."

One of her hands is red like a lotus, and the commentator interprets this to mean, "You should not fear the independence (*svātantrya*) of the Lord." The sound of its graceful bangles tinkling as Nappin̲n̲ai reaches to open the door brings life to those who hear it. Periyavāccān̲piḷḷai recalls in this context that the great *ācārya* Rāmānuja was especially fond of this verse, no doubt because of this focus on Pin̲n̲ai's mediating role: it was he who was chiefly responsible for declaring the necessity of the divine consort (Śrī in her several forms) in the equation of salvation.

Devotees depend upon a mediator and the commentator says that verse 19 makes this clear. They are dependents (*śeṣa*) of Nappin̲n̲ai, for she is the only one who can make Krishna available to them, and so when they find her hesitant to separate from Krishna to let them in, they berate her for going against her mediating role:

> If, because you will not bear to be separated from him even for a moment, we lose the means for attaining our goal of continuous union with him, that is certainly a perverse consequence. We do not speak out of ignorance. It is true. [Such behavior] is not your *dharma*. Such behavior does not fit your own nature or your own character. Nor does it fit your quality as an intercessor, nor your grace.

Nappin̲n̲ai does finally grant the girls access to Krishna, and then, the commentator says, she joins together with them in addressing him; she herself becomes one of the supplicants. In his introduction to verse 21 he observes, "Lady Nappin̲n̲ai says, 'When it comes to pleasure (*bhogam*) am I not only one woman among you? Please come and let us all together beg of Krishna.'" In the final analysis even Pin̲n̲ai, the bewitching beauty who engrosses Krishna's own consciousness, shares in the dependence (*śeṣatvam*) that all individual selves have in relation to the Lord of the Universe.[61]

Speculation on the Origin of Pin̲n̲ai

Having traced the story of Pin̲n̲ai from the fifth through the thirteenth centuries, we may appropriately consider the clues this story may contain as to her origin in Krishna lore. Let us begin by returning to the scene in the *Cilappatikāram* with which we began. Where did Pin̲n̲ai in this scene come from? Two answers seem plausible. One is that she appeared in Tamil literature through the assimilation of the North Indian Krishna story to the customs of Tamil cowherds, perhaps originally around Madurai. The purāṇic account of Krishna's conquest of the bull-demon Ariṣṭa could have become associated with a local practice among Tamil cowherds of grappling with bulls to gain brides. Such an assimilation would then require that Krishna have a bride, and in the Tamil kinship system she would ideally be his mother's brother's daughter. Even without the theme of the seven bulls, however, a society in which a boy grew up with an inherent claim on his maternal uncle's daughter would likely produce such a cousin-to-be-married for Krishna once he became thoroughly identified with Tamil cowherd experience.[62] And not only would she be the ideal bride for kinship reasons, she would also be ideally beautiful. Thus the origin of Pin̲n̲ai may lie in the assimilation of the Krishna story by Tamils to their own cowherd customs.

The second plausible answer is that Pin̲n̲ai is the Tamil form of a cowherd lover of Krishna already present in the Krishna-Balarāma cult when it was brought from North India prior to the fifth century A.D. The institutions through which the transmission of the cult occurred probably included vernacular dramas about Krishna's childhood: perhaps there was a story of Krishna's special love for one particular *gopī* that became the basis of the Pin̲n̲ai story in Tamil oral tradition. Her positioning in Tamil culture as Krishna's bride-to-be would then follow the pattern analyzed above.

Neither of these answers, however, clarifies whether this cowherd girl was originally that, later apotheosized, or originally a goddess who descended to be with Krishna and Balarāma. As we observed in the *ācāryas'* understanding of Pin̲n̲ai, her mediating position seems to be based in large measure on the fact that she is a human cowherd girl, a fact that may also explain why the *āl̲vārs* consistently refer to her in the supreme realm as the "Cowherd Lady." We also noted that such an "assumption" of a human to divine status is consistent with Tamil tradition; this may indeed be all there is to her origin.

For the purpose of creative speculation, however, let us explore the possibility that Pin̲n̲ai may have originated as cowherd lover of Krishna in North Indian lore who was herself the descended form of a goddess. Who might she be? Her own Tamil name does not offer many clues. Some scholars understand "Pin̲n̲ai" to mean "the younger one" The prefix *na*, "beautiful," would render her full name, "Nappinnai," to mean "the beautiful younger one"; or if the prefix is *nam*, "our," we would have "Nampinnai," "our younger one."[63] There is an ancient Tamil commentarial tradition,[64] however, that understands "Pinnai" to refer to her hair, specifically plaited hair, so that "Pinnai" means "she with the plaited hair." If *na* or *nam* is then understood in its old Tamil sense of "great,"[65] "Nappinnai" might also mean "she with an abundance of plaited hair." But these hints are too obscure to be of much immediate use.

There may be a clue, however, in the icon of the *kuravai* dance described in the *Cilappatikāram*, in which Pinnai stands between Krishna and Balarāma while Nārada drums. As Edholm and Suneson have noted, instructions for making images of a goddess standing between Krishna and Balarāma are contained in two Sanskrit texts on iconography dated around the time of the *Cilappatikāram* and *Paripāṭal*.[66] That goddess is called in Sanskrit Ekānaṃśā, "the single, portionless one." According to S. Ch. Mukherji,[67] by the time of the *Harivaṃśa* Ekānaṃśā was identified as an avatar of Durgā, herself the *śakti* of Viṣṇu (*vaiṣṇavī śakti*): she descended as the daughter of Nanda to protect the baby Krishna from Kaṃsa.[68] Is it possible that a non-purāṇic vernacular tradition might have understood this Durgā-Ekānaṃśā to be Krishna's sister at one time and his lover at another? Mukherji points out that just such a pattern is known in certain Vedic texts, where Ambikā first appeared as Rudra's sister and then as his consort.[69]

Further clues may be found by looking at the non-purāṇic versions of the Krishna story incorporated into a Sanskrit drama that probably originated in the South and possibly as early as the time of the *Cilappatikāram*. This is the *Bālacarita* attributed to the dramatist Bhāsa, one example of a *bālacarita nāṭaka*.[70] Charlotte Vaudeville has noted that it incorporates Krishna traditions from pastoral castes rather than from the Purāṇas, including a version that presents Durgā or Kātyāyanī as the slayer of Kaṃsa.[71]

The *Bālacarita* contains a number of suggestive variations of the Krishna story, but two are significant for our discussion. One is that after Durgā-Kātyāyanī assumes the form of a baby girl and is put in Krishna's place with Devakī, she reveals her true form to Kaṃsa and states that having already slain Śumbha, Niśumbha, and Mahiṣa (as Durgā), she has taken birth in the lineage of Vasudeva in order to ruin Kaṃsa's family.[72] She thus claims for herself the task that Krishna

FIGURE 11.

Ekānaṃśā between Balarāma and Krishna

Etah, U.P., ca. ninth century A.D.
(Courtesy, State Museum, Lucknow, G58.)
Photograph American Institute of Indian Studies.

himself, according to purāṇic tradition, was born to perform. Such a claim would not be contradictory, however, if she is understood to be the *vaiṣṇavī śakti*, for then Durgā-Kātyāyanī would be in some way Krishna's power to slay Kaṃsa.[73]

The second variation from the purāṇic norm is that once she proclaims this to Kaṃsa, instead of then ascending into the sky she and her four assistants go off in the guise of cowherds to Nanda's village in order to experience "Lord Viṣṇu's childhood exploits" (*bhagavato viṣṇor bālacaritam*).[74] The same guise had been assumed earlier in the play by Garuḍa and Vishnu's four weapons, and so as Krishna grows up his companions include forms of these ten deities.

Perhaps in the body of Krishna lore upon which the author of the *Bālacarita* drew there once existed a story, now lost, in which the Durgā-Kātyāyanī-Ekānaṃśā who returns to Gokula to experience Krishna's childhood exploits turns out to be his lover. Perhaps she was known in Tamil as Pinnai, the cowherd "girl with plaited hair," or as the girl born after Krishna (just as Balarāma was born before him: *tammuṉōṉ*) and thus "the younger one." The *Bālacarita* says that among the cowherds with whom Krishna grows up, one is named Kumbhadatta and one Dāmaka. Perhaps these names derive from the same non-purāṇic source as those appearing in the later *Harivaṃśa* interpolation: Kumbhadatta may be connected with Pinnai's father Kumbhaka, and Dāmaka with her brother Śrīdāman; indeed Pinnai's own Sanskrit name Nīlā may be connected with Kātyāyanī's male assistant Nīlā, "the dark one," who went in the guise of a cowherd to experience "Lord Viṣṇu's childhood exploits."

Keeping in mind this possible link between Pinnai and Durgā, let us return to the seventh-century Tamil verse by Poykai in which he describes for the first time the presence of the Cowherd Lady with the goddesses Śrī and Bhū. If we attempt to read that verse in its probable cultic context, several enticing facts emerge in both sculpture and liturgical texts. Let us consider the sculptural evidence first.

Durgā in Pallava sculpture is clearly a Vaiṣṇava deity. She is always presented as bearing Viṣṇu's conch and disk and is primarily associated with Vaiṣṇava temples. She is always portrayed as beautiful and is distinguished from other female figures by a specific type of band around her breasts (*kucha-bandha*) shared only with her female guardians.[75]

Two cave temples at Māmallapuram carved during the time of

Māmalla (630-668) portray three goddesses together with Nārāyaṇa. One is a temple of Varāha, where Bhū is present in the Varāha panel, Śrī is present in another panel as Gaja Lakṣmī seated on a lotus, and Durgā with four arms is present in a third, standing on a lotus *pīṭha*. Trivikrama is also portrayed but without an accompanying goddess.[76] The other temple portrays Durgā with eight arms slaying the buffalo demon Mahiṣa at one end of the hall, and Nārāyaṇa reclining on Śeṣa and worshipped by Bhū at the opposite end. The presence of Śrī is implied as an unmanifested aspect of the reclining Nārāyaṇa, and her explicit portrayal may have been intended as part of the central panel, which was never completed.[77] If one were to read Poykai's verse while standing inside these two temples, his references to Śrī and Bhū would have unambiguous iconic counterparts, while the third goddess, the Cowherd Lady, might have a referent in the icon of Durgā. It is quite possible, of course, that Poykai did not intend to refer to Durgā, and it must be admitted that none of the *āḻvārs'* descriptions of the Cowherd Lady even remotely suggest Durgā as she is best known, that is, as a terrifying warrior goddess. Their descriptions of Pinnai, however, do evoke the same beauty that Pallava sculpture bestows on Durgā as well as on Śrī and Bhū.

There is, however, another seventh-century cave temple at Māmallapuram that seems to link the Cowherd Lady and Durgā explicitly, if all the evidence here has been read correctly. In the *maṇḍapa* portraying Krishna's lifting of Mount Govardhana, Krishna stands with an arm upraised holding the mountain, and immediately to his left stands a *gopī* who is set apart from the others in the scene by her proximity to Krishna, her posture, and her hair style, features suggesting that she is Pinnai.[78] Yet the sculpture also suggests that she is linked with Durgā, for she alone among the other figures in the scene wears the breast band (*kucha-bandha*) that in every other Pallava sculpture is worn only by Durgā and her guardians.[79]

Turning now to liturgical texts, we find some suggestions of a link between Pinnai and Durgā in Vaikhānasa and Pāñcarātra texts associated with the South. They date in their present forms between the ninth and the twelfth centuries but probably contain traditions going back to the seventh century and earlier. One Vaikhānasa text, *Kāśyapa's Book of Wisdom,* contains this striking invocation to Durgā: "Durgā, the descendant of Kātyāyana, the Wife of Viṣṇu [!], the Habitant of Mount Vidhya."[80] Here the identification of Kātyāyanī as Viṣṇu's wife is explicit though startling in its context, as the translator's exclamation point indicates. In the Pāñcarātra texts Durgā is frequently presented as one of Nārāyaṇa's three consorts. In the *Lakṣmī Tantra,* for example, Mahālakṣmī calls herself Kālī, Durgā, and other "fierce" goddesses, as well as the wife of Nārāyaṇa. She makes repeated statements that while being the "I-hood" of Nārāyaṇa she brings forth the manifest universe by becoming three-fold, represented as three types of goddesses who can be grouped according to *guṇa* and function: Śrī (*rajas, śakti*), Bhū (*sattva, niyati*), and Durgā-Kālī-Yoganidrā (*tamas, kāla*).[81] Moreover, F.O. Schrader notes that in a Pāñcarātra *saṃhitā* of the twelfth century or later the three consorts of Nārāyaṇa are each portrayed as aspects of his *śakti* and play a role with regard to the three grades of souls, "the white Śrī taking care of the souls in which the Sattva Guṇa dominates, and red Bhū of the Rājastic ones, and the black (nīlā) Durgā of the Tāmasic ones. . . ."[82]

Taking this liturgical evidence and returning once again to Poykai's verse, we now see that he may in fact have been referring to a Pāñcarātra doctrine of Mahālakṣmī emanating herself into three goddesses, Śrī, Bhū, and Durgā. The verse could thus be paraphrased: "Though in his process of emanating the manifest universe Nārāyana unites with Śrī (*tirumakaḷ*), Bhū, and Nīlā Durgā (the Cowherd Lady) as forms of his *śakti* called Mahālakṣmī (*tirumakaḷ*), he remains all the while united with Mahālakṣmī, the primordial Śrī that is his own 'I-hood.' "

Such an interpretation presumes of course that Poykai understood Piṉṉai to be linked with Durgā, an understanding, if it ever in fact existed, that became lost to subsequent southern Bhāgavata tradition. Durgā recedes in Vaiṣṇava literature and sculpture in the South after the seventh century, while she becomes absorbed by the Śaivas, though even then retaining her conch and disk in Śaiva iconography. Perhaps a significant change in religious climate occurred in the Tamil South in the eighth century, which resulted in the loss of such non-purāṇic traditions about Krishna as those embodied in the *Bālacarita* and in the removal of Durgā from the place of importance in Vaiṣṇavism that Pallava sculpture so clearly shows she had. Such a change would also account for the loss in Tamil tradition of the memory of a link between Piṉṉai the cowherd lover of Krishna and the goddess Durgā, known also as Kātyāyanī and Ekānaṃśā, while it retained the memory of her link to Krishna as his sister.

The fact that Tamil Vaiṣṇava tradition does not itself connect Pinnai with Durga suggests strongly that such a connection never existed. The clues for it are slight and subject to interpretive ambiguity; I for one am not yet entirely persuaded by them. But the clues do exist, are difficult to explain, and suggest, I think, a fruitful area for new inquiry into the history of Krishna lore.

The Courtship of Vaḷḷi and Murugan: Some Parallels with the Rādhā-Krishna Story

BRENDA E.F. BECK

The tender eroticism of the Rādhā-Krishna love story is often thought to represent a uniquely Vaiṣṇava view of the divine. Śaiva traditions, by contrast, are sometimes said to emphasize the paradoxical and shocking, while downplaying more tender, beneficent glimpses of the godhead. Although the mythology surrounding Viṣṇu does contain some fearsome elements, it is the loving aspects of Krishna that are given central importance by most devotees. Krishna is generally remembered for his playful, seductive and gentle nature. Similar themes are not usually recognized as equally central to the Śaiva devotional tradition. The following essay attempts to outline some important parallels between the traditional love that surrounds Krishna and the popular literature depicting Śiva's second son, Murugan (also called Skanda).

In North India Skanda is considered a relatively minor figure in the pantheon; in the South, however, this is not the case. Indeed Murugan is perhaps the single most important divinity worshipped by Śaivites in Tamilnadu today. His cult has always been important in Tamil-speaking areas, but it has grown even more popular over the past hundred years.[1] It draws huge crowds in Kerala and Sri Lanka, as well as everywhere in Tamilnadu itself.

Murugan and Krishna

In his most celebrated form Murugan bears a striking resemblance to Krishna. Indeed, there are sufficient parallels to suggest that a basic pairing or complementarity in the distribution of their popular cults may be developing. Where Krishna is central in the pantheon, Murugan is peripheral or unknown, and vice versa. The acknowledgement of their similarities is rare, but underlying ostensible differences are many common themes.

Two of the most obvious parallels between the worship of Krishna and that of Murugan are the prominence of *bhakti* (personal demonstrations of devotion, hymn-singing, etc.) and the centrality of erotic themes in both mythologies. Worshippers in both cults use metaphors of ecstatic love to depict their devotional feelings, and devotees of both deities occasionally take the role of the Lord's mistress.[2] When they conceive of themselves as female they are better able to act out their desire for intimacy with one or the other of these two handsome and youthful gods. In both traditions, furthermore, these devotional thoughts and erotic images have found repeated expression in the tradition of a circular love dance.[3] Both cults celebrate the dance of a group of young maidens, who move together in a round formation while singing about their thoughts of divine love play. Such dances are still regularly performed in the South. In the villages of Tamilnadu unmarried girls can be seen singing songs to Murugan as they dance around a pile of overturned harvest baskets at local festivals.[4] Similar dances, dedicated to Krishna, are apparently practiced in the North.[5]

Many other parallels between Krishna and Murugan are also worthy of note. Looking to the mythology surrounding the two gods, for example, we find a number of striking similarities. Both deities enjoyed an infancy that is described by their devotees as playful, even mischievous. Murugan was so rambunctious, and upset so many things, that the gods mistook him for a demon (*asura*).[6] Krishna has a similar childhood reputation and is famous for stealing hanging pots of curds. Murugan is once reputed to have locked up Brahmā as a punishment for his excessive pride, just as Krishna once conducted a similar contest in order to earn the respect of this same divine colleague.[7] Both gods have a reputation, furthermore, for having defeated various sorts of demons as adolescents. Each use guile and trickery, coupled with extraordinary physical strength, in this work.

In addition to their childhood and adolescent feats, and more important for our theme, both Krishna and Murugan are famous as lovers. Each is youthful, handsome, and dark-complexioned. Each seeks after a woman who is socially "out of bounds," and makes her into his special mistress. Krishna takes Rādhā, usually considered a married woman, for his lovemate. Murugan takes Vaḷḷi, the low-caste daughter of a hunter, and woos her despite the immense difference of status between them. Although Vaḷḷi is unmarried, her father and brothers expect her to remain chaste. She imposes a strict code of decorum upon herself, furthermore, even when alone. Murugan breaks all the rules of normal interaction by approaching her so boldly; indeed, he already has a wife.

Murugan and Krishna also encounter their mistresses in similar settings. Each finds his mate in a forest. Neither maiden is entirely alone, however; each is accompanied by her female friends. What is more, in both cases these friends also fall in love with the godlike visitor. And in the loving interchanges between the primary mistress and her suitor, a certain equality or balance develops. Neither woman is a submissive spouse, rather both are playmates. Rādhā and Vaḷḷi, furthermore, are typically likened to honey, a sweet substance "stolen" from the forest. In these ways each tradition evokes a sense of sweet mutuality and tenderness. Each also celebrates a rejection of the world of formal hierarchies. And finally, at some point in these roughly parallel stories both women are pictured in a state of separation from their lovers. The poets celebrate their feelings of longing during such periods and describe with relish the madness that afflicts lovers.

Similarities between the Murugan and Krishna devotional traditions extend beyond mythology to the domain of iconography. For example, both Murugan and Krishna are commonly depicted as youthful adolescents in forest settings. Krishna carries a flute; Murugan, a spear. The shapes of these two objects are similar and both are gently held. More striking still, Krishna always wears a peacock feather in his crown, whereas Murugan has a peacock for a vehicle, which is almost always to be seen standing at his side.

One final point concerns a confusion over the identification of certain popular icons. The immensely sacred temple on Tirumalai hill in Andhra, for example, contains an image of Śri Veṅkateśvara, a dark young male understood to be a form of Viṣṇu. He is always shown in a standing position, bedecked in jewels that glow against a dark background. In the river that flows down this sacred hill is a place where Murugan is said to have done penance, and the story says that he manifested himself there without his weapons or extra hands. Interestingly the central icon depicting Veṅkateśvara is also "disarmed" in that it lacks the disc and conch, Viṣṇu's characteristic weapons. The image does, however, have matted locks, snake ornaments, and a crescent mark on its head, all familar details in the iconography of Śiva. Finally, some of the worship on this site is done with *bilva* leaves, an offering normally used only in Śaiva temples.[8] Since all hill sites in the South are sacred to Murugan, according to early Tamil literature, the earlier history of the Veṅkateśvara shrine could well have involved this Śaivite figure.

Murugan and Krishna are not simply allomorphs of one another, however; a number of motifs in the Murugan story recapitulate those associated with Śiva and bring him clearly within the Śaivite fold.[9] And there are basic differences between the Rādhā and Vaḷḷi courtship stories. Most central is the fact that Rādhā remains a mistress forever. Her story has no "ending." Krishna's divinity is glimpsed through the endless love-play in their repeated trysts. In Vaḷḷi's case, however, a clear progression occurs. Popular accounts normally start with Vaḷḷi's birth. They then progress through a period of seduction and love making, and end in Vaḷḷi's marriage, after which she ascends to the world of the gods at Murugan's side. In iconography, furthermore, Vaḷḷi is always pictured as she is late in the story: she is shown being wed to Murugan, or as his spouse. Rādhā, by contrast, is generally shown in a love tryst or yearning for Krishna's arrival. If, then, there are aspects of Murugan's story which suggest that of Krishna, we must also be aware that there are significant points of contrast.

The Courtship of Vaḷḷi

Keeping all this in mind, let us enter upon a brief analysis of one version of the well-known story of Murugan's courtship of Vaḷḷi. We may begin by breaking the account into three main stages. These are 1) Vaḷḷi's birth, childhood, and initial resistance to Murugan's advances; 2) Vaḷḷi's love of and receptivity to Murugan's advances (after he grasps her in order to prevent her from being harmed by a wild elephant); and 3) Vaḷḷi's wedding and subsequent role as a spouse (see figure 12). When we study these three phases in the Vaḷḷi-Murugan courtship we will see how each has become poetically embroidered with differing patterns of imagery. We will also see how the progression of stages can be understood as an allegory for the deepening attachment to the lord experienced by a true devotee.

The text upon which the following analysis is based, a small pamphlet I purchased in a local bazaar,[10] is only one of many accounts, but others tell essentially the same story. I have chosen this text for its popular style and also for the beauty and complexity of the thoughts conveyed by its poetic images. In its main outlines, at least, the sequence of events that lead up to Murugan's wedding with Vaḷḷi is familiar to nearly everyone of Hindu parentage in Tamilnadu over the age of ten. In rural areas, if the Coimbatore area is any indication, Vaḷḷi's story can be seen acted out and retold repeatedly. Here is the story in outline form.

Vaḷḷi's birth is said to have resulted from the chance union of a male ascetic with a spotted female deer. Vaḷḷi's deer-mother abandoned her at birth, however, in a hole formed by a sweet potato tuber. Soon the small baby was found by the king of a group of forest hunters. Vaḷḷi was adopted by this king and his wife, and raised in a small village. She grew up in the same mountainous, wild area where her parents had met. During her adolescence a forest wanderer Narathar (Skt Nārada), working as an assistant for the gods, came to know of Vaḷḷi's beauty. He took a drawing of the young girl to his guru, the god Murugan. The latter, a youthful and handsome divinity, became quickly infatuated by thoughts of this forest-dwelling maiden and went, dressed as a hunter, to look for her. Murugan found Vaḷḷi guarding a patch of millet in the forest, and proceeded to woo her with numerous amorous arguments. But he was unsuccessful. Later he tried a second disguise, that of a bangle-selling merchant. Still later he took the form of a very old sage. Vaḷḷi resisted each of these guileful approaches but was finally forced into Murugan's arms when the latter caused her to see, as a mirage, an attacking wild elephent. Afraid for her life, Vaḷḷi ran into the sage's arms. Then the great god relented and revealed himself in his "true" form, a young, virile male. Vaḷḷi was infatuated and yielded to him upon his promise of marriage. Vaḷḷi's father and brothers resisted this idea, but Murugan subdued them with arrows. They soon consented to the wedding and a great celebration was held three days later in the little village where Vaḷḷi was raised.

In this story there is an evident progression from low- to high-status behavior and from little cultured to highly cultured situational imagery. Murugan, for example, is first encountered in childlike form, as if he were a playful demon. Next he takes the disguise of a low-caste hunter (Vēṭar). Subsequently he becomes a somewhat higher status bangle merchant (Cēṭṭiyar), and then a still more respected old man (presumably a Brahman), a devotee of God. Thus the story is built, in part, around a progression of disguises. These masquerades outline a clear hierarchy of stages for the revelation of the true nature of the main character. There follows a wedding that unites a girl of low status background to a great god. Vaḷḷi has been raised in a forest by a family of hunters: she is said to have worn rags and to have slept on stones. But by the end of the story she is like a queen, and is seen dressed in beautiful clothes. By wedding her, Murugan also grants Vaḷḷi "immortality." At the end of the story she is more than a mortal: she has joined the ranks of the gods.

We can easily see the above sequence of events as a simple success story, not unlike a European fairy tale. The lowly maiden is married to the amorous prince and everyone lives happily ever after. Vaḷḷi is a classic low-caste Cinderella, and this dimension of the story is clearly important in explaining its appeal to the South Indian imagination. The Vaḷḷi theme equates low with high. It suggests that the path of devotion to Murugan is open to all, regardless of caste status. It is not surprising that this kind of social message, reinforced by the high intensity of romantic imagery, makes the story infinitely more popular with devotees than the description of Murugan's arranged marriage with his first wife, Dēvānai. That story, though not unknown, is always told very briefly. To my knowledge it is rarely elaborated upon, nor is it in popular demand.

There is more to Vaḷḷi's courtship story than the simple progression we have so far described. Let us now pay attention to the specific images and contours of the story to see what they tell us about the symbolic dimension of religious thought in a popular South Indian context. We begin by examining some of the natural images in this account that relate water to earth. We will also touch upon various references to animals, to wealth, and to immoral social actions. In conclusion we will discuss the role of kinship in the development of the Vaḷḷi-Murugan romance.

Natural Images

The images of water in this account begin with a description of Vaḷḷi's birth on an island. Just how an island can be found in a forest is never made clear. On the island or near it, however, is a fountain of the Ganges. The image seems to be one of a mountain stream that divides for a brief distance as it runs down an inclined forest floor. A small dry islet is thus formed and this is where Vaḷḷi is born.[11] Much later Murugan appears to the young girl in his disguise as a sage. He begs her for water to quench his thirst and Vaḷḷi shows him a spring where he can drink. We also learn that in a previous life Vaḷḷi used to meditate on Murugan while sitting beside a spring.

Murugan also attempts to woo Vaḷḷi by making use of water metaphors. He says at one point, "I will show you the sea of love, and sail a ship upon that sea." Then, when Vaḷḷi finally consents to become Murugan's mistress-wife, the narrator comments that "Murugan became as happy as a large ocean." At another point the narrator of the poem speaks of this god as "the son of the Ganges" (a reference to Murugan's father, Śiva, who has the river Ganges flowing from his hair). And Vaḷḷi's own father, upon meeting Murugan as an ascetic sage, says to him, "Your whole form is trembling. Perspiration runs like a river over you."

In a very general way, then, Vaḷḷi is depicted as born on an islet. Yet the associations with water go further. When the old man (Murugan) is later led to a spring, for example, he identifies this source of water with love itself. He says that he is "immersed in a spring of infatuation." He fears he will die by falling in. To save him Vaḷḷi has to grasp his hand and pull him back from the water's edge. A few stanzas later he finally unites physically with Vaḷḷi, while they still stand beside this spring, where water and land are in contact. Thus a spring lies at the center of many of the images that link them, and the scene of their meeting may also be likened to an islet or still point in the center of a river.

Other aspects of a natural landscape also enter into the story's imagery in a symbolic way. Vaḷḷi was born in a forest, in a hollow formed by a growing sweet potato tuber, and her mother was a spotted deer. In these ways she springs from natural things, far from cultivated, human surroundings. But Vaḷḷi is wooed, in the main, on the edge of an isolated millet field. Thus the love affair takes place in a spot that is undergoing human cultivation. Like Vaḷḷi herself, it is gradually being won over from the wild. Finally, Vaḷḷi is married in her own village, amongst her many relatives. At this point she is depicted for the first time in a fully social landscape. And finally there is a reference to the abode of the gods: the couple leave, after the wedding, for the habitat of the immortals.

A third progression in the imagery of this courtship story concerns the description of the principal characters' own bodily forms. Vaḷḷi is said at several points early in the text to resemble various species of birds. She is repeatedly referred to as a cuckoo, a peahen, and a swan.[12] Variations on this theme, such as a "cuckoo in a grove of mangoes," also occur. All these early references use passive images. Later, however, after Murugan unites with her, Vaḷḷi becomes a "dancing peacock." Paralleling this series are the several animal images used to refer to Murugan. At one point Vaḷḷi accuses him of being "like a snake that has encircled [her] leg." At another point her female friends speak of him as "as a tiger that came into the forest after a tender young creeper." Later, however, Vaḷḷi and Murugan are described without such metaphors. And at the wedding that seals their union, the initiative is more balanced between them. Murugan is no longer viewed as an aggressor vis-à-vis a physically passive (though verbally aggressive) creature. Physical desire has been contained and distributed within the socially acceptable institution of marriage, and in consequence we find fully human images of the lovers at the end of the account, which reflect their newly compassionate comportment toward one another.

One can find parallel progressions in the imagery of temperature and texture. Early in the story Vaḷḷi is accused by Murugan of having a "stony heart." He also describes her as having "a heart like iron."[13] By contrast, Murugan says of himself that a "hot sun" is burning him, and that his heart is melting. Vaḷḷi is cool and hard, resistent to his approaches, whereas he is excessively hot and soft.[14] Indeed, she is said at one point to be as cool as the moon, while Murugan is "boiling." Vaḷḷi accuses her suitor of having a mouth that is "like a pit of fire," and the narrator says at one point that Murugan looks like "a glowing coal" beneath his disguise as a sage.

When in the second stage of the story he shows his true form to her (just after she runs into his arms to avoid the elephant), however, he appears like a moon. His glance is now "cool." Furthermore, Murugan now approaches Vaḷḷi only at night (during the three-day interim between the elephant attack and the wedding). At this time the moon is properly "cool" and the cuckoos in the groves are said to sing. Vaḷḷi's softening is less obvious. Yet she does eventually allow Murugan to approach. Her words of consent are immediately preceded, furthermore, by the image of an attacking elephant. This beast is said "to pound and powder up all the trees" of the forest before her eyes. One might say, therefore, that a softening on her part is presaged by a background scene.

It is interesting to ask why this elephant attack is necessary. Simply put, it is a device used to keep Vaḷḷi's chastity and honor intact. Since Vaḷḷi believes that she is in mortal danger, she is justified in letting an old man protect her, even if this protection requires physical contact with him. But once the old man has his arms around her the situation abruptly changes. The old man is now her husband (symbolically), for he alone has embraced her. After this has occurred she may allow herself to be further wooed by him. Concurrently, he reveals himself in his "true" form as a handsome young man, as soon as she has passed his three "tests" of chastity. Therefore both Murugan and the poet use the elephant to bolster Vaḷḷi's moral reputation. She is not a loose woman who yields to any suitor. Murugan's disguises were designed simply to check on her character and mental attitudes. Vaḷḷi passes the tests, rejecting all three disguises, and finally the god must use the ruse of an elephant mirage to achieve his amorous ends.

This important elephant scene makes for a clear difference between the Rādhā and Vaḷḷi stories. Rādhā clearly transgresses social norms in her affair with Krishna. Vaḷḷi, however, cannot be accused of immorality at any point. Further evidence for this same contrast lies in the fact that only three days pass between Vaḷḷi's physical submission to Murugan and their wedding. The poet makes it clear that Murugan paid visits to Vaḷḷi at night during this period, and that they several times enjoyed intercourse together. Yet this phase of their love, parallels to which are given so much attention in the Rādhā-Krishna story, is quickly and briefly passed over in Vaḷḷi-Murugan accounts. Not only is their love-making never described in detail, but even the trysts themselves are barely mentioned. What descriptions the poet does provide for this period of love-making concern themselves only with Vaḷḷi's new character. She now yearns for Murugan's presence, whereas before she consistently rejected his approaches. She now loses her appetite and appears wan, while Murugan continues to suffer from excessive desire. Once Vaḷḷi's heart is won, she is all but consumed by love for her suitor. Now she is immensely loyal to him: now it is she who is "hot." But all this takes place, recall, as marriage approaches: the Vaḷḷi tradition seems to pay conscious attention to the maintenance of social norms, whereas the Rādhā story flouts social conventions. As if with the same attention to order, Vaḷḷi's moods are made to progress, whereas Rādhā's mental states oscillate. For her it is as if time were suspended.

Perhaps we can best view these differences against the differing sectarian traditions from which the two love stories stem. Each contrasts, in a sense, with the dominant pattern of its own milieu. True to the *bhakti* tradition, each story is radical relative to its own context. The Vaiṣṇava tradition can be said to embody a clearer "time" dimension than does the Śaiva milieu. Viṣṇu appears in time through a conventionally ordered series of avatar forms. Furthermore, we know that we are still in that time, as there is one avatar yet to come. The celebration of the Rādhā-Krishna love affair suspends this sense of progression. It gives us a glimpse of human interaction with the divine that stands beyond time. The story of Vaḷḷi, similarly, can be seen to contrast with the main principles of Śaiva mythology. There are no true avatars of Śiva and no clear time progression structures the myths about him. Instead, Śiva's activities pose a constant paradox. He is ascetic and householder, destroyer and creator, horrific and beautiful, all in one. There are alterations of episode, but there is no fixed sequence of events. Again, therefore, the popular, devotional tradition imbedded in this larger frame seems to have created its own counterpoint. The story of Vaḷḷi and Murugan is progressive. It has a beginning and an end. In addition, although Murugan retains elements of his father's character—madness, for instance, and the use of ruses—his behavior is not paradoxical. It is milder, more human, and has a clear life-cycle structure to it that makes him more popular with devotees.

Social Images

Let us now consider some further examples of this sense of ordered progression, such as the shift from material to spiritual wealth near the end of the story. At the beginning of the account Vaḷḷi is called a "golden little girl." Later she is said to be constituted of "pure gold" and to have precious stones decorating her arms, legs and breasts. Near the beginning she is also referred to as a "precious pearl" and as a "treasure that gives constant wealth." Furthermore, she is said to sit on a seat of coral, of gold, and of precious stones while she watches over the millet crop. Clearly these are metaphorical descriptions, since elsewhere her community is described as poverty-stricken and her people as dressed in rags: the poet praises Vaḷḷi by likening her to some form of material wealth.

Later, however, there is a shift. When Murugan comes disguised as a merchant selling bangles, Vaḷḷi asks how much they cost, allowing him to say, "You'll get six small bangles for money, but for your nature you'll get many great bangles." In addition, he says, "If you yield to me you will get even finer bangles, gems too precious to be priced." Presently he presses further, adding that "I have plenty of money . . . but money and coins are worth nothing, whereas the love of maidens is sugarcane." In this middle section of the story, then, physical beauty is of less value than is the right state of mind, as fed perhaps by some spiritual kind of food.

A complete transfer from the material to the spiritual perspective on beauty, however, occurs only at the end of the courtship story. After the wedding, when the father of Vaḷḷi sends his daughter off with Murugan to the abode of the gods, only Vaḷḷi's spiritual qualities are catalogued. She is now a daughter who is "very proper and good," a girl of "good character." These traits are then generalized. The story ends with a plea that all good mortals be showered with blessings.

Two more metaphors imbedded in the text of this love story remain to be explored. The first is a repeated set of references to the idea that Vaḷḷi is a kind of intoxicating substance, and the second that Murugan is a drunken reveler. Early in the tale Murugan is driven by a "fury of love." He is said to be like "one possessed." Love "dances within him like a demon." Disguised as a hunter, he skips and jumps and his body trembles. He is covered in perspiration. Later, as a sage, Murugan shouts to Vaḷḷi that he is dying, that he is suffering from a confusion of the mind. There the narrator says that he is "like a forest monkey possessed by a demon."

Murugan is not only a madman, however. He is also in a state in which he threatens societal moral norms. Initially this lover-god is referred to as a "demon child," "one who doesn't know the proper way." A little later he is someone "with bulging eyes, one who ogles." Murugan also fears that Vaḷḷi's brothers may catch him and beat him up as a "thief," recognizing his amorous designs.[15] And finally, the aging ascetic speaks of himself as a "black old man, a man fallen from good conduct." In all these ways Murugan is seen to transgress the boundaries of normal social behavior in his wooing of Vaḷḷi. He leaves the realm of correct conduct to court her, but eventually returns to it after their wedding. In the last lines of the poem, then, this god is seen as once again mentally stable, or sane. Now he participates in a major cultural rite. In this scene, by contrast with foregoing ones, Murugan is described as one who "has no deceit." The father and brothers of Vaḷḷi now fall at his lotus-red feet. He allows himself to be decorated and sprinkled with water, as the great bridegroom. And the last image of him is as he departs towards heaven to "live in great happiness . . . with his young ladies."[16]

There is also an important progression in the images of kinship. Vaḷḷi and Murugan first meet as two strangers in a forest. At first Vaḷḷi's

FIGURE 12.

The Marriage of Vaḷḷi and Murugan

Wall poster. The main figures, from left to right, are Sarasvatī, Vaḷḷi's father, Vaḷḷi, Murugan, Gaṇeśa, and Nārada. Brahmā tends the sacred fire in front of which the wedding takes place. Śiva and Pārvatī bless the couple from the upper left corner, and Viṣṇu and his wife Lakṣmī bless them from the right. Photograph Brenda E.F. Beck.

TABLE 1: PERCENTAGE OF QUATRAINS IN VAḶḶI'S STORY CONTAINING AT LEAST ONE REFERENCE TO GIVEN THEMES

Section of Poem:	I	II	III
Theme:			
Forest Imagery	23.5	17.8	0
Animal References	22.1	18.9	0
Immoral Behavior	15.7	0	0
Madness, Intoxication	13.7	13.0	0
Devotion to God	4.9	33.2	28.6
Happiness, Well-being, Longevity	2.0	39.1	71.4
Moral Behavior	4.4	12.5	28.8

relationship with her lover is very strained. She is understandably suspicious and angry. She dislikes the implications about her character contained in Murugan's repeated requests that she yield to his amorous advances. Thus Vaḷḷi complains that Murugan "talks wickedly" and that he is treating her "as one would treat a prostitute." But later she undergoes a change of heart. After Murugan manages to grasp her physically she begins to praise him. She now calls him "beautiful," a "husband fit for my love." Murugan speaks to Vaḷḷi earlier of separation from his own (first) wife and of his fear of dying while yet ununited with Vaḷḷi. She, too, is separated from others by her work as a guardian of crops planted in the forest. After she runs into his arms in fear, however, the imagery of union takes over. Vaḷḷi now speaks to Murugan, saying, "We will be great, (we will be) without any separation, ever."

This transformation of separation into union can also be viewed as a progression from stranger to close relative. But when Murugan approaches Vaḷḷi at the spring, just as she pulls him back from the water's edge, he turns and says "you are my proper granddaughter." A little later, after he has succeeded in fully embracing her, he says, "I am your cousin. . . . I am you own sun," meaning that he is a proper cross cousin, the correct marital partner. He then explains to Vaḷḷi that she is a daughter of Viṣṇu. The reader is assumed to know that according to common popular tradition Viṣṇu and Pārvatī (Murugan's mother) are considered siblings.[17] This makes Vaḷḷi a mother's brother's daughter in relation to her lover.[18] The first mention of kinship, the reference to a "granddaughter," seems a calculated ploy on Murugan's part to try to get Vaḷḷi to relax. He is an old man and she, a young girl: she should think of him as an aged relative. She has no cause to fear. But the second time the revelation of a kinship bond is more concrete and more accurate; an important transformation has occurred. These two lovers, initially strangers and inappropriate mates for one another, end up cross cousins, the ideal marital pair.

The next set of images to be considered concern the hunter/hunted theme. This imagery pervades much of the text. Such scenes are laden with irony: Vaḷḷi, the representative of a hunting caste, is featured here as the prey. Vaḷḷi describes herself to Murugan as belonging to a caste that traps wild birds while they dance. Yet he is attempting to capture her; and eventually she will "dance" in his embrace. Vaḷḷi understands the situation and asks him bluntly at one point, "Have you come as a hunter of animals or of women?" Hunting, furthermore, is also linked to food imagery. Just as the hunter is hungry, so Murugan is thin, like a starving man. The real prey that will satisfy his longing is the "bird-like" woman who arouses his passion, but she takes his complaints of hunger at face value. She tries to offer him her normal diet, raw millet flour mixed with honey. This food does not satisfy the visitor: it apparently has the opposite effect, for Murugan has a dizzy spell. He claims to have been poisoned and asks for water, and Vaḷḷi must lead him to a spring to drink.

Seeing the water, Murugan seems to fall toward it in a faint. Vaḷḷi stretches out her hand to catch him and the grasp that ensues is the first physical contact between the two.[19] Now Murugan is emboldened and begins to talk of the parallels between hunting and physical desire more directly. Thus he says, "You who satisfied my hunger, good pearl, Vaḷḷi pearl, please satisfy my infatuation. If you join me it will be fine."

The same kinds of analogy extend further into the text of the story by providing links to several metaphors of cooking. At the beginning of the encounter between these lovers, Vaḷḷi is called "red honey" by Murugan. Such imagery links her to a wild, naturally produced food that requires no cooking. Similarly, at other points she is called "nectar" and also the "juice of ripe fruit," both foods that are eaten raw. Murugan, on the other hand, is likened to a farmer and also to the of processes cooking more generally. He says to Vaḷḷi at one point, "I will raise a paddy crop of love," as if raw rice could be magically transformed into sexual desire. He is also very hot. His love, he says, "is boiling fast." Later, after the marriage, it is as if that "raw" desire had been modified and cooled after cooking. At the end the hunter is seen to have conquered the hunted. The hungry eater has obtained his desired food. These transformations are approached metaphorically, but at their root is a social perspective. Through marriage the intial sexual attraction that brought Vaḷḷi and Murugan together in the forest is transvalued and becomes a bond of social utility.

Table 1 is an attempt to summarize some of these progressive shifts of imagery. When the poem we have studied is divided into three successive parts that correspond to Vaḷḷi's resistance, capitulation, and marriage, a count can be made of references to various topics that occur in each section. Note that both forest imagery and animal descriptions decline in frequency in the later sections of the poem, as do references to madness, intoxication, and immoral behavior. All are absent completely after the wedding has taken place. By contrast, the poet's concern with devotion to God, well-being, longevity, and moral behavior all increase in frequency toward the end of the story. All are important elements in the final, post-marriage scene.

The progressive character of the love story of Vaḷḷi and Murugan, which all these images underscore, serves both to tame the god Murugan, bringing him into the world of proper social custom, and, in a different way, to tame his forest mistress. As an account of Vaḷḷi's life it can also be seen as an account of the progress of a human devotee toward merger with divinity. And just as some Vaiṣṇavas identify their experience with that of the *gopīs,* if not of Rādhā herself, Śaivites are apt to identify with Vaḷḷi in their attempt to appreciate the closeness of Murugan.[20] As in the case of Rādhā, too, an element of tension is introduced into the story once the union has been consummated. Another popular poem about Murugan that provides more information on his relationship with Vaḷḷi after their marriage shows the two in an argument.[21] Vaḷḷi tends to quarrel with Murugan, accusing him in a playful and seductive manner of ignoring her for her co-wife. Much of this poetry is in the blame-praise tradition, where insults are in fact hidden compliments. Vaḷḷi is forceful, in contrast to the mild, submissive woman that her co-wife Dēvānai represents, just as Rūpa Gosvāmī's Rādhā never becomes as submissive as her rival Candrāvalī.

In one of these arguments, Vaḷḷi begins to make fun of Murugan's

TABLE 2: MURUGAN AND KRISHNA AS BROTHERS-IN-LAW

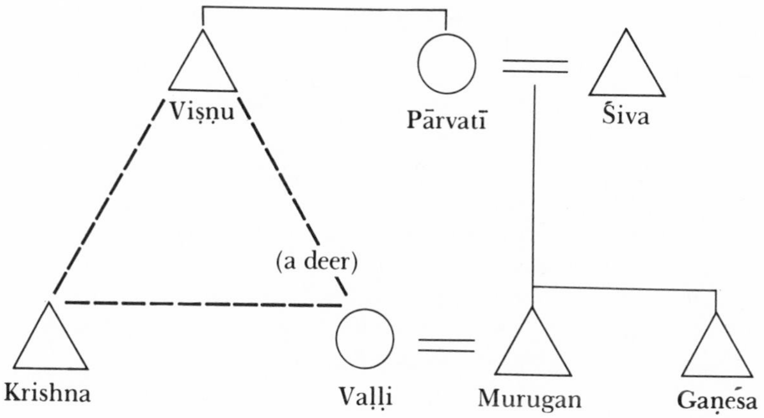

relatives and provides us with a clear statement of Murugan's relation to Krishna. She says, "Your brother [Ganeśa] . . . he of big stomach, sat on the riverbank . . . playing the drum. . . . Your brother-in-law [Krishna] was clapping in harmony." She refers here to the popular understanding of their relation in the South (table 2). This kin bond between the two gods fits well with their similar, yet distinct, sets of attributes: they are similar in broad outline but complimentary in detail.[22]

In sum, this popular version of Murugan's courtship story provides many parallels with familiar Krishna legends, but many contrasts as well.

Comments: The Divine Consort in South India

GLENN E. YOCUM

Sītā, Śrī, Piṉṉai, and Vaḷḷi—four Hindu goddesses, four consorts, all with the exception of Sītā associated with South India—an attractive array of divine personae, particularly in these four papers, each of which makes a distinctive contribution to our understanding of the particular consort upon whom attention is focused.

Cornelia Dimmitt's paper highlights the way in which the depiction of Sītā in Vālmīki's text parallels certain Vedic themes, particularly the Indra-Vṛtra myth. Although Sītā, whose name reflects the myth of her origin, has definite associations with fertility and the earth, I question whether these connections are strong enough to justify calling her a fertility goddess. Indeed Sītā does seem to personify nature at various points, and it is worth noting that it is always beneficent nature that she embodies, never the destructive, rampant nature of a Kālī or a pox goddess. But when nature echoes Sītā's actions and emotions, are these not just typical metaphorical devices being employed by Vālmīki that may well have no real theological point? In Indian literature it is not unusual for nature to be portrayed as sympathetically mirroring the situations and emotions of the protagonists. I was intrigued by the notion that Sītā is Rāma's *śakti,* but again one can ask whether Vālmīki was conscious of making such a theological statement in the passages cited. (It goes without saying that if there were no woman in this story, there would be no action.) Moreover, one might ask whether it is Sītā's feminine power, channeled by chastity and conjugal faithfulness, that is the motive for her (and *their*) comparison with the lifegiving aspects of nature, or whether it is the fact that she and Rāma together, in their union, guarantee prosperity, as the last sentence in Dimmitt's paper seems to suggest.

In Vasudha Narayanan's paper we are presented with quite a different world of thought, that of philosophical theology. Here one sees how Viṣṇu's consort Śrī, whose basic features first appear in myth and poetry, achieves philosophical legitimacy in Vedānta Deśika's attempt to incorporate her into a *viśiṣṭādvaita* system of doctrine. Śrī's mediating role, characterized by forgiveness and compassion, suggests that she represents the accessible aspect of the divine nature (*saulabhya*) as contrasted with the stern and more distant justice of the supreme Nārāyaṇa (*paratva*).[1] Perhaps, however, to use these categories is to make a sharper distinction than Vedānta Deśika himself intended. Be that as it may, what appears to characterize other Hindu goddesses who are firmly wedded to their husbands also is true of Vedānta Deśika's Śrī, namely, that she expresses the positive, compassionate side of the divine nature. It is worth emphasizing that for Vedānta Deśika, Śrī is neither *prakṛti* nor *śakti* in any general sense. Her primary role is soteriological rather than cosmogonic. Like Sītā, Śrī is never destructive or malevolent, and I would venture to say that here as before her benevolence and auspiciousness are closely related to her inseparability from and subservience to Viṣṇu, even though for Deśika her personality is distinct from that of the Lord. She is in every sense a proper and benign consort—a rightful dharmic wife of Nārāyaṇa and a compassionate mother of devotees.

Dennis Hudson formulates what I think is an exciting and plausible thesis suggesting that Piṉṉai is an incarnation of Durgā. But it raises, as he is aware, a fundamental question: if Piṉṉai is an *avatāra* of Durgā, then why has this fact been so thoroughly forgotten, why has she so completely lost all association with the more ferocious side of Durgā-Koṟṟavai's character? Is it that Vaiṣṇavism must domesticate its goddesses? Can it not tolerate the dark sides of a Durgā or a Koṟṟavai? And if so, why?

Brenda Beck's paper prompted me to reflect on some general questions of interpretation that arise in regard to all these papers, but before I explore these let me make a few particular remarks. The first is a caution against overinterpreting literary images. In regard to the text she has treated, one might at least raise the question of whether some of these images are selected because they reflect themes and conventions of *kuṟiñci* poems in classical Tamil Caṅkam literature.[2] Are there any residues here of this ancient symbolic tradition, which mixes nature and culture in a peculiarly Tamil manner? A further historical question is posed by the story of Murukaṉ's courtship of Vaḷḷi, namely, to what extent is Vaḷḷi's wooing by and marriage to Murukaṉ evidence of an integration (or a "Sanskritizing," i.e., a refining, a making cultured) of a local indigenous goddess into a pan-Indian Brahmanical system of meaning?[3]

But to come to the main point: if Beck is right in her contention that Vaḷḷi is at the beginning of her courtship homologized with nature, and that her wooing by Murukaṉ represents a progressive acquisition of culture on her part, then perhaps we many find the same dynamic operative in representations of other South Indian goddesses. Indeed this pattern may reflect a South Indian understanding of femininity in general. George Hart has argued that women as depicted in ancient Tamil poetry are repositories of a dangerous sacred power termed *aṇaṅku,* which has its principal locus in the breasts and loins of the mature female.[4] It is clear that this power is related to female sexuality and fertility. Unchecked, *aṇaṅku* is dangerous and can have grave social consequences. Controlled, however, it can be quite beneficial. The major way in which this female power is controlled, according to Hart, is through marriage, for marriage ideally brings a woman's faithfulness to her husband. Marriage controls sexual desire and guides the woman's reproductive capacity into clearly defined channels. In short, women must be domesticated. Fundamentally, a woman is a natural thing (like fire), which if brought under control ceases to be dangerous and is transformed into a source of great satisfaction.[5] The same, I think, can be said of goddesses in South India, and perhaps beyond.[6] Goddesses who are independent of male control—the village goddesses of smallpox are a good example—or who dominate their husbands tend to be ferocious, malevolent, dangerous.[7] However, when properly married, i.e., domesticated, enculturated, brought under male control, they are benevolent, compassionate, and accessible. The more firmly tied to a deity the goddess is, the more cultured, the more decorous her behavior.

In the Sanskritic tradition the association of the goddess with philosophical notions such as *śakti, prakṛti,* and *māyā* seems to convey a parallel insight. The goddess's fundamental being is natural. She is homologous with nature, and nature can be uncanny and destructive. Subjected to human control, however, nature is often a source of abundance. The ambiguity of nature itself seems to find expression in these female deities. Ambivalence about women (on the part of men, needless to say) is reflected in the ways goddesses are viewed. Women—natural creatures, full of power, whose most striking function has to do with the propagation of life itself—are viewed as being like the natural environment, essential and attractive but potentially dangerous. It is worth underlining in this regard that both Vaḷḷi and Piṉṉai are conceived in the South as married women; indeed they join their consorts in the most appropriate unions possible, cross-cousin marriages.

It seems that marriage to the god—both for his divine consorts and for his human devotees, who commonly consider themselves to be females vis-à-vis the god—is more necessary and desirable in South Indian *bhakti* than in the North. Is this because a view of femininity prevails in the South that differs from the one found in the North? Perhaps another factor is that Tamil *bhaktas,* particularly the Śaivas among them, conceive the god as an owner, a possessor, indeed, a subduer of his devotees. They in turn become his humble but intimate servants, and the best model for such service is wifely devotion. God tames his devotees in the South, a sometimes less than gentle process, though it should also be said that in the course of being tamed the devotees sometimes become "mad," an occurrence suggesting that divine "culture," particularly in the case of Śiva, is not always what humans have in mind. When God tames his devotees it sometimes has the effect of collapsing the typically elaborate Hindu social hierarchy into a simple superordinate-subordinate dyadic pair symbolized by marriage. If in that relation nature is transformed into culture, it is sometimes a very simplified culture, shorn of so many complexities that it becomes again almost natural.

If we are to understand the Goddess in terms of the human experience she signifies, we must pay close attention to the models a society presents for women. There is a close association, indeed an interaction, between images of human and divine femininity, and this seems to be particularly so with regard to female consorts, i.e., women viewed in relation to men. Here especially divine interactions present vivid models for more prosaic human realities. One can only lament that in regard to the goddesses and women under review here, as so often, we have access only to what are apparently male-formulated views of femininity.

Without implying any kind of ontological judgment about the reality of the gods, I want to conclude my remarks by saying what is perhaps obvious. Talk about God, Goddess, gods, and goddesses is talk about the self and the self in relation to its environment and to other selves. If God-talk is self-talk, and if self-talk is always in some sense social, then gods, goddesses, and divine consorts can be windows opening onto the self and onto what it means to be a male or female self in relation to other selves in a particular socio-cultural context.

IV.

Concluding Perspectives

Prolegomenon to a Psychology of the Goddess

DAVID M. WULFF

The complexity of religious phenomena and their centrality in the lives of devotees should give pause to any would-be interpreter. Such hesitancy ought to be characteristic especially of the psychologist, who knows full well how complex human motives can be and how common it is to misperceive and oversimplify them. The psychotherapist's principle that no interpretation should be accepted as true unless it has found corroboration in the patient's response might well be applied here. If our interpretation of a religious image or act does not somehow enrich the life of the devotee, if it does not in some sense lead the person forward, we might well suspect that we are wrong. Unfortunately, when dealing with mythic materials of a culture far distant in time or space, we often lack the opportunity for such a test of existential appropriation.[1] The risk of error is correspondingly greater, a fact that we must always keep before us.

Of the psychologists we shall consider in this essay, C.G. Jung above all has recognized both the complexities and the dangers. He strove to embrace a phenomenological viewpoint, to give "true expression" to all that he observed of the intricacies of human subjectivity. Moreover, he was profoundly concerned with the effect of psychological interpretations: what we do to the age-old images, he said, we do also to our own souls. Regrettably, few present-day psychologists seem to share Jung's caution.

Contemporary psychology is made up of a variety of sometimes contradictory viewpoints. It has yet to find a theoretical perspective that comprehends human experience in its fullness and at the same time meets the canons of scientific research. Moreover, much psychological discourse appears completely removed from the concrete realities of human experience and culture. Religion in particular is usually altogether absent from psychology textbooks, even those that are otherwise exceptionally comprehensive. There are signs, however, that the psychology of religion is regaining the momentum and visibility that it had earlier in the century. Yet it too is divided by essential differences in theory and method, and it likewise seems at times to ignore what is most fundamental.

Psychology's Neglect of the Goddess

Given the extraordinary qualities and inexhaustible richness of the imagery of the Goddess, one would expect psychologists of religion to be particularly fascinated by her. The case in fact is quite the opposite. Only one or two of the several dozen general works published in this field in the last two or three decades so much as mentions the Goddess, and none treats her at any length. There are at least two reasons for this neglect. One is the regrettable religious parochialism of most Western psychologists of religion, the majority of whom are of Protestant Christian background and limit themselves, by and large, to the phenomena and categories of that tradition. Another reason is the widely held conviction that empirical research in psychology must be based upon representative samples of persons and must consist of quantifiable responses subject to complex statistical evaluation. Given the paucity of Goddess devotees in America and Europe, as well as the apparent lack of interest among Indian psychologists in gathering data from worshippers of the Goddess, most Western psychologists of religion stand mute on the question of her psychological significance.

One can imagine without much difficulty the sort of study that might be carried out. Two sets of questions would be assembled. One set would measure religiousness, perhaps through inquiries like these: Do you believe in the Goddess? How often do you worship her? How much influence has she had in your life? What is the name of one of her sons? The other questionnaire might be designed to record the respondent's sex, socio-economic status, and educational level, or perhaps to measure certain personality or attitude dimensions. The two questionnaires would then be mathematically correlated, in the hope that the results would allow some generalizations on how persons relatively knowledgeable about and devoted to the Goddess differ from those less involved in Goddess-centered piety.

There is in fact a series of correlational studies carried out in America, Belgium, and France that bears indirectly on the question of Goddess worship. Using a variety of measurement devices, these investigators sought to test Freud's assumption that God "is nothing other than an exalted father" by correlating their subjects' concepts of God with their concepts of Father and Mother. The first of these studies[2] discovered that, for their Western subjects, deity concepts were actually more closely related to the Mother concept than to the Father. Further investigations[3] suggest two refinements: first, the closer association of God and Mother concepts can be predicted more reliably for males than for females, and second, for both sexes God is likely to be more strongly associated with the image of the preferred parent, whether mother or father. The data gathered by Vergote and his associates,[4] although interpreted by these researchers as reaffirming the age-old association of God and Father images, in actuality lend support to the God-Mother correlation, for it is only in terms of maternal characteristics, not paternal ones, that God and Father were judged by their Roman Catholic subjects to be similar. It appears, in sum, that whatever the traditional association may be, for a variety of Christian subjects God is more maternal than paternal.

Interesting though these findings may be, they do not take us far toward an understanding of the psychological dynamics of goddess images in India. More promising for our purposes are the depth psychologies of Freud and Jung. According to both these schools, religious myths are projections of psychological processes, although the two disagree on the nature of these processes and thus on the significance of the myths. Both schools have discovered that it is not uncommon for traditional mythic images to appear in the fantasies and dreams of patients previously unacquainted with such images. In particular, in some patients' experience the mother imago shows a radical split—the good, sheltering mother in contrast to the monstrous, terrifying mother[5]—just as the mother goddess is typically both benign creator and frightful destroyer. Daim[6] cites a case of a mother fixation in which the male analysand experienced the mother imago as a threatening and dangerous mother goddess whose gigantic proportions underscore her destructive omnipotence in the analysand's life (see figure 13). The arrows suggest movement toward the twisted cross and then toward the mother image, a movement that Daim interprets as a symbol of hope for salvation.

The Freudian View: The Goddess as Infantile Mother Imago

That reality as a whole should come to be perceived in personal terms, especially parental or familial ones, is no surprise to those psychoanalysts who follow Freud. After all, the child's first object-relations are with the parents, especially the mother. The infant's world in fact *is* the mother: reality as we first come to know it is thus fundamentally feminine. With time, of course, the father imago will ordinarily also come to play an important role, even a leading one. According to Freud, it is the adult's task to gain freedom from these parental images, and in the process to overcome the tendency to personalize reality. One could, however, maintain that the metaphor of the personal does indeed tell us something about reality, while still holding that psychoanalysis may serve as a means of uncovering distortions of this metaphor and of "purifying" our understanding of it.[7] In either case, one will look to childhood for clues to the complex imagery and practices that give form and structure to religious traditions.

Psychoanalysts are agreed that the infant lacks entirely the adult sense of reality and is governed, rather, by blindly insistent instinctual needs and wishes. Objects (including persons) at first lack coherence; indeed, in the beginning the infant has no sense of being separate from those parts of the world that impinge on him or her. Even when the inexorable process of ego development brings the child more intimately into relationship with reality, he or she remains subject to strange fantasies and powerful, sometimes devastating emotions. Infantile efforts to construe the surrounding reality—including especially the structure and functions of the human body, the nature of the parents' relationship, and the processes that brought the child and his or her siblings into the world—yield startlingly ill-informed theories in which the individual's sexual and aggressive wishes play a leading role.

Psychoanalysts are not in agreement, however, about the age at which these ideas and perceptions first take form. Child analyst Melanie Klein claims on the basis of her own work that some of the most significant ones appear in the first several months of life. It is during these months, she says, that destructive impulses, the projection of them onto others, and the splitting of impulses and objects are at their height. The frightening and persecutory figures that are the outcome represent, first of all,

> the frightening aspects of the mother and threaten the infant with all evils which he in states of hate and rage directs against his primal object. Although these figures are counteracted by love towards the mother, they are nevertheless the cause of great anxieties. From the beginning, introjection and projection are operative and are the basis for the internalization of the first and fundamental object, the mother's breast and the mother, both in her frightening and in her good aspects. It is this internalization which is the foundation of the superego. I tried to show that even the child who has a loving relation with his mother has also unconsciously a terror of being devoured, torn up and destroyed by her. These anxieties, though modified by a growing sense of reality, go on to a greater or lesser extent throughout early childhood.[8]

Such incorporative and sadistic fantasies, at whatever age they may first occur, are thought by psychoanalysts to be natural components of the oral stage of psychosexual development. The stages that follow represent further evolution of the child's discovery of the body as an object of pleasure as well as of profound emotional conflict. Although the socialization of the eliminative process during the anal stage may leave long-enduring tactics for impulse control, depending especially on parental attitudes, more momentous by far are the events of the phallic stage. Eager somehow to incorporate the genital sensations that come to the fore in this stage into his relation with his mother (the normal Oedipus complex) if not also into his relation with his father (the inverse Oedipus complex), the young boy is said to experience a terrifying mixture of longing, jealousy, and dread, fearing foremost punishment in the form of genital mutilation. The young girl is thought likewise to interpret the fact of sex differences as the outcome of castration, but for her the terrible event is already past, and thus the pressures toward the renunciation of Oedipal longings are less severe. Whether boy or girl, the child is said usually to resolve the Oedipus complex by identifying with the parents and their values, forming thereby the foundations for the superego (unless one assumes, with Klein, that the superego is functioning much earlier). With puberty, the unfulfilled sexual impulses will come once more to the fore, challenging the individual to achieve the mature, genital stage of development.

Whatever the degree of maturity attained, early childhood's strange, fragmentary, and pleasure-centered world remains to some degree alive in the unconscious. Evidence of its activity is most commonly found in dreams, which are the result of an elaborate process of transformation. By condensing several elements or objects into one, displacing the emphasis from the important to the unimportant, substituting an indifferent object or substance for a significant one, reversing elements into their opposites, and finally making some sense of the whole through secondary elaboration, the unconscious ego disguises the unacceptable latent dream content while yet allowing for a measure of wish-fulfillment.

The unconscious instinctual wishes and their vicissitudes in childhood are reflected as well in fairy tales and myths. These "shared dreams" are formed much as personal ones are, although in these stories the splitting of objects, especially the parent image, is perhaps more common than condensation, and secondary elaboration is undoubtedly more thorough, given the larger role of the conscious ego in their telling and retelling. The interpretaton of these shared dreams, therefore, is bound to be more difficult, for we are farther removed from the original wishes and fantasies. Moreover, the usual procedure of asking the dreamer for associations to elements in the dream cannot so easily be applied to "dreams" augmented or embellished by generations of "dreamers." On the other hand, we may assume that the themes and structural elements that have survived this process tell us something of the fears and wishes held in common by the people who cherish these stories and their associated images.

Freud himself undertook the task of interpreting religious myth, but he focused almost exclusively upon the traditions centering on a Father-God. God, he said, is the infantile father imago writ large, projected into the cosmos as a source of protection and consolation. Religion, Freud held, is primarily a product of the male psyche, and God reflects above all else the qualities of the boy's father imago during the Oedipal period—a father who is both loved and feared. Although he had very little to say about mother-goddesses, Freud did suggest that, in general, they probably preceded the father-gods; male deities first appeared, he speculates, as sons of the great mothers, and only later gained their more exalted rank. That mother-goddesses are sometimes androgynous can be explained, he adds, by recalling the young boy's image of the mother before he learns that there are beings without a genital organ like his own, the mother of the pre-Oedipal years.[9]

Freud's virtual silence about religious traditions that do not center on a Father-God is a significant limitation of his psychology of religion. It is also one that a few of his followers have sought to rectify. Harald and Kristian Schjelderup,[10] for example, identify three fundamental types of religiousness. *Father-religion* is characterized by the prominence of feelings of guilt and fear, as well as by a desire for atonement and submission. *Mother-religion* is marked by a longing for the divine, a yearning for nearness or even mystical union with God (or the Goddess), a desire for freedom and rest. *Self-religion,* finally, is identified by fantasies of being oneself divine. The Schjelderups assert that, in comparison with the father-motif, the mother-motif plays a role of equal or even greater importance in the religious attitude. Of the world's great religious traditions, they add, those of India best illustrate the two forms of piety that Freud neglected.

The Schjelderups' three forms correspond to three different stages of psychosexual development. The self-motif harks back to the earliest, narcissistic stage, before the formation of object-relations. The mother-motif signifies the pre-Oedipal period, when the relationship with the nurturing and protective mother is yet undisturbed by sexual feelings; it may also entail fantasies of returning to the mother's womb. The father-motif recalls the child's powerful feelings of ambivalence toward the father during the Oedipus complex. The three forms of religious attitude represent, accordingly, three different degrees of regression. How far back one goes in the "flight from reality" is dependent, say the psychoanalysts, on the character of one's experiences during the formative years as well as upon the contemporary circumstances that may prompt the regressive movement.

According to this theory, then, worship of the Goddess entails at least a moderately severe regression, to the pre-Oedipal mother-child relationship. Prerequisite to the recovery of symbiotic union with the mother is renunciation of one's own sexuality, a sacrifice that has sometimes taken the form of self-castration.[11] Although so literal a sacrifice is not unknown today,[12] the gesture has come to take, much as in dreams, a more symbolic form. The decapitation of sacrificial goats—always male—at the temple of Kālī in Calcutta represents the mechanisms both of substitution (the goat for the self) and of displacement (from the genitals to the head.)

The psychoanalytic principle of overdetermination, which asserts that, in principle, psychic events have a multitude of meanings or causes, is illustrated in a recent tragic variant on the worship of the Goddess.[13] In 1972 in Jullundur, the Punjab, a father decided to sacrifice his three sons to the Goddess as a means of assuring the peace of the soul of his own father, who had died some 15 years before. A night-long vigil of song and prayer culminated in the death and dismemberment of the one son, three and a half years old, who had not escaped. The boy's uncle had proclaimed that the Goddess would restore his life after the sacrifice. In this case we see not only an individual's denial of his own sexuality (by seeking to destroy the evidence of it, his three sons), in order to regain intimacy with the mother without rousing the wrath of the father, but also a quite literal playing out of a father's jealousy toward his Oedipal-age sons. The expectation of restoration reveals the omnipotence attributed by the infant to the parents, whose unlimited powers are later attributed to the divine and then symbolically incorporated through various religious rituals (including the undisguisedly cannibalistic rite of the Christian Eucharist). Restoration fantasies simultaneously provide assurance that the loss of virility (castration) is reversible. The element of dismemberment, common in myths of various cultures, underscores through repetition the fundamental meaning of the act at the same time that it disguises it through displacement.

As we know from both myths and dreams, however, the father is only one of the threatening figures in the child's life. The mother imago likewise has a destructive aspect, not only because the infant feels willfully deprived and even abandoned by the mother, but also because the child projects onto her the rage and destructive fantasies that she prompts through her aloofness or absence. Whereas the good Mother requires only a return to sexual (pre-Oedipal) innocence in order to regain her abiding love, the bad mother exacts the terrible price of castration and death.

The destructive mother imago is perhaps nowhere better illustrated than in the traditional image of Kālī. She is herself, first of all, a phallic being, the mother-with-a-penis: she stands triumphantly erect on Śiva's body, sword raised, fingers pointed, and eyes and tongue protruding. At the same time, draped with severed heads and hands, she is the bloodied image of the castrating and menstruating (thus castrated) female. Here again we find elements of repetition and overdetermination: the numerous heads and hands, for example, are both symbolic representations of the phallus and instruments in their own right of active sexuality. The plausibility of such an interpretation is underscored by the case of a graduate student I once counseled. Initially deeply troubled by his first acting out of long-suppressed homosexual impulses, he decided shortly thereafter to declare himself a homosexual at his army physical, to avoid induction. The almost immediate outcome of the fulfillment of this resolve was a terrifying paralysis and loss of feeling in his hands (an hysterical conversion reaction known as glove anesthesia) as well as in his mouth—the parts of his own body that played an active role in his sexual encounters. When guilt feelings from the superego failed to prevent the forbidden behavior, the unconscious ego effectively castrated him by removing his hands and mouth from his awareness and control. Although Carstairs[14] discerned evidence of repressed homosexual urges in his Hindu informants, the sexual renunciation demanded and symbolized by Kālī would seem to be general and thoroughgoing.

The unusual preeminence of castration anxiety in Hindu culture and the associated ambivalence toward women are responsible, argues Daly,[15] for a regression to concerns derived from the anal stage of development. In this way he explains the Hindu fear of pollution and the elaborate rituals of purification. Oral-stage interests are implicated simultaneously, for among the taboos observed by the Hindus those concerned with what and with whom one eats are among the most important. Unclean food pollutes the eater, who in turn pollutes anyone who touches him or her. Likewise, any leftover food that has touched the lips is polluting, unless it be from one's husband or father, or the *prasād* of one's guru or the deity.[16] Both oral and anal factors are also evident in the traditional preoccupation with the production and preservation of one's semen, which is thought to be stored in the head.

By Freudian psychoanalysts, in sum, the worship of the Goddess is interpreted as a complex, predominantly pre-Oedipal fixation that is reflected throughout Hindu culture. The associated wishes and fears are sometimes represented in startlingly transparent images and rites that seem to beg for a psychoanalytic interpretation. At the same time they can be traced in the exquisitely refined sublimations of spiritual disciplines and abstract philosophy. Evaluated in terms of existential appropriability, the psychoanalytic viewpoint will undoubtedly be judged inadequate. Yet the compelling concordance between certain of these mythic images and the main elements of Freudian theory suggests that something of reality-as-experienced has been captured in both.

The Jungian Perspective: The Goddess as Archetypal Image

Whereas the Freudians trace the origins of the Goddess to the ever-recurring experience of the personal mother, Jung and his followers view her, in all her diverse manifestations, as a transpersonal phenomenon issuing out of the deep, collective layers of the unconscious. Beneath the personal unconscious, Jung postulates, lies a reservoir of dynamic, impersonal forms, the archetypes. These universally inherited factors, themselves lacking specific content, are thought to predispose one to recognize or produce certain mythical ideas that are not rooted in one's own life-experience. First observing these recurrent images in the dreams and fantasies of his patients, Jung was startled to find them in the world's great mythic systems as well, including foremost its religious traditions.

As the result of painstaking study, especially of the syncretistic mystical doctrines of Gnosticism and, in much greater depth, the highly esoteric philosophical-religious symbolism of the alchemists, Jung came to focus upon the pattern and order formed by primordial images. The unconscious, he concluded, is a *process,* by means of which the psyche undergoes progressive transformation. He called this developmental trend individuation, and he designated its goal—expressed in symbols ranging from geometric patterns to heroic or divine personages—as the self.

Individuation is an unending and indeterminately complex process that entails gradual differentiation of psychic contents—both personal and collective—and subsequent integration. The psyche consists of a multitude of opposing tendencies, all of which must finally be recognized and brought into harmonious integration if the individual is to achieve wholeness. The promotion and direction of individuation, Jung asserts, has long been the province chiefly of the religious traditions, whose rites and symbols reflect and give shape to these archetypal tendencies. Furthermore, those symbolic expressions that are the central focus of religious interest—foremost, the God-image—are typically representations of the archetype of the self; accordingly, Jung refers to the self as the "God within us."

Among the chief archetypal elements encountered as the individuation process unfolds are two of special interest for an understanding of the Goddess: the anima and the mother. The anima represents first of all the man's unconscious femininity, the collective image of woman that forms the pole opposite to the male's conscious masculine attitude and exists in a relation compensatory to it. As an *a priori* category, the anima serves as a basis for a man's experience of a woman, in which form she frequently appears in dreams and myths. At the same time that the anima personifies the man's feminine "soul," she also represents the collective unconscious as a whole. Thus in myths and fairy tales she may serve either as the hero's guide into the unknown or as the goal of his heroic labors. She is commonly encountered, moreover, in the role of consort to a male deity, forming with him the divine syzygy, a symbol of the union of opposites.[17] From such a perspective we may view Rādhā: as the anima, she serves to mediate between individual consciousness (the devotee) and the highest possibilities of the collective unconsciousness (Krishna). Their union, then, represents the attainment of the self.

Like the anima, the mother archetype has many aspects within a bipolar structure of positive and negative meaning.

> The qualities associated with it are maternal solicitude and sympathy; the magic authority of the female; the wisdom and spiritual exaltation that transcend reason; any helpful instinct or impulse; all that is benign, all that cherishes and sustains, that fosters growth and fertility. The place of magic transformation and rebirth, together with the underworld and its inhabitants, are presided over by the mother. On the negative side the mother archetype may connote anything secret, hidden, dark; the abyss, the world of the dead, anything that devours, seduces, and poisons, that is terrifying and inescapable like fate.[18]

The mother archetype is commonly personified, especially as the mother goddess or the Great Mother. She may also appear, however, in a variety of impersonal forms, including city or country, earth, the woods, a tree, the moon, or the cow, on the positive side, and a witch, dragon, the grave, or deep water, on the negative. The three *guṇas* (attributes) ascribed by Sānkhya philosophy to *prakṛti*[19]—goodness, passion, and darkness (*sattva, rajas, tamas*)—are said by Jung to be elaborations of the mother archetype.[20]

We are indebted to Erich Neumann, one of the most distinguished of Jung's followers, for a detailed study of the emergence of both the Great Mother and the anima out of the archetypal feminine, which is itself at first an indistinguishable part of a larger whole. That totality is the psyche in its original state, the undifferentiated wholeness of which is symbolized by the uroboros, the circular snake or dragon devouring its own tail.[21] From out of the uroboros's womb-like containment, wherein lie the World Parents in perpetual union, gradually emerges the primordial archetype of the feminine. Essential to the feminine, according to Neumann, are two interpenetrating yet antagonistic characters. The maternal elementary character of the archetype represents the conservative tendency to hold fast and surround all that is born of it. By contrast, the transformative character, which only gradually escapes the domination of its opposite, is responsible for amplification, unrest, or change. Both characters retain the ambivalent quality of the archetypal feminine, an ambivalence found in all other archetypes as well.

As ego consciousness gradually emerges through the process of psychic differentiation, the archetypal feminine gives way to the more clearly delineated and predictable Great Mother, whose positive and negative attributes may be separately constellated in the Good Mother and the Bad Mother, as well as to the soul-like anima, "the vehicle par excellence of the transformative character."[22] The Great Mother and the anima represent the two bipolar axes that structure the world of the feminine. Insofar as the Great Mother promotes growth and development, by bearing and releasing, she appears as the Good Mother; on the level of spiritual transformation her activity is symbolized by vegetation mysteries. When, on the other hand, the Great Mother ensnares and holds fast, she is the Terrible Mother, who is associated with bloody dismemberment and death. The transformational axis of the anima is likewise bipolar: the functions of giving and of "sublimation" mark the positive end and those of rejection and dissolution, the negative. Although there are obvious correspondences between the positive and negative poles of these two axes, the difference between them yet remains: the axis of the Great Mother bespeaks primarily the corporeal-material development of the feminine, whereas the axis of the anima, the great instigator of change, refers more to the psychic-spiritual side. Here too, however, the indefiniteness and interpenetrability of the archetypes reign: however discriminable the Great Mother and the anima may be in principle, Jung thought that they are in actuality frequently implicated with one another.

Of the images giving form to the Terrible Mother, Kālī, "the blood-drinking goddess of death" who draws life back to herself, is identified by Neumann as the most grandiose. Nowhere is more vividly expressed the feeble ego's terror of sinking back into the unconscious, into the embrace of the bewitching, emasculating, and deadly Goddess. Yet Kālī has a positive aspect as well, in which she is "a spiritual figure that for freedom and independence has no equal in the West."[23] In Kālī is thus retained the paradoxical character of the underlying archetype of the Great Mother.

Intensification of an archetype's negative aspects, says Neumann, is evidence that the phase it governs is being transcended. Following a predominance, then, of the Great Mother's terrible aspects, one may expect the phase of the separation of the world parents and an evolution of the masculine companions who emerge with the Great Mother out of the male-female uruboros. Only when the father archetype takes form, however, and establishes itself as the antithesis to the mother archetype is the tension between the psyche's opposites—foremost, between conscious and unconscious—fully constellated.[24] Finally the stage is set for the drama of individuation to complete itself, a drama that will return at long last to the starting point.

> The same uroboric symbolism that stands at the beginning, before ego development starts, reappears at the end, when ego development is replaced by the development of the self, or individuation. When the universal principle of opposites no longer predominates, and devouring or being devoured by the world has ceased to be of prime importance, the uroboros symbol will reappear as the mandala in the psychology of the adult.[25]

As we noted earlier, the mandala is not the only symbol suggesting wholeness or completion. Divinity, especially in the form of the divine syzygy, is common as well.

The images thrown up by the unconscious, whether positive or negative, are said by Jung to redirect psychic energy away from dangerously regressive channels toward symbolically equivalent yet higher ones that will spiritualize the energy and thus lead the individual forward.[26] Unfortunately, the widespread devaluation of religion and the deposing of the gods have forced the corresponding psychological

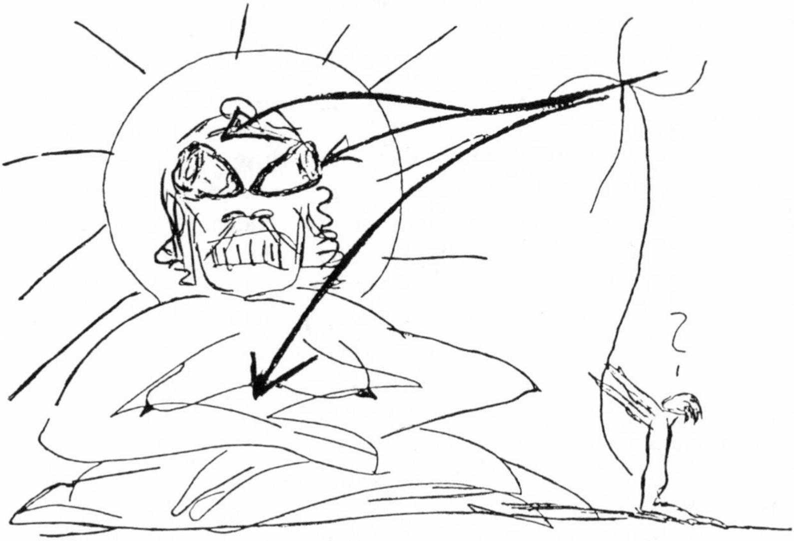

Figure 13.

A male patient's drawing in which the mother image has taken the form of the terrifying mother goddess. (From Depth Psychology and Salvation, *by W. Daim. Copyright 1963 by Frederick Ungar Publishing Co., Inc., New York. Used by permission.)*

functions to lapse, dissociated, into the unconscious. Yet recovery of naive belief in the traditional images is not the solution, given the history of mischief caused by the projection of the archetypes. What is required, says Jung, is growth into conscious awareness of the collective nature of the primordial images and strict differentiation of oneself from their suggestive powers.[27]

Eschewing every effort to explain away the archetypal factors and their effects, Jung saw his psychology as the substitution of a new set of metaphors, more accessible to the modern Western individual, for older, traditional ones. "The most we can do," he said, "is to *dream the myth onwards* and give it a modern dress."[28] Whether or not his psychology serves well those persons who retain a vivid appreciation for traditional mythic images and rites—and I suspect that it does not—there is no doubt that he has brought order and coherence to much that was once obscure.

Do we, then, accept Jung as our guide to these matters? The great majority of American psychologists have rejected his approach as "mystical" and "unscientific." Scholars of religion, for whom these epithets carry far less the intended opprobrium, might be well advised themselves to approach Jung with caution. Although his psychology is commonly contrasted with the reductionistic approach of Freud, the truth is that religion for Jung was no less a psychological phenomenon. Indeed, he explicitly rejects the possibility of metaphysics or theology, arguing that the psyche is all that we can know. Yet even if Jung's interest in religious symbols was ultimately derived from his fascination with the human psyche, there is no denying that he gives far more room than Freud to the paradoxes and polarities that confront the historian of religion. If a more adequate psychology of religion still lies on the horizon, there is little doubt that it will contain insights from the depth psychologies, especially those of Jung.

Types of Sexual Union and their Implicit Meanings

FRÉDÉRIQUE APFFEL MARGLIN

An attempt to analyze certain rituals and festivals that take place in and around the temple of Jagannātha in Puri, Orissa, revealed to me the crucial importance of discriminating among various forms of sexual union represented by different pairs of male and female deities.[1] I have been able to discriminate among three contrasting types of sexual union. I offer such a tripartite typology not as being exhaustive in a pan-Indian framework, but simply as representing the types of sexual union that I found in the iconographical, mythical, and ritual setting in Puri. I introduce the topic by presenting the cast of characters as they appear in iconography and then analyze the ritual and in some cases mythological settings in which these representations figure.

Three Types of Union

The first type of sexual union is that represented by the conjugal couple of Viṣṇu and Lakṣmī. In this pairing the woman is subordinate to the man. The hierarchical relationship is represented iconographically in such images as that of Nārāyaṇa or Viṣṇu as he sleeps on the serpent Ananta on the cosmic waters. In these images Lakṣmī is invariably represented massaging his legs, a most wifely occupation. Her size is markedly smaller than that of her Lord, a visual relation that expresses her subordination. Another popular representation of this conjugal couple in Puri is that of Lakṣmī Narasiṃha in which a diminutive Lakṣmī sits in the lap of a huge Viṣṇu in his incarnation as the Man-Lion (figure 14). The couple appears in the same hierarchical relation on the dais in the inner sanctum of the main temple of Jagannātha. On this dais there are three main deities, whose images, made of roughly carved and painted wood, stand some six feet in height. They represent, according to Vaiṣṇava tradition, a group of siblings: Jagannātha (Krishna), his sister Subhadrā, and his elder brother Balabhadra. Beside these is another wooden representation, in

FIGURE 14.

Lakṣmī in the Lap of Narasiṃha

Painted sculpture. Temple of Lakṣmī-Narasiṃha, Puri, Orissa.
Photograph Frédérique Appfel Marglin.

the shape of a pillar called Sudarśana, which is considered to be the formless aspect of the three deities. This wooden pillar is approximately the same height as the other three images. On either side of the image of Jagannātha are placed metal representations of his two wives: Lakṣmī on his left and Bhudevī, the earth goddess, on his right. This second wife of Jagannātha is considered by some to be Sarasvatī rather than Bhūdevī. These metal images are about a foot tall. The contrast between the stature of the wooden deities and that of the two wives of Jagannātha is striking and speaks eloquently of the status of the wife.

The second type of sexual union is represented by the Rādhā-Krishna couple and also by the image of Śiva Ardhanārīśvara. My reasons for classifying these two couples in the same category are not only certain iconographical parallelisms but certain sequences of ritual actions. What these two pairs share iconographically is the perfect equality of size and proportions between the male and the female. There is here no disparity in size and thus no statement about a possible hierarchical relationship between male and female. The traditional Oriya style of representing Rādhā and Krishna bears a striking resemblence to representations of Śiva Ardhanārīśvara: the pair is so depicted as to seem to be of one body (see figure 15).

The juxtaposition of these two couples is also made ritually. The last ritual of the day in Jagannātha's temple takes place just before the deities go to sleep for the night and the temple is closed. In this ritual a temple courtesan (*devadāsī*) who is standing on the threshold of the inner sanctum sings verses from the *Gītagovinda*. There is no representation of Rādhā either in the inner sanctum or elsewhere in the main temple. The song of the *devadāsī* is addressed not to the image of Jagannātha on the dais but to another figure—a small movable metal representation of Śiva Ardhanārīśvara that has been taken out of the storeroom for this ritual. The image is first placed on the bed that has just been put in front of Jagannātha by two Brahmin temple servants. It is then carried to the gate leading into the dance hall (*naṭa mandira*), all the while accompanied by the singing *devadāsī,* and there placed on a wooden stand in the shape of the *ḍamaru,* Śiva's drum. While the Brahmin priests make offerings of flowers and lighted lamps to this image, the *devadāsī* continues her song. The image is then put back in the storeroom, the lights in the temple are extinguished, and, after everyone has left the temple, the gates are locked and sealed for the night.

FIGURE 15.

Rādhā and Krishna Intertwined

Painting on cloth by the *citrakāras* of Puri district, Orissa.
Photograph Frédérique Appfel Marglin.

The third type of pairing is that of Kālī standing on a reclining image of Śiva, who is then called *śava* ("corpse"). In some pictorial representations of this pairing Śiva's erect penis is penetrating or about to penetrate the goddess (figure 7). Kālī is naked but for her ornaments, which include a garland of severed heads, a girdle of hands, and a corpse in each ear in lieu of earrings. Blood drips from her mouth. Her hair in unbound and dishevelled. In her lower left hand she holds a freshly cut head; in her upper left hand she holds a sword. Her two right hands display the "fear not" gesture and the "boon granting" gesture.

In the Śakta tradition, Jagannātha is considered to be Kālī, whose worship is performed secretly in a ritual called *śyāmā-pūjā*.(Śyāmā, "dark," is another name for Kālī). One of the mantras in the text used by the ritual specialist who performs this *pūjā* describes the image of Kālī to which worship is offered. In that *mantra* the description of Kālī is supplemented with the following specifications: she is in the cremation ground; she is surrounded by a pack of howling jackals; and she is engaged in inverse sexual union (*viparīta rati*) with Śiva, who is in this case called Mahākāla Bhairava. By "inverse sexual union" is meant that the female is above the male and that she rather than he is the active partner. Those familiar with the *Gītagovinda* will immediately recall that toward the end of the poem Rādhā is described as performing this inverse sexual union with Krishna. In fact, as Barbara Miller points out in her contribution to the present volume, Krishna calls Rādhā by the name Caṇḍī (a goddess bearing similarities to Kālī) twice in that context, and her friend also calls her by that same name once.[2]

The relation between Kālī and Śiva in this representation is in some ways the reverse of that between Lakṣmī and Viṣṇu. The asymmetry is not one of differential size but is expressed through the symbolism of the hierarchical relation among different parts of the body. The feet are the lowliest part of the body; thus placing one's feet on another's chest carries a rather strong message of differential dominance. Kālī's dominance expresses itself both through her stance and through her sexual behavior.

The Union of Equals

In order to deepen our understanding of these types of pairings we must move from the iconographical to the ritual setting. I will take as my point of departure the second type of union because it was through a study of the evening ritual in the temple and the interpretation of it given by certain participants that I began to understand what characterized the other two types of union.

Most of the exegesis of the evening ritual in the temple was given to me by one *devadāsī*, who belongs to the Gaudiyā Vaiṣṇava sect and is a faithful visitor to its local monastery. Her interpretations and comments were, however, heavily influenced by local Oriya tradition, an inevitable occurrence since her native tongue is Oriya and she is more familiar with the sixteenth-century Oriya *Bhāgavata* of Jagannātha Dās than with the writings of the Brindāvan *gosvāmīs*. One of the major differences between Gauḍiyā and Oriya Vaiṣṇavism is that Rādhā is not mentioned in the Oriya *Bhāgavata*. In this respect it follows the *Bhāgavata Purāṇa* text rather than the teachings of Caitanya.

The following words of the *devadāsī* succinctly capture how Vaiṣṇavas understand the evening ritual: "As the *gopīs* in dancing and singing in Brindāvan gave joy (*sukha*) to Krishna, here in Jagannātha's temple we give joy to Jagannātha through dancing and singing." This statement defines the setting of the ritual that the *devadāsī* went on to interpret. To explain *gopī bhāva* (the emotions, feelings of the *gopīs*) she contrasted this emotion with that existing between husband and wife. When Krishna left Brindāvan and went to the city of Dvāraka, he married eight queens. The *bhāva* of these queens, termed *svakīya*, is one appropriate to a contractual relation of mutual obligation. By marriage these queens belong to Krishna. The *gopīs*, by contrast, have *parakīya bhāva:* the emotion of a relation in which there is no ownership. The love between Krishna and the *gopīs* is referred to as "stolen love" (*corā prīti*). The *gopīs* playfully tease Krishna and brazenly call him "you thief" (*tu cora*), using the most familiar of the three forms of second person address. Krishna has stolen the love of the *gopīs* and it is in that stolen love that the greatest, most self-abandoned surrendering to him can occur. In the *svakīya bhāva* experienced by Krishna's eight queens there is always an element of ego feeling (*ahaṃkāra*). The queens say, "I have a husband," a statement that implies a feeling of possessiveness. Krishna does not belong to any one *gopī,* not even to Rādhā exclusively; his erotic dalliance is generously lavished on many women.

In the relationship between Krishna and the *gopīs,* there is not only a total absence of ego feeling, but also a complete disregard for status and hierarchy. Addressing him as "*tu cora*" would be unthinkable for a wife, who would only use the most respectful form of second person address when speaking to her husband. To illustrate the disregard of the *gopīs* toward the rules of behavior dictated by hierarchical considerations, my *devadāsī* friend told me many delightful stories. I will retell only one of these, which I feel is particularly appropriate:

> The sage Nārada not only did not understand this *parakīya bhāva* but he hated it as well. So Krishna decided to enlighten the sage. He caused himself to have a very high fever. Nārada was exceedingly grieved at the sight of Krishna's illness and immediately wanted to call all the doctors. Krishna told him that that would be useless and that the only cure for his fever would be for Nārada to bring him back the dust from the feet of some women. Nārada immediately embarked on a search for such a cure. He first went to the inner apartments of eight wives of Krishna and said: "Oh eight queens, my Lord and your husband is suffering from a high fever and the only cure for this ailment is the dust from your feet." The queen answered: "How can we possibly do such a thing? He is the master (*pati*), if we do this we will surely go to hell (*naraka*); it would be a sin (*pāpa*)." And so they refused. Nārada then left and sought out many women, but none would agree to give the dust from their feet. They all argued as follows: "Krishna is Brahman; he is the highest; it would be a sin to give dust from our feet." So Nārada in sorrow returned empty-handed to Krishna. Krishna asked him if he had brought the dust from the feet of any women. Nārada had to admit that he was returning empty-handed. Krishna asked him if he had gone everywhere. Nārada said that he had gone everywhere except to Brindāvan. Krishna sent him there. When the *gopīs* saw Nārada approaching they recognized him and realized that he must be bringing news from Krishna. Nārada said that Krishna was very sick and that he needed the dust from the feet of some women. All the *gopīs* immediately took the dust from their feet and put it in a cloth for Nārada. Nārada queried: "Oh *gopīs,* you know that Krishna is the highest; don't you feel it is a sin to do this?" The *gopīs* answered: "Oh Nārada, what he

> is we do not know; what we know is that he is from our village—our playmate. If he is suffering, we will do whatever is needed. If it is a sin we will go to hell; we are ready for that. He is everything to us." On his way back to Dvāraka where Krishna was, Nārada understood.

The story deals principally with hierarchy. Taking the dust from someone's feet is an expression of the high position of the person from whom the dust is taken and the low position of the person taking that dust. The lowliest portion of the higher person's body—the feet—is worthy of touching the highest portion of the lower person's body—the head. For the wives of Krishna to give him dust from their feet would be an infraction of the rules of hierarchy; it would be an action going against the grain, a *pratiloma* type of behavior. Such behavior threatens the very order of society and brings on worldly and/or other-worldly sanctions.[5] In their conduct the *gopīs* utterly disregard the rules of hierarchy; for them such considerations are irrelevant, though at one level not untrue. They know they might go to hell, but such a punishment is not what looms large in their minds. Their only concern is the welfare of Krishna; their actions are prompted solely by love.

The contrast between the *gopīs'* mode of behavior and that of Krishna's wives illustrates a central opposition in Vaiṣṇava thought, that between *aiśvarya* and *mādhurya*. The city of Dvāraka, where Krishna lives with his eight queens, is the realm of *aiśvarya,* "lordship." There the propriety and hierarchy appropriate to conjugal relationships hold sway. In striking contrast is the spontaneity of the *gopīs* in Brindāvan, the realm of *mādhurya* ("sweetness") where the divine play (*līlā*) of Krishna takes place. The *gopīs'* violation of societal norms in fact parallels Krishna's thievery. In Brindavan Krishna is not the supreme Lord of the universe but the mischievous child and the thief of love.[4]

Kāma and Prema

There remains a very important aspect of *parakīya* love to be explored, one that my informant considered to be of crucial importance: its utter imcompatibility with *kāma* ("desire" or "lust"). The *gopīs'* love is called *prema,* or sometimes *prīti,* and it is characterized by a complete absence of *kāma.* In view of the undeniably erotic and sensuous nature of the relationship between Krishna and the *gopīs,* especially as expressed in the *Gītagovinda,* I was at first taken aback by this assertion. My difficulty lay in placing this distinction in the framework of the erotic/ascetic dichotomy. Clearly this *prema* cannot be classified as either ascetic or erotic but seems to partake of both sides of the opposition. It was made clear to me that the absence of *kāma* does not mean chaste, platonic love. Krishna and the *gopīs* fondle, caress and embrace each other with abandon and show all the signs of sensual pleasure. What the absence of *kāma* specifically refers to is the fact that in his love-making Krishna does not spill his seed. One of the names of Krishna is Acyuta, usually rendered "unfallen"; according to the *devadāsī,* however, the more precise meaning of that name is "the one whose seed does not fall." The following two lines from the Oriya *Bhāgavata* express the same view: "Never does his juice (or essence) fall; that is why his name is Acyuta."[5]

What is the meaning of Krishna's retention of his seed? My informant delineated several levels of meaning. First, there is the testimony of everyday experience, in which sexual pleasure is only momentary. After orgasm the pleasurable erotic tension is gone; in such a manner one attains only temporary pleasure or happiness (*khyaṇika sukha*). Furthermore, by ejaculating one loses one's strength and becomes old. In this world, the world of *saṃsāra,* pleasure is brief and one begets children, whereas in the divine play of Krishna there is continuous (*nitya*) pleasure and no children. The *gopīs* are not impregnated. To illustrate the fact that the wheel of birth and death and rebirth is kept turning by *kāma* in this world, the *devadāsī* recited for me the following Sanskrit verse: "Again birth, again death, again sleep in the womb of the mother."[6] Continuity of pleasure is opposed to the discontinuity of birth and death. Furthermore, the opposition between the realm of lordship and the realm of sweetness is also expressed in this opposition between sexual love (*kāma*), which entails relinquishing the seed, and that other, continuous love (*prema*). *Kāma* exists between husband and wife and results in procreation. *Prema,* by contrast, is not restricted to erotic types of relationship; it is used to talk of the love between Krishna and Yaśodā, his foster mother, as well as that between Krishna and the *gopīs. Prema* is the reigning emotion in the realm of *mādhurya,* whereas *kāma* belongs in the realm of *aiśvarya.* The crucial element in the absence of *kāma* in the realm of *mādhurya* is that there are no consequences to the actions of the inhabitants of that realm. The shedding of the seed has ulterior consequences, i.e., a birth. Krishna's erotic dalliance with the *gopīs* has no ulterior purpose or consequence. It exists for itself, in itself. In the same way the *gopīs'* unconcern with the possibility that they might go to hell for giving the dust from their feet illustrates the same unconcern for consequences, a dwelling in immediacy, acting not with regard for the fruits of their actions but only for the action itself.[7]

We are now in a better position to understand both the import of the iconographical feature of the symmetry between male and female and the parallelism between Rādhā-Krishna and Śīva-Ardhanārīśvara. Śiva's union with his consort Pārvatī, represented in his form as half-man and half-woman, is the same as that between Krishna and the *gopīs:* neither male spills his seed.[8] Śiva's antagonism to Kāma, the god of desire and lust and perhaps more specifically the god of orgasm, is well known and forcefully expressed in the episode of Śiva's burning Kāma.

The differences between the two couples are of course great. First and foremost, Pārvatī is a wife and not a mistress. Moreover, Śiva is the great ascetic, whereas one could hardly characterize Krishna as an ascetic. It is not my intention to work out the implications of these differences and similarities in this paper. My aim in pointing out certain parallelisms between the two couples is rather to open some potentially fruitful areas of thought and research and pose some questions that must yet be answered.

In the foregoing discussion we have contrasted throughout the relation between Krishna and the *gopīs* with that between a husband and a wife. The latter is exemplified in the relationship between Viṣṇu and his consort Lakṣmī. However, in this contrast we have found not so much an opposition between the two modes of relating as an absence of commonality. *Prema* is not the opposite of *kāma;* it is simply other, different. *Kāma* and the *svakīya* relationship belong to the world of *saṃsāra,* where the discontinuity of life and death is as inescapable as the existence of a hierarchy that structures and maintains the world order.

Viṣṇu-Lakṣmī and Śiva-Kālī

Dominance and subordination and life and death are, in my judgment, the central themes in the other two types of sexual union, namely that between Viṣṇu and Lakṣmī and that between Kālī and

Śiva. Lakṣmī is the very embodiment of auspiciousness, as her name Śrī indicates. The opposition auspiciousness/inauspiciousness has unfortunately not received the attention it merits in the anthropological literature. I have shown elsewhere[9] that this opposition corresponds to that of life versus death as well as that of right versus left. These categories cut across rather than parallel the opposition between pure and impure. To illustrate this assertion let me indicate the way in which the life-cycle ceremonies are categorized as auspicious or inauspicious. The auspicious life-cycle ceremonies are weddings, initiations, temple dedications, ear-borings, births and birthdays, house-blessings, and some of the royal ceremonies. The inauspicious ceremonies are rites pertaining to death, to ancestor worship, and to illness. What one immediately observes from such a categorization is that the auspicious/inauspicious opposition does not correspond to that pertaining between pure and impure. Birth involves a period of impurity but is auspicious; offerings to the ancestors involve no period of impurity but are inauspicious. These findings are corroborated in the work of Veena Das on the right/left opposition in the *gṛhya sūtras* of Gobhila.[10] The opposition between right and left that she finds in these aphorisms corresponds to the one that we have noted.

From these classifications we can see that auspiciousness has to do with the creation and maintenance of life. In Puri, Lakṣmī is worshipped every Thursday during the month of Mārgaśīrsa (November-December), in the shape of a heap of newly harvested rice. Lakṣmī is the bountiful one, the giver of food, the embodiment of auspiciousness. She represents the married woman whose husband is alive (*ahya*), the woman who is sexually active and the primary feeder of the family: the giver as well as the maintainer of life. For such a woman, sexual intercourse is auspicious, for it belongs to marriage and leads to progeny. In other words, it is sexual intercourse with *kāma*. Lakṣmī's association with *kāma* is indicated on the mythological plane by the fact that when she appeared out of the churning of the milk ocean she was preceded by such symbols of auspiciousness as the *kāmadhenu,* the desire-fulfilling cow; the *apsarasas* (the heavenly *devadāsīs*); the physician of the gods, whose function is to remove inauspicious illness; jewels, which serve as tangible evidence of plenty; and the horse, which symbolizes the potency of the king.[11] Thus marriage, progeny, and the maintenance of life cannot be separated from *kāma;* and all these belong to the realm of *saṃsāra,* of life, death, and rebirth, which can only be maintained in a hierarchically structured world order.

Yet just as in the churning of the milk ocean poison is first separated from those things that usher in Lakṣmī and *amṛta,* the elixir of auspiciousness, so Lakṣmī herself is separated from inauspiciousness, that is, from the opposite of life, namely death. Life and death both belong to the same overall framework of *saṃsāra,* and they represent true opposites in a way that *prema* and *kāma* do not.

Let us now return to our third couple, Kālī and Śiva, and consider the kind of sexual intercourse that takes place between them. The *mantra* describing Kālī to which I referred earlier, which specifies that Kālī is engaged in inverse sexual union, does not provide any further details. However, the ritual text in which it is found[12] describes the successive actions of the specialist performing the worship. One of these actions is sexual intercourse (*maithuna*) which takes place between the officiant and a woman called a *śakti.* In the interpretation of this ritual given to me by its specialist it was made clear that this *śakti* is the living embodiment of the goddess Kālī, who is herself referred to as *śakti.* Like her she is naked. Nakedness carries with it certain specific meanings. I learned from other informants that at the time of marriage it is customary, at least among Vaiṣṇavas, for the couple to receive an initiatory *mantra* from a *guru.* This *mantra* is called the Krishna *mantra.* When receiving it the couple promise never to appear naked in front of each other, for it is believed that it is inauspicious (*amaṅgala*) for a husband to see his wife naked. One of the *devadāsīs* put it this way to me: "If I am seen naked, Lakṣmī will leave me" (*lakṣmī carī jibe*). Such meanings are in fact not wholly foreign to Westerners: the French word *dénué,* which means "poor" or "having nothing," is formed from the root *nu,* "naked."

The sexual intercourse that takes place between the ritual specialist and the *śakti* occurs early in the ritual as part of the preparation of the five substances (*pañcama tattva*) that are used later, in the worship proper. Sexual intercourse is engaged in for the purpose of procuring what is called "the fifth m" (*pañcama makāra*). This "fifth m" is the female sexual fluid called *raja.* This fluid is not menstrual blood—which in Oriya is designated by other terms—since the woman should not be menstruating at the time of this ritual. It is a colorless fluid that corresponds to semen in the male and like semen is believed to be secreted at the time of intercourse. In local theories of conception *raja* plays a role symmetrical with that of semen.

The ritual specialist, on the other hand, must not let his seed fall. The female sexual fluid is collected on a flower of a *bel* leaf (sacred to Śiva and the goddess) and along with a portion of the other four m's is placed in a conchshell half filled with purificatory water (*arghya*) and half with wine. This conchshell is then installed and given breath in the ceremony of *prāṇa-pratiṣṭhā* and is subsequently considered to be the goddess herself. During the worship proper (*pūjā*), which consists of a sixteenfold offering (*sodasopacāra*), the content of this conchshell is used for purifying the food offering. This offering is then consumed as the *prasāda* ("grace") of Kālī by the ritual specialist and shared with five or seven other men called *vīras,* who, along with their *śaktis,* join the worshipper after the main offering is completed. The ritual concludes with the specialist's draining the rest of the contents of the conchshell.

In this type of sexual union *kāma* is absent, since the man must not spill his seed. Yet this sexual union is also not one in which *prema* is supreme. What characterizes this type of sexual intercourse is that instead of the woman's receiving within her the male sexual fluid, the opposite process occurs: here it is the man who ingests the female sexual fluid. The rite is thus graphically and specifically the inverse of conjugal intercourse and well merits the appellation "inverse sexual intercourse."

It is now possible to ascertain with a greater degree of confidence that representations of Viṣṇu with Lakṣmī and of Kālī with Śiva belong in opposite categories. Such an opposition suggests that other and perhaps all features of the iconography as well as the ritual of this secret worship of Kālī symbolize inauspiciousness. Because inauspiciousness corresponds to death, illness, and ancestor worship, it was a logical step for me to turn my attention to texts describing the rites at the cremation ground, as well as to forms of ancestor worship. Such a step proved very rewarding.

In her study of the rites of ancestor worship as described in the *gṛhya sūtras* of Gobhila, Veena Das writes that "oblations to ancestors during the periodic ancestor worship have to be given with the left hand." She specifies further, "When the annual ancestor propitiation ceremony is being held, the left side predominates over the right side in the entire ritual."[13] The secret worship of Kālī is also referred to as the *vāmacāri* ("left-handed") ritual. Such an appellation reflects the fact that the left hand is dominant throughout. The text specifies that at many points during the offering the object offered, including food, must be given with the left hand. Another parallel between ancestor rites as described in the *gṛhya sūtras* and in the secret worship of Kālī is that the offering of food in each case consists of balls called *piṇḍa* or *bali,*[14] whereas the food offered to the gods in the daytime worship is known in the *gṛhya sūtras* as *agya.* In Puri the food offered during the annual ancestor propitiation rites (*śrāddha*) also consists of balls of food called *piṇḍas.* Although these are nowadays not offered with the left hand, the performer of the rites must, if he is a Brahmin, change his sacred thread from the left shoulder to the right shoulder, so that during the ritual it hangs from the right shoulder to the left waist, in the opposite direction from the usual way of wearing it.

Further resemblance between the secret worship of Kālī and ancestor worship may be seen in their common use of the terms *kula* and *vīra.* The secret worship of Kālī is referred to as the *kula-cakra,* "the circle of the *kula.*" The ritual specialist is called the *cakreśvara,* "the lord of the circle," and when the other five or seven men, the *vīras,* join the ritual with their *śaktis,* the moment is called "the entrance into the circle" (*cakra-praveśa*). This entrance takes place after the sixteenfold offering has been made to the goddess. Once the group of *vīras* and their *śaktis* have arrived and seated themselves "in order of seniority" in a semicircle, the main officiant performs *pūjā* to each of them in turn, offering incense, flowers and raw white rice to each. All the participants then take in their left hands and eat balls of food composed of the four m's (wine, meat, fish, and black gram cakes)—an action that is called *tarpaṇa*—after which they drink wine. The word *tarpaṇa* (literally, "satisfaction") is also used to refer to the offering of *piṇḍas* and water during the annual ancestor worship.

The term *kula,* usually rendered in English by the words "clan" or "lineage," "refers to a set of one's own people, taking a 'seed male' or 'ancestral male' (*bīja-puruṣa, pūrva-puruṣa*) and to 'ego' as its referent.... Such a lineage includes all the male descendants of a common ancestral male, together with their wives and unmarried daughters."[15] During the annual ancestor worship, the eldest son worships his deceased father, his father's father, and so on for seven generations, along with the wife of each. He must thus know the names of fourteen of his ancestors. If the worshipper is not a Brahmin, he offers food and water to five generations of ancestors. The offering is accomplished by the recitation of the ancestors' names in order of seniority. The ritual itself is also called *tarpaṇa,* for it is an act of "satisfying" the ancestors with offerings of food and water.

The evidence that we have reviewed seems clearly to indicate a connection between the annual ancestor rites and the secret worship of Kālī. In particular, there is a striking parallel between the seven (or sometimes five) male ancestors who are worshipped together with their wives in order of seniority by being offered balls of food in a ritual called *tarpaṇa,* in which the left side predominates, and the seven (or five) males with their *śaktis* who are seated in a semicircle and worshipped in order of seniority in the "entrance into the *cakra*" part of the secret rites to the Goddess, and who likewise partake of balls of food held in the left hand.

These men are called *vīras,* a word, usually translated "hero," that has other and for our purposes much more interesting meanings. In the Rig Veda and other ancient texts the word means male child, son. Its root (*vīr*) is the same as that of the Oriya word *bīrjya* (Skt *vīrya*), meaning semen. These *vīras* represent an unbroken line of male descent in which the continuity of the line is carried by the *bīrjya* and not by its female equivalent (the *raja*), since the wives come from other *kulas,* outside the male line. In genealogical terms semen represents continuity, and the equivalent female sexual fluid represents discontinuity. In those terms we can now restate the connection we made earlier between this ritual and inauspiciousness. Let me clarify: auspiciousness means among other things progeny, in particular male progeny, which assures the long life of the lineage, the *kula.* The auspiciousness of the wife is dependent on the life of her husband: when he dies she becomes an inauspicious widow. The male is of course equally dependent on the female for the production of male offspring. However, the female in herself cannot ensure continuity, she is only the instrument through which the continuous line of males, through a continuity of semen, is assured. Thus the female represented with a dead husband—Śiva as *śava*—is an eminently appropriate representation of discontinuity and thus of inauspiciousness.

I have used the term "continuity" both in the context of Kālī worship and while talking of the pleasure experienced in the erotic dalliance of Krishna and the *gopīs.* The former is a continuity in time, the smooth turning of the wheel of *saṃsāra,* whereas the latter refers to a continuity that is out of time, or, to put it another way, one in which time is suspended. It might have been wiser to use different terms for these two types of continuity, but none came to mind, and it is hoped that the preceding clarification will avert confusion.

In the anthropological literature we find mention of the worship by male agnates of clan goddesses called Kula-devī or Kula-mātā. This worship is said by one anthropologist to be secret.[16] Another, writing about society in Konku, says that these goddesses are "described as a special manifestation of a great goddess of some distant pilgrimage point, such a Conjeepuram or Madurai. . . . A frequently named clan goddess was AnkāLamman who was born in heaven as Pārvatī."[17] At least certain of these clan goddesses thus seem to be manifestations of Śiva's consort, and they can therefore be identified with Kālī.

Having noted certain prominent similarities between the secret worship of Kālī and ancestor worship, we may now consider parallels between the iconography associated with that ritual and certain passages of the *Bharadvāja Paitṛmedhika Sūtra,*[18] which describes the rites at the cremation ground. The wife of the deceased has a central role to play in these rites. Verse 1.5.14, which occurs just after the statement that the deceased husband has been placed on the pyre, reads as follows: "The uniting *(saṃveśana)* of the wife [with the deceased] and other rites should optionally be performed at this stage." *Saṃveśana* means coition, sexual union.[19] Thus it appears that the iconography of Kālī and Śiva-*śava* has roots in death rituals dating back at least to the period of the *gṛhya sūtra* literature.

We can now say with some confidence that the iconography of Kālī and Śiva and the rituals associated with it signify death and inauspiciousness. One of the important goddesses of Puri is called Maṅgalā, "the auspicious one." She is believed to have been born from Durgā's anger at the time of the slaying of the buffalo demon. Like Durgā and Kālī she receives blood sacrifices. Her name, in a manner parallel to that of Śītalā ("the Cool One"), goddess of fever and smallpox, indicates that she is propitiated for the avoidance of inauspiciousness. As the following *mantra* from the text of the worship of Kālī indicates, so long as the goddess is worshipped she will remain quiet, steady, and calm. The implication is that if one were not to propitiate her, she would stir things up and create havoc. The *mantra* is as follows: "Oh goddess, by my devotion you along with your family are available. As long as I worship, you stay here quietly and peacefully."[20]

Conclusion

In this paper I have set up a tripartite typology of types of sexual union and investigated the meanings implicit in their iconography, mythology and rituals. I have shown that the union of Viṣṇu and Lakṣmī and that of Kālī and Śiva represent opposite poles of the dichotomy between auspicious and inauspicious. In broad terms, this dichotomy was seen to correspond to the opposition between life and death rather than to that between pure and impure. The Rādhā-Krishna pair stands outside this opposition and partakes of elements from both sides of the dichotomy. Structurally this pair thus represents a mediating category. As a mediator between the auspicious and the inauspicious the pair can take on characteristics of either of the two couples.

This mediating role can best be illustrated by the *Gītagovinda*. In its twelve parts there is a progression from auspiciousness and sexual union in which the male is the active partner (Parts 1 and 2), through a middle portion (Parts 5 and 6) in which the symmetry of both partners is neatly expressed as each in turn suffers the pangs of separation, to the last portion, in which Rādhā is the active partner and performs "inverse sexual union." In Part 1 (Song 2) the poet says: "You rest on the circle of Śrī's breast."[21] This song is part of the initial "auspicious prayer"[22] and in that context Krishna is spoken of as the husband of Śri. In Song 6 in Part 2, Rādhā recalls her love-making with Krishna.[23] Except for the last part of the poem (in which Rādhā is called Caṇḍī), this is the only description of love-making between Rādhā and Krishna. In this song there is a line that echoes the one in Part 1; here Rādhā says, "He lies on my breast forever."[24] This is in clear contrast to the following line in the twelfth part (Song 23) in which Krishna, speaking of Rādhā's breasts, says to her, "Rest these vessels on my chest!"[25] The inverse nature of the union is introduced in the two previous parts (10 and 11) in which Rādhā is called Caṇḍī by the *sakhī*[26] and Krishna asks Rādhā to place on his head her foot, which he has likened to the hibiscus flower.[27] The hibiscus flower is the one to such offered bloodthirsty goddesses as Kālī and Caṇḍī.

Suggestive as this tripartite typology is, it should not be used without proper caution. The love of Rādhā and Krishna, for example, may be interpreted not as mediating between two poles, but as transcending the realm of auspiciousness and inauspiciousness entirely, as taking place outside time and the wheel of birth and death. I do not claim that the meanings I have discerned exhaust the richness of the myths, iconography, and rituals here considered. I propose this analysis simply as one fruitful perspective from which to look at Hindu hierogamies.

On Women Saints

A. K. RAMANUJAN

Love has long been a central metaphor for religious experience. A well-known passage in the *Bṛhadāraṇyaka Upaniṣad* likens the ultimate attainment of freedom and fearlessness to the sensation a man has in the embrace of his wife: so does a person, "when in the embrace of the intelligent Soul, [know] nothing within or without. . . . [H]is desire is satisfied, in which the Soul is his desire, in which he is without desire and without sorrow."[1] Philosophers continue the tradition, as does Yāmuna when he says, "Vision is *parabhakti:* union is *parajñāna:* fear of a new separation is *paramabhakti.*"[2] In *bhakti* poetry one finds new expressions of this old awareness. The word *prema* ("love"), for instance, which is rare in the Indian epic and becomes common in *kāvya* poetry, takes on a new life in the *bhakti* idiom. An espcially arresting aspect of the *bhakti* milieu, however, is the extent to which *bhakti* itself appears as "feminine" in nature, by contrast to Vedic sacrifice, which may be considered "masculine" in ethos, personnel, and language.[3] The chief mood of *bhakti* is the erotic (*sṛṅgāra*), seen almost entirely from an Indian woman's point of view, whether in its phase of separation or of union. Thus when saints both male and female address love poems to Krishna and Śiva and adopt such feminine personae as wife (*kāntā*), illicit lover (*parakīyā*), trysting woman (*abhisārikā*), even Rādhā herself, they are drawing on a long, rich history.

It is important, however, to distinguish between various kinds of saints. There are significant differences of life pattern between upper-caste and outcaste male saints, and between upper-caste male saints and all women saints. For upper-caste male saints the *bhakti* point of view effects a number of reversals when compared with normative Hindu views such as those represented in Manu's *Dharmaśāstra.* According to Manu the female is subordinate to the male and the outcaste to the upper-caste, but in the lives of the *bhakti* saints "the last shall be first": men wish to renounce their masculinity and to become as women; upper-caste males wish to renounce pride, privilege, and wealth, seek dishonor and self-abasement, and learn from the untouchable devotee. This reversal may be diagrammed as in table 3.

Table 3. Bhakti Reversals of Normative Hindu Patterns

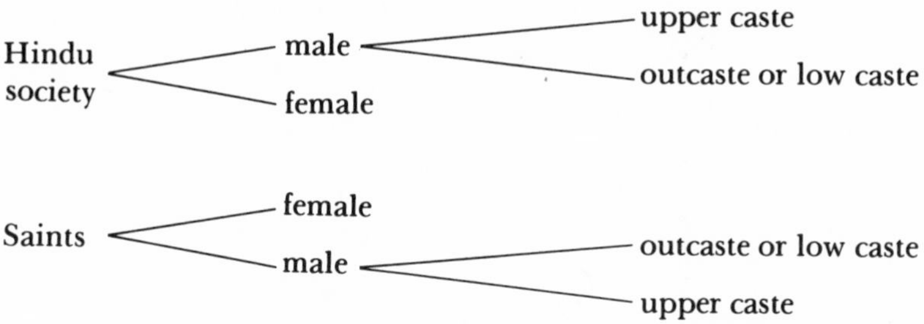

Elsewhere I have detailed various ways in which these reversals are accomplished, and speculated on the possible psychological patterns of such a desire for reversal.[4] Here I shall discuss another aspect of the same configuration: the way in which Indian women saints invert and even subvert the traditional ideals of womanhood embodied in such mythic figures as Sītā and Sāvitrī, adopting different patterns altogether.

I began my study of women saints by examining the detailed history of a Vīraśaiva woman saint, Mahādēviyakka, and then proceeded to look at the lives of several dozen women saints as given in the compendium of Ta. Su. Śāmarāya, the *Śivaśaraṇakathāratnakośa* ("Encyclopaedia of Vīraśaiva Saints").[5] I found a remarkable consensus among the Vīraśaiva examples. When I added the lives of women saints from other traditions and places in India (for instances, Bahiṇābāī of Maharashtra, Lallā of Kashmir, Mīrā of Rajasthan, Āṇṭāḷ of Tamilnadu), an extraordinary composite emerged before my eyes, in which the women saints' lives seem to display the following five phases in sequence.

Table 4. Stages of Life for Women Saints

- Her god is her first love; she undergoes no conversion; ➡
  - will marry no mortal; ➡
    - attains her god ➡
      - by becoming a courtesan and getting her god as her lover
      - OR
      - through love and sacrifice ➡
        - offering Him life or limb in worship (Rēkavve)
    - OR
    - escapes marriage ➡
      - by obstinately refusing to marry even Śiva in disguise (Goggavve)
      - OR
      - by being transformed into an unmarriageable ➡
        - male (Tilakavve)
        - OR
        - old woman (Avvai)
  - OR
  - marries a mortal, but ➡
    - gets rid of him ➡
      - by walking out on him (Mahādēvi)
      - OR
      - by terrifying him (Karaikkālammai)
    - OR
    - stays with him ➡
      - is widowed but refuses the state of widowhood ➡
        - by refusing "suttee" (Mīrābāī)
        - OR
        - by refusing widowhood rites (Gaurībāī)
      - endures a bad marriage, and ➡
        - has no children; sees her husband as her son in previous lives (Lallā)
        - OR
        - has children, but regrets them; considers them husbands in past lives (Bahiṇābāī)

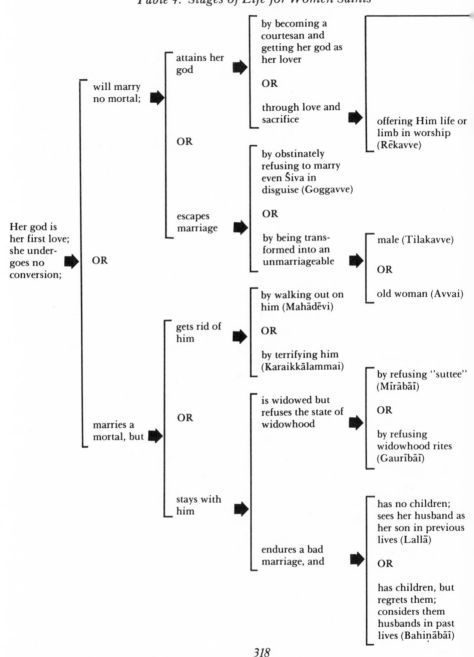

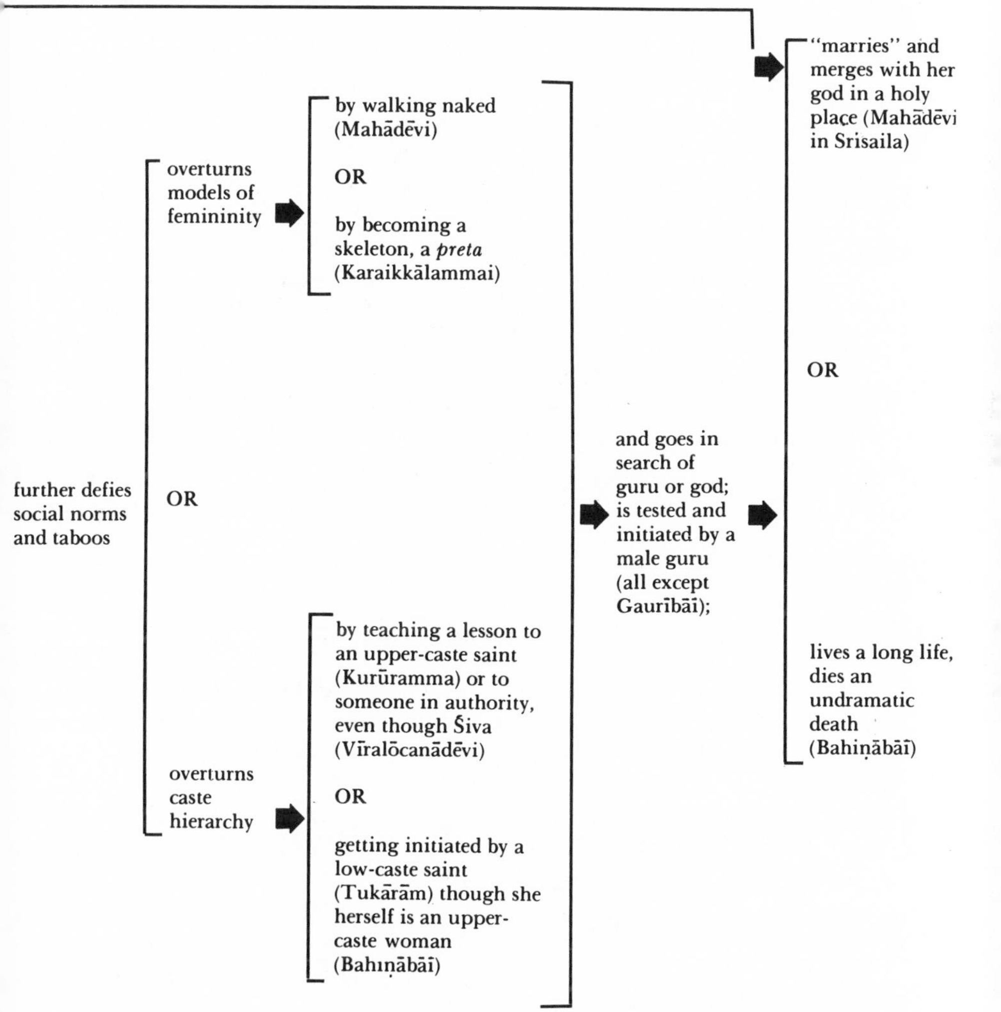

This chart presents a composite of the lives of Indian women saints. I have amused myself by presenting it as a "flow chart" of possibilities, indicating, from left to right, the sequence of life stages. At each stage different saints follow different options (e.g., either marrying a mortal or refusing to do so); each choice leads to further choices. These options are not the same as those for a male upper-caste saint, but are often similar to those of an untouchable male saint, especially when marriage is not the issue. These patterns deserve further inquiry. (Names in brackets are of saints whose lives illustrate specific options.)

A. Early Dedication to God

Manu says, in a notorious passage,[6] "In childhood a woman should be protected by her father, in youth by her husband, in old age by her son. Verily, a woman does not deserve freedom." The woman saint, however, is not typically bound to a man. Instead she is dedicated at an early age to God; God is her first love. Unlike upper-caste male saints, therefore, she need undergo no conversion. She defies her parents, escaping marriage in one of several ways. She may attain God by a single-minded love, as Āṇṭāḷ does, or win him by extreme forms of worship and sacrifice, as does Rēkavve, a Vīraśaiva who uses a piece of her own flesh to complete the Lord's garland because she cannot find a red flower. Or she may obtain her divine lover as a courtesan: this is how Vīrasaṅgavve manages to win Śiva. Another possibility is to become transformed into an unmarriageable old woman, like Avvai, or into a male by God's grace, as Tilakavve does. Finally, the woman may simply renounce marriage. Goggavve is so obstinate that she refuses to marry the disguised Śiva; even when he threatens to kill her she does not yield.

B. Denial of Marriage

Some women saints do get married, but in my sample of nearly a hundred women saints' lives there are only two women who endure a bad marriage, Lallā and Bahiṇā. Of these, only one, Bahiṇā, has a child, and contrary to everything Manu leads us to expect, she regrets it bitterly. Indeed, she attempts to deny her inescapable relation to her son by considering him a companion of former lives, thus transforming him in her mind. Lallā does the same in relation to her husband, viewing him as a son in a former life.

It is more common for a married woman saint to get rid of her husband than to endure him. She may walk out on him, leaving him for her only true lover, as Dālāyi deserts her husband while he is making love to her, at the call of Śiva; or she may terrify her husband by miracles, as does Kāraikkālammai. Another pattern is for her to be widowed, and in that case it is characteristic for the woman to treat her new status in such a way as to indicate that she denies the reality of having been married in the first place. Mīrā refuses *satī;* Gaurī and Veṅkamma refuse to shave their heads. It is as if she cannot be truly widowed, being married to God. Interesting in this connection is the fact that the Newars of Nepal marry all their young women first to Lord Nārāyaṇa; thus their earthly husbands are all second husbands, and they can never be widowed.[7]

C. Defying Societal Norms

In the next phase the woman saint further defies social norms and taboos. For instance, she rebukes men for their sexual advances, and teaches them a lesson when they treat her as "a sex object." Kāraikkāl-ammai turns into a skeleton before a lust-infatuated male. Mahādēvi throws away her clothes and with them the investment in society and the division between male and female that differential clothing signifies; abandoning modesty, she walks naked, covered only by her tresses. Some of her most poignant poems are in defense of her nudity.[8]

In this phase, like the untouchable and low-caste saint, the woman often defies caste hierarchy. She usually teaches a lesson to an upper-caste man, a priest, an elder, or even a senior saint, by some miracle or piece of wisdom. For instance, Kurūr Amma of Kerala was rebuked by no less a devotee than Vilvamaṅgaḷ, the great poet-saint, because he found her reciting the name of Viṣṇu during her menstrual period. She asks him, "Can you guarantee that we'll not die in a state of bodily impurity?" He is humbled by the truth of her feeling. Vīracoḷādēvi teaches even Śiva a similar lesson. Or if the saint is an upper-caste woman, she shocks the orthodox by taking initiation from a low-caste saint, as Bahiṇā does from Tukārām.

D. Initiation

Almost all woman saints, in this stage, are also questioned and tested by a male figure, as Mahādēvi was by Allama,[9] and/or initiated by him. This seems to be a concession to the general normative Hindu pattern: even in the lives of famous modern Indian women the mentor and initiator into public life is a male authority figure who legitimizes the unusual female role.[10]

E. Marrying the Lord

In the last phase the woman saint "marries the Lord." In the case of Mahādēvi a new, second family of saints arranges the marriage to the divine bridegroom and gives her away. Typically the woman saint merges with God in a temple or holy place, as does Mahādēvi in Srisaila, or Āṇṭāḷ in Srirangam. Of all the saints in my sample, only one, Bahiṇā, lives a long life of dedication and dies an ordinary, undramatic death.

The above phases of the woman saint's career may be presented in a flow chart, showing the different alternatives represented at each point by different lives. Some of the stages in the sequence are not found in some lives. This kind of stage-skipping could, however, be represented in a more complex diagram of the choices at each point: the sociolinguistic flow chart for the choice of appropriate terms of address (first name, kin term, nickname, etc.) would provide an appropriate model. For simplicity's sake, I shall present the less complex diagram (see Table 4).

Saints' Wives

A related pattern is to be found in the role of saints' wives. Even when women are not saints themselves but are married to saints, they still appear to be superior to their husbands, needing no conversion. They are the vehicles of divine grace for the male saint or poet. They come to see God, duty, and love effortlessly, even with a blessed blindness. I will content myself with one example.

In the story of Purandharadāsa's conversion,[11] Lord Viṭṭhala, disguised as a mendicant Brahmin, comes to Purandhara first, but finds him a hard-hearted money lender who turns him away. He then goes to Purandhara's wife and tells her that he needs money to get his daughter married. She has no money, but gladly gives him her nose ring. He promptly disguises himself as a rich diamond trader and takes it to Purandhara to sell it. The money lender recognizes it at once as his wife's, asks the Brahmin to wait in his shop, and goes inside his quarters. When he questions his wife, she is amazed to find that she has another, more splendid jewel of the same kind in her jewel box. She sees at once that it is a miracle, and that the Brahmin is none other than God himself. Purandhara runs back to his shop to see him, but he is gone, having left only a supernatural fragrance to fill the shop.

I would like to suggest that the contrast between the woman saint who rejects family and child, and the saint's wife who "out-saints" him, is parallel to the contrast between Mother goddesses and consort goddesses. The former are not really mothers at all and have no male consorts, or trample on them as well as on male demons. The consort goddesses, such as Lakṣmī and Umā, are benign (*saumya*), not fierce (*ugra*); they contain the power—they *are* power (*śakti*)—of the great gods.

A comparison with the typical male saint—though male saints are harder to typify, a point to which we shall return below—will help further to define the composite profile of the female saint. A figure such as Allama has a life that runs somewhat as follows:[12]

a) an early life of ease and pleasure;

b) abasement, loss, and subsequent awakening;

c) conversion, initiation at the hands of a guru;

d) the defying of orthodox authority and social norms;

e) the converting or defeating of people of other religions (e.g., Jainas) or sects;

f) the founding of his own sect;

g) merging with God.

Many of the male saints, for example, Basava and Dāsimayya, have families; they do not reject family life as most of the female saints do (or have to do) before they pursue their careers as saints. Whereas men may retain their families and in some instances direct their poetry toward social reform, women continue to choose love as the subject of their poetry, despite the enormity of the social protest implicit in their lives as they reject parents, husband, children, household, shelter, even clothes. In this respect they resemble the Rādhā who, as Karine Schomer tells us in the present volume, was so very distasteful to progressive Hindi poets of the 1930s; they asked her to forget her obsession with Krishna for a minute and think of social reform. Such an entreaty would have been equally necessary in the case of most women saints. They may give up their natal and conjugal families, but they substitute for them a second family composed of saints; and their poetry is still concerned, to use the excellent Tamil distinction, with private and interior (*akam*) themes.[13] Similarly, although these woman are highly respected as saints, and their poetry may be considered more deeply moving than that of their male counterparts, as in the case of Āṇṭāḷ or Mahādēvi, they never become gurus in the public realm as Basava, Kabīr, and Nammāḻvār do.

The upper-caste male's battle is with the system as a whole, often internalized as the enemy within, whereas the woman saint's struggle is with family and family values. She struggles not with her own temptations, but with husband and priest, and with her wifely and maternal roles. It is significant that Mahādēvi is called *akka,* "elder sister," for this name shows a concern with separating her from marital roles.

The males take on female personae: they are feminine, yearning, passive toward a male god. Before God all men are women. But no female saint, however she may defy male-oriented "relational" attitudes, takes on a male persona. It is as if, being already female, she has no need to change anything to turn toward God. Like the untouchable and the low-caste saint, she need shed nothing, for she has nothing to shed: neither physical prowess, nor social power, nor punditry, nor even spiritual pride. She is already where she needs to be, in these saints' legends.

The biographical legends imply that somehow women are secure in their identities, and hence do not need to undergo a conversion or change their sex. Anthropologists such as Margaret Mead[14] and Nancy Chodorow[15] have pointed out that males have elaborate initiation rites because they have to be weaned from their mothers and given a separate masculine identity in order to enter the male world. Men have to change to become "themselves"; only after the change may they long for the earlier feminine identification with the mother-figure.[16] Women, by contrast, may continue to identify with their mothers. The woman saint may fight the male in husband, priest, and elder; she may love a male god. But she remains feminine, and in her love poetry she rejoices intensely in this identity.

I wish to end where I began. The classical ideals embodied in Sītā and Sāvitrī are not the only models available to Indian women. In the context of *bhakti* a different track is opened for them, if the initial defiance of marriage and of other family pressures can be managed. Given the parallel contexts—the broadly "separate worlds" staked out for men and women in traditional societies[17]—such careers are not surprising, nor considered aberrant.

Notes

Krishna Gopāla, Rādhā, and the Great Goddess

Charlotte Vaudeville

[1]The French term *paredre* is a more precise translation of the Indian concept than the English term "consort," because it means "sitting by the side."

[2]As noted by C. Mackenzie Brown in his contribution to the present volume.

[3]In the *Devī-māhātmya* (a part of the *Mārkaṇḍeya Purāṇa,* Svāmī Jagadīsvarānanda, ed., Madras, 1953) 5.87-88, it is said that Ambikā (Durgā) came out of Pārvatī's body (lit. "physical sheath" [kosa]) and that after she had issued forth, Pārvatī became dark (*kṛṣṇa*) and was henceforth called Kālikā.

[4]This interpretation seems to fit the *yātrā* undertaken by Jagannātha, Subhadrā, and Baladeva to the Gundicā Devī temple on the day of the Śayanī festival. The primacy of Ādyakālī over all the gods, including Viṣṇu, and over all the other manifestations of Devī, is also implied in the first canto of the *Devī-māhātmya,* in which the eternal Goddess (*mahāmāyā*) appears first as the *yoganidrā* in which Viṣṇu is absorbed. Only through the intervention of the bright Goddess can the God be awakened. This fact probably accounts for the verse in the *Harivamśa* (hereafter cited as *HV*) hymn according to which the Goddess is "the eleventh day of the light *pakṣa* of the month," for the festival of *devotthāna* falls on this day in the month of Kārttika.

[5]This *amāvasyā* is dedicated to Lakṣmī-kuvera. Kuvera (Kubera) is the chief of the half-demon *yakṣas,* tree-spirits and guardians of hidden riches. Kuvera is the god of wealth. His wives are said to be Ṛddhi (prosperity) and Yakṣī. In the Hindu calendar the word Laksmī, which refers to the goddess of fortune, may have taken the place of the more abstract Ṛddhi. It is precisely as goddess of wealth that Lakṣmī is worshipped on that day.

[6]See Vaudeville, "The Govardhan Myth in Northern India," *Indo-Iranian Journal,* 22:1 (1980), pp. 1-45.

[7]In the popular imagery of the Vallabhite sect, whose cult centers on Śrī Govardhannāthjī or Śrī Nāthjī, "Śrī Yamunājī" is invariably represented as an exact replica of the latter in female form; in her raised hand she holds a lotus garland instead of the lifted hill.

[8]The Goddess is called Kālamātā, "Mother of Time" or "Mother of Death." *Kālarātrī* ("Night of Death") in the appendix to *HV* 47 refers to *pralayarātrī,* the night of the dissolution of all things; cf. the hymn to Ādyakālī in Arthur Avalon's *Hymns to the Goddess* (Madras: Ganesh & Co., 1964), p. 41, where the Goddess is called Kālamātā and Kālānalasamadyutī, "brilliant as the fire of *pralaya*" (*Ādyakālisvarūpastotram* from the *Mahānirvāṇa Tantra*).

[9]*Devī-māhātmya* 11.42: "Then I shall be born in the house of the cowherd Nanda, from Yaśodā's womb. Residing in the Vindhya mountains, I shall kill these two demons [Śumbha and Niśumbha]." The connection between Devī as Vindhyavāsinī and the Cowherd-god is not clear, unless we remember that Vindhyavāsinī-devī is the goddess "who resides on the peaks of fearful mountains, by rivers, and in caves, forests, and groves, much worshipped by the Śavara, Varvara, and Pulinda tribesmen" and "who with peacock-feathered flags traverses the world in all directions" (*HV,* app. I, 8.7-10). The Govardhana hill and the surrounding wooded areas, which serve as pasture land (*vraja*) for the nomadic tribe of Nandagopa, naturally come under the sway of that fearsome goddess of hills, jungles, and uninhabited tracts. It is probably from that hill goddess that Krishna Gopāla has inherited his peacock-feather crest.

[10]The *Mahābhāṣya* of Patañjali (on Pāṇini 3.1.26) alludes to dramatic representations of the *kaṃsa-vadha* episode. It is said that Kaṃsa's demon troops are *kāla-*

mukhaḥ ("black-faced") whereas Krishna's partisans are *raktamukhaḥ* ("red-faced"); red is the color of Devī in her *bhairavī* (ferocious) aspect.

[11]All hill goddesses are deemed black. According to the *Devībhāgavata Purāṇa,* Pārvatī, the spouse of Lord Śiva, was said to have originally been black, but to have acquired a resplendent golden complexion after she was burned by the fire of *yoga*. On the manifestation of Ambikā out of Pārvatī's body, see note 3 above.

[12]The Govardhana Hill is a black rock mountain that is said to have come from the Himalayas. According to legend, as reported in popular pamphlets, it was carried from the North by Hanumān at the time of the building of the bridge across the ocean by Rāma and dropped by the great monkey on the spot where it now stands.

[13]Kaśyapa is the water tortoise, an animal closely associated with the river Yamunā, which it symbolizes. Already in the Rig Veda, Aditi, "the unbroken, unimpaired one" (cf. Ekānaṃśā), the mother of the gods, symbolizes the eternal, infinite expanse. She is sometimes spoken of as the self-existing one or as the mother of Dakṣa. In the *Viṣṇu Purāṇa* she is the wife of Dakṣa and the mother of Viṣṇu in his dwarf incarnation (*vāmana-avatāra*).

[14]We find the same assertion in a hymn to the Goddess Kālī-Durgā in the *Mahābhārata (Bhīṣma-parva* 23), where the Goddess is called "younger sister of the chief of cowherds (*gopendra,* i.e. Krishna), but also "eldest one *(jyeṣṭā),* born in the family of the cowherd Nanda."

[15]The latter association underlies the link between the luminous form of the Goddess and Viṣṇu as a solar deity. On the eighth day of each bright *pakṣa* she manifests herself as the effulgent Durgā, and on the eleventh she appears with Viṣṇu as Śrī or Lakṣmī, his golden-skinned consort. The yearly celebration of Viṣṇu's marriage with Tulasī-devī takes place every year on Kārttika *śukla* 11, but it may be celebrated any day between the eleventh and the *pūrṇimā* of Kārttika (the day that marks the end of the *vrata* known as *kārttikasnāna,* which starts on the *pūrṇimā* of Aśvin, "Kojāgirī *pūrṇimā*").

[16]The account in *HV* 47, according to which Viṣṇu himself will be the seventh and eighth embryos born from Devakī, can be understood only as his "taking over" the two last "Durgās" (Bhramarī and Caṇḍikā) held in Kālī's womb. The Vaiṣṇava interpretation appears somewhat clumsily superimposed over the old myth.

[17]As in the case of the emergence of Ambikā from the sheath of Pārvatī's body; see note 3 above.

[18]See note 14 above.

[19]See note 13 above.

[20]Yamunā-devī and Devakī, the latter said to be an avatar of Aditi, appear closely related in the Cowherd-god legend. As dark goddesses and mother-figures, these two may be considered subsidiary forms of the primordial mother Kālī. Though she is supposed to be Yama's sister, Yamunā-devī also appears as a sort of twin sister to Krishna himself. (See note 7 above.)

[21]In tantric literature, the Goddess is said to be both mother and spouse of Maheśvara (Śiva), as in the hymn to Bhuvaneśvarī from the *Tantrasāra* (Avalon, *Hymns,* p. 32). Concerning the controversy about the relation of Subhadrā to Krishna-Jagannātha, see note 22 below.

[22]The Goddess Ekānaṃśā, a form of Durgā, was popular in ancient and medieval India. Said to be Krishna's sister, she was identified with Yaśodā's daughter, who saved Krishna's life; see S.C. Mukherji, "The Cult of Ekānaṃśā," *Indian Historical Quarterly* 35 (1959): 189-208. Some writers, quoting from the *Skanda Purāṇa,* consider Subhadrā (alias Ekānaṃśā) to be both sister and wife of Jagannātha. This interpretation is rejected by K.C. Misra in *The Cult of Jagannātha* (Calcutta: K.L. Mukhopadhyay, 1971, pp. 217-18). He says, "This idea is fantastic because in the realm of Hindu religion the concept of brother-sister worship is not a prevailing feature."

According to this author, "Subhadrā stands for Ādyaśakti or the primal energy of God and should be considered as the Śakti of Viṣṇu-Kṛṣṇa and not as a sister and wife at the same time." As consort of Jagannātha, Subhadrā should be placed on the male god's left side; and this is not the case in the Jagannātha trio. Yet in later representations in which Baladeva is absent, the goddess is found on the left side of the god—even when this goddess is clearly Durgā. An example is the painting found in the *bhogamaṇḍapa* within the Jagannātha temple, representing a double shrine: Jagannātha on the right and Durgā *mahiṣamardinī* on the left, the two standing on the same pedestal with a Śiva-*linga* in between (see Misra, *Jagannātha,* plate 36). Similarly, in joint images of Rādhā and Krishna, Rādhā stands at the left side of Krishna.

[23]The earliest purāṇic references to the *puruṣottama kṣetra* (Jagannātha-Puri)are found in the *Matsya Purāṇa* (ch. 13, *śloka* 35, and ch. 22, *śloka* 38), where Vimalā-devī is mentioned, but not Jagannātha. The male god is mentioned in later Purāṇas, such as the *Viṣṇu* and others. According to the tantric tradition, Vimalā-devī is "Bhairavī," the consort of Jagannātha, the latter being regarded as "Bhairava" (Śiva). She is worshipped in the tantric mode with the sacrifice of rams. The painting in the *bhogamaṇḍapa* of the Jagannātha temple, described above, seems to correspond to this Śaiva interpretation of the Jagannātha-Devī couple.

[24]On the influence of the tantric (Sahajiyā) tradition on the theology worked out by the *gosvāmīs* of Brindavan and especially on the development of Rādhā's identification with the *hlādinī śakti* of Lord Krishna, see E.C. Dimock, Jr., *The Place of the Hidden Moon* (Chicago: University of Chicago Press, 1966), pp. 81-83. According to Rūpa Gosvāmī in his *Ujjvalanīlamaṇī,* Rādhā is "established in the tantra" (*tantre pratiṣṭhitā*) as *hlādinī-mahāśakti.*

[25]Dimock's guess is that Kṛṣṇadāsa, the author of the *Caitanya-caritāmṛta,* had acquired from his gurus in Brindavan the notion of Rādhā and Krishna in the intimate relation of *śakti* and *śaktimān* and then put it in the mouth of Caitanya himself. Rāmānanda Rāya was called a "Sahaja Vaiṣṇava," that is, an adept of the Sahajiyā doctrine. This concept would originally have been a tantric view, borrowed later by orthodox Vaiṣṇavas (cf. ibid., pp. 148-49). This view of Rādhā is peculiar to the Gauḍīya sect; it has not been accepted by other non-Bengali Krishna sects.

[26]Among the eleven so-called *svarūpa* icons of Krishna Gopāla owned by the heads of the seven branches of the Vallabhite sect, only three are flanked by a female personage: (1) Śrī Viṭṭhalnāthjī (at Nāthdvārā, Rajasthan), clearly a replica of Viṭṭhala of Paṇḍharpūr; the worshipping female figure placed below the main icon on the left is probably Rukmiṇī (though the latter is not present within Viṭṭhala's shrine in Paṇḍharpūr); (2) Śrī Gokulnāthjī (at Gokul in Braj) and (3) Śrī Madanmohanjī (at Kāmban, Rajasthan). The latter two icons represent Krishna in the *muralīdhāraṇa* pose, as do the Gopinātha of Remuṇā and the Sākṣī-Gopāla of Kaṭak, and in both cases the god is flanked by two female—probably *gopī*—worshippers. Those are commonly identified as "Gopikā" and "Rādhikā" in Northern India and in the Gopālpur temple in Paṇḍharpūr. These two female figures are also present at the Gopinātha shrine visited by Caitanya, where they are known to have been added later.

[27]According to Maharashtrian tradition, Rukmiṇī-devī arrived at the Paṇḍharpūr *kṣetra* on her own, out of jealousy at Krishna's persistent attachment to Rādhā. Krishna is supposed to have come later, in search of her. In Paṇḍharpūr itself, Rukmiṇī's first residence was that of a local goddess, Masānī, the main goddess worshipped by the pastoral castes of Maharashtra. Rukmiṇī-devī is still worshipped there, together with Masānī, with whom she is identified. A similar story is told in Dvārakā, in connection with the old Rukmiṇī temple on the seashore, the most ancient temple in Dvārakā. The Goddess is said to have come before any of the other divine personages associated with it, and she has maintained her separate establishment to the present day.

NOTES

The Divine Duality of Rādhā and Krishna

Barbara Stoler Miller

[1]The entire discussion draws heavily on my study and translation of Jayadeva's *Gītagovinda*, published in *Love Song of the Dark Lord: Jayadeva's Gītagovinda* (New York: Columbia University Press, 1977); hereafter cited as *LSDL*. Section 5 of the Introduction gives a detailed account of references to Rādhā in literature antedating the *Gītagovinda*.

[2]This focus on the duality of Rādhā and Krishna in the *Gītagovinda* may offer a better insight into the religious perspective of Jayadeva's vision than I offer anywhere in *LSDL*. Most commentators on the *Gītagovinda* make the point that the word order of the dual compound *rādhā-mādhavau* is irregular in its priority (*pūrvanipāta*), like *naranārāyaṇau, umāmaheśvarau, kākamayūrau*, etc.

[3]Particuilarly relevant here are the analyses of memory (*smṛti*) in Indian epistemology and the interpretation of the concept of *pratyabhijñā*, "recognition," by Abhinavagupta. See Karl Potter, ed., *Indian Metaphysics and Epistemology* (Princeton: Princeton University Press, 1977), e.g., pp. 172-73, 219, 258, 297, 312-13; K.C. Pandey, *Abhinavagupta* (Varanasi: Chowkhamba, 1963), pp. 417-27.

[4]W.D. Whitney and R. Roth, eds., *Atharvaveda Saṃhitā* (Berlin: F. Dummler, 1856), 6.130.

[5]See Barbara Stoler Miller, *Phantasies of A Love-Thief* (New York: Columbia University Press, 1971); revised in *The Hermit and the Love-Thief: Sanskrit Poems of Bhartrihari and Bilhana* (New York: Columbia University Press: 1978).

[6]*Abhinavabharatī*, ed. Manavalli Ramakrishna Kavi (Baroda: Gaekwad Oriental Series, no. 36), 1:279-88. See Raniero Gnoli, *The Aesthetic Experience According to Abhinavagupta* (Rome: Instituto italiano per il medio ed estremo oriente, 1956) pp. 16, 74; J.L. Masson and M.V. Patwardhan, *Śāntarasa and Abhinavagupta's Philosophy of Aesthetics* (Poona: Bhandarkar Oriental Research Institute, 1969), pp. 57-58.

[7]E.g., *Bhagavadgītā* 7.14, where Krishna says that he is won by one who remembers him; *Viṣṇu Purāṇa* 2.6.40, where memory is said to dispel evil.

[8]See Rūpa Gosvāmī, *Bhaktirasāmṛtasindhu* 2.114, trans. Bon Maharaj (Vrindaban: Institute of Oriental Philosophy, 1965), vol. 1; based on the edition of D. Goswāmī (Benares, 1932) with the commentary *Durgasaṃgamanī* of Jīva Gosvāmī.

[9]*LSDL*, pp. 16-17, 50-51; also Suniti Kumar Chatterji, *Jayadeva* (New Delhi: Sahitya Akademi, 1973), pp. 15-17.

[10]Telang and Panshikar, eds. (Bombay: Nirnaya Sagara Press, 1899); see *LSDL*, pp. 187-88.

[11]In the language of Sanskrit aesthetics this involves the combination of the dreadful mood (*bhayānakarasa*) with the erotic mood (*śṛṅgārarasa*).

[12]V.G. Apte, ed., *Brahmavaivarta Purāṇa*, Kṛṣṇajanmakhaṇḍa 15 (Poona: Ānandāśrama Press, 1935); trans. R.N. Sen in *Sacred Books of the East* (Allahabad: Pānini Office, 1922), vol. 24.

[13]W.G. Archer, *The Loves of Krishna in Indian Painting and Poetry* (New York: Grove Press, 1958), plate 20.

[14]*LSDL*, pp. 18-24, 52-55.

[15]*LSDL*, pp. 3, 20, 23.

[16]*LSDL*, pp. 18, 28.

[17]*LSDL*, pp. 25.

[18]*LSDL*, pp. 3-6, 39.

[19]This triumph on one level follows the conventional image of *viparītarati*, in which the woman takes the man's role in love. See D.H.H. Ingalls, trans., *An Anthology of Sanskrit Court Poetry*, Harvard Oriental Series 44 (Cambridge: Harvard University Press, 1965), p. 200; *LSDL*, p. 222.

[20]*LSDL*, pp. 5, 17; John B. Carman, *The Theology of Rāmānuja: An Essay in Interreligious Understanding* (New Haven: Yale University Press, 1974); Per Kvaerne, *An Anthology of Buddhist Tantric Songs: A Study of the Caryāgīti* (Oslo: Universitets-forlaget, 1977). It should be noted that Rādhā is addressed as Caṇḍī at three critical points in the *Gītagovinda:* 10.11, 13; 11.7.

[21]The latter interpretation was formulated by C. Lassen in the Latin introduction to his 1836 edition of the *Gītagovinda,* based on the account in the *Bhaktamāl* of Nabhājī (see *LSDL*, p. 39, n. 2). It was translated into English by Edwin Arnold and quoted in the preface to his translation, entitled *The Indian Song of Songs* (London: Kegan Paul Trench Trübner, 1875; reprint ed., Bombay: JAICO, 1949). It has most recently been quoted at length by Marvin H. Pope in a section on the *Gītagovinda* in the Anchor Bible *Song of Songs* (New York: Doubleday, 1977), p. 86.

[22]Jogeshcandra Bagal, ed., *Bankim-racanāvalī* (Calcutta: Sahitya Samsad, 1969), 3:98; quoted from Chatterji, *Jayadeva*, pp. 50-51. See also Bankim's study of the life of Krishna, *Kṛṣṇacarita*, pp. 232 ff., and his articles in *Raṅgadarśana*, Chitra 1281, pp. 610-11, and *Sāhitya Pariṣat Patrikā* 45: 7-9, where he argues for Jayadeva's indebtedness to an "original version" of the *Brahmavaivarta Purāṇa* for his conception of Rādhā.

[23]See Mircea Eliade, *Patterns in Comparative Religion* (Cleveland: World, 1963), p. 421; and Stella Kramrisch, "The Indian Great Goddess," *History of Religions* 14 (May 1975): 258-62.

[24]J. Gonda, *The Dual Deities in the Religion of the Veda* (Amsterdam: North Holland Publishing Co., 1974).

[25]*LSDL*, p. 22.

[26]Throughout the *Mahābhārata* (Poona: Bhandarkar Oriental Research Institute, 1933), e.g., 1.219.15; also *Devībhāgavata Purāṇa, skandha* 4 (Bombay: Venkateśvara Press, 1919), containing the story of Nara and Nārāyaṇa.

[27]These verses are from the final two parts of the *Gītagovinda,* the opening couplets and refrains of songs 22 and 23 and *śloka* 12.1; *LSDL*, pp. 120-22.

A Sanskrit Portrait: Rādhā in the Plays of Rūpa Gosvāmī

Donna Marie Wulff

[1]In citing the VM, I follow the numbering of the Kāvyamālā edition: Bhavadatta Śāstrī and Kāśīnāth Pāṇḍurang Parab, eds., *The Vidagdha-mādhava of Śrī Rūpadeva Gosvāmī*, 2nd ed. (Bombay: Nirṇaya Sāgar Press, 1937) (Kāvyamālā 81). However, better readings of many passages are furnished by the two Bengali-script editions that I used extensively: Purīdās, ed., *Vidagdhamādhava-nāṭakam* (Mymensingh: Śacīnātha Rāyachaudhurī, 1947) and Satyendranāth Basu, ed., *Vidagdhamādhava* (Calcutta: Basumatī Sāhitya Mandir, n.d.).

For citations in the LM, I likewise follow the numbering of the Devanāgarī edition I used: Bābūlāl Śukla, ed., *Lalitamādhava-nāṭaka* (Varanasi: Chowkhamba Sanskrit Series Office, 1969) (Kashi Sanskrit Series 190). Again, however, better readings for many passages are found in the Bengali-script edition of Purīdās, *Lalitamādhava-nāṭakam* (Mymensingh: Śacīnātha Rāyachaudhurī, 1947).

For passages in the BRS, I follow the numbering of the following Bengali-script edition: Haridās Dās, ed., *Bhaktirasāmṛtasindhu*, 2nd ed. (Navadvīp: Haribol Kuṭī, 1961).

For passages in the UNM, I follow the divisions of the Kāvyamālā edition: Durgaprasād and Wāsudev Laxman, eds., *The Ujjwalanīlamaṇi by Shrī Rūpagoswāmī*, 2nd ed. (Bombay: Nirṇaya Sāgar Press, 1932) (Kāvyamālā 95).

For other editions of these and Rūpa's other works, see my thesis, "Drama as a

Mode of Religious Realization: The *Vidagdhamādhava* of Rūpa Gosvāmin," Harvard University, 1977.

[2]Rūpa's special debt to the *Bhāgavata* is unmistakable: although he departs radically from it in narrative detail, he repeatedly alludes to its themes and episodes. Moreover, many of his verses reflect its most characteristic stylistic device: the deliberate juxtaposition of apparently incongruous elements—as in the episode in which the baby Krishna opens his mouth to reveal the entire universe to his awestruck mother—in order to evoke a comparable sense of wonder in the devotee. On vernacular dramatic representations in the Mathurā region of the deeds of Krishna and their probable antiquity, see Norvin Hein, *The Miracle Plays of Mathurā* (New Haven: Yale University Press, 1972), esp. ch. 9.

[3]Here Rūpa implicitly contrasts two religious ideals, that of passionate devotion (*rāgānugā bhakti*) and that of ascetic renunciation of passion (*yoga, sannyāsa*). He clearly prefers the former.

[4]*VM* 6.21. The last two words of the verse, *jagad vismṛtam*, "the world forgotten," succinctly express a central goal of *yoga*, total obliviousness to the mundane realm.

[5]*VM* 2.47. The *tamāla* is black, like Krishna, and is thus closely associated with him. Rādhā's wish presupposes the conventional imagery of classical Sanskrit poetry, in which the (feminine) creeper and the (masculine) tree around which it is entwined represent the loving couple.

[6]Rūpa was clearly wrestling in the *Lalitamādhava* with a difficult theological problem posed by the *Bhāgavata* account: how was it possible for Krishna to leave the *gopīs*, and especially Rādhā, seemingly without regret? Did he have no notion of the grief that he would cause, or was he utterly heartless? And would he, too, not be consumed by grief?

[7]The classical model for this motif is Purūravas's anguished search for the nymph Urvaśī, as represented, for example, in Kālidāsa's *Vikramorvaśī*. The *gopīs'* search for Krishna when he disappears from their midst as narrated in the *rāsa* chapters of the *Bhāgavata Purāṇa* (10.30-31) is also clearly in the background.

[8]The parallel with one traditional account of Caitanya's death in the ocean at Puri is striking: he, too, is said to have entered the water because its waves appeared to him to be Krishna's dark form.

[9]See the list of practices found in Rūpa's *Bhaktirasāmṛtasindhu* (hereafter cited as *BRS*) 1.2.25 ff, especially "limbs" (*aṅgas*) 32-34: *gīta, saṅkīrtana* (in particular the first of its three subtypes, *nāmakīrtana*), and *japa*. See also Norvin J. Hein, "Caitanya's Ecstasies and the Theology of the Name," in Bardwell L. Smith, ed., *Hinduism: New Essays in the History of Religions* (Leiden: E.J. Brill, 1976).

[10]*VM* 3.4; 3.8.14-15; 5.14. Cf. 2.24. *Ekāgratā*, concentration on a single point, is a fundamental element of yoga.

[11]*VM* 2.48. The terms *jīvitapati* and the virtually synonymous *prāṇanātha* are reminiscent of several of the names of Viṣṇu enumerated, for example, at *MBh* 13.149, notably *jīvana, prāṇa, prāṇadā*, and *prāṇabhṛt*. See Jan Gonda, *Aspects of Early Viṣṇuism*, 2nd ed. (Delhi: Motilal Banarsidass, 1969), p. 18. In the *Vidagdhamādhava*, however, such terms assume a new significance, for the context is not a metaphysical one, but an emotional one of love and longing.

[12]*VM* 6.8.44. Viśākhā here calls Rādhā *premodbhrānte*, "you who are mad with love." Paradoxically, it is this "demented" condition that allows her to perceive metaphysical truth.

[13]*LM* 2.33.3; the designation is obviously a pun on her name, the diminutive of which is Rādhikā.

[14]In *LM* 7.16, Navavṛndā contrasts the worship of Krishna done with flowers and incense with the *gopīs' sevā*, which consists of the play (*līlā*) of sidelong glances and embraces.

[15]*VM* 5.41. *Āratī* is a graceful form of worship that is done by waving a tray of oil lamps in circular patterns.

[16]Cf. *LM* 6.36.

[17]*BRS* 3.2.

[18]*LM* 4.19; the word that he uses, *sārūpya,* "identity of form," is used in the Purāṇas to designate a kind of *mokṣa.*

[19]In Rūpa's *Ujjvalanīlamaṇī* (hereafter cited as UNM) *māna* is one of the four types of separation (*UNM, śṛṅgārabheda* 68 ff).

[20]*VM* 2.0.11; 6.8.44. See note 12 above.

[21]*UNM, sthāyibhāvaprakaraṇa.*

[22]For the use of the term *sahaja* among *sahajijā* Vaiṣṇavas, see Edward C. Dimock, Jr., *The Place of the Hidden Moon* (Chicago: University of Chicago Press), 1966.

[23]*UNM, sthāyibhāvaprakaraṇa* 79-83.

[24]The Sanskrit idiom is "the three worlds" (*tribhuvana, LM 4.12; trilokī, LM* 2.8.21-22).

[25]For *śakti* ("energy, power"), see Glossary.

[26]On Rādhā as Krishna's *hlādinī śakti,* see S.K. De, *Early History of the Vaiṣṇava Faith and Movement in Bengal,* 2nd ed. (Calcutta: K.L. Mukhopadhyay, 1961), pp. 279-281.

[27]Rūpa, *Saṃkṣiptabhāgavatāmṛta* 2.1; 2.43-44.

[28]The metaphor of tasting is central to *rasa* theory: aesthetic experience is referred to in works on poetics as *rasāsvāda,* "tasting *rasa.*"

[29]On the theological debate over whether the love of Rādhā and Krishna is *svakīyā rati* (married love) or *parakīyā rati* (extramarital love), see S.K. De, *Early History,* pp. 204-206, 348-351; Dimock, *Hidden Moon,* pp. 200-214. Noteworthy in this connection is the tenth act of the *Lalitamādhava,* in which Rādhā is married to Krishna in a grand ceremony of reunion.

[30]Rūpa explicitly contrasts these two religious ideals at several points in his theoretical writings. See, for example, *BRS* 1.1.4, in which he asserts that *bhakti* is incomparably superior to *mokṣa* (*mukti*).

A Vernacular Portrait: Rādhā in the *Sūr Sāgar*

John Stratton Hawley

[1]The pairing is explicit in both cases. In regard to sacred time it seems that Rādhā's birth festival (Rādhāṣṭamī) grew up to match the more venerable Kṛṣṇajanmāṣṭamī, of which the *Bhaviṣyottara Purāṇa* takes considerable note; it follows exactly a fortnight later. In regard to sacred place, however, Rādhā's town Barsānā has a preeminence that Krishna's nearby Nandagāõ only palely matches.

[2]Such scenes are witnessed in the *rādhācaranspars* (cf. also *naukā*) and *kākmāl līlās.*

[3]The claim made for the first time in the *Caurāsī Vaiṣṇavan kī Vartā* that Sūr took Vallabhācārya as his guru, thus joining the first ranks of the Vallabha Sampradāy, is doubted by few in Braj. Historically, however, it is probably inaccurate. See Charlotte Vaudeville, *Pastorales par Soûr Dās* (Paris: Gallimard, 1971), pp. 39 and 59; and Hawley, "The Butter Thief" (Ph.D. diss., Harvard University, 1977), pp. 269-74.

[4]For a brief review of manuscript information relating to the *Sūr Sāgar,* see John Stratton Hawley, "The Early *Sūr Sāgar* and the Growth of the Sūr Tradition," *Journal of the American Oriental American Society,* 99:1 (1979), pp. 62-72.

[5]This is a scruple not always observed. No less a critic than Hazārīprasād Dvivedī draws the culminating flourishes of his portrait of Sūr's Rādhā from a poem—Nāgarīpracāriṇī Sabhā (hereafter cited as NPS) 4911—in which her name is not mentioned.

The poem, as it happens, is old, but it was not until relatively recently that it came to be understood as descriptive of Rādhā's emotions when she met Krishna at Kurukṣetra. Indeed, there is no direct mention of the Kurukṣetra incident in the earliest instance of this poem to which I currently have manuscript access. Dvivedī, "Sūrdās kī Rādhā," in Harbanślāl Śarmā, ed., *Sūrdās* (Delhi: Rādhākṛṣṇa Prakāśan, 1969), pp. 202f.; 'Ratnākar,' *et al.*, eds., *Sūr Sāgar*, 2 vols. (Vārāṇasī: Nāgarīpracāriṇī Sabhā, 1972, 1976).

[6]Dvivedī, "Sūrdās kī Rādhā," pp. 193, 196, 198. Dvārkāprasād Mītal, *Hindī Sāhitya mẽ Rādhā* (Mathura: Javāhar Prakāśan, 1970), p. 300. Omprakāś, *Madhyayugīn Kāvya* (New Delhi: Arya Book Depot, 1973), pp. 83, 88 ff. In this Sūr is contrasted to Jayadeva, Caṇḍidās, and Vidyāpati, who only portray Rādhā as *vilāsinī*.

[7]NPS 1291. Here, as throughout, italics indicate the refrain (*ṭek*) when it comprises only that portion of a line of poetry in Braj Bhāṣā which would, in a full line, precede the caesura. If a full line functions as the refrain it is translated in two lines of English verse and no italics appear, though in performance at least its first phrase would normally be repeated. I am indebted to Mark Juergensmeyer for help in bringing the poems translated in this essay to their present form.

[8]Mītal, *Rādhā*, p. 301.

[9]Dvivedī, "Sūrdās," p. 200.

[10]Omprakāś, *Kāvya*, p. 92-93.

[11]NPS 1305.8, 1307.6.

[12]NPS 2786.

[13]NPS 2298.1, 4387.5.

[14]NPS 3399.1-2.

[15]NPS 4904 in the version given in Bikaner 156 (Bl).

[16]NPS 2320.6.

[17]NPS 2741.

[18]NPS 2379. Cf. NPS 3122 and 3136, but the woman is not named. A number of somewhat later poems (but still within 150 years of the poet's death) repeat the theme: NPS 3088, 3090, 3274, *pariśiṣṭ* 93.

[19]NPS 2742.

[20]NPS 4692, 4721, 4724.

[21]NPS 3217, 3399, 3432, 3434, 3435, 3440.

[22]NPS 2609. Critical reading based on Bikaner 156 and 157 and Allahabad 76 (Bl, B2, A1).

[23]NPS 3067.12.

[24]NPS 2732, 2736, 2802.

[25]NPS 3435.5 Cf. also NPS 3466.6.

[26]NPS 3399.

[27]NPS 3440.1.

[28]NPS 2522. Critical reading based on Bikaner 157 and 158 (B2, B3).

[29]NPS 1362 ff. Cf. also the necklace cycle, NPS 2584-2634, and individual, formulaic epithets in NPS 2519.2, 2624.1, 3070:7, 3106.6, etc. Interestingly, the parallel drawn between Krishna's cleverness and Rādhā's in NPS 3280.7 is a late alteration of an early poem. Early readings have *ātur ati kāmi* rather than *catur ati kāmini* (Bikaner 156 and Allahabad 76; B1, A1).

[30]NPS 1673.21-30, reading with Bikaner 158 (B4).

[31]NPS 1690 provides another instance, about equally early.

[32]NPS 2314. Critical readings based on Bikaner 156, 157, 158, and Udaipur 133 (Bl, B2, U2).

[33]*Śrīmadbhāgavata-mahāpurāṇa* 10.30.28 (Gorakhpur: Gita Press, 1962).

[34]Among numerous examples, NPS 2303, 2305, 2306, 2309, 2521, 2527, 2573, 2683 ff., *pariśiṣṭ* 5. There is a mention of *puruṣa* and *prakṛti* in an earlier poem, NPS 3434.7,

but it is no bald theological assertion. Rather it occurs in the context of an attempt by Rādhā's friend to draw her out of her angry sulking by assuring her of Krishna's faithfulness. Furthermore, it contrasts the sentiment (*ras*) of which the relation between Rādhā and Krishna is made with this more archaic relationship, and separates the two by two intervening relationships. In this early poem, then, a direct analogy between Krishna and Rādhā on the one hand and *puruṣa* and *prakṛti* on the other is not even established by Rādhā's friend, let alone by the poet.

[35]NPS 2379.6.

[36]NPS 3434.1. Cf. the ambiguous use of the word in NPS 4209.6.

[37]NPS 3073.17. Cf. the even earlier usage *nāgari nāgaravar* in 3435.5. The phrase *bām-aṅg* in NPS 1673.15 carries a hint of Rādhā's wifely status but is not used with precisely that intent. Similarly the term *suhāg*, occurring in the NPS version of 3280.8, suggests by its context a reference to Rādhā's good fortune as that of a married woman (*suhāginī*). Older versions of this poem, however, do not carry this implication so directly. The particle *su-* is separated from *bhāg* in the oldest MS at my disposal (Bikaner 156; B1) and is deleted in another (Udaipur 575; U1), appearing in more or less its NPS form only in Allahabad 76 (A1).

[38]For instance, *pati nāri* in NPS 2463.1.

[39]NPS 1690.30. In its first occurrence in the manuscripts (Bikaner 158) this poem introduces the whole body of poetry describing Krishna's dalliance (the editor calls it *śṛṅgār*) with Rādhā and the *gopīs*. It seems likely that it was constructed to fulfill just such a function.

[40]Such writers typically draw attention to NPS 1689:1-2, a passage from the later *Sūr Sāgar* that declares that the circle dance in which Rādhā and Krishna take part can be interpreted as a marriage rite of the informal *gāndharva* variety. See Mītal, *Hindī Sāhitya*, p. 289; Omprakāś, *Madhyayugīn Kāvya*, p. 85.

[41]The most familiar term is *kul kāni*, family respectibility.

[42]Other names, like Lalitā and Candrāvalī, occur only in later poems in the *Sūr Sāgar*, and very sparingly at that.

The Theology of Rādhā in the Purāṇas

C. Mackenzie Brown

[1]These lines are a summary of various passages in the *Brahmavaivarta Purāṇa*, reflecting the viewpoint of the latest textual layer of the Purāṇa. For an analysis of the textual history of the *Brahmavaivarta*, consult my study, *God as Mother: A Feminine Theology in India; An Historical and Theological Study of the Brahmavaivarta Purāṇa* (Hartford, Vt.,: Claude Stark & Co., 1974). The specific verses on which the summary is based are 2.1.9-12; 2.1.28-29; 2.35. 4-10; and 2.48.29-47. It should be noted that there are seeming discrepancies between some of these verses regarding the actual identity of the female being. My identification of her as Rādhā in the summary is in accord with one of the passages, and clearly represents the view of the final redactors of the text as a whole. All translations and summaries from the *Brahmavaivarta* are mine. The edition used, unless otherwise noted, is Bombay, Venkateśvara Press, 1930 (orig. pub. 1909-10).

[2]According to the *Brahmavaivarta*, Brahmā lives 108 years, each of which is equal to about 3.4×10^{14} human years.

[3]No explanation is given for this act of Rādhā's, other than that she was angry with the egg.

[4]This account is a summary of 2.2.30-2.3.60. For a more detailed summary, see my *God as Mother*, pp. 168-70.

[5]*Bhāgavata Purāṇa* 10.30.28, in *Śrīmad Bhāgavata Mahāpurāṇa with Sanskrit*

Text and English Translation (Gorakhpur: Gita Press, 1971). Cf. Edward C. Dimock, Jr., *The Place of the Hidden Moon* (Chicago: University of Chicago Press, 1966), p. 33.

[6]For a brief survey of some of the early references to Rādhā, see S.M. Pandey and Norman Zide, "Sūrdās and His Krishna-*Bhakti*," in Milton Singer, ed., *Krishna, Myths, Rites, and Attitudes* (Chicago: University of Chicago Press, 1968), pp. 182-83.

[7]For a discussion of Rādhā as *svakīyā* (Krishna's own) or *parakīyā* (another's), see Dimock, "Doctrine and Practice among the Vaiṣṇavas of Bengal," in Singer, *Krishna*, pp. 55-63.

[8]*Daśaśloki* 5 in *Dashashlokee*, Chowkhamba Sanskrit Series, No. 358 (Benares: Vidya Vilas Press, 1927). Translation mine.

[9]See Asoke Kumar Majumdar, "A Note on the Development of the Rādhā Cult," *Annals of the Bhandarkar Oriental Research Institute*, 36 (1955): 243.

[10]Parts of these works may be much older. Those sections which contain references to Rādhā, however, are invariably of relatively late date. Considerable work on the dating of the Purāṇas, including the later texts, has been done by R.C. Hazra in his *Studies in the Purāṇic Records on Hindu Rites and Customs* (University of Dacca: Bulletin No. 20, 1940).

[11]H.H. Wilson felt that the text came from a sect originating with Vallabhācārya and the Caitanya Gosvāmins; see his "Analysis of the Puráńas," in *Essays, Analytical, Critical, and Philological on Subjects Connected with Sanskrit Literature* (London: Trubner & Co., 1864), 1:120. J.N. Farquhar suggested that at least the fourth book of the Purāṇa (on the life of Krishna) was a Nimbārkite document; see *An Outline of the Religious Literature of India* (London: Oxford University Press, 1920), p. 240.

[12]For specific references to Rādhā in the other Purāṇas, see my *God as Mother*, pp. 33, 35, 158-62, 166; and A.K. Majumdar, "Rādhā Cult," pp. 244-47.

[13]Cf. H.H. Wilson, *Vishńu Puráńa, A System of Hindu Mythology and Tradition*, 3rd ed., (Calcutta: Punthi Pustak, 1972, p. 426.

[14]This earlier account appears in 1.3-6.

[15]See, for instance, 2.48.29-47.

[16]*Viṣṇu Purāṇa* 5.1; *Bhāgavata Purāṇa* 10.1.

[17]10.1.23.

[18]The *Brahmavaivarta* gives the usual reason for Krishna's incarnation in 4.4. Prefixed to this traditional account, in 4.2-3, is the disclosure of the "real" reason, and of how Rādhā herself descended to earth.

[19]Cf. Bimanbehari Majumdar, *Kṛṣṇa in History and Legend* (Calcutta: University of Calcutta, 1969), p. 195, for traditional interpretations of this episode in the *Gītagovinda*.

[20]The account of Rādhā's and Krishna's marriage appears in 4.15.

[21]See, for instance, 2.49.38-43, where it is also affirmed that this husband, Rāyāṇa, is in any case an emanation or fraction of Krishna himself. Elsewhere, as in the plays of Rūpa Gosvāmī, Rāyāṇa is known as Abhimanyu, which according to B. Majumdar, is "probably the Sanskritised form of the Prakrit word Ahibana, Āyāna or Rāyāna of the *Brahmavaivarta Purāṇa*" (*Kṛṣṇa*, p. 212).

[22]See *Viṣṇu Purāṇa with Ratnagarbha Bhaṭṭa's Commentary* (Bombay: Oriental Press, 1889), 1.2.21.

[23]E.g., 2.55.86; cf. 2.2.8.

[24]1.28.29-32.

[25]4.29.47; 4.67.76-77.

[26]4.6.208-12.

[27]4.15.62.

[28]2.54.92.

[29]2.55.77; 3.7.52. The *Brahmavaivarta* puts forth many views on the relationship of Krishna to *puruṣa* and Rādhā to *prakṛti*. At times, for instance, Krishna is equated

with *puruṣa* (or *puṃs*) in his highest form (2.54.109), whereas elsewhere he is above *puruṣa*, *prakṛti*, and whatever is neuter as well.

[30]See, for instance, 2.55.88-89; 4.15.59.

[31]Similarly, the analogies of substance and attribute overcome one of the serious limitations of the analogies of efficient and material cause, which suggest the distinct nature of the two principles, just as *puruṣa* and *prakṛti* were seen as distinct in the Sāṃkhya.

[32]1.28.23. Cf. 2.55.88.

[33]4.67.67-70. Cf. 2.2.74-76.

[34]For a brief discussion of these notions, see Heinrich Zimmer, *Myths and Symbols in Indian Art and Civilization* (Princeton: Princeton University Press, 1972), pp. 201-10.

[35]2.54.88-91; 2.55.52; 2.65.25. It is of interest that the name of the goddess Kālī occurs relatively rarely in the *Brahmavaivarta Purāṇa*. For one such reference, see 2.1.91 ff., where she is said to have arisen from the angered Durgā's brow and to have become black (*kṛṣṇa*) in color through contemplating Krishna.

[36]2.54.92.

[37]2.2.47.

[38]4.43.59.

[39]2.62.34.

[40]*The Bhagavad-Gītā, with the Commentary of Śrī Śankarācārya* (Poona: Oriental Book Agency, 1950), 7.13-14.

[41]See *Sāṃkhya Kārikā* 56-60, in S. Radhakrishnan and C.A. Moore, eds., *A Source Book in Indian Philosophy* (Princeton: Princeton University Press, 1957), pp. 442-44.

[42]4.6.

[43]This notion is well illustrated in the *Bhāgavata Purāṇa*, in the story of Krishna's revelation to his mother of the universe in his mouth. When she looked in to see if he had been eating earth, she beheld the entire cosmos. She immediately bowed down and worshipped her son as the Supreme Lord. Krishna then caused her to forget what she had seen and cast his *māyā* in the form of maternal affection upon her (10.8.35-45).

[44]4.110.4.

[45]2.62.32.

[46]4.15.70-72.

[47]See Donna Wulff and Shrivatsa Goswami in this volume, and Dimock, *Hidden Moon*, pp. 22-23.

[48]As pointed out to me by J.S. Hawley, given the prominence of the maternal theology in the *Purāṇa*, the more probable choice might have been the inverse form of *vātsalya*, in which God is worshipped as a parent. But the *Brahmavaivarta*, like the Bengali and Vallabhite theologians, gives no place to an inverted *vātsalya*, at least by that technical name. *Dāsya*, on the other hand, as used in the *Brahmavaivarta*, could easily include the affectionate adoration of a child for its parent.

[49]4.52.34-35.

[50]4.124.11.

[51]The Veṅkaṭeśvara edition reads *dhyānasādhyam* (attainable by meditation). The Vaṅgavāsī Press edition (Calcutta, 1890), however, has *dhyānāsādhyam* (unattainable by meditation), which seems the better reading in this context.

[52]Literally, "The Mother of Mahāviṣṇu." Mahāviṣṇu in the *Brahmavaivarta* is the deity born out of the cosmic egg and is responsible for creating the universe out of his own material being.

[53]2.54.28-31.

Rādhā: The Play and Perfection of *Rasa*

Shrivatsa Goswami

[1]Prabodhānanda Sarasvatī, *Śrī Rādhārasa-Sudhānidhiḥ*, ed. Purīdāsa (Vṛndāvana: Haridāsa Śarmā, 1953), verse 26, p. 3.

[2]Kṛṣṇadāsa Kavirāja, *Caitanya Caritāmṛta* (hereafter cited as *CC*), ed. Radha Govinda Nath, 4th ed. (Calcutta: Sadhana Prakashani, 1958), 2.8.54.

[3]*Bṛhadāraṇyaka Upaniṣad* (hereafter *BAU*) 3.6. *Kauśītakī Upaniṣad* 1.1; *Kaṭha Upaniṣad; Maitrī Upaniṣad* 1; *Praśna Upaniṣad.*

[4]*BAU* 3.7.1.

[5]Jīva Gosvāmī, *Prīti Sandarbha* (hereafter *PS*), ed. Purīdāsa (Vṛndāvana: Haridāsa Śarmā, 1951), *anu.* 1, p. 1.

[6]*Chāndogya Upaniṣad* (hereafter *CU*), 7.23.1.

[7]Jīva Gosvāmī, *Bhakti Sandarbha* (hereafter *BS*), ed. Purīdāsa (Vṛndāvana: Haridāsa Śarmā, 1951), *anu.* 1, p. 2. Also *PS, anu.* 1, p. 2.

[8]*Bhāgavata Purāṇa* (hereafter *BhP*), 1.2.11.

[9]Jīva Gosvāmī, *Bhāgavata Sandarbha* (hereafter *BhS*), ed. Purīdāsa (Vṛndāvana: Haridāsa Śarmā, 1951), *anu.* 1, p. 1.

[10]*BS, anu.* 170, p. 79; cf. *BhP* 11.20.6 *Jñāna* (knowledge) as a means of realization should not be confused with *jñāna* as ultimate knowledge. Jīva Gosvāmī, *Krama Sandarbha*, ed. Purīdāsa (Vṛndāvana: Harīdāsa Śarmā, 1952), 11.20.2, p. 425.

[11]Ibid. 3.32.36, p. 139.

[12]See T.R.V. Murti, "Knowing, Feeling and Willing as Functions of Consciousness," *Philosophical Quarterly* 9:4 (1934), pp. 47-65.

[13]*BS, anu.* 7, p. 5.

[14]*Taittirīya Upaniṣad* (hereafter *TU*), 2.1.1.

[15]*Raso vai saḥ, rasam hyevāyaṁ labdhvānandī bhavati, . . . esa hyevānandayati.* Ibid., 2.7.1.

[16]*Rig Veda* 10.90; *TU* 2.6.1; *BAU* 1.4.1-4; *BhP* 10.60.46; and Jīva Gosvāmī, *Kṛṣṇa Sandarbha* (hereafter *KṛS*), ed. Purīdāsa (Vṛndāvana: Haridāsa Śarmā, 1951), *anu.* 185, p. 114.

[17]*BhS, anu.* 98, p. 95.

[18]*Shree Brahma-Samhita* with commentary by Jeeva Goswami, ed. with English translation and purport by Bhakti Siddhanta Saraswati Goswami (Madras: Shree Gaudiya Math, Gaurabda 446, 1932), 5.1, p. 1.

[19]*BhP* 1.3.28.

[20]*BS, anu.* 3, p. 4.

[21]Rūpa Gosvāmī, *Ujjvalanīlamaṇi* (hereafter *UNM*), ed. with two commentaries by Purīdāsa (Vṛndāvana: Haridāsa Śarmā, 1954), 3.43-45, 48, pp. 22-23.

[22]*BS, anu.* 180, pp. 89-90.

[23]*BhP* 10.33.36.

[24]*KṛS, anu.* 28, p. 9.

[25]*Mahābhārata*, ed. Ramachandrasastri Kinjawadekar (Poona: Chitrashala Press, 1932), *Śānti-parva* 299.20, p. 596.

[26]Bimanbehari Majumdar, ed., *Caṇḍīdāser Padāvalī* (Calcutta: Baṅgīya Sāhitya Pariṣad, 1960), no. 85, p. 351.

[27]*Viṣṇu Purāṇa* 1.9.143.

[28]Indian thinkers foresaw and avoided the complications that would have been in ascribing cosmic functions directly to God: the puzzles of theodicy, determinism, and the like.

[29]*Vaidhī bhakti* comprises, broadly, nine phases (*BS, anu.* 235-308), pp. 116-56. Caitanya, however, established the supremacy among them of the *nāma saṃkīrtana.*

See Norvin J. Hein, "Caitanya's Ecstasies and the Theology of the Name," in Bardwell L. Smith, ed., *Hinduism* (Leiden: Brill, 1976), pp. 15-32.

[30]Jīva Gosvāmī, *Durgama Saṃgamanī*, in reference to Rūpa Gosvāmī, *Bhaktirasāmṛtasindhuḥ* (hereafter *BRS*) 1.2.1, ed. Haridāsa Dāsa (Navadvīpa: Haridāsa Dāsa, 1948), pp. 23-24.

[31]*BS, anu.* 310, pp. 157-79.

[32]Ibid.

[33]Cf. *PS, anu.* 110 ff., pp. 65 ff.

[34]Ibid, *anu.* 110-11, p. 67.

[35]*Brahma Saṁhitā* 5.56, p. 152.

[36]The basic text in this regard is the *Govindalīlāmṛta* of Kṛṣṇadāsa Kavirāja, in which 23 chapters are devoted to describing the daily *līlās* of Rādhā and Krishna.

[37]Raghunātha Dāsa Gosvāmī, *Stavāvalī*, ed. Purīdāsa (Meymensingh: Śacīnātha Rāyachaudhurī, 1947), 16.1, p. 41.

[38]*UNM*, 4.6-7, p. 24.

[39]Raghunātha Dāsa Gosvāmī, *Stavāvalī*, 15.1-10, p. 40.

[40]*UNM* 14.1-237, pp. 124-56.

[41]Ibid., 14.219, p. 155.

[42]*BRS* 2.1.230, p. 157.

[43]*UNM* 3.17-33, 5.10, pp. 17-19, 33.

[44]Cf. Jīva Gosvāmī, *Locana Rocanī* (hereafter *LR*), commenting on *UNM* 3.22, p. 18.

[45]*LR* 3.19, p. 17.

[46]*KṛS, anu.* 177, p. 104.

[47]Ibid., *anu.* 177, pp. 102-03; *anu.* 171, p. 92.

[48]Ibid., *anu.* 155, 182, 183, pp. 85, 109, 111. Also Jīva Gosvāmī, *Gopāla Campū* (hereafter *GC*), ed. Purīdāsa (Meymensingh: Śacīnātha Rāyachaudhurī, 1947), *pūrva* 33.13, p. 300.

[49]*BS, anu.* 320, p. 168; *PS, anu.* 41, p. 34.

[50]*BS, anu.* 320, p. 168.

[51]*BhP* 9.4.63; *PS, anu.* 61, 65, pp. 36-37.

[52]*KṛS, anu.* 189, p. 117.

[53]*Aphorisms on the Gospel of Divine Love or Nārada Bhakti Sutras*, ed. and trans. Swāmī Tyāgīśānanda (Madras: Śri Ramakrishna Math, 1967), no. 52., p. 15.

[54]Harivyāsa Deva, *Śrī Mahāvāṇī*, ed. Vrajavallabha Śaraṇa Vedāntācārya (Vṛndāvana: Śrī Nimbārka Śodha Maṇḍala, 1963), *Siddhāntasukha* 36, p. 314.

[55]*GC, pūrva* 33.8, p. 300; *KṛS, anu.* 189, p. 117.

[56]An anonymous *savaiyā*. The Moon of Vraja is Krishna.

[57]This process of maturity and reversal continued an additional step, however. In 1542 A.D. the worldly *līlā* of Caitanya was recreated in Vṛndāvana as his descent in the form of the deity of Śrī Rādhāramaṇa. In that supernal image Caitanya's light complexion became dark, his motion immovable, and his devotion the object of devotion. (*Śyāmācchabalam prapadye, śabalācchyāmam prapadye, CU* 8.13.1). On the process as whole, cf. *BAU* 4.3.21; *BhP* 11.5.32; and *KrS, anu.* 183, p. 111. In specific relation to Rādhāramaṇa, cf. Vanamālidāsa Śāstrī, *Rādhāramaṇa Śatakam* 2nd ed. (Vṛndāvana: Vanamālidāsa Śāstrī, 1975), pp. 40-60, and *Gurukṛpāradāna* (Calcutta; Pāṭhabāḍī Āśrama, 1969), 3:196-97.

[58]Cf. *BhP* 10.33.22.

[59]Rūpa Goswāmī, *Stavamālā*, ed. Purīdāsa (Meymensingh: Śacīnātha Rāyachaudhurī, 1946), "Śrī Caitanyadevasya dvitīyāṣṭakam" 3, p. 2.

[60]"The erotic *rasa* [i.e., *śṛṅgāra*] is shining dark (*śyāma*)," *Bharata Nāṭya Śāstra* 6.42, trans. J.L. Masson and M.V. Patwardhana, *Aesthetic Rapture* (Poona: Bhandarkar Oriental Research Institute, 1970), 1:48.

[61]*CC* 3.18.17.

[62]A *pada* of Harirāma Vyāsa in Bāsudeva Gosvāmī, *Bhaktakavi Vyāsajī,* ed. Prabhudayāla Mītal (Mathura: Agravala Press, 1952), *siddhānta* 31, p. 199.

[63]*GC, pūrva* 33.8, p. 300; *KṛS, anu.* 189, pp. 117-18.

[64]*KṛS, anu.* 181, p. 108.

Where Have All the Rādhās Gone?:
New Images of Woman in Modern Hindi Poetry

Karine Schomer

[1]*Kyūriyō Mārt mẽ Arjun kī talāś karte Śrīkṛṣṇa,* in Lakṣmīkānt Varmā, *Atukānt* (Varanasi: Bhāratīya Jñānpīṭh, 1968), pp. 18-19.

[2]See Kali C. Bahl, "Krishna Myth: Its Structure and Development in the Literatures of South Asian Languages," *Literature East and West,* forthcoming.

[3]Deben Bhattacharya, trans., *Love Songs of Chandidās: The Rebel Poet-Priest of Bengal* (London: George Allen & Unwin, 1967), p. 92.

[4]Edward C. Dimock, Jr., *et al., The Literatures of India: An Introduction* (Chicago: University of Chicago Press, 1974), p. 164.

[5]For a discussion of the important differences between Sanskrit poetic theory and theories developed by the *rīti* poets, see Bahl, "The Hindi *Rīti* Tradition and the *Rasikapriyā*of Keshavadasa: An Introductory Review," *Journal of South Asian Literature* 10:1 (1974), pp. 1-6.

[6]Viśvanāth Prasād Miśra, ed., *Keśav-granthāvalī,* 3 vols. (Allahabad: Hindustāni Academy, 1954), 1.68-75 (hereafter cited as *KG*).

[7]Nāgendra, ed., *Hindī sāhitya kā bṛhat itihās* (Varanasi: Nāgarī Pracāriṇī Sabhā, 1972), 7:134.

[8]Ibid., p. 157.

[9]KG, 1.8. [10]Ibid.

[11]Ibid., p. 11.

[12]Viśvanāth Prasād Miśra, ed., *Padmākar-granthāvalī* (Varanasi: Nāgarī Pracāriṇī Sabhā, 1958), p. 89.

[13]*KG,* 1.32.

[14]Ibid., p. 56.

[15]Barron Gregory Holland, "The Satsaī of Bihārī: Hindī Poetry of the Early *Rīti* Period; Introduction, Translation and Notes" (Ph.D. diss., University of California, Berkeley, 1969), p. 166.

[16]*Padmākar-granthāvalī,* p. 209.

[17]Nandadulāre Vājpeyī, ed., *Sūrsāgar,* 4th ed., 2 vols. (Varanasi: Nāgarī Pracāriṇī Sabhā, 1971), 2.1310.

[18]*KG,* 1.146-47.

[19]Holland, "Satsaī," p. 169.

[20]Sumitrānandan Pant, *Pallav,* 8th ed. (Delhi: Rājkamal Prakāśan, 1967), p. 22.

[21]Ibid., p. 20.

[22]Ibid., pp. 20-21. Satyavān is the husband whom the heroic Sāvitrī rescued from hands of death.

[23]Pant, *Pallav,* p. 31.

[24]Krishna's battle horn in the *Mahābhārata* war.

[25]Pant, *Pallav,* p. 16.

[26]Dhīrendra Varmā, *et al.,* eds., *Hindī sāhitya kośa,* 2nd ed., 2 vols. (Varanasi: Jñānmaṇḍal, 1962), 2.324.

[27]Śrīdhar Pāṭhak, "*Bhārat git,*" in Bālkṛṣṇa Rāv, ed., *Hindī kāvya saṃgraha* (Delhi: Sahitya Academy, 1968), p. 233.

[28]Subhadrā Kumārī Cauhān, "*Jhānsi kī rānī,*" in Sumitrānandan Pant, *et al.*, eds., *Kavi-bhāratī* (Chiragaon [Jhansi]: Sāhitya-Sadan, 1952), p. 201.

[29]*KG*, 1.135.

[30]Pāṭhak, "*Sāndhya-aṭan,*" in *Hindī kāvya saṃgraha*, p. 234.

[31]Ayodhyāsingh Upādhyāy 'Harioudh,' *Priyapravās*, 15th ed. (Varanasi: Hindī-Sāhitya-Kuṭīr, 1973), p. 244.

[32]Maithilī Śaraṇ Gupta, *Hindū*, 5th reprint ed. (Chiragaon [Jhansi]: Sāhitya-Sadan, 1969), p. 76.

[33]Ibid., pp. 76-77.

[34]Rāmnareś Tripāṭhī, "*Vidhvā kā darpaṇ,*" in Indranāth Madan, ed., *Kavitā aur Kavitā* (Delhi: Rājkamal Prakāśan, 1967), p. 68.

[35]Gupta, *Yośodharā* (Chiragaon [Jhansi]: Sāhitya-Sadan, 1972), p. 69.

[36]Mahādevī Varmā, *Sāhityakār kī āsthā tathā anya nibhanda*, 3rd ed. (Allahabad: Lokbhāratī Prakāśan, 1970), p. 67.

[37]Pant, *Vīṇā-Granthī* (Delhi: Rājkamal Prakāśan, 1972), p. 127.

[38] Varmā, *Raśmi*, 6th ed. (Allahabad: Sāhitya Bhavan, 1962), p. 21.

[39]Sūryakānt Tripāṭhī 'Nirālā,' *Anāmikā*, 7th ed. (Allahabad: Bhāratī Bhaṇḍār, 1969), p. 34.

[40]*Sūrsāgar*, 2.915.

[41]Pant, *Pallav*, p. 82.

[42]Nirālā, *Aparā*, 10th ed. (Allahabad: Bhāratī Bhaṇḍār, 1972), p. 15.

[43]Varmā, *Sāndhya-gīt*, 5th ed. (Allahabad: Bhāratī Bhaṇḍār, 1959), p. 59.

[44]Ibid., p. 26.

[45]Nāmvar Singh, *Chāyāvād*, 2nd ed. (Delhi: Rājkamal Prakāśan, 1968), p. 62.

[46]Jayśankar Prasād, *Kāmāyanī*, 16th ed. (Allahabad: Bhāratī Bhaṇḍār, 1973), p. 55.

[47]Pant, *Pallav*, p. 119.

[48]Nirālā, *Aparā*, p. 22.

[49]Varmā, *Nīhār*, 7th ed. (Allahabad: Sāhitya Bhavan, 1971), p. 15.

[50]Varmā, *Raśmi*, p. 57.

[51]Pant, *Chāyāvād: Punarmūlyānkan* (Allahabad: Lokbhāratī Prakāśan, 1965), pp. 35-36.

[52]Jagdīś Gupta, *Yugma* (Delhi: Bhāratīya Jñānpīṭh, 1973), p. 23.

[53]Ibid., p. 38.

[54]Dharmvīr Bhāratī, "*Pratham praṇay,*" in *Ṭhaṇḍā lohā*, 2nd ed. (Delhi: Bhāratīya Jñānpīṭh, 1970), pp. 72-73.

[55]Girijā Kumār Māthur, "*Mamatāõ kī sandhi par,*" in *Jo bandh nahī̃ sakā* (Delhi: Bhāratīya Jñānpīṭh, 1968), pp. 65-66.

[56]Duṣyant Kumār, "*O mere pyār ke ajeya bodh,*" in *Āvāzõ ke ghere* (Delhi: Rājkamal Prakāśan, 1963), pp. 25-26.

[57]Bhāratī, "*Dūsrā patra,*" in *Ṭhaṇḍā lohā*, pp. 39-42.

[58]Māthur, "*Tīsrā patra,*" in *Jo bandh nahī̃ sakā*, pp. 70-71.

[59]Kumār, "*Sūnā ghar,*" in *Āvāzõ ke ghere*, p. 38.

[60]Sarveśvar Dayāl Saksenā, "*Phir vasant ne mujhe ḍasā,*" in *Garm havāẽ* (Delhi: Rādhākṛṣṇa Prakāśan, 1969), p. 65.

[61]Bhāratī, "*Fīrozī hoṭh,*" in *Ṭhaṇḍā lohā*, pp. 18-19.

[62]Gupta, "*Pankti-setu,*" in *Yugma*, p. 9.

[63]Gupta, "*Surasundarī,*" ibid., p. 58.

[64]Jagdīś Caturvedī, "*Gũgõ kī bastī mẽ,*" in *Niṣedh* (Delhi: Jñān Bhāratī Prakāśan, 1972), pp. 30-31.

[65]Gupta, "*Yātanā kā nāgapāś,*" in *Yugma*, pp. 69-71.

[66]Gupta, "*Bindu se rekhā tak,*" ibid., p. 142.

[67]Gupta, "*Taras tum par nahī̃, apne par,*" ibid., p. 143.

[68]Bhāratī, "*Yah ātmā kī k͟hũk͟hār pyās,*" in *Ṭhaṇḍā lohā*, pp. 67-71.

[69]For an example of this, see Lakṣmīkānt Varmā's poem, "*Thaṇḍā sṭov, cāy kā ṭin aur khālī botal,*" in *Atukānt*, pp. 12-17.

[70]Prabhākar Machwe, "*Do namūne,*" in *Tel kī pakauḍiyā̃*, 2nd ed. (Delhi: Bhāratīya Jñānpīṭh, 1965), pp. 31-32.

[71]Gupta, *Yugma*, p. 36.

[72]Bhāratī, *Kanupriyā*, 4th ed. (Delhi: Bhāratīya Jñānpīṭh, 1972), p. 60.

Radha and Erotic Community

Norvin Hein

[1]Milton Singer, ed., *Krishna: Myths, Rites and Attitudes* (Honolulu: East-West Center Press, 1966), ch. 5.

The Shifting Balance of Power in the Marriage of Śiva and Parvatī

Wendy Doniger O'Flaherty

[1]A more extended version of this essay can be found in my book, *Women, Androgynes, and Other Mythical Beasts* (Chicago: University of Chicago Press, 1980) (hereafter cited as *WA*). I am deeply indebted to Richard Brubaker, William Mahony, David Shulman, and A.K. Ramanujan for their tactful but incisive comments on a very rough first draft.

[2]Robert Burton, *The Mating Game* (New York: Crown Publishing Co., 1976), p. 11. I am grateful to David Knipe for this source.

[3]Robert P. Goldman, "Mortal Man and Immortal Woman: An Interpretation of Three Ākhyāna Hymns of the Ṛg Veda," *Journal of the Oriental Institute of Baroda* 18.4 (June 1969), pp. 273-303.

[4]*Rig Veda* with the commentary of Sayana, ed. F. Max Muller, 4 vols. (London: Oxford University Press, 1890), 10.95.15; 1.179.4 Cf. Wendy Doniger O'Flaherty, *Asceticism and Eroticism in the Mythology of Śiva* (Oxford and London: Oxford University Press, 1973), pp. 52-55 (hereafter cited as *AEMS*).

[6]Ibid., 10.72.

[7]Ibid., 10.86.

[8]H. Jacobi, *Das Râmâyaṇa* (Bonn: F. Cohen, 1893).

[9]Valmiki, *Rāmāyaṇa* 6.103-06 (Baroda: Oriental Institute, 1960-65). Cf. O'Flaherty, *AEMS*, pp. 197-204.

[10]*Rāmāyaṇa*, 7.42.

[11]O'Flaherty, "The Indo-European Mare," in *WA*, ch. 6.

[12]*Rāmāyaṇa* 7, App. 13, lines 8 and 13.

[13]V.S. Suthankar, gen. ed., *Mahābhārata* (Poona: Bhandarkar Oriental Reseach Institute, 1933-69), 1.109-14.

[14]Alf Hiltebeitel, *The Ritual of Battle: Krishna in the Mahābhārata* (Ithaca: Cornell University Press, 1976), pp. 114-92 and 79-102.

[15]David Shulman, "The Murderous Bride: Tamil Versions of the Myth of Devī and the Buffalo Demon," *History of Religions* 16:2 (1976), pp. 120-47.

[16]See A.K. Ramanujan, in this volume.

[17]W. Norman Brown, "Change of Sex as a Hindu Story Motif," *Journal of the American Oriental Society* 47 (1927):3-24.

[18]This phenomenon is well documented. McKim Marriott informs me of the widespread practice in Maharashtra of transvestites worshipping the Goddess.

[19]*Brahmavaivarta Purāṇa,* 4 vols. (Poona: Ānandāśrama Sanskrit Series 102, 1935), 2.2.30-2.3.60.

[20]C. Mackenzie Brown, *God as Mother: A Feminine Theology in India, An Historical and Theological Study of the Brahmavaivarta Purāṇa* (Hartford, VT: Claude Stark & Co., 1974).

[21]Daniel H.H. Ingalls, *An Anthology of Sanskrit Court Poetry, Vidyākara's "Subhāṣitaratnakoṣa"* (Cambridge: Harvard Oriental Series 44, 1965), pp. 27-29.

[22]O'Flaherty, *AEMS,* pp. 11 and 231.

[23]*Skanda Purāṇa* (Bombay: Veṅkateśvara Press, 1967), 1.2.27-29; O'Flaherty, *Hindu Myths: A Sourcebook, Translated from the Sanskrit* (Harmondsworth, Eng.: Penguin Books, 1975), pp. 251-62. Cf. *AEMS,* pp. 186-90.

[24]O'Flaherty, "The Indo-European Mare," *WA,* ch. 6.

[25]*Kālikā Purāṇa* (Bombay: Veṅkateśvara Press, 1891), pp. 49-54. Cf. O'Flaherty, *AEMS,* pp. 205-09.

[26]O'Flaherty, *AEMS,* pp. 206-08.

[27]*Mahābhārata* 3.51-54; 3.122-23.

[28]Jayadeva, *Gītagovinda,* 12.10, ed. and trans. Barbara Stoler Miller, *Love Song of the Dark Lord* (New York: Columbia University Press, 1977).

[29]*Mahābhāgavata Purāṇa* (Bombay: Veṅkateśvara Press, 1913), pp. 9-11.

[30]Tulsī Dās, *Rāmacaritamānasa, dohas* 23-24 and 108-09, in W.D.P. Hill, *The Holy Lake of the Acts of Rāma* (London: Oxford University Press, 1952), pp. 310-11, 422-23.

[31]*Rig Veda* 10.17.1-2; *Bṛhaddevatā* of Śaunaka (Cambridge: Harvard Oriental Series 5, 1904), 6.162-63, 7.1-6; O'Flaherty, *AEMS,* pp. 60-70.

[32]Richard Lee Brubaker, "The Ambivalent Mistress: A Study of South Indian Village Goddesses and their Religious Meaning" (Ph.D. diss., University of Chicago, 1978), p. 153.

[33]Margaret Trawick Egnor, "The Sacred Spell and Other Conceptions of Life in Tamil Culture" (Ph.D. diss., University of Chicago, 1978), pp. 172 and 198.

[34]Moriz Winternitz, *A History of Indian Literature,* trans. H. Kohn (Calcutta: University of Calcutta, 1959), 3.40-44. Winternitz cites elaborate arguments on this subject, including those by Ānandavardhana (*Dhvanyāloka* 3.6, p. 137) and Mammaṭa (*Kāvyaprakāśa* 7, remarking on gods' loveplay like that of parents).

[35]*Bhāgavata Purāṇa* with the commentary of Śrīdhara (Bombay: Veṅkateśvara Press, 1832), 10.33.30-35. Cf. O'Flaherty, *The Origins of Evil in Hindu Mythology* (Berkeley: University of California Press, 1976), pp. 286-91.

[36]Frédérique Apffel Marglin, "Devadāsīs as Specialists in 'Auspiciousness,'" paper presented at the Symposium on Sexuality and Religion sponsored by the Conference on Religion in South India, Wilson College, Chambersberg, PA, 1978.

[37]O'Flaherty, *AFMS,* pp. 300-01.

[38]O'Flaherty, *Origins of Evil,* pp. 286-91.

[39]"The Shazam Syndrome, Or, The Banalization of the Hindu Gods," *WA,* ch. 3. See also *Origins of Evil,* p. 286-91.

Blood and Death out of Place:
Reflections on the Goddess Kālī

David Kinsley

[1]The *dhyāna-mantra* of *Śmaśāna-kālī* in Krsnānanda Āgamavāgīśa, *Tantrasāra,* 2 vols. (Calcutta: Basumatī Sahitya Mandir, 1934), 1:374.

[2]For example, the *Karpūrādi-stotra* describes her as young and beautiful (verse 1) and says that she has a gently smiling face (verse 18).

[3]The *Mānasāra-śilpaśāstra,* 9.289, says that Kālī's temples should be built far from

inhabited areas, near cremation grounds or near the dwellings of Caṇḍālas (out-castes who handle corpses).

[4]Kālī is associated with thieves as early as the *Bhāgavata Purāṇa* (ca. 10th century A.D.). See 5.9.12-20.

[5]*Devī-māhātmya,* chs. 7 and 8.

[6]*Linga Purāṇa* 1.106.

[7]Ibid., 1.72.66-68.

[8]*Vāmana Purāṇa,* chs. 25-29. In several late versions of the *Rāmāyaṇa* Kālī appears in her familiar role. On his return from Lanka, where he has just vanquished the mighty ten-headed Rāvaṇa, Rāma is confronted with an even more terrifying foe—a thousand-headed Rāvaṇa. When Rāma is unable to defeat this monster, his wife Sītā assumes the form of Kālī and handily slays the new menace. However, becoming drunk on the demon's blood, she begins to dance wildly and threatens to destroy the world. Śiva is summoned to stop her rampaging. The story is told in the *Adbhūta Rāmāyaṇa* (a Kashmiri *śākta* text), Sāralā Dāsa's Oriya *Rāmāyaṇa,* and the Bengali *Jaiminibhārata.* See Narendra Nath Bhattacharyya, *History of the Śākta Religion* (New Delhi: Munshiram Manoharlal, 1974), p. 149.

[9]Summarized in Arthur Avalon, ed., *Principles of Tantra: The Tantratattva of Śrīyukta Śiva Candra Vidyārnava Bhattācārya Mahodaya* (Madras: Ganesh & Co., 1960), pp. 208-13. See also *Skanda Purāṇa* 5.82.1-21, where Kālī is born when Satī, angry at Dakṣa's insult to Śiva, rubs her nose in wrath. I am grateful to Phyllis Granoff for calling my attention to this reference.

[10]C. Sivaramamurti, *Nataraja in Art, Thought and Literature* (New Delhi: National Museum, 1974), pp. 378-79, 384. See also M.A. Dorai Rangaswamy, *The Religion and Philosophy of Tēvāram* (Madras: University of Madras, 1958), bk. 1, pp. 442, 444-45; and R.K. Das, *Temples of Tamilnad* (Bombay: Bharatiya Vidya Bhavan, 1964), p. 195.

[11]Some renditions of Śiva's dance, in which the entire Hindu pantheon is shown as spectators or musicians, do include Kālī standing passively by (e.g., the painting at the Śiva temple at Ettumanur, 16th century, in Sivaramamurti, *Nataraja,* fig. 150, p. 282; and the scene from a 17th-century temple at Triprayār, Kerala, ibid., fig. 152, p. 284). In both scenarios Kālī rides a *preta* and her appearance is unchanged. It should perhaps be pointed out that the gaunt old woman who is so frequently shown attending upon Śiva while he dances, usually playing a pair of cymbals, is not Kālī, as is sometimes supposed, but the devotee Kāraikkālammaiyār, a famous saint who renounced her beauty in devotion to Śiva (pp. 353 ff.).

[12]That Śiva should have to resort to his *tāṇḍava* dance to defeat Kālī suggests the theme of Kālī's inciting Śiva to destructive activity. Śiva's *tāṇḍava* dance is typically performed at the end of the cosmic age and destroys the universe. Descriptions of the *tāṇḍava* dance often dwell on its destructive aspects. The chaotic dancing of Śiva, who wields a broken battle-axe, must be tempered by the soft glances of Pārvatī (Sivaramamurti, *Nataraja,* p. 138). In this aspect of his dance Śiva tends to get out of control, and in the legend of the dance contest with Kālī, it is she who provokes him to it.

[13]M.R. Kale, ed. and trans., *Bhavabhūti's Mālatīmādhava with the Commentary of Jagaddhara,* 3rd ed. (Delhi: Motilal Banarsidass, 1967), pp. 44-48.

[14]M., ed., *Gospel of Śri Ramakrishna,* trans. Swami Nikhilananda (New York: Ramakrishna-Vivekananda Center, 1942), p. 961.

[15]The theme of Pārvatī's acting as a restraining influence on Śiva is mentioned by Glenn E. Yocum, "The Goddess in a Tamil Śaiva Devotional Text, Māṇikkavācakar's *Tiruvācakam,*" *Journal of the American Academy of Religion* 45:1 (1977), supplement, p. K372.

[16]E.g., *Devī-māhātmya,* where she is called *mahāmāyā* (1.2.40-42, 45, 58, 73), *prakṛti* (1.59, 5.7), and *śakti* (1.63, 5.18); and the *Devī-bhāgavata, passim.*

[17]The practice of classical yoga aims precisely at disentangling the aspirant from the mesh of *prakrti* by reversing *prakrti's* natural evolution. Yoga is the devolution of matter, as it were, in which *prakrti* is tamed and stilled.

[18]The *Devī-bhāgavata,* while identifying Mahādevī with *prakrti* throughout, does not hesitate to affirm the binding nature of *prakrti* (*passim*).

[19]In *Purity and Danger: An Analysis of Concepts of Pollution and Taboo* (Baltimore: Penguin Books, 1970), Mary Douglas locates taboo in the idea of dirt out of place. In a sense Kālī may be regarded as taboo, a dangerous being out of place in the civilized sphere.

[20]Ibid., p. 193.

Consort of None, *Śakti* of All:
The Vision of the *Devī-Māhātmya*

Thomas B. Coburn

[1]F.E. Pargiter, trans., *The Mārkaṇḍeya Purāṇa* (Calcutta: The Asiatic Society, 1888-1904), pp. viii-xiii; V.V. Mirashi, "A Lower Limit for the Date of the *Devī Māhātmya,*" *Purāṇa* 6:1 (1964), pp. 181-84.

[2]Louis Renou, *L'Hindouisme: les textes, les doctrines, l'histoire* (Paris: Presses universitaires de France, 1958), p. 67; P.V. Kane, *History of Dharmaśāstra* (Poona: Bhandarkar Oriental Research Institute, 1930-62), 5:154-87, esp. pp. 154-56, 171-72. Cf. also P. Ghosha, *Durga Puja: With Notes and Illustrations* (Calcutta: Hindoo Patriot Press, 1871), pp. 20, 39.

[3]H.H. Wilson, *Works,* ed. R. Rost (London: Trübner and Co., 1862), p. 68.

[4]Shrivatsa Goswami has pointed out to me that Juan Roger Riviere is in error when he claims (in "European Translations of Purāṇic Texts," *Purāṇa* 5:2 [1963], pp. 243-50) that this translation of the *Devī-māhātmya* (hereafter cited as *DM*) is the first European translation of a Purāṇic text. The first such translation is in fact from the *Bhāgavata Purāṇa.* Daniel H.H. Ingalls alludes to it in his foreword to Milton Singer, ed., *Krishna: Myths, Rites and Attitudes* (Honolulu: East-West Center Press, 1966), p. viii. The full reference is: *Bagavadam ou Doctrine Divine, Ouvrage Indien, canonique; sur l'Être Supreme, les Dieux, les Géans, les hommes, les diverses parties de l'Univers, &c.,* traduit du Sanskrit d'après une version tamoule, par Méridas Poullé, un Malabare Chrétien (Paris: Foucher d'Obsonville, 1788).

[5]Full documentation of this point may be found in Thomas B. Coburn, "The Crystallization of the Worship of the Goddess: The Sources and Context of the *Devī-Māhātmya*" (Ph.D. diss., Harvard University, 1977), p. 82.

[6]Since there are neither capital letters nor articles in Sanskrit, while English employs both, the translation of *devī* by "the Goddess' can be misleading. In English, when we wish to speak of ultimate reality as masculine, of God with a capital "G," we automatically omit the article, in such phrases as "praise be to God." But if we wish to make the same statement about ultimate reality as feminine, it sounds odd to say "praise be to Goddess"; the language wants us to say, "praise be to *the* Goddess" or "to *a* Goddess." The *DM* would not allow such a qualification—not only on grammatical grounds, but also, as we shall see, on theological ones: she is not one goddess among others, but Goddess Supreme. In this essay I shall force Sanskrit to bear the brunt of a compromise by employing the term "Devī," with a capital. In the long run, however, we English speakers ought also to join in the compromise, by accustoming ourselves to such phrases as "praise be to Goddess."

[7]To facilitate reference to what is probably the most readily available English translation of the *DM* (V.S. Agrawala, *The Devī-māhātmya: The Glorification of the*

Great Goddess [Varanasi: All-India Kashiraj Trust, 1963]), I shall indicate in parentheses the verses in his edition, although my translations, which are based on multiple editions of the original, sometimes differ significantly from his.

[8]The crux of the merchant's dilemma is that, although abysmal abuse at the hands of his family prompted his retreat to the forest, he now finds that he yearns for news of them.

[9]"You are the great knowledge, the great illusion, the great insight, the great memory,
And (also) the great delusion, the great Goddess (*mahādevī*), the great Demoness (*mahāsurī*)" (58).

[10]In light of the interpretation of the *DM's* first episode that is offered below, one might say that one reason why Mahāmāyā has such power over the *asuras* is that, in a sense, she *is* the *asuras.*

[11]*Śvetāśvatara Upaniṣad,* 4.9-10.

[12]The same Sanskrit word, *māyā,* is also the concept that is so richly elaborated in the philosophical discussions of Vedānta.

[13]This reconstruction of the myth is based on consideration of all the epic variants. For a full translation of a particular version, see J.A.B. van Buitenen, ed. and trans., *The Mahābhārata* (Chicago: University of Chicago Press, 1975) 2:611-12 (3.194.8-30).

[14]The word for "power" is *śakti,* a designation of Devī to which we shall return.

[15]For instance, see 5.15, where Devī is affirmed to "abide in all creatures in the form of sleep (*nidrā*)."

[16]*Mānava Dharma Śāstra* 7.3-6, 10-11, in G. Bühler, trans., *The Laws of Manu* (New York: Dover Publications, 1969), pp. 216-17.

[17]Cf. 1.63, a portion of Brahmā's invocation of Devī that is quoted above. Cf. also 5.18, 11.8, 11.10. In Agrawala's translation, *śakti* is sometimes translated as "energy" or "might."

[18]The text here reads *caṇḍikā,* a name used throughout as synonomous with Devī, on which we shall comment below.

[19]The seven gods from whom they respectively emerge are: Brahmā, Śiva, Skanda (Kumāra), Viṣṇu, Viṣṇu's boar incarnation (Varāha), Viṣṇu's man-lion incarnation (Narasiṃha), and Indra.

[20]*Mahābhārata* (hereafter cited as *Mbh*) 14.43.14.

[21]Further confirmation of this interpretation may be found in the fact that the *DM* never employes the name Umā, and it uses the name Pārvatī on only three occasions, never with emphasis.

[22]Or "extraordinary powers": *vibhūtayaḥ.*

[23]The text here reads *ambikā,* a name that is used throughout as synonomous with Devī. See below.

[24]The exception is, as we might expect, in the *Devī-Bhāgavata Purāṇa.*

[25]Cf. 5.9, 5.26, 11.21, 12.36 for *lakṣmī,* 1.60, 4.4, 4.10 for *śrī.* The last of these instances indicates our text's awareness that there are ramifications to these epithets, for it identifies *śrī* as the one "whose sole abode is in the heart of Kaiṭabha's enemy," i.e., Viṣṇu. That it is content to leave them largely implicit provides further support for the interpretation offered here.

[26]On the basis of a comprehensive examination of the Sanskritic antecedents of the *DM's* epithets ("Crystallization," pp. 138-330), it seems to me that even the appearance of the epithet Nārāyaṇī in a *DM* hymnic refrain (11.7-23) may best be interpreted as part of the synthesizing endeavor. For an alternative interpretation of the relation between the *DM* and Vaiṣṇavism, see David R. Kinsley, *The Sword and the Flute* (Berkeley: University of California Press, 1975), p. 102, note, and his "The Portrait of the Goddess in the *Devī-Māhātmya," Journal of the American Academy of Religion,* 46:4 (1978, pp. 489-506).

[27]This assertion, made tentatively by Pargiter (*Mārkaṇḍeya Purāṇa*, p. xii), has been confirmed by my own inquiry into the Vedic and epic literature.

[28]Cf. *DM* 12.1-12.

[29]E.g., *Yajur Veda* 1.8.6; *Śatapatha Brāhmaṇa* 2.6.2.13-14.

[30]This account, to which the balance of this paragraph refers, is *Mbh* 3.207-221 (van Buitenen translation, 2:638-61). A second *Mbh* account of Skanda's birth (9.43-45) does not include the Mahiṣa story; the "Goddess motifs" that we are about to notice are also much less in evidence.

[31]Cf. W.D. O'Flaherty, *Asceticism and Eroticism in the Mythology of Śiva* (London: Oxford University Press, 1973), pp. 90-110, where Agni is discussed as one of the "Vedic antecedents" of the purāṇic Śiva.

[32]*Rig Veda* 10.5.5. Cf. also the material discussed in my "Crystallization," pp. 496-524, esp. pp. 500-02.

[33]J. Scheftelowitz, ed., *Die Apokryphen des Ṛgveda* (Breslau: M. und H. Marcus, 1906) and J. Scheftelowitz, "Srī Sūkta," *Zeitschrift der Deutschen Morgenländischen Gesellschaft* 75 (1921): 37-50.

[34]Cf. *DM* 4.10, 4.16, 5.10, 9.29, 11.24.

[35]E.g., *Viṣṇu Dharma Sūtra* 56.9; *Baudhāyana Dharma Śāstra* 4.3.8. Cf. also the quotation of *Rig Veda* 1.99 in the *Rātrī Khila* (in Scheftelowitz, *Apokryphen*, pp. 110-12).

[36]*Harivaṃśa* (critical edition) 47.49.

[37]*Viṣṇu Purāṇa* (Bombay: Oriental Press, 1889), readily available in H.H. Wilson's English translation (vols. 6-10 of his *Works*, frequently reprinted). *Bālacarita* (Delhi: Munshiram Manoharlal, 1959), translated in A.C. Woolner and L. Sarup, *Thirteen Trivandrum Plays Attributed to Bhāsa* (London: Oxford University Press-Humphrey Milford, 1930-31). Cf. also *DM* 11.38-51 where Devī, in describing five of her future appearances, announces that when two new demons, also named Śumbha and Niśumbha, have arisen, she will be born "in the house of the cowherd Nanda, in the womb of Yaśodā," in order to slay them.

[38]Cf. her "Aspects du mythe de *Kṛṣṇa-Gopāla* dans l'Inde ancienne" in *Mélanges d'Indianisme à la mémoire de Louis Renou* (Paris: Éditions de Boccard, 1968), pp. 737-61.

The Gaṅgā: The Goddess in Hindu Sacred Geography

Diana L. Eck

[1]Jagannātha, *Gaṅgā Laharī* (Varanasi: Thakur Prasad and Sons, n.d.) verse 1. Translations from this work and from the Vedic and Sanskrit sources below are my own.

[2]*Skanda Purāṇa*, Kāśī Khaṇḍa 27.22 (Calcutta: Gurumaṇḍala Granthamālāya no. 20, 1961), vol. 4. The Kāśī Khaṇḍa will hereafter be cited as KK.

[3]KK 27.30, 37, 105, 134.

[4]KK 27.18; 28.27-29.

[5]For a discussion of the way in which the Gaṅgā is an all-India agent of Sanskritization, see M.N. Srinivas, *Religion and Society among the Coorgs of South India*, (London: Oxford University Press, 1952), pp. 214 ff. Srinivas discusses the sanctity of the Kāverī and, in an appendix, recounts the Kāverī's myth of origin.

[6]For a discussion of what I have termed "spatial transposition," see my "Banāras, City of Light: The Sacred Places and Praises of Kāśī" (Ph.D. diss., Harvard University, 1976), pp. 15 ff.

[7]Raj Bali Pandey, *Varanasi: The Heart of Hinduism* (Varanasi: Orient Publishers, 1969), p. 30.

[8]Śrī Rāmpratāp Tripāṭhī, *Purāṇõ mẽ Gaṅgā* (Prayāg: Hindī Sāhitya Sammelan, 1952), p. *jha*.

[9]Ibid., p. *ga*.

[10]From Jawaharlal Nehru's Will and Testament, quoted in Eric Newby and Raghubir Singh, *Gaṅgā: Sacred River of India* (Hong Kong: The Perennial Press, 1974), p. 9.

[11]*Rig Veda* 10.90.

[12]See *Rig Veda* 10.82 and 10.121.

[13]See, for example, *Kūrma Purāṇa* 1.9. *Bhāgavata Purāṇa* 2.5.6 and *Mārkaṇḍeya Purāṇa* 45-47 also contain accessible accounts of the transformation of the Hiraṇyagarbha motif.

[14]Betty Heimann, *Facets of Indian Thought* (London: George Allen and Unwin, 1964), p. 107, in the essay entitled "Indian Metaphysics." I am also deeply indebted to another essay in this posthumous collection, "India's Biology," which develops the notion of a biological world-view.

[15]See, for example, *Atharva Veda* 10.7 and *Rig Veda* 10.130.

[16]*Bṛhadāraṇyaka Upaniṣad* 3.6 and 3.8.

[17]The esoteric symbolism of the two rivers is elaborated by Heinrich von Stietencron in his work *Gaṅgā und Yamunā* (Weisbaden: Otto Harrassowitz, 1972). He deals primarily with the river goddesses as they appear to the right and left of medieval temple entrances in northern India.

[18]*Mahābhārata* 13.111.16.

[19]"Ayodhyā, Mathurā, Māyā (Hardwar), Kāśī, Kāñcī, Avantikā (Ujjain), and the city of Dvārāvatī (Dvārakā)—these seven give *mokṣa*." This verse describing the *saptapurī* is found in many Purāṇas and is known to practically every literate Brahman.

[20]The four are Purī in the East, Rāmeśvaram in the South, Dvārakā in the West, and Badrināth in the North.

[21]See D.C. Sircar, *The Śākta Pīṭhas* (Delhi: Motilal Banarsidass, 1973; orig. pub. 1928).

[22]*Rig Veda* 7.49.

[23]The seven are mentioned repeatedly as a group. See, for example, *Rig Veda* 1.32.12, 1.34.8, 1.35.8, 2.12.12, 4.28.1. *Rig Veda* 10.75 mentions the Gaṅgā, but she does not figure among the seven.

[24]The seven: Gaṅgā, Yamunā, Godāvarī, Sarasvatī, Narmadā, Kāvērī, and Sindhu.

[25]Amarasiṃha, *Amarakośa* (Varanasi: Chowkhamba Sanskrit Series no. 198, 1970).

[26]Jagannātha, *Gaṅgā Laharī*, verse 20.

[27]Rāmpratāp Tripāṭhī, *Hinduõ ke vrat, Parva, aur Tyauhār* (Allahabad: Lokbhāratī Prakāśan, 1971), p. 86.

[28]See W. Norman Brown, "The Creation Myth of the Rig Veda," *Journal of the American Oriental Society* 62:2 (1942). See also, for example, *Rig Veda* 1.32, 2.12.

[29]*Bhāgavata Purāna* 5.17; *Devībhāgavata Purāṇa* 8.7. Sculpture depicts this myth as well. C. Sivaramamurti in *Gaṅgā* (New Delhi: Orient Longman, 1976) has two plates from 12th-century Mysore in which Brahmā is pouring the Gaṅgā from his water pot upon Vāmana-Viṣṇu's upraised foot.

[30]*Kūrma Purāṇa* 1.44; *Brahmavaivarta Purāṇa,* Kṛṣṇajanma Khaṇḍa 34; *Bhāgavata Purāṇa* 5.17; *Viṣṇu Purāṇa* 2.2.8.

[31]*Rāmāyaṇa,* Bāla Khaṇḍa 38-44; *Mahābhārata* 3.104-108; *Skanda Purāṇa,* Kāśī Khaṇḍa 30; *Bhāgavata Purāṇa* 9.8-9; *Brahmavaivarta Purāṇa,* Prakṛti Khaṇḍa 10; *Devībhāgavata Purāṇa* 9.11. K. Damodaran Nambiar lists many others in "The Nārada Purāṇa: A Critical Study," *Purāṇa* (July 1973). In several accounts of the *avataraṇa* it is Krishna to whom appeal is made by Bhagīratha.

[32]The *Mahābhārata* account of the *avataraṇa,* for instance, immediately follows the story of Agastya's swallowing the ocean.

[33]"Śrī Gaṅgāṣṭaka," verse 1, in *Nityakarma Vidhi tathā Devapūjā Paddhati* (Varanasi: Ṭhākurdās Surekā Cairitī Phaṇḍ, 1966).

[34]See C. Mackenzie Brown, *God as Mother: A Feminine Theology in India* (Hartford, Vermont: Claude Stark and Company, 1974), pp. 161-67.

[35]*Brahmavaivarta Purāṇa,* Prakṛti Khaṇḍa 11; *Devībhāgavata Purāṇa* 9.13.

[36]*Brahmavaivarta Purāṇa,* Prakṛti Khaṇḍa 6; *Devībhāgavata Purāṇa* 9.6.

[37]*Brahmavaivarta Purāṇa,* Prakṛti Khaṇḍa 10; *Devībhāgavata Purāṇa* 9.12.

[38]Sivaramamurti, *Gaṅgā,* fig. 6.

[39]Jagannātha, *Gaṅgā Laharī,* verse 12.

[40]Sivaramamurti, *Gaṅgā,* pp. 21-24, figs. 7 and 8.

[41]KK 27.182-84.

[42]Tripāṭhī, *Hinduõ ke Vrat,* p. 95.

[43]Kālidāsa, *Kumārasambhava* 10.26.

[44]KK 27.8-9.

[45]For other elaborations of the *agni-soma* polarity and resolution, see Wendy Doniger O'Flaherty, *Asceticism and Eroticism in the Mythology of Śiva* (London: Oxford University Press, 1973), pp. 286 ff.

[46]KK 28.84.

[47]KK 27.157-58.

[48]Jagannātha, *Gaṅgā Laharī,* verse 1 quoted above.

[49]*Rig Veda* 10.75.

[50]*Rig Veda* 10.9.

[51]O'Flaherty, *Asceticism,* pp. 93-110, describes the many myths of the birth and multiple motherhood of Skanda.

[52]*Mahābhārata* 1.95-100 describes her marriage to Śantanu and the birth of the Vasus and Bhīṣma. *Mahābhārata* 13.154.18-25 tells of Gaṅgā's lament at the death of Bhīṣma.

[53]*Mahābhārata* 13.27.49.

[54]*Mahābhārata* 13.27.48, 50, 51 and 52.

[55]The legend is well known, at least among the traditionally educated of Kāśī. It has several variants. In English, Lakshman Ramachandra Vaidya related something of Jagannātha's life and legend in his introduction to the Sanskrit text of another of Jagannātha's poems, the *Bhāminī Vilāsa* (Bombay: Bhāratī Press, 1887).

[56]These sentences summarize some of the sentiments of *Gaṅgā Laharī,* verses 13, 28, 29, and 45.

[57]*Gaṅgā Laharī,* verse 24.

[58]KK 28, 84, and 88.

[59]KK 27.19.

A Theology of the Repulsive:
The Myth of the Goddess Śītalā

Edward C. Dimock, Jr.

[1]The text has been translated by Ralph W. Nicholas and Aditinath Sarkar under the title "The Great Śītala Mangal, or The Drama of Śītala for which People Stay Awake All Night," and discussed by the same authors in a paper entitled "The Fever Demon and the Census Commissioner"; see the *Proceedings* of the Eleventh Bengal Conference, ed. Marvin Davis (East Lansing: Center for Asian Studies, 1976). As the authors point out, Nityānanda was a courtier of the Rāja Rājanārāyaṇa of Kāśijora,

who ruled from 1756 to 1770. The text has been printed by Taracand Das and Sons, Calcutta, n.d.; the quotation is from the introductory section called *Śītalār janma.*

[2]Kṛṣṇarām-dās was a poet of the late 17th century; one of his poems shows the chronogram 1676 A.D. His *Śītalār-maṅgal,* a short text, can be found in Satyanārāyaṇ Bhaṭṭācārya, ed., *Kavi kṛṣṇarām dāser granthāvalī* (Calcutta: Calcutta University, 1958), pp. 251-85.

[3]*Journal of the American Oriental Society* 61:2 (1941), p. 99.

[4]Thomas Burrow, *The Sanskrit Language* (London: Faber and Faber, 1955), p. 72.

[5]E.g, *Śatapatha Brāhmaṇa* 2.3.3.5; 3.2.4.2, 3.

[6]Quoted by Sukumar Sen, *Bāṅglār sāhityer itihāsa,* 1st ed. (Calcutta: Eastern Publishers, 1948), 1:994.

[7]The terms "endemic" and "epidemic" are somewhat loosely used in the context, although the metaphor is I think valid. According to the *Oxford English Dictionary,* endemic disease is "habitually prevalent in a certain country and due to permanent local causes," whereas epidemic disease is "prevalent among a people or community at a special time and produced by some special cause." In fact, in 1865, malaria was endemic to Dinajpur, Rangpur, and some other districts, but not to the west bank of the Hughli, i.e., Burdwan. It was new to Burdwan at the time of the first census (1872), but over the following decades became prevalent, and by 1938 Radhakamal Mukherjee could write in *The Changing Face of Bengal: A Study in Riverine Economy* (Calcutta University, 1938) that "seventeen out of twenty-eight districts are now malarious in Bengal. At least 60,000 of the 86,618 villages in Bengal are more or less seriously affected by the malady, which levies an annual toll of 350,000" (p. 80). In any case, the terms are used to mean "latent" and "manifest."

[8]E.g., Gaston Machelard, *The Psychoanalysis of Fire* (Boston: Beacon Press, 1964), esp. ch. 4.

[9]Coomaraswamy, "Līlā," p. 99.

[10]New York: Harper and Brothers, 1899.

[11]In Marvin Davis, ed., *Proceedings* of the Eleventh Bengal Conference (East Lansing: Center for Asian Studies, 1976).

[12]Another that is possibly locatable in historical time is the *Rāy-maṅgal,* a poem of the god of tigers prevalent in southern Bengal. There is a strong possibility that the central episode in this *maṅgal,* a great battle between armies of tigers and crocodiles, headed by a Hindu general called Dakṣin Rāy on the one hand and on the other by a Muslim general simply called Gāzi, has some basis in historical fact. There was in the early 16th century a Hindu ruler in Jessore district called Mukuṭ Rāy, who had a Brahman general called Dakṣin Rāy, and who warred against the Muslims. Satiścandra Mitra, *Yaśoharakhulnera itihāsa,* 3rd ed. (Calcutta: Dasgupta and Company, 1963), 1:433.

[13]J. Rennell, *The Provinces of Bengal Situated on the West of the Hooghly River* (London: J. Rennell, published according to Act of Parliament, October 1779). See also Edward C. Dimock, Jr. and Ronald Inden, "The City in Pre-British Bengal, according to the *maṅgala-kāvyas,*" in Richard Park, ed., *Urban Bengal, Proceedings* of the Fifth Bengal Conference (East Lansing: Center for Asian Studies, 1970). See also the portion of the *Manasā-maṅgal* translated in Edward C. Dimock, Jr., *The Thief of Love* (Chicago: University of Chicago Press, 1963). Many of the *maṅgal* poems tell the story of a trading voyage that originates in one or another of the river ports of Bengal and carries the protagonist, usually the chief merchant, presumably bound for Sri Lanka or Southeast Asia, out into the open sea of the Bay of Bengal. It is in the course of the voyage that the goddess is encountered.

[14]*Vidyādharīs* are female divine beings said to dwell in the Himalayas and attend upon Śiva. See J.A.B. van Buitenen, "The Indian Hero as Vidyādhara," in Milton

Singer, ed. *Traditional India: Structure and Change,* constituting the *Journal of American Folklore* (71:281 (1958), pp. 303-11.

[15]The text has *virakani,* which would mean "warlike dress" or "warlike music."

[16]The form, *śiśujal,* is odd and the translation therefore open to some doubt. It is true, however, that many of the goddesses, including Manasā, are depicted with children. See Edward C. Dimock, Jr., "The Goddess of Snakes—Part I," in *History of Religions,* 1:2 (1962), pp. 307-21.

[17]*Chāni.*

[18]The referent is unclear; presumably the palace is meant.

[19]The name is usually applied to Sarasvatī or Durgā.

[20]Bhaṭṭācārya, ed., *Kavi kṛṣṇarām,* pp. 281-8.

[21]Sukumar Sen, ed., *Kavikankan viracita candimangal* (New Delhi: Sahitya Akademi, 1975), p. 200.

[22]*Patterns in Comparative Religion* (New York: Sheed and War, 1958), p. 419.

[23]Ibid., p. 420.

[24]From a song of an anonymous Baul, recorded by me in Calcutta in 1963.

[25]*The Interpretation of Dreams,* sect. 6, in A.A. Brill, ed., *The Basic Writings of Sigmund Freud* (New York: The Modern Library, 1938), p. 342.

[26]Nicholas and Sarkar, "The Fever Demon," *passim.*

[27]In the *Mahābhārata,* the younger brother of Dhṛtarāṣṭra and Paṇḍu, and depicted in that epic as one of the wisest of men. See, for example, J.A.B. van Buitenen, ed. and trans., *The Mahābhārata,* bk. 2 (Chicago: University of Chicago Press, 1975), p. 114.

[28]I.e., Hanumān.

[29]Nityānanda, *Śītalā-mangal,* the section called "Śītalā's Counseling with Fever, the Three-headed One, and Pox About Establishing Her Worship on Earth"; unpublished translation by Ralph Nicholas and A.N. Sarkar.

[30]This curious creature was born from the sweat of the forehead of the meditating Śiva, and was a threat to the gods. Viṣṇu therefore commanded his discus to cut him into three pieces. Brahmā revived him, but by that time each of the three parts had grown head and limbs. Thus Jvarāsura comes to have three heads, three feet, and the remarkable ability to move in all directions at once. See the introductory section *"Jvarāsurer janma"* in Nityānanda's *Śītalā-mangal.*

[31]"The bloody one," Śītalā's lady-in-waiting.

[32]Interestingly, these are the colors of the four ages in Vaiṣṇava mythology.

[33]I.e., innumerable diseases.

[34]Nityānanda, *Śītalā-mangal,* "The Advent of Śītalā in the Capital of Virata in the Form of Fever and Her Causing the King Terrifying Dreams," in Nicholas and Sarkar, trans., unpublished paper.

[35]Nityānanda, *Śītalā-mangal,* pp. 43-44.

[36]Freud, *Interpretation of Dreams, passim.*

[37]"The Poet as Mouse and Owl: Reflections on a poem by Jibānananda Dās," *The Journal of Asian Studies* 33:4 (1974), pp. 603-10.

[38]*Proceedings* of the Eleventh Bengal Conference, p. 35.

[39]"For whenever of the right/A languishing appears, son of Bharata/A rising up of unright,/Then I send Myself forth.//For protection of the good,/And for destruction of evil-doers,/To make a firm footing for the right,/I come into being in age after age.//" Franklin Edgerton, trans., *The Bhāgavad Gītā* (New York: Harper and Row, 1964), p. 23.

[40]Sylvia Thrupp, ed. (New York: Schocken, 1970).

[41]Ibid., pp. 215-17.

[42]"Revitalization Movements," *American Anthropologist* 58 (1956); *The Death and Rebirth of the Seneca* (New York: Knopf, 1970), and other writings.

[43]*The Holy Bible: Revised Standard Version* (New York: Thomas Nelson, 1946).

[44]His article "Millenium" in *Encyclopedia Britannica,* 1961 edition.

[45]"Medieval Millenarianism: Its Bearing on the Comparative Study of Millenarian Movements," in Thrupp, ed., *Millenial Dreams*, pp. 31-43.

[46]Ibid., p. 31.

[47]*Disaster and the Millenium* (New Haven: Yale University Press, 1974), p. 36.

[48]Ibid., pp. 36-37.

[49]Ibid., pp. 79-80.

[50]Ibid., p. 54.

[51]*The Sacred and the Profane* (New York: Harper and Row, 1959), p. 79.

[52]"The Utopian Side of the Indian Uprising," in David W. Plath, ed., *Aware of Utopia* (Urbana: University of Illinois Press, 1971), p. 112.

[53]Albert Camus, *La Peste* (Paris: Gallimard, 1947), p. 337.

The Goddess and the Polarity of the Sacred

Richard Brubaker

[1]Claude Lévi-Strauss, *The Savage Mind* (Chicago: University of Chicago Press, 1966), p. 10.

[2]*Devī-māhātmya,* line 39, trans. Thomas Coburn.

[3]So, more ambiguously and more humanly, is Pārvatī/Tārāvatī. Although here the devotee is female and her divine lover male, their union is decidedly non-hypergamous and "out of place," inasmuch as she is a queen and he a gruesome Kāpālika. She shows us both possibilities: as the unenlightened Tārāvatī she is devastated by the encounter, but as Pārvatī, who knows who she really is, she welcomes it "with great joy."

[4]See Richard L. Brubaker, "The Ambivalent Mistress: A Study of South Indian Village Goddesses and Their Religious Meaning" (Ph.D. diss., University of Chicago, 1978), esp. ch. 6.

Śītā: Mother Goddess and *Śakti*

Cornelia Dimmitt

[1]G. Buhler, trans., *The Laws of Manu* (London: Oxford University Press, 1886).

[2]Quotations from the *Rāmāyaṇa* are translated from the critical edition: *The Vālmīki Rāmāyaṇa* (Baroda: Oriental Institute, 1960-75). Corresponding references in translation by Shastri are given second in each case within the same parentheses and designated "Sh": *The Ramayana of Valmiki,* trans. Hari Prasad Shastri (London: Shantisadan, 1962).

[3]The same story occurs in 1.65, Sh.1.66, but some scholars, most notably H. Jacobi, have concluded on the basis of both content and style that Bks. 1 and 7 of the Vālmīki *Rāmāyaṇa* consist principally of later additions to the original text. See H. Jacobi, *Das Rāmāyaṇa,* trans. S.N. Ghosal (Baroda: Oriental Research Institute, 1960), pp. 20-24.

[4]R.T.H. Griffith, trans., *Hymns of the Ṛgveda* (Varanasi: Chowkhamba Sanskrit Series, 1963). Note that Sītā is also mentioned in the *Gobhila Gṛhyasūtra* 4.4.29 and *Taittirīya Brāhmaṇa* 2.3.4.1 and 2.3.10.1; and that Rāma is found in *Rig Veda* 10.93.14, *Śatapatha Brāhmaṇa* 4.6.1.7, and *Aitareya Brāhmaṇa* 8.34.

[5]M. Bloomfield, ed., *The Kauśika Sūtra of the Atharva Veda* (New Haven: American Oriental Society, 1939), 9.14.106.1-9. Quotations are from verses 7c, 7g, and 6.

[6]O. Loth, ed., *Abhandlungen für die Kunde des Morgenlandres* (Leipzig: G. Kreysing, 1876), 6:2; *Parāskara Sūtra* 2.17.1-19. Quotations are from verse 9.

[7]Rāmanārāyaṇadatta Shāstrī, ed., *Harivaṃśa* (Poona: Bhandarkar Oriental Research Institute, 1977), 2.3.

[8]Sītā does not actually die, for she is taken back into the earth on a throne; this is described in 7.88/Sh.7.97, which may be a later addition to the text (see note 3 above).

[9]Griffith, *Ṛg Veda* 1.32.

[10]*Rig Veda* 10.108.1, 2. Note the analogy between the captive cows in the *Rig Veda* story and the captive Sītā in the epic. Both are imprisoned beyond a body of water that must be crossed in order to rescue them, and both are rescued by battle.

[11]Research used here on the relation between Sītā and the plants, and below on the relation between Sītā and the animals, was done by Anna Mathew, Georgetown University, 1975.

[12]Here and elsewhere the argument presented is somewhat circular, for nature mourns and rejoices at the departure and return of both Rāma and Sītā from Ayodhyā, not Sītā alone. If, however, one accepts Sītā's role as Rāma's *śakti*, the source of power (see below), then it is her absence that causes Ayodhyā to be bereft, and her return that is responsible for the rejoicing of plants, animals, and humans.

[13]This passage was not included in the Baroda edition of the epic; perhaps it should be discounted entirely. It is, however, a good example of the use of simile, a poetic technique employed abundantly in *kāvya*. Some of the evidence in this paper for Sītā's qualities as a goddess is of this kind, but this need not detract from the argument. For it appears likely that the ultimate source of this kind of poetic convention as regards Sītā is her earlier nature as a fertility deity, and that Vālmīki, the *ādikavi*, has concealed her divine origins to some degree through his use of poetic technique in order to transform her into a loyal and dutiful wife.

[14]This theme is also found in the famous myth "The Churning of the Ocean," which is told in Vedic literature, both epics, and numerous Purāṇas, for example, *Rāmāyaṇa*, 1.44/Sh.1.45; *Mahābhārata* 1.15.17; and *Viṣṇu Purāṇa* 1.9.

[15]Sītā frequently reminds Rāma of his duty (*dharma*), e.g. in 3.8-9, Sh.3.9.10.

[16]This theme is reminiscent of a motif that occurs in epic and purāṇic myths, that the powers won by the *tapas* of a seer are dependent on the purity of his wife, and conversely, that a lapse in her virtue will destroy the strength of his *tapas;* see, for example, the story of Paraśurāma in *Bhāgavata Purāṇa* 9.15-16, and the "Sages of the Pine Forest" myth in *Brahmāṇḍa Purāṇa* 1.2.27.

[17]After Sītā enters into the earth following a second ordeal in Book 7, Rāma fashions a golden image of her that remains his companion for the rest of his days; this fact seems to demonstrate the same point, that her presence is necessary to the success of his reign.

The Goddess Śrī: The Blossoming Lotus and Breast Jewel of Viṣṇu

Vasudha Narayanan

[1]"Tiruvāymoḻi," in *Nālāyira tivyap pirapantam*, ed. P.P. Aṇṇaṅkarācāriyar (Madras: V.N. Tēvanāthan, 1971), 6.10.10, p. 522. All translations are my own. I am indebted to J.S. Hawley for his help in revising the first draft of this paper.

[2]"Śrī Stuti," verse 1, in *Śrī Tecika Stotramala* (hereafter cited as *STS*), ed. Śrī Rāmatēcikācāryar (Kumbakonam: Oppiliyappan Sanniti, 1970), 2:691. "Śrī Devanāyaka Pañcasat," verse 4, *STS*, 1:422. Indic terms cited in this essay are normally Sanskrit; where this is not the case they will be indicated as Tamil or Maṇipravāla.

[3]"Śrī Stuti," verse 23, *STS* 2:722.

[4]This matter is discussed in greater detail in my doctoral dissertation. See V. Rajagopalan, "The Śri Vaiṣṇava Understanding of Bhakti and Prapatti" (University of Bombay, 1978), pp. 435-37.

[5]Deśika, *Catuḥślokibhāṣyam* (hereafter cited as *CSB*), in Chettaloor V. Srivatsankacharyar, ed., *Catuḥślokibhāṣyam, Stotraratnabhāṣyam, Gadhyatrayabhāṣyañca*

(Madras: Venkatesa Agraharam, 1968), p. 14.

[6]Deśika, *Rahasyatrayasāram* (hereafter cited as *RTS*), ed. Śrī Rāmatēcikācāryar Svāmi (Kumbakonam: Oppiliyappan Sanniti, 1961), 2:16, 183.

[7]"Śrī Stuti," verse 24, *STS*, 2:723.

[8]"Yatiraja Saptati," verse 2, *STS*, 2:1015.

[9]*CSB*, p. 10.

[10]*CSB*, pp. 1, 8.

[11]*Rahasya Ratnāvaḷi Hṛutayam*, in Śrī Rāmatēcikācāryar, ed., *Cillarai Rahasyaṅkaḷ* (hereafter cited as *CR*) (Kumbakonam: Oppaliyappan Sanniti, 1972), 1:107-08.

[12]*CSB*, p. 12.

[13]*Vālmīki Rāmāyaṇa* 5.27-44, 45, 58-88, quoted in *Śaraṇāgatigadyabhāṣyam* (hereafter cited as *SGB*), pp. 134-35; *Rahasya Ratnāvaḷi Hṛutayam, CR*, 1:107; *RTS*, 1:125.

[14]"Śrīguṇaratnakośa," verse 50, quoted by Deśika in *RTS*, 1:126.

[15]*RTS*, 2:180. Also *CSB*, p. 3, following *Āhirbudhnya Saṃhita*, 21-8.

[16]*Rahasyatraya Culakam-tvayātikāram, CR*, pp. 234-35.

[17]"Śrī Suktam," verse 4, quoted by Deśika in *SGB*, p. 132. See also Rāmānuja's *Śaraṇāgatigadya*, verse 1.

[18]"Śrī Suktam," verse 9, ibid., p. 131. See also *CR*, 1:49.

[19]*Viṣṇu Purāṇa*, 1.9.100, 103, 115. Deśika quotes from this section several times, especially in *SGB*, pp. 131-32.

[20]Ibid., p. 132.

[21]*CSB*, p. 16. Śrī Vaiṣṇavas make a theoretical distinction between the Lord's personal form (*divyamaṅgala-vigraha*), and His all-pervasive form in which the whole universe forms his body (*divyātma-śarīra*). Deśika makes clear that Śrī too has a personal form, which resides in the Lord, and an all-pervasive nature in which the universe forms her—and the Lord's—body. The equality of Śrī with Viṣṇu and the insistence that she is the perfect consort in every way are thus reiterated.

[22]*CSB*, p. 4.

[23]From the *Lakṣmī Sahasranāma*, quoted in Deśika, *Rahasya Ratnāvaḷi Hṛutayam, CR*, p. 106.

[24]Ibid., pp. 105-06.

[25]"Śrīguṇaratnakośa," verse 58, quoted in *RTS*, 2:18.

[26]*CSB*, p. 15.

[27]*SGB*, p. 131.

[28]"Śrī Stuti," *STS*, verse 1.

[29]Cf. also *RTS*, 2:20, and Yāmuna's line, *"śrīrityeva ca namate bhagavati,"* from "Catuḥśloki," verse 1. Bhaṭṭar's "Śrīguṇaratnakośa," verse 29, is also quoted by Deśika at this point; *RTS*, 2:185.

[30]*CSB*, pp. 4-8.

[31]"Śrīguṇaratnakośa," verses 31 and 34, quoted in Deśika, *RTS*, 2:20-21.

[32]*CSB*, p. 5.

[33]*Bhagavadgītā* 18.66. The word "dharma" in this context is interpreted in a special sense by the Śrī Vaiṣṇavas. Deśika, for instance, says that the word refers to the scriptural prescriptions of the several mediate ways that one may adopt to reach the Lord. *RTS*, 2:216.

[34]*Rāmāyaṇa* 6.114-15. Quoted in *RTS*, 1:37.

[35]*RTS*, 2:186.

[36]*RTS*, 1:36-38.

[37]*RTS*, 2:258-61 and 20.

[38]See Rāmānuja, *Vedārtha Saṃgraha*, in P.P. Aṇṇaṅkarācāryar, ed., *Śrīmad Rāmānuja Granthamāla* (Kāñci: V.N. Tevanāthan, 1974), pp. 20-21.

[39]"Śrī Stavam," verse 1, quoted by Deśika, *RTS*, 2:18.

[40]*RTS*, 2:22.

[41]Ibid.

[42]*SGB*, pp. 133-34.

[43]In Śrī Vaiṣṇava temples there is also a separate shrine for Āṇṭāḷ, a woman mystic of about the 7th century A.D. Āṇṭāḷ is held in devotional writings to be an incarnation of Bhū and Nīlā. On a popular level, however, Āṇṭāḷ is seen as a human being who longed to be a bride of Viṣṇu and whose longing was fulfilled, a paradigm of a human soul who is also the bride of the Lord.

[44]"Periya Tirumoḻi" 2.7.1, in P.P. Aṇṇaṅkarācāryar, ed., *Nālāyira Tivyap pira-pantam,* p. 184.

[45]"Śrīguṇaratnakośa,' verse 51, quoted in *RTS,* 2:183.

[46]Cf. Dennis Hudson, "Bathing in Kṛṣṇa," *Harvard Theological Review* 73:1-2 (1980), pp. 537-564.

[47]"Śaraṇāgati Dīpikā," verse 5, *STS,* 1:308.

Piṉṉai, Krishna's Cowherd Wife

Dennis Hudson

[1]K.V. Zvelebil, *Tamil Literature,* vol. 10, fasc. 1, of J. Gonda, ed., *A History of Indian Literature* (Wiesbaden: Otto Harrassowitz, 1974), p. 132. Zvelebil's chronology will be followed in this study.

[2]Āycciyar kuravai," ch. 17, book 2, in *Cilappatikāra mūlamum nāvalar paṇṭita Na. Mu. Veṅkaṭacāmi Nāṭṭāravarkaḷ iyaṟṟiya uraivum* (Tirunelvēli: Śaiva Siddhānta Works Publishing House, 1966), pp. 396-415. It has been translated by Alain Daniélou in Prince Ilangô Adigal, *Shilappadikaram (The Ankle Bracelet)* (New York: New Directions, 1965), pp. 112-21.

[3]"The Seven Bulls and Kṛṣṇa's Marriage of Nīlā/NappiNNai in Sanskrit and Tamil Literature," *Temenos: Studies in Comparative Religion* 8 (1972): 29-53. I have used this article extensively as the basis for this research.

[4]Zvelebil places it in the 4th-5th centuries (*Tamil Literature,* p. 48).

[5]"Mullaik kali," ch. 103, verses 1-79, in *Kalittokai maturaiyāciriyar pārattuvāci Nacciṉārkkiniyaruraiyuṭaṉ* [*Iḷvaḷakaṉār ārāycci muṉṉuraiyum uraiviḷakkamum aṭaṅkiyatu*] (Tirunelvēli: Saiva Siddhānta Works Publishing House, 1967), pp. 315-21. Ch. 103, lines 1-55 have been translated by K.V. Zvelebil in "Bull-Baiting Festival in Tamil India," *Annals of the Náprstek Museum* 1 (1962): 191-99, translation on pp. 193-94. Lines 69-79 have been translated by Edholm and Suneson, "The Seven Bulls," p. 45.

[6]*Harivaṃśa* (critical ed.) 63.26-28; *Prose English Translation of Harivamsha* by M.N. Dutt (Calcutta, 1897), 75.26-28, p. 317. *Viṣṇu Purāṇa* 5.13; *The Vishnu Purana,* trans. H.H. Wilson (Calcutta: Punthi Pustak, 1961; orig. pub. 1840, 1888), p. 424. In his critical edition P.L. Vaidya dates the oldest part of *Harivaṃśa* to about 300 A.D. See *The Harivaṃśa,* ed. P.L. Vaidya (Poona: Bhandarkar Oriental Research Institute, 1969), 1:xv, xxix, xxxix. The date of the *Viṣṇu Purāṇa* may be closer to that of the *Cilappatikāram.* W.D. O'Flaherty places it at approximately 450 A.D. in her *Hindu Myths* (Baltimore: Penguin, 1975), p. 18.

[7]Edholm and Suneson, "The Seven Bulls," p. 44.

[8]Norvin Hein, *The Miracle Plays of Mathurā,* (New Haven: Yale University Press, 1972), pp. 257-59; 270-71.

[9]The distinction between Mathurā in the North (*vaṭamaturai*) and Mathurā in the South (*teṉmaturai*) is made frequently in Tamil Vaiṣṇava literature and is suggested as early as Āṇṭāḷ's *Tiruppāvai,* where in verse 5 she refers to Krishna as in "everlasting northern Mathurā" (*maṉṉu vaṭa maturai*).

[10]The description of Madurai in the *Cilappatikāram* alludes to temples of Krishna

and Balarāma inside the city, and Friedhelm Hardy has noted "in the classical strata of *caṅkam* literature a specific link between the Pāṇṭiya kings and Viṣṇu. . . ." See "Ideology and Cultural Contexts of the Śrīvaiṣṇava Temple," *The Indian Economic and Social History Review*, 14:1 (1977), pp. 119-51, esp. p. 132.

[11]Zvelebil, *Tamil Literature*, p. 141.

[12]Ch. 19, lines 62-65. I have used U. Ve Cāminātaiyar, ed., *Maṇimēkalai*, āṛām patippu (Ceṉṉai: Maturai kulavāṇikan Cīttalaiccātaṉar, 1965); and *Maṇimēkalai*, Na. Mu. Vēṅkaṭacāmi Nāṭṭār and Auvai Cu. Turaicāmippiḷḷai, eds. (Tirunelvēli: Śaiva Siddhānta Works Publishing House, 1964; orig. pub. 1946).

[13]Zvelebil, *Tamil Literature*, p. 89.

[14]François Gros, *Le Paripāṭal: texte tamoul*, Institut français d'Indologie pub. no. 35 (Pondichéry, 1968), pp. li-lii.

[15]Discussed by P.L. Vaidya, *Harivaṃśa*, l:xliii-xliv; by Edholm and Suneson, "The Seven Bulls," pp. 32-33 and note 10; and by J. Filliozat, *Un texte tamoul de devotion Vishnouite: le Tiruppāvai d'Āṇṭāḷ*, Institut français d'Indologie pub. no. 45 (Pondichéry, 1972), pp. xvi-xix. The Sanskrit text is reprinted in Vaidya 2:54-62.

[16]For a discussion of this kinship term see Filliozat, *Un texte*, pp. 49-50, note XVIII, 7.

[17]According to Adalbert Gail, *Bhakti im Bhāgavatapurāṇa* (Weisbaden: Münchener Indologische Studien, 1969), 6:9-16.

[18]*Bhāgavata Purāṇa* 10.30.21-44, in J.M. Sanyal, trans., *The Srimad-Bhagavatam*, 2nd ed. (Calcutta, n.d.) 4:127-29. She is also found in *Viṣṇu Purāṇa* 5.13 (Wilson translation, pp. 424-25). This suggests a development separate from Piṉṉai.

[19]*Bhāgavata Purāṇa* 10.57.41-48 (Sanyal translation, p. 250).

[20]Ibid.

[21]Citations given by K.R. Srinivasan, *Some Aspects of Religion as Revealed by Early Monuments and Literature of the South* (Madras: Archaeological Survey of India, 1960), p. 16; and M.A. Dorai Rangaswamy, *The Religion and Philosophy of Tēvāram*, bk. 1 (Madras: University of Madras, 1958), p. 203. Edholm and Suneson, "The Seven Bulls," p. 30, note that Cuntarar (c. 780-830 A.D.) also made at least one reference to her.

[22]Zvelebil, *Tamil Literature*, p. 91.

[23]All *āḻvār* verses in which reference is made to Piṉṉai and/or to the seven bulls can be found in the appendix to this study.

[24]Pūtam in *Iraṇṭāntiruvantāti* 63, and Pēy in *Mūṉṟāntiruvantāti* 49.

[25]*Mutaltiruvantāti* 42.

[26]Zvelebil, *Tamil Literature*, p. 102. Two *āḻvārs* do not mention Piṉṉai or the seven bulls at all: Toṇṭaraṭippoṭi (c. 825 A.D.) and Tirupāṇ (700-850? A.D.). See Zvelebil, *Tamil Literature*, p. 101.

[27]*Perumāḷ Tirumoḻi* (hereafter cited as *PT*) 4.1. Two references may be to Krishna's conquest of Ariṣṭa: 2.3 and 2.5.

[28]*Harivaṃśa* 64 (Dutt translation, ch. 77, pp. 319-21).

[29]Zvelebil, *Tamil Literature*, p. 106.

[30]Three verses may refer to Ariṣṭa: *PT* 8.6.8, 10.2.2, and 10.7.13.

[31]*PT* 3.4.4, 1.2.3, 5.9.8.

[32]*PT* 8.8.8.

[33]*PT* 6.6.9, 8.6.6, 10.4.7, 11.2.5.

[34]*PT* 2.3.5. Out of 13 references to her by name, this is the only time he calls her "Nappiṉṉai" rather than "Piṉṉai."

[35]*PT* 3.3.9.

[36]*PT* 4.4.5, 6.6.9, and 10.47, respectively.

[37]Zvelebil, *Tamil Literature, p. 101.*

[38]*Tiruccanta Viruttam* p. 101.

[39]Zvelebil, *Tamil Literature*, p. 102.

[40]Ibid., p. 103.

[41]These verses (18-20) are translated following the commentary of Periyavāccāṉpiḷḷai, *Tirupāvai mūvāyirappati ārāyirappaṭi viyākkiyāṉaṅkaḷutaṉ kuṭiyatu* (Kāñcī: P.B. Aṇṇaṅkarācāriyar, 1970), pp. 105-24.

[42]Zvelebil, *Tamil Literature,* p. 107.

[43]*Tiruvāymoḻi* 1.7.8. Translations of *Tiruvāymoḻi* are made with reference to two works: Nammāḻvāraruḷicceyta, *Tiruvāymoḻi,* 10 vols., Śrī Kāñci pirativāti payaṅkaram Aṇṇaṅkarācāriyar iyaṟṟiya tivyārttattīpikai yuraiyuṭaṉ kūṭiyatu, 1st, 2nd, 3rd eds. (Kāñci: Granthamala, 1953-57); and B.P. Purushothama Naidu, *Bagavat Vishayam Tiruvāymoḻi Īttiṉ Tamiḻākkam,* 9 vols., 3rd ed. (Madras: University of Madras, 1971).

[44]*Tiruvāymoḻi* 6.4.2.

[45]*Tiruvāymoḻi* 8.1.7 and Purushothama Naidu, *Īttiṉ Tamiḻākkam,* 8:33.

[46]*Tiruviruttam* 3; *Tiruvāymoḻi* 1.9.4, 5.6.11, 6.5.10, 7.2.9, and 8.3.1.

[47]*Tiruvāymoḻi* 1.9.4.

[48]*Tiruvāymoḻi* 8.3.1.

[49]Piṉṉai continued to appear in non-Vaiṣṇava literature at this time. For example, the 10th century Jain author of the *Cīvakacintāmaṇi* uses Krishna and Piṉṉai as exemplars of proper intracaste marriage and refers to their erotic relationship with the question," . . . did not the husband of Lady Earth drink elixir from the mouth—like the *ilavi* flower—of her with the long, plaited and abundant hair (*nīṇirai nappiṉṉai*)?" The South Indian Sanskrit poet Vāsudeva, also of the 10th century, drew upon the Nīlā story interpolated into the *Harivaṃśa* for his courtly epic *Śaurikathodaya.* See verse 482 of Tirutakkatēvar, *Cīvakacintāmani* Mūlamum . . . Naccinārkkiṉiyaruraiyum, ed. U. Vē. Cāminātaiyaravarkaḷ, 7th ed. (Ceṉṉai: Kabeer Printing Works, 1969), pp. 242-45; and Edholm and Suneson, "The Seven Bulls," p. 31.

[50]In personal correspondence. I am greatly indebted to her generous assistance in the collection of materials and their interpretation for this section.

[51]In the *Śaraṇāgatigadya,* sect. 4. See Periyavāccāṉpiḷḷai, *Katya vyākyānankaḷ* (Tirrucci: Vijaya), pp. 24-25.

[52]In his *Sundarabāhustava,* verse 70. Se Kūruttāḻvan, *Suntarapāhustava viyāke kiyāṉam,* ed. P.B. Aṇṇaṅkarācāriyar (Kāñcī: P.B. Aṇṇāṅkarācāriyar, 1976), pp. 70-71.

[53]According to K.K.A. Venkatachari, he was a disciple of Rāmānuja, the eldest of two sons of Rāmānuja's foremost disciple Kūrattāḻvān or Kūreśa. See "The Maṇipravala Literature of the Śrivaisnava Ācaryas 12th to 15th Century A.D." (Proefschrift . . . aan de Rijksuniversiteit de Utrecht, 1975), p. 69.

[54]Trans. Zvelebil, *Tamil Literature,* p. 104, n. 33.

[55]In his *Śrīguṇaratnakośa,* verse 26. See Parāśara Bhaṭṭar, "Śrīguṇaratnakośa" in *Stotramala,* ed. P.B. Aṇṇaṅkarācāriyar (Kāñcī, 1969); and U. Vē. Ki Śrīnivāsayyaṅkār Svāmi, *Tiruppāvai,* 2nd ed. (Tirucci, 1960?), p. 170.

[56]Venkatachari, "Maṇipravāḷa Literature," pp. 75-92.

[57]The following references to the *Ītu* will be based on Purushothama Naidu's "Tamilized" version, *Bagavat Vishayam Tiruvāymoḻī Īṭṭin Tamiḻākkam,* with reference to the "Maṇipravāḷa" original as found in Cē. Kiruṣṇamācāriyar, ed., *Śrī Pakavatviṣayam:* Tiruvāymoḻi mūlamum, āṟāyirappaṭi, onpatiṉāyirappaṭi, paṉṉīrāyirappaṭi, irupattiṉālāyirappaṭi, īṭu muppattāṟāyirappaṭi, vyākkiyāṉaṅkalum cīyar arumpatavurai, pramāṇattiraṭṭu, travitopanisatsankati, travitopanisattatparyaratnavali, tiruvaymolinurrantati ivaikalutan, 10 vols. (Cennai: Ganesha Press, vols. 1 and 2, n.d.; vols. 3 ff., 1924-30).

[58]Purushothama Naidu, *Īṭṭin Tamilākkam,* pp. 227-31.

[59]The commentary on 9.10.4 in *Īṭu* refers to Nappiṉṉai as having "femininenessand other such qualities of the Self" (*strītvam mutalāna ātmakunankalaiyutaiva nappiṉṉaippirāṭṭi*). In verse 96 of *Śrīvacaṇa Bhuṣaṇam* by Piḷḷai Lōkācārya, the chief qualities of the Self are listed as *sama* and *dama.* I have referred to Piḷḷai Lōkācāryar, *Śrī Vacaṉa Pūṣaṇam,* Maṇavāḷa Māmuṉikaḷ viyākkiyāṉam—Tamiḻ ākkam (Katalūr, 1970), p. 214;

and to Sri Satyamurthi Swami, *Srivacana Bhushanam by Sri Pillai Lokacharya: An English Glossary* (Gwalior: S. Satyamurthi Ayaangar, 1972), pp. 21-22.

[60]This portion of Periyavāccāṉpiḷḷai's commentary is amplified here by reference to the parallel commentary of Āḻakiyamaṇavālapperumaḷ Nāyaṉār, "The Six Thousand Grantha Commentary."

[61]By the time of Vaṭakkutiruvītippiḷḷai's second son, Āḻakiyamaṇavālapperumaḷ Nāyaṉār, in the 14th century, the three goddesses and their avatar forms had been assimilated to the Pāñcarātra *vyūha* doctrine. In his "Six Thousand Grantha Commentary" on *Tiruppāvai* where he introduces verse 18, he notes, "In the Supreme Realm (*paratacai*) one should invoke the aid of all three Ladies (*nāyccimār*) . . . In the Vyūha Realm (*vyūhāvastai*) one should invoke the aid of the two Ladies [Śrī and Bhū]. . . . In the descent of Rāma the Great Lady lives as only one person [Sītā]. In the manifestation of Śrī Varāha, invoke the aid of the Lady Śrī Bhūmi. In the descent of Krishna she is the pre-eminent queen and therefore they [the *gopīs*] invoke the aid of Lady Nappiṉṉai." See *Tiruppāvai*, ed. Aṇṇaṅkarācāriyar, p. 105; and Mu. Aruṇācalam, *Tamiḻ ilakkiya varalāru: nūṟṟāṇṭu 14* (Thiruchitrambalam, Māyūram, Tanjore DT: Gandhi Vidyalayam, 1969), pp. 286-88.

[62]David Shulman notes that Piṉṉai fits into a pattern of double wives in Tamil mythology "one senior and orthodox [Śrī], one local and better loved [Piṉṉai]." See David Dean Shulman. *Tamil Temple Myths: Sacrifice and Divine Marriage in the South Indian Śaiva Tradition* (Princeton: Princeton University Press, 1980), pp. 267-97, esp. pp. 285-86.

[63]Zvelebil gives this interpretaiton in *Tamil Literature*, p. 103 and n. 32, as do J. Filliozat, *Un texte tamoul*, p. xvi, and N. Subrahmanian, *Pre-Pallavan Tamil Index* (Madras, 1966), p. 570.

[64]Followed, for example, by Mu. Irākavaiyaṅkār, *Ārāyccittokuti* (Cennai: Pari Nilayam, 1964), p. 56, note; referred to by Filliozat, *Un texte tamoul*, p. xvi, note; and continued by Edholm and Suneson, "The Seven Bulls," p. 38.

[65]Dorai Rangaswamy, *Tēvarām*, bk. 1, p. 219.

[66]The *Viṣṇudharmottara Purāṇa* of about the 5th century and important in the South, and the *Bṛhat saṃhitā* by Varāhamihira of about the 6th century. See Edholm and Suneson, "The Seven Bulls," pp. 51-52, and P.L. Vaidya's critical note on ch. 48 in *The Harivaṃśa*, 1:794.

[67]S. Ch. Mukherji, "The Cult of Ekānamśā," *Indian Historical Quarterly* 35 (1959):189-208.

[68]Mukherji, "Ekānamśā," pp. 192-94.

[69]Ibid., p. 195. Lynn Ate provides a provocative discussion of the meaning of "Piṉṉai," of the positioning of Piṉṉai during the *kuravai* dance, and of the possibility that she was initially identified as Krishna's sister and with Durgā. Moreover Ate notes, that in the Buddhist version of the Rāma story, the "Dasaratha Jātaka," Sītā is described as both the sister of Rāma and his wife. David Shulman also shows examples of brother-sister marriage in Tamil myths. See Lynn Marie Ate, *Periyāḻvār's Tirumoḻi—A Bāla Krsna Text From the Devotional Period in Tamil Literature* (Ph.D. diss., University of Wisconsin-Madison, 1978), pp. 385-92; and Shulman, *Tamil Temple Myths*, pp. 172-73; 252-59.

[70]Bhāsa, *Bhāsa's Two Plays Avimāraka and Bālacharita*, trans. Bak Kumbae (Delhi: Meharchand Lachhmandas, 1968). The play seems to have originated in the South between the 3rd and the early 8th centuries. The Daṇḍin who wrote the *Kāvyadarśa* at approximately the beginning of the 8th century quotes a stanza from the *Bālacarita*. Daṇḍin was associated with Kāñcī. It is not certain that Bhāsa wrote the *Bālacarita;* but if he did, it may have originated as early as the 3rd century according to J.L. Masson, who assigns that date to the *Avimāraka*, also attributed to Bhāsa. See Bak Kunbae, *Bhāsa's Two Plays*, pp. 5-6; S.K. De, "The Prose Kāvyas of Daṇḍin, Subandhu and Bāṇa" in *A*

Volume of Studies in Indology Presented to Prof. P.V. Kane (Poona, 1941), pp. 119-20; and Bhāsa, *Avimāraka (Love's Enchanted World)*, trans. J.L. Masson and D.D. Kosambi (Delhi: Motilal Banarsidass, 1970), pp. 6-7.

[71]Charlotte Vaudeville, "Aspects du mythe de *Kṛṣṇa-Gopāla* dans l'Inde ancienne" in *Mélanges d'Indianisme à la mémoire de Louis Renou* (Paris: Éditions de Boccard, 1968), pp. 757-59.

[72]Act 2.

[73]Such a tradition is contained in the *Cilappatikāram* where she is understood to be Krishna's sister and is identified with the Tamil goddess of war, Koṟṟavai. In 2.12 ("Veṭṭuva vari") she is described as the one who pulled down two Maruta trees, kicked Śaṭaka, and appeared because of the evil deeds of her uncle Kañcaṉ. The editor of the text says that these and similar references to her activities which are associated with Śiva indicate that she is the *kriyā-śakti* of the Lord. In this song Koṟṟavai is stated to be the younger sister of Krishna who himself seems to be understood as the *śakti* of Śiva. See *Cilappatikāram*, Veṅkaṭacāmi edition, pp. 281, 295.

[74]Act 3.

[75]This and the following discussion of Durgā in Pallava sculpture is based on extensive conversations with Marylin Rhie of the Department of Art, Smith College, who very generously brought this material to my attention and helped me think it through; and on the studies of K.R. Srinivasan, *Cave-Temples of the Pallavas* (New Delhi: Archaeological Survey of India, 1964), and J. Ph. Vogel, "The Head-offering to the Goddess in Pallava Sculpture," *Bulletin of the School of Oriental Studies* 6 (1930-32): 538-43.

[76]Srinivasan, *Cave-Temples*, p. 141-48. He makes the following suggestion as to the intention of these carvings during Māmalla's reign: "Characteristically enough by the side of the Varāha panel is Śrīdevī symbolic of *Rājya-Śrī* and prosperity while by the side of the Trivikrama panel is shown Durgā the goddess of victory or *vijaya-śrī*. Probably all these were after Māmalla's conquest of Bādāmi and therefore late in his reign" (p. 148). He suggests that the cave-temple follows the Vaikhānasāgama.

[77]Srinivasan, *Cave-Temples*, pp. 148-56. This temple appears to have started out Vaiṣṇava, but it was never completed, and the present Somaskanda panel in the main shrine was carved later. This is suggested by Srinivasan and confirmed by Michael Lockwood, Gift Siromoney and P. Dayanandan, *Mahabalipuram Studies* (Madras: The Christian Literature Society, 1974), pp. 7-17. The unmanifest presence of Śrī in the reclining figure of Nārāyaṇa worshipped by Bhū is suggested by K.V. Soundara Rajan, "The Typology of the Anantaśayī Icon," *Artibus Asiae* 29 (1967): 79.

[78]Srinivasan, *Some Aspects*, p. 17.

[79]The only possible exception to this is in the Varāha panel discussed earlier where the figure of Bhū has a cloth hanging over her right thigh and behind her hip. Srinivasan identifies this as a *kucha-bandha* which has fallen, but it seems too long to be her breast-band and does not conform to other Pallava representations of her. See *Cave-Temples*, p. 146. It is true, however, that in late Chola sculpture Bhū does wear a *kucha-bandha*, though there is also a tradition in which Śrī should wear it, but not Bhū (Hariṇī). See *Kāśyapa's Book of Wisdom*, trans. T. Goudriaan (The Hague: Mouton, 1965), p. 125 and n. 9.

[80]*Kāśyapa's Book*, p. 219. The text gives prescriptions for making images of Krishna seated with his Kṣatriya queens Rukmiṇī and Satyabhāmā on either side. Rukmiṇī is understood as an aspect of Śrī and Satyabhāmā as an aspect of Bhū. See pp. 254-55, and Jan Gonda, *Aspects of Early Viṣṇuism*, p. 125, cited in *Kāśyapa's Book*, p. 255, n. 5. Such a statement does leave open the logical possibility that if Krishna's wife in his life as a cowherd were to become important in the Vaisnava cult, she would be understood as an aspect of the third goddess, Durgā-Kātyāyanī.

[81]*Lakṣmī Tantra: A Pāñcarātra Text,* trans. Sanjukta Gupta (Leiden: E.J. Brill, 1972), pp. 28, n. 4; 40; 49; 64-65; 88; 137-40; 155 ff; 356 ff; xxiii.

[82]F.O. Schrader, *Introduction to the Pāñcarātra and the Ahirbudhnva Saṃhitā* (Madras: Adyar Library, 1916), p. 54, n. 7.

Appendix: References to Piṉṉai and/or the seven bulls in the poems of the āḻvārs.

Poykai, *Mutal Tiruvantāti* 42; 83.
Pūtam, *Iraṇṭan Tiruvantāti,* 62; 63.
Pēy, *Mūṉrāṉ Tiruvantāti* 25; 49; 85.
Kulacēkara, *Perumāḷ Tirumoḻi* 2.3; 2.5; 4.1.
Tirumaḻicaippirāṉ, *Nāṉmukaṉ Tiruvantāti* 23; 33.
Tirumaḻicaippirāṉ, *Tiruccanta Viruttam* 13; 33; 40; 41; 42; 55; 92; 99.
Tirumaṅkai, *Periya Tirumoḻi* 1.2.3; 1.4.6; 1.10.7; 2.2.4; 2.3.5; 2.4.1; 2.9.9; 2.10.7; 3.1.5; 3.2.7; 3.3.5; 3.3.9; 3.4.4; 3.7.7; 3.8.9; 3.10.10; 4.4.4; 4.4.5; 4.5.3; 4.5.4; 5.9.8; 6.5.4; 6.5.5; 6.6.8; 6.6.9; 7.7.7; 7.8.8; 8.3.3; 8.6.6; 8.6.8; 8.6.9; 8.7.1; 8.7.2; 8.9.3; 10.4.7; 10.7.13; 11.2.2; 11.2.5; 11.2.10; 11.7.9.
Tirumaṅkai, *Tiruneṭuntāṇṭakam* 29.
Tirumaṅkai, *Ciṟiya Tirumaṭal* 11 (?).
Tirumaṅkai, *Periya Tirumaṭal* 118.
Periyāḻvār, *Tirumoḻi* 1.5.3; 1.5.7; 2.4.9; 2.5.1; 2.7.6; 3.3.3; 4.1.4.
Āṇṭāḷ, *Tiruppāvai,* 18; 19; 20.
Nammāḻvār, *Tiruviruttam* 3; 21.
Nammāḻvār, *Periya Tiruvantāti* 48.
Nammāḻvār, *Tiruvāymoḻi* 1.5.1; 1.7.8; 1.8.7; 1.9.4; 2.5.7; 3.5.4; 3.9.8; 4.2.5; 4.3.1; 4.8.4; 5.6.11; 5.7.9; 6.4.2; 6.4.6; 6.5.10; 7.2.9; 8.1.7; 8.1.8; 8.3.1; 9.8.2; 9.8.4; 9.10.4; 10.4.3.

The Courtship of Vaḷḷi and Murugan:
Some Parallels with the Rādhā-Krishna Story

Brenda E.F. Beck

[1]Fred Clothey, *The Many Faces of Murugan* (The Hague: Mouton, 1977), pp. 1-4, and Gananath Obeyesekere, "The Fire-Walkers of Kataragama: The Rise of Bhakti Religiosity in Buddhist Sri Lanka," *The Journal of Asian Studies,* 27:3 (1978), pp. 457-76.

[2]For example, a lovely poem by Arunakiri (a male poet who lived in the first half of the 15th century) reads in part:

From the murderous arrows of Maṉmataṉ
rescue this woman with creeper-like waist
from being destroyed in sorrows
You, adorned with the *kura* flower,
grant me your garland of *kaṭappa* blossoms
strung round your wide arms!

The poem is addressed to Murugan and expressed the poet's views of himself as female in relation to this "Lord with the spear." Trans. S. Kokilam, quoted from Kamil Zvelebil, *The Smile of Murugan* (Leiden: E.J. Brill, 1973), p. 245.

[3]An early and very important reference to this theme in the South appears in Prince Ilangô Adigal, *Shilappadikaram: The Ankle Bracelet,* trans. Alain Daniélou

(London: George Allen & Unwin, 1967), p. 149. For a parallel in the Krishna tradition, see *Bhāgavata Purāṇa* 10.29-33.

[4]These occur in the villages of Coimbatore District, particularly the Pollachi area. One book on South Indian folk dances describes similar circular dances performed by women to songs praising either Murugan or Krishna, Hildegard Spreen, *Folk Dances of South India* (Bombay: Geoffrey Cumberlege, 1945), pp. 32-37, 85-91.

[5]A Gujarati dance called the *rās* has links to Krishna's courtship of the *gopīs*. Interestingly, it is performed mainly by men. "Banwari, Folk Dance of Gujarat," *Mārg* 13:1 (1959), pp. 32-33.

[6]R. Dessigane and P.Z. Pattabiramin, trans., *La Légende du Skanda*, Institut français d'Indologie pub. no. 31 (Pondichéry, 1967).

[7]Ibid., pp. 22-24, and *Bhāgavata Purāṇa* 10.13-14.

[8]Pidatala Sitapati, *Sri Venkateswara: Lord of the Seven Hills, Tirupati* (Bombay: Bharatiya Vidya Bhavan, 1972), pp. 22-23.

[9]E.g., R. Dessigane, P.Z. Pattabiramin, and J. Filliozat, *La Légende des jeux de Çiva à Madurai,* Institut français d'Indologie pub. no. 19 (Pondichéry, 1960), story no. 32. Here Murugan, in his pursuit of love, assumes disguises that are reminiscent of Śiva's—a point to which Wendy O'Flaherty has alerted me.

[10]*Vaḷḷiyammaṉ Kummi* (Madras: R.G. Pati Company, 1964). I am indebted to Mrs. Vaija Ragunāthan for help with reading and analyzing the Tamil text.

[11]Islets have been considered sacred places for centuries, as the very beginnings of Tamil literature attest. A.K. Ramanujan's translation of a Sangam poem makes mention of rituals being performed on islets of this kind. *The Interior Landscape: Love Poems from a Classical Tamil Anthology* (Bloomington: Indiana University Press, 1967), Kuṟ 263, p. 78.

[12]All these are common poetic images for women in Tamil. The point here is not originality, but rather the poet's choice of where in the story to use such metaphors, and how extensively.

[13]This, again, is a common expression. What is significant is its placement in a progression.

[14]In one famous southern story, Śiva is also said to have softened his body to help the goddess Pārvatī conquer her fear of him. R. Dessigane, P.Z. Pattabiramin, and J. Filliozat, *Les Légendes çivaites de Kāñcipuram,* Institut français d'Indologie pub. no. 27 (Pondichéry, 1964), story no. 63, p. 90.

[15]Here the parallel with Krishna, the love thief, is evident.

[16]In other words, in harmony with both Vaḷḷi and his previous wife, Dēvānai, who in fact gives her consent to her husband's second wedding.

[17]This "fact" is common knowledge among Southerners of Śaivite persuasion. I have encountered innumerable references to this relationship in literature and folk drama alike. Sometimes Pārvatī is Viṣṇu's elder sibling; at other times she is portrayed as the younger.

[18]Cross-cousin marriage, especially marriage with the mother's brother's daughter, is highly approved throughout southern India.

[19]Again there is a parallel with the behavior of Murugan's father, Śiva, who once extended his hand to a doubting devotee after the latter had been burnt by Śiva's third eye and had jumped into a pool of water. R. Dessigane, et al., *La Légende des jeux de Çiva à Madurai,* story 53.

[20]This tradition is widespread in popular literature, where girls are said to "swoon" and fall down in a faint when struck by love for Murugan. Paṟanicāmi Pulavar, *Alakumalai Kuṟavañci* (Tiruppur: South India, 1969), pp. 22-24. Similar literature exists describing girls who fall in love with Śiva. I quote one particularly striking passage where Śiva is given an amorous role precisely parallel to that usually accorded his son:

Lots of girls came to watch Śiva as he was paraded through the town (at a temple festival). The girls fell in love with him and forgot such simple things as putting their bangles on. One girl first tied her blouse around her hips, she was so distracted. Some girls ran with their eye make-up in hand, or with eye make-up on only one eye. Some were trying to talk with him. Some thought of hugging him and wondered what was the use of having breasts if they could not touch them to him. . . . In this state Śiva looked at her (Vasanta-vaḷḷi). At this moment all her bangles fell off. After this she became thin with love. She became angry and sad because her love was unattainable.

Tirukūṭarācappakavirāyar, *Tirukuttrala Kuṟavañci* (Tirunelveli: Saiva Sidhanta Publishing Works, 1968).

[21]Brenda E.F. Beck, "A Praise Poem for Murugan," *The Journal of South Asian Literature* 11:1-2 (1975), pp. 95-116.

[22]Kamil Zvelebil makes the same point in regard to the very earliest strata of Tamil literature, offering broadly similar descriptions of these two gods, in "The Beginnings of *Bhakti* in South India," *Temenos* 13 (1977): 223-57.

The Divine Consort in South India

Glenn E. Yocum

[1]On these concepts in Rāmānuja's thought, see John B. Carman, *The Theology of Rāmānuja: An Essay in Interreligious Understanding* (New Haven: Yale University Press, 1974).

[2]On Tamil Caṅkam poetry and its conventions, see especially A.K. Ramanujan, trans., *The Interior Landscape: Love Poems from a Classical Tamil Anthology* (Bloomington: Indiana University Press, 1967); Kamil Zvelebil, *The Smile of Murugan: On Tamil Literature of South India* (Leiden: E.J. Brill, 1973), pp. 65-118; and Kamil Veith Zvelebil, *Tamil Literature* (Wiesbaden: Otto Harrassowitz, 1974), pp. 7-47.

[3]Fred W. Clothey alludes to such a process in his discussion of the Murukaṉ-Vaḷḷi myth; see *The Many Faces of Murukaṉ: The History and Meaning of a South Indian God* (The Hague: Mouton, 1978), pp. 83-85.

[4]On *aṇaṅku* and its meaning in early Tamil culture, see the following publications by George L. Hart, III: *The Poems of Ancient Tamil: Their Milieu and Their Sanskrit Counterparts* (Berkeley: University of California Press, 1975), pp. 93-119; "Women and the Sacred in Ancient Tamilnad," *Journal of Asian Studies* 32:2 (1973), pp. 233-250; "Some Aspects of Kinship in Ancient Tamil Literature," *Kinship and History in South Asia,* ed. Thomas R. Trautmann (Ann Arbor: Center for South and Southeast Asian Studies, The University of Michigan, 1974), pp. 29-60; and "Some Related Literary Conventions in Tamil and Indo-Aryan and their Significance," *Journal of the American Oriental Society* 94:2 (1974), pp. 157-167.

[5]For this image, see Hart's translation and interpretation of *Aiṅkuṟunūṟu* 405 in *Poems of Ancient Tamil,* pp. 111-112.

[6]See my article "The Goddess in a Tamil Śaiva Devotional Text, Māṇikkavācakar's *Tiruvācakam,*" *Journal of the American Academy of Religion* Supplement 45:1 (1977), pp. 369-390.

[7]On goddesses in the Chhattisgarh region of Madhya Pradesh, see Lawrence A. Babb, *The Divine Hierarchy: Popular Hinduism in Central India* (New York: Columbia University Press, 1975), pp. 215-246; and "Marriage and Malevolence: The Uses of Sexual Opposition in a Hindu Pantheon," *Ethnology* 9:2 (1970), pp. 137-148.

NOTES

Prolegomenon to a Psychology of the Goddess

David M. Wulff

[1]Wilfred Cantwell Smith, "A Human View of Truth," *Studies in Religion* 1 (1971), pp. 6-24.

[2]Marven O. Nelson and Edward M. Jones, "An Application of the Q-Technique to the Study of Religious Concepts," *Psychological Reports* 3 (1957): 293-297.

[3]Jean-Pierre Deconchy, "God and Parental Images. The Masculine and Feminine in Religious Free Associations," in A. Godin, ed., *From Cry to Word: Contributions Toward a Psychology of Prayer* (Brussels: Lumen Vitae Press, 1968), pp. 85-94; Marven O. Nelson, "The Concept of God and Feelings Toward Parents," *Journal of Individual Psychology* 27 (1971): 46-49; Orlo Strunk, Jr., "Perceived Relationships Between Parental and Deity Concepts," *Psychological Newsletter* 10 (1959): 222-226.

[4]Antoine Vergote, Alvaro Tamayo, Luiz Pasquali, Michel Bonami, Marie-Rose Pattyn, and Anne Custers, "Concept of God and Parental Images," *Journal for the Scientific Study of Religion* 8 (1969): 79-87.

[5]Julien Bigras, *Les images de la mère* (St-Jérôme, Canada: Hachette, 1971); Nicole Fabre, "La mère aux deux visages," *Études Psychothérapiques* No. 22 (1975), pp. 227-232.

[6]Wilfried Daim, *Depth Psychology and Salvation,* (New York: Frederick Ungar, 1963).

[7]Roy S. Lee, *Freud and Christianity* (London: James Clark, 1948); Oscar Pfister, *Christianity and Fear,* trans. W.H. Johnston (London: George Allen and Unwin, 1948).

[8]Melanie Klein, *Our Adult World and Other Essays* (London: William Heinemann, 1963), p. 25.

[9]Sigmund Freud, *The Standard Edition of the Complete Psychological Works,* trans. James Strachey (London: Hogarth Press, 1953-1974), 13:149; 23:83; 21:94-95.

[10]Harald Schjelderup and Kristian Schjelderup, *Über drei Haupttypen der religiösen Erlebnisformen und ihre psychologische Grundlage* (Berlin: Walter de Gruyter, 1932).

[11]Edith Weigert-Vowinckel, "The Cult and Mythology of the Magna Mater from the Standpoint of Psychoanalysis," *Psychiatry* 1 (1938): 347-378.

[12]A.W. Kushner, "Two Cases of Auto-castration Due to Religious Delusions," *British Journal of Medical Psychology* 40 (1967): 293-298.

[13]"Inhuman Ritual Murder of Babe," *Northern India Patrika,* April 4, 1972, p. 1.

[14]G. Morris Carstairs, *The Twice-Born; A Study of a Community of High-Caste Hindus* (London: Hogarth Press, 1957).

[15]C.D. Daly, "Hindu-Mythologie und Kastrationskomplex," *Imago* 13 (1927): 147-198.

[16]Carstairs, *The Twice-Born,* p. 80.

[17]Carl G. Jung, *Collected Works,* trans. R.F.C. Hull (Princeton: University Press, 1953-1979); vol. 7, *Two Essays on Analytical Psychology* (2nd ed., 1966); vol. 9, pt. 1, *The Archetypes and the Collective Unconscious* (2nd ed., 1968).

[18]Jung, *Collected Works,* vol. 9, pt. 1, p. 82.

[19]Ibid.

[20]The common definition of *prakṛti* as matter is somewhat misleading; see Glossary.

[21]Erich Neumann, *The Origins and History of Consciousness,* trans. R.F.C. Hull (New York: Pantheon, 1954).

[22]Erich Neumann, *The Great Mother: An Analysis of the Archetype,* trans. Ralph Manheim (New York: Pantheon, 1955), p. 33.

[23]Ibid., pp. 150, 332.

[24]Erich Neumann, *The Child: Structure and Dynamics of the Nascent Personality*, trans. Ralph Manheim (New York: G.P. Putnam's Sons, 1973).

[25]Neumann, *Origins*, p. 36.

[26]Jung, *Collected Works*, vol. 5, *Symbols of Transformation* (2nd ed., 1967), pp. 226, 263.

[27]Jung, *Collected Works*, vol. 7.

[28]Jung, *Collected Works*, vol. 9, pt. 1, p. 160.

Types of Sexual Union and their Implicit Meanings

Frédérique Apffel Marglin

[1]This work is based on field work carried out in Puri from October 1975 to July 1976 with the generous help of a grant from the American Institute of Indian Studies, and again in the summer of 1977 with the help of a grant from the Center for the Study of World Religions, Harvard University.

[2]Barbara Stoler Miller, *Love Song of the Dark Lord* (New York: Columbia University Press, 1977), pp. 116, 123. She translates Caṇḍī as "fierce Rādhā."

[3]For examples in the *dharmaśāstra* and the epic literature illustrating the terrible consequences of *pratiloma* (against-the-grain) actions, see my paper "Power, Purity and Pollution: Aspects of the Caste System Reconsidered" in *Contributions to Indian Sociology*, n.s., 11:2 (1977).

[4]For an insightful treatment of the dichotomy of *aiśvarya* and *mādhurya*, see John Stratton Hawley, "The Butter Thief" (Ph.D. diss., Harvard University, 1977), ch. 9.

[5]*Jāhāra nahĩ rasa cyuta/teṇu tānāmati acyuta.* Jagannātha Dās, *Śrīmad Bhāgabata* 10:34 (Behrampur: Samnyasi Press, 1954), p. 172.

[6]*Punar api janma, punar api maraṇam, punar api jananī jathare śayanam.*

[7]In commenting on Caitanya and his understanding of *kāma* and *prema*, Jan Gonda expresses the view that is generally held in this tradition: "[*Bhakti*] is crowned by love (*prema*) in which the soul melts into the divine. This love is diametrically opposed to human passion (*kāma*), devoid of eroticism. . . . Ecstatic in nature, it is a communion of the soul with God, who makes it grow and develop in such a way that the soul loves all mankind as a reflection of God" [my translation]. *Les Religions de l'Inde* (Paris: Payot, 1965, 1:194. The view of *prema* as selfless emotion and *kāma* as an emotion that ties one to ego-based desires and passions is not far from the Orissan interpretation I have presented here. The major difference is in excluding eroticism from *prema* and attributing it exclusively to *kāma*. The selflessness of *prema* is well illustrated in the story of Nārada's quest for the dust of the women's feet.

[8]Wendy Doniger O'Flaherty, *Asceticism and Eroticism in the Mythology of Śiva* (Delhi: Oxford University Press, 1975), pp. 261-77.

[9]Frédérique Apffel Marglin, "Auspiciousness and the Devadāsīs," paper presented at the ninth annual workshop of the Conference on Religion in South India, Chambersburg, Pennsylvania, May 1978.

[10]Veena Das, "On the Categorization of Space in Hindu Ritual," in Ravindra K. Jain, ed., *Text and Context: The Social Anthropology of Tradition* (Philadelphia: Institute for the Study of Human Issues, 1977), pp. 9-27.

[11]For textual references to the myth of the churning of the milk ocean, see J. Bruce Long, "Life out of Death: A Structural Analysis of the Myth of the Churning of the Ocean of Milk," in Bardwell L. Smith, ed., *Hinduism: New Essays in the History of Religions* (Leiden: Brill, 1976), pp. 171-207.

[12]This is an unpublished manuscript entitled *Śyāmāpūjā Vidhi*. The language is Sanskrit, the script Oriya. It is the possession of the ritual specialist in Puri who performs this worship and who was my main informant on the *śākta* tradition. This per-

son gave me a copy of the text along with a translation and a commentary. The translation was jointly produced by him and my research assistant in Puri, Purna Chandra Mishra. The written material was supplemented by oral exegesis given to me as we discussed the ritual.

[13]Veena Das, "Categorization of Space," pp. 11, 13.

[14]Ibid., p. 15.

[15]Ronald B. Inden and Ralph W. Nicholas, *Kinship in Bengali Culture* (Chicago: University of Chicago Press, 1977), p. 4.

[16]Adrian C. Mayer, *Caste and Kinship in Central India* (Berkeley: University of California Press, 1973), pp. 167, 184-88. Brenda E.F. Beck, *Peasant Society in Konku* (Vancouver: University of British Columbia Press, 1972), p. 99.

[17]Beck, *Peasant Society*, p. 99.

[18]This passage is found in the *Sūtras of Bharadvāja*, pt. 2, ed. and trans. C.G. Kashikar (Poona: Vaidika Saṁśodhana Maṇḍala, 1964), pp. 460-501.

[19]I am indebted to Edward Hale for reading and explaining the Sanskrit text to me.

[20]*Deveśi bhaktisulabhe parivāra samanvite/yāvat tvām pūjayiṣyāmi tāvat tvam susthirābhāva.*

[21]Miller, *Love Song*, p. 72.

[22]Ibid., p. 73.

[23]In the version of this song that my Oḍissi dance guru taught me, the hand gestures, the accompanying explanation, and the translation of this song say that Rādhā is recalling at this point her first love-making with Krishna. The first line of paragraph no. 12 (translated by Miller as, "I shy from him when we meet," p. 80) is, in the version I was taught, rendered by gestures and translation as: "at our first meeting, I was shy." This rendering reinforces the structural opposition that I perceive between the love-making at the beginning of the poem and that at the end.

[24]Ibid., p. 80.

[25]Ibid., p. 116.

[26]Ibid., pp. 112, 113.

On Woman Saints

A.K. Ramanujan

[1]*Bṛhadāraṇyaka Upaniṣad*, 4.3.21, trans. R.E. Hume, *The Thirteen Principal Upanishads* (London: Oxford University Press, 1931).

[2]Quoted from Charlotte Vaudeville's excellent article, "Evolution of Love-symbolism in Bhagavatism," *Journal of the American Oriental Society* 82:1 (1962), p. 40.

[3]"Masculine" and "feminine," of course, imply well-known cultural stereotypes: active/passive, instrumental/expressive, public/private, etc. Hence my quotation marks around the words. Part of the intent of this paper is to examine these stereotypes in Hindu culture, and to discern how both males and females conform to, struggle with, contradict, vary, or enlarge these stereotypes.

Freud considers all religion to express a regressive longing for the security of the infantile relation to the parent. For him, as Philip Rieff has said, religion is a "feminine" preoccupation; religious man, like a woman, is "forced to obey unconditionally," to be passive, compliant, dependent. See Rieff, *Freud: The Mind of the Moralist* (New York: Anchor Books, 1961), p. 293.

[4]"Men, Women, and Saints," lecture given at the colloquium of the Center for the Study of World Religions, Harvard University, April 1977.

[5]Ta. Su. Śāmarāya's *Śivaśaraṇa Kathāratnakośa* (Mysore: Taḷukina Venkaṇṇayya Smāraka Grantha Māle, 1967), is an encyclopedia in Kannada that summarizes material from more than 200 sources about nearly 1,000 Śaiva saints. Of these, about 100 are

women. The entries vary in length from a single line to a couple of pages. Most of the saints are not given dates. My materials regarding the following Kannada Vīraśaiva saints' legends come from this source: Tilakavve, Vīrasaṅgavve, Dālāyi, Goggavve, Rēkavve, and Vīracōḷādēvi. The life of Mahādēviyakka has received more elaborate treatment in the works of Harihara and in the *Śūnyasampādane*. I have summarized her life and three others' in my *Speaking of Śiva* (Baltimore: Penguin, 1973). For outlines of other Indian women saints' lives, I have relied on *Women Saints of East and West* (London: Ramakrishna Vedanta Centre, 1955). The book contains short articles on the following women saints: Avvaiyār (Tamil, Śaiva), Kāraikkāl Ammaiyār (Tamil, Śaiva), Āṇṭāl (Tamil, Vaiṣṇava), Lallā or Lalleśvari (Kashmiri, Śaiva), Mīrā Bāī (Hindi, Vaiṣṇava), Bahiṇābāī (Marathi, Vaisnava), and Gaurībāī (Gujarati, Vaiṣṇava). Well-known works like *Periyapurāṇam* (Tamil) and *Śrī Mahābhaktavijayam* (available in Hindi, Marathi, and Tamil versions) should also be mentioned. For the sake of brevity I have used only 15 examples, which I consider representative and structurally typical in this paper.

I have looked at these saints' life stories not for the truth of historical fact, but for patterns in what is presented by the narrators.

[6]*The Laws of Manu* 9.3, trans. G. Buhler (Oxford: Clarendon Press, 1886). The whole chapter on the duties of husband and wife should be read with the lives of the women saints: rule after rule is broken. See especially 9.13, 21-22, 26-28, 83.

[7]Robert Levy, lecture given at the University of Chicago, May 1978.

[8]For example, the following poem:

People,
male and female,
blush when
a cloth covering their shame comes loose.
    When the lord of lives
lives drowned without a face
in the world, how can you be modest?

When all the world is the eye of the lord,
onlooking everywhere, what can you
cover and conceal?

Trans. Ramanujan, *Speaking of Śiva*, p. 131.

[9]Ibid., pp. 112-13.

[10]Eleanor Zelliott, lecture given at Carleton College, spring 1978.

[11]From *Śrī Mahābhaktivijayam* (Tamil version by Kukapriyai, Madras, 1958), pp. 100-13. According to one text, Purandharadāsa's name, before conversion, is Raghunātharāv; his wife's name is Lakṣmībāyi. He is a Kannada Vaiṣṇava saint and composer who probably lived in the sixteenth century. Independently, R. Blake Michael has pointed to a similar pattern in the lives of two Vīraśaiva saints' wives. "Kayakave Kailasa," unpublished paper, 1979.

[12]For a brief life of Allama, see *Speaking of Śiva*, pp. 143-48.

[13]For the distinction between *akam* ("interior, self, household," etc.) and *puram* ("exterior, other, public space," etc.), see my *The Interior Landscape* (Bloomington: Indiana University Press, 1967), p. 101.

[14]Margaret Mead, *Male and Female* (New York: William Morrow, 1949), p. 119. The theme of male envy of the female, which Mead, Bettelheim, and others have studied, is not treated here. See "Men, Women, and Saints," note 4 above.

[15]N. Chodorow, "Family Structure and Feminine Personality," in M. Rosaldo

and L. Lamphere, eds., *Women, Culture, and Society* (Stanford: Stanford University Press, 1974).

[16]Such patterns of secure continuity with the mother-figure might be relevant to the fact that in many cultures, including the American and the Indian, the male is the "marked" category, the female the "unmarked." The male, in differentiating himself, cannot take over female clothing, whereas females can don variations of male clothing. Male saints, however, take on female personae (often clothing) and attitudes, because they are in a very special context of great intensity. The lack of security may also account for the wide variety of stances in male saint figures, as if they were casting about for identities. This makes a composite type harder to specify.

[17]See H. Papanek, "Purdah: Separate Worlds and Symbolic Shelter," *Comparative Studies in Society and History* 15:3 (1973), pp. 289-325, and Lloyd A. and Margaret C. Fallers, "Sex Roles in Edremit," in J.G. Péristiany, ed., *Mediterranean Family Structures* (New York: Cambridge University Press, 1976).

Glossary

abalā "without strength"; word for woman that connotes her weakness and helplessness.

ācārya person of exemplary conduct and authoritative doctrine; title given by Śrī Vaiṣṇavas (q.v.) to a guru who provides initiation into the practices and teachings of the community and authoritative expositions of sacred knowledge. Also an honorific title for several Śrī Vaiṣṇava theologians.

acit that which is not conscious; considered threefold in Śrī Vaiṣṇava theology: "matter," consisting of the three *guṇas* (q.v.), *śuddha sattva,* the pure substance of which the Lord's body and abode are formed, and *kāla,* time; cf. *cit.*

advaita "non-dual," a philosophy declaring the complete unity of the godhead and all its "creation," associated especially with Śaṃkara (ca. 800 A.D.) and his school.

Ādyakālī the primordial form of the Goddess in her dark aspect.

ahaṃkāra "the I-maker," egocentricity, individualized identity, the notions of "I" and "mine."

aiśvarya "lordliness, majesty"; the exalted aspects of divinity largely veiled by the sweet beauty (*mādhurya,* q.v.) of Krishna as a child and youth in Braj (q.v.).

āḻvār one who is submerged in the qualities of the Lord (*bhagavān*); title given by Śrī Vaiṣṇavas to the twelve poet-saints of the 7th-10th centuries whose 4,000 Tamil verses they acknowledge to be the vernacular equivalent of the Sanskrit Vedas.

amaṅgala inauspicious; cf. *maṅgala.*

amṛta "immortal," the nectar of immortality, for which the gods and the demons contended and which the gods won.

ānanda "bliss"; with *sat* (being) and *cit* (consciousness), one of three predicates of *brahman* (q.v.) considered by Advaita Vedāntins to constitute the essence of ultimate reality; viewed by *bhaktas* (q.v.) both as an essential characteristic of the Lord and as the fruit of spiritual realization.

anuloma "with the grain," of actions that accord with the rules of hierarchy; cf. *pratiloma.*

apsaras water nymph, heavenly courtesan at the court of Indra.

āratī a graceful form of worship (*pūjā,* q.v.) in which an officiant waves a tray of lighted oil lamps or another object (e.g., a fan) in circular patterns before the deity, often to the accompaniment of a song or the ringing of a bell.

aṣṭamī the eighth lunar day (*tithi,* q.v.) of each lunar fortnight (*pakṣa,* q.v.), consecrated to the Goddess.

aśubha inauspicious; cf. *śubha.*

asura "lord" among men or gods; demon, enemy of the gods; the great feat of Durgā (q.v.) celebrated on Dassera (q.v.) is her vanquishing of the water-buffalo demon Mahiṣāsura (q.v.).

aurat the most unmarked Perso-Arabic word for woman in Hindi; the term is frequently used by contemporary poets.

avatar (Skt *avatāra*) "descent," i.e., of a deity, who assumes an embodied form. The *avatāras* of Viṣṇu are his numerous divine "descents" into the phenomenal world. Cf. *avataraṇa.* Compare incarnation.

avataraṇa "descent"; the act of descending, as that of the river Gaṅgā from heaven to earth.

Baladeva "deity possessing strength," a name of Krishna's elder brother, also known as Balarāma and Saṃkarṣaṇa; ancient snake deity (*nāga,* q.v.) worshipped at Purī together with Jagannātha (q.v.) and Subhadrā (q.v.).

Balarāma the elder brother of Krishna, also called Saṃkarṣaṇa and Baladeva (q.v.)

bhagavān "venerable one," "lord"; applied especially to Krishna; for Gauḍīya Vaiṣṇavas, ultimate reality (said by Jīva Gosvāmī to be higher than *brahman* [q.v.] and *paramātman*), source and maintainer of the universe, and abode of all *śaktis* (q.v.).

Bhāgavata one devoted to the Lord (*bhagavān*); a movement of such devotees which began perhaps as early as 200 B.C. in North India and whose cultic focus was on supremely transcendent Nārāyaṇa identified with Viṣṇu and Krishna, and called *bhagavān;* the movement spread to South India in the early centuries A.D.

Bhāī-dūj (Skt Bhrātṛ-dvitīya) the second day of the bright half of Kārttika, on which the goddess Yamunā is worshipped with lighted oil lamps, theoretically with her brother Yama.

bhairavī "frightful," the terrible aspect of the Goddess.

bhakta devotee, one who loves and worships a personal deity, often passionately.

bhakti loving devotion; a spiritual path advocated by Krishna in the *Bhagavadgītā* that flowered into a popular movement throughout India in medieval times. Its main forms are Vaiṣṇava (directed toward Viṣṇu, often in one or another of his two major *avatāras,* Krishna or Rāma); Śaiva (directed toward Śiva), and Śākta (directed toward the Goddess).

bhāva emotional state; in Sanskrit aesthetic theory, that which, evoked and refined through an aesthetic medium, serves as the basis for *rasa* (q.v.), ultimate aesthetic experience; one of the devotional modes exemplified by the close associates of Krishna in Vraja (q.v.). Rūpa Gosvāmī and others enumerated five such *bhāvas—śānta, dāsya* (q.v.), *sakhya, vātsalya,* and *mādhurya* (q.v.)—and these have continued to serve as the basis of much Gauḍīya Vaiṣṇava devotion down to the present day.

brahman the absolute; ultimate reality, usually understood as impersonal (the word is neuter) and without attributes (*nirguṇa,* q.v.), although it is also described as pure being (*sat*), consciousness (*cit*), and bliss (*ānanda,* q.v.).

Braj (Skt Vraja) the pastoral country around Mathurā, in present-day U.P., in which Braj Bhāṣā is spoken. The entire region is a pilgrimage center for Vaiṣṇavas, for it is identified with the purāṇic Vraja, the place of Krishna's childhood and youth. The term is also shorthand for the language of Braj (Braj Bhāṣā).

Brindāvan (Skt Vṛndāvana) town and pilgrimage center near Mathurā in the heart of Braj (q.v.), to which Caitanya is said to have deputed the six *gosvāmīs* (q.v.). The town is filled with Vaiṣṇava temples and devotees of Krishna. Also written Vrindāban.

Caitanya a passionate devotee of Jagannātha whose ecstatic devotion touched off a wave of *bhakti* (q.v.) throughout eastern India and resulted in the establishment of the Gauḍīya Vaiṣṇava sect. He has been regarded variously as an incarnation of Krishna, of Rādhā, and of the two together in the closest possible embrace.

Caṇḍī "the fierce one," a name of Durgā especially in the form in which she destroyed the water buffalo demon Mahiṣāsura (q.v.), a deed celebrated in the *Devī-māhātmya* or *Caṇḍī-pāṭha* and in the festival of Dassera (q.v.).

Caṇḍidās the name given to three or more Bengali poets who wrote on the love of Rādhā and Krishna, especially the earliest of these, Baḍu Caṇḍidās, the author of the *Śrīkṛṣṇakīrtan.*

cātaka a bird that drinks only rainwater and whose poignant cry, "piu, piu," is heard from springtime to the coming of the monsoon rains.

Chāyāvād a group of romantic Hindi poets in the 1920's and 30's who wrote of spiritual love and portrayed woman in correspondingly abstract and universal terms, as *nārī* (q.v.).

cit that which is conscious; cf. *acit.*

Dassera (Skt *Daśahara*) the culminating festival of Navarātrī (q.v.), in which Durgā (q.v.) is honored as the slayer of the water buffalo demon Mahiṣāsura (q.v.).

dāsya "servitude," the devotional attitude in which the Lord is regarded as a beloved master; one of the five primary emotional relations (*bhāvas,* q.v.) enumerated by Rūpa Gosvāmī; considered by Gauḍīya Vaiṣṇavas to be an essential element in all true devotion; in the *Brahmavaivarta Purāṇa* it is the attitude most emphasized.

Devakī wife of Vasudeva and mother of Krishna.

devī "goddess," the most general name for feminine divinity; often used to refer to the wife of Śiva (Pārvatī, Kālī, etc.) but applied to other goddesses as well; or specifically, *the* Goddess, ultimate reality conceived as feminine.

Devī-māhātmya a medieval text, part of the *Mārkaṇḍeya Purāṇa,* narrating the victory of Devī or Durgā over the water buffalo demon Mahiṣāsura (q.v.); also called the *Caṇḍī-pāṭha,* this text is recited during the festival of Navarātrī (Durgā-pūjā).

dhām (Skt *dhāma*) "abode," one of many places of pilgrimage where the deity is said to have a permanent abode.

dharma righteousness, virtue, duty, "law," the social and spiritual obligations of every Hindu; the order of the cosmos, including norms of social and ritual action.

Dīvālī (a short form of the Sanskrit Dīpāvalī, "row of lights") the festival of lights, a cluster of feasts named from the offering of lighted oil lamps to Yama (q.v.), god of death. During this festival the goddess of wealth, Lakṣmī (q.v.), is worshipped along with Kuvera, (q.v.), her male counterpart.

Durgā "the inaccessible one," the fair war-goddess spouse of Śiva whose victory over the water buffalo demon Mahiṣāsura (q.v.) is celebrated in the festival of Dassera (q.v.). The celebration of this event, known especially in Bengal as Durgā-pūjā, is the most important festival of the year in Bengal.

ekādaśī the eleventh lunar day (*tithi,* q.v.) of each lunar fortnight (*pakṣa,* q.v.), a fast day for many Hindus.

Ekānaṃśā "the single, portionless one," the name of the new moon and of a deity identified with Durgā (q.v.).

Gaṇeśa the elephant-headed son of Śiva and Pārvatī, invoked by Hindus especially at the beginning of all undertakings as the lord who removes obstacles.

Gauḍīya Sampradāya "Bengali" school or sect of Vaiṣṇavas established by Caitanya (q.v.) and his immediate disciples in the early sixteenth century; Gauḍīya Vaiṣṇavas are especially numerous in Greater Bengal and in Brindāvan (q.v.).

Gaurī "fair one," a name of the wife of Śiva in her radiant form. It is the goddess Gaurī who presides over the festival of Annakūṭa or Govardhana-pūjā.

ghāṭ "step," the steps leading down to a sacred river or temple tank, a place pilgrims may bathe.

ghī clarified butter, poured into the fire as a ritual offering in Vedic ceremonies.

Gītagovinda the twelfth-century dramatic lyrical poem of Jayadeva (q.v.) that celebrates the love of Rādhā and Krishna. It inspired a stream of poetic and dramatic compositions in Sanskrit and the North Indian vernacular languages during the medieval period.

gopa "protector of cows," cowherd, used especially to refer to the men and boys of the pastoral community in which Krishna grows up.

Gopāla "protector of cows," cowherd; an epithet of Krishna, used in particular to designate the hero of a cycle of purāṇic stories centering on Krishna's childhood and youth among the cowherds of Braj (q.v.), as opposed to the prince of the *Mahābhārata* account.

gopī cowherd woman of Vraja (q.v.); in the Purāṇas (q.v.) and later poetry and dramas these woman lavish maternal affection upon the baby Krishna and become the amorous companions of his youth. Their intense longing for their beloved in his absence represents and inspires the yearning of the human soul for the divine. Preeminent among the *gopīs* is Rādhā.

gosvāmī "lord of cows," "master of the senses"; honorific title applied especially to six learned disciples of Caitanya who lived in Brindāvan (q.v.) in the sixteenth century and wrote the major authoritative Sanskrit treatises of the Gauḍīya Sampradāya (q.v.), and also to subsequent revered teachers of that school.

Govardhana the mountain in Braj (q.v.) that was lifted by Krishna to protect the cowherds and cattle from the torrential rain unleashed by Indra; terms Girirāj, "king of mountains," and worshipped especially by the pastoral castes in the festival of Annakūṭa or Govardhana-pūjā.

guṇa "thread," "quality"; in Sāṃkhya philosophy, one of three constituents or qualities of the phenomenal world (*prakṛti*, "nature," q.v.): *sattva* (goodness, purity), *rajas* (passion, energy), and *tamas* (darkness, lethargy). Ultimate reality is often said to be devoid of *guṇas* (*nirguṇa*, q.v.).

hlādinī śakti "blissful potency," the bliss-filled and joy-giving quality of the Lord (*bhagavān*, q.v.); identified with Rādhā in certain tantric works and by the Brindāvan *gosvāmīs* (q.v.).

īśvara "lord," whether earthly or divine; a personalistic designation of ultimate reality used especially of Śiva; the term emphasizes the Lord's power and supremacy. Cf. *bhagavān*.

jagadambā "mother of the universe," an epithet of the great Goddess.

Jagannātha "Lord of the world," an epithet of Viṣṇu especially in the primitive iconic form in which he is worshipped at Purī, together with his brother Baladeva (q.v.) and his sister Ekānaṃśā-Durgā, also called Subhadrā.

Jayadeva twelfth-century court poet of Lakṣmaṇa Sena of Bengal; author of the Sanskrit *Gītagovinda* (q.v.), a literary masterpiece that served as the fountainhead of a stream of Sanskrit and vernacular works celebrating the love of Rādhā and Krishna.

jīva an individual self or soul. In Śrī Vaiṣṇava (q.v.) theology, these are of three types: bound, liberated, and eternally liberated.

Kālā "the black one," the dark form of the Goddess, also called Kālarūpiṇī or Kālī. (q.v.).

Kālī "the black one," the Goddess in a fearsome dark form, usually depicted with lolling tongue, a garland of human heads, and a girdle of human hands.

kāma desire, lust, orgasmic eroticism; personified as Kāmadeva, the god of love whose flower-arrows affected even the great Lord Śiva as he sat in meditation in the Himalayas.

kāma-śāstra "the science of erotics," a genre of textbooks on the art of erotic love.

kāminī "lovely one"; word for woman that emphasizes her desirability.

Kaṃsa tyrant king of the Mathurā region at the time of Krishna's birth, according to the purāṇic accounts; regarded as a demon (*asura*, q.v.) and slain by Krishna.

karma "action, work," one means or path to salvation (*karmamārga*); according to the law of *karma*, every action has its inevitable fruit (*phala*), either in this lifetime or in a future one.

Kātyāyanī a name of Durgā. It is Kātyāyanī to whom the *gopīs* (q.v.) in the purāṇic accounts pray and perform a penance in order that they may win Krishna as their husband.

kṛpā compassion, grace; an important aspect of Rādhā's redemptive role in the *Brahmavaivarta Purāṇa*. In Śrī Vaiṣṇava (q.v.) theology, the Lord's or Śrī's innate grace which is spontaneously bestowed on all creation; it is the initial grace with which the Lord creates the universe; cf. *prasāda*.

kṛṣṇa "dark," the second half (*pakṣa*, q.v.) of each lunar month, from full moon to new moon; cf. *śukla*.

Kuvera (also Kubera) god of wealth and guardian of the northern region; chief of the half-demon *yakṣas*, tree-spirits who guard hidden treasure; worshipped together with Lakṣmī (q.v.) during the festival of Dīvālī (q.v.).

lakṣaṇa-grantha genre of medieval Hindi poetic works, each of which consists of a list of definitions and illustrations of various elements in poetic theory.

Lakṣmī "good fortune," the goddess of wealth and beauty, in later mythology regarded as the wife of Viṣṇu or Nārāyaṇa; worshipped throughout India, especially by the Vaiśyas, during the festival of Dīvālī (q.v.).

līlā "play"; spontaneous, effortless action, especially that of the Lord in creating and maintaining the universe. The term is used especially by Vaiṣṇavas to designate the graceful actions of Krishna as well as dramas representing these actions. The Krishna plays performed by troupes from Braj are called *rās līlās*.

liṅga "characteristic," the male sexual organ; in particular, the phallic representation of Śiva, understood as symbolizing his transcendent, formless nature.

mādhurya "sweetness," the graceful beauty of divinity considered to be most fully manifest in Krishna's form and actions among the cowherds of Braj (q.v.); also the amorous emotion (*bhāva*, q.v.) represented especially by the *gopīs* (q.v.) in their love for the youthful Krishna.

Mahābhārata the longer of the two great Sanskrit epics, composed ca. 300 B.C. - 300 A.D. In some 100,000 verses, it narrates the story of the great war between the Pāṇḍavas and the Kauravas.

mahāmāyā "great illusion"; one possessed of great deluding and creative power (*māyā*, q.v.); identified with Devī (q.v.) in the *Devī-māhātmya*.

māhātmya "greatness," a genre of epic and purāṇic literature that extols the greatness and power of a deity, a ritual observance, or a place of pilgrimage.

Mahiṣāsura the water buffalo demon, the great adversary of Durgā (q.v.) whose death at her hands is celebrated in the *Devī-māhātmya* (or *Caṇḍī-pāṭha*) and in the festival of Dassera (q.v.), the culmination of Navarātrī (q.v.) (Durgā-pūjā).

maithuna "forming a pair," an erotic couple; sexual union.

mantra sacred Vedic formula. These have been employed in a variety of ritual and meditative contexts from the time of the Rig Veda (ca. 1200 B.C.E.).

māyā the mysterious (female) creative power of the Lord, sometimes personified as his consort; in Advaita Vedānta (q.v.), the illusory superimposition of the phenomenal universe onto the one absolute reality (*brahman*, q.v.); a force represented as both deluding and redemptive; identified with Rādhā in the *Brahmavaivarta Purāṇa*.

mokṣa "liberation, release," in some Hindu contexts, salvation, freedom from *saṃsāra* (q.v.), the endless round of birth, death, and rebirth. The last of the four goals of a human being (*puruṣārtha*), the remaining three being righteousness (*dharma*, q.v.), material well-being (*ārtha*), and pleasure (*kāma*, q.v.). Certain theistic groups in India modify or reject the ideal of *mokṣa*, replacing it with *bhakti* (q.v.) or *prema* (q.v.).

Murugan (Murukaṉ) probably the most ancient major god of the Tamil people and the most important single recipient of personal devotion in local Tamil cult activities today. Long assimilated into the Sanskritic pantheon as Skanda or Kārttikeya, yet far more important in the religious life of the South than Skanda has ever been in the North.

nāga "snake"; a class of ancient Indian aquatic deities, serpents who dwell in pools, streams, and tanks and control the realms of water. Balarāma (q.v.), the elder brother of Krishna, is represented as a *nāga.*

nakh-śikh a literary genre consisting of poems describing the human figure "from the toe to the top of the head."

Nanda foster father of Krishna; chief of the cowherd community in which Krishna grows up.

nārī the most abstract Hindi and Sanskrit word for woman; the term preferred by the Chāyāvād poets (q.v.).

Naṭarāja "king of the dance," an epithet of Śiva as the Lord whose cosmic dance creates, sustains, and destroys the universe.

Navarātrī "nine nights," the most important festival in honor of the great Goddess. It culminates in the celebration of Dassera (q.v.), in which Durgā is honored as Mahiṣāsuramardiṇī, the slayer of the water buffalo demon Mahiṣāsura (q.v.). In Bengal and elsewhere the festival as a whole is referred to as Durgā-pūjā.

nāyaka hero, ideal courtly lover; identified with Krishna in *rīti* poetry (q.v.) and by Gauḍīya Vaiṣṇavas (q.v.) beginning with Rūpa Gosvāmī.

nāyikā heroine, ideal courtly lover; identified with Rādhā in *rīti* poetry (q.v.) and by Gauḍīya Vaiṣṇavas (q.v.) beginning with Rūpa Gosvāmī.

nirguṇa "without qualities (*guṇas,* q.v.)"; a designation commonly applied to ultimate reality, whether that reality is conceived as transpersonal (i.e., as the neuter *brahman,* q.v.) or as personal (e.g., as Viṣṇu or Krishna); in a Vaiṣṇava context, *nirguṇa* is usually understood to mean devoid of *limiting* attributes (e.g., by Rāmānuja, 11th-12th c.).

pakṣa "wing, side," half a lunar month (cf. *kṛṣṇa, śukla*). Each *pakṣa* consists of fifteen lunar days (*tithi,* q.v.).

Pañcarātra: a tantric liturgical and theological school (*āgama*) providing rituals for the devout service of the Glorious One; a branch of the Bhāgavata movement that in general was socially inclusive and thus "popular."

parakīyā "belonging to another," a woman married to someone other than her lover; a type of heroine in Sanskrit poetics. Rādhā is usually depicted in Indian literature as a *parakīyā* heroine, although theologians such as Rūpa Gosvāmī and his nephew Jīva point out that in reality Rādhā belongs to Krishna eternally as his *hlādinī śakti* (q.v.). Cf. *svakīyā.*

pati lord, master, husband.

piṇḍa ball of food offered to the ancestors (*pitṛ,* q.v.) in the *śrāddha* ceremony (q.v.).

pīṭha "seat," one of many sites of the worship of the Goddess.

pitṛ "father," an ancestor to whom water libations and food offerings are made, in ceremonies known as *śrāddha*.

prakṛti "nature," the phenomenal world; in Sāṃkhya philosophy, insentient yet active matter, as opposed to quiescent spirit (*puruṣa*, q.v.), but also including much of what in the West is termed psychological (e.g., emotions, dispositions, motives). It has three constituents (*guṇas*, q.v.). The term is feminine, in contrast to *puruṣa* (q.v.), which is masculine, and it is often personified; the *Brahmavaivarta Purāṇa* identifies the goddess Prakṛti with Rādhā.

prasāda "purity," grace; food left over after being offered to a deity or deities, distributed to devotees. Śrī Vaiṣṇavas (q.v.) use the term to designate salvific grace, as distinct from initial grace (*kṛpā*, q.v.), except in Śrī, in whom the two are identical.

pratiloma "against the grain," of actions that violate the rules of hierarchy; cf. *anuloma*.

prema love, affection; specifically, love devoid of egocentricity, hierarchy, and fertility.

Purāṇa "ancient"; any of numerous medieval Sanskrit compendia of myth and ritual lore. The Purāṇas have been important "scriptural" sources for *bhakti* communities throughout India.

puruṣa "the male"; in Sāṃkhya philosophy, pure sentience or unchanging Spirit, in contrast with the evolving phenomenal world (*prakṛti*, q.v.). The liberation of each individual's *puruṣa* from *prakṛti* is the goal of the classical systems of Sāṃkhya and Yoga.

puruṣakāra mediator; for Śrī Vaiṣṇavas (q.v.) Śrī is the ultimate *puruṣakāra*.

Rādhā consort of Krishna; the most celebrated of the *gopīs* (q.v.) and the one most favored by Krishna; interpreted theologically especially by Gauḍīya Vaiṣṇavas (q.v.) as his *hlādinī śakti* (q.v.).

rajas colorless female sexual fluid produced during intercourse; menstrual blood; the atmosphere; the second of the three *guṇas* (q.v.), that of passion.

ramaṇī "delightful one"; Hindi and Sanskrit word for woman that emphasizes her enjoyableness.

Rāmāyaṇa the shorter of the two great Sanskrit epics, composed ca. 200 B.C.-200 A.D. and attributed to the poet Vālmīki. It narrates the story of Rāma's search for his wife, Sītā, who is abducted by the demon Rāvaṇa and kept captive in Laṅkā.

rās (Skt *rāsa*) the circle dance of Krishna with Rādhā and the other *gopīs* (q.v.); enacted by troupes from Braj (q.v.) in performances known as *rās līlās* (q.v.).

rasa "flavor, liquid extract"; aesthetic experience; for the eleventh-century Kashmir Śaiva Abhinavagupta, one of nine universal human possibilities evoked by an aesthetic medium that prefigure the ultimate state of universal consciousness. Rūpa Gosvāmī (16th c.) analyzed the highest form of *bhakti* (q.v.) as *rasa,* delineating five primary *bhaktirasas* that correspond to five emotional relations (*bhāvas,* q.v.) of the devotee to the divine.

Rig Veda the most ancient sacred book of India (ca. 1200 B.C.). It contains more than a thousand hymns to a variety of gods, many of them closely connected with natural phenomena, prominent among whom are Indra, god of the thunderstorm, Agni, fire, and Soma, the intoxicating, hallucinogenic drink made from the Soma plant.

rīti a stylized school of secular court poetry in Braj (q.v.) that employed the theme of the love between Rādhā and Krishna, but treated it in a completely non-devotional manner.

Rohiṇī mother of Krishna's elder brother, Balarāma.

Śākta pertaining to Śakti, the Goddess; worship of the Goddess; a devotee of the Goddess.

śakti energy, power, especially the creative energy that generates and continues to activate the universe. Conceived as female and often personified as the consort of a male deity or as the dynamic, independent Goddess.

saṃsāra the phenomenal universe; the endless round of birth, death, and rebirth from which Hindus seek release, *mokṣa* (q.v.).

saṃskāra one of the numerous Hindu life-cycle rituals that stretch from before birth to after death.

saṃyoga "union"; love-in-union, the state of being united with one's beloved. As a term for union with God, *saṃyoga* also represents the goal of certain forms of *bhakti* (q.v.).

śaraṇāgati taking refuge in the Lord, surrendering oneself, also used for the cultic act of initiation into the Śrī Vaiṣṇava (q.v.) community.

Satī "virtuous woman"; the wife of Śiva, who burned herself upon the death of her husband. Anglicized as suttee, the term came to signify the practice of self-immolation by a widow on the funeral pyre of her husband.

śeṣa "remainder"; one who is owned, a vassal, slave. Used by Śrī Vaiṣṇavas (q.v.) to designate the human soul, who is owned by the Lord.

śeṣī "owner," used by Śrī Vaiṣṇavas (q.v.) to designate Viṣṇu. Vatakalai Śrī Vaiṣṇavas apply the term to Śrī as well.

sevā "service," as that rendered by a servant to a master or mistress; an important component of *bhakti* (q.v.) as represented in the Purāṇas and later devotional texts; especially prominent in the devotional attitude of servitude (*dāsya,* q.v.).

Smārta a follower of Brāhmaṇical tradition, especially that of Śaṃkara;

these worship five great deities: Durgā, Śiva, Gaṇeśa, Viṣṇu, and Sūrya.

śrāddha ceremony performed periodically in honor of the ancestors (*pitṛ*, q.v.), in which they are offered balls of food (*piṇḍa*, q.v.).

Śrī "radiance, splendor," the deity and consort of Viṣṇu who embodies the qualities of prosperity and beauty; worshipped especially by the Śrī Vaiṣṇavas as inseparable from Viṣṇu.

Śrī Vaiṣṇava: one who seeks access to Viṣṇu by first approaching his divine consort, Śrī or Lakṣmī; an initiate into the tantric sect of that name, which acknowledges the authority of the *ālvārs*, their Tamil poems, the Pañcarātra liturgical school, and the unbroken lineage of *ācāryas* who descend down to the present from the Lord himself; the first of the human *ācāryas* was Nāthamuni and the most important was Rāmānuja.

śṛṅgāra rasa the erotic "mood" (*rasa*, q.v.), the first and especially for drama most important of the eight *rasas* enumerated by Bharata in the *Nāṭyaśāstra* (q.v.). Transmuted in the theory of Rūpa Gosvāmī into *madhura bhaktirasa*, the "sweet devotional mood" realized in the love of Krishna and the *gopīs*, especially Rādhā.

stotra hymn of praise to a deity, written in verse and often sung or recited metrically.

strī the most unmarked Sanskrit word for woman in Hindi, much used in contemporary poetry.

śubha auspicious; cf. *aśubha*.

Subhadrā epic name of Durgā (q.v.) or Ekānaṃśā (q.v.), the third deity, with Jagannātha (q.v.) and Balarāma (q.v.), of the trio worshipped in the great temple of Jagannātha in Purī.

śukla "bright, light," the first half (*pakṣa*, q.v.) of each lunar month, from new moon to full moon; cf. *kṛṣṇa*.

svakīyā "one's own," a woman who is the wife of her lover; a type of heroine in Sanskrit poetics. Cf. *parakīyā*.

svarūpa "essential form," the true form of a deity. Certain representations of Krishna are known as *svarūpa* icons.

tāṇḍava one of the styles of dance performed by Śiva. Unlike its opposite, the slow, graceful *lāsya*, the *tāṇḍava* is an energetic style danced by Śiva at the destruction of the universe.

tantra a "left-hand" form of religion, often purposely unorthodox, in which the devotee visualizes himself or herself as the deity; tantric practice often involved esoteric sexual rituals and the worship of the Goddess (cf. Śākta).

tapas "heat," the fervor of a meditating seer won through intense self-discipline, a source of great spiritual and physical power.

Thug one of a caste of stranglers who murdered travellers in India and worshipped the goddess Kālī.

tīrtha "ford, crossing," a sacred pilgrimage place where the river of earthly life may be forded to reach the "far shore."

Tiruvāymoḻi one of the four works of Nammāḻvār and probably the single most important work in the collection of the *āḻvārs'* hymns.

tithi a lunar day (thirtieth part of a lunar month of somewhat more than twenty-seven solar days); the eighth (*aṣṭamī,* q.v.) *tithis* of the dark and the bright fortnights (*pakṣa,* q.v.) are consecrated respectively to Kālī and Durgā (qq.v.).

Tulasī a plant (the basil shrub) sacred to Viṣṇu; a goddess whose marriage to Viṣṇu is celebrated shortly after the festival of his awakening from sleep (Devotthāna or Prabodhinī), at the end of the rainy season.

upāya the way or means ordained for securing the result that one desires. Of two types according to Deśika: that which is undertaken by the individual (*sādhyopāya*) and that which is ever present in the form of Viṣṇu's or Śrī's grace (*siddhopāya*).

Vaikhānasa a non-tantric, "Vedic" liturgical and theological school (*āgama*) for the devout service of the Lord; a branch of the Bhāgavata movement that was socially exclusive and strictly speaking not Śrī Vaiṣṇava, though it provided the liturgy for many Śrī Vaiṣṇava temples.

Vaḷḷi a South Indian goddess of ancient origin, sweetheart and later wife of the god Murugan; although a secondary spouse, she is much loved by the populace of Tamilnadu.

vāmācāra "left-handed" practice or way; cf. *tantra.*

Vasudeva father of Krishna.

Vāsudeva "son of Vasudeva," a name of Krishna.

Vedānta "end of the Veda" in two senses: the final portion and ultimate significance; name given to the Upaniṣads and philosophies derived from them, which usually have a mystic, monistic vision of God and the universe.

Vidyāpati Maithili poet of the fifteenth century who wrote graceful lyrics on the love of Rādhā and Krishna; especially prominent in eastern India, particularly in Bengal and Bihar.

viparītarati inverse sexual union.

vīra hero; male child, son; among the Coorgs of South India, an ancestor who has died a violent death.

viraha separation from one's beloved; a condition of Rādhā and Krishna described in minute detail by devotional and secular poets.

vīrya manliness, heroism; male seed, semen.

viyoga "separation; love-in-separation," the state of being apart from one's beloved, characterized by intense yearning and eager anticipation. As a religious ideal the term is contrasted with *yoga* by a number of *bhakti* poets, including Sūr Dās (16th c.).

Vraja cowherd settlement; in the Purāṇas, the term designates the cowherd village of Nanda, in which Krishna grows up. Cf. Braj.

Vṛndāvana name of a forest near Gokula in Braj where, according to tradition, Krishna played his enchanting flute, luring the *gopīs* (q.v.) from their homes to frolic with him in the field and groves. Cf. Brindāvan.

yakṣa a class of ancient Indian life-energy deities, ordinarily associated with vegetation, particularly trees.

Yama "twin"; the god of death, the inauspicious deity who presides over the ancestors (*pitṛ*, q.v.); regarded as the first human being, the son of Vivasvat (the sun) and his wife Saraṇyū; worshipped with lighted lamps during the festival of Dīvālī (q.v.).

Yamunā (also Jumna) with the Ganges one of two great sacred rivers that flow eastward across the plains of North India; it waters the Braj country and is closely associated with Krishna, whose dark color it shares and many of whose childhood exploits take place near or in its blessed waters. It is revered especially by Vaiṣṇavas as Yamunā-devī.

Yaśodā a cowherd woman (*gopī*, q.v.) of Vraja (q.v.), wife of Nanda and foster mother of Krishna. Her adoring love serves as the highest model of parental affection (*vātsalya bhāva*).

yogamāyā the female embodiment of the divine power of emanation manifest in the phenomenal world; personified as a goddess and identified with Durgā. Cf. *yoganidrā*.

yoganidrā "the sleep of yoga," Lord Viṣṇu's state of consciousness during the universal dissolution at the end of each cosmic cycle; personified as a goddess and identified with Durgā. Cf. *yogamāyā*.

yoni female sexual organ, a representation of the Goddess; the *yoni* in conjunction with the *liṅga* (q.v.) symbolizes the female aspect of the universe, the *śakti* (q.v.) of the great Lord Śiva.

Selected Bibliography

Note: The bibliography has been compiled from entries submitted by the contributors to the volume. Initials indicate the source of the comments for each annotated entry; DMW represents Donna Wulff, DW represents David Wulff.

1. Primary Sources in Indian Languages

Bhāgavata Purāṇa, with the commentary of Śrīdhara. Bombay, 1832.

Bhāgavata Purāṇa. Bombay: Veṅkaṭeśvara Press, 1910.

Deśika, Vedānta. *Catuḥślokibhāṣyam, Stotraratnabhāṣyam, Gadyatraya-bhāṣyañ ca.* Edited by Chettaloor V. Srivatsankacharyar. Madras: Venkatesa Agraharam, 1968. Deśika's thirteenth-century Sanskrit commentary on two hymns of the tenth-century *ācārya* Yāmuna, one of which is to Śrī, and on the *gadyas* of Rāmānuja. (VN)

Deśika, Vedānta. *Cillarai Rahasyaṅkal.* Volume 1. Edited by Śrī Rāmatēcikācāryar Svāmī. Kumbakonam: Oppiliyappan Sanniti, 1972. The "minor secrets," brief works expounding the three verses of "secrets" sacred to Śrī Vaiṣṇavas, in *Maṇipravāla* in a combination of Tamil and Sanskrit scripts. (VN)

Deśika, Vedānta. *Rahasyatrayasāram.* 2 volumes. Edited by Śrī Rāmatēcikācāryar Svāmī. Kumbakonam: Oppiliyappan Sanniti, 1961. A basic manual of Śrī Vaiṣṇava theology, in *Maṇipravāla* in a combination of Tamil and Sanskrit scripts. Relatively inaccessible, but by far the best edition of this important work. (VN)

Deśika, Vedānta. *Śrī Tēcika Stotramālā.* 2 volumes. Edited by Śrī Rāmatēcikācāryar Svāmī. Kumbokonam: Oppiliyappan Sanniti, 1970. Sanskrit hymns of Deśika with a Tamil commentary by the editor. (VN)

Jīva Gosvāmī. *Bhāgavata-sandarbha.* 2 volumes. Edited by Purīdās. Brindavan: Haridās Śarmā, 1951. Contains the six treatises popularly known as *Ṣaṭ-sandarbha,* which constitute the central work of Gauḍīya Vaiṣṇava philosophy. The first four treatises deal with the nature of Absolute Reality and its various manifestations; the fifth details the path of *bhakti;* and the last describes the *summum bonum—prīti—*the transcendental aesthetic experience. (SG)

Jīva Gosvāmī. *Gopāla Campū.* Edited by Purīdās. Mymensingh: Sacīnātha Rāyacaudhurī, 1947. An elaborate work in mixed prose and verse, describing the life of Krishna from his celestial manifestation in Goloka through his childhood and adolescence in Vraja to his adult life as the ruler of Dvārakā and his ultimate return to Vraja. (SG)

Kṛṣṇadāsa Kavirāja. *Caitanyacaritāmṛta.* Edited with a commentary by Rādhāgovinda Nāth. 6 volumes. Fourth edition. Calcutta: Sadhana Prakashani, 1958.

Mahābhārata. Poona: Bhandarkar Oriental Research Institute, 1933-69. The critical edition of the Sanskrit text, including its "appendix," the *Harivaṃśa.* (DMW)

Mārkandeya Purāṇa. Edited by Swāmī Jagadīśvarānanda. Madras, 1953.

Matsya Purāṇa. Edited by Rāma Śarmā Ācārya. Bareli: Saṃskṛti Saṃsthāna, 1970.

Nālāyira Tivyap Pirapantam. Edited by P.P. Annankaracaryar. Madras: V.M. Tēvanātan, 1971. A collection of approximately 4,000 Tamil verses by the twelve *āḻvārs.* (VN)

Rāmāyaṇa [The Vālmīki Rāmāyaṇa]. Baroda: Oriental Institute, 1960-75. The critical edition of the Sanskrit text. (CD)

Rūpa Gosvāmī. *Bhaktirasāmṛtasindhu,* with the commentaries of Jīva Gosvāmī, Mukundadāsa Gosvāmī, and Viśvanātha Cakravartī. Second edition. Edited by Haridās Dās. Navadvīp: Haribol Kuṭī, 1961. (Original edition 1948). Rūpa's *magnum opus* on *bhakti,* conceived in a fresh manner through the elaborate categories of Sanskrit poetics. The pervasive influence of this work especially on Gauḍīya Vaiṣṇava religious life continues to the present day. (DMW)

Rūpa Gosvāmī. *Lalitamādhava-nāṭaka.* Edited by Purīdās. Mymensingh: Sacīnātha Rāyacaudhurī, 1947.

Rūpa Gosvāmī. *Ujjvalanīlamaṇi,* with the commentaries of Jīva Gosvāmī and Viśvanātha Cakravartī. Edited by Purīdās. Brindavan: Haridās Śarmā, 1954. A supplement to Rūpa's *Bhaktirasāmṛtasindhu,* this work, the basic treatise of Vaiṣṇava aesthetics, explores the love of the supreme hero and heroine, Krishna and Rādhā, through all their varied moods. (SG)

Rūpa Gosvāmī. *Ujjvalanīlamaṇi [The Ujjvalanīlamaṇi by Shrī Rūpagoswāmī],* with the commentaries of Jīvagoswāmī and Vishvanātha Chakravarty. Edited by Durgaprasād and Wāsudev Laxman. Second edition. Kāvyamālā 95. Bombay: Nirṇaya Sāgar Press, 1932.

Rūpa Gosvāmī. *Vidagdhamādhava-nāṭaka [The Vidagdhamādhava of Śrī Rūpadeva Gosvāmī,* with a commentary*].* Edited by Bhavadatta Śāstrī and Kāsīnāth Pāṇḍurang Parab. Kāvyamālā 81. Second edition. Bombay: Nirṇaya Sāgar Press, 1937. (Original edition, 1903).

Sarasvatī, Prabodhānanda. *Śrī Rādhārasasudhānidhi.* Edited by Purīdās. Brindavan: Haridās Śarmā, 1953. A collection of 272 verses in praise of Rādhā, describing her nature, personality, and diverse moods. (SG)

Sūr Dās. *Sūr Sāgar.* Edited by 'Ratnākar' *et al.* 2 volumes. Varanasi: Nāgarīpracāriṇī Sabhā, 1972, 1976.

Viṣṇu Purāṇa, with the commentary of Śrīdhara. Calcutta: Vaṅgavāsī Steam Machine Press, 1887.

Viṣṇu Purāṇa, with the commentary Vaiṣṇavākūṭacandrikā. Bombay: Gopala Narayana and Co., 1902.

2. Primary Sources in Translation

Āḻvārs. Hymns of the Āḻvārs. Translated by J.S.M. Hooper. Calcutta: Association Press, 1929.

Bhagavadgītā. Translated by Franklin Edgerton. Harvard Oriental Series, Volumes 38 and 39. Cambridge, Massachusetts: Harvard University Press, 1944.

Bhagavadgītā [The Bhagavad-Gītā, with a Commentary based on the original sources*].* Translated by R.C. Zaehner. London: Oxford University Press, 1969.

Bhāgavata Purāṇa [Le Bhāgavata Purāṇa]. 5 volumes. Translated into French by Eugène Burnouf *et al.* Paris: Imprimerie Royale, 1840-98.

Bhāgavata Purāṇa [The Srimad Bhagvatam of Krishna-Dwaipayana Vyasa]. Second Edition. 2 volumes. New Delhi: Munshiram Manoharlal, 1973. (Original edition in 5 volumes, 1929.)

Bhāgavata Purāṇa. Translated by Ganesh Vasudeo Tagare. Volumes 7-10 of *Ancient Indian Tradition and Mythology,* edited by J.L. Shastri. New Delhi: Motilal Banarsidas, 1976-1978. Especially *skandha* 10, chapters 29-33 (Krishna's love-making with the *gopīs*). (WDO)

Bihārī. *Satsaī.* Translated by Barron Holland. "The Satsaī of Bihārī: Hindi Poetry of the Early Rīti Period; Introduction, Translation, and Notes." Ph.D. Dissertation, University of California, Berkeley, 1969.

Brahmavaivarta Purāṇa. Translated by Rajendra Nath Sen. Volume 24 of the *Sacred Books of the Hindus.* Allahabad: Rajendra Nath Sen, 1920-1922. Reprinted by the AMS Press, New York, 1974. 2 volumes. The only available English translation; it is readable, but suffers from poor English style and syntax. Especially 1.15-22, the seduction of Tulasī; 3.1-20, the birth of Gaṇeśa and Skanda; 4.33-46, the marriage of Śiva and Pārvatī. (WDO)

Chandidās. *Love songs of Chandidās.* Translated by Deben Bhattacharya. London: George Allen & Unwin, 1967. More than a hundred poems written over the signature Chandidās are rendered in readable English poetry in this valuable anthology. Bhattacharya's substantial introduction helps sort out the various "Chandidāses" and relates the songs to other poetry in Bengal, to the musical notations found in Jayadeva's *Gītagovinda,* and to the Sahajiyā movement. (DMW)

*Devībhāgavata Purāṇa [*The Sri Mad Devi Bhagavatam*].* Translated by Swami Vijnanananda. Volume 26 of the *Sacred Books of the Hindus.* Allahabad: Suhindra Nath Vasu, 1921-1923. A long mythological text extolling the Hindu great Goddess in her various forms. (DRK) Especially 6.2-18, the killing of Mahiṣa, and 9.15-25, the marriage of Tulasī. (WDO)

Devī-māhātmya [Devī-māhātmya: The Glorification of the Great Goddess] Translated by Vasudeva S. Agrawala. Varanasi: All-India Kashiraj Trust, 1963. The most famous Hindu text celebrating the deeds of the great Goddess. In the third episode, Kālī is portrayed as a helpmate of the Goddess. (DRK) The most readily available English translation of the *Devī-māhātmya;* one should be wary of the "symbolic interpretation" offered in the notes. (TBC)

Devī-māhātmya [Célébration de le Grande Déesse, Devī-māhātmya]. Translated by Jean Varenne. Paris: Les Belles Lettres, 1975. A useful book containing the Sanskrit text, a readable translation, a short but substantial introduction, and a clear analysis of the three main episodes of the text. (CV)

Harivaṃśa. [A Prose English Translation of the Harivamsha].

Translated by Manmatha Nath Dutt. Calcutta: H.C. Dass, 1897.

Hindi poetry. *Modern Hindi Poetry: An Anthology*. Translated by Vidya Niwas Misra. Bloomington: Indiana University Press, 1965.

Hindu Myths: A Sourcebook. Translated from the Sanskrit by Wendy Doniger O'Flaherty. Harmondsworth: Penguin Books, 1975. A judicious selection of Vedic, epic, and purāṇic passages, including several myths of consorts. The translations are accurate and readable, and the introductions provide valuable perspectives on individual myths and the interrelations among them. (DMW)

Illangô Adigal. *Shilappadikaram (The Ankle Bracelet)*. Translated by Alain Danielou. New York: New Directions, 1965. Readable translation of the fifth-century Tamil epic, *Cilappatikāram*. (DH)

Jayadeva. *Gītagovinda [Love Song of the Dark Lord: Jayadeva's Gītagovinda]*. Translated by Barbara Stoler Miller. New York: Columbia University Press, 1977. A textual study and translation of Jayadeva's twelfth-century Sanskrit lyric drama, dedicated to the god Krishna. The text portrays the love of Rādhā and Krishna in a rite of spring. The book includes extensive notes and bibliography. (BSM) The detailed text-critical work, the substantial introduction and explanatory notes, and the masterful, lyrical English rendering of the poem make this an exceptionally valuable study. (DMW)

Karpūrādi-stotra. Hymn to Kālī. Translated by Arthur Avalon. Third edition. Madras: Ganesh & Co., 1965. A hymn in praise of Kālī set in the context of tantric ritual. (DRK)

Keśavadāsa. *Rasikapriyā [The Rasikapriyā of Keshavadāsa]*. Translated by K.P. Bahadur. Delhi: Motilal Banarsidass, 1972.

Kṛṣṇadāsa Kavirāja. *Caitanyacaritāmṛta*. Translated by Edward C. Dimock, Jr. Harvard Oriental Series. Cambridge, Massachusetts: Harvard University Press, forthcoming. The standard Bengali biography of Caitanya, dating from the late sixteenth century, provides an accessible summary of the philosophical and religious views of the Caitanya school. (SG)

Kuṟuntokai. *The Interior Landscape: Love Poems from a Classi-*

cal Tamil Anthology. Translated by A.K. Ramanujan. Bloomington: Indiana University Press, 1967.

Mahābhārata. Translated by Manmatha Nath Dutt. 7 volumes. Calcutta: H.C. Dass, 1895-1905.

Mahābhārata. Translated by Pratap Chandra Roy. 11 volumes. Second edition. Calcutta: Oriental Publishing Company, 1927-32.

Mahābhārata. Translated by J.A.B. van Buitenen. 3 volumes. Chicago: University of Chicago Press, 1974-78. Fluent, reliable translation based on the critical edition, with helpful introductions to each book. (JSH)

Mārkaṇḍeya Purāṇa. Translated by F. Eden Pargiter. Calcutta: The Asiatic Society, [1888-] 1904. Variously reprinted. The standard, generally reliable translation of the Purāṇa that contains the *Devī-māhātmya*. (TBC)

Matsya Purāṇa [Matsya Puranam]. Translated by S.V. Sastri. Delhi: Oriental Publishers, 1972.

Nirālā. *A Season on the Earth: Selected Poems of Nirālā*. Translated by David Rubin. New York: Columbia University Press, 1976.

Padāvalī. *In Praise of Krishna: Songs from the Bengali*. Translated by Edward C. Dimock, Jr., and Denise Levertov. New York: Doubleday, 1967, and London: Jonathan Cape, 1968. A brief but judiciously chosen and beautifully rendered selection of Vaiṣṇava lyrics from the medieval period, arranged in order of the successive phases in the love of Rādhā and Krishna. The book contains original woodblock prints and an evocative introduction to the medieval Vaiṣṇava poetry of Greater Bengal. (DMW)

Purāṇas. *Classical Hindu Mythology: A Reader in the Sanskrit Purāṇas*. Translated by Cornelia Dimmitt and J.A.B. van Buitenen. Philadelphia: Temple University Press, 1978.

Rāmāyaṇa [The Rāmāyaṇa of Vālmīki]. Translated by Hari Prasad Shastri. 3 volumes. London: Shantisadan, 1962. A very readable translation. (CD)

Rāmprasād. *Rama Prasada's Devotional Songs: The Cult of Shakti*. Translated by Jadunath Sinha. Calcutta. Sinha Publishing House, 1966. A short biography and many of the hymns of a famous Bengali saint and worshipper of Kālī in the eighteenth century. (DRK)

Śākta lyrics. *Bengali Religious Lyrics, Śākta.* Translated by Edward J. Thompson and Arthur Marshman Spender. Calcutta: Association Press, 1923. Most of the hymns are addressed to the goddess Kālī. (DRK)

Śākta lyrics. *Hymns to the Goddess.* Translated by Arthur Avalon. Madras: Ganesh & Co., 1964.

Sanskrit Poetry. *The Hermit and the Love-thief: Sanskrit Poems of Bhartrihari and Bilhaṇa.* Translated by Barbara Stoler Miller. New York: Columbia University Press, 1978. A critical essay and translations provide an introduction to classical Indian poetry, whose ideas and aesthetics are relevant to much later devotional literature. Especially important is the function of memory in the poems attributed to Bilhaṇa. (BSM)

Śiva Purāṇa. Translated into English by J.L. Shastri. Volumes 1-4 of *Ancient Indian Tradition and Mythology.* Delhi: Motilal Banarsidass, 1970. Especially *Rudrasaṃhitā* 2-5 (the marriage of Śiva and Pārvatī and the birth of Skanda). (WDO)

Song of Songs. Translated by Marvin Pope. *The Anchor Bible.* New York: Doubleday, 1977. The introduction to this new translation makes special reference to the *Gītagovinda.* The arguments, though suggestive, are based on uncritical translations. (BSM)

Subhāṣitaratnakosa [An Anthology of Sanskrit Court Poetry]. Translated by Daniel H.H. Ingalls. Harvard Oriental Series, Volume 44. Cambridge, Massachusetts: Harvard University Press, 1965. The elegant translations and detailed notes and introduction to the individual sections of this important anthology, together with the fine general introduction, make this work a comprehensive guide to the multi-faceted *kāvya* literature. The sections on love are especially important for understanding the symbolic conventions of the Rādhā-Krishna lyrics. (DMW)

Sūr Dās. *Pastorales par Soûr Dâs.* Translated by Charlotte Vaudeville. Paris: UNESCO, 1971. Lovely translations of selected poems from the *Sūr Sāgar,* with an insightful and sometimes controversial introduction. (JSH)

Sūr Dās. *Poems to the Child-God: Structures and Strategies in the Poetry of Sūrdās.* Translated by Kenneth E. Bryant. Berkeley: University of California Press, 1978. Vivid renderings of selected poems from the *Sūr Sāgar*, with an especially high proportion drawn from sections depicting Krishna as a child. (JSH)

Tulsī Dās. *Rāmcaritmānas [The Holy Lake of the Acts of Rāma].* Translated by W. Douglas P. Hill. London: Oxford University Press, 1952. (Reprinted Bombay, 1971.) Tulsī Dās's Hindi poem, the most famous "translation" of the *Rāmāyaṇa* in India, is of immense importance for understanding medieval as well as contemporary Vaiṣṇava *bhakti*. (WDO and DMW)

Upanishads [The Thirteen Principal Upanishads]. Translated by Robert Ernest Hume. Second Edition. London: Oxford University Press, 1931.

Vidyāpati. *Love Songs of Vidyāpati.* Translated by Deben Bhattacharya, with an introduction and notes by William G. Archer. London: George Allen & Unwin, 1963. This fine volume contains translations of a hundred poems of the Maithili poet Vidyāpati, whose portrayal of the love of Rādhā and Krishna has inspired secular lover and *bhakta* alike. Archer's excellent introduction places the poems in the tradition of Sanskrit courtly and devotional verse as well as in Vidyāpati's immediate historical context. Black-and-white reproductions of 31 Pahari miniatures complement the textual portraits of the lovers. (DMW)

Viṣṇu Purāṇa [The Vishnu Purāṇa]. Translated by Horace Hayman Wilson. 5 Volumes. Edited by Fitzedward Hall. London: Kegan Paul, Trench, Trübner, 1864-1877. Reprinted Calcutta: Punthi Pustak, 1972.

3. Secondary Sources

Agrawala, P.K. "Skanda in the Purāṇs and Classical Literature." *Purāṇa*, 8:1 (1966), pp. 135-158.

Archer, William G. *Indian Paintings from the Punjab Hills.* Two volumes. London: Sotheby Parke Bernet, 1973.

Archer, William G. *The Loves of Krishna in Indian Painting and Poetry.* London: George Allen and Unwin, 1957. Unusual for its integration of visual materials into a general introduction to Krishna. (JSH)

Babb, Lawrence A. *The Divine Hierarchy: Popular Hinduism in Central India.* New York: Columbia University Press, 1975.

Babb, Lawrence A. "Marriage and Malevolence: The Uses of

Sexual Opposition in a Hindu Pantheon." *Ethnology* 9:2 (1970), pp. 137-148.

Bahl, Kali. "The Hindi *Rīti* Tradition and the *Rasikapriyā* of Keshavadāsa: An Introductory Review." *Journal of South Asian Literature* 10 (Fall, 1974), pp. 1-38.

Barrett, Douglas and Basil Gray. *Indian Painting*. London: Macmillan, 1978.

Barrett, Douglas and Basil Gray. *Painting of India.* Geneva: Albert Skira, 1963.

Beane, Wendell Charles. *Myth, Cult and Symbols in Śākta Hinduism: A Study of the Indian Mother Goddess.* Leiden: E.J. Brill, 1977. The dissertation of a disciple of Eliade, who is also indebted to Przyluski, valuable for the data presented, but tendentious, and sometimes clearly erroneous, in its interpretation. (TBC)

Beck, Brenda E.F. "A Praise Poem for Murugan." *Journal of South Asian Literature,* 11:1 & 2 (1975), pp. 95-116.

Bharati, Agehananda. *The Tantric Tradition.* London: Rider, 1965; New York: Doubleday, 1970.

Bhattacharyya, Narendra Nath. *History of the Śākta Religion.* New Delhi: Munshiram Manoharlal, 1973 [1974]. An historical outline of the most important goddesses in the Hindu religious tradition, including some comments on village goddesses. (DRK) A welcome effort to identify the sociological factors involved in the worship of Devī, but one marred by Marxist jargon and a slighting of textual material. (TBC)

Brown, C. Mackenzie. *God as Mother: A Feminine Theology in India; An Historical and Theological Study of the Brahmavaivarta Purāṇa.* Hartford, Vermont: Claude Stark & Co., 1974. An analysis of the emerging feminine theology of Rādhā/Prakṛti in the *Brahmavaivarta Purāṇa,* against the background of the generally masculine-oriented Vaiṣṇava tradition as a whole. (CMB)

Bryant, Kenneth E. *Poems to the Child-God: Structures and Strategies in the Poetry of Sūrdās.* Berkeley: University of California Press, 1978. The finest analysis in any language of structural principles governing the composition of a great many poems in the *Sūr Sāgar.* (JSH)

Brown, W. Norman. "Change of Sex as a Hindu Story Motif."

Journal of the American Oriental Society 47:1 (1927), pp. 3-24. Much Freudian material, no Freudian analysis. (WDO)

Carman, John Braisted. *The Theology of Rāmānuja: An Essay in Interreligious Understanding*. New Haven: Yale University Press, 1974. An important source for the historical context and thought of the most significant Śrī Vaiṣṇava *ācārya*. (DH) Chapter 18 contains a sensitive discussion of Rāmānuja's understanding of Śrī. (VN) This study is helpful for understanding traditional Vaiṣṇava commentaries on the *Gītagovinda* and related texts. (BSM)

Carstairs, G. Morris. *The Twice-Born; A Study of a Community of High-Caste Hindus*. London: Hogarth Press, 1957. A psychiatrist-physician and social anthropologist whose own childhood was spent in Rajasthan, Carstairs suggests that the personal and social trends of his Hindu informants, as well as the terrifying imagery of the Mother-Goddess, can be traced back to infantile nuclear fantasies resulting from a nearly perfect early childhood clouded by the infant's own aggressive wishes (à la Melanie Klein) and finally shattered by the father's claims on the mother, the withdrawal represented by weaning, and the mysterious danger of the mother's periodic menstrual impurity. (DW)

Chakravarti, Sudhindra Chandra. *Philosophical Foundation of Bengal Vaiṣṇavism*. Calcutta: Academic Publishers, 1969. A fair treatment of the philosophy of the Caitanya school. (SG)

Chandra, Pramod. "Ustād Sāliuahana and the Development of the popular Mughal Style." *Lalit Kalā* 8 (1960), pp. 25-46.

Chandra, Pramod, and Daniel J. Ehnbom. *The Cleveland Tuti-Nama Manuscript and the Origins of Mughul Painting*. Cleveland: Cleveland Museum of Art, 1976.

Clothey, Fred W. "Chronometry, Cosmology and the Festival Calendar of the Murukan Cultus." *Interludes: Festivals of South India*. Edited by Guy Welbon. New Delhi: Manohar Books, 1979.

Clothey, Fred W. *The Many Faces of Murukan: The History and Meaning of a South Indian God*. The Hague: Mouton, 1978.

Clothey, Fred W. "Pilgrim Centers in the Tamil Cultus of Murukan." *Journal of the American Academy of Religion* 40:1 (1972), pp. 79-95.

Clothey, Fred W. "Skanda-Ṣaṣṭi: A Festival in Tamil India." *History of Religions* 8:3 (1969), pp. 236-259.

Coomaraswamy, A.K. *Catalogue of the Indian Collections in the Museum of Fine Arts, Boston.* Part 5, *Rajput Painting.* Boston: Museum of Fine Arts, 1927. (Whole in six volumes.)

Coomaraswamy, A.K. "The Eight Nāyikās." *Journal of Indian Art and Industry* 16 (1914), pp. 99-116.

Coomaraswamy, A.K. *Rajput Painting.* London: Humphrey Milford and Oxford University Press, 1916.

Coomaraswamy, A.K. *Yakṣas.* New Delhi: Munshiram Manoharlal, 1971.

Daly, C.D. "Hindu-Mythologie and Kastrationskomplex." *Imago* 13 (1927), pp. 145-198. An orthodox psychoanalytic study that finds in the image of Kālī and certain Hindu rites evidence of the Oedipal longings and fears of the young child in its relations with its parents, especially the fear of castration and, by association, of menstruating women. An analysand of Freud and Ferenczi, Daly served for some years as an officer in the Indian Army. (DW)

Darian, Steven G. *The Ganges in Myth and History.* Honolulu: The University Press of Hawaii, 1978. A very readable study of the mythology and symbolism of the Ganges in Indian culture from ancient times to the present. (DLE)

Das, Veena. *Structure and Cognition: Aspects of Hindu Caste and Ritual.* Delhi: Oxford University Press, 1977.

Dasgupta, Shashi Bhushan. *Bhārater Śakti-sādhana o Śākta Sāhitya* (Bengali). Calcutta: Sāhitya Saṃsad, 1961. A detailed history of goddesses in the Hindu tradition with special reference to Bengal. (DRK)

Dasgupta, Shashi Bhushan. "Evolution of Mother-worship in India," in his *Aspects of Indian Religious Thought.* Calcutta: A. Mukherjee & Company, 1957, pp. 42-106. A general history of the most important goddesses in the early Hindu tradition. (DRK) Contains a powerful exegesis of the Śākta worldview. (TBC)

Dasgupta, Shashi Bhushan. *Obscure Religious Cults.* Third edition. Calcutta: K.L. Mukhopadhyay, 1962.

De, Sushil Kumar. *Early History of the Vaiṣṇava Faith and Movement in Bengal from Sanskrit and Bengali Sources.* Calcutta:

General Printers and Publishers, 1942. Second edition: Calcutta: K.L. Mukhopadhyay, 1961. An excellent account of the life and teachings of Caitanya and his followers, with a brief introduction to the historical and religious setting of Bengal Vaiṣṇavism. (CMB)

Dimock, Edward C., Jr. "Doctrine and Practice among the Vaiṣṇavas of Bengal," in Milton Singer, ed., *Krishna: Myths, Rites, and Attitudes.* Chicago: University of Chicago Press, 1968, pp. 41-63. A brief but insightful sketch of selected theological and literary developments in Bengal Vaiṣṇavism; offers an illuminating discussion of the *svakīyā* and *parakīyā* ideals of love. (CMB)

Dimock, Edward C., Jr. *The Place of the Hidden Moon: Erotic Mysticism in the Vaiṣṇava-sahajiyā Cult of Bengal.* Chicago: University of Chicago Press, 1966. An extended account of the history, doctrines, and literary-poetic symbolism of the orthodox and heterodox Vaiṣṇava sects of Bengal. (CMB)

Dimock, Edward C., Jr., *et al.*, eds. *The Literatures of India: An Introduction.* Chicago: University of Chicago Press, 1974. An important collection of seminal chapters on various aspects of Indian literature, including sections on several of the most important regional languages of the subcontinent. (DMW)

Dowson, John. *A Classical Dictionary of Hindu Mythology and Religion.* Tenth edition. London: Routledge & Kegan Paul, 1961.

Dvivedī, Hazārīprasād. "Sūrdās kī Rādhā," in Harbanślāl Śarmā, ed., *Sūrdās.* Delhi: Rādhākṛṣṇa Prakāśan, 1969, pp. 192-203. A short statement about Sūr Dās's portrayal of Rādhā by one of the great contemporary Hindi critics. (JSH)

Edholm, Erik Af and Carl Suneson. "The Seven Bulls and Kṛṣṇa's Marriage of Nīlā/NappiNNai in Sanskrit and Tamil Literature." *Temenos: Studies in Comparative Religion* 8 (1972), pp. 29-53. An important starting point for future studies of Krishna lore in the Tamil South. (DH)

Eidlitz, Walther. *Kṛṣṇa-Caitanya: Sein Leben and Seine Lehre.* Stockholm: Almqvist & Wiksell, 1968. A scholarly and sensitive study that surveys the scriptural background of the Caitanya school and the life and teachings of Caitanya. (SG)

Eliade, Mircea. *Yoga: Immortality and Freedom.* Bollingen Series.

Princeton: Princeton University Press, 1973. (Original edition, 1958).

Eschmann, A., H. Kulke and G.C. Tripathi, eds. *The Cult of Jagannātha and the Regional Tradition of Orissa.* Delhi: Manohar, 1978.

Filliozat, Jean. *Un Texte Tamoul de Dévotion Vishnouite: Le Tiruppāvai d'Āṇṭāḷ.* Pondichéry: Publication de l'Institut Français d'Indologie No. 45 (1972). A thorough critical treatment of an *āḻvār* poem crucial for understanding the Śrī Vaiṣṇava approach to devotion; contains copious notes and a Sanskrit commentary on the poem in translation. (DH)

Gerow, Edwin. *A Glossary of Indian Figures of Speech.* The Hague: Mouton, 1971. Although it concentrates on the earlier authors of Indian treatises on poetics, this glossary is a fairly broad survey of Sanskrit figures of speech that serves as an important aid to deciphering the stylistic conventions of much *bhakti* literature. (DMW)

Gnoli, Raniero. *The Aesthetic Experience According to Abhinavagupta.* Rome: Instituto Italiano per il Medio ed Estremo Oriente, 1956. Text, translation, and critical introduction to the tenth-century critic Abhinavagupta's commentary on the *rasa-sūtra* of Bharata's Nāṭyaśāstra, a text of central importance for the aesthetics of devotional literature. (BSM)

Goldman, Robert P. "Mortal Man and Immortal Woman: An Interpretation of Three Ākhyāna Hymns of the Ṛg Veda." *Journal of the Oriental Institute of Baroda* 18:4 (June, 1969), pp. 273-303. Three Vedic hierogamies deciphered. (WDO)

Gonda, Jan. *Aspects of Early Viṣṇuism.* Utrecht: N.V.A. Oosthoek's Uitgevers Mij, 1954. Second edition: Delhi: Motilal Banarsidass, 1969. An intensive treatment of important facets of Viṣṇu as he is portrayed especially in Vedic and epic texts. (DMW)

Hardy, Friedhelm. "Ideology and Cultural Contexts of the Śrīvaiṣṇava Temple." *The Indian Economic and Social History Review* 14 (January-March, 1977), pp. 119-151. Useful survey of the emergence of the Vaiṣṇava cult in the Tamil South and of Tamil devotion generally. (DH)

Hart, George L., III. *The Poems of Ancient Tamil: Their Milieu and Their Sanskrit Counterparts.* Berkeley: University of California Press, 1975.

Hart, George L., III. "Some Aspects of Kinship in Ancient Tamil Literature." *Kinship and History in South Asia,* edited by Thomas R. Trautmann, pp. 29-60. Ann Arbor: Center for South and Southeast Asian Studies, the University of Michigan, 1974.

Hart, George L., III. "Some Related Literary Conventions in Tamil and Indo-Aryan and their Significance." *Journal of the American Oriental Society* 94:2 (1974), pp. 157-167.

Hart, George L., III. "Women and the Sacred in Ancient Tamilnad." *The Journal of Asian Studies* 32:2 (February, 1973), pp. 233-250.

Hawley, John Stratton. "The Butter Thief." Ph.D. Thesis, Harvard University, 1977. A comprehensive and penetrating analysis of the motif of the child Krishna's thievery as it appears in the purāṇas and other early Sanskrit texts, in sculpture, and in the poems of Sūr Dās and the plays of Brindavan. (DMW)

Hawley, John Stratton. "The Early Sūr Sāgar and the Growth of the Sūr Tradition." *Journal of the American Oriental Society* 99:1 (1979), pp. 64-72. An introduction to manuscripts of the *Sūr Sāgar* and to the development of the collection of poems that came to be called by that name. (JSH)

Hazra, Rajendra Chandra. *Studies in the Purāṇic Records on Hindu Rites and Customs.* Dacca: University of Dacca, Bulletin No. 20, 1940. Includes a thorough historical, text-critical analysis of the major purāṇas, with useful descriptions of their contents especially as related to rituals and customs, but also with reference to more purely theological and philosophical matters. (CMB)

Heimann, Betty. *Facets of Indian Thought.* London: George Allen & Unwin, 1964. A series of provocative essays on elements of the Hindu world view. (DLE)

Hein, Norvin. *The Miracle Plays of Mathurā.* New Haven: Yale University Press, 1972. A comprehensive study of dramatic forms in the Mathurā area of North India, especially the *līlās* depicting events in the lives of Rāma and Krishna. A brilliant historical chapter assembles diverse evidence for the antiquity of vernacular Krishna dramas in this region. (DMW)

Hopkins, E. Washburn. *Epic Mythology*. Strassburg: Karl J. Trübner, 1915. Includes a discussion of fertility themes found in the epic. (CD)

Hudson, Dennis. "Bathing in Krishna: A Study in Vaishnava Theology." *Harvard Theological Review* 73:1-2 (1980), pp. 537-564. Examines the Śrī Vaiṣṇava understanding of Āṇṭāḷ's *Tiruppāvai* by focusing on the Maṇipravāḷa commentary of the thirteenth-century *ācārya* Periyavāccānpiḷḷai. (DH)

Ingalls, Daniel H. H. "The *Harivaṃśa* as a *Mahākāvya*." *Mélanges d'Indianisme à la Mémoire de Louis Renou*. Paris: É. de Boccard, 1968. An illuminating essay on the earliest extant account of Krishna's boyhood and youth among the cowherds of Vraja and his later adventures in Mathurā and Dvārakā. (DMW)

Jacobi, Hermann. *Das Rāmāyaṇa*. Translated into English by S.N. Ghosal. Baroda: Oriental Institute, 1960. (Original German edition, 1893.) Offers a theory of the origins and growth of the Rāma legend in India before Vālmīki and refutes Albrecht Weber, emphasizing the Vedic origin of epic themes. (CD)

Kakar, S. *The Inner World: A Psycho-analytic Study of Childhood and Society in India*. Delhi: Oxford University Press, 1978. Writing with the knowledgeable sensitivity of one born and raised a Hindu and drawing especially on Erikson's epigenetic model and Kohut's analysis of narcissism, New Delhi psychotherapist Kakar suggests that a variety of factors—including the sexual attitudes and the psycho-social diffusion within the extended family; the intense social and emotional significance of the male child for the Hindu mother; the extended intimate relation of mother and son; the sudden reversal from unchecked indulgence to inflexible standards with entry into the masculine world; and the emotional restraint between father and son—conspire together to reinforce the fusion-oriented Hindu world image, among the elements of which is the Great Mother, whose longed-for affirming presence is at the same time experienced as sexually demanding and destructive of individuality. (DW)

Kinsley, David R. *The Sword and the Flute—Kālī and Kṛṣṇa*. Berkeley: University of California Press, 1975. Part II deals with the history of Kālī and some of the ways in which she expresses fundamental Hindu ideas. (DRK)

Kumar, Pushpendra. *Sakti Cult in Ancient India (With Special Reference to the Puranic Literature)*. Varanasi: Bhartiya

Publishing House, 1974. A series of paraphrases of purāṇic and Tantric material pertaining to the names, rituals, and theologies of Devī, with little explicit analysis of the material. (TBC)

Kramrisch, Stella. "The Indian Great Goddess." *History of Religions* 14:4 (1975), pp. 235-265.

M. [Mahendranath Gupta]. *The Gospel of Sri Ramakrishna.* Translated by Swami Nikhilananda. New York: Ramakrishna-Vivekananda Center, 1942. The biography of a famous nineteenth-century saint and worshipper of Kālī, containing many recorded conversations of Ramakrishna. (DRK)

Majumdar, Asoke Kumar. "A Note on the Development of the Rādhā Cult." *Annals of the Bhandarkar Oriental Research Institute* 36 (1955), pp. 231-257. Provides helpful historical references, but the tone of the author is often unsympathetic and even condescending. (CMB)

Majumdar, Bimanbehari. *Kṛṣṇa in History and Legend.* Calcutta: University of Calcutta, 1969. Though arguing at times for questionable historical hypotheses (e.g., the purely Aryan origin of Krishna), the author presents considerable literary and archaeological evidence for his views, and provides two important chapters on Rādhā. (CMB)

Maury, Curt. *Folk Origins of Indian Art.* New York: Columbia University Press, 1969. An excellent treatment of non-scriptural sources of the goddess traditions. (DLE)

Meyer, Johann Jakob. *Sexual Life in Ancient India.* New York: Dutton, 1930. Epic materials on puberty, marriage, childbirth, in classical texts. (WDO)

Miller, Barbara Stoler. "Rādhā: Consort of Kṛṣṇa's Vernal Passion." *Journal of the American Oriental Society* 95:4 (1975), pp. 655-671.

Mishra, V. *Rasikapriyā kā Priya Prasāda Tilaka* (Hindi). Banaras, 1964.

Mītal, Dvārikāprasād. *Hindī Sāhitya me Rādhā.* Mathurā: Javāhar Pustakālay, 1970. A compendious introduction to the figure of Rādhā in Sanskrit and Hindi literature. The Hindi section is organized according to *sampradāy.* (JSH)

Monier-Williams, Sir Monier. *Indian Epic Poetry.* London: Williams and Norgate, 1893.

Mukherjee, Prahbat. *The History of Medieval Vaishnavism in Orissa.* Calcutta: R. Chatterjee, 1940.

Neumann, Erich. *The Great Mother: An Analysis of the Archetype* (2nd edition). Translated by R. Manheim. New York: Pantheon, 1963. A profusely illustrated study of the structure and manifestations of the Great Mother archetype by perhaps the most gifted of Jung's associates. (DW)

Obeyesekere, Gananath. "The Fire-walkers of Kataragama: The Rise of Bhakti Religiosity in Buddhist Sri Lanka." *The Journal of Asian Studies* 37:3 (1978), pp. 457-476.

O'Flaherty, Wendy Doniger. *Asceticism and Eroticism in the Mythology of Śiva.* Oxford and London: Oxford University Press, 1973. A penetrating analysis of Śiva as the ithyphallic yogi and husband of Pārvatī, carried out in part through the conceptual framework provided by Claude Lévi-Strauss. (DMW)

O'Flaherty, Wendy Doniger. *Women, Androgynes, and Other Mythical Beasts.* Chicago: University of Chicago Press, 1980. Especially Chapters 2 (sexual fluids), 4 (hierogamies), and 9 (androgynes). (WDO)

Pandey, S.M. and Norman Zide. "Sūrdās and His Krishna-*bhakti*," in Milton Singer, ed., *Krishna: Myths, Rites, and Attitudes.* Chicago: University of Chicago Press, 1968, pp. 173-199. Includes a brief overview of the role of Rādhā in medieval Hindi devotional poetry, especially in the poems of Sūr Dās. (CMB)

Payne, Ernest A. *The Śāktas: An Introductory and Comparative Study.* London: Oxford University Press, 1933. A history of Hindu goddesses with some attempt to relate goddess-worship to climate and politics. (DRK) A biased but not entirely outdated study. (TBC)

Rādhā Aṅk. Bhakta Bhārat 7:1 (January, 1972). Edited by Rāmdāsa Śāstri. Brindavan: Cār Sampradāy Āśram, 1972.

Raghavan, V. *The Greater Rāmāyaṇa.* Varanasi: All-India Kashiraj Trust, 1973. A survey of the Rāma legend as it appears in the *Mahābhārata,* the *Harivaṃśa,* the Purāṇas, and the Upapurāṇas. (CD)

Rajagopalan, Vasudha [Narayanan]. "The Śrī Vaiṣṇava Understanding of *bhakti* and *prapatti:* From the *Āḻvārs* to Vedānta Deśika." Ph.D. dissertation, University of Bombay, 1978. Discusses the Śrī Vaiṣṇava *ācāryas'* understanding of Śrī as a refuge to the devotee and focuses on her mediating role. (VN)

Randhawa, M.S. *Basohli Paintings.* New Delhi: Publications Division, Ministry of Information and Broadcasting, Government of India, 1959.

Randhawa, M.S. *Kangra Paintings of the Bhāgavata Purāṇa.* New Delhi: National Museum, 1960. Includes Sanskrit and English of textual passages. (DMW)

Randhawa, M.S. *Kangra Paintings of the Gītagovinda.* Introduction by William G. Archer. New Delhi: National Museum, 1963.

Randhawa, M.S. and S.S. Bhambei. "Basohli Paintings of Bhanuratta's Rasamanjari." *Roopa Lekha,* 36:1-2 (1967), pp. 1-124.

Ruben, Walter. *Kṛṣṇa: Konkordanz und Kommentar der Motive seines Heldenlebens.* Istanbul: Istanbul Yazilari, 1944.

Sahai, Bhagwant. *Iconography of Minor Hindu and Buddhist Deities.* New Delhi: Abhinav Publications, 1975. Excellent chapters on Mahiṣamardiṇī, Chāmuṇḍā, and Sapta-Mātṛkā. (TBC)

Śaktyaṅka. Kalyāṇa. 97:1 (August, 1934). Edited by Hanuman Prasad Poddar and Chimanlal Goswami. [Gorakhpur: Gita Press, 1934.] An encyclopedic survey of the female principle (*śakti-tattva*) and its manifestations, covering the history, iconography, temples, and forms of worship of the goddesses of India, including numerous photographs, diagrams, charts, and maps. (SG)

Sankalia, H.D. *Rāmāyaṇa: Myth or Reality?* New Delhi: People's Publishing House, 1973. Discusses historical aspects of the epic based on the author's archaeological investigations in North and South India. (CD)

Śarmā, Rāmprasād. *Śakti Tattva Darśan.* Birlagram, M.P.: Śivatattva Darśan Granth Prakāśan Samiti, 1977. A voluminous work in Hindi on goddesses, their traditions and worship, complete with photographs and diagrams. (SG)

Schomer, Karine. "Mahadevi Varma and the Chayavad Age of Modern Hindi Poetry: A Literary and Intellectual Biography." Ph.D. Dissertation. Chicago: University of Chicago, 1976.

Sharma, R. *A Socio-Political Study of the Vālmīki Rāmāyaṇa.* Delhi: Motilal Banarsidass, 1971. Surveys Aryan social customs related to the epic, including family life, marriage customs, and the position of women in society as wives and mothers. (CD)

Shastri, V.S. Srinivasan. *Lectures on the Rāmāyaṇa.* Madras: S. Viswanathan, 1949. Collection of detailed interpretive lectures on the important episodes and themes of the epic by an Indian scholar and devotee. (CD)

Shulman, David. "The Murderous Bride: Tamil Versions of the Myth of Devī and the Buffalo Demon." *History of Religions* 16:2 (November, 1976), pp. 120-147. Essential to an understanding of the Sanskrit myths of Devī. (WDO)

Siegel, Lee. *Sacred and Profane Dimensions of Love in Indian Traditions as Exemplified in the Gītagovinda of Jayadeva.* Delhi: Oxford University Press, 1978. A comparative study of love as a universal theme in religious and secular literature, using Jayadeva's *Gītagovinda* as the focal text. (BSM)

Sircar, D.C. *The Śākta Pīthas.* Delhi: Motilal Banarsidass, 1973. (Original edition, 1948.)

Sircar, D.C. (ed.). *The Śakti Cult and Tārā.* Calcutta: University of Calcutta, 1971. Excellent short papers that examine various facets of the Indian view of feminine divinity, though the volume lacks a satisfactory synthesis of these facets. (TBC)

Sivaramamurti, C. *Gaṅgā.* New Delhi: Orient Longman Limited, 1976. A study of the images and myths of the Gaṅgā, based primarily upon Indian sculpture dating from the second to the twelfth centuries. (DLE)

Spink, Walter M. *Krishnamaṇḍala: A Devotional Theme in Indian Art.* Ann Arbor, Michigan: Center for South and Southeast Asian Studies, The University of Michigan, 1971.

Spratt, P. *Hindu Culture and Personality: A Psycho-Analytic Study.* Bombay: Manaktalas, 1966. Indulgent child-rearing practices among the Hindus are said in this work to yield the narcissistic personality, which beyond devotion to mothers and mother symbols—e.g., water, cows, sweets, and of course goddesses—and weak repression of early anal attachments, may in its highest form become the "projective extrovert type," who, in identifying ego with the world, finally directs its all-consuming self-love outward upon the whole world and thereby achieves its admirable ideals. (DW)

Śrī Rādhā Aṅk. Śrī Sarveśvara 23:7-12 (1975). Edited by Govind Śaran Śāstrī *et al.* Salemabad, Rajasthan: A. Bhā. Nimbārkācārya Pīth, 1975.

Srinivas, Mysore N. *Religion and Society Among the Coorgs of*

South India. New York: Asia Publishing House, 1965. (Original edition, 1952).

Upādhyāy, Baladev. *Bhāratīya Vāṅmay mẽ Śrīrādhā.* Patna: Bihar Rāṣṭrabhāṣā Pariṣad, 1963. An account of the history and development of the conception of Rādhā from the Vedas to the present, drawing on nearly all the literary languages and religious traditions of India. (SG)

Vaudeville, Charlotte. "Aspects du Mythe de *Kṛṣṇa-Gopāla* dans l'Inde Ancienne," in *Mélanges d'Indianisme à la Mémoire de Louis Renou.* Paris: É. de Boccard, 1968. A seminal article, fundamental for understanding the worship of both Krishna and Devī. (TBC)

Vaudeville, Charlotte. "Evolution of Love-symbolism in Bhāgavatism." *Journal of the American Oriental Society* 82:1 (1962), pp. 31-40.

Vaudeville, Charlotte. "The Govardhan Myth in Northern India." *Indo-Iranian Journal,* 22:1 (1980), pp. 1-45.

Venkatachari, K.K.A. *The Maṇipravāḷa Literature of the Śrīvaiṣṇava Ācāryas, 12th to 15th Century A.D.* Utrecht: Profeschrift . . . aan de Rijksuniversiteit de Utrecht, 1975. Most recent and authoritative discussion of the early *ācāryas* and their commentaries on the *āḻvār* poems. (DH) Discusses the nature of Śrī in the Śrī Vaiṣṇava *maṇipravāla* works and focusses on the *ācārya* Periyavāccāṉ Piḷḷai. (VN)

Von Stietencron, Heinrich. *Gaṅgā und Yamunā.* Wiesbaden: Otto Harrassowitz, 1972. A discussion of the symbolic dimensions of the two river goddesses, particularly as they appear on the doorways of medieval temples. (DLE)

Weber, Albrecht. *On the Rāmāyaṇa.*Translated by D.C. Boyd. London: Trubner & Co., 1873. Raises the issues of the origin of the Rāma legend in the Buddhist Jātakas and its possible relationship with Greek tradition. (CD)

White, Charles S.J. *The Caurāsī Pad of Śrī Hit Harivaṃś.* Honolulu: University Press of Hawaii, 1977.

Wilson, Horace Hayman, "Analysis of the Puráṅas," in his *Essays, Analytical, Critical, and Philological on Subjects Connected with Sanskrit Literature.* Collected and edited by Reinhold Rost. London: Trubner & Co., 1864, 1, pp. 1-155. The earliest extended description and analysis of the *Brahma-*

vaivarta Purāṇa; the interpretation frequently reflects the author's animosity toward the text. (CMB)

Woodroffe, Sir John [Arthur Avalon]. *Shakti and Shākta.* Fifth edition, 1959. New York: Dover Publications, 1978.

Wulff, Donna M. "Drama as a Mode of Religious Realization: The *Vidagdhamādhava* of Rūpa Gosvāmin." Ph.D. Thesis, Harvard University, 1977.

Yocum, Glenn E. "The Goddess in a Tamil Śaiva Devotional Text, Māṇikkavācakar's Tiruvācakam." *Journal of the American Academy of Religion* Supplement 45:1 (1977), pp. 369-390.

Young, Katherine K. "Beloved Places (ukantaruḷiṉanilaṅkaḷ): The Correlation of Topography and Theology in the Śrīvaiṣṇava Tradition of South India." Ph.D. thesis, McGill University, Montreal, 1978. Very useful for the cultic context of the *āḻvārs* and *ācāryas.* (DH)

Zimmer, Heinrich. *The King and the Corpse.* New York: Pantheon Books, 1948. Reprinted in paperback, Princeton: Princeton University Press, 1971. Especially Part 2, on the birth, marriage, and death of Satī. (WDO)

Zimmer, Heinrich. *Myths and Symbols in Indian Art and Civilization.* Edited by Joseph Campbell. Bollingen Series 6. New York: Pantheon Books, 1946. Reprinted in paperback, Princeton: Princeton University Press, 1971. Especially Chapter 5, on the Goddess. (WDO)

Zvelebil, Kamil V. "A Guide to Murukan." *Journal of Tamil Studies* 9 (1976), pp. 1-22.

Zvelebil, Kamil V. *The Smile of Murugan: On Tamil Literature of South India.* Leiden: E.J. Brill, 1973.

Zvelebil, Kamil V. *Tamil Literature.* Volume 10, Fascicle 1 of *A History of Indian Literature.* Edited by Jan Gonda. Wiesbaden: Otto Harrassowitz, 1974. The most recent, complete, and authoritative history of Tamil literature to date. (DH)

Zvelebil, Kamil V. "Vaḷḷi and Murugan—A Dravidian Myth." *Indo-Iranian Journal* 19 (1977), pp. 227-246.

Contributors

Brenda E.F. Beck is Professor of Anthropology at the University of British Columbia and the author of several books and papers on South Indian symbolic tradition. Her research interests are social organization, regional cultures in relation to national traditions, folklore, ceremonial, and the role of metaphor in expressing social values. Her current work involves the analysis of a South Indian oral epic.

C. Mackenzie Brown, Associate Professor of Religion and Chairman of Asian Studies at Trinity University, has interests in comparative religious sexual symbolisms and in purāṇic literature. His publications include *God as Mother, The Development of a Feminine Theology in India* (Claude Stark, 1974).

Richard L. Brubaker, Assistant Professor of Religion at Davidson College, is preparing for publication his University of Chicago dissertation, "The Ambivalent Mistress: A Study of South Indian Village Goddesses and Their Religious Meaning." His articles include "Barbers, Washermen, and Other Priests: Servants of the South Indian Village and Its Goddess," *History of Religions* 19:2 (1979).

John B. Carman, Professor of Comparative Religion and Director of the Center for the Study of World Religions at Harvard University, has specialized in the study of South Indian religion. His books include *Village Christians and Hindu Culture* (with P.Y. Luke, Lutterworth Press, 1968), and *The Theology of Rāmānuja* (Yale University Press, 1974).

Thomas B. Coburn, Associate Professor of Religious Studies and Classical Languages, St. Lawrence University, has interests in purāṇic religion, the Sanskritization of Devī, and religious pluralism. He has written on methodological and theological issues in the study of scripture, and in the study of the feminine, and is currently working on a study of the commentaries and abridgements of the *Devī-māhātmya.*

Vishakha N. Desai, Keeper of Indian, Southeast Asian and Islamic collections, and Head of Exhibition Resources at the Museum of Fine Arts, Boston, is completing her dissertation on "Early Rasikapriyā Paintings in Rajasthan" for the University of Michigan. She has lectured widely on love themes in Indian art and dance styles and is currently working on the role of Rādhā as a secular heroine in Rasikapriyā paintings.

Cornelia Dimmitt, Associate Professor of Theology, Georgetown University, Washington, D.C. teaches in the field of History of Religions (Hindu and Buddhist traditions), does research in comparative mythology, and is co-translator of a reader in the Hindu Sanskrit Purāṇas: *Classical Hindu Mythology* (Temple University Press, 1978).

Edward C. Dimock, Jr., currently President of the American Institute of Indian Studies, is Distinguished Service Professor at the University of Chicago. His publications concerning Bengali Vaiṣṇavism include *The Place of the Hidden Moon* (University of Chicago Press, 1966) and a forthcoming edition and translation of the *Caitanya-Caritāmṛta.*

Diana L. Eck is Associate Professor of Sanskrit and Indian Studies at Harvard University. She has worked in the comparative study of religion, with particular emphasis on pilgrimage and sacred geography. Her book *Banāras, City of Light* will be published in 1982.

Shrivatsa Goswami, currently completing his Ph.D. dissertation on the philosophy of Jīva Gosvāmī at Banaras Hindu University, is a member of the family of priests at Śrī Rādhāramaṇa Temple, Brindavan, and is academic director of the Śrī Caitanya Prema Sansthāna there. A contributor to the *Bhāratīya Darśana Kośa* (Government of India, forthcoming), he was Visiting Scholar at the Center for the Study of World Religions, Harvard University in 1977-78.

John Stratton Hawley is Assistant Professor of Asian Languages and Literature (Hindi) at the University of Washington. His publications include textual and art historical studies relating to Krishna, articles on medieval Hindi literature, and a book written in association with Shrivatsa Goswami: *At Play with Krishna: Pilgrimage Dramas from Brindavan* (Princeton University Press, 1981).

Norvin Hein is Professor of Comparative Religion in the Yale University Divinity School and Director of Graduate Studies in the Department of Religious Studies there. His principal writing in the area of North Indian religion is *The Miracle Plays of Mathurā* (Yale University Press and Oxford University Press, 1972).

D. Dennis Hudson, Professor of Religion, Smith College, teaches the religious history of India and has research interests in the relations between the religions of South India and in the Tamil poetry of the Āḻvārs and their medieval commentaries. An article relevant to this volume, "Bathing in Krishna: A Study in Vaiṣṇava Hindu Theology," can be found in the *Harvard Theological Review* 73:3-4 (July-October 1980).

David Kinsley is Associate Professor of Religious Studies at McMaster University. He is the author of a number of articles and of three books: *The Sword and the Flute — Kālī and Kṛṣṇa* (University of California Press, 1975); *The Divine Player: A Study of Kṛṣṇa Līlā* (Motilal Banarsidass, 1979); and *Hinduism: A Cultural Perspective* (Prentice-Hall, 1981). His current research is focused on goddesses in medieval Sanskrit literature.

Frédérique Apffel Marglin is Assistant Professor of Anthropology at Smith College. Her interests include ritual and myth, anthropology and literature, women in symbolic roles, and kingship. She has written several articles on kingship, power, and the use of multiple media in rituals. A book entitled *Wives of the God-King: The Rituals of Hindu Temple Courtesans* (Oxford University Press, Delhi) is forthcoming.

Barbara Stoler Miller is Professor of Oriental Studies at Barnard College, Columbia University. Her recent publications include *Love Song of the Dark Lord* (Columbia University Press, 1977), *The Hermit and the Love-Thief* (Columbia University Press, 1979), and *Sombraventadora/Shadowinnower,* translations from the Spanish poetry of Agueda Pizarro (Columbia University Press, 1979). She is currently translating Sanskrit dramatic literature.

Vasudha Narayanan, Assistant Professor of Religious Studies at DePaul University, is a member of the Śrī Vaiṣṇava community of South India and has recently completed a dissertation on "The Śrī Vaiṣṇava Understanding of *Bhakti* and *Prapatti*" (University of Bombay, 1978). She is a contributor to *The Abingdon Dictionary of Living Religions.*

Wendy Doniger O'Flaherty, Professor of History of Religions, University of Chicago, has done research in comparative religion and the ancient Indian tradition, with particular focus on mythology. Her publications include *The Origins of Evil in Hindu Mythology* (University of California Press, 1976), *Women, Androgynes, and Other Mythical Beasts* (University of Chicago Press, 1980), *Śiva, The Erotic Ascetic* (Oxford, Galaxy, 1981), and *The Rig Veda* (Penguin, 1981). She is now working on a book about dream myths.

Joyce M. Paulson, an appraiser of oriental art and a contemporary art consultant, was formerly Curatorial Assistant in the Department of Asiatic Art of the Museum of Fine Arts, Boston, where she cared for the Indian and Islamic collections. She has particular interests in Mughal painting and Indian sculpture. Her publications include *From River Banks and Sacred Places: Ancient Indian Terracottas,* a catalogue for an exhibition commemorating the one hundredth anniversary of the birth of Ananda K. Coomaraswamy.

A.K. Ramanujan is Chairman of the Department of South Asian Languages and Civilizations, and Professor of Dravidian Studies at the University of Chicago. A noted poet in English and Kannada, he has translated from the literature of South India in *The Interior Landscape* (Indiana, 1967); *Speaking of Śiva* (Penguin, 1972); *Samskara* (Oxford University Press, 1977); *Hymns for the Drowning: Poems for Viṣṇu by Nammāḻvār* (Princeton, 1981); and in several forthcoming works including *Kurinji* (classical Tamil Poetry), and a volume on Kannada folktales.

Karine Schomer, Assistant Professor of Hindi, University of California, Berkeley, has published translations of Hindi short stories and written articles on medieval and modern Hindi poetry and on the folklore of the Hindi area. Her book on the modern Hindi poet Mahadevi Varma and the Chhayavad movement of modern Hindi poetry is forthcoming (University of California Press), and she is currently co-editing a volume on the Sant tradition of India, to appear in the Berkeley Religious Studies Series.

Charlotte Vaudeville, Professor at the Sorbonne and Director of Studies in the IVth Section of École Pratique des Hautes Études, is a specialist in the literature and religion of medieval and modern North India. Her recent works include *Le Rāmāyaṇ de Tulsī-dās* (Belles Lettres, Paris 1978) and *Kabīr* (Oxford University Press, 1974). She has also written a series of four articles on Braj culture and the cult of the Govardhan hill, published in the *Indo Iranian Journal,* vols. 18 (1976) and 22 (1980).

Jitendrasinh of Wankaner comes from an old Rajput family and is a connoisseur and scholar of Indian art. He has received M.A. degrees from the University of California at Los Angeles and from Harvard University. At Harvard he has been associated with the Fogg Art Museum and the Center for Near Eastern Languages. His central interest is in Vaiṣṇava symbolism in Mughal and Rajput painting.

David M. Wulff is Associate Professor of Psychology, Wheaton College, Norton, Massachusetts. Interested especially in European contributions to the psychology of religion, he is the author of a forthcoming work that surveys this field as it has developed since before the turn of the century in Europe and America.

Donna Marie Wulff is Assistant Professor of Religious Studies at Brown University. Her Harvard dissertation (1977) deals with the dramatic works of Rūpa Gosvāmī, and in recent papers she has studied the evolution of Sanskrit drama and aesthetic theory. Her current research examines a variety of contemporary Bengali dramatic and musical expressions, especially Vaiṣṇava *kīrtan*.

Glenn E. Yocum, Associate Professor of Religion, Whittier College, has a special interest in the religious traditions of South India. His publications include several articles on Tamil *bhakti* poetry, contributions to two volumes of essays on South India which he also co-edited, and a forthcoming book on Māṇikkavācakar, *Hymns to Śiva Naṭarāja,* (New Delhi: Heritage Publishers).

Index

abalā, 97-104
Abhimanyu, 27, 35, 41
Abhinavagupta, 14-15
Ādiśakti, 10
Agni, 164-65, 172, 180, 185, 192, 217, 221
Aiśvarya, 39-40, 77, 252-53, 305-06
ālvārs, 127, 224, 234, 236, 238, 242-43, 248, 250, 255
Annapūrṇā, 119
Āṇṭāḷ, 246, 248, 250, 253, 317, 322, 324
Arjuna, 26, 46, 122, 192
ātman, 41
aurat, 111-15
auspiciousness, 225, 228, 232, 307-14
avatar. See *avatāra*
avatāra, 18, 77, 123, 171, 174-76, 189, 195, 246, 279
avataraṇa, 166, 177, 207
Bahiṇābāi, 317, 320-21
Bālacarita. See *Bhāsa*
Baladeva, 3, 9-10
Balarāma, 238-41, 255, 258
Barkum, Michael, 200
Baul, 190
Bengal, 10-12, 27-28, 77, 89, 144, 147, 184-203
Bergman, Ingmar, 202
Bhagavān, 18-19, 73-74, 82
Bhāgavata cult, 10, 18, 240-42, 260, 370
Bhāgavata, Oriya. See Dās, Jagannātha
Bhāgavata Purāṇa, 8, 15, 24-25, 27, 35, 40, 58, 95, 114, 138, 242, 303
Bhagavad-Gītā, 68, 122-23, 197, 231-32
bhakti, 28-41, 73, 78, 81, 125-28, 132, 263, 281, 324; and the sexes, 142-43, 316-24; rejection of, 126. See also Rādhā, as paradigm of devotion
bhaktirasa, 28, 36, 63, 82. See also *rasa*
Bhaktirasāmṛtasindhu, 36
Bhānu Miśra, 91, 93
Bharadvāja Paitṛmedhika Sūtra, 313
Bharata, 91
Bhāratī, Dharmvīr, 113-14
Bhāsa, 8, 256, 258, 260
Bhaṭṭar, Parāśara, 227, 230, 236, 250
bhāva, 28, 79, 81-83, 91, 303-04. See also *mahābhāva*
Bhavabhūti, 147
Bhū, 235, 238, 244-46, 250, 259-60, 300. See also earth
Brahmā, 65, 157-58, 182, 217; in *trimūrti,* xi
bhramaragīta, 16.
brahman, 41, 73, 179
Brahmavaivarta Purāṇa, 53, 57-71, 138, 176
Braj, 28, 42, 45, 54, 76, 79, 82-83, 87, 118
Brindāvan, 11, 19, 27, 30, 37, 42, 51, 62-63, 66, 76, 114, 192, 303, 305
Bṛṣabhānu, 45, 76, 80, 94
buffalo demon. See Mahiṣa; Mahiṣāsura

Caitanya, 10-11, 27-28, 31, 42, 72, 84, 87, 90, 137, 192, 303
Caitanya Sampradaya. See Gauḍīya
calendar: Hindu, 2-5
Camus, Albert, 202
Caṇḍī, 5, 162-63, 187, 189-90, 302, 314
Caṇḍidās, 45, 61, 76
Caṇḍikā. See Caṇḍī
Candrāvalī, 27, 30, 32, 38-39, 276
Carstairs, Morris, 291
caste, 316, 321
Center for the Study of World Religions, Harvard University, xi
Chatterji, Bankim Chandra, 25
Chāyāvād, 104-15
Chodorow, Nancy, 324
Christianity, 55, 122, 127-28, 186, 199, 284-85, 290
Cilappatikāram, 238-42, 245, 255-56
Cohn, Norman, 199
Coomaraswamy, A.K., 184, 186
cosmogony, 57-58, 65-66, 118, 169, 294
courtesan. See *devadāsī*
cowherd, 4

Daim, Wilfried, 285
Daly, C.D., 291
Dance. See *kuravai; rāsalīlā*
dān līlā, 138
Dās, Jagannātha, 303, 306
Dās, Keśav, 90-91, 95, 123
Das, Veena, 308, 310
dāsya, 28, 36, 79
death, 212, 308, 315
demon, 5, 145-48, 154-65, 184, 187, 194, 208, 244, 255, 263, 272. See also Mahisa; Mahiṣāsura; Nisumbha; Śumbha

INDEX

Deśika, Vedānta, 224-237, 278
devadāsī, 300, 303-04, 306, 309
Devakī, 6, 9, 165
Devī, 1-12, 61-62, 68, 71, 100, 133-45, 153-65, 205-07
Devī-bhāgavata, 61, 71, 176
Devī-māhātmya, 5, 145, 153-65, 204-05
dharma, 38, 123, 151-52, 204-06, 222, 230-31, 234, 254, 279, 305, 316, 321
disease, 184-203, 208, 278
drama, 27-41. See also perspective
Draupadī, 97, 114, 131
duality: of Rādhā and Krishna, 13-26
Durgā, 2-3, 8-12, 62, 68, 120, 145, 153, 165, 260; and Nappiṉṉai, 256-61, 279
Durgā-Kātyāyanī, 6
Durgā-pūjā, 5
Dvārakā, 27, 36, 30, 46, 303, 305

earth, 214, 235, 238, 243, 245-46, 249, 278, 300. See also Bhū
Edholm, Erik Af, 239
Ekānaṃśā, 3, 10, 256, 258
Ekānaṃśā-Durgā, 10
Eliade, Mircea, 189, 202
erotic community, 116-24
erotic love. See love
eschatology, 197-203

faith, 51-52
father: God as, 118, 285, 288-89
feminity, 252
fertility, 211-18, 222, 278, 280
fire. See Agni
Fogg Art Museum, Harvard University, xviii
Freud, Sigmund, 191, 195, 285-86

Gaṇeśa, 4, 277
Gaṅgā. See Ganges
Gaṅgā Laharī, 174, 181
Ganges, 99, 109, 166-83, 187, 207-08, 268
Garuḍa, 51, 258
Gauḍīya, 10-11, 31, 40, 72, 303
Gaurī, 4, 135, 146, 178
geography, 166-83, 184-88
Gītagovinda, 11, 13-27, 58, 61, 64, 127, 138, 300, 302, 306, 314
goddess: as archetype, 292; as mediator, 135-43, 253-54; as mediator (Rādhā), 293; as mediator (Śrī), 224-25, 236-37; as mother of universe, 57; dominant, 131-32, 147; hegemony of, xi; non-Aryan origin, 163; psychology of, 283-97; supreme, 153-65
Goloka, 62-63, 65, 71, 120
gopī, 9, 27, 35, 37, 40, 54, 58, 63, 75, 82, 102, 238, 242, 303-04, 307
gosvāmī, 10, 27-41, 55, 303
Gould, Harold, 202
Govardhana, 4, 6, 10-11, 259
grace, 32, 62, 69, 78, 184-86, 192, 255-26, 228, 230, 291, 310
Graduate Theological Union, xviii
gṛhya sūtras, 308, 310-11
Gupta, Maithilī Śaraṇ, 101, 183
Gupta, Jagdīś, 112

Hanumān, 216-17, 219-20, 227
Harioudh, 102, 114
Harivaṃśa, 5-6, 27, 58, 165, 211-12, 240-42, 244-45, 256, 358
Harnack, Adolf von, 199
Hart, George, 280
Hein, Norvin, 240
hlādinī śakti, 1-2, 12, 40, 75-76, 80-81, 84

Indra, 161, 175, 212-14, 217-18
International Society for Krishna Consciousness, 42

Jagannātha, 3, 10, 18, 23, 298, 300, 302-03
Jaṭilā, 27
Jayadeva, 11, 13-26, 121
jīva, 75
Jīva Gosvāmī, 73
jñāna, 73
Jumna, 13, 17, 110, 166-67, 170
Jung, C.G., 283, 292-297
Jvarāsura, 184

Kabīr, 324
Kaitabha, 154, 156-57, 163
Kālī, 2, 5-7, 68, 119, 144-52, 204, 207-08, 278, 290, 302, 307-15
Kālidāsa, 109, 141, 178
Kalittokai, 239-40
Kali Yuga, 167, 182, 195
kāma (Kāma), 14, 46, 91, 93, 120, 138, 272, 305-07
kāminī, 93, 97-100, 104
Kaṃsa, 7-9, 18, 192, 256
karma, 68, 73, 227
Kāvērī, 167
kinship, 236, 272, 275, 277. See also marriage
Klein, Melanie, 286-87

Krishna: as *bhagavān*, 18, 74; as father of universe, 70; as Gopāla, 1-11, 165, 238; as paradigm of devotion, 37; childhood of, 42-47; devotion to Rādhā, 31, 39; love for Rādhā, 37; marriage to Rādhā, 65; non-Aryan origins of, 165; supreme, 57
kṛpā, 62, 69, 225. See also grace
kuravai, 238-41, 256, 263
Kurukṣetra, 45-46
Kurur Ammā, 321

Lakṣmaṇa, 101, 214, 216, 219
Lakṣmī, 5, 8-9, 61, 80, 131, 141, 177, 216, 223, 230, 236-37, 251, 253, 259-60, 298, 300, 307-15; and Viṣṇu, 302, 307-14, 322. See also Śrī
Lalitamādhava. See Rūpa Gosvāmī
Lalla, 317-20
Lévi-Strauss, Claude, 204
līlā, 37, 64-65, 76, 79, 83, 184-90, 195, 201, 208, 234, 253, 305. See also *rāsalīlā*
liṅga, 134, 171, 207, 302
lotus, 224, 228-32
love, 77-84, 316; courtly, 89-97; erotic, 89-124; sexual, 106, 110. See also *bhakti; kāma; prema*
love-god. See *kāma* (Kāma)
Machwe, Prabhakar, 114
Madhu, 154, 156-57, 163
mādhurya, 28, 39, 40, 77, 79, 305-06
madness, divine, 31, 38, 272-77, 281
Mahābhārata, 18, 25, 89, 97-98, 102, 114, 131, 156, 171, 175, 180
mahābhāva, 11, 28, 55, 80-81
Mahadēviyakkā, 317, 321-22, 324
māhātmya, 153-65, 167, 171, 174, 179
Mahiṣa, 138, 154, 158, 256
Mahiṣamardinī, 5
Mahiṣāsura, 5, 145
māna, 38, 64, 94, 119
Maṅgal, 184-203
Manu, 210, 316, 320
marriage, xii, xvi, 53, 210, 236, 255, 262-77, 298-324; divine-human, 137, 281-324; of Śiva and Pārvatī, 129-43. See also kinship; *svakīyā*
mātṛkā. See mothers
matter. See *prakṛti*
māyā, 62, 68-69, 148, 150, 152, 154-55, 187-88, 190, 193, 249, 280
Mead, Margaret, 324
memory, 14, 15
millenarianism, 197-203
Mīrā, 317
Miśra, Bhānu, 91, 93
mokṣa, 41, 152, 167, 182, 199, 204-06, 225, 227, 230-31
mother, 2-3, 7, 65, 70, 118, 324; earth as, 214; Gaṅgā as, 166-68, 176, 180; god as, 285; goddess as, 8, 118-19, 132-33, 286-93; Kālī as, 152; of time, 2; Sītā as, 211; Śītalā as, 191, 196, 201; Śrī as, 224-26, 227, 235-36, 270; Viṣṇu as, 249
mothers (*mātṛkā*), 162, 164
Murugan, 262-77, 279. See also Skanda
Murukaṉ. See Murugan
Museum of Fine Arts, Boston, xviii

nakh-śikh, 92, 97-99, 114
Nanda, 17, 44, 64, 76, 253, 258
Nāndīmukhī, 28, 30, 35
Nappiṉṉai, 235, 238-61
Nārada, 188, 239, 305
Nārada Bhakti Sūtras, 84
Narasiṃha, 298
Nārāyaṇa, 244, 246, 248, 253, 260, 279, 298, 321. See also Viṣṇu
nārī, 104-11, 113
nature, 170; Vaḷḷi and, 276-71. See also *prakṛti*
Nāṭyaśāstra. See Bharata
Navarātrī, 5, 7, 376
nāyaka, 96-101, 105
nāyikā, 89-115, 91, 96, 97, 99-102, 105
Nehru, Jawaharlal, 168
Neumann, Erich, 294-95
Nicholas, Ralph, 187, 191, 197-98
nidrā, 165. See also *yoganidrā*
Nīlā Devī. See Nappiṉṉai
Nimbārka, 61
Nirālā, 105-06, 109
nirguṇa, 67-68, 70
Niśumbha, 145-46, 154, 160, 165, 205, 256
non-dual, 73-74

Orissa, 298-324

Pañcarātra, 248, 259-60
Pant, Sumitrānandan, 97-98, 104, 110
parakīyā, 41, 53, 82-83, 93-94, 303-04, 316
Paripāṭal, 241, 256
Pārvatī, 100, 129-43, 145-46, 178, 207, 307, 313
Pāṭhak, Śrīdhar, 101

INDEX

Paurṇamāsī, 28-35, 40
Periyavāccāṉpiḷḷai, 253
perspective, 27-41, 46-47, 54
phallus. See *liṅga*
Piṉṉai, 238-61
play. See *līlā*
pollution, 152, 291
power. See *śakti*
prakṛti, 25, 57, 62, 65-67, 70, 148, 150, 152, 155, 158, 170, 176, 179, 230-31, 279-80
Prasād, Jayśankar, 108
prasāda. See grace
prema, 81, 305-07, 316
psychology, 283-97
Purāṇas, 51, 57-71, 131, 135, 142, 146, 175, 218, 256
Purandaradāsa, 322
Purī. See Jagannātha
puruṣa, 25, 65-67, 70, 156, 169, 171
puruṣa and *prakṛti*, 52, 66
Rādhā, 43, 238; ambiguous position of, xii, 53; and Vaḷḷi, 276; as a young girl, 43; as anima, 293; as consort, xii; as *gopī*, 9-12, 54-55, 58, 63, 94; as mistress, 53 (see also *parakīyā*); as mother, 2, 118; as mother of universe, 70; as *nāyikā*, 90-97; as *nirguṇa*, 70; as paradigm of devotion, 28-31, 51, 55, 119; as paradigm of love, 25; as *prakṛti*, 57-65; as redeemer, 69-71; as *śakti*, 40, 67-68, 74 (see also *hlādinī śakti*); as wife, 44, 53 (see also *svakīyā*); beauty of, 48-52; childhood of, 42-45; divinization of, 2; emergence of, 9-12; evolved from Krishna, 57-63; exaltation of, 47-52, 55, 58, 63-65; in the Purāṇas, 57-71; jealousy of, 64; marriage to Krishna, 65; object of devotion, 31-36; queen of *rasa*, 63; rejection of, 89-115, 127; supreme, 26, 32, 39, 42, 56; theology of, 57-88, 117, 122, 125, 128
Rādhā-Krishna, 84; and androgyne Śiva, 307; and Gaṅgā, 176-77, 182; and Vaḷḷi-Murugan, 262-65; as mediating, 314; dramas, 27-41 (see also *rāsalīlā*); in the form of Caitanya, 87; marriage, 65; parity, 65, 67; sexual liaison, 24-25, 46, 66; union of, 53, 83
rāgānugā bhakti, 78
Rāma, 98-101, 131, 142, 192, 194, 210-23, 236, 251, 253, 278
Rāmānanda Rāya, 72
Rāmānuja, 126, 224, 226, 227, 234, 250
Rāmāyaṇa, 102, 130, 175, 210-23, 227, 236, 252-53, 278-81
Rānī of Jhansi, 100
rasa, 27, 63, 73-88, 91, 107. See also *bhaktirasa; śṛṅgāra rasa*
rāsa, 19
rāsalīlā, 20, 37, 42, 44, 56, 63-65, 177, 238, 263. See also *rāsa*
Rasamañjarī. See Bhānu Miśra
Rāvaṇa, 210, 214-15, 217, 219-20, 227
relationship, 56, 120
Rig Veda, 129-30, 155, 164-65, 169, 172, 175, 185, 211, 212, 218
rīti, 89-115
romanticism, 104-111
Rukmiṇī, 12, 45, 47, 252
Rūpa Gosvāmī, 27-41, 53, 80, 91, 276

sacrifice, 290, 313, 316
saints, 316, 324
sakhya, 28, 36, 79
śakti, xi, 1, 10, 40, 62, 65, 67-69, 74, 82, 133, 143, 148, 150, 152, 160-166, 177, 205, 207-08, 219-23, 260, 278-80, 310-12
salvation, 118, 224
Śāmarāya, Ta. Su., 317
Sāṃkhya, 65, 68, 132, 293
Sarasvatī, 177, 212
Sarkar, Aditinath, 187, 191, 197-98
Śītalā, 184-203, 208
Satī, 98, 134, 146, 331
Sāvitrī, 97, 114, 165, 212, 317, 324
Schjelderup, Harald and Kristian, 289
Schrader, F.O., 260
separation, 18, 29, 35, 93, 95, 106, 110, 274
service. See *sevā*
sevā, 32, 62
sexuality, 24, 26, 119, 132-43, 206, 280, 298-324; and community, 120, 123
Shiva. See Śiva
Singer, Milton, 124
Sītā, 98, 114, 119, 131, 134, 142, 210-23, 227, 236, 251-53, 278, 317, 324
Śītalā, 184-203, 278, 280, 313
Śiva, 23, 47, 52, 67, 100, 129-43, 146, 159-61, 164, 166, 175, 177-79, 181-82, 187, 192, 206-07, 218, 268, 271, 316, 321; as androgyne, 300-02, 307; and Kālī, 145-48, 157, 307-14; in *trimūrti*, xi. See also Vīraśaiva
Skanda, 179-80, 262. See also Murugan
smallpox, 184

INDEX

smallpox goddesses, 280. See also Śītalā
Smara. See memory
South India, xii, xvi, 127, 146, 167, 208, 224-81
spirit. See *puruṣa*
Śrī, 8, 20, 24, 52, 131, 178, 216, 223, 224-37, 243, 245, 246, 249, 250, 252, 260, 278, 314. See also Lakṣmī
Śrī Vaiṣṇava, 224, 227-28, 231-32, 236, 238, 244
śṛṅgāra rasa, 80, 91, 94-95, 97, 316
strī, 111-15
Śumbha, 145-46, 154, 160, 162, 165, 205, 256
Suneson, Carl, 239
Sūr Dās, 43-56, 90, 95
Sūr Sāgar, 42-56, 121
suttee, 221. See also Satī
svakīyā, 53, 82, 94, 303
symbol, 170

Tagore, 104
Taittirīya Upaniṣad 74
Tamil Nadu, 227-31, 238-77
tantra, 9-10, 80, 208, 309-13
tantric, 10
Tārāvatī, 135-37
theology, Śrī Vaiṣṇava, 224-37
time, 187-203, 208; goddess as, 186
tīrtha, 166, 168, 171, 176
Tiruppāvai. See Āṇṭāḷ
Tripāṭhī, Rāmnareś, 103
Tukārām, 321
Tulsī Dās, 98

Uddhava, 16, 40, 47
Ūdhō. See Uddhava
Ujjvalanīlamaṇi, 36-38, 91
Umā, 323
union, 18, 26, 53, 83, 95, 106, 137, 206, 274, 298-324
Upaniṣads, 41, 155-56, 164, 170, 185, 316
Urmilā, 101
Urvaśī, 130

vaidhi bhakti, 78-79
Vallabha, 11, 61
Vaḷḷi, 279-80
Vālmīki. See *Rāmāyaṇa*
Varmā, Laksmīkānt, 89
Varmā, Mahādevī, 107
Vāsudeva, 9, 20
vātsalya, 28, 35-36, 79, 226
Veda 51, 129-30, 136, 172, 213, 316. See also Rig Veda
Vedic, 62, 214, 217, 222
Vergote, Antoine, 285
Vidagdhamādhava. See Rūpa Gosvāmī
Vidyāpati, 45, 89
Vilvamaṅgal, 321
viraha, 95. See also separation
Vīraśaiva, 316-24
Virāta, 192-94
Vishnu. See Viṣṇu
Viṣṇu, 18, 114, 141, 156-60, 175, 182, 207, 218, 223, 244, 298, 307-14; in relation to Śrī, 224-37, 250; in *trimūrti*, xi
Viṣṇu Purāṇa, 8, 27, 58, 228, 240
Vraja. See Braj
Vṛndā, 28, 32, 35
Vṛndāvana. See Brindāvan
Vṛṣabhānu. See Bṛṣabhānu
Vṛtra, 212-14, 216-18
vyūha, 55, 63, 120
Vyāsadāsa, 88

Wallace, Anthony, 198, 201
widow, 103
wife, 316; Śītā as, 210; Śrī as, 224-37; of saint, 322; Vaḷḷi as, 262-77
woman: helpless, 97-104; as saint, 316-24; as widow, 103; ideal, 117; realistic, 111-15; universal, 104-11

Yama, 212
Yamunā, 4, 7, 30, 226. See Jumna
Yaśodā, 6, 7, 35, 76, 165, 241, 307
Yaśodharā, 107, 253
yoga, 28, 31, 206
Yoganidrā, 156-57, 165, 206, 208, 260